MOBILITY, SHOCK, AND FIREPOWER

The Emergence of the U.S. Army's Armor Branch, 1917–1945

by

Robert Stewart Cameron

Center of Military History
United States Army
Washington, D.C., 2008

Library of Congress Cataloging-in-Publication Data

Cameron, Robert Stewart.
Mobility, shock, and firepower : the emergence of the U.S. Army's armor branch, 1917–1945 / by Robert Stewart Cameron.
p. cm. — (Army historical series)
Includes bibliographical references and index.
1. United States. Army. Armored Force—History. I. Title. II. Series.

UA30.C36 2008
358'.18097309041—dc22 2007045505

CMH Pub no. 30–23–1

For sale by the Superintendent of Documents, U.S. Government Printing Office
Internet: bookstore.gpo.gov Phone: toll free (866) 512-1800; DC area (202) 512-1800
Fax: (202) 512-2104 Mail: Stop IDCC, Washington, DC 20402-0001

ISBN 978-0-16-079417-9

UNITED STATES ARMY HISTORICAL SERIES

CONTENTS

Table

Charts

Maps

Illustrations

Page

Page

Illustrations courtesy of the following: front cover, pp. 2, 6, 8, 10, 14, 19, 20, 22, 23, 29, 32, 33, 35, 39, 51, 52, 53, 54, 58, 59, 63, 65, 69, 71, 76, 105, 111, 115, 117, 120, 121, 124, 126, 128, 130, 132, 135, 136, 147, 148, 150, 152, 153, 154, 155, 156, 157, 158, 161, 162, 164, 172, 175, 178, 190, 193, 195, 203, 211, 213, 215, 219, 227, 231, 242, 244, 249, 256, 260, 263, 266, 269, 272, 274, 276, 280, 285, 286, 289, 300, 306, 327, 332, 345, 347, 350, 372, 377, 382, 409, 410, 416, 420, 424, 426, 436, 440, 441, 443, 444, 446, 447, 450, 452, 456, 458, 459, 464, 466, 469, 475, 476, 477, 478, 483, 485, 487, 490, 494, 496, 498, 499, 500, 502, 504, 506, back cover, Patton Museum of Cavalry and Armor; 4, 16, 24, 26, 28, Virginia Military Institute; 81, 83, 87, 92, 94, 169, 198, 201, 209, 222, 246, 363, 392, 406, 419, U.S. Army Military History Institute; 86, 96, 98, 180, 185, 186, 205, 225, 233, 235, 238, 302, 336, 367, 370, 386, 399, 413, 449, 454, 461, 467, 468, 472, 479, 492, 503, *Armor* magazine; 91, 100, 102, 354, U.S. Army 1st Cavalry Division Museum; 303, 417, 422, 428, 430, 432, U.S. Army 4th Infantry Division Museum; 322, 389, 395, 482, 505, U.S. Army Center of Military History.

FOREWORD

Dr. Robert Cameron's *Mobility, Shock, and Firepower: The Emergence of the U.S. Army's Armor Branch, 1917–1945* captures the multifaceted development of the Armored Force from its inauspicious beginnings in World War I to its fully mature, operational status at the close of World War II. Through analysis of the Armor Branch's early years, it provides an excellent case study in force transformation. The development of new armor doctrines and organizations to exploit emerging technologies, concepts, and missions is the heart of this work. How that transition was accomplished during the brief space of about twenty years—the accepted duration of a single generation—is a story worthy of careful examination as our Army gropes with managing similar transformations today.

In relating the transition of the Armored Force from a tiny tactical organization in 1918 to one of the major components of the U.S. Army in 1944, the author addresses issues that resonate with all military organizations. These include the impact of new technology upon force structure; the influence of theoretical and actual threats on force design; the allocation of resources between current and future needs; and the impact of combat operations upon doctrine, organization, training, and materiel development. Also analyzed are relevant policy debates among senior Army leaders, military intelligence assessments of foreign mechanized trends, and the influence of broader national defense issues. Together, they provide a rich tapestry for a complex, compelling tale.

Since 1945, America's military leaders have relied increasingly on advanced technologies, more effective organizational structures, and greater focus on specialized military education and training, consciously breaking from the industrial-age armies of the past with their mass-produced weapons and mass-produced soldiers. For the Army, such policies have placed greater attention on the acquisition process, on tactical and operational force design, on the Army schoolhouse, and on more effective battlefield decision making. Yet, after a sometimes tortuous process, the leaders of the Army's Armored Force had successfully addressed all these complex issues by the end of World War II. Consequently, *Mobility, Shock, and Firepower* has many practical insights for today's military leaders that should not be ignored. While offering a major scholarly contribution to the literature treating the U.S. Army and America's unique concepts of armored warfare, it also speaks to those issues currently being vigorously debated today.

Washington, D.C.
22 July 2008

JEFFREY J. CLARKE
Chief of Military History

THE AUTHOR

Robert Cameron holds a B.A. in economics and history from Binghamton University, New York. In 1994 he received his Ph.D. in modern military history from Temple University, Pennsylvania. He taught undergraduate history at several colleges in the Philadelphia area, including Temple University, Camden County College, and Manor Junior College. In 1996 he joined the civil service and became the U.S. Army Armor Branch historian. He continues to serve in this capacity, providing historical support to the Armor community. His publications include a comprehensive guide to the Civil War battle of Perryville and many articles related to armored warfare trends and issues. His last article appeared in the March–April 2007 issue of *Armor* magazine and detailed the fielding and operational problems associated with scout platoons equipped with high mobility multipurpose wheeled vehicles. He is currently working on a study of mounted reconnaissance organizations from the interwar years to the present.

PREFACE

The following pages provide a narrative analysis of the U.S. Army's development of armored organizations and their related doctrine, materiel, and training activities in the period 1917–1945. This period marked the emergence of clear principles of armored warfare that became the underpinnings of the Armor Branch, influencing armored developments long after World War II ended. A unique style of mounted maneuver combat emerged that reflected a mix of tradition and innovation. In the process, American military culture changed, particularly through the adoption of combined-arms principles. Conversely, political actions, budgetary considerations, and senior leadership decisions also shaped the course of armor development.

The emergence of an American armored force involved more than simply tank development. It included the creation of an armored division structure steeped in combined-arms principles, organizational flexibility, and revolutionary command and control processes. Parallel developments included the establishment of specialized units to provide antitank, reconnaissance, and infantry support capabilities. Several Army branches played a role in determining the precise path of armored development, and one of them—the Cavalry—became a casualty as a result.

Between 1917 and 1945 Army concepts of armored warfare grew from a platform focus and a narrowly defined mission into a broad capability. This change influenced the evolutionary path from the tank battalions of World War I to the armored divisions of World War II. While the former constituted little more than a collection of tanks intended to breach fortified lines, the latter included an integrated team of tanks, infantry, mechanized cavalry, artillery, engineers, and combat service support elements. The term armor became synonymous with combined-arms operations; rapid, decisive action; flexible organizations and command and control measures; and a broad mission set. Similarly, the armored divisions offered more to the Army's warfighting ability than simply a means to overcome enemy entrenchments.

This transformation occurred in three phases. The first included the World War I experience and the years immediately following this conflict. During this period of exposure, the Army identified the need for tank organizations and established its first tank force. The foreign origins of the tank and the absence of American tanks or the related doctrine and training institutes made the Army initially dependent upon French and British support. The resulting American tank force supported offensive operations in the closing months of World War I. After the war, however, the focus of armored development shifted to the retention of this tank force amid demobilization and a restructuring of the Army's force structure. The early 1920s marked the institutionalization of the tank's wartime infantry support role and ensured its permanency as an Army asset.

The second phase lasted from the late 1920s until the large-scale introduction of American armor into combat in late 1942. This period witnessed significant pioneering efforts in armored doctrine, organization, training, and materiel. Discussions regarding possible uses of the tank quickly transcended the infantry support role assigned. The late 1920s marked deliberate efforts to test the viability of employing tanks in other roles. The mechanized cavalry emerged from those efforts. Its activities in the 1930s resulted in revolutionary concepts of tactical organization, doctrine, battle command, and the related employment of signal communications. The onset of World War II and Germany's lightning campaigns against Poland and France triggered a widespread expansion of the Army's armored might and the consolidation of development responsibility. Armored divisions resulted that built upon the mechanized cavalry experience and provided an American equivalent to the German panzer division.

However, this pioneering phase of armored development reflected the realities of the American interwar military experience. The constrained military budgets of the Great Depression years led the Army to emphasize personnel retention over the fielding of new organizations and technology, thereby slowing armored development. Financial constraints also fostered competition among the various branches, particularly over the allocation of personnel and funding. Political action shaped the nature of the Army in the interwar years and established the administrative context for armored development. Foreign mechanized developments received considerable attention, but the absence of any consensus on the structure and use of armored formations abroad simply provided validation for the competing viewpoints within the Army regarding the proper course of American armored development. Uncertainty regarding the pace and extent of mechanization encouraged prolonged debates and study that often resulted in the deferment of key decisions. At issue was the degree to which the Army should adopt new, unproven concepts based on technology rather than rely on traditional and proven organizations. The Cavalry came to embody this issue as it sought to determine the right mix of horse and mechanized cavalry.

Between 1940 and 1942, the Army undertook widespread modernization and mobilization. The onset of World War II encouraged these actions and largely eliminated financial constraints from armored development. However, the need to rapidly prepare tactical organizations for combat led to the influx of senior leadership ideas of training, organization, and doctrine that sometimes contradicted existing patterns of development. Deployment needs also forced reductions in armored organizations that eroded their self-sufficiency on the battlefield. The establishment of the Armored Force as a central organ for armored development did not solve the question of antitank operations, resulting in the creation of the tank destroyer, whose development occurred separate from armored tactics and doctrine. Similarly, mechanized cavalry organizations optimized for reconnaissance emerged independent of armored formations. Separate tank battalions existed to provide infantry support, but their development lacked the centralized focus of the armored divisions. Consequently, armored organizations by 1943 reflected compromise solutions between conflicting needs and did not yet constitute an integrated team.

The final phase of armored development constituted one of refinement. Imbued with doctrinal principles pioneered during the interwar years and manned by personnel still learning their craft, the Army's mounted forces entered combat in every theater of operation. They made their largest impression in the years 1943–1945, when the Army reached its peak strength in mechanized cavalry, separate tank battalions, tank destroyers, and armored divisions. Combat provided the most important field test. It demonstrated the fallacy of some concepts while validating others, most notably those associated with command and control. Where possible, units in the field improvised solutions to deficiencies; often their actions led to stateside changes. Combat resolved the uncertainties of the interwar years and underscored the importance of tactically versatile organizations. The degree of specialization embedded in tank destroyer and mechanized cavalry units, for example, did not survive contact with the enemy.

The World War II battlefields demonstrated the importance of combined-arms doctrine, organizations, and training. Teamwork provided the flexibility and agility necessary to adapt to the unexpected, particularly when guiding doctrine proved weak or nonexistent. The war years highlighted the need for armored units to be able to operate routinely in complex terrain, including cities, jungle, forest, and mountains. These terrain types underscored the value of close cooperation of mounted and dismounted organizations at the small-unit level. Moreover, such cooperation permitted armored units to overcome resistance and situations for which they were neither equipped nor configured to perform. By war's end the experiences of the battlefield had become the dominant influence on armored development, eclipsing the theories of the prewar years. The lessons learned provided enduring principles of employment for mounted organizations.

Some readers may question the need for another work on U.S. armored developments, given the large body of literature already available. However, this work constitutes an institutional history of early armored-force development in the U.S. Army. It encompasses the entire period from the first creation of an American tank unit in World War I through the defining crucible of World War II. Whereas many works address only a particular event, combat operation, unit, or select piece of the American armored experience, this work offers a holistic interpretation. It attempts to show how technology, doctrine, training, leadership, and organization interacted within a context shaped by political considerations, the Army's corporate nature, and a view of warfare in flux to create a uniquely American way of armored warfare. In the process, this work provides a case study of the Army in transition from its constabulary nature at the start of World War I to the global influence achieved by the conclusion of World War II.

This study is not a battle history. It does not offer detailed accounts of combat operations. In fact, it gives more attention to training maneuvers conducted in the interwar period than to any one battle in either world war. This disproportionate focus reflects the widespread availability of published literature on armored combat, as well as the shaping influence of prewar developments on wartime activities. Combat actions are addressed for the lessons that were derived and used to refine training, doctrine, organization, and materiel development.

Similarly, the source material for this work reflects not only senior leaders, but the reports, memorandums, and correspondence of the majors, lieutenant colonels, and colonels associated with armored development since World War I. Many of these individuals gradually faded from the pages of history, but their activities provide a more accurate depiction of the thinking and decision making associated with armored development. They also provide a means with which to assess the impact of senior-leader policy decisions. Armored development in these pages appears as a complex process that often posed more questions than it resolved. Opponents of armored developments had valid concerns that proponents were hard pressed to address until combat operations provided the necessary data. Until then, many developments that seem obvious with the advantage of hindsight were in fact clouded in uncertainty. Despite the plethora of ideas surrounding tank operations, it was not clear how to build armored organizations to conduct a variety of missions against an uncertain foe on an unknown battlefield. World War II provided a degree of clarity, but analysis of the work done during the interwar period offers many useful insights to those individuals charged with the design of new tactical organizations built around emerging technology for use against a wide range of possible threats.

Many organizations and individuals proved instrumental in the research and development of this work. The staff at the U.S. Army Military History Institute provided invaluable assistance in identifying and understanding much of the source material used. I received similar support from the staffs at the George C. Marshall Foundation Library Archives and Museum, the York County Historical Society, the U.S. National Archives and Records Administration, the U.S. Army 1st Cavalry Division Museum, the U.S. Army 4th Infantry Division Museum, *Armor* magazine, and the Patton Museum of Cavalry and Armor. The Publishing Division at the U.S. Army Center of Military History also deserves special thanks for its support in publishing this work. Inspiration for these pages came from the work and memory of Dr. Russell F. Weigley, whose selfless dedication to the profession of history and the analysis of military affairs established the high standard of excellence to which the rest of us can only aspire.

Fort Knox, Kentucky
22 July 2008

ROBERT STEWART CAMERON
Branch Historian
U.S. Army Armor Center and Fort Knox

MOBILITY, SHOCK, AND FIREPOWER

The Emergence of the U.S. Army's Armor Branch, 1917–1945

1

AMERICA ADOPTS THE TANK

World War I introduced the U.S. Army to the tank. In that conflict American forces struggled to build and field tank combat units, relying on foreign ideas and equipment. The years following the Great War marked a transition in which the tank became an accepted part of the U.S. Army. Political and budgetary considerations slowed this integration. Little experimentation in tank usage occurred beyond the wartime role of infantry support. Only through the direct intervention of the secretary of war in the late 1920s was the Army driven to consider alternatives. The Mechanized Force emerged as a tactical laboratory intended to determine the optimal organization and doctrine for a combat unit built around the tank. Despite this promising development, by 1931 the Mechanized Force represented a conundrum for the Army. It symbolized the growing desire to explore varied missions and organizations for the tank, but it also portended the creation of a separate mechanized branch—a controversial step the existing combat arms generally opposed.

The Tank Corps

Two dominant influences shaped the U.S. Army's World War I experience: America's decision to employ large numbers of troops on the Western Front and the need for their rapid deployment there. In 1917 the weakening of Russian resistance to Germany coupled with manifestations of war weariness among the French, British, and Italian Armies created an imperative for immediate reinforcement by American military forces. In 1918 Russia's withdrawal from the war and the German spring and summer offensives on the Western Front intensified this imperative. The consequent frenzied effort to employ the American Expeditionary Forces (AEF) in a combat role preempted careful, deliberate preparations by the U.S. Army for its battlefield debut. Nevertheless it endeavored to equip, train, and transport large numbers of troops to an overseas combat theater and adapt itself to the new military technologies in use there. For American ground forces, the tank represented one of the most important technologies.[1]

---

[1] David M. Kennedy, *The First World War and American Society* (New York: Oxford University Press, 1980), pp. 169–70; Edward M. Coffman, *The War To End All Wars: The American Military Experience in World War I* (Madison: University of Wisconsin Press, 1986), pp. 50, 55–56, 84; Timothy K. Nenninger, "American Military Effectiveness in the First World War," in *Military Effectiveness*, 3

French-built Renault light tank in American service on the Western Front

The tank emerged as a technological solution to the problem of overcoming heavily fortified positions. Too often British and French offensives on the Western Front foundered with great loss of life while trying to penetrate German trenches protected by mines, barbed wire, and machine guns. Attacking forces that actually reached the German lines found themselves disorganized, unable to communicate effectively with supporting artillery, and subjected to well-timed counterattacks that negated any gains they made. In response, the British developed the tank, employing it for the first time during the Somme Offensive of 1916. The French followed suit, but not until the following year did French tanks enter combat. Both nations soon found the tank to be an indispensable asset in the trench warfare of the Western Front, and they developed their own distinct doctrines for its employment.[2]

The U.S. Army studied these early tank operations as it deployed American soldiers to France. In July 1917, it established the Tank Board to review French

vols., ed. Allan R. Millett and Williamson Murray (Boston: Allen and Unwin, 1988), 1: 124, 129–30, 134; George C. Reinhardt and William R. Kintner, *The Haphazard Years: How America Has Gone to War* (Garden City, N.Y.: Doubleday and Co., 1960), p. 101.

[2] See Kenneth Macksey, "The Tank Story," in *Tanks and Weapons of World War I* (London: BPC Publishing, 1973), pp. 88–94; Richard M. Ogorkiewicz, "The French Tank Force," in *Tanks and Weapons of World War I*, pp. 95–101.

light and British heavy tank usage on the Western Front. In September, the board recommended the creation of a separate American tank arm directly subordinate to the AEF commander and equipped with both British heavy and French light tanks. Another study conducted by two Ordnance officers and submitted in November 1917 included a plan for tank production commensurate with the high expectations of American industrial potential.[3]

Following these preparations, General John J. Pershing, commander of General Headquarters American Expeditionary Forces, established the Tank Corps within the existing AEF infrastructure in December 1917. Together with the earlier creation of the Air Service and the Chemical Warfare Service, this action marked the conclusion of an Army effort to incorporate new military technologies into the American Expeditionary Forces. Col. Samuel D. Rockenbach, a Cavalry officer, became chief of the Tank Corps, which by Christmas 1917 numbered only three officers including its chief.[4]

In the absence of any American experience with tanks, the Tank Corps needed French and British assistance in training tank crews; but doctrinal differences between these two allies resulted in a bifurcated American effort. The British emphasized a heavy tank that preceded assaulting infantry, destroying wire obstacles and enemy strong points. The French employed light tanks to accompany their infantry, providing direct fire support as needed. Rockenbach believed American tank doctrine should integrate both concepts, which required separate training efforts under British and French tutelage.[5]

To train Tank Corps personnel in the tactical use of the light tank, Pershing authorized activation of the Light Tank School in Bourg, France, near a much larger AEF training center established in Langres to train soldiers newly arrived from the United States. Lacking any experience with tanks, the instructors of the new tank school, including its head, Capt. George S. Patton Jr., first had to attend introductory classes at the French Light Tank Training Center in Chamlieu before assuming their own educational duties.[6] However, the American tank school benefited from its inclusion in the general AEF school system. The training environment encouraged analysis of tank operations under realistic conditions, while the school's proximity to the front gave instructors direct access to allied tank officers in the field.[7]

---

[3] Robert L. Collins, "Report on the Development of the Tank Corps," in *The United States Army in the World War, 1917–1918, Reports of Commander-in-Chief, A.E.F., Staff Sections and Services* (Washington, D.C.: U.S. Army Center of Military History, 1948), p. 220; Dale E. Wilson, *Treat 'Em Rough! The Birth of American Armor, 1917–20* (Novato, Calif.: Presidio Press, 1989), pp. 10, 12.

[4] Wilson, *Treat 'Em Rough*, pp. 23, 26; Nenninger, "American Military Effectiveness," p. 138.

[5] Joseph W. Viner, *Tactics and Techniques of Tanks* (Fort Leavenworth, Kans.: General Service Schools Press, 1920), pp. 4–5; S. D. Badsey, "The American Experience of Armour," in *Armoured Warfare*, ed. J. P. Harris and F. H. Toase (New York: St. Martin's Press, 1990), p. 126.

[6] Collins, "Development of the Tank Corps," p. 221; S. D. Rockenbach, "Tanks," Lecture at Tank School, 4 Jun 23, p. 36, U.S. Army Military History Institute (MHI), Library, Carlisle Barracks, Pa.; Martin Blumenson, *The Patton Papers*, 2 vols. (Boston: Houghton Mifflin Co., 1972), 1: 438, 445, 465.

[7] Wilson, *Treat 'Em Rough*, pp. 39, 41; Blumenson, *Patton Papers*, 1: 537–38.

Colonel Rockenbach, December 1917

In Britain, the Americans established a training camp to familiarize Tank Corps personnel with heavy tanks. Under British tutelage, using British equipment, and isolated from the combat theater and the American Expeditionary Forces, the American tank training center in Britain simply trained tank personnel. Little incentive existed for the students to analyze tank operations in the fashion of their counterparts at the Light Tank School, nor did their subsequent combat experience exert the same degree of influence on the doctrinal development of the AEF Tank Corps. Employed under British control, only one heavy tank battalion entered combat with the British Expeditionary Force, far removed from the St. Mihiel and Meuse-Argonne Offensives where much of American wartime and postwar military attention focused.[8]

Despite the formulation of American tank tactics derived from French and British ideas, the American Expeditionary Forces never implemented them as intended. The absence of American-made tanks throughout the war forced the Tank Corps to remain dependent on the French and British for tanks, but the latter proved reluctant to divert tanks to an unproven American tank force. Thus, the British equipped the American 301st Heavy Tank Battalion with the proviso that it be deployed in a British combat sector.[9]

Without tanks, the training of personnel who had never seen a tank could not advance beyond a rudimentary level. Not until March 1918 did the Light Tank School receive its first ten tanks. In the United States, a separate effort to train Tank Corps personnel resulted in the creation of a headquarters in Washington, D.C., led by Col. Ira C. Welborn to manage recruitment and tank production. In addition, several training centers were established to prepare soldiers for assignment to tank units. Capt. Dwight D. Eisenhower commanded the Camp Colt training center near Gettysburg, Pennsylvania. Training effectiveness there also suffered from the absence of tanks, forcing Eisenhower to focus on basic training and the prevention of boredom. Some relief from the tedium occurred through machine-gun training on nearby Gettysburg National Military Park. One unarmed light tank arrived in June

---

[8] Collins, "Development of the Tank Corps," p. 221; Wilson, *Treat 'Em Rough*, pp. 51, 54–60.

[9] Rockenbach, "Tanks," 4 Jun 23, pp. 42, 54; Blumenson, *Patton Papers*, 1: 482; Wilson, *Treat 'Em Rough*, p. 56.

1918, but the outbreak of Spanish influenza in September disrupted the minimal tank training.[10]

The dearth of American-made tanks resulted from the failure to mobilize industry early enough to meet the outpouring of military demands that accompanied the nation's entrance into the war. Industry proved unable to convert existing plants rapidly from commercial to war goods production. Neither the government nor the military possessed any central coordinating body to match available industrial output with the Army's prioritized needs, and widespread shortfalls of materiel resulted.[11]

The War Department also lacked a vertical command structure. Composed of numerous bureaus under the nominal control of the secretary of war, the department gave no one bureau overall responsibility for supply and procurement of army needs. Instead, five separate bureaus controlled the supply services and partially duplicated each other's activities. Lack of standardization among equipment even as basic as blankets, harnesses, and shovels needlessly multiplied procurement, accounting, and storage problems. Worse, the horizontal nature of the War Department organization generated competition among its bureaus for the attention of manufacturers.[12]

The American Expeditionary Forces suffered as a consequence. In the case of motor vehicles, over two hundred different types, with concomitant maintenance problems, saw service with the American Expeditionary Forces. Tank production fared even worse, since lack of experience with such relatively complex platforms compounded existing administrative and organizational problems.[13]

Neither AEF planners nor the War Department General Staff (WDGS) comprehended the inability of the existing administrative organization to address AEF needs effectively. While the AEF staff gradually increased the number of combat divisions deemed necessary to achieve victory to one hundred, expansion of war materiel production occurred at a much slower pace. Even had American industry produced enough materiel to equip the formations the American Expeditionary Forces considered necessary, the ships necessary to transport this equipment to France did not exist. Indeed, military planners in the American Expeditionary Forces and War Department General Staff initially paid little attention to shipping requirements. Consequently, throughout the war the American Expeditionary Forces remained dependent largely on French and British equipment. While America ultimately manufactured 7 million tons of war materiel, it purchased 10 million

---

[10] Blumenson, *Patton Papers*, 1: 508; Dwight D. Eisenhower, *At Ease: Stories I Tell to Friends* (Garden City, N.Y.: Doubleday and Co., 1967), pp. 146–50; Merle Miller, *Ike the Soldier: As They Knew Him* (New York: G. P. Putnam's Sons, 1987), p. 170; Wilson, *Treat 'Em Rough*, pp. 65–66.

[11] James E. Hewes Jr., *From Root to McNamara: Army Organization and Administration, 1900–1963* (Washington, D.C.: U.S. Army Center of Military History, 1975), pp. 23, 30; Nenninger, "American Military Effectiveness," p. 120; Reinhardt and Kintner, *Haphazard Years*, pp. 83–85.

[12] L. R. Wolfe, "Standardization," *Quartermaster Review* XIX, no. 6 (May-June 1940): 30; Peyton C. March, *The Nation at War* (Garden City, N.Y.: Doubleday, Doran and Co., 1932), pp. 163–68.

[13] Coffman, *The War To End All Wars*, p. 37; Wolfe, "Standardization," p. 30; Edmund B. Gregory, "Motor Transport—Today," *Quartermaster Review* XXI, no. 3 (November-December 1941): 37.

British Mark V heavy tank in World War I

from the French and British. Britain shouldered the responsibility for transporting nearly half of all AEF personnel to France.[14]

In this environment, American tank production suffered severe delays. Expectations bore no resemblance to realizable goals. The Tank Board report of July 1917 advocated production of two thousand light tanks and two hundred heavy tanks. The Ordnance Department endeavored to attain this goal by implementing the subsequent production plan recommended in November by two of its officers detailed to study the matter. They suggested production of the French FT–17 light tank under license by the United States and a joint American-British program to design and produce a heavy tank. The latter, subsequently designated the Mark VIII, would mount an American Liberty engine and carry weapons and armor provided by the British. Final assembly would occur in France, where the tank was to be employed. The Liberty engine was initially designed for aircraft, and the American Air Service desired large quantities for new aircraft. Unfortunately, American manufacturers could not meet the demands of both the Tank Corps and the Air Service. They gave priority to the Air Service, triggering widespread delays in the production and delivery of the engines to the Tank Corps. The cessation of the

---

[14] March, *Nation at War*, p. 91; Leonard P. Ayres, *The War with Germany: A Statistical Summary* (Washington, D.C.: Government Printing Office, 1919), p. 41; Nenninger, "American Military Effectiveness," pp. 121, 125; Coffman, *The War To End All Wars*, pp. 40, 178–81.

heavy tank program resulted shortly before the armistice and before the assembly of the first tank.[15]

Wartime production of the FT–17 foundered on the Ordnance Department's decision to modify the design before production. The vehicle's proven combat record, the Tank Corps' pressing need for tanks, and the absence of American experience with tank design did not deter the Ordnance Department. Not surprisingly, the intended modifications to the turret, main armament, and gun mounting proved more complicated than anticipated. Multiple committees of military personnel and civilian engineers were formed to oversee the tank program, but disputes among the committees over design details further retarded progress. For example, although the vehicle could attain a maximum speed of only five miles per hour, time-consuming debates surrounded the question of whether the tank's speedometer should indicate miles or kilometers per hour.[16]

The Ordnance Department further increased the chaos characteristic of American tank production in World War I through its support of a new tank design for which no requirement existed. The Ford Motor Company captured the attention of the Ordnance Department with a 3-ton tank design and promises of rapid mass production, low cost, and mechanical reliability. The resultant vehicle received the designation M1918. Several were sent to France for field testing by Tank Corps personnel, who found the tank unsuited for the combat environment of the Western Front. They demanded exclusive production of the FT–17. The Ordnance Department, however, had already granted Ford a contract for fifteen thousand vehicles. Yet U.S. companies managed to produce only fifteen Ford and ten Renault tanks by war's end. None saw combat.[17]

These negligible production figures reflect the difficulties inherent to the design, development, and manufacturing of new technology during wartime conditions. The tank represented a complex weapon with which American engineers possessed no experience. The discrepancy between Ford's promised mass production and actual output of the M1918 reflects the realization that tank production fundamentally differed from that of the automobile. Similarly, the tyranny of committees that dominated efforts to build the FT–17 reflected the Army's inexperience with the management and organization of tank programs.

In general, the ability to provide war materiel commensurate with military needs improved by war's end. Although only 3 percent of ordnance contracts had been completed, the foundations for a large-scale industrial effort had been laid. This change became possible only with the creation of the War Industries Board to coordinate supply, procurement, and production of war materiel and

---

[15] Collins, "Development of the Tank Corps," pp. 221–22, 224; Frederick Palmer, *Newton D. Baker: America at War*, 2 vols. (New York: Dodd, Mead and Co., 1931), 2: 166; Robert J. Icks, "Four Decades of Mechanization: Our Record of Combat-Vehicle Development," *Army Ordnance* XVII, no. 102 (May-June 1937): 333–34.

[16] Wilson, *Treat 'Em Rough*, pp. 82–84; Icks, "Four Decades of Mechanization," p. 334.

[17] Collins, "Development of the Tank Corps," pp. 222–23; Rockenbach, "Tanks," 4 Jun 23, p. 40; Viner, *Tactics and Techniques of Tanks*, pp. 15–16; Icks, "Four Decades of Mechanization," p. 335; Wilson, *Treat 'Em Rough*, pp. 85–86.

Tank Corps FT–17 negotiating a ditch in France

the appointment of Bernard Baruch, a prominent financier and businessman, as its chairman. Concurrently, Secretary of War Newton D. Baker supported the aggressive exercise of executive authority by Chief of Staff General Peyton C. March to create a unified, vertical command structure for which the Overman Act of May 1918 provided the necessary legislative underpinning.[18] Through these measures, the War Department transformed itself from a collection of bureaus into a rationalized, vertical structure designed for efficiency and organized on the basis of prevailing scientific management principles.

The Tank Corps benefited from these improvements. In the months following the armistice, American-made FT–17s, designated the M1917, finally began to roll off assembly lines in appreciable numbers. By March 1919, the Tank Corps had accepted delivery of 618 light tanks. In addition, it received sufficient pieces with which to assemble 100 Mark VIII heavy tanks. A further 213 French FT–17s and 32 British Mark V heavy tanks accompanied the AEF on its return to the United States.

[18] March, *Nation at War*, pp. 168–69; Constance McLaughlin Green, Harry C. Thomson, and Peter C. Roots, *The Ordnance Department: Planning Munitions for War*, U.S. Army in World War II (Washington, D.C.: U.S. Army Center of Military History, 1955), pp. 25–27; Nenninger, "American Military Effectiveness," pp. 120–21.

Collectively, these machines provided the materiel basis for America's postwar tank force, greatly exceeding the Tank Corps' wartime vehicle strength.[19]

The Tank Corps' Demise

In November 1918, the AEF Tank Corps consisted of some twelve thousand officers and enlisted men, while Tank Corps members in the United States numbered nearly eight thousand two hundred. This apex of Tank Corps strength could not be maintained in the face of the postwar demobilization. Congress reduced the Tank Corps to an establishment of three hundred officers and five thousand enlisted men in March 1919. However, with fewer personnel and more tanks, this action eliminated the wartime discrepancy between too many men and too few vehicles.[20]

Yet the war's end did not provide the Tank Corps with an opportunity to evaluate its own experiences and identify those lessons that should shape postwar development. Demobilization, the American Expeditionary Forces' return from France, the relocation of the Tank Corps to Camp George G. Meade, Maryland, and the general uncertainty created by the Army's pending reorganization effectively precluded effective analysis or the formulation of new doctrine. The Tank Corps chief, now Brig. Gen. Samuel D. Rockenbach, remained in France until August 1919 supervising the repatriation of AEF Tank Corps elements. These duties prevented him from leading any serious study of tank operations.[21]

Even after completion of demobilization and the American Expeditionary Forces' return to the United States, personnel issues continued to preclude analytical efforts. In July Congress further reduced Tank Corps strength to 154 officers and 2,508 enlisted men. This cut represented a serious loss of trained personnel whose experience with tanks could not be replaced. Those who remained found their professional futures clouded by rumors of a War Department intention to subordinate the Tank Corps to the Infantry.[22]

Army-wide grade reductions returned most officers to their prewar ranks. This action gutted the Tank Corps' leadership. Many of its officers had been commissioned from the ranks during the war, and these leaders now lost their commissions altogether. Regular Army officers had been promoted rapidly. Patton and Eisenhower both had risen from captain to colonel. While their influence had risen with their rank, it now similarly declined. Patton, again a captain, could not retain command of the

---

[19] U.S. Congress, House Document 863, "Report of the Chief of the Tank Corps," 30 Jun 20, in *War Department Annual Reports, 1920*, 66th Cong., 3d Sess., 3 vols., 1921, 1: 1891. For wartime tank strength, see chart in Collins, "Development of the Tank Corps," p. 223; Ayres, *Statistical Summary*, p. 80.

[20] U.S. Congress, House Document 426, "Report of the Chief of the Tank Corps," 13 Oct 19, in *War Department Annual Reports, 1919*, 66th Cong., 2d Sess., 3 vols., 1920, 1: 4375; "Report of the Chief of the Tank Corps," 30 Jun 20, 1: 1891; Rockenbach, "Tanks," 4 Jun 23, pp. 39–40.

[21] Congress, "Report of the Chief of the Tank Corps," 30 Jun 20, 1: 1893; "Report of the Chief of the Tank Corps," 13 Oct 19, vol.1; Blumenson, *Patton Papers*, 1: 705–06.

[22] Congress, "Report of the Chief of the Tank Corps," 30 Jun 20, 1: 1892; Wilson, *Treat 'Em Rough*, p. 222.

Remains of an FT–17 after direct hit by artillery

tank units he had led in battle. In deference to Patton's wartime role, Rockenbach assigned officers of equal or junior rank and seniority to his unit, but such measures could not hide the Tank Corps' declining ability to control its own affairs. Some officers left the Army altogether, while others left service with tanks to return to their previous branch. The Tank Corps' future appeared very much in jeopardy.[23]

While the Tank Corps endeavored to adapt to peacetime conditions, Congress embarked on restructuring the Army. It sought to avoid the chaos that plagued the wartime mobilization and overseas deployment of American soldiers. Against the backdrop of the Red Scare, the debate over American involvement in the League of Nations, and widespread labor unrest, members of Congress pondered and debated the proper size and structure of the armed forces. They also considered whether to retain the Air Service, Chemical Warfare Service, and Tank Corps as separate, independent arms.[24]

Tank Corps personnel supported retention of their independent status despite their limited combat experience. American tanks had not been able to emulate the massive British employment of tanks during the fighting around Cambrai and Amiens, France, that shattered German resistance. Terrain, weather, mud, mechanical unreliability, and lack of tanks limited the effectiveness of American tanks during the principal American offensives of St. Mihiel and the Meuse-Argonne in the autumn of 1918. (*See Map 1.*) Many tanks became separated from their accompanying

[23] Congress, "Report of the Chief of the Tank Corps," 13 Oct 19, 1: 4374; Blumenson, *Patton Papers*, 1: 739; Wilson, *Treat 'Em Rough*, p. 227.

[24] Allan R. Millett and Peter Maslowski, *For the Common Defense: A Military History of the United States of America* (New York: Free Press, 1984), p. 366.

infantry, wandering about the battlefield attacking targets of opportunity until they were mired, knocked out by enemy fire, or simply broke down.[25]

Nevertheless, Tank Corps officers prepared a literary justification for the permanence of their arm based on the tanks' wartime use. Patton's role as a tank instructor and combat commander provided him with a degree of experience not shared by most Tank Corps officers, but his postwar writing revealed the limits of that experience. In an article published by the *Infantry Journal* in May 1920, Patton argued that enthusiasm for the tank suffered from inadequate knowledge of its use and potential. Accordingly, he endeavored to educate officers in the value of the tank by drawing an image of war in the future that differed from the trench battles of World War I. He did not postulate a new theory of warfare in which the tank predominated. Instead, he simply combined the prevailing desire to avoid trench warfare with the demonstrated value of tanks supporting infantry. In the world's underdeveloped regions, he envisioned combatants clashing over wide frontages that would prevent the dense concentrations of artillery and infantry typical of the Western Front. In the absence of massed friendly artillery support, an attacking force thus needed tank support to overcome enemy machine guns and exploit success.[26]

These views differed little from those of Rockenbach. The latter stressed the valuable contribution of the tank to the defeat of Germany. He believed this usefulness a function of the morale erosion among defending soldiers that the tank's physical presence generated. He also believed that the tank's future tactics should include the same merging of British and French concepts advocated during the war. Rockenbach perceived the tank's principal function as one of infantry support, but he also supported its potential use in other roles, including exploitation, pursuit, interdiction of enemy movement, raids in conjunction with horse cavalry, and advance guard.[27]

Despite the Tank Corps' public emphasis on infantry support, members acknowledged the potential of the tank to perform a variety of roles. They believed that the tank's proper role and mission had yet to be determined. They considered the tank a weapon valuable to all arms and saw an independent Tank Corps as the best means to explore how to exploit the tank's capabilities. Conversely, they did not believe the tank would realize its full potential if its development were subordinated to an existing combat arm.[28]

---

[25] Anon., "U.S. Army Expeditionary Force, France, 1917–1919: Report Operations Tank Corps, 1918," apps. 4, 6, 8, MHI Library; Ken Steadman, "The Evolution of the Tank in the U.S. Army," Combat Studies Institute, Rpt no. 1, pp. 2–3, Fort Leavenworth, Kans., 21 Apr 82; Mildred H. Gillie, *Forging the Thunderbolt: A History of the Development of the Armored Force* (Harrisburg, Pa.: Military Service Publishing Co., 1947), p. 14.

[26] George S. Patton Jr., "Tanks in Future Wars," *Infantry Journal* XVI, no. 11 (May 1920): 958–62.

[27] S. D. Rockenbach, "Cooperation of Tanks with Other Arms," *Infantry Journal* XVI, no. 7 (January 1920): 533, 543, and no. 8 (February 1920): 662–68, 670; S. D. Rockenbach, "The Tank Corps," Lecture to WDGS Members, 19 Sep 19, p. 7, MHI Library.

[28] Patton, "Tanks in Future Wars," pp. 958–62; Rockenbach, "Cooperation of Tanks with Other Arms," no. 7, pp. 533–45, and no. 8, pp. 662–73; Dwight D. Eisenhower, "A Tank Discussion," *Infantry Journal* XVII, no. 5 (November 1920): 453–58; George F. Hofmann, "The Demise of the U.S. Tank

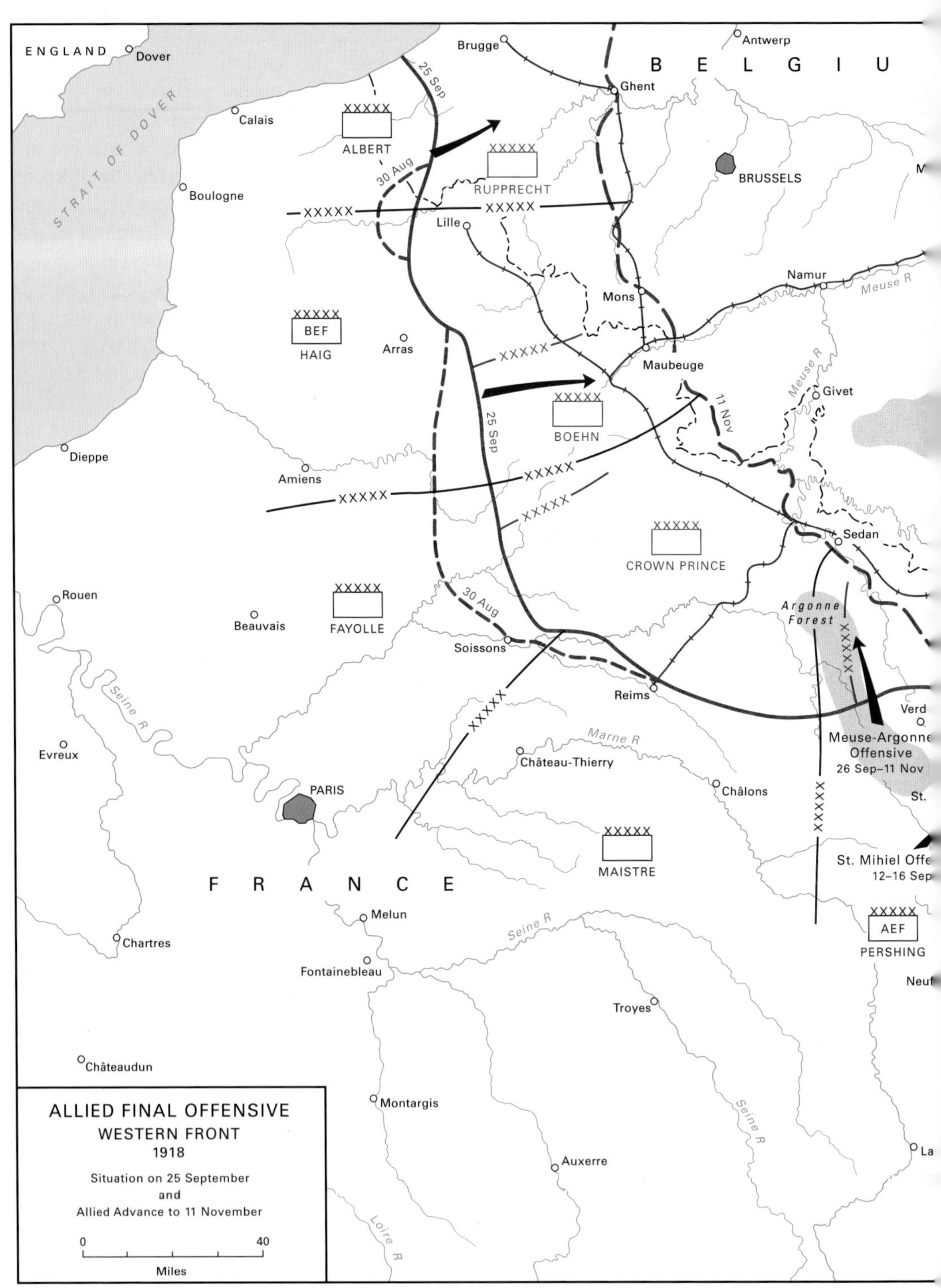
ALLIED FINAL OFFENSIVE
WESTERN FRONT
1918
Situation on 25 September
and
Allied Advance to 11 November
0
40
Miles
ENGLAND
Dover
STRAIT OF DOVER
Calais
Boulogne
Dieppe
Brugge
Antwerp
Ghent
BRUSSELS
ALBERT
RUPPRECHT
BEF
HAIG
FAYOLLE
BOEHN
CROWN PRINCE
MAISTRE
AEF
PERSHING
Lille
Arras
Amiens
Mons
Maubeuge
Namur
Meuse R
Givet
Sedan
Rouen
Beauvais
Soissons
Reims
Evreux
PARIS
Château-Thierry
Marne R
Châlons
Argonne Forest
Meuse-Argonne
Offensive
26 Sep–11 Nov
Seine R
Melun
Fontainebleau
Chartres
Troyes
Châteaudun
Montargis
Auxerre
Loire R
F R A N C E
25 Sep
30 Aug
11 Nov

Map 1

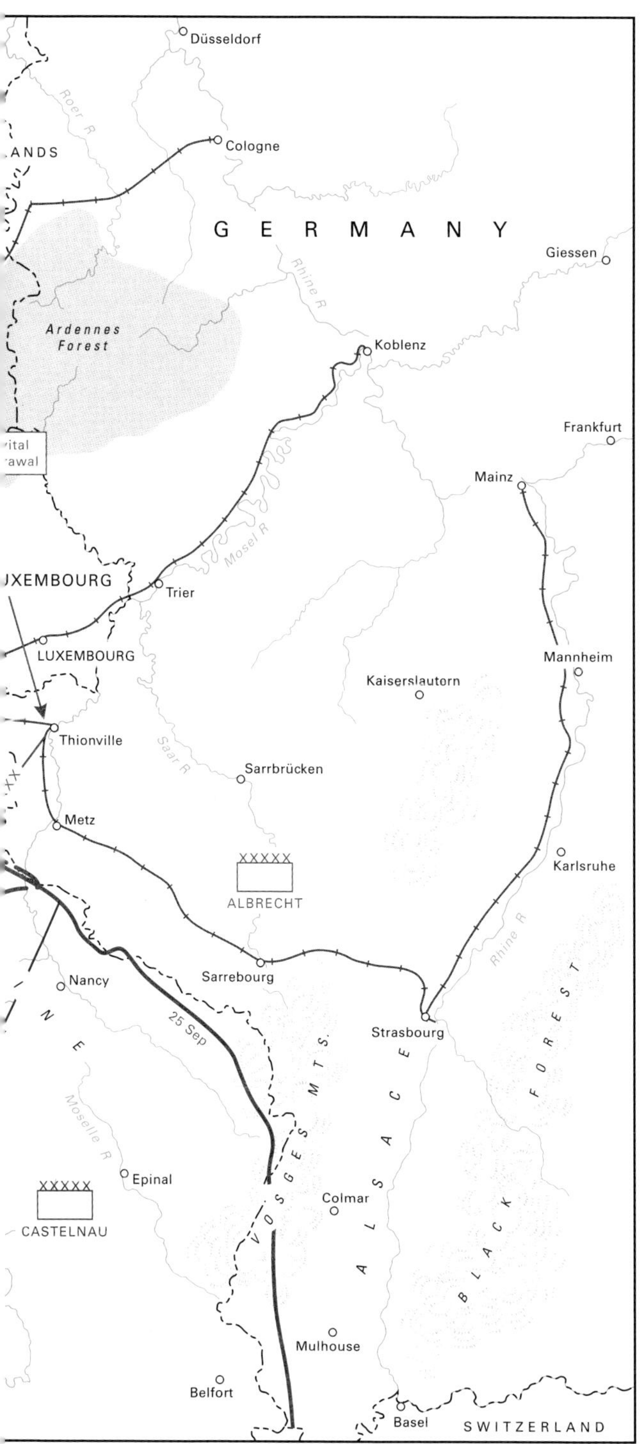

These efforts to justify retention of the Tank Corps as an independent entity failed to leverage foreign ideas and experiences. French tank design initially sought to provide a mobile artillery platform. Later designs, including the FT–17, focused on direct support of the infantry and greater mobility and survivability. Vehicle design and tactical ideas began to move beyond the trenches, focusing on more mobile pursuit and exploitation operations. In March 1918 the British fielded the Whippet tank, specifically designed to exploit breaches in German lines made by the heavier Mark IV and Mark V tanks. J. F. C. Fuller, a British tank officer who would gain worldwide attention for his postwar writings on the use of the tank, in 1918 formulated a strategy for defeating the Germans. In "Plan 1919," Fuller advocated the use of armored vehicles to strike deep into the enemy's rear area to destroy headquarters and lines of supply/communication. Such havoc aimed at undermining Germany's ability to mount an effective defense.[29]

Corps and Medium Tank Development Program," *Military Affairs* XXXVII, no. 1 (February 1973): 21.

[29] D. J. Fletcher, "The Origins of Armour," in Harris and Toase, *Armoured Warfare*, p. 18; Michael Carver, *The Apostles of Mobility: The Theory and Practice of Armoured Warfare* (New York: Holmes and Meier Publishers, 1979), pp. 31–33. "Plan 1919" can be found as an appendix in J. F. C. Fuller, *Memoirs of an Unconventional Soldier* (London: Nicholson & Watson, 1936).

Ford M1918 3-ton tank

The American Tank Corps largely dismissed these developments. Indeed, Rockenbach boasted of the absence of impractical British theoretical influences on the organization and doctrine of the Tank Corps and the absence of any French influence on tank design concepts. Fuller's views regarding tank operations were depicted as futuristic and unsuited to the technological and financial realities of the postwar era.[30]

Ironically, Fuller's vision of fast-moving armored columns striking deep into enemy territory offered a clear role for the tank that the American Tank Corps might have used to justify its continued existence. Instead, the Tank Corps disappeared amid congressional restructuring of the Army. Congress sought the views of the military in determining how best to incorporate the tank within the Army's force structure. In testimony before Congress, Tank Corps members failed to present clear doctrinal roles for the tank other than infantry support, while General Pershing recommended the tank's subordination to the Infantry. Congress opted to cease financing the administrative overhead costs of an organization whose demonstrated function clearly demanded association with the Infantry. The passage of the National Defense Act of 1920 formally abolished the Tank Corps.[31]

The War Department and the National Defense Act of 1920

During the interwar period American military development proceeded according to policies established by the War Department and within the structure and organizational functions defined by the National Defense Act of 1920. These twin influences provided regulatory and legal parameters for military activity. They established the framework within which the branches of service would interact and how branch-specific developments, including tank development, would occur.

The American military consisted of two major elements: a field army of regionally designated components and a War Department located in Washington. The latter provided the administrative link between the field forces and the civilian government. The regional forces possessed an internal unity of command, but the War Department functioned as a "hydra-headed holding company, an arrangement industrialists were finding increasingly wasteful and inefficient."[32] A civilian

[30] Rockenbach, "Tanks," 4 Jun 23, pp. 67–70; S. D. Rockenbach, "Discussion," *Infantry Journal* XXX, no. 5 (May 1927): 465–68; Charles Messenger, *The Blitzkrieg Story* (New York: Charles Scribner's Sons, 1976), p. 48.

[31] U.S. Congress, House, *Hearings Before Committee on Military Affairs*, 66th Cong., 1st Sess., 2 vols., 1919, 1: 529–30; Timothy K. Nenninger, "The Development of American Armor, 1917–1940," Master's Thesis, University of Wisconsin, 1968, p. 62; Steadman, "Evolution of the Tank," p. 3.

[32] Hewes, *Root to McNamara*, p. 5.

Chart 1—War Department Bureau System, 1917

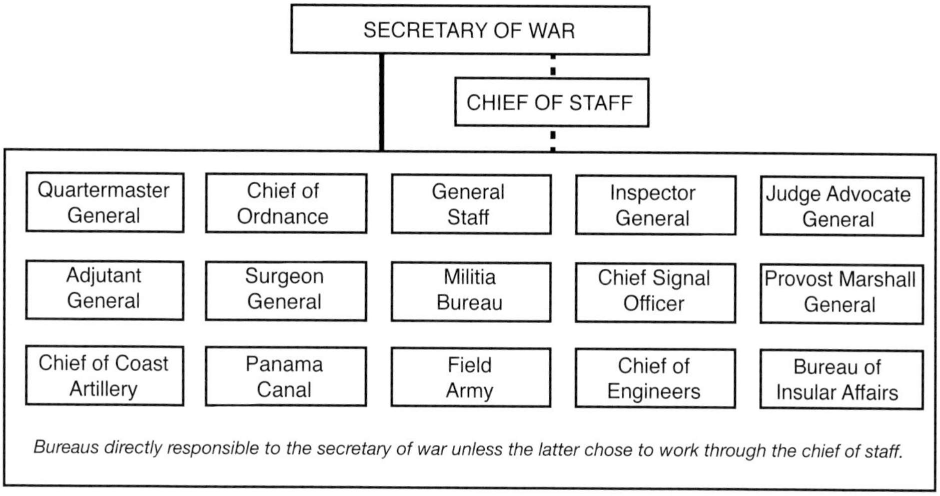

SECRETARY OF WAR

CHIEF OF STAFF

Quartermaster General	Chief of Ordnance	General Staff	Inspector General	Judge Advocate General
Adjutant General	Surgeon General	Militia Bureau	Chief Signal Officer	Provost Marshall General
Chief of Coast Artillery	Panama Canal	Field Army	Chief of Engineers	Bureau of Insular Affairs

Bureaus directly responsible to the secretary of war unless the latter chose to work through the chief of staff.

secretary of war headed the War Department, but he relied on a collection of bureau chiefs for advice on military affairs. Each bore responsibility for specific areas of military administration (*Chart 1*).[33]

The War Department General Staff stood apart from the bureau chiefs. Its purpose lay in planning and preparation for future conflicts. The chief of the General Staff was intended to be the senior and ranking officer in the U.S. Army and to serve as the sole military adviser to the secretary of war. He would provide the central guidance necessary to coordinate bureau activities and prevent a recurrence of the administrative conditions that nearly spelled disaster for the Army in the Spanish-American War. Congress made the General Staff and its functions law on 14 February 1903.[34]

The bureau chiefs, however, refused to relinquish their independence. Through their intransigence, they undermined the chief of staff's authority, reducing his position to little more than an arbiter of petty administrative disputes. They also forced the secretary of war to choose between the chief of staff and the bureau chiefs for his principal military advice. In doing so the bureau chiefs refused to acknowledge the chief of staff's primacy and ignored the purpose of the General Staff's creation. They opposed the authority of the chief of staff in order to retain their own independence and to secure the interests of their bureaus.[35]

---

[33] Graham A. Cosmas, *An Army for Empire: The United States Army in the Spanish-American War* (Columbia: University of Missouri Press, 1971), pp. 14–15; Mark Skinner Watson, *Chief of Staff: Prewar Plans and Preparations*, U.S. Army in World War II (Washington, D.C.: U.S. Army Center of Military History, 1950), p. 57.

[34] Millett and Maslowski, *For the Common Defense*, pp. 263, 310; Watson, *Chief of Staff*, pp. 57–58; Palmer, *Newton D. Baker*, 1: 29–31, 67.

[35] Hewes, *Root to McNamara*, pp. 10–11; Palmer, *Newton D. Baker*, 1: 33–35; Watson, *Chief of Staff*, p. 58.

General Rockenbach (*second from left*) with Tank Corps officers in France. George S. Patton Jr., a wartime colonel, is on *far right*.

The administrative strength of the bureau chiefs lay in bureaucratic precedent and the permanence of their tenures. Immune to the political fluctuations affecting the chief of staff and secretary of war, theirs was an influence recognized by its longevity. Their permanency enabled the accumulation of a wealth of specialized knowledge unmatched by the chief of staff or the War Department General Staff. Only the continuous support of succeeding secretaries of war for the chief of staff and exclusive reliance on him for advice in military affairs could have created a new bureaucratic structure enabling the chief of staff to fulfill the responsibilities legally assigned him. However, between 1904 and 1917, only one secretary of war, Henry L. Stimson, worked through the chief of staff.[36]

The bureau chiefs manipulated the willingness of succeeding secretaries of war to bypass the chief of staff and embarked on their own legislative effort to further curb the power of the entire War Department General Staff. The National Defense Act of 1916 recorded their triumph, precluding the chief of staff and General Staff from interfering in bureau actions and reducing the size of the latter. Popular fears of militarism and a political heritage of antipathy toward a standing army aided their efforts by creating a political climate unreceptive to the administrative rationalization of the War Department.[37] Moreover, the bureau system seemed to work. It proved

[36] Hewes, *Root to McNamara*, pp. 5, 13–14; Cosmas, *Army for Empire*, p. 36. Henry L. Stimson is more commonly remembered as President Franklin D. Roosevelt's secretary of war from July 1940 to September 1945, but he also served in this capacity from May 1911 until March 1913 under President William Howard Taft.

[37] United States, *National Defense Act Approved June 3, 1916*, 1918, sec. 5, pp. 3–4; Hewes, *Root to McNamara*, pp. 19–21; Watson, *Chief of Staff*, p. 58; March, *Nation at War*, pp. 44–46.

adequate for the administration of a small army stationed for the most part within the United States.

America's entrance into World War I exposed the weaknesses of the bureau system. The U.S. Army proved incapable of mobilizing and sustaining the large-scale overseas deployment mandated by American strategy. The confusion and chaos that plagued the Army in the Spanish-American War reemerged on a larger scale, and only the materiel aid of the British and French prevented the complete bankruptcy of the American war effort in 1917. Acknowledgment of this failure led Secretary of War Newton D. Baker to abandon his own reliance on the bureau chiefs and support the chief of staff's efforts to subordinate the bureau chiefs to his authority.[38]

By November 1918, the chief of staff controlled, coordinated, and supervised the military through the General Staff, itself organized on a functional basis in the form of directorates (*see Chart 2*). The chief of staff was free to establish guiding principles and policy measures that the directors implemented. The Directorate of Purchase, Storage, and Traffic was perhaps the most important, since it provided the link between the War Department and industry and exerted a central influence over supply and procurement matters. The emergence of the directorates, however, did not eliminate the bureau chiefs.[39]

After the war, legislative concern over the administrative problems that weakened the American war effort became interwoven with broader questions concerning the unsatisfactory relations between the National Guard and the federal Army; the need for a federal reserve separate from the National Guard; and whether to establish the Army as a professional cadre capable of expansion through wartime conscription. The congressional response to these questions was the National Defense Act of 4 June 1920. It provided for an Army of two hundred eighty thousand men divided into corps areas within the United States, a closer affiliation of the National Guard with the federal Army, and the creation of a federal reserve.[40]

The 1920 act reflected the continued faith placed in the traditional and familiar horizontal structure of the War Department. The wartime imperative to rationalize the War Department organization ended with the armistice, and its absence stimulated the renewed opposition of the bureau chiefs to the authority of the chief of staff. The War Department returned to its prewar bureau organization, and the power of the bureau chiefs was restored. A permanent assistant secretary of war assumed responsibility for military procurement and industrial mobilization, relying on the advice of the

---

[38] Hewes, *Root to McNamara*, p. 39; March, *Nation at War*, pp. 49–50, 191; Reinhardt and Kintner, *Haphazard Years*, p. 63.

[39] Hewes, *Root to McNamara*, pp. 45, 49; March, *Nation at War*, pp. 40, 187–89; Watson, *Chief of Staff*, p. 61.

[40] U.S. War Department (WD), *The National Defense Act Approved June 3, 1916 as Amended by Act Approved August 29, 1916; Act Approved July 9, 1918; Act Approved February 28, 1919; Act Approved July 11, 1919; Act Approved September 29, 1919; Act Approved June 4, 1920*, 1920, secs. 2 and 3, p. 5; Millett and Maslowski, *For the Common Defense*, pp. 366–67; Ronald Spector, "The Military Effectiveness of the U.S. Armed Forces, 1919–1939," in Millett and Murray, *Military Effectiveness*, 2: 71.

Chart 2–War Department Rationalization, 1918

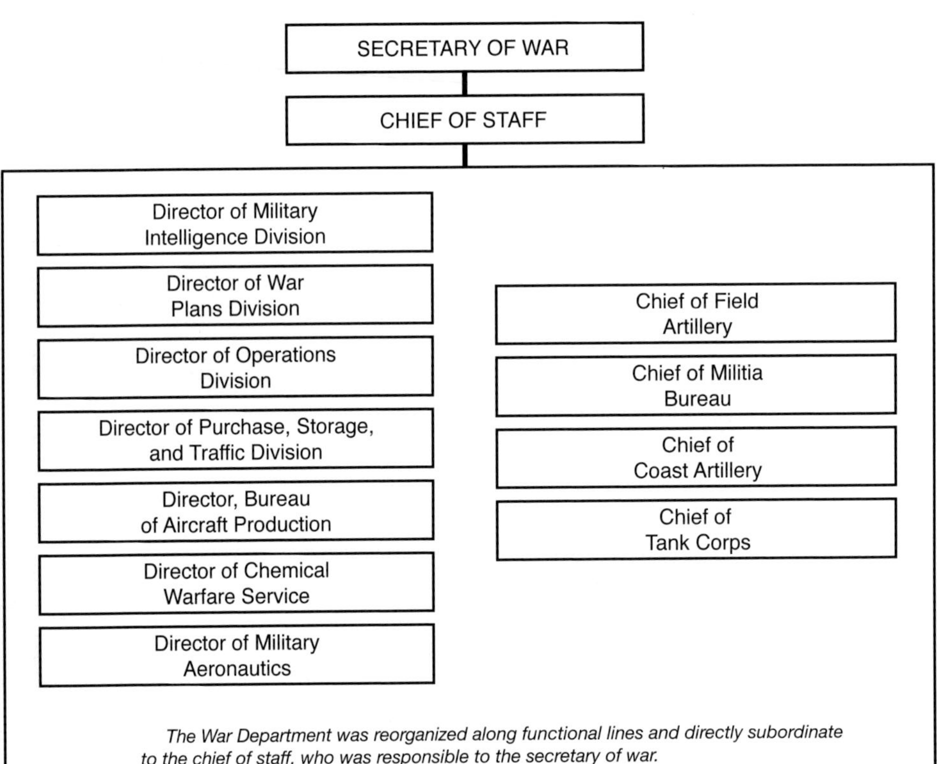

The War Department was reorganized along functional lines and directly subordinate to the chief of staff, who was responsible to the secretary of war.

reorganized Supply Services. This change simply refined the bureau system to permit the coordination of industrial capacity and the Army's wartime needs.[41]

In effect, the General Staff became a de facto bureau among many that reported directly to the secretary of war. Its duties, under the guidance of the chief of staff, included mobilization, strategic planning, and training. The National Defense Act of 1920 also restricted the number of General Staff officers that could be assigned to Washington and prohibited them from becoming involved in the affairs of any established bureau. Neither the chief nor the General Staff possessed any authority over the bureau chiefs; nor did they constitute the secretary of war's principal source of military advice. The chief of staff had the authority to provide general guidance to the bureaus, but he had no means to ensure its implementation.[42]

The dramatic curtailment of the General Staff's influence stemmed from the confluence of popular fears of militarism and antiwar sentiment. The resultant polit-

---

[41] WD, *The Work of the War Department of the United States* (Washington, D.C.: Government Printing Office, 1924) p. 11; Watson, *Chief of Staff*, p. 63.

[42] WD, *National Defense Act*, 1920, sec. 5, p. 10.

Tank Corps assembly area in France, September 1918

ical climate ensured widespread suspicion of an efficient, vertically organized War Department. The inefficient, horizontally organized bureau system found acceptance in the postwar period precisely because it posed no danger to civilian government and permitted detailed congressional supervision of military spending.[43]

During the interwar period, the fiscal policy of succeeding administrations with respect to military spending remained generally one of parsimony. The president's financial policy, not military needs, determined the level of military appropriations requested of Congress and undermined military efforts to maintain an army realistically capable of defending national interests. In this atmosphere bureau chiefs within the military availed themselves of the congressional access afforded by the House and Senate committee hearings on military appropriations to emphasize the importance of their particular arm of service and, by their testimony, to encourage Congress to channel additional funds directly to their own bureaus. Consequently, bureau competition acquired financial and political undertones that emerged in the testimonies given by the chiefs of the service arms before congressional committees.[44]

Given the lack of any significant military threat to the United States, the traditional American aversion to a large professional army, and an increase in antiwar

---

[43] Ibid., pp. 9–10; Hewes, *Root to McNamara*, p. 50; Watson, *Chief of Staff*, p. 63.

[44] Spector, "Military Effectiveness, 1919–39," pp. 71–73; Watson, *Chief of Staff*, pp. 21–22; Green, Thomas, and Roots, *Ordnance Department*, p. 48. The annual reports of succeeding secretaries of war also reveal the weakened state of the Army and the impact of underfunding.

Tank Corps FT–17s being readied for rail transport

sentiment, Congress did not assign military spending a high priority. The Senate's rejection of the Versailles Treaty also eliminated the need to retain a large army capable of rapid deployment to Europe to enforce actions taken by the League of Nations. Consequently, military spending remained low throughout the 1920s and spurred the War Department bureaus to compete for the limited financial resources available.[45]

The extension of the bureau system into the field army and the elimination of the army's unity of command constituted congressional reaffirmation of the administrative principles inherent in the bureau system. Under the National Defense Act of 1920, separate chiefs of the Cavalry, Infantry, Air Service, and Chemical Warfare Service complemented the already existing chiefs of Field Artillery, Coast Artillery Corps, and Corps of Engineers; but their tenure was limited to four years in contrast to the permanency of the prewar bureau chiefs. The proliferation of bureau chiefs mandated an assignment of purpose by the War Department to each one, appropriately worded to prevent duplication of effort and overlapping spheres of influence. Consequently, each chief received a mission assignment governing the tasks for which his bureau was responsible. Applied to the combat arms, the missions predicated peacetime courses of development. In wartime they prescribed the manner in which the combat arms would function on the battlefield. In both cases each combat arm would pursue its own mutually exclusive goal.[46]

A professional and personal imperative reinforced this separation of interests. The National Defense Act of 1920 provided for one promotion list for the entire Army; but beneath the rank of brigadier general, officers were still identified according to branch of service and their assignment derived from this branch affiliation. Branch

[45] John R. M. Wilson, "The Quaker and the Sword: Herbert Hoover's Relations with the Military," *Military Affairs* XXXVIII, no. 2 (April 1974): 41–47.

[46] WD, *National Defense Act*, 1920, sec. 4C, p. 8; Hewes, *Root to McNamara*, p. 51.

affiliation was further enhanced by the June 1920 grade reduction and the generally slow rate of promotion during the interwar period. Most officers beneath the rank of colonel waited at least ten years before promotion. Thus a majority of officers in the interwar period remained in junior grades within their parent branch learning how to implement the missions assigned to that combat arm more effectively. Upon their ability to do so rested their chances for promotion.[47]

In applying the compartmentalization of the War Department's bureau system to the field forces, Congress discouraged any analysis of combat operations and doctrine that transcended bureau mission assignments. These missions collectively represented traditional views of warfare modified through creation of the Air Service and the Chemical Warfare Service. They did not provide an elasticity enabling the U.S. Army as a whole to respond mentally to a combat environment changing in accord with the emergence of new military technologies. Instead, the National Defense Act of 1920 created an administrative barrier to interarm cooperation and the development of the modern combined-arms concept. No incentive existed for an officer to circumvent or ignore the mission orientation of his parent arm in pursuit of a different and perhaps more effective manner of conducting battle.

Section 17 of the National Defense Act of 1920 assigned responsibility for tank development to the newly created chief of Infantry, thereby creating an obstacle to the future expansion of the tank's role beyond infantry support and discouraging officers from developing new perceptions of warfare in which the tank played a prominent, if not dominant, role on the battlefield. The Tank Corps comprised personnel whose sole professional interest was the effective use of the tank on the battlefield. This organization tended to safeguard the continued existence of the weapon and encouraged further analysis of its potential. Its subordination to the chief of Infantry meant that tank development would be governed by roles assigned to the Infantry on the basis of that arm's traditional mission.[48]

Infantry Tank Development

Reflecting their new legal role as infantry support weapons, American tanks were deployed throughout the United States in small concentrations with parent Infantry units. The Tank School, with now-Colonel Rockenbach as its commandant, remained at Camp Meade with one heavy tank battalion; one light tank battalion; and affiliated repair, salvage, and maintenance elements.[49] Infantry divisions received one tank company each; and the Infantry School at Fort Benning, Georgia, became host to a tank battalion for instructional purposes. In a parallel distribution, the National Guard received fifteen light tank companies dispersed among Guard formations throughout the United States.[50]

---

[47] WD, *National Defense Act*, 1920, sec. 24C, p. 20; Spector, "Military Effectiveness, 1919–39," p. 77.

[48] WD, *National Defense Act, 1920*, sec. 17, p. 15.

[49] Rockenbach, like every other officer promoted during the war years, reverted to his prewar rank following the war's end.

[50] Rockenbach, "Tanks," pp. 59–60; Steadman, "Evolution of the Tank," p. 10.

FT–17s being loaded onto truck carriers in the 1920s

This new administrative arrangement originated from Rockenbach's earlier recommendations for a postwar Tank Corps structure. It differed from Rockenbach's intent only in its limited scale and the permanent subordination of the tank to the Infantry. As a component of the Infantry, the tank force did not require a separate body to determine the tank's function. Consequently, the Tank Board disappeared. Its duties concerning the creation of training and doctrinal manuals became Tank School responsibilities.[51]

As the principal and senior tank officer within the Army, Rockenbach's presence ensured continuity between the World War I experience and postwar developments. The appointment of Maj. Sereno E. Brett, an instructor and tank brigade commander during the war, to command the tank battalion stationed at the Infantry School further reinforced this continuity. Their service offset the loss of many ex–Tank Corps officers, including Patton and Eisenhower. The former transferred back to the Cavalry in 1920, and the latter to the staff of Brig. Gen. Fox Conner's infantry brigade in Panama in 1922.[52]

The Tank School at Camp Meade remained the focal point of tank developments throughout the 1920s. It provided instruction to Regular Army, Organized Reserve, and National Guard officers. It collated information and data collected from tank officers throughout the United States and redistributed it to tank officers in the form of pamphlets entitled "Tank Notes." Through the efforts of the Tank School, interested officers kept abreast of tank activities in the United States and received some indication of parallel foreign activities. The high cost of fuel and maintenance, however, greatly curtailed field maneuvers. The limitations of the tanks themselves resulted in exercises in which Mark VIII tanks towed M1917 light tanks through predetermined lanes to compensate for the latter's poor engine power.[53]

---

[51] Rockenbach, "Tank Corps," 19 Sep 19, pp. 10–11; Messenger, *Blitzkrieg Story*, p. 50; Nenninger, "Development of American Armor," pp. 62, 68.

[52] Nenninger, "Development of American Armor," p. 62; Wilson, *Treat 'Em Rough*, pp. 227–31; Blumenson, *Patton Papers*, 1: 740–41.

[53] "Report of the Chief of the Tank Corps," 30 Jun 20, 1: 1896; Nenninger, "Development of American Armor," pp. 62, 68, 73; Miller, *Ike*, p. 185; Eisenhower, *At Ease*, pp. 170–71.

Combined tank and infantry training at Fort Benning

Within the Infantry, ideas governing tank use stemmed from Tank Corps experience and the mission emphasis of the military. The purpose of the tank was to assist the advance of the infantryman and prevent the degeneration of an offensive war of movement into positional warfare. In fulfilling this task, tanks were expected to function in two primary roles. First, breakthrough tanks would support the main offensive and bear responsibility for clearing obstacles to the infantry's advance. Second, accompanying tanks moving with the infantry would directly assist them to achieve their objectives. In the tank force of the day, the Mark VIII would perform the first role and the M1917 the second. This conception of the tank's function originated from Tank Corps efforts in World War I to blend French and British tank tactics into a single, unified doctrine. It found official sanction in a pamphlet entitled *The Employment of Tanks in Combat*, published as a text for use at the Command and General Staff School at Fort Leavenworth, Kansas, in 1925.[54]

The postwar refinement of earlier doctrinal concepts reflected the Tank Corps' early dependence on the French for much of its training and equipment, as well as the continued respect within the U.S. Army for the French military. The tactical roles assigned to American tanks paralleled those performed by their French counterparts. Rockenbach considered the similarity between French and American postwar tank doctrines indicative of the correctness of American efforts.[55]

---

[54] R. H. Allen, "A Resume of Tank Development in the United States," Lecture at U.S. Army War College (AWC), 27 Oct 29, pp. 2–3, AWC Curricular Archives, MHI Archives; Rockenbach, "The Tank Corps," 19 Sep 19, p. 27; General Service Schools (GSS), *The Employment of Tanks in Combat* (Fort Leavenworth, Kans.: General Service Schools Press, 1925).

[55] Allen, "Resume of Tank Development," 27 Oct 29, pp. 10–11; Notes of Discussion Following Lecture by Maj. Gen. George A. Lynch, Chief of Infantry, p. 5, 20 Sep 38 (hereafter cited as Lynch Discussion Notes), AWC Curricular Archives; Rockenbach, "Tank Corps," 19 Sep 19, pp. 10–11.

Tank School instruction at Fort George G. Meade in the 1920s

Despite the efforts of the Tank School, however, development of tank use within the Infantry remained slow throughout the 1920s. No organization exclusively performed the study and preparation of training manuals or conducted theoretical studies as the Tank Board had done. The tasks previously fulfilled by the board devolved on training officers whose duties precluded full-time devotion to this additional task. A Tank Board was recreated in 1924, but its four members were expected to treat board responsibility as a part-time endeavor. Not until 1928 did the board grow to three full-time Infantry officers: the commandant and assistant commandant of the Tank School and one officer from the Ordnance Department.[56]

The tanks themselves contributed to the slow progress of tank development. The large number of M1917 light tanks and Mark VIII heavy tanks created an illusion of tank strength that hid the need for funding new designs suited to the Army's contemporary needs rather than those of the Western Front. The number of vehicles also did not address the tank fleet's poor mechanical condition. The M1917 suffered from major defects that required an estimated 225 man-hours per tank to rectify. The FT–17s and Mark Vs brought to the United States with the returning American Expeditionary Forces also required major overhauling. No tanks were battle ready when the National Defense Act of 1920 became law.[57]

---

[56] Messenger, *Blitzkrieg Story*, p. 50; Nenninger, "Development of American Armor," p. 74.

[57] "Report of the Chief of the Tank Corps," 30 Jun 20, 1: 1891, 1894; Hofmann, "Demise of the Tank Corps," p. 21.

The available vehicles dissatisfied Rockenbach. Too few Mark Vs existed; the Mark VIII was too heavy, too long, and exceptionally slow; the M1917 possessed limited firepower and poor visibility, and it was too small. Both the Mark VIII and M1917 proved mechanically unreliable, and the continuous investment in money and man-hours to maintain them constituted an onerous financial drain. Maintenance expenses for these vehicles further reduced the already limited funding available for the development of new tanks. To control these expenses, tank participation in field exercises was reduced.[58]

Between 1920 and 1932, the Army budget for mechanization was $2 million, or approximately $167,000 per year. The total cost of a Mark VIII was $85,000, and Ordnance Department budgets for tank development allowed for building only one experimental model per year between 1925 and 1931.[59] The Army's tank fleet thus became more obsolescent and more expensive to maintain with each passing year.

The development of better tanks suffered from financial restraints and the apparent apathy of the General Staff. The effective design, development, and production of a tank necessitated the cooperation of the Ordnance Department, the Infantry, and the General Staff; but not until 1922 did the latter issue guidelines for tank development. Indeed, the field service regulations of 1923 disavowed widespread usage of tanks because of their exclusive suitability to positional warfare. This perception of the tank, however, stemmed from the General Staff's failure to establish requirements for new tank designs suited to the current operational environment.[60]

Despite the tardiness of the General Staff in establishing tank requirements, Rockenbach continued to develop his own design ideas. He envisioned the design and development of a tank as a two-step process: 1) determination of the tank's function and 2) creation of a compatible design. From his wartime experience Rockenbach perceived the former as assisting an infantry advance through artificial obstacles and defensive lines. Consequently, tanks should be designed to accompany the infantry everywhere, negotiate prepared defenses, and withstand small-arms fire.[61]

Like most American officers Rockenbach considered the trench deadlock of the Western Front an aberration of warfare rather than an indication of future trends. He rejected the Mark VIII heavy tank as the basis for design evolution because it had been built exclusively for the conditions of the Western Front. Tanks required greater cross-country mobility. Mexico, not Flanders, figured prominently in the 1920s as a likely battlefield for American troops.[62]

---

[58] Rockenbach, "American Tanks Since the World War," 1923, p. 2.

[59] Badsey, "American Experience of Armour," p. 127; Icks, "Four Decades of Mechanization," pp. 335–36; Steadman, "Evolution of the Tank," p. 4.

[60] WD, *Field Service Regulations, United States Army*, 1923; Green, Thomson, and Roots, *Ordnance Department*, pp. 190–91; Hofmann, "Demise of the Tank Corps," p. 24; Messenger, *Blitzkrieg Story*, pp. 49–50; Steadman, "Evolution of the Tank," p. 4.

[61] Rockenbach, "Tank Corps," 19 Sep 19, p. 7.

[62] Rockenbach, "American Tanks Since the World War," 1923, pp. 2–3.

M1917 reconfigured as a communications vehicle

Rockenbach devoted himself to the design of a medium tank capable of performing both leading and accompanying tank roles. By merging these capabilities in a single platform, he sought to reduce development costs. He established twenty-nine characteristics for a medium tank that included movement under its own power on and off the battlefield; a top speed of twelve miles per hour; an armament of one cannon and two machine guns; a 360-degree field of fire; the ability to cross a nine-foot-wide trench; and armor sufficient to resist .50-caliber ammunition. The entire vehicle could not weigh more than fifteen tons, which was considered the maximum weight limit of highway and pontoon bridges.[63]

These requirements reflected Rockenbach's assessment of combat operations and future battlefield requirements. Realizing all these requirements in a single, 15-ton platform, however, exceeded the level of American tank expertise and related technology in the 1920s. Between 1921 and 1925 the Ordnance Department built three medium tank models, but none incorporated all of Rockenbach's requirements. They all exceeded fifteen tons and proved unsatisfactory.[64]

Design tradeoffs followed. Ordnance Department engineers reassessed Rockenbach's original requirements to determine which of them must be

---

[63] Ibid., pp. 3–4; Rockenbach, "Weight and Dimension of Tanks," Feb 23, MHI Library; Allen, "Resume of Tank Development," 27 Oct 29, pp. 2–3.

[64] Icks, "Four Decades of Mechanization," pp. 336–37; Steadman, "Evolution of the Tank," p. 5; Hofmann, "Demise of the Tank Corps," p. 24.

retained. To fight in the envisioned war of maneuver, the engineers did not believe tanks needed the heavy firepower, armor, and trench-crossing ability associated with the British wartime tanks or the Mark VIII. These characteristics added materially to the overall weight of the design. Compromises in these areas yielded a lighter vehicle able to keep pace with the tempo of infantry operations. The reduced weight mitigated engine stress and offered the promise of greater mechanical reliability. Consequently, the Ordnance Department began to embrace a light tank concept that also received the support of Chief of Infantry Maj. Gen. R. H. Allen.[65]

The T series of light tanks resulted. Designed as a light, fast tank suitable for portage by a 5-ton commercial truck, the first model fulfilled a collaborative effort between the Ordnance Department and the Society of Automotive Engineers. It embraced the newest advances in automotive technology, including the link-type springless suspension and use of an all-purpose chassis to facilitate standardization. Armament consisted of a 37-mm. cannon and a machine gun. First demonstrated in October 1927, the T–1 light tank proved unexpectedly rugged and reliable. These qualities suggested the ability to build tanks that would not depend on tank carriers for movement to and from the battlefield.[66]

Further encouragement for the Army's shift toward light tank designs came from the publicity awarded the tanks designed and built by inventor J. Walter Christie. Between 1919 and 1928, Christie's tanks achieved cross-country speeds of forty miles per hour, forded rivers, moved on either wheels or tracks, and went forward and backward at equal speeds. They also did not depend on a special transport vehicle. Nevertheless, the Army never adopted any of Christie's tanks for standardization, since they proved too expensive and ill suited for the harsh conditions of field operations. Christie's own personality also discouraged close association. Convinced of his own inventive genius, he showed little interest in working alongside Ordnance Department engineers. Moreover, he expected to retain patent rights and reap a financial reward for any design the Army adopted. Even so, the Ordnance Department showed consistent interest in Christie's work throughout the 1920s and purchased several tank models for study.[67]

Christie's designs highlighted the technological strides made since the war's end. Improvements in vehicle reliability in particular eliminated the tank's dependence on special carriers. During the war tanks relied on railways and trucks for movement everywhere except on the battlefield. However, the movement of a column of tank-laden trucks barely exceeded three miles per hour, which greatly restricted tank usage in an environment other than that of positional warfare. A tank that could

---

[65] Icks, "Four Decades of Mechanization," p. 337; Allen, "Resume of Tank Development," 27 Oct 29, pp. 3–4.

[66] Icks, "Four Decades of Mechanization," pp. 337–38; Allen, "Resume of Tank Development," 27 Oct 29, pp. 4–5.

[67] Allen, "Resume of Tank Development," 27 Oct 29, pp. 2–3; George F. Hofmann, "A Yankee Inventor and the Military Establishment: The Christie Tank Controversy," *Military Affairs* XXXIX, no. 1 (February 1975): 9–10.

A Mark VIII and M1917s execute an attack on a defended trench during training in the 1920s.

safely rely on its own engine both on and off the battlefield increased the versatility of the weapon and reduced road congestion. Tank units that did not require organic tank carriers also reduced the cost and personnel necessary for such a unit and eased the task of maintenance, all without loss of combat value. The erstwhile carriers themselves could be released for logistical purposes.[68]

Reconsidering the Tank's Battlefield Role

Despite passage of the National Defense Act of 1920, many officers continued to speculate about alternate tank uses. Collectively, they concluded that the tank would not reach its potential if restricted to an infantry support role. Yet aside from this commonly stressed point little else bound these individual viewpoints together. They did not represent the official views of any particular branch, nor did they possess any uniformity in their conception of alternate uses and organizations for the tank. The individual efforts of various officers in no way resembled the clarity of intent expressed by the infantry support role assigned the American tank force.

The service journals provided the primary outlet for viewpoints concerning tank use. In 1921 Maj. Bradford G. Chynoweth, an Infantry tank officer, submitted to the *Cavalry Journal* an article emphasizing the applicability of tanks for cavalry missions and their potential to enhance the cavalry trooper as they had the rifleman.

[68] GSS, *Employment of Tanks in Combat*, p. 8; Hofmann, "Christie Tank Controversy," p. 14.

The T–1 light tank, 1929

Other articles advocated tanks as supply carriers, self-propelled artillery, communications vehicles, and a host of other tasks throughout the combat arms.[69]

Outside the service journals, Capt. Joseph Viner, a former Tank Corps member now serving with the Cavalry, authored a provisional manual for the General Service Schools at Fort Leavenworth. He addressed the Tank Corps' history, training measures, and several special missions that tanks might fulfill in addition to the primary role of infantry support. These included raids, pursuit, and advance and rear-guard activities. Despite his leadership of the Infantry's tank force, Rockenbach also continued to suggest the wider applicability of the tank. He specifically recommended the assignment of a tank battalion to the Cavalry School at Fort Riley, Kansas, and a tank company to each Cavalry division.[70]

In 1921 a conference of representatives of the General Service Schools met to discuss tactics and organization of the Infantry tank force. The ensuing discussion quickly embraced a variety of tank applications beyond the scope of the Infantry's mission. The written report of the conference suggested tank support of cavalry, creation of a combined tank and machine-gun unit, and the apportionment of tanks between the division and higher command echelons.[71]

---

[69] Bradford G. Chynoweth, "Cavalry Tanks," *Cavalry Journal* XXX, no. 124 (July 1921): 247–51.

[70] Viner, *Tactics and Techniques of Tanks*; "Report of the Chief of the Tank Corps," 30 Jun 20, 1: 1896; Nenninger, "Development of American Armor," p. 84.

[71] Nenninger, "Development of American Armor," pp. 65–66.

For their efforts to constructively and openly discuss methods of employing the tank, the members of the conference received the criticism of The Adjutant General's Office for deviating from the conference's purpose. Other officers, including Eisenhower, also incurred censure for advocating ideas contravening official tank policy. These incidents exemplified the lack of encouragement for officers to advocate new ideas departing from the mission of their parent branch.[72]

In 1920 the wartime British campaigns in Palestine prompted interest in the use of tanks to perform cavalry roles. Although only a small provisional squadron from the 2d Cavalry Regiment saw combat in World War I, after the war the *Cavalry Journal* stressed the importance of cavalry in the campaigns of the belligerent armies, particularly the British in the Middle East.[73] Field Marshal Viscount Edmund H. H. Allenby, who commanded British forces in Palestine, acknowledged this attention in a written response to the editor of the *Cavalry Journal* published in 1921. He defended the value of horse cavalry in all theaters of operation, including Western Europe, but acknowledged the increase in cavalry effectiveness that might be achieved through the use of trucks, armored cars, and tanks in cooperation with horse cavalry. He freely admitted the obsolescence of horse cavalry in strategic reconnaissance missions compared to aircraft performing the same function. Hardly a statement of doctrine, his two-page letter identified the primary concern of American cavalry in the interwar era: achieving balance between modern mechanical means and the horse.[74]

For much of the decade, however, Cavalry experiments with vehicles focused on armored cars, despite the interest of individual officers in tanks. The exclusive assignment of tanks to the Infantry mandated by Section 17 of the National Defense Act of 1920 limited Cavalry expressions of interest in tanks to the personal opinions of individual officers to which the chief of Cavalry could not give official support. Armored cars were a cheaper and politically simpler alternative to the tank.[75]

The mounted arm's traditional emphasis on firepower and mobility led to the study and acceptance of the armored car as an integral cavalry weapon despite

---

[72] Ibid., p. 67; Stephen E. Ambrose, *Eisenhower*, 2 vols. (New York: Simon and Schuster, 1983), 1: 10; Eisenhower, *At Ease*, p. 97.

[73] Ernest N. Harmon, "The Second Cavalry in the St. Mihiel Offensive," *Cavalry Journal* XXX, no. 124 (July 1921): 282. For examples of the *Cavalry Journal*'s interest in British Cavalry operations in Palestine, see George E. Mitchell, "The Rout of the Turks by Allenby's Cavalry," *Cavalry Journal* XXIX, no. 119 (April 1920): 28–43; George E. Mitchell, "The Rout of the Turks by Allenby's Cavalry," *Cavalry Journal* XXIX, no. 120 (July 1920): 174–205; Edward Davis, "The British Cavalry in Palestine and Syria," *Cavalry Journal* XXXI, no. 127 (April 1922): 123–29 (see Bibliography for Davis' article in subsequent issues); J. R. H. Cruikshank, "From Acre to Aleppo with Allenby," *Cavalry Journal* XXXIII, no. 134 (January 1924): 52–62.

[74] E. H. H. Allenby, Ltr to Editor, *Cavalry Journal* XXX, no. 122 (January 1921): 1–2.

[75] Typical of this interest are G. S. Patton Jr., "Armored Cars with Cavalry," *Cavalry Journal* XXXIII, no. 134 (January 1924): 5–10; W. B. Bradford, "Cavalry Armored Cars: Filling the Gap at Amiens in March, 1918," *Cavalry Journal* XXXIV, no. 140 (July 1925): 299–302; H. S. Hawkins, "The Importance of Modern Cavalry and Its Role as Affected by Developments in Airplane and Tank Warfare," *Cavalry Journal* XXXV, no. 145 (October 1926): 487–99; C. C. Benson, "Armored Car Design," *Cavalry Journal* XXXVIII, no. 155 (April 1929): 196–204.

its relative lack of tactical mobility in comparison with the horse. As mechanical reliability increased, so too did the Cavalry's interest. In 1926 the Cavalry School issued a provisional training manual for armored cars and accepted the armored car as a reconnaissance vehicle.[76] By 1927 the 1st Cavalry Division—the only Cavalry formation whose real strength and organization even approximated that of a division—had been assigned an armored car company. In 1928 the War Department constituted three armored car squadrons on paper and activated one troop.[77] In October 1929 the 1st Cavalry Division used one company in maneuvers along the Mexican border. Although the company's use there reflected problems of command and control, lack of aggressiveness, and the relative ease of disabling the armored car, their rapid speed suited the Cavalry's emphasis on maneuver rather than direct assaults on enemy strongpoints. Secretary of War Dwight F. Davis authorized the joint Cavalry/Ordnance procurement and development of a Christie chassis as an armored car. He soon revoked this authorization in January 1930 because of problems in contract negotiations with Christie.[78]

The publicity that the service journals gave to British experiments with tanks fueled the interest of Cavalry officers in the possibilities of tank use. The British maneuvers of 1925, which introduced the Vickers medium tank, received wide exposure in the service journals and stimulated interest in the tank's viability to perform some Cavalry roles. Despite the demonstrated usefulness of the wheeled armored car, its limited cross-country mobility restricted its ability to maintain the rapid tempo of Cavalry operations. The armored car indicated how mechanical means might be used to enhance performance of Cavalry missions, but its road-bound nature prevented maximum realization of this enhancement. Awareness of new British tank designs and the Christie tanks suggested the tank as a possible successor.[79]

In 1927 Secretary of War Davis acted on a proposal by Chief of Cavalry Maj. Gen. Herbert B. Crosby and assigned a tank unit, an armored car unit, and an Air Corps observation squadron to Cavalry divisions. But this action occurred on paper and contradicted the intent of Section 17 of the National Defense Act of 1920. The following year a platoon of Renault light tanks transported in trucks was used in the 1st Cavalry Division maneuvers; but the tank's slowness reinforced the desire for a light, fast tank independent of any carrier.[80]

---

[76] Cav Sch, Academic Div, "Armored Cars," Fort Riley, Kans., 1926, MHI Library.

[77] U.S. Adjutant General's Office, *Official Army Register* (Washington, D.C.: Government Printing Office, 1931), p. 1294.

[78] E. C. McGuire, "Armored Cars in the Cavalry Maneuvers," *Cavalry Journal* XXXIX, no. 160 (July 1930): 386–99; George S. Patton Jr., "The 1929 Cavalry Division Maneuvers," *Cavalry Journal* XXXIX, no. 158 (January 1930): 9–10; George S. Patton Jr., "Tactical Lessons Derived from the Cavalry Division Maneuvers, October, 1929," 27 Nov 29, in Blumenson, *Patton Papers*, 1: 865.

[79] C. C. Benson, "Mechanization—Aloft and Alow," *Cavalry Journal* XXXVIII, no. 154 (January 1929): 61–62; Chynoweth, "Cavalry Tanks," pp. 247–51; Kenyon A. Joyce, "The British Army Maneuvers 1925," *Cavalry Journal* XXXV, no. 142 (January 1926): 17–28; Messenger, *Blitzkrieg Story*, p. 51; William J. Woolley, "Patton and the Concept of Mechanized Warfare," *Parameters* XV, no. 3 (Autumn 1985): 75–76.

[80] Nenninger, "Development of American Armor," p. 84; George Dillman, "1st Cavalry Division Maneuvers," *Cavalry Journal* XXXVII, no. 150 (January 1928): 63.

Christie T–3 tank, 1932

The Experimental Mechanized Force

In 1927 the British Army created the Experimental Mechanised Force to develop concepts to guide the organization and employment of a combat force built around tanks and armored vehicles. Secretary of War Davis observed the activities of this force during a visit to England the same year. The experience so impressed him that upon his return to the United States he ordered the establishment of a similar American force. It would test the viability of using tanks in roles other than infantry support and marked a belated awareness that accompanying riflemen into battle might not constitute the tank's definitive role.[81]

Hence, the American Experimental Mechanized Force assembled at Camp Meade, where it measured its brief existence from 1 July to 20 September 1928. Its strength centered on its tanks, supported by cavalry and infantry elements. War Department guidance directed that the unit be considered a special force for select missions rather than an organic division asset.[82]

As a combat organization the Experimental Mechanized Force posed no significant military threat. The tanks on which its fighting power depended included the same Mark VIIIs and M1917s that Rockenbach had already rejected as unsuitable for the postwar Army. The other vehicles included nearly thirty different types

---

[81] Adna R. Chaffee, "The Status of the Mechanized Combat Organization and the Desired Trend in the Future," Lecture at AWC, 19 Sep 29, pp. 1–2, AWC Curricular Archives; Badsey, "American Experience of Armour," p. 128; Millett and Maslowski, *For the Common Defense*, p. 382.

[82] Hist Sec, Army Ground Forces (AGF), Army Ground Forces Studies no. 27, "The Armored Force, Command and Center," 1946, pp. 1–2, U.S. Army Center of Military History, Washington, D.C. (CMH); Benson, "Mechanization—Aloft and Alow," pp. 58–60.

of widely varying ages. Mechanical failures plagued these vehicles and seriously undermined the value of their activities. Without replacements or additional funding to maintain and operate its tanks, the American Experimental Mechanized Force disbanded after less than three months in existence.[83]

Sereno E. Brett, shown here as a captain, following the Army-wide rank reduction mandated after World War I

The creation of the force nevertheless indicated a change in the official perception of tank use and organization and marked the first authorized departure from the National Defense Act of 1920. Significantly, the change in policy was the result of the secretary of war's reaction to foreign developments and not a response to the collective views of individuals within the Army. The bureau system of the War Department provided neither institutional encouragement for ideas that transcended designated missions nor the ability to respond to internal stimuli.

To study the experience of the Experimental Mechanized Force and to determine whether the force should be a permanent organization, the War Department established the Mechanized Board. It convened on 15 May and submitted its final report on 1 October 1928, shortly after the disbandment of the Experimental Mechanized Force. The Mechanized Board recommended the establishment of a permanent mechanized force in fiscal year 1931. This force would include 131 officers and 1,896 enlisted men drawn from several combat arms. It would receive modern equipment over a three-year period, and its supply and support components would be entirely motorized. This force would function as the Army's technical and tactical test bed for mechanized development. Although not intended as a separate branch, the proposed unit was also not to be affiliated with any existing combat arm. Its purpose lay in determining the optimum use and organization of tanks for the Army, not in supplanting the combat arms.[84]

---

[83] Memo, Col J. W. Anderson to Brig Gen Leonard T. Gerow, sub: Development of Mechanization and Armored Units in the U.S. Army, 5 Dec 40, p. 1, Item 1479, Reel 36, National Archives Project, George C. Marshall Library (GCM), Lexington, Va.; Benson, "Mechanization—Aloft and Alow," pp. 58–59; Steadman, "Evolution of the Tank," pp. 3–4; Messenger, *Blitzkrieg Story*, p. 53; Gillie, *Forging the Thunderbolt*, p. 22.

[84] Memo, Mechanized Board to The Adjutant General (TAG), sub: A Mechanized Force, 1 Oct 28, pp. 30–36, File 84–20, AWC Rcds Sec, MHI; Hist Sec, AGF, "Armored Force, Command and Center," p. 2.

Like the earlier advocates for the retention of the Tank Corps' independent status, the Mechanized Board members perceived the use of the tank as an asset to combat arms other than the Infantry and sought its integration with the traditional cavalry-infantry-artillery team. The board was not, however, envisioning the combined-arms team of later years. It simply sought to create an effective tool with which to study tank roles and uses.[85]

The Bureau System Versus Mechanization

In the late 1920s a new generation of officers began to emerge as the leaders of American mechanized development, gradually replacing ex–Tank Corps members in this capacity. The latter had labored under the constraints of the National Defense Act of 1920 and their own limited wartime experience. Consequently, tank development tended to focus on the platform rather than on a broader set of guiding ideas to govern its organization and employment with other arms. Secretary of War Davis' willingness to consider a role for the tank other than infantry support, however, encouraged more attention to concepts unfettered by the intellectual constraints of the War Department's mission orientation. The term mechanization became much more commonplace, denoting as it did a range of functions and platforms rather than just the tank.

In this encouraging climate, Adna R. Chaffee Jr. emerged as one of the new leaders of American mechanized development. He graduated thirty-first of seventy-eight from the U.S. Military Academy in 1906. He attended the Cavalry School at Fort Riley, Kansas, and in 1912 the French Cavalry School in Saumur. During World War I he served as an instructor at the AEF General Staff College in Langres and also as a member of General Pershing's staff. Following the war he taught at the Command and General Staff School at Fort Leavenworth before attending the Army War College. In June 1927 Major Chaffee was posted as a staff officer to work in the G–3 (Operations and Training) Division of the War Department General Staff, where he became immersed in the study and development of tanks. In 1928 he was appointed to serve on the Mechanized Board.[86]

Possessing little knowledge of tanks, Chaffee entered the scene of mechanized development without the background or experience ex–Tank Corps members possessed. He epitomized the new generation of officers who had remained largely removed from postwar tank development. Their comparatively late arrival to mechanized development coincided with the War Department's changing attitude toward the tank that encouraged rather than censured new ideas concerning its optimal employment.

To compensate for his lack of experience with tanks, Chaffee undertook a personal study of mechanization and its developments since the World War.

[85] Ibid.

[86] George W. Cullum, *Biographical Register of the Officers and Graduates of the U.S. Military Academy*, 9 vols. (Chicago, Ill.: R. R. Donnelly and Sons Co., 1930), 7: 719; Gillie, *Forging the Thunderbolt*, pp. 27–29.

M1917 conducting field demonstration at Fort Meade in 1929

His appointment to the Mechanized Board fueled this interest. He especially sought information on British mechanization efforts, paralleling the interest of Secretary of War Davis and reflecting the general belief that the British Army led the world in concepts of mechanized warfare. In this endeavor he benefited from his friendship with Maj. Charles G. Mettler, the American military attaché to Great Britain.[87]

In December 1928 Chaffee submitted to the War Department a proposal advocating the creation of a separate mechanized branch. He based his proposal on conclusions formulated from his personal study and his participation on the Mechanized Board. Chaffee outlined a four-year program with an estimated cost of $4 million and an implementation date in fiscal year 1931. Initially, he felt this mechanized force should function as a test bed to determine the optimum organization, equipment, and role for a mechanized regiment. Subsequently, it would evolve into a separate branch of service composed of several mechanized regiments, each a union of all arms whose tank elements would consist of light, fast tanks.[88]

Chaffee's recommendations reflected many of the concepts the British were already demonstrating in maneuvers that he was in a unique position to evaluate through his contact with the American military attaché in London. But willingness to

---

[87] Nenninger, "Development of American Armor," pp. 90, 92–93.

[88] Chaffee, "Status of the Mechanized Combat Organization," 19 Sep 29, pp. 5–9; Hist Sec, AGF, "Armored Force, Command and Center," p. 2; Messenger, *Blitzkrieg Story*, p. 5.

advocate a separate mechanized arm also reflected the interest demonstrated by Brig. Gen. Frank Parker, assistant chief of staff, G–3, Chaffee's immediate superior.

Earlier in 1928, in a memorandum to the chief of staff, Parker had outlined a long-range mechanization program that embraced the notion that the tank would restore the element of decisiveness to the battlefield through its combination of firepower and mobility. While he considered entirely mechanized armies inconceivable, he did believe that mechanized elements could assist the traditional ground forces by attacking the enemy's flank and rear. Parker's recommended mechanized force included fully mechanized formations and self-propelled artillery. Its purpose was the formulation of tactical and strategic roles for permanently established mechanized units.[89]

Yet these ideas seemed conservative compared to those of the Tank School commandant and commanding officer at Fort George G. Meade, Col. James K. Parsons, who succeeded Rockenbach.[90] Parsons submitted proposals for a mechanized development program that included six tank divisions formed from elements of all combat arms. Each field army would receive one division. As self-contained formations with support elements organic to them, Parsons considered these divisions capable of extended, independent operations.[91]

None of these ideas could be realized without substantial financial and manpower allocations from Congress and the acquiescence of the combat-arms chiefs. Congressional unwillingness to expand military appropriations or consent to an increased personnel establishment made the support of the branch chiefs a necessary condition, but they did not have Parsons' level of familiarity with the tank to warrant such unconditional support. The development programs of Chaffee and Parker represented the perspective of the G–3 Division of the War Department General Staff, whose purpose was to prepare for future conflict and whose position within the War Department organization elevated it above the mission orientation of the combat arms. The combat-arms chiefs, however, bore a responsibility to the interests of their particular arms of service and to the specific missions of their arms that would be undermined by the creation of a separate mechanized arm or a large-scale expansion of the existing tank force.

Without an increase in personnel, the War Department could create a new force only by diverting soldiers and funding from the existing combat arms. The specter of losing appropriations and personnel to a mechanized force—whose very nature undermined the dominance of the traditional services on the battlefield—prompted the members of the threatened bureaus to oppose such a force and to renew emphasis on the importance of their own arms.[92]

---

[89] Memo, Assistant Chief of Staff (ACS), G–3, Brig. Gen. Frank Parker, to Chief of Staff (CS), sub: A Mechanized Force, 20 Mar 28, AWC Rcds Sec, MHI Archives.

[90] Camp George G. Meade became Fort George G. Meade in 1929.

[91] Brief of Memo, Col James K. Parsons to TAG, sub: Mechanized Forces, 17 Apr 30, AWC Rcds Sec, MHI Archives; Nenninger, "Development of American Armor," p. 97.

[92] The Mechanized Board recognized this danger and did not recommend diverting money and manpower from the existing service arms for precisely this reason. Memo, Mechanized Board to TAG, 1 Oct 28, pp. 30–36.

Chief of Infantry Maj. Gen. Stephen O. Fuqua responded to the idea of a separate mechanized force by reaffirming the importance of the infantry as the decisive force on the battlefield and the only element capable of seizing and holding ground. To him, the tank's usefulness derived from its value as an auxiliary weapon enabling the infantry to achieve its assigned mission more effectively. The establishment of a mechanized force for the study of the tank's potential also threatened the infantry's dominant influence on tank design. Fuqua feared that tanks developed outside the context of the infantry mission would prove unable to provide effective support to the rifleman.[93]

Fuqua sensed a parallel between these new proposals concerning the tank and the ongoing efforts of the Air Corps to become independent of the Army. The prior establishment of the Air Corps as a separate bureau within the War Department did not lead to more capable close air support as intended. Instead, it engendered development of strategic bombers designed to achieve victory independent of ground forces. The Air Corps Tactical School similarly emphasized strategic bombardment over ground-support operations in its instruction. The chasm between air and ground forces widened after passage of the Air Corps Act of 1926 and further expansion of the Air Corps at the expense of the combat arms.[94]

The Infantry remained unconvinced of the war-winning ability of strategic bombing but proved unable to channel Air Corps efforts into the development of an effective ground-support capability. The Air Corps argument that strategic bombing assisted the ground forces by destroying the enemy's will and means to fight meant to Infantry personnel that they could not depend on the Air Corps to provide a protective umbrella in the theater of operations.

Thus, from Fuqua's perspective, the suggestion that a separate mechanized force be established to determine the best use of the tank carried an implicit threat. Already faced with a deficiency in the support rendered to it in the air, the Infantry rallied around Section 17 of the National Defense Act of 1920 to ensure that it would not also lose the benefits of the armored vehicle on the ground. While individual Infantry officers might support expansion of the tank's role beyond that of infantry support, none advocated that the Infantry relinquish its tanks altogether.

The Cavalry responded to the proponents of a stronger or separate mechanized arm by reasserting the Cavalry's irreplaceable value to the U.S. Army in the past, present, and future, simultaneously stressing the tank's limitations. These views flowed directly from the Office of the Chief of Cavalry, which established Cavalry policy and controlled publication of the *Cavalry Journal*. At the end of the 1920s, when the controversy concerning a separate mechanized force came to a head, Maj. George S. Patton Jr. was the officer charged with enunciating the view of the chief of Cavalry in memorandums and articles. Patton served as the head of the Plans

[93] Nenninger, "Development of American Armor," p. 95.

[94] Robert Frank Futrell, *Ideas, Concepts, Doctrine: A History of Basic Thinking in the United States Air Force, 1907–1964* (Maxwell Air Force Base, Ala.: Air University Press, 1971), pp. 31–32, 34, 44; Spector, "Military Effectiveness, 1919–1939," p. 83; Millett and Maslowski, *For the Common Defense*, p. 371; James N. Eastmen Jr., "The Development of Big Bombers," *Aerospace Historian* XXV, no. 4 (1978): 212–13.

and Training Division within the Office of the Chief of Cavalry from May 1928 until September 1931. His extensive service with the Tank Corps enabled him to evaluate the tank's realizable potential with a familiarity possessed by few officers outside the Infantry tank force.[95]

Patton believed the tank's effectiveness derived in part from the technology embodied in its design. As technology improved, so too must the tank to maintain its relative combat value. Patton concluded that the continuous evolution in military technology thus mandated continuous tank replacement, a costly and time-consuming process ill suited to the political and social climate of 1920s America. Without such replacement, the tank's combat value sank. In Patton's view, the American tank force of the day possessed no combat value because its tank strength derived from vehicles nearly identical to those he had commanded while in the Tank Corps. The Infantry's pride in maintaining them in working order simply indicated the futility of creating a large tank force that would be allowed to lapse into obsolescence but through rigid maintenance present an illusion of fighting power.[96]

To these considerations Patton added terrain limitations, visibility restrictions, and dependence on a fixed line of supply for gasoline and spare parts. These aspects of tank operations he had experienced firsthand, but they also reflected the state of tank development in the late 1920s. No tank of that era was capable of replacing the horse in all or even most of its roles. The tactical mobility of the horse could not be matched by any tank. Bridges allowed tanks to pass river obstacles but could not be presumed to remain standing during combat. Hence, the tank's mobility was restricted still further.[97]

Patton flatly rejected as unrealistic the visionary ideas embedded in Britain's mechanization efforts. He especially criticized the writings of J. F. C. Fuller and Basil H. Liddell Hart.[98] Fuller's writings during and after World War I stressed the dominant role that armored vehicles would possess, almost to the exclusion of other combatants such as the infantry and artillery. Liddell Hart's writings similarly articulated a future battlefield on which mechanized means would have a disproportionate influence. His advocacy of the indirect approach (assail the enemy's weaknesses and undermine his ability to fight) offered a potentially decisive role for mechanized columns relying on speed and firepower to achieve decisive effect. The writings of both Fuller and Liddell Hart proved influential in many armies during the interwar period.[99]

---

[95] Woolley, "Patton and the Concept of Mechanized Warfare," p. 75.

[96] G. S. Patton Jr. and Clarence C. Benson, "Mechanization and Cavalry," *Cavalry Journal* XXXIX, no. 159 (April 1930): 234–40; Blumenson, *Patton Papers*, 1: 872–73; Messenger, *Blitzkrieg Story*, p. 53.

[97] Patton and Benson, "Mechanization and Cavalry," pp. 234–40.

[98] Messenger, *Blitzkrieg Story*, p. 48.

[99] For examples of Fuller's writings, see *On Future Warfare* (London: Sifton Praed & Co., 1928); *Lectures on Field Service Regulations II* (London: Sifton Praed & Co., 1931); *Lectures on Field Service Regulations III* (London: Sifton Praed & Co., 1932). To understand the interwar influence and ideas of Liddell Hart, see Brian Bond, *Liddell Hart: A Study of His Military Thought* (New Brunswick, N.J.:

An M1917 is unloaded from its carrier for use with the Mechanized Force.

Patton, however, denigrated Fuller and Liddell Hart as military thinkers: "Surely the remarks of Col. J. F. C. Fuller (British Army) who during the course of four years' war replete with opportunities attained only the rank of Lieutenant-Colonel, or the opinions of such a hack-writer as Captain Lyle [*sic*] Hart seem puerile when compared with the forceful statements of the elite of the military world."[100] Patton accused Liddell Hart of historical determinism, but underneath the personal criticisms he disbelieved the viability of large mechanized forces dominating the battlefield. Parsons' six-division tank force he similarly considered too large and unnecessary for the United States and, like the Fullerian concepts from whence it derived, impractical. These views were echoed throughout the Cavalry.[101]

Patton's opinions represented a mixture of personal views regarding tanks and the influence of the War Department's organization. As a Cavalry officer whose professional career depended on the continuing relevance of the Cavalry as a separate arm, he was impelled to challenge the more extreme advocates of mechanization. His position in the Office of the Chief of Cavalry mandated that he evaluate the

---

Rutgers University Press, 1977). See also Basil Liddell Hart, *Paris, or the Future of War* (London: Kegan Paul, 1925), and *The Remaking of Modern Armies* (London: John Murray, 1927).

[100] Quote from Blumenson, *Patton Papers*, 1: 860.

[101] Memo, Maj Raymond E. McQuillen to Asst Commandant, AWC, 1 Mar 31, p. 23, AWC Curricular Archives; Chaffee, "Status of the Mechanized Combat Organization," 19 Sep 29, p. 4; Blumenson, *Patton Papers*, 1: 872–73, 877.

merits and weaknesses of a separate mechanized force and its relation to the Cavalry while simultaneously emphasizing the Cavalry's importance.[102]

The Cavalry neither rejected the tank nor remained blindly loyal to the nobility of the horse. Cavalry officers continued to perceive roles for horse cavalry that the tank simply could not perform as effectively. These included raiding, reconnaissance, delaying actions, and security missions in all weather over any type of terrain.[103] Nor did the Cavalry espouse the mounted charge above the use of firepower and mobility. Saber charges were reserved for extraordinary situations such as surprise attacks and the pursuit of a broken enemy. Tables of organization and equipment included increasing numbers of automatic weapons. Training stressed dismounted fighting, reflecting the Cavalry's emphasis on the horse as a means of tactical transport rather than a combat platform.[104]

Cavalry emphasis on its own importance when confronted with the specter of a separate mechanized force also stemmed from a fear for its existence as a combat arm. The War Department proposed consolidation of the Cavalry, Field Artillery, and Coast Artillery to save money. The Cavalry responded by curtailing unit movements and training maneuvers to reduce expenses. Fear of amalgamation created turmoil among Cavalry officers whose professional ambitions hung in the balance. Consequently, their writings and public statements stressed the relative cheapness of maintaining horse units and contrasted the proven worth of horse cavalry with the largely theoretical value of the tank.[105]

The dual threat of amalgamation and the creation of a new bureau siphoning men and money from the mounted branch prompted Cavalry officers to rally to their chief's standard. When merged with the individual statements and views of officers, the controversies surrounding the issue of a separate mechanized force became personalized and diverted attention from the administrative obstacles to change within the bureau system. The Cavalry's defense of itself at the expense of a mechanized force obscured the Cavalry's demonstrated interest in the application of mechanical means to Cavalry roles. The Cavalry possessed an interest in experimentation with tanks, but not at the cost of its own already deficient manpower, its appropriations, or its independence.

The Mechanized Force

At the urging of Chief of Staff General Charles P. Summerall, in 1930 Congress responded to these conflicting hopes and fears by authorizing the creation of the

---

102 Woolley, "Patton and the Concept of Mechanized Warfare," p. 75.

103 Patton and Benson, "Mechanization and Cavalry," pp. 234–40; Benson, "Mechanization—Aloft and Alow," pp. 60–61; Hawkins, "Importance of Modern Cavalry," pp. 487–99.

104 R. J. Fleming, "Mission of the Cavalry School with Comments on Modern Cavalry and Cavalry Training," *Cavalry Journal* XXXVIII, no. 154 (January 1929): 41, 51, 53–54. Colonel Fleming was assistant commandant of the Cavalry School during this period, and this article was originally a lecture delivered to students there.

105 Memo, ACS, G–3, Maj Gen Edward L. King, to CS, G–3, sub: Consolidation of Coast Artillery, Field Artillery, and Cavalry, 3 Oct 31, Ofc of the Ch of Cav, Gen Corresp, Record Group (RG) 177, National Archives and Records Administration (NARA); Blumenson, *Patton Papers*, 1: 882.

Mechanized Force as a test unit combining elements from nine combat and service arms.[106] The Mechanized Force essentially embodied the recommendations of the Mechanized Board's 1928 report. Established at Fort Eustis, Virginia, the new organization was charged with "the temporary assembly of a mechanized force with the object of studying questions of tactics and technique and to service test certain equipment."[107] The War Department further directed that its initial activities focus on organization, equipment, and individual training before progressing to unit training and field exercises.[108]

Command of the Mechanized Force was given to Col. Daniel Van Voorhis, a Cavalry officer whose organizational and administrative abilities were deemed especially important in the creation of the new force. Van Voorhis' executive officer was Major Brett, whose involvement with tanks during and since World War I provided a foundation of practical experience. Several other officers in the force were also Cavalry, and the armored-car squadron was a Cavalry unit. However, the overall mix of Infantry and Cavalry personnel in the Mechanized Force reflected the shared interests of these branches in mechanized development and helped to allay respective branch fears concerning the new force.[109]

The small size of the Mechanized Force and the low level of congressional appropriations further diminished resistance from the bureau chiefs. Congress appropriated $284,000 for the Mechanized Force, a fraction of the $4 million Chaffee had thought necessary for his program. Personnel assigned to the Mechanized Force remained members of their parent branches but on temporary, detached service, thereby ensuring that the existing bureaus would not lose personnel.[110]

The Mechanized Force that assembled at Fort Eustis consisted of a headquarters company; the Army's only active armored-car troop; a company of infantry tanks; a machine-gun company; a self-propelled artillery battery; an engineer company; an ordnance company; and detachments of Signal, Chemical Warfare, and Quartermaster troops. It included 36 officers and 648 men but only 23 tanks and 11 armored cars among its 167 vehicles. Despite its small size, the Mechanized Force included 44 different types of vehicles. Its tanks were primarily M1917s, and World War I–vintage trucks towing artillery pieces represented its self-propelled artillery. Only one armored car and four trucks possessed radios.[111]

The lack of standardized, modern equipment severely restricted the activities and value of the Mechanized Force, but its motley and obsolescent composition

---

[106] Hist Sec, AGF, "Armored Force, Command and Center," p. 2; Badsey, "American Experience of Armour," p. 128; Gillie, *Forging the Thunderbolt*, p. 36.

[107] Memo, McQuillen to Asst Commandant, AWC, 1 Mar 31, p. 25.

[108] Ibid., p. 26; Robert W. Grow, "The Ten Lean Years: From the Mechanized Force (1930) to the Armored Force (1940)," p. 10, Robert W. Grow Papers, MHI Archives.

[109] Grow, "Ten Lean Years," p. 5; Gillie, *Forging the Thunderbolt*, pp. 38–39; Blumenson, *Patton Papers*, 1: 881.

[110] Badsey, "American Experience of Armour," p. 128; Hist Sec, AGF, "Armored Force, Command, and Center," p. 2.

[111] Grow, "Ten Lean Years," pp. 10–11; Hist Sec, AGF, "Armored Force, Command and Center," 1946, p. 2, CMH.

reflected the state of available equipment. The Mark VIII remained in service until finally declared obsolete in 1932.[112] This condition prompted one cavalry officer to assert, "It must be recognized that with obsolete and make-shift equipment but little of real value can be learned as to the proper tactics and technique in the employment of a modern mechanized force."[113]

Despite this state of affairs, some theoretical development did occur from the simple collocation of personnel from different arms. The Mechanized Force helped to establish a common basis of experience for officers throughout the Army. It brought them together as representatives of their parent branches to determine how best to coordinate their efforts and missions while housed in the same unit. It provided an unprecedented opportunity to escape the compartmentalization of the bureau system and to share ideas freely. Although the exceptionally high number of different vehicle types greatly hindered their coordination, maintenance, and ability to conduct field exercises, several insights did emerge. These included the necessity for a mix of towed and self-propelled artillery (the latter an artillery piece mounted on the chassis of a light tank) and the desirability of a light tank as the primary attack component.[114]

The tactical roles outlined for the Mechanized Force represented the consolidation of the unfocused views on tank use other than infantry support that had appeared during the previous decade. The limited experience of the Experimental Mechanized Force and the Mechanized Force helped to transform these vague notions into a clearer, but still tentative, path of doctrinal development. The roles now being recommended included the seizure and temporary holding of important, distant objectives, enveloping movements, counterattack, flank protection, rearguard action, breakthrough and exploitation, and possible use in a sustained independent action.[115] These functions marked the Mechanized Force's gravitation toward employing the tank in the Army's only mobile role—cavalry. Impetus in this direction also came from Van Voorhis' cavalry background and the replacement of Major Brett by Major Chaffee in July 1931.[116]

Outside the Mechanized Force, officers also began to accept the notion of tanks acting in cavalry roles, given certain favorable conditions. Prominent among them was Army War College Commandant Maj. Gen. William D. Connor, who introduced mechanized elements into all student problems in 1929 at the War Department's request. He also conducted his own study of mechanization and concluded that, although mechanized formations could not yet entirely replace horse cavalry, cavalry missions largely constituted their future function.[117]

The Mechanized Force represented the emergence of new thinking regarding the organization and employment of tanks. It marked an important departure from

---

112 Icks, "Four Decades of Mechanization," p. 339.

113 Memo, McQuillen to Asst Commandant, AWC, 1 Mar 31, p. 26.

114 Ibid., pp. 27–28.

115 Ibid., pp. 26–28; Grow, "Ten Lean Years," p. 10.

116 Grow, "Ten Lean Years," p. 14.

117 Memo, AWC Commandant, Maj Gen William D. Connor, to TAG, sub: The Mission and Composition of a Mechanized Force, 12 Mar 30, AWC Rcds Sec, MHI Archives.

the restrictive National Defense Act of 1920. However, the Mechanized Force's existence did not symbolize a radical departure in American views regarding tanks. No American Fuller emerged to advocate the creation of combined-arms formations built around the tank and reliant on radio communications. The Army tended to perceive the tank not as a dominant weapon but as an auxiliary one. No desire for creating an entirely mechanized army existed.[118]

Experience and understanding of mechanized units was still in its infancy in the United States. Beginning to emerge, however, was a theoretical foundation from which principles concerning the tactical use and organization of the tank were being formulated and experimented with, albeit ineffectively, by the two mechanized forces created at the end of the 1920s. The depiction of tanks in American cavalry missions represented the way in which this formulation occurred.

---

[118] Ibid.; Grow, "Ten Lean Years," p. 11.

2

EARLY DEVELOPMENT OF THE MECHANIZED CAVALRY

The early 1930s marked the end of efforts to pursue mechanization independent of the combat arms. The 7th Cavalry Brigade (Mechanized) replaced the Mechanized Force, an action that symbolized the alignment of mechanization with the Army's existing mission orientation and organization. A new mechanization policy emerged to remove the Infantry's monopoly on tank development without threatening the tank's infantry-support mission. This policy permitted the Cavalry to develop its own mechanized component and determine the related organization and doctrine. The 7th Cavalry Brigade thus served as a test bed for cavalry concepts applied to a combat unit built around the tank. Maneuver experience and continued interest led to the expansion of the mechanized cavalry, but the latter's evolution began to raise questions as to its future role and status within the Cavalry Branch.

Demise of the Mechanized Force

On 31 October 1931, the Mechanized Force disbanded. Rumors of its demise had circulated throughout the summer, hastening its officers to complete a final report on the unit's activities. This report recommended retention of the Mechanized Force as an independent organization and further study of the employment of mechanized units in cavalry roles. Previously, Tank Corps members had sought to keep the tank force unaligned with any one combat arm, but they could not articulate a role other than infantry support. Similarly, the interest Mechanized Force personnel showed in cavalry missions—partially a reflection of the predominance of Cavalry officers within the unit—undermined arguments for the unit's independence. The War Department therefore abolished the Mechanized Force.[1]

Financial considerations played a role in this decision. The limited funds initially allocated to the Mechanized Force were soon exhausted, but efforts to redistribute

[1] Robert W. Grow, "The Ten Lean Years: From the Mechanized Force (1930) to the Armored Force (1940)," pp. 10, 12, 15, Robert W. Grow Papers, U.S. Army Military History Institute (MHI) Archives, Carlisle Barracks, Pa.; C. C. Benson, "Mechanization—Aloft and Alow," *Cavalry Journal* XXXVIII, no. 154 (January 1929): 61–62; Adna R. Chaffee, "The Status of the Mechanized Combat Organization and the Desired Trend in the Future," Lecture at U.S. Army War College (AWC), 19 Sep 29, pp. 10–11, AWC Curricular Archives, MHI Archives.

money from other branches of service aroused the opposition of the combat- and service-arm chiefs. Additional appropriations could not be obtained amid the onset of the Great Depression.[2] Indeed, the initial reaction of President Herbert Hoover's administration to the financial crisis lay in reducing government spending. The War Department possessed the largest budget of any federal activity. It became a natural target for funding cuts, particularly since the president considered the Navy the principal means of national defense. In his view the Army needed only a small force to patrol the country's borders.[3]

War Department funding cuts coincided with a growing need to replace equipment either worn out or simply obsolete. The depletion of wartime equipment surpluses forced the consideration of new purchases to meet the Army's basic needs. Unfortunately, development and production costs had risen steadily since World War I, thereby reducing the dollar's ability to purchase military strength.[4]

General Douglas MacArthur became chief of staff of the Army on 21 November 1930, and he applied himself to the worsening financial situation. Aware that he could not prevent a reduction in War Department appropriations, he sought to lessen its impact by lowering funding requests for nonessential programs. He further sought to distribute budget cuts evenly throughout the combat and service arms. Congress proved unsympathetic, imposing even more severe budget reductions than MacArthur anticipated; but it spared Air Corps funding. Congressional budget guidance thus further strained relations between the Army's air and ground components.[5]

MacArthur feared that the Army's small size and budget would undermine its effectiveness in a national emergency. He therefore made the retention of personnel his primary objective throughout his tenure as chief of staff. He refused to condone reductions in the Regular Army establishment and consistently opposed efforts to reduce the officer corps, furlough officers at half pay, or instigate forced retirements. By acquiescing in base closings, cancellation of field maneuvers, limitations on the Army's general activity level, and reductions in the research and development of new weapons, MacArthur succeeded in preserving the Army's personnel base.[6]

---

[2] S. D. Badsey, "The American Experience of Armour," in *Armoured Warfare*, ed. J. P. Harris and F. H. Toase (New York: St. Martin's Press, 1990), p. 128.

[3] John R. Wilson, "The Quaker and the Sword: Herbert Hoover's Relations with the Military," *Military Affairs* XXXVIII, no. 2 (April 1974): 41–47; D. Clayton James, *The Years of MacArthur*, 3 vols. (Boston: Houghton Mifflin Co., 1970), 1: 363.

[4] U.S. Congress, House, Subcommittee of the Committee on Appropriations, *War Department Appropriation Bill for 1931 Military Activities, Hearings*, pt. 1, 71st Cong., 2d Sess., 1929, p. 10; Wilson, "The Quaker and the Sword," pp. 41–47; John W. Killigrew, "The Impact of the Great Depression on the Army, 1929–1936," Ph.D. Diss., Indiana University, 1960, pp. 6–8, 17–18; James, *Years of MacArthur*, 1: 357–58, 363–64.

[5] James, *Years of MacArthur*, 1: 354–56, 378–79; Killigrew, "Impact of the Great Depression," p. III-11.

[6] James, *Years of MacArthur*, 1: 355, 359, 427–28; Allan R. Millett and Peter Maslowski, *For the Common Defense: A Military History of the United States of America* (New York: Free Press, 1984), p. 378; William Manchester, *American Caesar: Douglas MacArthur, 1880–1964* (Boston: Little, Brown, and Co., 1978), pp. 147–48; Douglas MacArthur, "Modernization of the Army," in *A Soldier Speaks:*

MacArthur also permitted the disbandment of the Mechanized Force. He felt that this organization was a luxury the Army could not afford during a period of fiscal restraint. Nor did he consider the Mechanized Force the best means of promoting mechanization throughout the Army. MacArthur feared that the concentration of mechanized development in a single, independent organization would reduce its importance to the traditional combat arms.[7] He did not believe the benefits of tracked and wheeled vehicles should be confined to any one arm. Instead, he envisioned the use of mobile columns containing cavalry, infantry, tanks, and artillery, all relying on vehicular transport.[8]

In his vision of the future battlefield, MacArthur did not envision large tank masses playing a dominant role. Instead, he expected tanks to be "difficult to procure in large numbers, particularly in the early stages of any war. Opportunities for their best employment on the battle front must be carefully selected, both as to time and as to place. They are assault weapons only, to be used for relatively short periods of time, under favorable opportunities. Consequently, they would be used as corps, army, and General Headquarters elements."[9] In May 1931 MacArthur outlined a plan for Army mechanization that reflected these views. This plan evolved into a War Department directive: "Every arm is authorized to conduct research and experiment with a view of increasing its own power to perform promptly the missions it has been especially organized and developed and to carry it out. Every part of the Army will adopt mechanization and motorization as far as practicable and desirable."[10]

This policy statement governed Army mechanized development until 1940, reflecting the alignment of MacArthur's ideas with the administrative organization established by the National Defense Act of 1920. By distributing responsibility for mechanized development to all combat arms and eliminating the Mechanized Force, MacArthur reconciled mechanization with the preexisting bureau system. The chiefs of the combat arms now controlled the pace and extent of mechanization, which no longer posed a threat to their traditional independence. Consequently, MacArthur ended the jurisdictional debates concerning a separate mechanized force.

He also provided more detailed guidance on the establishment of a cavalry mechanization program. MacArthur believed the tank capable of supporting select cavalry actions: reconnaissance, seizure of key objectives, pursuit, delay, exploitation, and reserve. He considered horse cavalry necessary for operations in rough terrain and mechanized cavalry a vehicle-based, general-purpose unit for use

---

Public Papers and Speeches of General of the Army Douglas MacArthur, ed. Vorin E. Whan Jr. (New York: Frederick A. Praeger, Inc., 1965), pp. 55–56; Killigrew, "Impact of the Great Depression," pp. IV-13, 15–17.

[7] U.S. Congress, House, Subcommittee of the Committee on Appropriations, *War Department Appropriation Bill for 1933 Military Activities, Hearings*, pt. 1, 72d Cong., 1st Sess., 1932, pp. 17–18.

[8] Chief of Staff (CS) Gen Douglas MacArthur, "General Principles To Govern in Extending Mechanization and Motorization Throughout the Army," 1 May 31, pp. 1–2, Willis D. Crittenberger Papers, MHI Archives.

[9] Ibid., pp. 3–4.

[10] Maj Gen James F. McKinley, "War Department Policies for Mechanization," 5 Apr 35, p. 1, Crittenberger Papers.

in suitable environments. To stimulate development of the latter, he ordered the reorganization of the Mechanized Force into the nucleus for a mechanized cavalry regiment. To avoid the legislative barrier posed by Section 17 of the National Defense Act of 1920 that legally restricted tanks to the Infantry, tanks assigned to the Cavalry would be known as combat cars.[11]

The War Department further defined the Cavalry's mechanization program in a directive dated 3 October 1931. The Cavalry was to determine the powers and limitations of a self-contained tactical and administrative mechanized unit in the performance of those missions identified by MacArthur. One mechanized cavalry regiment would be created to determine tactical principles and organization. Subsequently, units from other arms would be attached to develop effective means of coordination and further mechanized cavalry regiments would be established.[12]

Significantly, no rapid mechanization of horse regiments would occur. Instead, the War Department outlined a long-term program, allowing a gradual expansion of mechanized units commensurate with the acquisition of practical experience. The program possessed a clear logic and suited the Army's chronic lack of funding, personnel, and equipment while permitting a maximum of doctrinal experimentation. Moreover, the collectively broad nature of the missions deemed suitable for mechanized cavalry encouraged organizational and doctrinal flexibility. Because no regulatory or doctrinal precedent existed for mechanized cavalry, the missions assigned assumed the nature of guiding objectives rather than constraints.

The new mechanization policy and the specific guidance governing the creation of a mechanized cavalry force met with opposition from Chief of Infantry Maj. Gen. Stephen O. Fuqua. He opposed the assignment of tanks to the Cavalry because it violated the National Defense Act of 1920. Because MacArthur's policy did not threaten the Infantry's tank force, Fuqua's position likely represented a reaction to the criticism implicit in MacArthur's statement that "the tank itself may never become a piece of equipment assigned to an infantry regiment."[13] The chief of staff's comment echoed prior comments from a variety of sources denouncing infantry tank development as unprogressive. From the Infantry's perspective, the National Defense Act of 1920 subordinated tank development to the infantry mission, mandating an exclusive emphasis on infantry support.[14]

Mechanized Force personnel offered the strongest opposition to the new direction of mechanized development. The unit's commander, Col. Daniel Van Voorhis, argued that it would restrain tank development and subject it to branch rivalry, undermining the achievements of the Mechanized Force in establishing a sound foundation for further mechanized development. He believed that only an independent organization could determine how the tank might effectively assist

---

[11] Guy V. Henry Jr., "A Brief Narrative of the Life of Guy V. Henry, Jr.," p. 65, n.d., Guy V. Henry Jr. Papers, MHI Archives; MacArthur, "General Principles," pp. 3–4.

[12] McKinley, "War Department Policies," p. 1; Daniel Van Voorhis, "Mechanization," Lecture at AWC, 13 Oct 37, p. 7, AWC Curricular Archives.

[13] MacArthur, "General Principles," p. 3.

[14] Timothy K. Nenninger, "The Development of American Armor, 1917–1940," Master's Thesis, University of Wisconsin, 1968, pp. 110–11.

each combat arm. Yet he could not dispel the fears of the combat-arms chiefs and the General Staff that the Mechanized Force would evolve into a separate arm that followed its own independent doctrinal goals in the manner of the Air Corps. Subsequently, Van Voorhis and Mechanized Force personnel attributed the demise of their organization to conservative and unprogressive individuals within the War Department rather than to the inability of the bureau system to absorb administrative changes stemming from technological evolution.[15]

Outside the Mechanized Force, however, MacArthur's mechanization policy received widespread support because it suited the existing War Department organization and reinforced the findings of the Caliber Board. The latter, headed by Brig. Gen. William I. Westervelt, had been created in December 1918 to study ordnance, ammunition, and Field Artillery transport. Among its findings, submitted in a report of May 1919, the board stressed the importance of mechanical means of transport for all military purposes.[16] Twelve years later, the Army seemed poised to realize the board's recommendations.

The Cavalry especially welcomed the new mechanization policy because it provided an opportunity to explore the viability of using tanks in cavalry roles. The barrier posed by the National Defense Act of 1920 to such experimentation had been removed. Moreover, the transfer of Mechanized Force personnel into the new mechanized cavalry would ensure a continuity of ideas and experience. Although the tank was not thought capable of supplanting the horse completely, Chief of Cavalry Maj. Gen. Guy V. Henry Jr. considered such replacement possible in the future.[17] First, however, a mechanized cavalry regiment had to be established.

Birth of the Mechanized Cavalry

In accordance with the new mechanized policy, a small remnant of cavalry personnel and armored cars from the Mechanized Force was renamed the Detachment for Mechanized Cavalry Regiment on 1 November 1931. It relocated to Camp Knox, Kentucky, the same month. There it was absorbed into the 1st Cavalry Regiment, subsequently renamed the 1st Cavalry Regiment (Mechanized). Colonel Van Voorhis accompanied the transfer of Mechanized Force personnel and assumed command of the new mechanized regiment. Adna R. Chaffee Jr., now a lieutenant colonel, served as his executive officer.

---

[15] Hist Sec, Army Ground Forces (AGF), AGF Study no. 27, "The Armored Force, Command and Center," 1946, p. 3, U.S. Army Center of Military History, Washington, D.C.; Nenninger, "Development of American Armor," p. 110; Grow, "Ten Lean Years," pp. 7–8, 15.

[16] Gen William Westervelt, Gen Robert E. Callan, and Col Walter P. Boatwright, "Westervelt Board Report: A Study of the Armament, Calibers and Type of Material, Kinds and Proportion of Ammunition, and Methods of Transport of Artillery To Be Assigned to a Field Army," MHI Library, 1919, pp. 43–52; Constance McLaughlin Green, Harry C. Thomson, and Peter C. Roots, *The Ordnance Department: Planning Munitions for War*, U.S. Army in World War II (Washington, D.C.: U.S. Army Center of Military History, 1955), pp. 169–70, 192.

[17] Henry, "Brief Narrative," p. 65; Nenninger, "Development of American Armor," p. 111.

The Cavalry attempted to man and equip the 1st Cavalry Regiment (Mechanized) at full strength by shifting personnel and materiel from other units. However, many cavalry units were already below their peacetime establishment, severely limiting the influx of officers and enlisted personnel. Administrative obstacles and funding shortages similarly obstructed the procurement of combat vehicles. General Henry noted, "there seems to be more or less 'cold feet' developing in the expenditure of funds to equip the regiment with two combat car troops and, in addition, a scout troop with light, fast tanks." Consequently, Cavalry officers drafted plans to improvise a scout car by adding a gun shield and a machine gun to a commercial automobile.[18]

Plans to develop mechanized cavalry went beyond the creation of the 1st Cavalry Regiment (Mechanized). In December 1931 the War Department also ordered the activation of the 7th Cavalry Brigade (Mechanized) by the following May. General Henry developed a table of organization for the brigade headquarters, but the latter was not established nor the 1st Cavalry Regiment formally assigned to it until March 1933. Although little more than a single regiment subordinated to a small command cell, the brigade's establishment symbolized the War Department's embracement of mechanized cavalry and the likelihood of its future expansion.[19]

Camp Knox's large size made it a logical site for the new mechanized cavalry. With thirty-three thousand acres and varied terrain, it was one of the largest installations in the country. Camp Knox saw little military activity except for some training in the summer months and thus was considered superior to Fort Eustis, Virginia, as a site for mechanized development. The assignment of the 1st Cavalry Regiment (Mechanized) and the 7th Cavalry Brigade (Mechanized) also elevated the installation's status, denoted by its name change from Camp to Fort Knox in January 1932.[20]

Infrastructure improvements soon followed. The post lacked permanent housing; many of its existing structures lay in a state of disrepair, having been unused since World War I. Soil conditions created a serious drainage problem, and the numerous creeks on the military reservation necessitated extensive bridging projects. New buildings and garages soon arose, but rain and cold weather interfered with these projects. The use of inmates from local prisons provided necessary labor: "We are making the lives of the prisoners at the rock crusher quite miserable."[21]

Despite these preparations, the 1st Cavalry Regiment did not leave Fort Russell in Marfa, Texas, for Fort Knox until 1 January 1933. The chairman of the House

---

[18] Ltr, Guy V. Henry to Col Daniel Van Voorhis, 7 Dec 31, Ofc of the Ch of Cav, Gen Corresp, Record Group (RG) 177, National Archives and Records Administration (NARA).

[19] Memo, Ch of Cav Maj Gen Guy V. Henry to Commanding Officer (CO), Headquarters Detachment, Mechanized Force, sub: Tables of Organization for Cavalry Brigade, Mechanized, 15 Jan 32, and 1st End, HQ for Mechanized Cav Rgt to Ch of Cav, 27 Jan 32, and 11th End, Ofc of the Ch of Cav to TAG, 14 Oct 32; all in Ofc of the Ch of Cav, Gen Corresp, RG 177, NARA.

[20] Grow, "Ten Lean Years," p. 16; Nenninger, "Development of American Armor," pp. 133–34.

[21] Ltr, Lt Col Adna R. Chaffee to Maj Robert W. Strong, 17 Dec 31, Ofc of the Ch of Cav, Gen Corresp, RG 177, NARA.

1st Cavalry Regiment (Mechanized) departing Texas en route to Fort Knox, 1933

Committee on Military Appropriations for fiscal year 1934, Mississippi Democrat Ross Collins, blamed the War Department for the delay and charged that it finally moved the regiment only to avoid the prying questions of his committee.[22] In actuality, the 1st Cavalry Regiment's immobility stemmed from a debate between Kentucky and Texas Congressmen intensified by the Great Depression and the presidential election of 1932. The Texas Congressmen argued that the mechanized cavalry should be stationed near the Mexican border, while the Kentucky Congressmen urged the speedy transfer of the 1st Cavalry Regiment to Fort Knox. Movement of the 1st Cavalry Regiment to Kentucky meant the loss of economic activity associated with Fort Russell but a corresponding increase at Fort Knox.[23]

Kentucky won the dispute, but the efforts of newly elected President Franklin D. Roosevelt to combat the Great Depression diverted the attention of the 1st Cavalry Regiment away from mechanized development. Roosevelt persuaded Congress to create the Civilian Conservation Corps (CCC) on 31 March 1933 to provide employment in landscaping, reforestation, and other public works projects. Initially, the Labor, Agriculture, and Interior Departments controlled the program, but their inability to recruit and equip CCC members on the scale demanded by the president resulted in the War Department's assuming control. The War Department

[22] U.S. Congress, House, Subcommittee of the Committee on Appropriations, *War Department Appropriation Bill for 1934 Military Activities, Hearings*, pt. 1, 72d Cong., 2d Sess., 1933, pp. 380–81; Nenninger, "Development of American Armor," p. 134.

[23] Mildred H. Gillie, *Forging the Thunderbolt: A History of the Development of the Armored Force* (Harrisburg, Pa.: Military Service Publishing Co., 1947), pp. 56–57; Nenninger, "Development of American Armor," pp. 137–38.

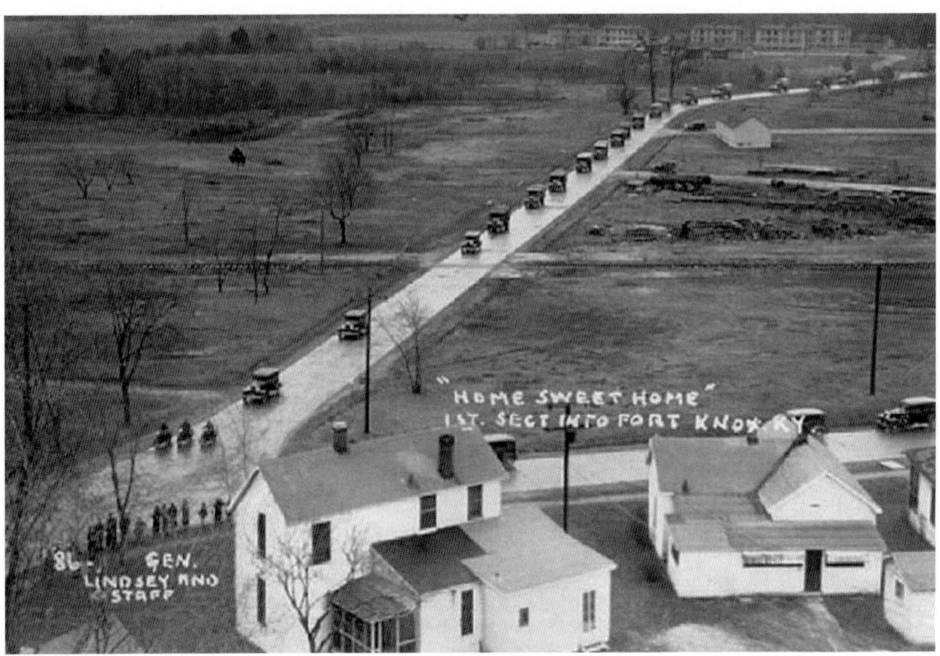

1st Cavalry Regiment (Mechanized) arriving at Fort Knox, 1933

presented its mobilization plan and between 12 May and 1 July succeeded in meeting Roosevelt's CCC national recruitment levels, mobilizing 275,000 men in 1,315 camps.[24]

The War Department met its CCC mobilization goals by diverting energy and personnel to the mission. It drastically curtailed military activities in general and training in particular. Officers attending military schools were graduated early, and the Cavalry School temporarily closed. Large numbers of officers were removed from normal duties to oversee CCC mobilization in a diversion of effort that military planners believed could be sustained only at the cost of national security. Worse, the higher pay available to men joining the Civilian Conservation Corps adversely affected Army recruitment and triggered a rise in desertion.[25]

The 1st Cavalry Regiment (Mechanized) became responsible for 144 CCC camps in the V Corps Area, which included Kentucky. Still struggling to complete its transformation from a horse to a mechanized unit, the regiment now temporarily

---

[24] WD, "Annual Report of the Chief of Staff, United States Army, for the Fiscal Year Ending June 30, 1933," in *Report of the Secretary of War to the President*, 1933, pp. 3–8; *Years of MacArthur*, 1: 421–24.

[25] WD, "Annual Report of Chief of Staff," pp. 8–9; Oral History of General Robert W. Porter Jr., p. 108, Senior Officers Oral History Program, 1981, MHI Archives; Oral History of General Bruce Palmer Jr., pp. 74–75, Senior Officers Oral History Program, Dec 75–Apr 76, MHI Archives; Robert K. Griffith Jr., "Quality Not Quantity: The Volunteer Army During the Depression," *Military Affairs* XLIII, no. 4 (December 1979): 174.

Supporting the Civilian Conservation Corps

lost officers and enlisted soldiers to support CCC activities. The latter included direct supervision of the work camps, managing supply depots for the camps, delivering coal supplies, and repairing roads. Colonel Van Voorhis, commanding the 1st Cavalry Regiment, reported a personnel readiness of only 65 percent after deductions for sickness, furloughs, and detached duty—principally with the Civilian Conservation Corps. The absence of many officers particularly obstructed efforts to conduct training and develop doctrine. The leadership shortage restricted training activities to platoon-size exercises. In effect, the Army's only mechanized cavalry unit found itself only marginally involved with mechanized development.[26]

The Army also provided motor transport and maintenance services for the CCC camps. At Fort Knox, these tasks absorbed the vehicle and maintenance assets intended for the mechanized cavalry. The 28th Motor Repair Section, for example, assumed responsibility for maintaining those vehicles detached on CCC duties. This unit lacked major repair equipment—promised by the War Department but never delivered—and many of its motley collection of vehicles dated back to the World War. Nevertheless, it became immersed in nonstop maintenance activities. Comments within the War Department suggesting that the unit had little work at

[26] Leon Kromer, Address at Cav Sch, 1934, p. 4, Leon B. Kromer Papers, MHI Archives. Ltrs, Col Daniel Van Voorhis to Ch of Cav Maj Gen Guy V. Henry, 29 Jun 33, p. 5, and Col Daniel Van Voorhis to Ch of Cav Maj Gen Guy V. Henry, 11 Jul 33, p. 3, both in Ofc of the Ch of Cav, Gen Corresp, RG 177, NARA. Gillie, *Forging the Thunderbolt*, p. 60.

President Roosevelt's New Deal resulted in new facilities at Fort Knox during the 1930s, including the barracks pictured here.

Fort Knox and should be reassigned resulted in a lengthy rebuttal from the post commander, Brig. Gen. Julian R. Lindsey.[27]

The post infrastructure, however, benefited from the mechanized cavalry's support for the Civilian Conservation Corps. The Works Projects Administration allocated construction funds to Fort Knox for new housing. In July 1933 Colonel Van Voorhis reported the near completion of a motor park for the 1st Cavalry Regiment (Mechanized). The development of facilities also helped make possible the conduct of training in the remaining summer months.[28]

Aside from the diversion of personnel to CCC activities, the mechanized cavalry also suffered from the lack of suitable vehicles and equipment. Continual delays obstructed delivery of the T–4 combat car and personnel carriers. The regiment possessed no 4-wheel-drive armored cars for off-road reconnaissance and depended on an assortment of twenty experimental radio sets for communication. Experiments with different truck types throughout 1933 led to advocacy of the U.S. Army standard 2-ton truck for cargo purposes in the regiment. Though lacking 4-wheel drive, it was deemed satisfactory for mechanized cavalry, which was expected to operate near available road nets.[29]

The Academic Section of the Cavalry School provided the doctrinal foundation of the mechanized cavalry in a 1933 pamphlet. This work presented theoretical principles for the tactical development of the mechanized cavalry but cautioned:

---

[27] Note, Ch of Cav Maj Gen Guy V. Henry to Brig Gen Julian R. Lindsey, 3 Aug 33; Ltr, Brig Gen Julian R. Lindsey to Ch of Cav Maj Gen Guy V. Henry, 7 Aug 33; both in Ofc of the Ch of Cav, Gen Corresp, RG 177, NARA.

[28] Kromer, Address at Cav Sch, 1934, p. 4; Ltrs, Van Voorhis to Henry, 29 Jun 33, p. 5, and 11 Jul 33, p. 3; Gillie, *Forging the Thunderbolt*, p. 60.

[29] Ltr, Van Voorhis to Henry, 29 Jun 33; Note, Maj Robert W. Grow to Maj R. W. Strong, 15 Feb 33; Ltr, Maj Robert W. Strong to Maj Robert W. Grow, 20 Feb 33, Ofc of the Ch of Cav, Gen Corresp, RG 177, NARA.

"Aside from an armored car troop the cavalry service has had no experience in the development of mechanization in our army. The principles enunciated in this pamphlet are based on studies of foreign mechanization, on the experience gained by the mechanized forces of 1928 and 1930–31, and on some experimentation by the Detachment for Mechanized Cavalry Regiment in 1932."[30]

The Cavalry School pamphlet emphasized rapid movement and firepower. The former enabled the mechanized cavalry to move to covered positions close to the enemy, whom it would destroy through firepower. Armored car operations received the most detailed coverage, reflecting cavalry experimentation in the 1920s. Discussion of the combat car focused on its detractions: terrain sensitivity, limited visibility, and purely offensive mission. These limits and the growing threat of antitank weapons led the Cavalry School to conclude that the combat car would have to depend on support from other arms to achieve its maximum effectiveness. Despite the lack of historical precedent, the Cavalry School also envisioned mechanized cavalry in an antimechanization role because its capabilities matched those of other mechanized formations proliferating throughout the world.[31]

Work on the mechanized cavalry's organization began shortly after the disbandment of the Mechanized Force. In February 1932 the regiment consisted of a headquarters and headquarters troop; one machine-gun troop for use as a holding force; a covering squadron of one armored-car troop for distant reconnaissance and one scout-car troop for close reconnaissance and security; and a combat-car squadron of two troops for assault (*see Chart 3*). This structure served as the regiment's baseline organization until field experience and analysis could determine a more effective one.[32]

Such study began even before the arrival of the 1st Cavalry Regiment (Mechanized) at Fort Knox, but proposed modifications routinely met with disapproval outside the Cavalry because they included organic maintenance and repair elements. The mechanized cavalry was expected to depend on Quartermaster Corps and Ordnance units for towing and maintenance. The General Staff reminded Van Voorhis, "Our Cavalry Regiments (Mechanized) must be kept stripped—and if we make any errors they must be on the side of cutting out vehicles rather than adding a single one, no matter how very valuable the particular vehicle might be under certain conditions."[33] The financial stringency of the postwar era, intensified by the Great Depression, encouraged the Army's organizational emphasis on highly

---

[30] Academic Div, Cav Sch, "Mechanized Cavalry," Fort Riley, Kans., 1932–1933, p. 45.

[31] Cav Sch, "Mechanized Cavalry," pp. 41–42, 83. For other examples of the Cavalry's view of combat-car usage, see Hamilton S. Hawkins, "Cavalry and Mechanized Force," *Cavalry Journal* XL, no. 167 (September-October 1931): 19–25; George Grunert, "Cavalry in Future War," *Cavalry Journal* XLII, no. 177 (May-June 1933): 5–10; F. T. Bonsteel, "The Employment of a Mechanized Cavalry Brigade," *Cavalry Journal* XLII, no. 179 (September-October 1933): 19–26.

[32] Leon B. Kromer, "The Cavalry Maneuvers, Fort Riley, Kansas, May 1934," Jun 34, p. 2, Kromer Papers; Cav Sch, "Mechanized Cavalry," p. 47; Ltr, Van Voorhis to Henry, 29 Jun 33.

[33] Ltr, Maj Gen Geo. Van Horn Moseley to Col Daniel Van Voorhis, 16 Feb 33, Ofc of the Ch of Cav, Gen Corresp, RG 177, NARA.

Chart 3–Mechanized Cavalry Regiment, 1932

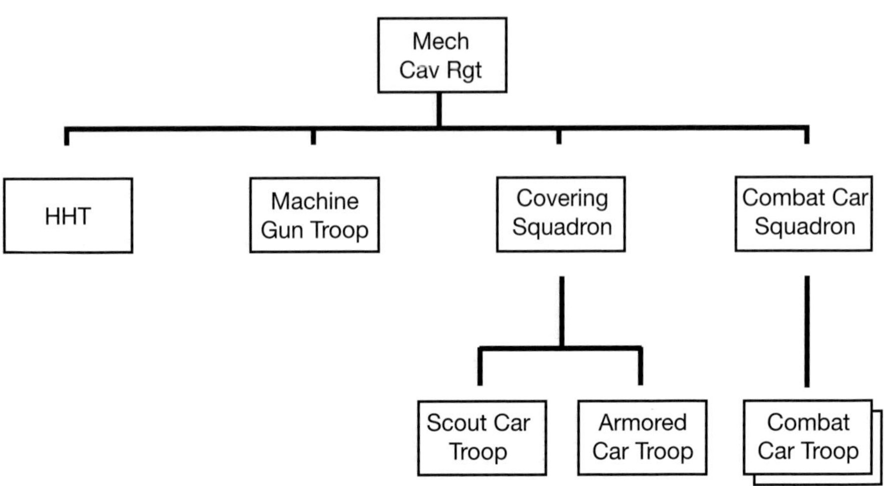

specialized units oriented on their branch's exclusive mission and possessing the minimum of personnel and materiel assets.

Throughout 1933 work on a permanent table of organization for the mechanized cavalry continued. The principal focus lay in preserving the existing number of soldiers assigned to the regiment and minimizing equipment requirements. Funding uncertainties also spurred alternate organizations that assumed the absence of combat cars, but the Cavalry generally preferred to assume their availability. Moreover, planners at Fort Knox favored an increase in combat-car crew size to facilitate operations and maintenance. To permit the breakdown of the regiment into smaller tactical groups, they also included detachable command and control cells within the regimental headquarters. By 1934, however, organizational design efforts had not established a satisfactory organization, partially due to the absence of any actual experience in the operation of mechanized cavalry.[34]

The 1934 Fort Riley Maneuvers

In March 1934 General Henry completed his tenure as chief of Cavalry. Normally, the termination of such an assignment would result in the officer's resuming the rank of colonel. Army Chief of Staff General MacArthur retained Henry as a brigadier general, and he assumed command of the 7th Cavalry Brigade

[34] Ltrs, Van Voorhis to Henry, 29 Jun 33, 11 Jul 33; Grow, "Ten Lean Years," p. 54.

(Mechanized). Later he became the Cavalry School commandant.[35] Maj. Gen. Leon B. Kromer succeeded General Henry as chief of Cavalry. Kromer supported MacArthur's mechanization and motorization program and welcomed mechanized development within the Cavalry, but he did not consider the horse obsolete. In his view, mechanization complemented but did not supplant horse cavalry.[36]

In May the mechanized cavalry participated in maneuvers at Fort Riley in conjunction with horse cavalry elements stationed there.[37] Earlier recommendations from the G–3 (Operations and Training) Division of the War Department General Staff to use the mechanized cavalry in maneuvers at the Infantry School met with disapproval from Maj. Gen. George Van Horn Moseley, the deputy chief of staff. He explained his reasons to Colonel Chaffee, commander of the 1st Cavalry Regiment (Mechanized): "But for one, I do not intend to see our first regiment (mechanized) killed off in a close-in tactical problem for which they are not equipped or organized. I told them in effect that if they will get up a problem where we may have overnight missions involving a couple of hundred miles, we will send the Cavalry Regiment (Mechanized) to take part for under such circumstances appropriate missions could be assigned."[38]

Joint preparation by Cavalry School faculty, who would provide the umpire staffs, and mechanized cavalry officers for the Fort Riley maneuvers began in the autumn of 1933. The 1st Cavalry Regiment (Mechanized) lacked equipment, vehicles, and personnel. It possessed 189 vehicles, but 103 were for supply and maintenance. Of its 24 combat cars, 18 had to be represented by other vehicle types. To extend the reconnaissance zone of the horse regiments participating, the Cavalry School improvised scout cars from salvaged wrecks.[39]

For the maneuvers, a motorized artillery battery and one flight of observation aircraft were attached to the 1st Cavalry Regiment (Mechanized). The nonmechanized force included the 2d and 13th Cavalry Regiments, both permanently posted at Fort Riley. These two regiments constituted the Cavalry School Brigade, which during the maneuvers also included a battalion of attached horse artillery, a troop of motorized engineers, a mechanized chemical platoon, and a flight of observation aircraft.[40]

In the first scenario, the 1st Cavalry Regiment (Mechanized) undertook a reconnaissance mission over multiple river lines while the Cavalry School Brigade conducted counterreconnaissance. Heavy rains delayed 1st Cavalry Regiment

---

[35] Maj. Gen. Charles P. Summerall as chief of staff had instigated a policy of no reappointments of any service-arm chief, which MacArthur continued. Normally an officer either retired with the grade of major general or continued in service as a colonel. Henry, however, had been elevated from colonel to chief of Cavalry despite his reluctance and the lack of any precedent for such a promotion. Upon completion of his tenure as chief of Cavalry, he was allowed to become a brigadier general and assigned to command the 7th Cavalry Brigade (Mechanized).

[36] Kromer, Address at Cav Sch, 1934, pp. 2–5.

[37] Kromer, "Cavalry Maneuvers," p. 1.

[38] Ltr, Moseley to Van Voorhis, 16 Feb 33, p. 1.

[39] Grow, "Ten Lean Years," pp. 47–48; Kromer, Address at Cav Sch, p. 5.

[40] Kromer, "Cavalry Maneuvers," p. 1.

An armored car of the 1st Cavalry Regiment (Mechanized) during the 1934 maneuvers at Fort Riley

operations while it prepared its wheeled vehicles to negotiate the mud. To circumvent simulated bridge demolitions, the regiment conducted a 35-mile night march without lights to another bridge that umpires had erroneously reported clear of demolitions.[41]

In the second scenario the 1st Cavalry Regiment (Mechanized) confronted the 2d Cavalry Regiment in a daytime encounter. Both units sought a centrally located hill as their common objective, but the firepower of the mechanized regiment dominated the battle area.[42] The performance of the combat cars inspired the commandant of the Cavalry School, Brig. Gen. Abraham G. Lott, to remark to horse cavalry personnel: "Look at them. They have 52 caliber .50 guns on fixed mounts. Those are all machine guns protected by armor, and they could run all over that place and burn you up."[43]

The third scenario began at dusk with the mechanized force acting as an advance guard charged with securing bridges against Cavalry School Brigade counter efforts. The horse cavalry interposed itself between the mechanized force and the bridges during a confused night melee and launched a dawn attack while the mechanized cavalry endeavored to concentrate. The 1st Cavalry Regiment (Mechanized) acknowledged the likelihood of its defeat.[44]

---

[41] Ibid., pp. 6–7; Academic Div, Cav Sch, "Report of Maneuvers, The Cavalry School, April–May 1934," 2 vols., MHI Library, 1934, 1: 62.

[42] Kromer, "Cavalry Maneuvers," pp. 9–10.

[43] Cav Sch, "Report of Maneuvers," 1: 108.

[44] Kromer, "Cavalry Maneuvers," pp. 10–11; Cav Sch, "Report of Maneuvers," 1: 2, 143.

Early combat cars of the mechanized cavalry in 1934

The fourth scenario lasted three days and employed the mechanized cavalry on a flanking maneuver designed to obstruct the retreat of an imaginary enemy army using the Cavalry School Brigade as a rearguard. Col. Bruce Palmer commanded the horse cavalry and dispersed his force across a front of forty miles. The motorized engineer unit was broken into numerous demolition teams charged with destroying every bridge conceivably accessible to the mechanized cavalry, ultimately completing sixty simulated destructions. The scout car units of each horse cavalry located and tracked the mechanized cavalry in conjunction with aerial reconnaissance. The rest of the brigade adjusted its positions in accordance with the intelligence received.[45]

The 1st Cavalry Regiment (Mechanized), finding its path repeatedly barred by blown bridges, detoured across the state of Nebraska, covering 460 miles in thirty-six hours. It found a crossing site, but insufficient fuel supplies and personnel fatigue prevented an immediate attack. The Cavalry School Brigade thus gained valuable response time.[46]

In the final three scenarios, the horse and mechanized cavalries operated together against a simulated enemy. The most significant results illustrated the problems posed to a commander of a horse and mechanized unit due to the difference in mobility and

[45] Kromer, "Cavalry Maneuvers," pp. 12–13; Cav Sch, "Report of Maneuvers," 1: 2, 185, 188, 197.

[46] Kromer, "Cavalry Maneuvers," pp. 12–13; Cav Sch, "Report of Maneuvers," 1: 196–98; Grow, "Ten Lean Years," pp. 50–51.

the limits of terrain that restricted mechanized movement.[47] Maneuver restrictions limited the lessons learned. Restrictions on the use of private property prevented simulated combat or off-road movement outside the military reservation. Thus, only during the second scenario, occurring on Fort Riley, did extensive simulated combat occur. Preset time conditions terminated maneuver activity when opposing forces made tactical contact. Curious civilian observers obstructed movement, and radio unreliability beyond short distances led to accusations of signal jamming. Many of the mechanized cavalry components, dependent on radio for command purposes, simply drove out of communication range. At night, units tended to fire before confirming target identification, resulting in numerous friendly fire losses.[48]

The Cavalry's conclusions from the maneuvers, drawn from the reports of participating and observing officers (including General Henry, Colonel Palmer, and Colonel Chaffee) summarized the Cavalry's understanding of mechanization. Noting the bottleneck effect of bridges on the movement of mechanized forces, Cavalry officers considered mechanized units exceptionally terrain sensitive, a condition aggravated by the use of demolitions. They considered mechanized cavalry unsuited for night combat, vulnerable to ambuscade while conducting distant vehicular reconnaissance, subject to personnel fatigue generated by long road marches, and dependent on careful planning of fuel requirements to prevent inaction at critical moments. Yet the strategic mobility, road reconnaissance efficiency, and ability of the mechanized cavalry to negotiate mud and rain at night impressed them.[49]

The officers reviewing the maneuvers noticed an inverse relation between horse and mechanized cavalry. They concluded that combined operations by mechanized and horse units increased overall cavalry effectiveness. The horse elements allowed action at night and in rough terrain and could secure gains made by the mechanized elements. The similarity of fundamental doctrine and training ensured a level of cooperation superior to that possible between elements of different combat arms.[50]

The maneuvers did not demonstrate the need to eliminate horse cavalry or subordinate its development to that of the mechanized cavalry. Instead, they reinforced a prior tendency within horse cavalry regiments to rely on motor vehicles for administrative and support roles and on the horse for tactical transport. In September 1933 the Cavalry completed plans to provide trucks, motorcycles, automobiles, and scout cars to all horse cavalry organizations, subject to budgetary restrictions. The maneuvers encouraged recommendations to completely motorize the supply trains of the horse cavalry regiments and provide truck transport to improve their strategic mobility. The Cavalry believed that lack of terrain sensitivity made the horse the most effective form of tactical transport, but the maneuvers encouraged continued experimentation with motor vehicles in a strategic reconnaissance role that would enable horse cavalry units to monitor the rapid movements of mechanized units.[51]

---

[47] Kromer, "Cavalry Maneuvers," p. 14; Cav Sch, "Report of Maneuvers, April–May 1934," 1: 2.

[48] Cav Sch, "Report of Maneuvers," 1: 62–63, 200; 2: 407.

[49] Kromer, "Cavalry Maneuvers," pp. 8, 18–20.

[50] Cav Sch, "Report of Maneuvers," 2: 412–14.

[51] Ltr, Guy V. Henry to Col C. F. Martin, 27 Sep 33, Ofc of the Ch of Cav, Gen Corresp, RG 177, NARA; Kromer, "Cavalry Maneuvers," pp. 17–20.

The faster tempo of mechanized action required "constant attention . . . to horsemanship and horse mastership in order that the Horsed Cavalry may continue to operate over an extended period of time." Inclusion of the .50-caliber machine gun—considered the antidote to mechanization—in Cavalry rifle troops would provide protection against mechanized units.[52]

The maneuvers also provided an opportunity to test the .50-caliber machine gun, as well as combat cars T–4 and T–5, in an antitank role. The Cavalry accepted the T–5 and requested production of twenty-eight. The .50-caliber's ability to be assembled or disassembled rapidly for transport via horse pack and its armor penetration, rated at ½-inch at 1,100 yards and ¾-inch at 600 yards, resulted in a request for 350 to equip horse cavalry units; but cost considerations reduced the anticipated delivery rate to only 29 before 1936.[53]

Reorganization of the Mechanized Cavalry

A series of personnel changes within the mechanized cavalry followed the Fort Riley maneuvers. General Henry remained in command of the 7th Cavalry Brigade (Mechanized) into 1935. Colonel Palmer, the former assistant commandant of the Cavalry School, replaced Colonel Van Voorhis as commander of the 1st Cavalry Regiment (Mechanized) after commanding the Cavalry School Brigade during the Fort Riley maneuvers. Palmer's staff included Lt. Col. Henry Baird as executive officer and Lt. Col. Willis D. Crittenberger as operations officer responsible for tactics development. Colonel Van Voorhis departed for service in Hawaii.[54]

Colonel Chaffee became the chief of the Budget and Legislative Planning Branch in the Office of the Deputy Chief of Staff. He continued to monitor mechanized cavalry activities and retained close ties with those officers directly responsible for its development. Chaffee's own duties included oversight of War Department financial matters. In this capacity he acted as a de facto liaison officer for Cavalry mechanization. He helped to ensure funding availability and used his direct access to General Staff members and the combat- and service-arms chiefs to promote mechanized cavalry development. In turn, Cavalry officers routinely consulted him on matters of mechanization. In this manner Chaffee became a central influence on mechanized cavalry affairs.[55]

After the Fort Riley maneuvers, the mechanized cavalry found few opportunities to practice its craft beyond the military reservation at Fort Knox. A General Headquarters (GHQ) command post exercise held in New Jersey in September 1934 included mechanized and horse cavalry operating as components of a provisional cavalry corps. However, it involved only commanders and their staffs. Conclusions from this exercise underscored the value of using mechanized and horse cavalry

---

[52] Kromer, "Cavalry Maneuvers," pp. 20–21.

[53] Grow, "Ten Lean Years"; Kromer, "Cavalry Maneuvers," pp. 3–4, 16, 22.

[54] Henry, "Brief Narrative," pp. 64, 67; Grow, "Ten Lean Years," pp. 47, 55; Nenninger, "Development of American Armor," p. 146.

[55] Gillie, *Forging the Thunderbolt*, p. 89; Nenninger, "Development of American Armor," p. 148.

together. The latter's better cross-country mobility offset the road-bound nature of the former. Plans to include mechanized cavalry in army-level maneuvers in 1935 ended when the War Department cancelled all large-scale training because of insufficient funds. In June of that year a small detachment from the 1st Cavalry Regiment (Mechanized) traveled to the U.S. Military Academy at West Point to introduce the cadets to mechanized cavalry.[56]

In the absence of large-scale maneuver participation, many mechanized cavalry officers gained invaluable command experience supervising CCC activities in Kentucky. They worked in varied weather and terrain conditions far from major road nets, towns, and cities. They organized and managed supply conduits from railheads to work camps. To coordinate the actions of scattered work parties, they built communications networks using radios and messengers to compensate for the absence of telephones lines. They also honed personal leadership skills while directing the daily activities of work parties. These experiences instilled an understanding of command, communications, and supply flow that benefited officers responsible for leading mobile combat formations over broad frontages.[57]

At Fort Knox, the 1934 maneuvers became the subject of analysis intended to improve the organization of the mechanized cavalry regiment. An informal board of officers convened with the chief of Cavalry's approval to address this issue. A formal War Department board, requiring special authorization and subject to the concurrence of the chiefs of the combat and service arms and the General Staff, was not considered necessary or desirable.[58]

Despite the avoidance of potential War Department interference, however, a shortage of officers at Fort Knox hindered the board's work. The lack of regulatory precedent for mechanized cavalry increased the routine workload of the few commissioned officers available. Noncommissioned officers unaccustomed to the standard operating procedures of mechanized cavalry could not assume such responsibilities as they did in horse cavalry units. CCC support continued to draw officers away from Fort Knox, while normal duty rotations created additional, temporary losses until replacements arrived for those officers departing to new assignments.[59]

Nevertheless, the Mechanized Cavalry Board developed a number of proposals. Board members considered their primary goal the creation of the smallest unit commensurate with desired increases in combat power. Their recommendations included the addition of a motorized engineer unit to assist river crossings, a support

---

[56] Cav Sch, "Report of Maneuvers," 2: 419; MacArthur, "Modernization of the Army," p. 60; Ltr with "Extracts of Reports on New Jersey Command Post Exercises," Ch of Cav Maj Gen Leon B. Kromer to Col Ben Lear, 4 Mar 35, Ofc of the Ch of Cav, Gen Corresp, RG 177, NARA; Press Release, "Cadets To Receive Instruction in Mechanization," 4 Jun 35, RG 177, NARA.

[57] H. Jordan Theis, "Yet Another Treasure and Problem for the Army," *Cavalry Journal* XLV, no. 4 (July-August 1936): 292–95; Ronald Spector, "The Military Effectiveness of the U.S. Armed Forces," in *Military Effectiveness*, 3 vols., ed. Allan R. Millett and Williamson Murray (Boston: Allen and Unwin, 1988), 2: 72.

[58] Ltrs, Ch of Cav Maj Gen Leon B. Kromer to Brig Gen Guy V. Henry, 12 Jul 34, and Brig Gen Guy V. Henry to Ch of Cav Maj Gen Leon B. Kromer, 19 Jul 34, both in Ofc of the Ch of Cav, Gen Corresp, RG 177, NARA.

[59] Ltr, Henry to Kromer, 19 Jul 34.

M1 combat car of the 1st Cavalry Regiment (Mechanized), ca. 1935

unit to secure seized ground, new tactical formations less vulnerable to antitank fire, and the inclusion of mortars to suppress antitank weapons. In all of its proposals, however, the board carefully avoided any personnel reduction.[60]

To increase the unit's tactical flexibility the board prepared five variations of the existing table of organization and equipment for the 1st Cavalry Regiment (Mechanized). Significantly, all included the provision of one or two squadron headquarters detachments, command nodes through which the regimental commander decentralized control of combat assets. These headquarters detachments facilitated operation of the regiment as a collection of independently operating components. On the basis of the regiment's mission, the regimental commander assigned tasks to each one. Collective accomplishment of these smaller objectives simultaneously fulfilled the regiment's mission.[61]

These ideas presaged the later combat command arrangement and derived from Cavalry doctrine. The Cavalry envisioned the use of horse regiments, not as rigid blocks of men and horses in the fashion of Napoleonic cuirassiers, but as a collection of small groupings dispersed throughout the battle area. The replacement of the

[60] Kromer, "Cavalry Maneuvers," pp. 17–20; Memo, Brig Gen Guy V. Henry to CO, 1st Cav (Mechanized), sub: Reorganization, 1 Aug 34, Ofc of the Ch of Cav, Gen Corresp, RG 177, NARA.

[61] Ltr, Lt Col Adna R. Chaffee to Maj I. G. Walker, 15 Aug 34, Ofc of the Ch of Cav, Gen Corresp, RG 177, NARA.

Chart 4–Proposed Mechanized Cavalry Regiment, 1935

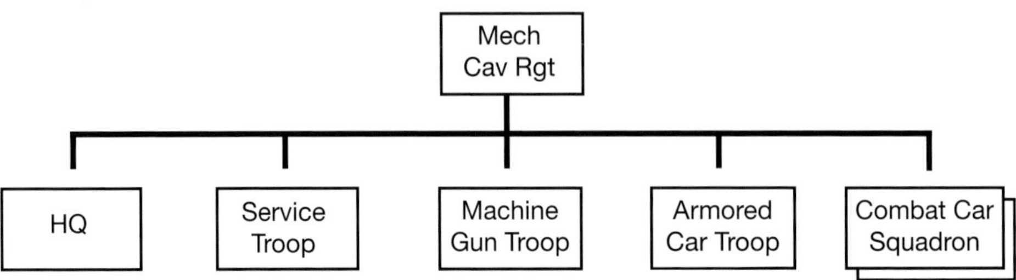

horse by motor vehicles increased the extent and rate of this dispersion, mandating a flexible organization. All the plans created by the Fort Knox board reflected these ideas, but none prescribed how the regiment should break down into smaller components. This responsibility belonged to the regimental commander, based on his assessment of the tactical situation.

Chief of Cavalry Kromer endorsed the ideas of the Fort Knox board. He requested its approval and the rapid implementation of proposed organizational changes to the mechanized cavalry regiment (*Chart 4*). The latter constituted a major restructuring of the unit. Supply and maintenance responsibilities within the regiment moved from the headquarters to a separate service troop. This eliminated the previous practice of assigning too many functions to the headquarters troop commander. The regiment lost a scout-car troop but gained a second combat-car squadron, which raised the total number of combat cars from thirty-six to fifty-six. Combat-car platoons shrank from five vehicles to three, the maximum number thought controllable by a single platoon commander. However, the total number of platoons increased in an effort to provide greater command flexibility. The machine-gun troop's defensive capability improved through the addition of more light machine guns, a cavalry rifle platoon, and .50-caliber machine guns for use in an antitank role.[62]

Overall, the changes reflected in Chart 4 marked a significant improvement in offensive and defensive capabilities. The mechanized cavalry regiment gained firepower, assets to secure ground seized, and better command and control. Implementation mandated a personnel increase of 6 officers and 139 enlisted men and the addition of 20 combat cars, 62 trucks, and nearly 200 machine guns ranging from .30- to .50-caliber. The chief of Cavalry considered the benefits worth the additional cost.[63]

---

[62] Draft Memo, Ch of Cav Maj Gen Leon B. Kromer to TAG, sub: Continuation of Development of Mechanized Cavalry, 28 Mar 35; Memo, Ch of Cav Maj Gen Leon B. Kromer to TAG, sub: Modifications of Procurement Program for the 1st Cavalry (Mecz.), 4 Apr 35, both in Ofc of the Ch of Cav, Gen Corresp, RG 177, NARA.

[63] Draft Memo, Kromer to TAG, 28 Mar 35; Memo, Kromer to TAG, 4 Apr 35, pp. 4–5.

Mechanized cavalry armored car, 1936

Kromer also supported further mechanized cavalry experimentation with a platoon of six 4.2-inch mortars mounted in 4-wheel-drive trucks. The mortars laid smoke to cover combat-car advances and to blind hostile antitank guns. The platoon would be assigned to the headquarters troop for support of subordinate units as necessary and manned by cavalry personnel to ensure continuity of doctrine. This seemingly straightforward proposal, however, brought the chief of Cavalry into direct conflict with the chiefs of the Field Artillery and the Chemical Warfare Service. The latter contended that the release of any chemical agent, including smoke, was the mission of the Chemical Warfare Service. Hence the platoon should be a chemical unit attached but not assigned to the 7th Cavalry Brigade (Mechanized). The chief of Field Artillery argued that all mortar missions properly belonged to the artillery. Therefore Field Artillery should be the proponent for development of any mortar unit.[64]

[64] Ibid.; Memo, Ch of Cav Maj Gen Leon B. Kromer to Assistant Chief of Staff (ACS), G–3, sub: Mortar Platoon, 1st Cavalry (Mecz), 27 Mar 35, Ofc of the Ch of Cav, Gen Corresp, RG 177, NARA; Memo, Kromer to TAG, 4 Apr 35, p. 2; Draft Memo, ACS Brig Gen John H. Hughes to CS, sub: Organization, Equipment, and Funds for the 1st Cavalry, Mechanized, n.d., p. 1, Ofc of the Ch of Cav, Gen Corresp, RG 177, NARA.

The mortar debate symbolized the shortcomings of the bureau system. It could not easily accommodate developments that tended to merge the separate missions of the combat arms. Moreover, the atmosphere of financial stringency ensured that such debates quickly escalated into internecine strife among the branches. The General Staff served as an arbiter of sorts in these conflicts, but too often its decisions reflected a desire to reconcile the bureaus rather than to impart decisions on them—even when it lay in the Army's interest to do so.

The Bureau System and Mechanized Cavalry Reorganization

Initially, the General Staff favorably received General Kromer's proposals. The G–3 Division concurred with them, noting their underlying tendency to transform the mechanized cavalry regiment from "a light, mechanized reconnaissance unit, towards a heavy self-contained mechanized striking force." The G–3 accepted this change, believing it to be an appropriate modernization of the Cavalry's tradition of combining shock action and close combat. He cautioned, however, that mechanized cavalry must not be designed to perform all potential mechanized activities. The G–3 stressed the importance of specialization, following the British example of creating different mechanized units to perform separate tasks. Nevertheless, he noted that "Since mechanization induces specialization, and intensifies the differences between specialties, it creates the necessity for an increasing flexibility in the organization of specialized means for an end." Cavalry efforts to improve the mechanized cavalry's command and organizational flexibility seemed to make it better able to fulfill the specific missions assigned to it in 1931.[65]

The General Staff's early support for the Cavalry proposals waned, however, in light of their impact on existing branch relationships. The G–3 expected the changing nature of cavalry mechanization to undermine efforts to coordinate mechanization throughout the combat arms. Therefore, he considered the creation of a GHQ mechanized force patterned on the GHQ Air Force established on 1 March 1935. The GHQ Air Force centralized control of Air Corps combat elements but left responsibility for technical development, procurement, administration, and schooling to the chief of the Air Corps. Similarly, the GHQ mechanized force would centralize control over the Army's mechanized assets.[66]

The GHQ mechanized force would not include any regiments. Instead, to enhance organizational flexibility, smaller tactical mechanized units drawn from the combat arms, each functionally organized to perform a specific type of mechanized activity, would operate together under specially created group headquarters.[67] In effect this concept preserved the combat arms' independent influence on mechanized development without establishing a rival branch. The G–3 considered the creation of a new branch but rejected this action due to its likely disruptive impact on the bureau system:

---

[65] Draft Memo, Hughes to CS, n.d., p. 1.

[66] Ibid., pp. 2–3; MacArthur, "Modernization of the Army," p. 56.

[67] Draft Memo, Hughes to CS, n.d., pp. 4–5.

> There is much to be said for the creation of a mechanized arm. It would serve to focus public attention on the fact that the Army faces a problem of modernization on the ground as well as in the air. On the other hand, it would add overhead. Above all there would unquestionably be serious difficulty in coordinating this new arm with all other arms. The entire personnel situation would be thrown into confusion. . . . To place all mechanization under a single arm also would have advantages. On the other hand, there would unquestionably be aroused much inter-branch friction which would be most unfortunate. It seems unnecessary to disturb the existing friendly relations to such an extent.[68]

These considerations led the G–3 to recommend the disapproval of General Kromer's proposals. He further recanted his office's earlier enthusiasm for the recommended changes to the mechanized cavalry regiment. The Cavalry was now criticized for deviating from War Department mechanization policy through the creation of a unit capable of accomplishing battlefield tasks normally distributed among the combat arms. The G–3 also recommended restrictions on cavalry tank usage and the limitation of cavalry mechanization toward the use of light, fast, and inexpensive personnel carriers. Otherwise, "it might easily happen that these expensive, hard to procure combat cars (tanks) might become worn out in the preliminary tasks of combat and therefore be not available when the opportunity presented itself for the use of their striking force and fire power."[69]

Ironically, the G–3's criticism did not highlight the organizational deviation of the mechanized cavalry regiment from the views of Chief of Staff General MacArthur. The latter emphasized the enhancement of speed and mobility as the principal aim of all changes to tables of organization and equipment. He believed these characteristics would prevent future military operations from devolving into a static war of attrition. Therefore, he sought to minimize the equipment deemed necessary for combat units:

> Difficulty in movement mounts rapidly with the size of the command, and the effort must be to reduce every echelon to the smallest possible size consistent with requisite power in shock and fire action. Homogeneity promotes mobility. The small units of the front lines—certainly to include the battalions of infantry—must abandon the attempt to include within themselves every type of tactical power of which they may have occasional need. Emergency and special fires must be furnished by supporting troops separately organized so that the front line unit and its commander may concentrate on one objective and one type of problem and carry their own tasks swiftly to completion. Each portion of the whole command must trust

[68] Ibid., p. 4.

[69] Memo, ACS Brig Gen John H. Hughes to the CS, sub: Organization, Equipment, and Funds for the 1st Cavalry (Mecz.), 17 Apr 35, quote from p. 3, Ofc of the Ch of Cav, Gen Corresp, RG 177, NARA.

> every other portion to perform its own missions properly and promptly. Our whole tactical organization must be developed in this concept.[70]

MacArthur's views reflected and reinforced the Army's organizational emphasis on separation by branch mission and battlefield function. His belief in the importance of a homogeneous organization effectively precluded the creation of a combined-arms unit that integrated weapon types and actions normally distributed among several combat arms. Given the mission orientation of the Army, such a unit was superfluous and unnecessarily duplicated the tactical responsibilities of the combat arms.

Yet the Cavalry considered the proposed mechanized cavalry regiment organization ideal precisely because the regiment could perform multiple functions without external support. The original tasks assigned to mechanized cavalry in 1931 included reconnaissance, pursuit, exploitation, envelopment, the rapid seizure of key terrain in advance of main-force elements, and service as a mobile reserve. To meet this range of activity, mechanized cavalry regiment design gravitated toward a multipurpose, self-sufficient organization capable of independent operations. The inclusion of organic mortar, maintenance, and supply elements in organizational tables reflected this emphasis.[71]

MacArthur expected the mechanized Cavalry to "speedily support air operations and sustain the opportunities created by it until additional forces can come into action."[72] This role also had been recommended during the command post exercise of September 1934. However, it necessitated operations in advance of an attacking army, reinforcing the desire for self-sufficiency in vehicle maintenance to avoid leaving along the line of march a trail of disabled vehicles awaiting removal to repair facilities far to the rear.[73]

The divergence of the mechanized cavalry from established organizational trends, however, does not appear to have excited much comment or criticism except from the G–3. The mechanized cavalry constituted only a small fraction of Army activities, and no doctrinal precedent existed for mechanized cavalry regiments or brigades. Therefore, the War Department continued to view cavalry mechanization as largely experimental and adhered to its original program to gradually expand the extent of this effort.

In April 1935 the War Department assigned the 1st Battalion, 68th Field Artillery Regiment (Mechanized), to Fort Knox for combined training and to provide fire support for the 7th Cavalry Brigade (Mechanized) to which it was attached. The former was charged with developing suitable tactics and techniques for the effective support of a mechanized unit and determining "the most efficient organization and types of equipment and armament for mechanized field artillery units." Although

[70] MacArthur, "Modernization of the Army," pp. 49–50.

[71] Memo, Maj Willis D. Crittenberger to CG, Seventh Cav Bde, sub: Tables of Organization, T/O 423 P (Mecz), 5 Jul 35, pp. 7–10, Ofc of the Ch of Cav, Gen Corresp, RG 177, NARA.

[72] MacArthur, "Modernization of the Army," p. 53.

[73] Ltr, Kromer to Lear, 4 Mar 35; Memo, Crittenberger to CG, Seventh Cav Bde, 5 Jul 35, and 1st End, Brig Gen Guy V. Henry to Ch of Cav, 6 Jul 35; all in RG 177, NARA.

Early halftracks used by the mechanized cavalry

the mechanized cavalry and artillery had separate development goals, together they were expected to develop the principles for effective tactical coordination.[74]

The arrival of an artillery unit at Fort Knox accelerated the organizational trend of the mechanized cavalry toward independence and self-sufficiency. It also served to distinguish the mechanized cavalry from the rest of the branch. The attachment of the 1st Battalion, 68th Field Artillery Regiment (Mechanized), to the 7th Cavalry Brigade (Mechanized) underscored this process, because the latter became the Army's only combined-arms unit. Outside Fort Knox, units from different combat arms operated together only during maneuvers and periodic tactical field exercises; they were not permanently stationed together.

The same directive that collocated artillery at Fort Knox also charged the commanding general, V Corps Area, with the further development of the 7th Cavalry Brigade (Mechanized). In effect, the War Department loosened the administrative and supervisory bond between the chief of Cavalry and the only mechanized cavalry force. Symbolically, the War Department referred to the 7th Cavalry Brigade (Mechanized) and the 1st Battalion, 68th Field Artillery Regiment (Mechanized), collectively as the Mechanized Force, the same name given the independent mechanized formation created in 1930. However, the War Department did not seek the creation of a separate mechanized arm. Instead, it acted to discourage the perception that development of both mechanized artillery and cavalry was the responsibility of any single branch chief.[75]

---

[74] TAG, "War Department Policies," 5 Apr 35, p. 2.

[75] Grow, "Ten Lean Years," pp. 58–59; TAG, "War Department Policies," 5 Apr 35, p. 3.

Additional impetus to mechanized development occurred on 26 April 1935, when both the chief of staff and deputy chief of staff approved General Kromer's proposals to modify the organization of the mechanized cavalry regiment. Colonel Chaffee influenced this decision by submitting to the deputy chief of staff a memorandum that emphasized the fiscal viability of the proposed changes and the regiment's need for additional materiel to accomplish its assigned missions. Chaffee also refuted the G–3's criticisms and argued against any limitation on combat-car use by the cavalry.[76]

Mechanization of a Second Cavalry Regiment

Despite the acceptance of MacArthur's mechanization and motorization program in 1931, the Cavalry had been unable to obtain from the War Department a clear statement regarding the desirable proportion of horse to mechanized cavalry regiments. Nor had it received guidance as to when a second mechanized regiment should be formed. Nevertheless, Cavalry planning for a second mechanized regiment had begun simultaneously with the establishment of the 1st Cavalry Regiment (Mechanized). Following the 1934 Fort Riley maneuvers, this planning intensified. The Cavalry formally broached the subject with the General Staff in February and again in November 1935. By 1936 the development of the 1st Cavalry Regiment (Mechanized) was considered sufficiently advanced to warrant creation of a second mechanized regiment to complete the 7th Cavalry Brigade (Mechanized). The assignment of the 1st Battalion, 68th Field Artillery Regiment, at Fort Knox strengthened this belief. The related issues of which regiment would be mechanized and where it would be stationed, however, delayed War Department action.[77]

Initially, the Cavalry planned to mechanize the 4th Cavalry Regiment, stationed at Fort Meade, South Dakota, and relocate it to Fort Knox. There it would benefit from the experience and tutelage of 1st Cavalry Regiment (Mechanized) personnel and enable all elements of the 7th Cavalry Brigade (Mechanized) to train as one. Fort Knox already possessed the base facilities and post administration for support of a mechanized unit whereas Fort Meade did not, necessitating expenditures for construction and overhead. In addition, the Cavalry considered the retention of the 4th Cavalry Regiment at Fort Meade unnecessary, because it performed no special function there.[78]

---

[76] Memo, Lt Col Adna R. Chaffee to Deputy Chief of Staff, 1st Cav M, sub: Organization, Equipment, and Funds for the 1st Cavalry (Mecz.), 22 Apr 35, Ofc of the Ch of Cav, Gen Corresp, RG 177, NARA; Memo, ACS to CS, 17 Apr 35, penciled note.

[77] Henry, "Brief Narrative," p. 65; Memo, Col A. M. Miller to Col Adna R. Chaffee, sub: Station and Housing for the Second Mechanized Regiment of Cavalry, 25 Apr 36, p. 3, Ofc of the Ch of Cav, Gen Corresp, RG 177, NARA.

[78] Ltr, Van Voorhis to Henry, 29 Jun 33, p. 1. Memo, Miller to Chaffee, 25 Apr 36, and 2d End of Unknown Document Encl with this Memo, Ofc Ch of Cav to ACS, G–3, 27 Feb 35; Memo, C. L. Scott, sub: Mechanization of a Second Regiment of Cavalry, 4 May 36; all in Ofc of the Ch of Cav, Gen Corresp, RG 177, NARA.

Christie light tank in use by the mechanized cavalry

But moving the 4th Cavalry Regiment to Fort Knox meant closing Fort Meade and halting the related economic activity, a consequence some congressmen were unwilling to countenance, especially in an election year. The resultant political opposition forced the abandonment of the effort to mechanize the 4th Cavalry Regiment.[79]

To avoid similar political opposition, mechanized cavalry officers next proposed activating a currently inactive cavalry regiment, the 15th Cavalry Regiment, at Fort Knox. Older vehicles from the 1st Cavalry Regiment (Mechanized) and a portion of its new deliveries would provide the vehicular nucleus for the 15th Cavalry Regiment (Mechanized). Personnel requirements for the latter would be met with drafts from existing horse cavalry regiments, new recruits, and the transfer of personnel from the 1st Cavalry Regiment to provide a cadre of trained mechanized personnel.[80]

This plan foundered on the opposition of the War Department General Staff Divisions G–1 (Personnel), G–3 (Operations and Training), and G–4 (Supply). The heads of these divisions argued that activating the 15th Cavalry Regiment would upset the current mobilization plans by creating an additional cavalry regiment not

[79] Memo, Scott, 4 May 36; Memo, Col Charles L. Scott to General Kromer, sub: Data on the Mechanization of Second Regiment of Cavalry, 8 May 36, p. 1, Ofc of the Ch of Cav, Gen Corresp, RG 177, NARA.

[80] Memo, Col Bruce Palmer to Ch of Cav, sub: Plan for Reactivation of the 15th Cavalry (Mechanized), 29 Apr 36, Ofc of the Ch of Cav, Gen Corresp, RG 177, NARA.

encompassed in these plans, incur added housing construction costs, and mandate added personnel and overhead expenses. Although Kromer had earlier endorsed activation of the 15th Cavalry Regiment, he was temporarily hospitalized and unavailable to answer the criticisms of the General Staff. The Cavalry unsuccessfully tried to communicate its views through Colonel Chaffee, again acting in his unofficial role as mechanized cavalry liaison, to the deputy chief of staff and chief of staff. On 4 May the General Staff formally disapproved reactivation of the 15th Cavalry Regiment or any other inactive cavalry regiment, forcing reconsideration of how to mechanize a second cavalry.[81]

Through Chaffee mechanized cavalry advocates learned that the chief of staff's disapproval of the 15th Cavalry Regiment action stemmed from its potential disruption of negotiations with Congress concerning an increase in the Army's establishment. Upon Kromer's return to duty, Cavalry officers urged him to confer personally with the chief of staff and advocate a reconsideration of the 15th Cavalry Regiment option. They felt, "We are certain to *arouse* a lot of *political* opposition no matter what regiment we may move away from its present station."[82] Kromer was also encouraged to consult Van Voorhis, now a brigadier general and thought to have considerable influence on the chief of staff. The emphasis on immediate action was necessary: "If not, with the present trend of thought in Congress and in the War Department we open ourselves to the criticism of being *reactionary* and lukewarm to progress in this important problem—and thus play into the hands of those persons who wish to confine cavalry mechanization to scout cars and armored cars."[83]

Nevertheless, the chief of staff still disapproved activation of the 15th Cavalry Regiment; but the efforts to make him reconsider reflect a perception of Cavalry mechanization as a struggle against conservative minds within the War Department and as a way to deflect congressional criticism of the Cavalry as obsolete. To prevent further obstructions to the mechanization of a second cavalry regiment, the Cavalry adopted what previously had been only a contingency measure. It would mechanize one of the two regiments stationed at Fort Riley and transfer it to Fort Knox, reassigning some of its personnel to the remaining regiment to increase its establishment to war strength. Although this action reduced the number of troops available to the Cavalry School, it alleviated the overcrowding at Fort Riley due to its shortage of permanent housing. An anticipated congressionally approved increase in Cavalry personnel would compensate for any shortfalls resulting in either regiment. The Cavalry also noted that a precedent for creating a war-strength unit at a service school already existed within both the Infantry and the Field Artillery.[84]

---

[81] Ltr, Col A. M. Miller Jr. to Maj Gen Leon B. Kromer, 25 Apr 36, Ofc of the Ch of Cav, Gen Corresp, RG 177, NARA; Memo, Acting ACS, Brig Gen Duncan K. Major Jr. to Ch of Cav, sub: Second Mechanized Regiment of the 2nd Cavalry Brigade, Mechanized, 4 May 36, Ofc of the Ch of Cav, Gen Corresp, RG 177, NARA; Note, Col A. M. Miller Jr. to Col Bruce Palmer, 320.2/__th Cavalry, 5 May 36, Ofc of the Ch of Cav, Gen Corresp, RG 177, NARA.

[82] Memo, Scott to Kromer, 8 May 36, quote from p. 1.

[83] Ibid., p. 1.

[84] Ibid., pp. 3–4; Memo, Col A. M. Miller Jr. to Ch of Cav, sub: Mechanization of an Additional Regiment, 7 May 36, Ofc of the Ch of Cav, Gen Corresp, RG 177, NARA; Memo, Scott, 4 May 36;

Because this plan affected only the Cavalry, opposition remained limited to members within that combat arm. This opposition focused on the need to transfer the prospective mechanized cavalry regiment to Fort Knox. Opponents of the move, led by Cavalry School Commandant General Henry, who had previously commanded the 7th Cavalry Brigade (Mechanized), argued that removing either Cavalry School regiment would be "fatal to the continued practical instruction at this school of all cavalry components of the Army of the United States." The presence of a mechanized and a horse cavalry regiment, however, would stimulate development of mechanized cavalry doctrine and familiarize the cavalry arm with mechanization. Henry believed that the 7th Cavalry Brigade (Mechanized) should be concentrated at Fort Knox, but not at the expense of Fort Riley.[85]

Forced to choose between overruling the commandant of the Cavalry School or engaging in a prolonged battle with congressmen and the General Staff that he might easily lose, the chief of Cavalry opted for the former. The 13th Cavalry Regiment would mechanize and relocate to Fort Knox. Such action did not impact political concerns, disrupt branch relations, upset mobilization planning, or require additional personnel. It mandated some construction at Fort Knox, but it did not require substantially altering the Cavalry's budget. Consequently, the 13th Cavalry Regiment was authorized to transfer to Fort Knox in September 1936, under the command of Col. Charles L. Scott. Despite the housing shortage at Fort Knox and the high percentage of married men whose families would have to relocate, the personnel of the 13th Cavalry Regiment opted to remain with their regiment.[86]

The machinations culminating in the mechanization of the 13th Cavalry Regiment helped establish Fort Knox as the center of mechanized cavalry activity. Generals Kromer and Van Voorhis, Colonel Chaffee, and several mechanized cavalry officers strongly supported concentration of the elements of the 7th Cavalry Brigade (Mechanized). Much of this emphasis derived from the logic of concentrating for training purposes the elements of the unit, reinforced by the financial considerations of preparing another cavalry station for mechanized operations. Cavalry mechanization's exclusive association with Fort Knox, however, marked the emergence of the mechanized cavalry's separate identity from the rest of the cavalry arm, symbolized by the 750 miles separating Fort Knox and Fort Riley, the center for cavalry education and doctrinal development.

Memo, Ch of Cav Maj Gen Leon B. Kromer to ACS, G–3, WD, sub: Second Mechanized Regiment of the 7th Cavalry Brigade (Mechanized), 15 May 36, Ofc of the Ch of Cav, Gen Corresp, RG 177, NARA.

[85] Memo, Miller to Ch of Cav, 7 May 36; Memo, Commandant Brig Gen Guy V. Henry to Ch of Cav, sub: Completion of the Organization of the 7th Cavalry Brigade (Mecz.) by Mechanizing One Horse Regiment at Fort Riley, Kansas, 9 May 36, Ofc of the Ch of Cav, Gen Corresp, RG 177, NARA.

[86] Memo, Ch of Cav to ACS, G–3, WD, 15 May 36; Memo, TAG to Ch of Cav, sub: Mechanization of a Second Regiment of Cavalry, 2 Jun 36; Memo, TAG to CG, V Corps Area, sub: Mechanization of a Second Regiment of Cavalry, 2 Jun 36; Note, Col A. M. Miller Jr. to Maj Gen Leon B. Kromer, 3 Aug 36; Immediate Action Memo, TAG to Ch of Cav, sub: Mechanization of the 13th Cavalry, 14 Aug 36; Ltr, Capt J. H. Claybrook to Col Charles L. Scott, 21 Jul 36; all in Ofc of the Ch of Cav, Gen Corresp, RG 177, NARA.

Second Army Maneuvers of 1936

The Second Army maneuvers of August 1936 marked the first interaction between mechanized cavalry and other combat arms on an appreciable scale. The mechanized cavalry therefore spent much of the period from autumn 1935 to August 1936 preparing for its participation. It especially emphasized the use of night marches to exploit its superior strategic mobility and use of brief, fragmentary orders in lieu of the standard five-paragraph written form stipulated in Army regulations. Mechanized cavalry officers were also encouraged to continue to perceive the subunits of the mechanized cavalry regiment as basic ingredients to be assembled into combinations appropriate to changing tactical situations.

The maneuvers included two phases, the first at Fort Knox and the second in the vicinity of Allegan, Michigan. From the Cavalry's perspective, the maneuvers tested the latest developments of the mechanized cavalry and the ability of motorized infantry to assist mechanized units. Commanded by Colonel Palmer, the mechanized contingent consisted of the 7th Cavalry Brigade (Mechanized), including the 1st Cavalry Regiment (Mechanized); the 1st Battalion, 68th Field Artillery Regiment (Mechanized); an additional motorized artillery battalion temporarily attached; a squadron of observation aircraft; a motorized infantry battalion; and service units.[87]

The Fort Knox phase of the maneuvers included three scenarios in which the mechanized cavalry fought against forces from a fictitious country dubbed Blue. The first two scenarios required the mechanized cavalry to delay a Blue infantry corps and a horse cavalry brigade advancing in three columns south from the town of West Point, Kentucky, toward Elizabethtown. In both cases Palmer used the armored-car troop and observation aircraft to pinpoint enemy troop movements. After locating the Blue force, he deployed task forces of motorized infantry and artillery to obstruct its advance while enveloping it with the 1st Cavalry Regiment (Mechanized) supported by artillery. Several Blue infantry units were overrun as a result.[88]

In the third scenario, the strategic situation was altered by the assumption that another nation had declared war on Blue, mandating the rapid withdrawal of its forces to the Ohio River. The mechanized cavalry mission focused on disrupting this retreat. Palmer opted for a night flank march that almost bogged down in rough terrain, muddy roads, and a stream that required motorized infantry detachments to prepare a crossing site for vehicles. Despite these obstacles, the mechanized cavalry reached the front of the withdrawing Blue forces and launched a dawn attack before they could deploy.[89]

During the Allegan, Michigan, phase, the mechanized cavalry operated with motorized and nonmotorized infantry and a horse cavalry regiment against a Blue

---

[87] Bruce Palmer, "Mechanized Cavalry in the Second Army Maneuvers," *Cavalry Journal* XLV, no. 6 (November-December 1936): 461.

[88] Ibid., pp. 463–67.

[89] Ibid., pp. 467–69.

infantry corps supported by a horse cavalry squadron. The 7th Cavalry Brigade (Mechanized) repeated its envelopment tactics, but the limited size of the maneuver area coupled with private property restrictions kept the fast-moving columns on roads and precluded an assault by the entire 1st Cavalry Regiment. Nevertheless, the latter employed aggressive reconnaissance and small-scale flanking movements to get into the Blue rear area, theoretically poised for a decisive blow.[90]

The 7th Cavalry Brigade returned to Fort Knox on 22 August, and evaluation of its maneuver experience commenced. The use of motorized infantry in conjunction with mechanized cavalry was considered a success. Motorized infantry pinned opposing forces while the mechanized cavalry enveloped them. The infantry then secured the ground taken and the cavalry continued its advance. In both cases the mobility of the motorized infantry permitted it to keep pace with the cavalry.[91]

Throughout the maneuvers, National Guard units provided the motorized infantry. Their successful performance vindicated MacArthur's earlier policy of emphasizing motorization in the National Guard to a greater extent than the Regular Army. The National Guard was expected to reinforce Regular Army forces only after the outbreak of hostilities; thus it could rely on road nets for rapid movement to the front. The Regular Army, however, required horse mobile units for operations in rough terrain and for any activities in which animal transport held advantages over motor transport, including actions against potential guerrillas.[92]

The maneuvers also confirmed the basic conception of tactical movement for the mechanized cavalry: displacement from one dominant terrain feature to another, each chosen to allow multiple actions. Such tactical handling enabled a mechanized cavalry commander to retain his freedom of action and sustain the rapid tempo of action considered vital to success. Despite land use restrictions, the congestion created by curious civilian spectators, and the need to halt activities temporarily while umpires conferred, the mechanized cavalry had achieved its objectives at an unprecedented rate.[93] This accomplishment derived in part from extensive use of radios despite numerous associated technical problems. In addition to command purposes, large numbers of radio-equipped observers ensured prompt fire support to any part of the mechanized cavalry from mobile batteries advancing on a central axis.[94]

Following the Second Army maneuvers, recommendations emerged for further mechanized cavalry expansion. Plans included augmentation of the 7th Cavalry Brigade (Mechanized) with cavalry rifle units for dismounted action, observation aircraft for command and reconnaissance, an engineer troop for road repairs and demolition work, a signal detachment for communication purposes, an ordnance

---

[90] Palmer, "Second Army Maneuvers," pp. 470–74; Grow, "Ten Lean Years," p. 66.

[91] Palmer, "Second Army Maneuvers," pp. 475–76.

[92] MacArthur, "Modernization of the Army," pp. 50–51.

[93] Palmer, "Second Army Maneuvers," p. 478; Bruce Palmer, "The Cavalry," Lecture at AWC, 12 Oct 36, AWC Curricular Archives.

[94] Palmer, "Second Army Maneuvers," pp. 475–77.

The 13th Cavalry Regiment (Mechanized)

company for light repairs within the brigade, and a quartermaster squadron for supply. These proposals sought to increase the mechanized brigade's self-sufficiency.[95]

General Kromer endorsed most of these recommendations, but he considered an increase in the rifle strength of the mechanized cavalries undesirable until personnel carriers capable of greater cross-country mobility became available. The Cavalry intended to create fully mechanized regiments unrestricted in their operations by the presence or absence of roads. Consequently, any increase in the number of wheeled vehicles in the regiment met with opposition. The issue of increased rifle strength was deferred until the 7th Cavalry Brigade (Mechanized) had received its complete equipment set and had participated in at least one maneuver as a complete brigade.[96]

By the end of 1936 the mechanized cavalry had become something more than an experimental force. Clear doctrinal and organizational ideas had emerged that made the 7th Cavalry Brigade (Mechanized) distinctive. The emphasis on tactical versatility, self-sufficiency, and the integration of battlefield functions in a single unit made it unique to the U.S. Army. At Fort Knox, the mechanized cavalry possessed

---

[95] Draft Memo, Col Guy Kent to General Kromer, sub: Report of Mechanized Force in the 1936 Second Army Maneuvers, 15 Dec 36, Ofc of the Ch of Cav, Gen Corresp, RG 177, NARA.

[96] Memo, Brig Gen Daniel Van Voorhis to Ch of Cav, sub: Revision of Tables of Organization, 19 Dec 36; Draft Memo, Maj Robert W. Grow to Col Kent, sub: Memo from G–3, Attached, 21 Dec 36; both in Ofc of the Ch of Cav, Gen Corresp, RG 177, NARA.

a distinct doctrinal and bureaucratic identity that could potentially shatter the unity of command and purpose previously existing within the Cavalry.

Although not yet considered capable of supplanting the horse, mechanized cavalry had brought about definite conceptions as to its role, use, and future development. The mechanized cavalry regiment included four tactical groups capable of four separate, coordinated functions: reconnaissance, combat, antitank-weapons neutralization, and machine-gun and rifle support. The combat car provided the primary combat weapon, but all the tactical groups were capable of integrated action. Combat car usage differed from infantry tank doctrine in its emphasis on the firefight rather than on overrunning the objective.[97]

Outside Fort Knox, most Cavalry officers perceived horse and mechanized cavalry as necessary complements. The mechanized cavalry's terrain sensitivity, its dependency on fixed supply lines for gasoline and oil, and the difficulties associated with maintaining peak vehicle strength during sustained operations suggested the importance of joint operations with horse cavalry units, largely insensitive to terrain and possessing similar doctrine. Combat cars could disrupt enemy fire and seize objectives, which horse cavalry could then secure. The increase in motor vehicle use by horse cavalry regiments, especially motorization of their trains, also reflected the Cavalry's appreciation for motorized assets, encouraged by the activities of its mechanized component. The Cavalry could correctly proclaim: "Our present day cavalry has adopted modern means to extend its sphere of action, the speed of performance of its missions, and the power of its attacks. These means include, besides a very powerful armament, the use of motor vehicles wherever practicable to assist horse cavalry and the complete substitution of mechanization for a part of the horse cavalry."[98]

In 1936 this assessment was correct. Mechanized combat units suffered from a variety of limitations, most notably their terrain sensitivity and mechanical fragility. They simply could not perform the full range of tactical activities associated with horse cavalry. The latter remained an all-weather, all-terrain force. However, the great strides in effectiveness the mechanized cavalry had made since 1931 portended still further improvements in the future. How long horse cavalry organizations would retain their primacy remained problematic.

---

[97] Palmer, "Cavalry," 12 Oct 36.

[98] W. W. Gordon, "The Role of Modern Cavalry," Lecture at AWC, 9 Sep 36, quote from p. 13, AWC Curricular Archives.

3

MECHANIZATION: THE CHIEF OF CAVALRY'S RUNAWAY HORSE

In the 1930s mechanized and horse cavalry development diverged. To prevent the Cavalry Branch's complete disintegration, successive chiefs of Cavalry worked to restore centralized coordination over all cavalry development. Their efforts met with opposition from the mechanized cavalry, as well as War Department inaction. In the areas of personnel assignments, materiel development, and doctrinal development, they failed to assert the primacy of the Office of the Chief of Cavalry. Consequently, their ability to direct mechanized development remained limited. Horse cavalry modernization became the principal recipient of their leadership. Hence, this period featured major improvements in the combat effectiveness of horse units, including widespread motorization of assets, greatly increased firepower, and expanded tactical versatility. Unfortunately, a growing perception of obsolescence overshadowed the increased capability of horse cavalry and undermined the chief of Cavalry's influence.

American Cavalry in the 1930s

Throughout the interwar years, the Cavalry included fifteen active horse cavalry regiments. By 1937 two of these had been mechanized and formed the 7th Cavalry Brigade (Mechanized).[1] One regiment was stationed in the Philippines, and twelve were assigned to posts in the continental United States.[2] The 9th and 10th Cavalry Regiments were composed of African American enlisted personnel led by white officers. These units possessed distinguished combat records that dated to the Indian wars of the nineteenth century. Nevertheless, in the interwar period they were regarded with some suspicion because of alleged cowardice

---

[1] U.S. Congress, House, Subcommittee of the Committee on Appropriations, *War Department Appropriation Bill for 1931 Military Activities, Hearings*, pt. 1, 71st Cong., 2d Sess., 1929, p. 620; Mary Lee Stubbs and Stanley R. Connor, *Regular Army and Army Reserve: Armor-Cavalry*, U.S. Army Lineage Series (Washington, D.C.: U.S. Army Center of Military History, 1984), p. 53.

[2] "Conversations Between General James H. Polk, U.S.A., Ret., and Lt. Col. Roland D. Tausch, U.S.A.," pp. 20–21, Senior Officers Debriefing Program, 1971–1972, U.S. Army Military History Institute (MHI) Archives, Carlisle Barracks, Pa. (hereafter cited as Polk/Tausch Conversations).

during a skirmish in the 1916 Punitive Expedition.[3] They were broken into service units, performing essentially noncombat duties. The 9th Cavalry Regiment received the honorific assignment of running the presidential stables in addition to acting as servants and laborers at Fort Riley, but neither regiment received much attention in the *Cavalry Journal*, the principal medium for highlighting unit activities.[4]

The remaining ten regiments constituted the core of the Cavalry's active strength within the continental United States. They were scattered across the country from Vermont to Arizona in regimental and smaller increments. Four regiments occupied posts along the Mexican border as part of the 1st Cavalry Division, the Army's only active cavalry division.[5]

Cavalry regiments possessed an average strength of 33 officers and 575 enlisted men, which was beneath the authorized peacetime establishment.[6] Deficiencies in personnel strength interfered with combat training. After assignment of officers and enlisted ranks to various administrative duties, squadron and in some cases troop-level training was not feasible.[7] During the initial period of Civilian Conservation Corps mobilization, formal training activities effectively stopped.[8]

Officer shortages made those available responsible for a wide range of activities in addition to their normal duties. They conducted the regiments' administrative affairs and when possible field exercises and combat training. They also supervised instruction of Army Reserve and National Guard personnel. Junior officers attended regimental schools where they received instruction in weapons, equitation, horseshoeing, and veterinary skills. Cavalry posts frequently possessed more horses than men, but overseeing animal care permitted junior officers to apply the animal husbandry skills they learned.[9]

The dearth of officers led most regiments to rely on noncommissioned officers to govern daily routines. Regular Army cavalry NCOs frequently possessed ten to twenty years of service and had acquired an understanding of the duties of junior officers despite their lack of officer training. They could and did assume the duties

---

[3] Ibid.

[4] Ibid.; Lucian K. Truscott Jr., *The Twilight of the U.S. Cavalry: Life in the Old Army, 1917–1942* (Lawrence: University Press of Kansas: 1989), pp. 77, 78, 87.

[5] "Conversations Between General Bruce Palmer Jr. and Lt. Cols. James E. Shelton and Edward P. Smith," p. 60, Senior Officers Debriefing Program, December 1975–April 1976, MHI Archives (hereafter cited as Palmer/Shelton/Smith Conversations).

[6] Congress, *Appropriation Bill for 1931*, p. 620.

[7] Polk/Tausch Conversations, pp. 15–16; Palmer/Shelton/Smith Conversations, pp. 65–66.

[8] H. Jordan Theis, "Yet Another Treasure and Problem for the Army," *Cavalry Journal* XLV, no. 4 (July-August 1936): 292–95.

[9] Polk/Tausch Conversations, pp. 15–16; Palmer/Shelton/Smith Conversations, pp. 65–70; Oral History of General Robert W. Porter Jr., pp. 124–26, Senior Officers Oral History Program, MHI Archives, 1981 (hereafter cited as Porter Oral History); Oral History of General John K. Waters, p. 99, Senior Officers Oral History Program, MHI Archives, 1980 (hereafter cited as Waters Oral History).

Newly promoted Maj. Gen. Guy V. Henry Jr. (*left*) taking the oath of office as chief of Cavalry in 1930

of junior officers in addition to their own responsibilities and familiarized new officers with their command responsibilities.[10]

The NCOs' value derived from their accumulated experience with combat formations whose purpose and nature remained stable. The dramatic transformation of cavalry regiments in the 1930s that resulted from the introduction of the motor vehicle, new weapons and equipment, and new tactics depreciated the value of this past experience. Officers assumed responsibility for routine duties previously left to NCOs, exacerbating the problem of insufficient commissioned personnel. The 7th Cavalry Brigade (Mechanized) especially suffered from an insufficient officer complement and a deficit of NCOs experienced in the operations, maintenance, and drills of motor vehicles.[11]

[10] "Conversations Between General George R. Mather, U.S.A., Ret., and Col. James H. Shaha, U.S.A.," p. 6, Senior Officers Debriefing Program, 1972, MHI Archives (hereafter cited as Mather/Shaha Conversations); Palmer/Shelton/Smith Conversations, p. 66; Porter Oral History, pp. 105, 107; Waters Oral History, p. 104.

[11] Ltr, Brig. Gen. Guy V. Henry to Ch of Cav Maj. Gen. Leon B. Kromer, 19 Jul 34, Ofc of the Ch of Cav, Gen Corresp, Record Group (RG) 177, National Archives and Records Administration (NARA).

Throughout the interwar era, Cavalry officers faced stagnant promotion opportunities until the country began to revitalize national defense in the late 1930s. Newly commissioned second lieutenants in the Cavalry retained their rank for years before promotion to first lieutenant and had a similar wait before attaining their captaincy. Yet the slow advancement rate enabled officers to develop a detailed comprehension of the regimental duties associated with their rank. They spent three to four years in the same regiment before reassignment, learning the command responsibilities of each squadron, troop, and platoon; the basic skills required of enlisted personnel; and a wide variety of administrative, logistical, and educational functions that suited them for multiple tasks in the event of mobilization.[12]

Competitiveness dominated cavalry service. Lengthy endurance rides over rough, sparsely populated country were a common test of stamina and skill in varied terrain and climate conditions. Competition within and among the regiments—especially in the form of polo, riding contests, and shooting matches—encouraged officers and enlisted personnel to improve their efficiency. The emphasis given to equestrian talents sustained physical conditioning and offset the heavy drinking prevalent on some posts. More important, every cavalry activity, including polo, emphasized the need and ability for rapid decisions.[13]

Attending the Cavalry School, the Cavalry's academic center, provided further education in equitation and mounted tactics. Located at Fort Riley, Kansas, the Cavalry School replaced the Mounted Transport School during the reorganization that followed passage of the National Defense Act of 1920. Its instructors were all graduates of the Command and General Staff School at Fort Leavenworth, Kansas, and some possessed General Staff experience or had graduated from the Army Industrial College. The Cavalry School also favored the use of instructors trained at foreign cavalry schools to incorporate the best features of foreign equitation training into its curriculum.[14]

All students possessed a minimum of three years of service before attending the Cavalry School. Its curriculum covered a variety of topics related to cavalry activity, including intensive training in gunnery, machine-gun use, and cavalry tactics up to the brigade level. Later additions included technical instruction in vehicle engines and signal communications.[15] Student assignments focused on knowledge of the cavalry field manuals and application of the concepts represented. The principal opportunity to employ these techniques and procedures occurred during field exercises conducted at Fort Riley. These events employed the 2d and 13th Cavalry Regiments stationed there until the latter's transfer to Fort Knox, Kentucky, in 1936.[16]

---

[12] Polk/Tausch Conversations, pp. 14, 31.

[13] Ibid., pp. 15–17; Palmer/Shelton/Smith Conversations, pp. 67–70; Porter Oral History, pp. 124–26; Waters Oral History, p. 99.

[14] Waters Oral History, p. 94; Truscott, *Twilight of the U.S. Cavalry*, pp. 75, 79.

[15] Porter Oral History, pp. 146–47, 154; Mather/Shaha Conversations, p. 18, Clarence Lininger, "Some Trends at the Cavalry School," *Cavalry Journal* XLVII, no. 3 (May-June 1938): 233–35; Truscott, *Twilight of the U.S. Cavalry*, pp. 80–83.

[16] Porter Oral History, p. 134.

Cavalry School classroom at Fort Riley

The Cavalry School also functioned as the higher institute for learning equitation, with a principal objective "to produce a horse and rider capable of fast and long continued movement and ability to perform successfully the missions that fall to the lot of Cavalry in war."[17] The pinnacle of equitation training was the Advanced Equitation Course in which each student bore responsibility for transforming four horses into trained cavalry mounts.[18] The course's emphasis on horse care and skills inspired one graduate's recollection that "We didn't do a damn thing but ride four horses a day."[19]

Graduates of the Advanced Equitation Course qualified as equitation specialists entrusted to teach their skills throughout the Cavalry in addition to their other duties. The most successful students became members of the U.S. Olympic Equestrian Team and the Army Horse Show Team.[20] The constant riding essential to the course, however, led to numerous accidents and broken bones. Student officers found obtaining accident insurance difficult because of repeated claims on their policies.[21]

In addition to its educational responsibilities, the Cavalry School compiled drafts of texts, field manuals, and drill regulations to be used at the school subject

[17] Lininger, "Some Trends at the Cavalry School," p. 232.

[18] Polk/Tausch Conversations, p. 30; Mather/Shaha Conversations, p. 18; Truscott, *Twilight of the U.S. Cavalry*, p. 80.

[19] Polk/Tausch Conversations, p. 30.

[20] Waters Oral History, pp. 112–13; Polk/Tausch Conversations, p. 30.

[21] Polk/Tausch Conversations, p. 30.

to War Department approval. It also coordinated tactical instruction between the horse and mechanized cavalry.[22] Utilizing the mounted units stationed at Fort Riley, the Cavalry School faculty assisted in conducting tests and experiments of new organizations, equipment, weapons, and tactics.[23]

The Problem of the Cavalry's Image

During the 1930s successive chiefs of Cavalry worked to improve the effectiveness of both mechanized and horse cavalry. However, the public's inability to distinguish horse cavalry from the image of saber-wielding horsemen charging machine guns affected Congress' willingness to allocate funds to the War Department for cavalry purposes. The public's understanding of war derived from the publicity afforded the American Expeditionary Forces and their role in a war dominated by trenches, machine guns, artillery, and airplanes. American horse cavalry did not seem suited to such an environment, and its general absence from the expeditionary forces reinforced this belief.[24]

The spectacle of a uniformed equestrian seemed anachronistic in a society increasingly enamored with machines. Automobiles, barnstormers, air shows, and the proliferation of backyard aviators striving to build their own airplanes offered visions of the future more appropriate to a belief in American technical ingenuity than the cavalry's continued reliance on the horse. The Great Depression also encouraged a rejection of the aristocratic values that the cavalry's tradition of fox hunting and polo seemed to embrace.

Public awareness of the cavalry was shaped through interaction. Cavalry regiments performed horse shows in nearby communities or conducted polo matches that pitted troopers against local civilians or National Guard cavalry.[25] The cavalry also appeared at county fairs and rodeos, offered riding classes for women, and performed at charitable events.[26]

The 3d Cavalry Regiment, stationed at Fort Myer, Virginia, received the most publicity. Located near Washington, D.C., the regiment's personnel provided honor guards for the White House, diplomatic functions, and the Tomb of the Unknown Soldier, routinely participating in parades in the capital.[27] Ceremonial functions also included burials at Arlington National Cemetery.[28] One officer recalled, "We were burying people all the time. . . . So I became quite an expert on funerals, because on

---

[22] Porter Oral History, p. 145; Lininger, "Some Trends at the Cavalry School," pp. 232–34.

[23] Truscott, *Twilight of the U.S. Cavalry*, p. 82.

[24] Guy V. Henry, "The Trend of Organization and Equipment of Cavalry in the Principal World Powers and Its Probable Role in Wars of the Near Future," *Cavalry Journal* XLI, no. 170 (March-April 1932): 7–9

[25] Polk/Tausch Conversations, p. 25; Palmer/Shelton/Smith Conversations, p. 86.

[26] Porter Oral History, p. 100; Waters Oral History, p. 84.

[27] Waters Oral History, pp. 71–72, 76–77; Polk/Tausch Conversations, p. 33.

[28] Truscott, *Twilight of the U.S. Cavalry*, pp. 110–12.

some days you had as many as 12–15 funerals to supervise."[29] The extent of ceremonial functions distinguished the 3d Cavalry Regiment from other regiments.

Not all communities near cavalry posts shared a widespread interest in equestrian activities. Poverty sometimes accounted for disinterest, but other situations contributed to less than favorable reactions.[30] For example, at Fort Meade, South Dakota, 4th Cavalry Regiment personnel alienated local farmers by establishing a pig farm and selling the meat to local markets in competition with the farmers.[31]

Generally, Cavalry activities fostered a benign public image that did not have a uniform appeal across the nation. Nor did the cavalry's domination of the Army Horse Show Team and the U.S. Olympic Equestrian Team suggest a different perception. Members of both teams included officers from the Cavalry School, and student officers considered acceptance onto either team a crowning achievement.[32] In 1936, while Cavalry School Commandant Maj. Gen. Guy V. Henry Jr. led the U.S. Olympic Equestrian Team to the Olympic Games in Germany, the 7th Cavalry Brigade (Mechanized) acquired its second regiment.[33]

The principal public display of the cavalry's martial ability was its participation in dispersing the Bonus March of 1932. Elements of the 3d Cavalry Regiment, commanded by Maj. George S. Patton Jr., in conjunction with the 12th Infantry Regiment, evicted the Bonus Marchers from Washington. They operated in the streets of the city, burning the shelters of the demonstrators and pursuing them with drawn sabers across the Anacostia Bridge. The Cavalry considered the operation a success and praised the performance of its personnel, but suppressing civilian demonstrations did not improve the Cavalry's image or suggest that American cavalry differed substantially from the Cossacks of czarist Russia.[34]

Congress reflected the public perception in its hesitancy to allocate funds to the Cavalry. In successive hearings before the House Subcommittee on Military Appropriations, congressmen subjected Cavalry representatives to a barrage of criticism concerning the supposed obsolescence of the cavalry. Mississippi Democrat Ross Collins epitomized the anti-Cavalry viewpoint and became the nemesis of the Cavalry. He considered the pace of Cavalry mechanization too slow and rejected that arm's continued attention to horse regiments, drawing unfavorable comparisons between American and British Cavalry mechanization programs.[35] In particular, he found polo a waste of the taxpayer's money and repeatedly endeavored to trap the Cavalry representative into admitting its irrelevance. Collins considered civilians

---

[29] Polk/Tausch Conversations, pp. 33–34.

[30] Palmer/Shelton/Smith Conversations, p. 86.

[31] Porter Oral History, pp. 113–14.

[32] Ibid., pp. 142–45; Waters Oral History, p. 113.

[33] Guy V. Henry Jr., "A Brief Narrative of the Life of Guy V. Henry, Jr.," p. 69B, Guy V. Henry Jr. Papers, MHI Archives.

[34] Waters Oral History, pp. 64–65, 68–69; Truscott, *Twilight of the U.S. Cavalry*, pp. 120–30.

[35] U.S. Congress, House, Subcommittee of the Committee on Appropriations, *War Department Appropriation Bill for 1933 Military Activities, Hearings*, pt. 1, 72d Cong., 1st Sess., 1932, pp. 679–80.

Elements of the 1st Cavalry Division during the interwar years

more progressive than the cavalry because of their greater reliance on motor vehicle transport.[36]

Collins' depiction of the Cavalry as unprogressive found support from other congressmen who criticized the cavalry for not emulating civilian cattlemen in the use of trucks for horse transport. In fact, however, the cavalry had begun experimenting with modified commercial trucks. Truck transport of horse cavalry suggested the possibility of combining the strategic mobility of the motor vehicle with the tactical mobility of the horse. However, the funding priority given to the 7th Cavalry Brigade (Mechanized) prevented the rapid development of portee cavalry.[37] As late as October 1939, portee cavalry experimentation continued to suffer from the lack of a standardized horse transport vehicle suitable for military use. Instead, the Cavalry relied on the unsatisfactory expedient of modified commercial vehicles.[38]

Collins' criticisms reflected a general ignorance of Cavalry affairs. In 1933 he proposed consolidation of the Cavalry and the Field Artillery because he saw no difference in their functions and a potential cost savings in overhead. General Henry, serving as chief of Cavalry at that time, refuted the proposal. He endeavored to explain the difference between the two arms and the nature of the bureau system established by the National Defense Act of 1920, which specifically separated the

---

[36] Congress, *Appropriation Bill for 1931*, pp. 616–18, and *Appropriation Bill for 1933*, pp. 676–78.

[37] U.S. Congress, House, Subcommittee of the Committee on Appropriations, *War Department Appropriation Bill for 1936 Military Activities, Hearings*, pt. 1, 74th Cong., 1st Sess., 1935, p. 355; *War Department Appropriation Bill for 1937 Military Activities, Hearings*, pt. 1, 74th Cong., 2d Sess., 1936, pp. 19–20.

[38] L. W. Cramer, "Portee Cavalry: An Experiment with Commercial Trucks," *Cavalry Journal* XLIX, no. 3 (May-June 1940): 254–55.

Riding hall at the Cavalry School

combat arms by function.[39] Had amalgamation occurred, the Cavalry would have ceased to exist.

Succeeding chiefs of Cavalry responded to congressional criticism by reasserting the value of the cavalry to the Army in the past, present, and future.[40] They anticipated this value to rise in relation to the increasing emphasis on firepower and motorization within horse regiments.[41] They considered the cavalry indispensable as the Army's only mobile ground arm.[42] They also cited the developments and activities of the mechanized cavalry at Fort Knox as further proof of the Cavalry's progressive nature, noting the proportional similarity between British and American cavalry mechanization efforts.[43] They defended the value of polo in developing

[39] U.S. Congress, House, Subcommittee of the Committee on Appropriations, *War Department Appropriation Bill for 1934 Military Activities, Hearings*, pt. 1, 72d Cong., 2d Sess., 1933, pp. 384–85.

[40] U.S. Congress, House, Subcommittee of the Committee on Appropriations, *War Department Appropriation Bill for 1935 Military Activities, Hearings*, pt. 1, 73d Cong., 2d Sess., 1934, p. 302; *War Department Appropriation Bill for 1938 Military Activities, Hearings*, 75th Cong., 1st Sess., 1937, pp. 396–98; *War Department Appropriation Bill for 1939 Military Activities, Hearings*, 75th Cong., 2d Sess., 1938, pp. 401–03.

[41] Congress, *Appropriation Bill for 1931*, p. 622.

[42] Congress, *Appropriation Bill for 1935*, pp. 302–03.

[43] U.S. Congress, House, Subcommittee of the Committee on Appropriations, *War Department Appropriation Bill for 1932 Military Activities, Hearings*, 71st Cong., 3d Sess., 1930, p. 642; *Appropriation Bill for 1933*, p. 679; *Appropriation Bill for 1935*, pp. 302–03; *Appropriation Bill for 1936*, p. 351.

physical stamina, rapid decision making, and equestrian ability under all conditions. As chief of Cavalry, General Henry also cited an article written by Colonel-General Hans von Seeckt emphasizing the training value of polo.[44] Von Seeckt commanded the German *Reichswehr* in the 1920s and established it as an elite, expansible force that formed the basis of the later *Wehrmacht*.[45]

Yet the Cavalry faced a quandary. It needed favorable publicity to support its assertions of importance with respect to the other combat arms and to attract congressional funding. Exclusive emphasis on the mechanized cavalry might have achieved these goals, but such a policy contradicted the Cavalry's own beliefs and experience suggesting the continued viability of horse cavalry. Thus, in testimony before Congress, in lectures delivered at the Army's schools, and in formal memorandums, the chiefs of Cavalry endeavored to inform the public as to the true nature of American horse cavalry. Because American cavalry had lacked a significant combat role since the Spanish-American War and the Philippine Insurrection, they relied on military history and the exploits of foreign cavalry in the World War to demonstrate the value of horse cavalry. They also used the *Cavalry Journal* as a forum for defending horse cavalry and encouraged similar articles in the civilian press.[46] Emphasis on past cavalry exploits, however, did little to deflect criticism of the Cavalry as unprogressive and traditionalist.

The Office of the Chief of Cavalry and the Bureau System

Before World War I the chiefs of Field Artillery, Coast Artillery, Ordnance, Engineers, and Signal Corps together with the chief surgeon constituted the primary influences on Army needs and policies. After the war senior Army officers successfully convinced legislators of the need for similar advisers for the combat arms to ensure military effectiveness in a national emergency.[47] The National Defense Act of 1920 provided War Department representation of the combat arms through the creation of the chiefs of Infantry, Cavalry, Air Corps, and Chemical Warfare Service. In the horizontal organization of the War Department that Congress favored, each combat arm possessed an equal voice and opportunity to secure its needs.

---

[44] Congress, *Appropriation Bill for 1931*, pp. 616–18, and *Appropriation Bill for 1933*, pp. 676–78.

[45] See James S. Corum, *The Roots of Blitzkrieg: Hans von Seeckt and the German Military Reform* (Lawrence: University Press of Kansas, 1992).

[46] Leon B. Kromer, "Cavalry," Lecture at U.S. Army War College (AWC), 1 Oct 37, AWC Curricular Archives, MHI Archives; Memo, Ch of Cav Maj Gen J. K. Herr to The Adjutant General (TAG), 16 Aug 38, p. 2, Ofc of the Ch of Cav, Gen Corresp, RG 177, NARA; John K. Herr, "The Cavalry," Lecture at AWC, 19 Sep 38, AWC Curricular Archives; Memo, Ch of Cav Maj Gen John K. Herr to Chief of Staff (CS), 17 Oct 38, p. 2, Ofc of the Ch of Cav, Gen Corresp, RG 177, NARA. Ltrs, Robert B. Phillips Jr. to Gen Kromer, 1 Jan 39; John K. Herr to Leon B. Kromer, 1 Feb 39; Leon B. Kromer to Robert B. Phillips Jr., 18 Feb 39; all in Leon B. Kromer Papers, MHI Archives.

[47] Memo, Ch of Cav Maj Gen Leon B. Kromer to Assistant Secretary of War (ASW), sub: Office of the Chief of Cavalry and National Defense, 26 Aug 37, pp. 2–3, Ofc of the Ch of Cav, Gen Corresp, RG 177, NARA.

However, the regulations governing the chiefs of the combat arms transformed each arm into a microcosm of the War Department bureau system, possessing the same lack of administrative rationalization. The chiefs of the combat arms did not wield command authority over their respective branches. Although each directly controlled the activities of his branch school and board, he could only recommend measures concerning his branch to the adjutant general. Thus, a combat-arm chief could not implement actions concerning unit organization, training policies, or equipment development solely on his own authority.[48]

A branch chief might informally propose such a measure during a personal consultation with the chief of staff or at a meeting of the General Council. The latter, under the jurisdiction of the chief of staff, included the deputy chief of staff, the heads of the General Staff divisions, the Army War College commandant, the chief of the National Guard Bureau, the executive for Reserve Officers, and all branch chiefs. Either approach enabled a combat-arm chief to assess the viability of a desired measure, but no formal action occurred until receipt of a recommendation by the adjutant general.[49]

The adjutant general categorized a recommendation according to the interests represented by the G–1 (Personnel), G–2 (Intelligence), G–3 (Operations and Training), G–4 (Supply), and War Plans Divisions of the General Staff and referred it to the appropriate division or divisions for study. The latter analyzed the recommendation, evaluating its value and consequences, and sought the concurrence of the other General Staff divisions and the branch chiefs. The completed study was then submitted to the Army chief of staff with the division's recommendations and a full presentation of any dissenting or nonconcurring views. The chief of staff recommended a course of action to the secretary of war, who rendered the final decision subject to congressional approval. The adjutant general then communicated the result to the initiating branch chief.[50] Finances exerted a major influence in the final ruling.[51]

Process for Implementing Branch Recommendations

1. A branch chief proposed action to the chief of staff;
2. The General Council reviewed the proposal;
3. Accepted proposals were forwarded to the adjutant general;
4. The adjutant general referred proposals to the General Staff for study;
5. Comments of other staff sections and branch chiefs were sought;
6. Study findings were submitted to the chief of staff;

---

[48] U.S. War Department (WD), Army Regulation (AR) 70–5, *Chiefs of Combatant Branches*, 1927.

[49] Congress, *Appropriation Bill for 1934*, pp. 24–25; L. D. Gasser, "The War Department General Staff," Lecture at AWC, 16 Sep 38, p. 3, AWC Curricular Archives.

[50] Robert McC. Beck Jr., "The Organization and Functions of the G–3 Division, War Department General Staff," Lecture at AWC, 17 Sep 38, pp. 1–2, AWC Curricular Archives; Congress, *Appropriation Bill for 1934*, p. 24.

[51] Beck, "Organization and Functions of the G–3 Division," 17 Sep 38, p. 3.

7. The chief reviewed the findings and suggested a course of action to the secretary of war;
8. The secretary of war rendered his decision.

This procedure symbolized the importance American society attached to the free exchange of ideas and the subordination of the Army to the civilian political leadership. Unfortunately, it also maximized the potential for criticism and obstruction of a recommended measure. It encouraged interbureau rivalry and necessitated a prolonged time lag between initiation of a request and final action that increased in proportion to the related fiscal and personnel considerations. This process also discouraged branch chiefs from recommending actions for which they perceived little chance of approval.

The chief of Cavalry acted as the chief of staff's principal adviser on Cavalry affairs.[52] He supervised branch activity through the Office of the Chief of Cavalry. His executive officer performed a role similar to that of the deputy chief of staff, administering the work of the Office of the Chief of Cavalry and acting for the chief of Cavalry in his absence. The executive officer also controlled the flow of correspondence to and from the chief of Cavalry, although the latter often handled personnel matters directly.[53]

The Office of the Chief of Cavalry included eight officers distributed among the Personnel, Intelligence, Operations, and Supply and Fiscal Sections. Their functions paralleled those of the War Department General Staff. In addition to surveying military attaché reports on foreign cavalry developments, the Intelligence Section oversaw publication of the *Cavalry Journal*. The latter responsibility tended to overshadow the former because the section had only one officer and one enlisted man.[54]

The separation of interests responsible for cavalry development, however, undermined the chief of Cavalry's authority. The Cavalry Board, located at Fort Riley, bore responsibility for developing tactics, revising tables of organization and equipment, and testing new materiel. Directly subordinate to the chief of Cavalry, it provided him with information to support recommendations submitted to the adjutant general.[55] To conduct field tests of organizational and tactical principles up to the brigade level, the Cavalry Board used the two horse regiments stationed at Fort Riley. A second board duplicated Cavalry Board responsibilities at the division level. The 1st Cavalry Division commander controlled the 1st Cavalry Division Board, which was located at Fort Bliss, Texas, the home of the 1st Cavalry Division. Elements

52 WD, AR 70–5, p. 1.

53 Ltr and Encl, Ch of Cav Maj. Gen. Leon B. Kromer to Col. John K. Herr, 7 Mar 38, Ofc of the Ch of Cav, Gen Corresp, RG 177, NARA.

54 Memo, Ch of Cav Maj. Gen. Leon B. Kromer to ASW, sub: Commissioned Personnel of the Office of the Chief of Cavalry, 27 Aug 37, Ofc of the Ch of Cav, Gen Corresp, RG 177, NARA; Ltr and Encl, Kromer to Herr, 7 Mar 38; Memo, TAG to Ch of Cav, sub: Survey of Military Intelligence Organization Duties and Functions in the Office of the Chiefs of Arms and Services, 9 Mar 38, and 1st End, Col G. Kent to TAG, 11 Mar 38, Ofc of the Ch of Cav, Gen Corresp, RG 177, NARA.

55 Ltr, Ch of Cav Maj Gen Leon B. Kromer to Brig Gen Daniel Van Voorhis, 19 Nov 37, Ofc of the Ch of Cav, Gen Corresp, RG 177, NARA.

Horse cavalry conducting machine-gun training

of this formation, deployed along the border with Mexico, could be temporarily concentrated for 1st Cavalry Division Board field tests. This board could also conduct limited experimentation in developing the organization of a cavalry corps.

Under Army regulations the chief of Cavalry exercised direct supervision and control only of the Cavalry Board at Fort Riley. Its activities took precedence over those of the 1st Cavalry Division Board, but no formal subordination existed. Nor did the chief of Cavalry possess the authority to communicate directly with the president of the 1st Cavalry Division Board. Instead, formal communications were routed through the adjutant general and the commander of the VIII Corps Area—which included the 1st Cavalry Division—before submission to the 1st Cavalry Division Board.[56]

A personal agreement could shorten this communications path. Thus, while chief of Cavalry, General Henry arranged with the division commander to be informed of all 1st Cavalry Division Board activities. Such an arrangement, however, violated Army regulations and depended on the willingness of the division commander to cooperate, in part because the latter held equivalent rank to the chief of Cavalry. Henry's arrangement ended with the appointment of Maj. Gen. Ewing E. Booth to command of the 1st Cavalry Division. General Booth gradually ceased direct communication with the Office of the Chief of Cavalry. Instead he submitted recommendations concerning division organization directly to the adjutant general without informing the chief of Cavalry. When Maj. Gen. Leon B. Kromer succeeded Henry as chief of Cavalry, no improvement in relations occurred, and the 1st Cavalry

---

[56] Memo, Kojassar to Col Kent, sub: Relations of the Office of the Chief of Cavalry with the 1st Cavalry Division Board, 5 Jul 38, Ofc of the Ch of Cav, Gen Corresp, RG 177, NARA.

General Henry in 1932

Division and 1st Cavalry Division Board assumed a quasi-independent status with respect to the Cavalry arm.[57]

Unfortunately, the 1st Cavalry Division did not always abide by Cavalry doctrine and training methods developed at Fort Riley and approved by the War Department. As a remedy, Henry recommended to Kromer that the cavalry division commander and his brigade commanders be encouraged to visit the Cavalry School to establish a closer working relationship. In case this diplomacy failed, he advocated a different course of action:

> If necessary, at the proper time, when the Division Commander changes, to report to the War Department that the employment of the supporting weapons in the Division has not been in accord with the teachings at the

[57] Memo, Kojassar to Kent, 5 Jul 38; Memo, Ch of Cav Maj Gen Leon B. Kromer to President, Cavalry Board, sub: Mechanized Cavalry Board, 1 Jul 37, and 1st End, Brig Gen Guy V. Henry to Ch of Cav, 30 Jul 37, p. 2; all in Ofc of the Ch of Cav, Gen Corresp, RG 177, NARA.

> Cavalry School and War Department publications, and request that the Division adhere to the instructions given throughout the rest of the Army as a whole, including both the National Guard and Organized Reserve.[58]

Mechanization further eroded the chief of Cavalry's control of the tactical and technical development of his arm. By the end of 1936 Cavalry officers became increasingly aware that the path of mechanized cavalry development diverged from that of horse cavalry. One executive officer warned that lack of mechanized cavalry at Fort Riley encouraged this divergence and prevented the coordinated development of horse and mechanized cavalries.[59] During his tenure as Cavalry School commandant, General Henry warned the chief of Cavalry:

> If this rift is permitted to exist and develop, the time is not far distant when an attempt will be made to separate mechanized cavalry from horse cavalry completely. A relatively few years ago the Artillery Corps was split up into the Coast Artillery and Field Artillery. An attempt was made immediately after the war to divorce the tanks from the Infantry. Even some experienced machine gunners advocated the formation of a machine gun corps separate from both the Infantry and Cavalry. The separation of the Air Corps from the Signal Corps was a logical step but current attempts to make the Air Service into a third service with the Army and Navy are no more malicious than would be an attempt to split up the Cavalry.[60]

The chief of Cavalry found coordination of mechanized and horse cavalry development hindered by the paucity of vehicles at Fort Riley. Cavalry School troops included only horse units. The absence of mechanized cavalry precluded the introduction of a mechanized cavalry course at the school and limited mechanized instruction to theoretical paper exercises and technical instruction in motor-vehicle engines. Occasional visits by mechanized cavalry personnel did not eliminate this problem.[61] The lack of mechanized representation also prevented the Cavalry Board from testing equipment and tactics and improving doctrine for both horse and mechanized cavalries.[62] The transfer to Fort Knox and mechanization of the 13th Cavalry Regiment in September 1936 further reduced the school's ability to function as an effective laboratory for horse cavalry beyond the regimental level.[63]

---

[58] Ltr, Brig Gen Guy V. Henry to Ch of Cav Maj Gen Leon B. Kromer, 10 Mar 36, p. 3, Ofc of the Ch of Cav, Gen Corresp, RG 177, NARA.

[59] Memo, Col A. M. Miller Jr. to Ch of Cav, sub: Cavalry Board and School Troops, 1 Sep 37, Ofc of the Ch of Cav, Gen Corresp, RG 177, NARA.

[60] Memo, Kromer to President, Cav Board, 1 Jul 37, and 1st End, Henry to Ch of Cav, 30 Jul 37, quote from p. 1.

[61] Polk/Tausch Conversations, p. 28.

[62] Memos, Miller to Ch of Cav, 1 Sep 37; Ch of Cav Maj Gen John K. Herr to TAG, sub: Mechanized Cavalry Board, 13 Apr 38, Ofc of the Ch of Cav, Gen Corresp, RG 177, NARA.

[63] Memo, Commandant Brig Gen Guy V. Henry to Ch of Cav, sub: Completion of the Organization of the 7th Cavalry Brigade (Mecz.) by Mechanizing One Horse Regiment at Fort Riley, Kansas, 9 May 36, Ofc of the Ch of Cav, Gen Corresp, RG 177, NARA.

Classroom instruction at Fort Riley

Consequently, the 7th Cavalry Brigade (Mechanized) at Fort Knox assumed the roles of the Cavalry School and Cavalry Board as they related to cavalry mechanization because it possessed vehicles, maintenance facilities, and personnel familiar with mechanization.

However, a War Department directive of April 1935 authorizing the assignment of the 1st Battalion, 68th Field Artillery Regiment (Mechanized), to Fort Knox for combined training with the 7th Cavalry Brigade (Mechanized) included the statement: "The Commanding General, Fifth Corps Area, under direction of the War Department, is charged with carrying out the program announced above and with the development of the 7th Cavalry Brigade (mecz.), reinforced, in accordance with the above approved policies and principals."[64] In part this statement derived from Fort Knox's status as a V Corps Area training center rather than as a cavalry post.[65] Consequently, Army regulations barred direct, formal communication between

[64] TAG, "War Department Policies for Mechanization," 5 Apr 35, p. 3, Willis D. Crittenberger Papers, MHI Archives. This new arrangement limited the influence of the chief of Cavalry on his two most important field elements, the 1st Cavalry Division and the 7th Cavalry Brigade (Mechanized). The former came under the jurisdiction of the VIII Corps Area commander, and the V Corps Area commander controlled the latter. The Chief of Cavalry's influence was subject to the acquiescence and approval of the corps area commanders.

[65] Draft Memo, Maj Robert W. Grow to Ch of Cav, sub: Relationship Between the Chief of Cavalry and Cavalry Mechanized Units, 25 Jun 37, p. 2, Ofc of the Ch of Cav, Gen Corresp, RG 177, NARA.

the chief of Cavalry and the 7th Cavalry Brigade (Mechanized) commander. Correspondence had to be routed through the adjutant general and the V Corps Area commander, an arrangement analogous to that of the chief of Cavalry and the 1st Cavalry Division. Consequently, the chief of Cavalry faced similar coordination problems with both the 1st Cavalry Division and the mechanized cavalry.[66]

To some extent the chief of Cavalry could mitigate the divergent tendencies of the 1st Cavalry Division and 7th Cavalry Brigade (Mechanized) through control of Cavalry personnel. The Army regulations governing the chiefs of the combat arms made them responsible for recommending appointments, assignments, transfers, and retirements of commissioned and warrant officers within their respective branches.[67] Generally, their recommendations encountered little opposition from the War Department.

To correct the deviation in 1st Cavalry Division tactical training from approved Cavalry doctrine, the chief of Cavalry could recommend the appointments of the formation's chief of staff, G–3 officer, and brigade and regimental commanders, since these officers oversaw the division's tactical training and employment. Thus, the chief of Cavalry could ensure the division's conformity to established Cavalry doctrine through personnel manipulation. Henry employed such a practice while chief of Cavalry and recommended a similar policy to his successor, Kromer.[68] The Army's special interest in mechanization and the dearth of experienced mechanized cavalry officers, however, prevented implementation of a similar policy in the 7th Cavalry Brigade (Mechanized).

Efforts to coordinate cavalry development faced threats from within the War Department. In April 1937 the adjutant general proposed that responsibility for personnel matters be removed from the chiefs of the combat arms and centralized in the Adjutant General's Office in order that the chiefs of the combat arms "might have more time and leisure for the consideration of 'other large questions of branch interest.'" In response Kromer stressed the importance of assigning officers to tasks commensurate with their ability to ensure combat-arm efficiency and continued progressive development. He considered the combat-arms chiefs especially suited to discharge this responsibility. He echoed the views of all branch chiefs:

> The Chief of Cavalry has not requested any relief from his responsibilities for personnel matters, nor does he consider that they are unduly onerous or taking up too much of his time. On the contrary he believes that to take them away would lesson his power to accomplish the tasks contemplated by law and regulations with no compensating advantages.[69]

---

[66] Memo, Herr to TAG, 13 Apr 38; Draft Memo, Grow to Ch of Cav, 25 Jun 37.

[67] WD, AR 70–5, p. 2.

[68] Ltr, Henry to Kromer, 10 Mar 36.

[69] Memo, Ch of Cav Maj Gen Leon B. Kromer to TAG, sub: Personnel Matters, 29 Apr 37, quote from p. 1, Ofc of the Ch of Cav, Gen Corresp, RG 177, NARA.

The 6th Cavalry Regiment conducting a river crossing

No implementation of the adjutant general's proposal occurred, but a subsequent recommendation of the assistant secretary of war posed a more serious threat to the chief of Cavalry's administrative authority. The assistant secretary suggested the removal of the offices of the chiefs of the combat arms from the War Department building in Washington to their respective service schools.[70]

Kromer believed that the effectiveness of the War Department's administrative organization depended on the ability of the General Staff and the combat- and service-arm chiefs to coordinate their efforts. The collocation of the General Staff and the branch chiefs within the War Department building facilitated this cooperation. Kromer warned that these benefits would be lost should the combat-arms chiefs be removed to their respective schools and that the War Department would relapse into the administrative chaos that had plagued American military activities during the World War.[71]

In general, Kromer believed that implementation of the assistant secretary of war's suggestion would effectively eliminate the chiefs of the combat arms because their administrative representation would be reduced. Thus he elaborated on their importance and praised the National Defense Act of 1920 for creating

---

[70] Memo, Ch of Cav Maj Gen Leon B. Kromer to ASW, sub: Office of the Chief of Cavalry and National Defense, 26 Aug 37, p. 1, Ofc of the Ch of Cav, Gen Corresp, RG 177, NARA.

[71] Ibid.

them, concluding that "It must be evident that the Offices of the Chiefs of Combat Arms—and specifically that of the Chief of Cavalry—are indispensable in the War Department organization."[72]

In fact, Kromer was correct. As long as the War Department embraced the bureau system, any agency that lacked representation on an equal or superior basis with that of the existing branch chiefs could not secure for itself the political, financial, or personnel resources necessary for its continued bureaucratic existence, as indicated by the fate of the Mechanized Force. Conversely, the success of the Air Corps in expanding and publicizing its importance demonstrated the advantages of representation and lobby power in legislative and military spheres of influence.

The Mechanized Cavalry Board

General Kromer sought to establish the Office of the Chief of Cavalry as the central influence on all cavalry development. Only by doing so could he prevent the dissolution of the branch into three separate pieces: the Cavalry School, the 1st Cavalry Division, and the 7th Cavalry Brigade (Mechanized). Blocked by regulation from direct communication with the mechanized cavalry or the 1st Cavalry Division and unable to shape the former through manipulation of personnel assignments, Kromer now sought to achieve his aim through the subordination of all technical developments to the Cavalry Board. The latter lay under the direct control of the chief of Cavalry. Unfortunately, the lack of mechanized assets at Fort Riley prevented the Cavalry Board from providing the materiel and doctrinal guidance for the mechanized cavalry. The 7th Cavalry Brigade (Mechanized) therefore had assumed these functions through the use of informal boards at Fort Knox.

This seeming impasse did not deter Kromer. Instead, he noted: "The situation is analogous to that which confronted the Infantry when the tank school and 66th Infantry (tanks) were at Fort Meade [Maryland]. There was an Infantry Board and a Tank Board. The former has now absorbed the latter."[73]

Inspired by the Infantry precedent, in the spring of 1937 Kromer considered establishing a permanent mechanized cavalry board at Fort Knox. Doing so required War Department approval and a reappraisal of the relationship between the chief of Cavalry and the 7th Cavalry Brigade (Mechanized). Kromer's advisers, who included General Henry, the Cavalry School commandant, urged him to seek supervisory authority over mechanized cavalry development. They supported the creation of a mechanized cavalry board but only as an extension of the Cavalry Board. They accepted the need to establish the mechanized cavalry board at Fort Knox, pending the development of appropriate facilities at Fort Riley and the stationing of a mechanized unit there. Similarly, they wanted the 1st Cavalry Division Board subordinated to the Cavalry Board.[74]

---

[72] Ibid., quote from p. 6.

[73] Draft Memo, Grow to Ch of Cav, 25 Jun 37, quote from p. 2.

[74] Draft Memo, Grow to Ch of Cav, 25 Jun 37; Memo, Kromer to President, Cav Board, sub: Mechanized Cavalry Board, 1 Jul 37, and 1st End, Henry to Ch of Cav, 30 Jul 37, quote from p. 3; Draft

Horse cavalry training at Fort Riley

These recommendations would have considerably strengthened the chief of Cavalry's influence over branch developments. Kromer, however, opted to pursue a lesser goal, perhaps dissuaded from the more aggressive stance by the difficulty of sustaining it amid the War Department's committee nature. Instead he proposed the creation of a small cell, or sub-board, at Fort Knox with the chief of Cavalry responsible for coordinating its activities with those of the Cavalry Board. He also began the formal process of changing Army regulations to permit direct communication with the sub-board.[75] He presented these actions as merely an extension of the existing relationship between the Cavalry Board and the chief of Cavalry.[76]

Kromer's advisers considered his decision unlikely to prevent the continued divergence of horse and mechanized cavalry development.[77] Brig. Gen. Daniel Van

Memo, Col G. Kent to Ch of Cav, sub: Change in AR 80–10 (Cavalry Board), 10 Aug 37, Ofc of the Ch of Cav, Gen Corresp, RG 177, NARA; Draft Memo, Lt Col Karl S. Bradford to the Executive, sub: Sub-boards of the Cavalry Board, 12 Aug 37, Ofc of the Ch of Cav, Gen Corresp, RG 177, NARA; Draft Memo, Maj Robert W. Grow to Exec Ofcr, sub: Sub-boards of the Cavalry Board, 12 Aug 37, Ofc of the Ch of Cav, Gen Corresp, RG 177, NARA; Memo, Miller to Ch of Cav, 1 Sep 37.

[75] Memo, TAG to Ch of Cav, 4 Aug 37, and 1st End and Encl, Ch of Cav Maj Gen Leon B. Kromer to TAG, 16 Nov 37, Ofc of the Ch of Cav, Gen Corresp, RG 177, NARA.

[76] Ltr, Ch of Cav Maj Gen Leon B. Kromer to Brig Gen Daniel Van Voorhis, 19 Nov 37, Ofc of the Ch of Cav, Gen Corresp, RG 177, NARA.

[77] Draft Memo, Bradford to the Executive, 12 Aug 37.

Voorhis, commanding the 7th Cavalry Brigade (Mechanized), confirmed this fear through his efforts to create an independent mechanized cavalry board at Fort Knox under his direct authority.[78] Previously, he had created informal boards of part-time members from the mechanized cavalry to study particular issues. The number of such boards, however, tended to increase without tangible benefits. Their separate efforts lacked coordination, and their activities diverted scarce officers from training.[79]

Van Voorhis thus sought additional officers for the 7th Cavalry Brigade to provide a full-time staff for a single board dedicated to mechanized developments.[80] He did not consider horse cavalry personnel qualified to test materiel or to assess doctrinal and organizational matters related to mechanized cavalry. Therefore, in his view, association with the Cavalry Board was unnecessary and undesirable.[81] Moreover, he considered any such linkage harmful to the Cavalry's public image:

> From a point of view of psychology and public sentiment, both within the Army and on the outside, it is hardly desirable to subordinate within the cavalry service the mechanized cavalry activities to those of the horse cavalry. This is contrary to the spirit of the times . . . it certainly would subject the cavalry arm of the service to criticism if it can be interpreted that we are disregarding this modern trend in new and future installations by inaugurating a Mechanized Cavalry Board which appears to be subordinate to a horse cavalry board.[82]

The opposing views of Van Voorhis and Kromer resulted in mutual recriminations. Van Voorhis criticized the effectiveness of officers trained at the Cavalry School and insinuated that mechanized development would suffer under tighter control by the chief of Cavalry. He accused Kromer of seeking to circumvent the V Corps Area commander's influence on mechanized cavalry development. In response, Kromer outlined the ongoing modernization of the Cavalry School curriculum and the success of the chief of Cavalry in securing over $4 million in materiel for the mechanized cavalry.[83]

In March 1938 Maj. Gen. John K. Herr succeeded Kromer as chief of Cavalry. He inherited the unresolved mechanized board issue but reached a compromise with Van Voorhis and his two regimental commanders, Cols. Bruce Palmer and Charles L. Scott. This agreement called for the creation at Fort Knox of an independent mechanized cavalry board whose activities the chief of Cavalry would coordinate

---

[78] Memo, Kromer to President, Cav Board, 1 Jul 37.

[79] Synopsis of Memo, Col Karl S. Bradford to Ch of Cav, sub: Cavalry Board, 1 Jul 38, Ofc of the Ch of Cav, Gen Corresp, RG 177, NARA.

[80] Memo, Brig Gen Daniel Van Voorhis to Ch of Cav, sub: Establishment of Board on Mechanized Cavalry at Fort Knox, Kentucky, 27 Nov 37, Ofc of the Ch of Cav, Gen Corresp, RG 177, NARA.

[81] Ibid.

[82] Ibid., quote from p. 2.

[83] Draft Memo, Ch of Cav Maj Gen Leon B. Kromer to CG, 7th Cav Bde (Mech), sub: Instruction in Mechanization and Mechanized Board, 2 Dec 37, pp. 1–4, quote from p. 5, Ofc of the Ch of Cav, Gen Corresp, RG 177, NARA.

Horse cavalry during a pause in training, 1939

with those of the Cavalry Board.[84] Like Kromer, Herr considered an independent mechanized board at Fort Knox a temporary expedient until the establishment of facilities at Fort Riley to support mechanization.[85]

In order to coordinate board activity at Fort Knox and Fort Riley, Herr needed the ability to communicate directly with the 7th Cavalry Brigade (Mechanized). Some degree of responsibility for the unit's development had also to be shifted from the V Corps Area commander to the chief of Cavalry. These alterations to Army regulations and policy required War Department authorization.[86] In July 1938 the War Department approved direct communication between the chief of Cavalry, the Cavalry Board, and the commander of the 7th Cavalry Brigade (Mechanized). Herr also requested and received similar authority for communication with the 1st Cavalry Division.[87]

---

[84] Synopsis of Memo, Col G. Kent to General Kromer, sub: Mechanization Board and Course, n.d., Ofc of the Ch of Cav, Gen Corresp, RG 177, NARA.

[85] Ltr, Johnnie Herr to Col Dorsey R. Rodney, 6 May 38, Ofc of the Ch of Cav, Gen Corresp, RG 177, NARA.

[86] Memo, Herr to TAG, 13 Apr 38.

[87] Ibid., and 2d End, Col G. Kent to TAG, 6 Jul 38, and 1st End to 2d End, TAG to Ch of Cav, 15 Jul 38, Ofc of the Ch of Cav, Gen Corresp, RG 177, NARA; Memo, TAG to CG, 7th Cav Bde, sub: Mechanized Cavalry Board, 15 Jul 38, Ofc of the Ch of Cav, Gen Corresp, RG 177, NARA; Ltr and Encl, Johnnie Herr to Brig Gen Ben Lear, 18 Jul 38, Ofc of the Ch of Cav, Gen Corresp, RG 177, NARA.

These actions improved the chief of Cavalry's ability to communicate with principal Cavalry components but not his control of them. The War Department disapproved his proposal for a special mechanized cavalry board. Nor would it consider any reallocation of development responsibility for the 7th Cavalry Brigade away from the V Corps Area commander. The failure to do so marginalized the chief of Cavalry's influence on a critical component of his branch and ensured the quasi-independent status of the mechanized cavalry.[88]

At Fort Knox, Van Voorhis created an independent board. He used his authority as a unit commander to do so without requiring War Department action. The new body became the Mechanized Cavalry Board. Technically, it was an entity of the 7th Cavalry Brigade (Mechanized) and therefore directly subordinate to him. Van Voorhis intended this board to be solely responsible for materiel testing and experimentation with organizational and doctrinal issues. It would replace the multiplicity of informal boards previously convened, consolidating their work into a single body under the supervision of the brigade commander.

Staffing, however, obstructed the realization of this goal. Van Voorhis desired full-time board members, but the 7th Cavalry Brigade (Mechanized) lacked sufficient numbers of officers. Those available were already split between training and post administration duties. Consequently, by October 1938 the Mechanized Cavalry Board existed largely on paper and its members had yet to be designated.[89] This situation improved in November with the permanent assignment of four additional officers to the board.[90] The following month they were reduced to part-time membership because the War Department could not decide how board assignments should be classified for career considerations. This change in status undermined the board's effectiveness. Van Voorhis strove unsuccessfully to restore the officers' full-time status and secure additional members.[91] Ironically, it was the chief of Cavalry who offered some relief. In October 1939 Herr indicated that the pending disbandment of the Cavalry's Olympic teams would free two officers for assignment to the Mechanized Cavalry Board.[92]

The Cavalry School and Mechanization

The debates surrounding the creation of a mechanized cavalry board stemmed partly from the lack of mechanized assets at Fort Riley. The Cavalry Board could not

---

[88] Memo, Herr to TAG, sub: Mechanized Cavalry Board, 13 Apr 38, and 1st End, TAG to Ch of Cav, 1 Jun 38, Ofc of the Ch of Cav, Gen Corresp, RG 177, NARA.

[89] Synopsis of Memo, Bradford to Ch of Cav, 1 Jul 38; Ch of Cav Maj Gen John K. Herr, "Remarks re Conference with Assistant Chief of Staff, G–3," 10 Oct 38, Ofc of the Ch of Cav, Gen Corresp, RG 177, NARA.

[90] Maj B. Morrow, "Special Orders No. 41," 22 Nov 38, Ofc of the Ch of Cav, Gen Corresp, RG 177, NARA.

[91] 1st End to Unknown Ltr, Brig Gen Adna R. Chaffee to Ch of Cav, 9 Dec 38, Ofc of the Ch of Cav, Gen Corresp, RG 177, NARA.

[92] Memo, Brig Gen Adna R. Chaffee to Ch of Cav, sub: Commissioned Personnel, Mechanized Cavalry Board, 6 Oct 39, and 1st End, Lt Col Karl S. Bradford to CG, 7th Cav Bde, 9 Oct 39, Ofc of the Ch of Cav, Gen Corresp, RG 177, NARA.

Horse artillery in the interwar era

effectively address technical matters related to the mechanized cavalry. Similarly, the Cavalry School could not provide effective instruction in mechanized operations. This inability added a training dimension to the growing schism between horse and mechanized cavalry already evident in doctrine and materiel development.

General Henry served as the Cavalry School commandant from 1935 to 1939. Previously chief of Cavalry and commander of the 7th Cavalry Brigade (Mechanized), he understood the break emerging between the horse and mechanized cavalries. He tried to prevent a complete rupture through revision of the Cavalry School's curriculum to include both cavalry types. His efforts focused on creating a mechanization course to parallel the Advanced Equitation Course, and he received active support from both Kromer and Herr.[93]

The War Department, however, blocked such action. No opposition existed to theoretical instruction in mechanized cavalry tactics or technical instruction in engines, only to training related to combat cars. The assistant chief of staff, G–3, for example, supported an advanced automotive course at the Cavalry School if it involved no instruction or demonstration of the combat car. Herr considered the matter a "tempest in a teapot," but no advanced mechanized course had received War Department approval by October 1938.[94]

Beyond a special mechanized course, the Cavalry School expanded the training time given to a variety of skills associated with combat vehicles. It increased the time

---

[93] "Conference: General Kromer and General Henry," 16 Nov 37, Ofc of the Ch of Cav, Gen Corresp, RG 177, NARA.

[94] Herr, "Remarks re Conference," 10 Oct 38.

allotted to signal communications and motor vehicles. Mechanized cavalry tactics were taught by instructors who had served in the 7th Cavalry Brigade (Mechanized). Additional training in radio and motor-vehicle operations was considered for the Advanced Equitation Course.[95] Training assignments and visits to Fort Knox were arranged when funding was available.[96] However, similar action to detail mechanized cavalry personnel to Fort Riley for instruction failed.[97]

Cavalry School mechanized instruction remained unsatisfactory. Graduates assigned to the 7th Cavalry Brigade (Mechanized) required further instruction in the brigade before assuming their command responsibilities.[98] In reporting on the state of mechanized instruction for the 1937–1938 academic year, the assistant commandant of the Cavalry School noted: "The instruction is of necessity entirely theoretical except as regards that for scout cars, a few motorcycles and an armored car."[99]

The Cavalry School's inability to provide effective mechanized training coupled with the establishment of the independent Mechanized Cavalry Board prompted fears that a separate mechanized cavalry school would be created.[100] Herr, however, noted a parallel between cavalry and infantry mechanization. Infantry tanks had been stationed at Fort George G. Meade, Maryland, separate from the Infantry School at Fort Benning, Georgia. Problems of coordination similar to those now facing the Cavalry resulted. Concentration of infantry and tank school facilities, coupled with the assignment of a tank unit at Fort Benning, eliminated the problem. Herr desired a similar solution for the cavalry.[101]

Initial plans for establishing a mechanized cavalry unit at Fort Riley centered on the 2d Cavalry Regiment. This regiment was already stationed at Fort Riley and supported the Cavalry School. It was to be reorganized to include a combat-car squadron.[102] This plan was never enacted because of the limited number of combat cars available within the Army, most of which were assigned to the 7th Cavalry Brigade (Mechanized). Cavalry School personnel proved willing to use substitute vehicles, but the reorganization still did not occur.[103]

In December 1937 the chief of staff of the Army approved plans to organize a combat car squadron after the 13th Cavalry Regiment (Mechanized) had received its full complement of combat vehicles. However, the Cavalry was prohibited from any reorganization activity until the vehicles became available and directed to

---

[95] Memo, Kromer to CG, 7th Cav Bde (Mech), 2 Dec 37.

[96] Congress, *Appropriation Bill for 1938*, pp. 395–96; Memo, Lt Col H. J. M. Smith to Col A. M. Miller Jr., 2d Cav, 17 Feb 37, Ofc of the Ch of Cav, Gen Corresp, RG 177, NARA.

[97] Memo, Col A. M. Miller Jr. to Ch of Cav, sub: Mechanized Cavalry at the Cavalry School, 16 Feb 37, Ofc of the Ch of Cav, Gen Corresp, RG 177, NARA.

[98] Memo, Smith to Miller, 17 Feb 37.

[99] Synopsis of Annual Rpt of Asst Commandant of Cav Sch for Sch Year 1937–1938, 1 Jul 38, Ofc of the Ch of Cav, Gen Corresp, RG 177, NARA.

[100] Herr, "Remarks re Conference," 10 Oct 38.

[101] Ibid.

[102] Ibid.

[103] Memo, Miller to Ch of Cav, 16 Feb 37.

expect fielding delays.[104] In August 1938 Herr received notice that lack of funding and personnel would prevent organization of the new squadron until 1940.[105] Consequently, Cavalry planning focused on other sources of personnel and materiel. These included using 2d Cavalry Regiment personnel, activating a squadron from the 15th Cavalry Regiment, employing the African American soldiers of the 10th Cavalry Regiment, and directly converting another existing horse squadron into a combat-car squadron.[106]

In early 1940 Cavalry aspirations were partially realized with War Department approval of the creation of the Separate Combat Car Squadron. Combat-car deliveries were not to begin until March and then only at the rate of two or three per month because Fort Knox received fielding priority.[107] Once the cars arrived, the Separate Combat Car Squadron would appear a successful conclusion to three years of Cavalry effort. On 10 July 1940, however, the squadron became part of the Armored Force and ceased to be a Cavalry unit.[108]

On paper the Cavalry possessed another potential source of combat cars. Since 1927 the cavalry division table of organization and equipment had included a light tank company. In 1933 light tank companies were abolished from infantry divisions. The tanks were concentrated in tank regiments for use as General Headquarters elements. The Cavalry opposed any similar reduction to cavalry formations, since it did not believe General Headquarters tank units capable of providing effective support for fast-moving and far-ranging cavalry operations. Hence the Cavalry would consider the removal of light tank units from mounted divisions only if they were replaced with combat-car units. The name change effectively altered the branch alignment of these units from Infantry to Cavalry.[109]

However, in November 1938 the War Department deferred any action on this issue until ongoing revisions of the table of organization and equipment for cavalry divisions had been completed and approved.[110] Despite the passage of almost six

---

[104] Synopsis of Memo, G–3, sub: Tanks and Mechanized Units, 25 Oct 37, Ofc of the Ch of Cav, Gen Corresp, RG 177, NARA.

[105] Synopsis of Annual Rpt, 1 Jul 38.

[106] Memo, Lt Col Willis D. Crittenberger to Ch of Cav, 13 Sep 39, Ofc of the Ch of Cav, Gen Corresp, RG 177, NARA.

[107] Ltr, Lt Col Karl S. Bradford to Lt Col Thoburn K. Brown, 1 Mar 40, Ofc of the Ch of Cav, Gen Corresp, RG 177, NARA.

[108] 2d End of Unknown Doc Referenced as 322.02(7–11–40), Col K. S. Bradford to CG, 1st Armd Corps, 16 Jul 40, Ofc of the Ch of Cav, Gen Corresp, RG 177, NARA.

[109] Draft Memo, Acting ACS, G–3, Col Duncan K. Major Jr. to Chiefs of Inf, Cav, and Ord for Comment, sub: Utilization of Tanks During Mobilization, 27 Feb 33; Memo, Ch of Cav Maj Gen Leon B. Kromer to Ch of Inf, sub: Light Tank Company in Cavalry Division, 14 Feb 35, and 1st End, Ch of Inf Maj Gen Edw. Croft to Ch of Cav, 15 Feb 35; Memo, Ch of Cav Maj Gen Leon B. Kromer to Ch of Inf, sub: Light Tank Company in Cavalry Division, 14 Feb 35, and 1st End, Ch of Inf Maj Gen Edw. Croft to Ch of Cav, 15 Feb 35; Memo, Ch of Cav Maj Gen Leon B. Kromer to Ch of Inf, sub: Light Tank Company in Cavalry Division, 14 Feb 35, and 1st End, Ch of Inf Maj Gen Edw. Croft to Ch of Cav, 15 Feb 35; all in Ofc of the Ch of Cav, Gen Corresp, RG 177, NARA.

[110] Memo, Maj Gen R. M. Beck Jr. to Ch of Cav, sub: Combat Car Troop in the Cavalry Division, 10 Nov 38, and 2d End, ACS, G–3, Maj Gen R. M. Beck Jr. to Ch of Cav, 21 Dec 38, Ofc of the Ch of Cav, Gen Corresp, RG 177, NARA.

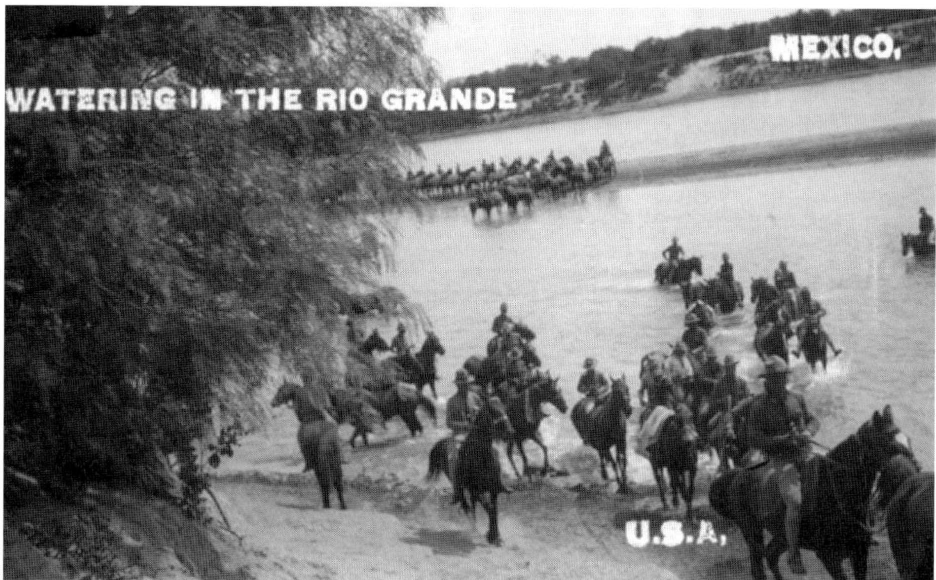

Horse cavalry on the border with Mexico

years, the tanks of the cavalry division remained under the jurisdiction of the chief of Infantry. Only at Fort Knox did the Cavalry possess a significant combat-car formation, but not under the direct authority of the chief of Cavalry.

The Chief of Cavalry and Cavalry Modernization

In matters other than combat cars or the mechanized cavalry, the Office of the Chief of Cavalry proved a progressive influence on the mounted arm. Subject to funding limitations, cavalry modernization proceeded steadily throughout the 1930s. A collective determination to ensure troopers' survival and viability on the battlefield guided the efforts of successive chiefs of Cavalry. One result lay in the steady increase in firepower. By 1938 troopers no longer carried sabers. Instead, the array of weapons at their disposal included light and heavy machine guns (including the .50-caliber), submachine guns, 60-mm. mortars, and 37-mm. guns. These weapons complemented the more traditional semiautomatic rifles and pistols carried by every mounted soldier. In terms of the weapons used, little distinguished cavalry from infantry units. Indeed, the cavalry adopted infantry drill to train troopers in dismounted operations.[111]

Doctrinal changes also improved cavalry effectiveness. These included increased reliance on smoke usage and aerial reconnaissance. Artillery support

[111] Memo, Kromer to ASW, 26 Aug 37, p. 4; Congress, *Appropriation Bill for 1936*, p. 351; Memo, Herr to TAG, 16 Aug 38, pp. 2–3; "Notes of Discussion Following Lecture by Major General John K. Herr," 19 Sep 38, pp. 5–6, AWC Curricular Archives (hereafter cited as Herr Discussion Notes).

procedures became more integral to mounted operations. New march formations and antiaircraft tactics developed to reduce the vulnerability of cavalry organizations to air attack. [112] Radio communications expanded and became more effective.[113] Training improvements included efforts to conduct combined exercises with attached infantry and aircraft, but lack of available personnel generally precluded the presence of the former.[114]

Cavalry interest in motorization began in the immediate aftermath of World War I and continued throughout the interwar period. The War Department acknowledged this interest in its Army motorization program. Under this program, Cavalry objectives included the creation of seven separate armored car troops for use in mobilization with Regular Army and National Guard cavalry divisions; inclusion of a scout-car platoon in every horse cavalry regiment; complete motorization of all division, brigade, and regimental headquarters; and motorization of all horse cavalry field trains (though some animals were to be retained for combat supply).[115] The Cavalry further undertook to include motorized artillery in the cavalry division.[116]

The Cavalry accomplished most of these objectives by the late 1930s. Horse regiments benefited from the integral presence of scout cars and motorized field trains. Headquarters motorization extended down to the troop level.[117] In the 1st Cavalry Division, motorization led to analysis of how best to coordinate the actions of motor vehicles and horses.[118] Interest in motorcycle usage led to extensive experimentation, but the utility of this vehicle remained limited. Designs remained too fragile for off-road movements or operations in inclement weather.[119]

Improvements to weapons, tactics, and organizations up to the brigade level occurred at Fort Riley under the direction of the Cavalry Board and the Cavalry School faculty. In 1931 the 2d Cavalry Regiment became the Project Regiment when it was reorganized to test proposed changes to the regiment's structure. Subsequently, the regiment served as the Cavalry's field laboratory.[120] It developed tactics for new weapons (including the .50-caliber machine gun in an antitank role) and methods

---

[112] Memo, Asst Commandant, Cav Sch, Col Bruce Palmer, to Commandant, Cav Sch, sub: Comments on Proposed Experimental 1933 Tables of Organization, 2d Cav, 19 Apr 33, Ofc of the Ch of Cav, Gen Corresp, RG 177, NARA.

[113] Memo, Kromer to ASW, 26 Aug 37, p. 4; Congress, *War Department Appropriation Bill for 1936*, p. 351.

[114] Congress, *Appropriation Bill for 1931*, p. 623.

[115] Memo and Encl, Deputy Chief of Staff Maj Gen Hugh A. Drum to ACS, G–4, sub: Motorization, Mechanization, and Air Corps Policies Resulting from War Department Studies, Including Those Associated with Public Works, 2 Nov 33, Ofc of the CS, Gen Corresp, RG 165, NARA; Congress, *Appropriation Bill for 1938*, p. 3.

[116] Ltrs, Frank Richmonds to Col Willis Crittenberger, 26 May 38, and Lt Col John A. Considine to Karl [Col Karl S. Bradford], 21 May 39, both in Ofc of the Ch of Cav, Gen Corresp, RG 177, NARA.

[117] Memo, Herr to TAG, 16 Aug 38, pp. 2–3; Herr Discussion Notes, 19 Sep 38, pp. 5–6; Ltr, Richmonds to Crittenberger, 26 May 38.

[118] Memo, Palmer to Commandant, Cav Sch, 19 Apr 33.

[119] Congress, *Appropriation Bill for 1932*, p. 635.

[120] Memo, Col A. M. Miller Jr. to General Kromer, sub: Chronology of Project Regiment at Fort Riley (2d Cavalry), 27 May 36, Ofc of the Ch of Cav, Gen Corresp, RG 177, NARA.

for coordinating mechanized and horse cavalry operations and participated in radio designs. The 2d Cavalry Regiment bore responsibility for demonstrating the viability of motorizing horse cavalry field trains. It also experimented with different organizational establishments for horse regiments, developed scout car tactics, and sought to improve the ability of horse cavalry to operate independent of field trains through altering the type and distribution of food rations.[121]

Through use of the Project Regiment and simulating tracked vehicles with wheeled ones, the Cavalry Board experimented with horse cavalry operating with and against mechanized combat units.[122] The Cavalry's dual nature stimulated analysis of antitank tactics. The Cavalry considered antitank measures vital to any future combat role because of the proliferation of mechanized and motorized combat units throughout the world. Tactical experiments with scout and armored cars revealed their versatility and value but also their vulnerability to ambush.[123]

The steady improvements and changes to cavalry organizations and doctrine provided a stark contrast to the public's perception of the mounted arm. Consequently, the branch had little difficulty attracting young officers throughout the decade. At the U.S. Military Academy, graduating cadets with sufficient academic performance were permitted to choose their branch of service. The Corps of Engineers, considered the Army's intellectuals, drew the greatest number of qualified cadets—followed by the Cavalry.[124] This steady influx of West Point graduates provided the Cavalry with a talent pool from which many future combat commanders would emerge.

---

[121] Memo, Col Selwyn D. Smith to Ch of Cav, sub: Experimental Organization, 5th Quarterly Report, 20 Apr 33, Ofc of the Ch of Cav, Gen Corresp, RG 177, NARA.

[122] Ibid.

[123] Memo, Palmer to Commandant, Cav Sch, 19 Apr 33.

[124] Waters Oral History, p. 105; Palmer/Shelton/Smith Conversations, p. 52.

4

THE INFANTRY AND MECHANIZATION

In the 1930s infantry tank development occurred amid a backdrop of change and uncertainty. Doctrinal confusion and reorganization of the division structure directly impacted related efforts to improve the use of support weapons including the tank. Nevertheless, tank doctrine remained largely consistent in its emphasis on the close coordination of the tank and the rifleman. Related tactics and techniques became the focus of training and doctrine. The clear subordination of the tank to the foot soldier ensured that infantry mechanization did not pose a threat to branch unity. Infantry tank development adhered to the branch mission, although in so doing it sometimes incurred criticism as being unprogressive.

Army Doctrine in the 1930s

Throughout the interwar period, the Infantry constituted the Army's largest branch. Its mission included the destruction of hostile forces and the seizure and occupation of key geographic objectives. Army doctrine and concepts of battle focused on infantry formations, with other combat assets performing a supplementary role. The rifleman was expected to be in the forefront of any significant military action and to play a dominant role, much as he had since the Revolutionary War.

The tactics, techniques, and procedures related to infantry operations derived from Army doctrine. In general terms, offensive action based on maneuver was preferred in lieu of the static, positional nature of World War I. No senior leader advocated trench warfare. However, the Army's doctrinal base proved confusing and contradictory. It did not provide a clear vision of how the next war should be fought. Instead, Army doctrine embraced two opposing tactical philosophies.

After World War I the War Department studied its wartime experiences. It updated its doctrine based on the lessons learned from that conflict. This work resulted in *Field Service Regulations, United States Army*, published in 1923.[1] This manual emphasized reliance on maneuver, envelopment, and retention of the initiative to threaten enemy vital areas. Operations based on these means sought to

---

[1] U.S. War Department (WD), *Field Service Regulations, United States Army*, 1923; Memo, Lt Col George A. Lynch to Commandant, U.S. Army War College (AWC), sub: Tactical Doctrine Governing the Employment of Large Units: Its Relation to the Tactics of Small Units, 1 Mar 30, p. 1, George A. Lynch Papers, Archives, U.S. Army Military History Institute (MHI), Carlisle Barracks, Pa.

force a predictable reaction that could be addressed without sacrificing initiative or momentum.[2] The field service regulations envisioned "the concentrated and simultaneous launching of force in a battle of annihilation; we admit, of course, cases in which a lesser objective should be sought."[3] The preference for a concentration of force to achieve rapid destruction of the enemy reflected a desire to avoid positional warfare and the influence of German ideas.[4]

In 1930 the War Department published *A Manual for Commanders of Large Units (Provisional)*. This manual addressed the operations of divisions, corps, and armies. The War Department intended it to supplement the field service regulations, which the War Department believed offered insufficient guidance for higher command echelons. The manual for commanders expounded the concept of a careful, deliberate approach to battle. It emphasized the importance of linear operations and maintaining an unbroken, continuous front. Offensives entailed not the overwhelming application of force outlined in the field service regulations but a series of low-intensity attacks that escalated as the enemy's disposition was determined. A careful, deliberate attack then commenced to destroy the enemy through high concentrations of firepower rather than maneuver and envelopment. Command and control measures favored extensive use of rigid timetables and phase lines coupled with highly centralized direction.[5]

These principles contradicted those included in the field service regulations. The discrepancy originated in the manual's foreign origins. It proved little more than a translation of the French *Instruction Provisoire sur l'Emploi Tactique des Grandes Unités* published by the French War Ministry in 1922. Army War College students reviewing a draft of the War Department's manual advised against its publication. They preferred an update to the field service regulations and the Army-wide application of its principles. The War Department General Staff overruled these objections and published the manual.[6]

Army doctrine thus failed to provide a uniform vision of how to fight. Worse, the simultaneous adoption of conflicting tactical principles generated confusion in training programs and practical application. This unsatisfactory situation led to repeated calls for a complete revision of Army doctrine to eliminate the discrepancies and accommodate newer weapons and technologies. Foremost among these

---

[2] George A. Lynch, "The Infantry," Lecture at AWC, 20 Sep 38, pp. 11, 17, Army War College Lectures, 1938–1939, pt. 1, AWC Curricular Archives, MHI Archives.

[3] Memo, Lynch to Commandant, AWC, 1 Mar 30, p. 12.

[4] Col G. A. Lynch, "Conference, Officers School, 15th Infantry," p. 3, Lynch Papers.

[5] Memo, Lynch to Commandant, AWC, 1 Mar 30; Lynch, "Infantry," 20 Sep 38, pp. 11, 13–14, 17; George A. Lynch, "The Tactics of the New Infantry Regiment," Address at Command and General Staff School (CGSS), 14 Mar 39, p. 3, Lynch Papers; WD, *A Manual for Commanders of Large Units (Provisional)*, 1930; William O. Odom, *After the Trenches: The Transformation of U.S. Army Doctrine, 1918–1939* (College Station: Texas A&M University Press, 1999), pp. 118–20.

[6] "Notes of Discussion Following Lecture by Maj. Gen. George A. Lynch, Chief of Infantry," 20 Sep 38, p. 5, AWC Curricular Archives (hereafter cited as Lynch Discussion Notes); George A. Lynch, "Final Report of Major General George A. Lynch: A Summary of Infantry Developments During His Term of Office," 30 Apr 41, p. 9, MHI Library.

M1917 at Fort George G. Meade, Maryland

reformers was Maj. Gen. George A. Lynch, who served as chief of infantry from May 1937 until April 1941.

Earlier, as a lieutenant colonel, Lynch had been one of the principal authors of the field service regulations. He considered the principles they embodied appropriate to the U.S. Army and the preferred basis for doctrinal reform. In 1930, while attending the Army War College, he had proven one of the most outspoken critics of *A Manual for Commanders of Large Units (Provisional)*. As chief of Infantry, however, his principal concern lay in the lack of uniform Army doctrine to guide branch modernization. He therefore prodded the War Department to adopt a single vision of how to fight.[7]

The General Staff proved largely unresponsive to Lynch's views. It belatedly undertook a revision of the field service regulations without consulting the branch chiefs. Instead the General Staff worked directly with the Command and General Staff School to produce *Field Service Regulations: Operations (Tentative)* in October 1939. This publication met with widespread criticism throughout the Army when it was finally released for comment. Consequently, it did not become the capstone document desired and underwent further revision. In May 1941 this work finally resulted in Field Manual (FM) 100–5, *Field Service Regulations: Operations*.

[7] Memo, Lynch to Commandant, AWC, 1 Mar 30, pp. 12–13; Lynch, "Infantry," 20 Sep 38, pp. 7–8; Lynch, "Final Report," pp. 9–10.

Unlike its predecessor, this new manual did provide an effective statement of how the Army expected to fight and offered common guidance for the separate branch development efforts.[8]

Until publication of the 1941 regulations, branch chiefs were largely left to struggle with the conflicting views represented by the 1923 field service regulations and *A Manual for Commanders of Large Units (Provisional)*. Lacking General Staff guidance, the branches and the Command and General Staff School all developed their own tactical procedures related to their specific missions. This trend undermined efforts at cooperation among the combat arms.[9] In this doctrinal vacuum, the Command and General Staff School assumed that its tactical developments applied Army-wide. Such a belief was not shared throughout the Army. More than one officer noted that "Many a recent Leavenworth graduate has come to grief by a not too tactful reference as to how they do it at Leavenworth."[10]

Independent branch actions were necessary for training. Limited in scope, they nevertheless required War Department approval before implementation. The G–3 (Operations and Training) Division of the General Staff bore responsibility for the publication of field manuals and regulations governing doctrine and tactics. The understaffed G–3 could not keep pace with the deluge of projects that increased throughout the 1930s and required analysis and action. Hence, branch efforts to secure approval for doctrine and training developments encountered prolonged delays. In the meantime, the branch schools compromised between teaching old ideas that might soon be superseded and training new concepts that might not receive War Department approval. Limited funding further obstructed the publication even of approved training literature.[11]

Infantry Motorization

The confused state of Army doctrine posed a stumbling block for Infantry efforts to incorporate motor vehicles into combat organizations. In 1931 the 34th Infantry Regiment experimented with motorization and found that providing vehicular transport for riflemen greatly enhanced their mobility. However, their vulnerability to hostile action increased, limiting their employment. These tests generated interest in an armored carrier that protected its passengers while in transit. The optimal role for the carriers lay in reserve, where they could exploit their mobility to move

[8] Lynch, "Final Report," pp. 9–10, 68–69, 75; WD, *Field Service Regulations: Operations (Tentative)*, 1939, and FM 100–5, *Field Service Regulations: Operations*, 1941.

[9] Rpt of Committee no. 4, sub: Modernization of Tactical Doctrines and Tactical Organization, Development of Weapons, 25 Sep 39, p. 15, AWC Curricular Archives; Bradford G. Chynoweth, "Modernization," pp. 2–3, 15, 1935, Bradford G. Chynoweth Papers, MHI Archives; Memo, Lt Col A. C. Gillem Jr. to Asst Commandant, Inf Sch, sub: Coordination Between Special Service Schools, Infantry and Field Artillery, 6 Feb 39, Alvan C. Gillem Jr. Papers, MHI Archives.

[10] Rpt of Committee no. 4, 25 Sep 39, pp. 15–16, quote from p. 14.

[11] The Adjutant General (TAG), "Training Literature," 1 May 39, p. 2, Tab C of Memo, Maj H. J. Matchett to Asst Commandant, AWC, sub: War Department Training Literature, 8 Nov 39, AWC Curricular Archives; Rpt of Committee no. 4, 25 Sep 39, p. 16.

quickly to a threatened area or reinforce an attack. The absence of adequate vehicles, however, limited the scope of the 34th Infantry Regiment's experimentation.[12]

The following years witnessed a growing interest in motorized infantry and its potential employment. Wheeled vehicles were not generally considered a viable means of tactical transport due to their poor cross-country mobility and lack of protection. By 1937 four types of infantry regiments existed. Each reflected a different degree of motorization. No consensus existed regarding the optimal allocation of vehicles to infantry units or their employment. The uncertainty surrounding the organization and employment of motorized units effectively prevented the creation of standard tactics, techniques, and procedures to guide operations and training.[13]

During the Great Depression, the Army faced the prospect of suppressing domestic disturbances triggered by economic hardship. In order to reach potential crisis areas, understrength infantry units scattered across the country would have to travel long distances. Greater reliance on motorization, however, meant they could exploit the nation's road net and at least achieve parity with the mobility of expected agitators using private and commercial vehicles.[14]

Motor vehicle use in the Spanish Civil War, 1936–1939, suggested that their principal value lay in the movement of men, supplies, and equipment. However, their susceptibility to air attack, small-arms fire, and natural and artificial obstacles restricted their combat usage. These experiences raised questions about the wisdom of building fully motorized formations.[15] The Infantry therefore opted to motorize regimental supply and support assets, leaving its rifle companies to march and fight on foot. For rapid movement to and from the battlefield, division or corps truck companies could provide additional transport.[16]

For much of the 1930s, however, Infantry motorization plans remained little more than paper concepts. They could not be realized given the state of the Army's vehicle pool, which included a multiplicity of makes and models with a corresponding diversity of parts.[17] Many of these vehicles had become obsolete and needed replacement. The mechanized cavalry fared little better. By 1936, 7th Cavalry

---

[12] F. C. Phelps, "The Tactical Employment of Motorized Infantry," Lecture at Tank Sch, 16 Dec 31, pp. 21, 28, in "Tank Notes," Mar 32, MHI Library.

[13] George A. Lynch, "Current Infantry Developments," Lecture at AWC, 4 Oct 37, pp. 5–6, Lynch Papers; Lynch, "Final Report," p. 8.

[14] Memo, Col W. S. Drysdale to CG, 5th Inf Bde, sub: Request for Class A Motorization of 4th Infantry, 24 Jun 37, Item 4960, Reel 315, National Archives Project, George C. Marshall Library (GCM), Lexington, Va.

[15] Suppl no. 2 to Rpt of Committee no. 2, sub: The Spanish Revolution, 24 Jan 38, pp. 5, 11, AWC Curricular Archives; Emilio Canevari, "Forecasts from the War in Spain: Lessons Based on Technical and Tactical Experience," *Army Ordnance* XVIII, no. 107 (March-April 1938): 275–76.

[16] Editor, "Truck Tactics," *Infantry Journal* XLIV, no. 6 (November-December 1937): 511.

[17] U.S. Congress, House, Subcommittee of the Committee on Appropriations, *War Department Appropriation Bill for 1938 Military Activities, Hearings*, 75th Cong., 1st Sess., 1937, p. 43; Daniel R. Beaver, "Politics and Policy: The War Department Motorization and Standardization Program for Wheeled Transport Vehicles, 1920–1940," *Military Affairs* XLVII, no. 3 (October 1983): 106; Harry C. Thomson and Lida Mayo, *The Ordnance Department: Procurement and Supply*, U.S. Army in World War II (Washington, D.C.: U.S. Army Center of Military History, 1960), p. 269.

Brigade (Mechanized) personnel were scouring the junkyards of major industrial cities seeking spare parts no longer commercially produced.[18]

Modernization of the Army's vehicle fleet faced several obstacles. Automotive manufacturers resisted demands to produce vehicles specifically for military service. They preferred instead to build vehicles to meet commercial and private needs, thus ensuring a reliable profit margin.[19] The Quartermaster Corps, responsible for motor-vehicle procurement, used the best commercial components and assembled its own trucks for Army use.[20]

Congress ended this practice in 1933 by forcing the War Department to rely on private manufacturers to meet motor vehicle needs. The Army was required to accept commercially produced vehicles and prohibited from influencing their design specifications. Similarly, Congress permitted the military little role in the selection of a manufacturer. As the effects of the Great Depression worsened, War Department contracts were distributed among many manufacturers to help them remain in business. Consequently, small firms often underbid larger and more established ones to secure a contract, regardless of their ability to provide the best product. Vehicles produced often did not match military needs or expectations.[21]

The Army could not afford to replace aging vehicles and purchase additional ones. The War Department therefore gave priority to the replacement of antiquated vehicles. Hence, in 1937 a request to motorize the entire 5th Infantry Brigade to permit its early response to possible riots and demonstrations was refused. The War Department sympathized with the proposal's intent, but it could not afford the measure. Therefore, the brigade was directed to either rely on corps area truck assets or hire locally available vehicles.[22]

By 1939 the conditions facing the Army's vehicle fleet started to improve. Automotive manufacturers began commercial production of large, multi-wheel-drive trucks with interchangeable components. These vehicles had direct military applications and were designed in part for Army use. Manufacturers had at last come to the realization that the Army represented a stable and lucrative market. As numbers and types of the new trucks increased, the War Department limited

---

[18] Ltr, Col Charles L. Scott to Maj Robert W. Grow, 23 Sep 36, p. 2, Ofc of the Ch of Cav, Gen Corresp, Record Group (RG) 177, National Archives and Records Administration (NARA).

[19] Beaver, "Politics and Policy," p. 104.

[20] Ibid.; Thomson and Mayo, *Ordnance Department*, p. 268.

[21] Memo, Quartermaster General Maj Gen L. H. Bash to Asst Sec of War, sub: Comptroller General's Decisions nos. A–53405 and A–54540, P.W.A. Motorization Program, 28 Apr 34, p. 1, Ofc of the Quartermaster General, Gen Corresp Decimal File, 1922–1935, RG 92, NARA; Thomson and Mayo, *Ordnance Department*, pp. 266–67; Beaver, "Politics and Policy," pp. 104–05.

[22] Memo, Col W. S. Drysdale to CG, 5th Inf Bde, sub: Request for Class A Motorization of 4th Infantry, 24 Jun 37; 2d End, Brig Gen W. C. Sweeney to CG, 5th Inf Bde, 30 Jun 37; 3d End, Brig Gen George C. Marshall to CG, 3d Div, 15 Jul 37; 7th End, Ofc of the Ch of Inf Exec, Col J. B. Woolnough, to TAG, 18 Oct 37; Memo, TAG to CG, IX Corps Area, sub: Request for Class A Motorization of 4th Infantry, 3 Nov 37; all on Item 4960, Reel 315, National Archives Project, GCM. Beaver, "Politics and Policy," pp. 104–05.

Kentucky National Guard tanks at Camp Knox

the number of different chassis types deemed necessary for the military to simplify parts accessibility and maintenance.[23]

Division Redesign

In 1935 the War Department undertook the redesign of the infantry division. This effort sought to reduce the size of the formation while increasing its mobility. The new organization would incorporate a high level of motorization despite the poor state of the Army's vehicle fleet. Analytical work over the next two years led to the design of a triangular division that differed significantly from the square divisions of World War I. On the battlefields of France, the latter provided the manpower necessary to penetrate fortified positions. The triangular division, however, reflected the interwar emphasis on mobility and maneuver. Field tests of the new formation began in 1937 and continued into 1939. A year later the new division type characterized all Regular Army infantry divisions; the National Guard retained the square structure.[24]

The triangular division reflected the War Department's emphasis on organizations that possessed only those components essential to their mission. To the greatest extent possible, support assets, including tanks, were removed from the division and pooled in units assigned to corps and army commands. From there they could be temporarily assigned to support the execution of a particular mission. An increase in firepower resulted from the adoption of the M1 Garand semiautomatic rifle.

---

[23] Beaver, "Politics and Policy," pp. 106–07; Thomson and Mayo, *Ordnance Department*, p. 270.

[24] Mark Skinner Watson, *Chief of Staff: Prewar Plans and Preparations*, U.S. Army in World War II (Washington, D.C.: U.S. Army Center of Military History, 1950), pp. 156–58, 160.

The War Department therefore concluded that rifle units could be reduced in size without sacrificing combat power. Similarly, command flexibility improved through elimination of the brigade headquarters. Collectively, these measures gave the triangular division a strength of 13,500, compared to the square division's 22,000. The former, however, possessed much greater mobility through widespread reliance on motor vehicles for supply and support functions.[25]

The organization of the triangular division reflected the Army's struggle to strike a balance among combat capability, mobility, and size. However, the minimization tendency evident in the new formation's composition raised concerns about its combat effectiveness. The American formation was similar in strength to the German infantry division. In the number of accompanying weapons and overall firepower, however, the German formation appeared considerably superior. In 1938 the chief of Field Artillery noted that should the new American division engage the German formation in combat, "we would contend with it on very unequal terms."[26]

Controversy surrounded the structure of the regiment. The War Department preferred three identical rifle battalions and one motorized battalion with all of the regiment's support weapons, including machine guns. Rifle battalions limited to small arms would presumably be capable of faster tactical maneuver and possess greater flexibility of command.[27] Maj. Gen. Edward Croft supported this concept during his tenure as chief of Infantry from May 1933 until April 1937.[28]

His successor, Maj. Gen. George A. Lynch, did not, and he came to embody a broad range of concerns about the nature of the triangular division. Lynch considered the fourth battalion "a conglomerate of incongruous weapons." He disagreed with the inherent assumption that the support weapons would always be available when needed. He also doubted their ability to coordinate effectively with the rifle battalions under fire, citing the experiences of machine-gun units in World War I. Machine guns had been organized separately and only temporarily assigned to support rifle units. Too often this support proved inadequate in terms of timeliness, effectiveness, and cohesion. Lynch therefore preferred the permanent integration of support weapons into each rifle battalion. Similarly, he disagreed with the elimination of basic regimental components to reduce overhead, since the functions of these elements would still have to be performed. The elimination of the regiment's reconnaissance detachment,

---

[25] Memo, Chief of Staff (CS) General Malin Craig, sub: Reorganization of the Division and Higher Units, 5 Nov 35, Ofc of the Ch of Cav, Gen Corresp, RG 177, NARA; Lynch, "Final Report," pp. 37–38; WD, *Table of Organization* no. 7-P, *Infantry Division (Triangular), Consolidated Table*, 1 Oct 39, MHI Library; Ronald Spector, "The Military Effectiveness of the U.S. Armed Forces, 1919–39," in *Military Effectiveness*, 3 vols., ed. Allan R. Millett and Williamson Murray (Boston: Allen and Unwin, 1988), 2: 80; Odom, *After the Trenches*, pp. 112–13.

[26] Memo, Ch of Field Arty Maj Gen U. Birnie Jr. to CS, sub: Comparative Strength and Armament—German and Proposed United States Infantry Divisions, 11 Nov 38, Item 4852, Reel 313, National Archives Project, GCM.

[27] "Infantry Digest," *Infantry Journal* XLII, no. 5 (September-October 1935): 450; T. J. Camp, "The Fourth Battalion," *Infantry Journal* XLIII, no. 3 (May-June 1936): 201–07.

[28] Edward Croft, "Developments in Organization, Armament and Equipment of Infantry," Lecture at AWC, 18 Sep 34, pp. 4–6, "Lectures, Army War College, 1934–1935," AWC Curricular Archives.

M1917s moving through wooded terrain

for example, permitted a reduction in the regiment's size. However, the need for a reconnaissance capability necessitated rifle companies' diverting combat strength to this task.[29]

For similar reasons, Lynch remained critical of the triangular division structure. It relied too much on the provision of external support assets, creating at the division level problems similar to those associated with the fourth battalion idea. Temporary attachments of specialized units to support division actions seemed to overlook the tactical coordination problems likely to result from mixing units whose debut as a team occurred on the battlefield. Lynch shared the view of many field commanders who desired more versatile combat formations with the means to adapt to changing tactical conditions without relying on external organizations.

He supported the emphasis on increased command flexibility and mobility, but he disagreed with the drastic reductions in personnel strength taken to achieve these goals. He considered the resultant division weak in offensive power and largely the result of paper analysis rather than extensive field tests. These criticisms paralleled

[29] Lynch, "Current Infantry Developments," 4 Oct 37, pp. 9–10; George A. Lynch, "Infantry," p. 4, 20 Sep 39, Lynch Papers; Lynch, "Final Report," pp. 37–38, 40–41.

Chart 5–Triangular Division, 1939

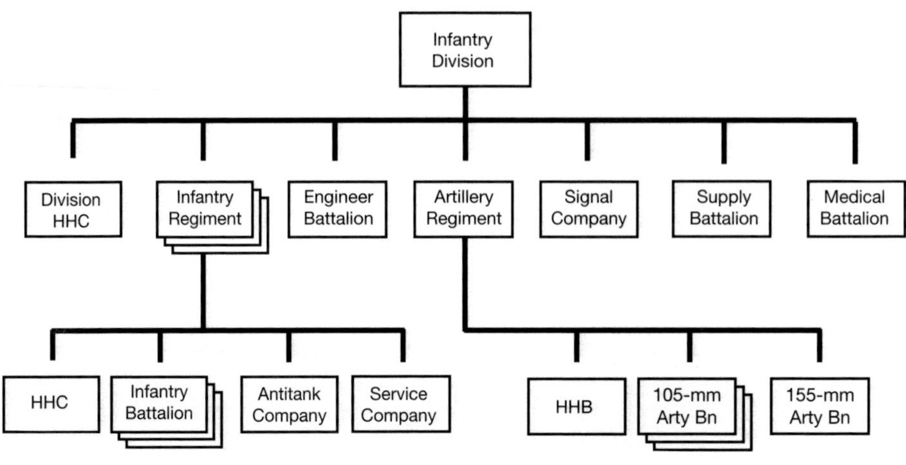

his disparagement of the 1939 revision of the field service regulations. In both cases, he considered the absence of branch chief input—especially that of the chief of Infantry—at least partially responsible for what he considered flawed products.[30]

The outbreak of war in Europe in September 1939 altered the focus of the War Department. Instead of developing new concepts for future combat, the Army increased its emphasis on immediate readiness. Lynch accordingly worked to support the fielding of the triangular division (*Chart 5*), despite his reservations about its efficacy. He also sought to defer any further changes to the formation's organization until they could be based on field experience. During spring maneuvers in 1940, the triangular division made its debut and the experience Lynch desired began to accumulate.[31]

The development of the new formation and the revision of the field service regulations symbolized a change within the War Department. The limited influence of the branch chiefs on these actions, which impacted the entire Army, marked a transition in the military's decision-making process. With the threat of war growing, the War Department gravitated toward a more vertical command structure through expansion of the chief of staff's authority at the expense of branch chief influence. This development paralleled events in World War I, but it also signaled the decline of the chief of Infantry's ability to influence his branch's activities.

[30] Lynch, "Final Report," pp. 37–39, 54.

[31] Ibid., pp. 37–39, 54.

The Foundations of Infantry Tank Doctrine

Infantry tank development occurred amid the backdrop of the triangular division, motorization, and the Army's doctrinal duality. While these efforts suffered from uncertainty and controversy, infantry tank development remained remarkably consistent throughout the 1930s. The Infantry's tank force did not pose a threat to branch unity, and it remained closely linked to the branch's nonmechanized component. Infantry tanks lacked the administrative autonomy of the mechanized cavalry, and their mission ensured the convergence of tank and foot-soldier development. Consequently, tank doctrine developed in concert with the branch's general focus and War Department intent.

Unlike the variety of tactical roles assigned to the mechanized cavalry, infantry tanks had a singular purpose—direct support of the foot soldier. In his May 1931 mechanization policy, Chief of Staff General Douglas MacArthur provided the following guidance for infantry tank development:

> The infantry mission is to close with the enemy, and its ability and power to accomplish this makes infantry the decisive arm. Its success is a prerequisite to army success; consequently, its efforts must not be dispersed in the performance of auxiliary and supporting missions that can be carried out by other arms. As one of the principal duties of the tank will be to support infantry, it should be trained with it to develop the most efficient type of machines and most applicable methods of tank support for infantry units.[32]

In general, infantry tank development did strive to improve the coordination of the tank and the rifleman. The Infantry Board considered envelopment of obstacles to the foot soldier's advance preferable to the frontal assaults practiced in the World War, but it considered sweeping flank marches to be cavalry operations.[33] This view also accorded with the emphasis of the field regulations of 1923 on maneuver rather than potentially costly frontal assaults that did not promise a decisive result.

The precise manner in which tanks would be employed on the battlefield reflected the principles established by Tank School Commandant Col. Samuel D. Rockenbach. He served as the chief of the Tank Corps in World War I, achieving the rank of brigadier general before the Army's postwar rank reduction returned him to his prewar rank of colonel. From 1920–1924 he commanded the Tank School until again promoted to brigadier general and reassigned.[34]

---

[32] Douglas MacArthur, "General Principles To Govern in Extending Mechanization and Motorization Throughout the Army," 1 May 31, p. 3, Willis D. Crittenberger Papers, MHI Archives.

[33] Timothy K. Nenninger, "The Development of American Armor, 1917–1940," Master's Thesis, University of Wisconsin, 1968, pp. 126–27.

[34] WD, Special Orders no. 248–0, 21 Oct 20; no. 20, 24 Jan 24; no. 33, 8 Feb 24; all in Samuel D. Rockenbach Papers, Virginia Military Institute (VMI) Archives, Lexington, Va.

Reserve officer tank orientation, ca. 1932

Rockenbach advocated the use of leading and accompanying tanks to support infantry operations. During the war these notions represented little more than a merging of British and French ideas to provide a doctrinal basis for the Tank Corps. After the war Rockenbach continued to refine these concepts, and they remained integral to infantry tank doctrine long after he had left the tank force.

The Infantry field manual of 1931, for example, included guidance for tank units that addressed the separate roles of leading and accompanying tanks. Leading tanks preceded the infantry assault, eliminating potential obstacles to the main effort. A second wave of accompanying tanks followed, advancing immediately in front of the foot infantry, targeting enemy machine guns. A third set of tanks advanced with the riflemen and provided direct fire support against remaining resistance. Additional tanks exploited breaches made in the enemy's defenses. A special paragraph in the field manual, entitled "Crushing," encouraged tanks to overrun enemy obstacles, weapons, and personnel. It noted the likely demoralization of soldiers when confronted by a huge steel box intent on driving over them.[35]

Two schools of thought surrounded leading tank operations. One emphasized the use of light, fast tanks to make a rapid penetration of enemy defenses, relying on speed to minimize losses. The quick disruption of resistance was believed to facilitate the action of riflemen advancing behind the leading tanks. These foot soldiers could avoid heavy casualties and consolidate the gains of the tanks. Critics believed that

[35] WD, *Infantry Field Manual*, 2: 181, 208, 211–16.

A Mark VIII of the 67th Infantry Regiment conducting demonstration at the U.S. Military Academy in 1934

using light tanks in this manner would make them vulnerable to destruction before they could be supported by infantry or artillery. Therefore, the action of tanks should be coordinated closely with all supporting forces. This viewpoint prevailed.[36]

The emphasis given to coordination of all arms suited infantry needs whether maneuvering in the open or assaulting fortified positions. In the former case, tanks helped to rupture enemy defenses. They then used their firepower and mobility to prevent the creation of new defensive positions. They would also perform the role of supporting fire until artillery assets displaced forward to assume this mission. The tanks would then return to support further infantry advances. In this manner tanks would help sustain offensive momentum and prevent operations from devolving into the trench warfare of the World War.[37]

In April 1938 a War Department directive offered additional refinements to tank doctrine. The directive stressed the importance of coordinated action among tank and nonmechanized assets. Tanks were to be assigned common objectives with foot soldiers and employed on terrain suited to their mobility. The War Department expected tanks to function as part of a team. Therefore, its directive described how it expected tanks to interact with other combat assets:

---

[36] William C. Lee, "Fast Tanks as Leading Tanks and Exploiting Tanks," Lecture at Tank Sch, 12 Jan 32, pp. 2, 14, in "Tank Notes," Mar 32, MHI Library.

[37] Lynch, "Final Report," pp. 60–61.

> The infantry takes advantage of the tank action to advance promptly and occupy each successive intermediate objective. The tanks are supported by the use of artillery, heavy infantry weapons, smoke, and combat aviation for neutralizing hostile antitank weapons and artillery which may threaten the tank advance. Observation aviation will cooperate in the detection of tank obstacles. Whenever the necessity for their services can be foreseen, engineer troops may be attached to tank units for assisting their advance.[38]

Tanks assigned to support a formation would subordinate themselves to the latter's commander, who assumed coordination responsibility.[39] The subordination of tank units to nonmechanized commanders conformed to the Infantry's view of the tank as simply one of many support weapons available to assist the advance of the riflemen. This practice also discouraged independent action by tank units. It reflected the War Department's guidance that "The mission of the tanks is determined by their power to contribute to the execution of the Infantry mission."[40]

In general, however, guidance concerning tank employment still embraced the use of leading and accompanying tanks massed at the point of contact. Hence, the War Department directive included:

> In the attack, the leading echelon advances closely behind the supporting fire of the artillery and heavy infantry weapons. These tanks, with the support of the other weapons, have the mission of dominating the antitank guns. The second echelon, closely followed by the foot troops, advances with the mission of dominating the enemy's machine guns. These are the accompanying tanks that break into the hostile position with the infantry.[41]

In many respects infantry tank doctrine reflected the World War I battlefield. Certainly, the War Department's guidance seemed more attuned to Tank Corps operations on the Western Front than to the fast-moving war of maneuver envisioned by many senior leaders. The mechanization directive seemed to favor the principles embedded in *A Manual for the Command of Large Units (Provisional)* rather than those of the field service regulations.

Nevertheless, the War Department's emphasis on coordinated action reinforced the Infantry's own efforts to ensure the integrated action of all available support weapons—including tanks. This doctrinal emphasis on the integrated action of tank and nonmechanized assets led to a proposal that both be included in tank units.

---

[38] Ibid., p. 4.

[39] Memo, TAG, sub: Policies Governing Mechanization, and the Tactical Employment of Mechanized Units, 6 Apr 38, pp. 3–4, Crittenberger Papers.

[40] Ibid., p. 4.

[41] Ibid., p. 3.

Maj. Sereno E. Brett, a Tank Corps veteran who continued to serve with tanks throughout the interwar period, considered the most effective tank unit to be one with a balanced combination of tanks, self-propelled antitank guns, antiaircraft weapons, engineers, reconnaissance, and supply and maintenance echelons. Brett's views reflected over ten years' experience with tank operations and development, including the Mechanized Force.[42]

By 1933 Infantry tank officers had promulgated plans for revising the table of organization and equipment for a tank battalion to include tanks, armored cars, and a machine-gun force to be transported by halftrack. Supporters of the organization considered it superior in cohesiveness and combat effectiveness to one that included only tanks, armored cars, or foot infantry; but questions emerged concerning the ability to maintain and supply such a diverse unit. Nor did a consensus exist regarding the relative merits of a unit that mixed different tactical functions.[43]

The uncertainty reflected another clash of the divergent organizational principles that afflicted the triangular division's evolution. The War Department emphasized streamlined units designed for a singular mission. The branches strove to build combat units that organically included a variety of capabilities, symbolized by the Infantry's prospective tank battalion and the mechanized cavalry. In so doing they blurred the distinctions among branch missions and called into question the distribution of responsibility inherent to the bureau system. Hence, the War Department generally rejected organizational proposals that merged functional responsibilities distributed among more than one branch.

Tank Development and the Infantry School

The Infantry maintained a separate Tank School at Fort Meade, Maryland, from 1920 until 1932. This school remained separate from the Infantry School at Fort Benning, Georgia. However, in January 1932 the Tank School relocated to the latter post and became the Tank Section of the Infantry School.[44] This change centralized doctrinal development and training under the direct control of the chief of Infantry. Students attending the Infantry School were exposed to both the tank and nonmechanized aspects of the branch. Consequently, the Infantry avoided the type of administrative obstacles that blocked the Chief of Cavalry's influence on Cavalry mechanization.

Fort Benning occupied a 97,000-acre military reservation with a variety of hills, valleys, streams, rivers, forests, and open clearings.[45] The purpose of the Infantry School was to teach tactics and techniques and to act as the chief of Infantry's agency for the development of Infantry doctrine and equipment. Though all Infantry matters

[42] Sereno E. Brett, "Tank Reorganization," *Cavalry Journal* XXXIX, no. 158 (January 1930): 30.

[43] Notes of Discussion Following Lecture, Maj Oswald H. Saunders at AWC, "Status of Mechanization—1933," pp. 25–27, 18 Sep 33, AWC Curricular Archives (hereafter cited as Saunders Discussion Notes).

[44] Nenninger, "Development of American Armor," pp. 128–29.

[45] Inf Sch, "Preparation of a Field Maneuver," 1935–1936, p. 5, Gillem Papers.

An M2A1 light tank of the 66th Infantry Regiment at Fort Benning in 1935

including tanks received attention, the Tank Section suffered from a shortage of instructors that worsened as the number of classes increased.[46]

A special course addressed tank operations, but the secretary of war required attending officers to first receive instruction in the fundamentals of Infantry doctrine. Although this requirement shortened the tank course from twelve to five months, it ensured that tank officers possessed the same doctrinal background as other Infantry officers, reinforcing a close affiliation between tanks and non-mechanized Infantry components.[47]

The Weapons Section of the Infantry School emphasized the value of moving fire. Tank officers were taught to aim rapidly and fire the tank's armament with the tank in motion. Theoretically, the continuous motion made the tank a more difficult target for antitank weapons; but it also hindered accurate target acquisition by the tank, especially given the tank's limited visibility.[48] As long as the tank's main

[46] Alvan C. Gillem Jr., "Introduction to the Course in Tactics," pp. 2, 6, 1938–1939, Gillem Papers; Severne S. MacLaughlin, "History of the Tank School," pp. 26–27, in "Tank Notes," May 32, MHI Library.

[47] Nenninger, "Development of American Armor," p. 129.

[48] Inf Sch, "Notes on Tank Marksmanship," 1936–1937, pp. 2–3, Gillem Papers.

armament consisted of a machine gun, its high rate of fire allowed some compensation for inaccuracy.

However, in 1939 American tanks began to carry a slower-firing 37-mm. antitank gun. Additionally, analysis of tank operations during the Spanish Civil War, 1936–1939, revealed the ineffectiveness of tanks' firing while in motion. Only by stopping to fire could gunners register any significant effect on the target. The failure of unsupported Nationalist and Republican tank attacks, however, supported the existing emphasis of the Infantry on the coordinated action of tanks, riflemen, and artillery, as well as their concentration at a decisive point.[49] Reports on tank use in Spain indicated that these principles were generally violated at the expense of men, materiel, and mission.[50]

During the academic year 1939–1940, the Infantry School began to base tank instruction on "Tank Combat Principles (Tentative)." This manual reflected the last refinement of the Infantry's tank doctrine during the interwar period. In substance it remained consistent with earlier concepts. Tanks supported riflemen by attacking in successive waves until resistance collapsed. They did not act alone or independent of foot soldiers. Medium tanks performed the leading tank function, primarily focused on antitank weapons. Light tanks followed, moving with the infantry and destroying machine guns encountered. Additional tanks constituted a reserve force, ready to exploit initial success and preempt efforts to establish new defensive lines.[51]

The manual did not exclude maneuvering for an advantageous position. Similarly, it did not bar the use of tanks in pursuit, flanking, or encirclement movements. In these cases, tanks sought the destruction of enemy reserves, headquarters, support weapons, and communications. These actions were considered exceptional, since they fell more appropriately within the cavalry mission. Likewise, tanks were to engage counterattacking mechanized forces, but only if no other antitank means existed.[52]

Defensive operations employed tanks as a general reserve that used fire and maneuver to destroy targets. They also fulfilled a counterattack role, which might result in encounters with enemy mechanization. In these circumstances, the manual stressed the importance of moving from one covered firing position to another and engaging targets when most vulnerable. Generally, however, tanks were not expected to function in an antitank role. Infantry formations were expected to rely on special antitank units for defense against enemy mechanization.[53] In 1939 such units did not exist.

---

[49] Lynch, "Current Infantry Developments," 4 Oct 37, p. 4; George A. Lynch, Address Before CGSS, 5 May 38, p. 7, Lynch Papers; Suppl no. 2 to Rpt of Committee no. 2, 24 Jan 38, pp. 10–11.

[50] J. F. C. Fuller, "The Tank in Spain: Tactics Still Fail To Keep Pace with Technics," *Army Ordnance* XIX, no. 109 (July-August 1938): 27; Henry J. Reilly, "Proving Ground in Spain: Armament Trends as Revealed by the Civil War," *Army Ordnance* XIX, no. 114 (May-June 1939): 335; Canevari, "Forecasts from the War in Spain," p. 275.

[51] Inf Sch, "Tank Combat Principles (Tentative)," 1939–1940, pp. 2–4, Gillem Papers; Lynch, "Final Report," pp. 59–62.

[52] Inf Sch, "Tank Combat Principles," pp. 2–4, 16–17; Lynch, "Final Report," pp. 59–62.

[53] Inf Sch, "Tank Combat Principles," p. 18.

Divisional tank company at Fort Houston in 1937

Detailed command and control measures underscored the importance of coordinating tank and infantry actions. The manual retained the practice of subordinating tank units to the commander of a supported formation. Moreover, all relevant command personnel, including those responsible for artillery support, were expected to collectively develop a tactical plan and ensure that any necessary reconnaissance occurred. Preset boundaries defined zones of action for each tank unit and the extent to which tanks could advance without establishing contact with friendly infantry.[54] Timetables controlled the pace of operations.

These methods, though acknowledged as time-consuming, were considered necessary to ensure the effective employment of tanks, especially against a prepared defensive position. Against hastily organized resistance, tank commanders were encouraged to use their own initiative without prolonged deliberation.[55]

Tank commanders controlled their units through oral and fragmentary orders communicated via radio. Coordination of all activities generally occurred through this medium, although signal flags and carrier pigeons served as contingency measures. Radio was considered ineffective as a tool to coordinate tanks in combat due to its technical limitations and security considerations. Indeed, tank company commanders were considered unlikely to exert much control over their platoons once combat began. The preset coordination measures prescribed in the training manual were thus intended to ensure the coordinated action of tanks and other combat units even amid the chaos of the battlefield.[56]

With the issuance of "Tank Combat Principles (Tentative)," the Infantry Branch effectively translated the War Department's 1938 directive into tactical doctrine. This manual provided detailed guidance regarding the nature of tank operations in different tactical environments. It clearly bore the imprint of the World War experience on the Western Front. However, the emphasis given to command and control measures marked an effort to prevent tanks from acting alone and being

[54] Ibid., p. 15.
[55] Ibid., pp. 7, 13–16.
[56] Ibid., pp. 7–8, 30, 35.

destroyed—the fate of many Nationalist and Republican tank units fighting in Spain. The attention given to exploitation or possible antitank roles, together with the use of oral fragmentary orders, reflected the realities of the more open style of warfare generally favored in the Army.

The prospective manual also mirrored the viewpoint of Chief of Infantry General Lynch. He stressed the importance of tanks and infantry working together:

> It ought to be clear that infantry tanks must be brought into the closest possible relation with foot infantry. For the two elements stand in complementary relations. Neither can function independent of the other. Foot infantry can take advantage of the cover of the terrain where tanks must expose themselves. Tanks are immune to hostile small-arms fire but are vulnerable to gun fire. They need the support of infantry flat-trajectory weapons to neutralize the hostile anti-tank guns. Terrain interdicted to tanks by natural or artificial obstacles must frequently be captured by foot infantry before a tank attack can be launched. . . . Together these two elements form a perfect team.[57]

Lynch's views regarding the relative importance of the foot soldier and the tank paralleled the Cavalry's emphasis on the collective value of horse and mechanized cavalries. In both arms, the awareness of the benefits accruing from the combined use of mechanized and nonmechanized elements led to efforts to integrate their development. Both arms, however, were prevented from completely integrating mechanized and nonmechanized elements in July 1940, when the former became part of the newly created Armored Force. Consequently, the Infantry's manual, with its emphasis on the coordination of tanks and foot soldiers, was never approved by the War Department.[58]

Infantry Tank Organization

In 1931 the Infantry tank force consisted of a light tank regiment, a heavy tank regiment, and thirteen individual tank companies. The Tank School also possessed a small tank force. Most of these units, including both regiments, existed only on paper. Only seven of the tank companies were active, and some of these possessed only a single platoon. The companies were stationed with the infantry divisions to whom they would be attached on mobilization. All tank units, whether active or inactive, traced their lineage to the Tank Corps.[59]

The National Guard also included tank units. In 1920 the War Department planned to establish four light tank battalions composed of tank companies drawn from twelve states. No battalion headquarters existed, since National Guard officers could command only units from their own state unless federalized. Before

---

57 Ibid., p. 61.

58 Ibid., p. 59.

59 The Adjutant General's Office, *Official Army Register*, 1931, pp. 1303–04.

Tanks of the 66th Infantry Regiment pass in review, 1938.

implementation of this plan, the National Guard underwent reorganization in 1921. Eighteen National Guard divisions resulted, and each was to include a light tank company. By 1931 fifteen of these companies existed, and the remainder entered service before 1939. Despite these units' company designation, most possessed only two tanks for training purposes. Like their parent divisions, they were scattered across the United States.[60]

The War Department planned to gradually increase the strength of the Regular Army and National Guard tank units. It intended to fully equip a regiment of light tanks, a regiment of medium tanks, and seven light tank companies for use with infantry divisions.[61] This plan remained in effect until 1938, when it increased to include eight divisional light tank companies and six tanks for Infantry School use. The National Guard also anticipated increasing the strength of its divisional

---

[60] Bruce Jacobs, "The Evolution of Tank Units in the Pre–World War II National Guard and the Defense of Bataan," *Military Collector and Historian*, XXXVIII, no. 3 (Fall 1986): 125–26.

[61] Memo and Encl, Deputy Chief of Staff Maj Gen Hugh A. Drum to Assistant Chief of Staff (ACS), G–4, sub: Motorization, Mechanization, and Air Corps Policies Resulting from War Department Studies, Including Those Associated with Public Works, 2 Nov 33, Ofc of the CS Corresp, RG 165, NARA.

companies to four tanks by 1940. The paper strength of the Guard companies lay at eighteen, but four was considered the minimum necessary for effective training.[62]

Fielding plans did not match the financial realities of the Great Depression. For much of the 1930s the actual strength of Army tank units fell far below even their peacetime establishments. In 1937 Army budget planners hoped to secure funding for 235 out of 306 light tanks required to complete the light tank regiment and partially outfit the Regular Army's individual tank companies. The medium regiment required a total of 162 tanks, but the Army did not expect to have more than 36 available by 1940, enough to equip a battalion.[63]

The cost of producing even these limited numbers of tanks led to congressional scrutiny and efforts to reduce costs. The Army generally purchased major tank components from automotive manufacturers and assembled them at Rock Island Arsenal in a manner similar to earlier Quartermaster Corps efforts to secure suitable wheeled vehicles. This practice reflected the private sector's unwillingness to incur the expenses of building tanks without the prospect of recurring contracts and a profit. The War Department could guarantee neither of these conditions. Hence the Army sought to build its own vehicles, using commercially available products.[64]

In 1938 this practice became the target of criticism from Mississippi Democrat Ross Collins during congressional hearings on military appropriations. He depicted the tanks produced as patchwork affairs made from a grab bag of automobile parts. He believed the Army could acquire better and cheaper vehicles by purchasing completed tanks from the private sector. As an example, he cited the tank design work of inventor J. Walter Christie, whose vehicles did indeed mark significant technological strides in tank development. Collins considered the Army's light tank to be a substandard copy of a Christie design.[65]

Collins' view, however, did not suggest any comprehension of the problems encountered by the Army in its dealing with the egocentric Christie. The inventor proved unwilling to cooperate with Ordnance Department officers responsible for tank development. Nor had he acceded to Army requests to improve battlefield effectiveness by incorporating modifications in his tank designs. Although his early T-model tanks generated interest among tank and mechanized cavalry officers, rather than cultivate this interest, Christie abandoned these models in favor of a flying tank of dubious viability.[66]

Christie signed contracts with the War Department to produce limited numbers of prototype tanks. Before completing these obligations, however, he embarked on more lucrative work for foreign military powers. Consequently, Christie's credibility with the War Department, especially the Ordnance Department, reached a nadir. It did not improve when the inventor asserted that only he knew how to produce

---

[62] U.S. Congress, *Appropriation Bill for 1938*, pp. 3, 35–36.

[63] Ibid., pp. 35–36.

[64] Ibid., pp. 44–45.

[65] Ibid.

[66] Ltr, Aubrey Lippincott to Maj N. B. Briscoe, 15 Aug 32, Ofc of the Ch of Cav, Gen Corresp, RG 177, NARA.

T–5 medium tank

modern tanks. The Army lost interest in Christie's designs, and Christie found himself near bankruptcy by 1934.[67]

The impasse with Christie and periodic confrontations with Congress regarding the cost of tanks did not resolve the discrepancy between the number of tanks desired and those available. The difficulty of securing additional tanks coupled with a belief that tanks should be concentrated for maximum battlefield effect led to a reorganization of tank units in 1938. The Army eliminated divisional tank companies in the Regular Army, though they remained in National Guard formations.[68] The tank companies thus abolished were reorganized into General Headquarters tank battalions and regiments that could be temporarily attached to infantry divisions as needed.[69]

---

[67] George F. Hofmann, "A Yankee Inventor and the Military Establishment: The Christie Tank Controversy," *Military Affairs* XXXIX, no. 1 (February 1975): 12–18.

[68] Draft Memo, Acting ACS, G–3, Col Duncan K. Major Jr., to Chiefs of Inf, Cav, and Ord for Comment, sub: Utilization of Tanks During Mobilization, 27 Feb 33, Ofc of the Ch of Cav, Gen Corresp, RG 177, NARA.

[69] Memo, TAG, pp. 3–4; Draft Memo, Major to Chiefs of Inf, Cav, and Ord for Comment, 27 Feb 33; Memo, ACS, G–3, Maj Gen R. M. Beck Jr., to Ch of Cav, sub: Combat Car Troop in the Cavalry Division, 10 Nov 38, Ofc of the Ch of Cav, Gen Corresp, RG 177, NARA.

Reconfigured, the Infantry tank force included the National Guard tank companies; the 66th Infantry Regiment (Light Tanks) and the 67th Infantry Regiment (Medium Tanks); and two separate light tank battalions. The headquarters of the 66th Infantry Regiment (Light Tanks), however, existed only on paper, and its three component battalions were dispersed among Fort Meade, Maryland; Fort Benning, Georgia; and Fort Devens, Massachusetts. Before October 1939 only one company of the 67th Infantry Regiment (Medium Tanks) existed. In that month a battalion headquarters, a headquarters company, and an additional medium tank company were activated at Fort Benning; but the regiment still lacked the components for its other two battalions.[70]

Infantry tank regiments included a regimental headquarters, a headquarters company, a maintenance company, and three tank battalions. The latter consisted of a battalion headquarters, headquarters company, and three tank companies. The unit organizations included minimal maintenance elements to prevent mobility from being retarded by a train of repair vehicles and equipment. Major overhauls required removing a tank to rear-echelon repair shops. Because tanks were intended to operate in close proximity to infantry formations, such dependence on rear-area facilities was not considered a liability.[71]

The new tank organization contained an inherent confusion that reflected the War Department's own uncertainty regarding the proper configuration of a tank unit. Despite its creation of tank regiments, the War Department increasingly considered tank battalions the largest administrative and tactical tank unit. It expected that larger groupings of tanks could be created as needed by combining tank battalions.[72] Such an expectation explains why the 66th Infantry Regiment (Light Tanks) was dispersed among three Infantry posts rather than concentrated for training purposes and tactical development. In 1938 the War Department announced its decision to form only medium tank battalions, rather than regiments; but it nevertheless activated part of the 67th Infantry Regiment (Medium Tanks) in 1939.[73]

The confusing state of tank organization attracted the attention of mechanized cavalry leaders. Brig. Gen. Daniel Van Voorhis, commander of the 7th Cavalry Brigade (Mechanized), made the following observation during an address at the Army War College: "I do not want to create the impression that the infantry is not thoroughly sensitive to the development and employment of the tank. However, I cannot but feel that the infantry has not had at its disposal a clear cut directive commensurate with the modern trend of mechanization development."[74]

Other mechanized cavalry officers proved much less sympathetic to infantry tank developments. They considered their infantry counterparts inhibited and unprogressive

---

[70] Memo, Maj Stanley J. Grogan to Chairman, Subcommittee no. 1 of Committee no. 5, Suppl no. 3, 10 Oct 39, p. 2, AWC Curricular Archives.

[71] Ibid., pp. 6, 11.

[72] Daniel Van Voorhis, "Mechanization," Lecture at AWC, p. 17, 29 Sep 38, Army War College Lectures, 1938–1939, pt. 1, AWC Curricular Archives.

[73] Ibid.; George A. Lynch, "The Infantry," Notes of Lecture at AWC, 20 Sep 39, p. 7, Lynch Papers.

[74] Van Voorhis, "Mechanization," Lecture at AWC, 29 Sep 38, p. 13.

M2 medium tank

with respect to mechanization. In December 1939 the Infantry School sought information on the mechanized cavalry's use of radios to control tactical operations. One Cavalry officer reacted to the query with the comment:

> The Infantry, with 260 tanks on their hands, are now becoming interested in matters of control and communications! Perhaps the quickest way to prove the superiority of mechanized cavalry in the mechanized field, is to concentrate 260 Infantry tanks and try to employ them in mass—or move them all at once in any direction! Unless I am wrong we are several years ahead of them.[75]

Indeed, Cavalry officers eagerly awaited the 1940 opening of spring maneuvers involving mechanized cavalry and infantry tanks, considering the former superior in every conceivable facet of mechanized activity. They expected that "In the coming exercises we may be presented with the chance of proving to the rest of the Army as well as to the public the Cavalry's superiority in the mechanized field."[76]

---

[75] Inquiry from Ofc of Commandant of Inf Sch Through Adjutant General's Office to CG, 7th Cav Bde (Mech), sub: Use of Prearranged Message Codes, 18 Dec 39, and Handwritten Comment on Same, Lt Col Willis D. Crittenberger, Crittenberger Papers.

[76] Ltr, Lt Col Willis D. Crittenberger to Col Charles L. Scott, 22 Dec 39, Crittenberger Papers.

Infantry Tanks

For much of the interwar period the difficulties and costs associated with procuring new vehicles forced the Infantry to rely on an antiquated tank fleet. A 1933 General Staff study listed the Army's tank force as 916 light tanks and 90 Mark VIII heavy tanks. The weight of the Mark VIII made it dependent on rail transportation and limited its use to stabilized battlefield conditions. Declared obsolete in 1932, its use nevertheless was considered likely in the event of a national emergency. War plans did not include the start of tank production until seven months after mobilization. Hence, the Infantry would go to war with the tanks on hand, no matter how outdated.[77]

The light tanks included American-built versions of the wartime Renault FT–17. This platform remained the mainstay of the Infantry's tank strength until gradually replaced by newer models during the 1930s. However, it continued to equip National Guard units as late as 1941. It possessed an operational radius of only thirty miles and depended on truck transport to and from the battlefield. It proved mechanically frail; once employed, it "deteriorate[d] quickly." Although some light tanks had their engines modified to increase power and reliability, they remained obsolete.[78]

Suggestions that they be given to the police forces of major cities for riot duty met with skepticism. One National Guard tank officer, who had performed a similar duty, noted that the tank represented an excessive use of military force. The light tank's frail nature would only embolden angry mobs once they realized they could disable it with a crowbar and that the tank's crew was unlikely to fire indiscriminately into civilian crowds.[79]

Officers familiar with the light tanks considered them a hazard to their crews if used in combat. They recommended their rapid replacement with tanks reflective of 1930s technology. Major Brett considered the "best solution for the present mechanized means of the U.S. Army is to get the biggest transport we have, load it all on, and dump it into the middle of the Atlantic Ocean."[80] Brett considered the presence of nearly one thousand obsolete tanks a hindrance to acquiring new ones, because they presented a false image of nonexistent fighting power.[81]

War Department requests for additional funding to begin quantity tank production repeatedly failed. In the financially austere climate of the Great Depression, the Army placed retention of personnel over materiel procurement. It could not afford both, nor would Congress substantially increase military appropriations while the

---

[77] Draft Memo, Major to Chiefs of Inf, Cav, and Ord for Comment, 27 Feb 33.

[78] Ibid.; Robert J. Icks, *Tanks and Armored Vehicles* (New York: Duell, Sloan and Pearce, 1945), p. 50; Robert J. Icks, "Four Decades of Mechanization: Our Record of Combat-Vehicle Development," *Army Ordnance* XVII, no. 102 (May-June 1937): 339.

[79] Charles S. Canby, "Tanks and Riot Duty," *Infantry Journal* XLII, no. 2 (March-April 1935): 162.

[80] Saunders Discussion Notes, 18 Sep 33, p. 24.

[81] Ibid., pp. 23–24.

Depression continued.[82] Initial War Department requests that substantial sums for Army mechanization be provided from Public Works Administration funds also met with failure, despite the Army's successful administration of the Civilian Conservation Corps.[83] Branch rivalry also helped discourage large expenditures on Infantry tank production.

In the absence of quantity production, the Army focused on the development of small numbers of prototype vehicles. These were subjected to prolonged field-testing and modification to ensure their effectiveness and incorporation of the latest technological developments. Continuous refinement sought to provide a quality vehicle that could be mass-produced upon mobilization.[84] This policy led to a widening gap between intended tank doctrine and actual capability. It forced reliance on obsolescent tanks and a mixture of experimental models that obscured comprehension of the tank's potential combat value. Consequently, it slowed the development of tactics and related command and control techniques.

The status of the Infantry's tank fleet improved slowly. By 1939 it included 280 modern light tanks with an additional 18 medium tanks in production.[85] The light tanks included the M2A1, M2A2, and M2A3. These vehicles possessed similar armor, weighed about ten tons, and carried one .50-caliber and two .30-caliber machine guns. The A2 and A3 versions possessed two limited-traverse turrets, each mounting either a .50-caliber or .30-caliber machine gun in addition to a bow-mounted .30-caliber machine gun. The appearance of the twin turrets led crews to nickname this configuration Mae West. The principal differences in the A2 and A3 lay in the latter's slightly thicker frontal armor and better transmission.[86]

All three vehicles represented a vast improvement in tank design, particularly in their more robust suspensions and engines that permitted speeds in excess of thirty miles per hour. However, they were still intended largely for training purposes, pending the development of the M2A4.[87] This tank increased armament to a 37-mm. gun mounted in a single turret. In addition, it had four machine guns mounted in the hull front coaxially with the main gun and in two hull sponsons. This array of weaponry marked a dramatic improvement in armament. Armor increased to one inch, and overall weight rose to nearly twelve tons. Yet the M2A4 retained the automotive reliability and general mobility of the A2 and A3 models. The new

---

[82] U.S. Congress, House, Subcommittee of the Committee on Appropriations, *War Department Appropriation Bill for 1934 Military Activities, Hearings*, pt. 1, 72d Cong., 2d Sess., 1933, p. 28; WD, *Report of the Secretary of War to the President*, 1933, pp. 20, 30.

[83] U.S. Congress, House, Subcommittee of the Committee on Appropriations, *War Department Appropriation Bill for 1935 Military Activities, Hearings*, pt. 1, 73d Cong., 2d Sess., 1934, p. 15.

[84] Congress, *Appropriation Bill for 1934*, p. 26; Rpt of Committee no. 4, 25 Sep 39, pp. 11, 14; Nenninger, "Development of American Armor," p. 123; Watson, *Chief of Staff*, pp. 31–35.

[85] Lynch, "Infantry," 20 Sep 39, p. 7.

[86] George Forty, *United States Tanks of World War II* (New York: Sterling Publishing Co., 1983), pp. 34–35, 38.

[87] Lynch, "Infantry," 20 Sep 39, pp. 6–7; Memo, Maj Stanley J. Grogan to Chairman, Subcommittee no. 1 of Committee no. 5, Suppl no. 3, 10 Oct 39, p. 6; Lynch, "Final Report," pp. 16–17.

Maintenance on an M2A2 light tank, 1939

vehicle also benefited from a periscope device that improved visibility, especially when operating with the hatches closed.[88]

Development of the M2A4 coincided with the onset of war in Europe and related efforts to increase the modernization of the U.S. Army. Additional funds became available not only for tank development but also for production. Consequently, in October 1939 the American Car and Foundry Company received a contract to produce 329 M2A4s. This contract marked the first significant production order placed since World War I. In contrast to tank production in that war and despite the greater design complexity of the M2A4, deliveries began in April 1940 and finished by March 1941.[89]

Medium tanks remained in short supply. The preference given to light tanks since the 1920s, coupled with the difficulties associated with building a heavier vehicle, slowed medium-tank development in the 1930s. In 1939 the Army assembled eighteen M2 mediums at Rock Island Arsenal. This vehicle possessed one-inch armor and weighed seventeen tons. It was scheduled for replacement by the heavier and

---

[88] Lynch, "Infantry," 20 Sep 39, pp. 8–9; Memo, Grogan to Chairman, Subcommittee no. 1 of Committee no. 5, Suppl no. 3, 10 Oct 39, pp. 6–7.

[89] Nenninger, "Development of American Armor," p. 121; Forty, *United States Tanks*, pp. 14–15.

Many M1917s ultimately were consigned to the scrap yard.

better-protected M2A1, which weighed 18.5 tons. Its five-man crew operated a total of six .50-caliber machine guns in addition to the turret-mounted main armament of a 37-mm. gun.[90]

Despite the medium tanks' heavier weight and better armor, they offered only slight improvements in capabilities. The M2A1 medium tank, for example, carried the same main armament as the M2A4 light tank. The 37-mm. gun carried by both vehicles did not offer any particular advantage to the medium tank. The weapon possessed an effective range of 1,000 yards, the same distance at which a similar gun could theoretically destroy the tank. To engage targets, it had to close to ranges that made it vulnerable. In financial terms, the $50,000 medium tank could be destroyed by a $4,000 antitank gun firing a round valued at $5. Such considerations did not encourage mass production.[91] Reports of European tank battles in 1939 and 1940 led the Ordnance Department to seek a tank more powerful than the M2A1 and to cancel production plans for the latter.[92]

Ongoing development of medium and light tanks marked important changes in infantry tank design. Tanks remained subject to weight limitations intended to

---

[90] Memo, Grogan to Chairman, Subcommittee no. 1 of Committee no. 5, Suppl no. 3, 10 Oct 39, pp. 7–8.

[91] Ibid.

[92] Nenninger, "Development of American Armor," p. 122.

permit them to cross standard highway and pontoon bridges without difficulty. Within these restraints, however, the Infantry sought greater firepower and protection. The antitank gun replaced the machine gun as the main armament in the M2 medium and M2A4 light tanks. Chief of Infantry Lynch considered the increase in armament necessary because he considered tank-versus-tank engagements likely on any future battlefield. In particular, he expected attacking American forces to be met with counterattacks by enemy armor. Hence, these vehicles reflected a preference for larger tank crews and turreted weapons, which would make these tanks more effective despite an increase in weight.[93]

The Infantry no longer equated speed with survivability. In the 1920s tank speed was considered the best protection from antitank weapons. It simultaneously enabled the tank to rapidly penetrate enemy lines, keep pace with a retreating foe, and prevent the creation of new defensive barriers. The Spanish Civil War, however, demonstrated the fallacy of fast, lightly armored tanks equipped only with machine guns.[94] American military intelligence revealed that antitank guns used in Spain accounted for a much higher proportion of tank casualties than anticipated, partially because of the ease with which light tanks could be destroyed.[95]

An Army War College study of the conflict testified to the value of the antitank gun and the relative ineffectiveness of light tanks attacking defended positions. The light tank could not apply its speed while negotiating numerous natural and artificial obstacles. It became an easy target for antitank fire that its armor was not designed to deflect. Conversely, light tanks lacked an effective means of delivering accurate fire while moving. Stopping to deliver more precise fire only increased their vulnerability.[96]

Analysis of tank battles between Soviet tanks supplied to the Republicans and the German and Italian light tanks delivered to the Nationalists favored the more powerfully armed and armored Soviet vehicles.[97] German and Italian light tanks had limited value as reconnaissance vehicles and poor cross-country mobility.[98] They became bogged in mud or mired while crossing the innumerable natural obstacles that characterized the Spanish countryside. Upon entering combat their insufficient armor could not protect them from antitank weapons that their machine-gun armament could not eliminate.[99]

---

[93] Lynch, "Infantry," 20 Sep 39, pp. 8–9; Memo, Grogan to Chairman, Subcommittee no. 1 of Committee no. 5, Suppl no. 3, 10 Oct 39, p. 7; Lynch, "Final Report," pp. 59–62.

[94] Lynch, "Final Report," p. 7.

[95] Col Stephen O. Fuqua, U.S. Mil Attaché, Spain, Rpt no. 6862, sub: Analysis of Tank Casualties—Spain, 25 Jul 38, Crittenberger Papers.

[96] Suppl no. 2 to Rpt of Committee no. 2, 24 Jan 38, pp. 5, 10; Memo, ACS, G–2, Col E. R. W. McCabe, to AWC Commandant, sub: Comment on Committee Study, "The Spanish Revolution, Committee #2, A.W.C., January 24, 1938," 22 Apr 38, AWC Curricular Archives; Canevari, "Forecasts from the War in Spain," p. 275.

[97] Suppl no. 2 to Rpt of Committee no. 2, 24 Jan 38, pp. 3–4; Reilly, "Proving Ground in Spain," p. 335.

[98] Suppl no. 2 to Rpt of Committee no. 2, 24 Jan 38, pp. 3–4.

[99] Basil Liddell Hart, "Lessons of the Spanish War: An Estimate of the Military Factors: Men and Matériel," *Army Ordnance* XVIII, no. 106 (January-February 1938): 201–02.

One Italian officer noted that light tanks possessed little combat value unless equipped with flamethrowers.[100] Ultimately, both Nationalists and Republicans condemned the light tank as a failure on the battlefield.[101] Consequently, the Army War College study anticipated that military powers would abandon the light, fast tank in favor of more heavily armed and armored ones and that they would invest more in antitank guns, mines, and artificial obstacles.[102]

The study characterized the Spanish Civil War as too specialized to permit generally applicable conclusions to the future conduct of war, but it did recommend the integrated use of tanks with infantry and artillery. The tendency of the Nationalists and the Republicans to commit tanks in small numbers to unsupported attacks against fortified lines resulted in the rapid ruination of the attacking tank force without any appreciable gain.[103]

Consequently, analysis of the Spanish Civil War reinforced the Infantry's emphasis on close coordination of all support weapons, including tanks. The conflict appeared to confirm existing trends in Infantry tank development, particularly the preference for a tank force designed for direct support of the foot soldier and capable of sustained combat—even in the presence of enemy antitank guns. Mechanized cavalry officers might consider this focus myopic; but it suited infantry needs, reflected available information from a foreign war, and progressively refined earlier Tank Corps tactics.

---

[100] Canaveri, "Forecasts from the War in Spain," p. 275.

[101] Reilly, "Proving Ground in Spain," p. 335.

[102] Suppl no. 2 to Rpt of Committee no. 2, 24 Jan 38, pp. 10–11.

[103] Ibid.

5

THE VIEW FROM ABROAD

By the 1930s U.S. Army mechanization had expanded from the exclusive infantry support role of World War I. The creation of the 7th Cavalry Brigade (Mechanized) symbolized efforts to build a more versatile organization. However, the separate development efforts of the Infantry's tank force and the mechanized cavalry raised questions concerning the proper role and organization of mechanized units in general. The Army sought answers in the related developments of foreign powers. It relied on information gathered by the Military Intelligence Division (MID) or the G–2 (Intelligence) Section of the War Department General Staff. This information derived largely from military attachés posted abroad. Despite limitations in their effectiveness, these attachés obtained valuable insights into the activities of the principal military powers associated with mechanization, especially Britain, France, and Germany. However, it soon became clear that no international consensus existed regarding the proper organization and use of mechanized combat forces. Therefore, American observers tended to see in foreign developments confirmation of their own sometimes contradictory notions.

The Military Intelligence Division and Its Military Attachés

The Military Intelligence Division tracked foreign developments through its military attachés. Alternate sources of information either proved limited or were intentionally ignored. American companies abroad, for example, remained untapped as intelligence sources. Nor did the Military Intelligence Division employ secret agents for espionage. Indeed, attachés attempting to employ covert agents or purchase confidential information faced immediate recall and discredit. The Military Intelligence Division believed that such activities discouraged foreign governments from exchanging military information with the United States and undermined the credibility of American attachés.[1]

---

[1] F. H. Lincoln, "The Military Intelligence Division, War Department General Staff," Lecture at Army War College (AWC), 5 Jan 37, p. 5, File G–2#5, 1937; Notes of Discussion Following Lecture of Col E. R. Warner McCabe at AWC, "The Military Intelligence Division, War Department General Staff," 4 Jan 38, p. 2, (hereafter cited as McCabe Discussion Notes); McCabe Discussion Notes, 4 Jan 39, p. 1, File G–2#5, 1939; Committee no. 12, Suppl no. 1, "Collection of Foreign Military Intelligence by Non-military Personnel," 28 Jan 39, p. 1, File 2-1939-120; all in AWC Curricular Archives, U.S. Army Military History Institute (MHI) Archives, Carlisle Barracks, Pa. Bruce W. Bidwell, *History*

Military Intelligence considered the civilian press and foreign military publications valid sources, but the quality of such publications varied. Moreover, a language barrier limited the value of non-English material. The Army possessed only two translation organizations: the Operations Branch Translation Section within the Military Intelligence Division and the Army War College Translation Section. The latter, composed of one officer (whose duties prevented full-time devotion to the section) and two sergeants, faced a perpetual backlog of work for the Army War College. No other school possessed a translation office, though the Command and General Staff School (CGSS) relied on the voluntary and extracurricular efforts of attending officers and its librarian. Much of the Army's translation work therefore devolved on the Military Intelligence Division's Translation Section. With 1 part-time officer, 1 clerk, and 3 underpaid civilian translators, it could not keep pace with the number of translation requests from Army and other government offices.[2]

Officers selected for military attaché duty reported to the Military Intelligence Division to prepare for their assignment abroad and to receive instruction concerning the Military Intelligence Division's basic organization, nature, and operating procedures. This preparatory period lasted one month. After this training, attachés deployed overseas to begin collecting information on the economic, political, and military status of their host countries. Abroad, each attaché was assigned to the American embassy in the host nation, where he also represented the War Department and served as military aide.[3]

Despite the importance of military attachés to the acquisition of military intelligence, they functioned under a number of difficulties. These officers possessed little prior knowledge of their intelligence-gathering responsibilities or their host nation. Few officers sought attaché assignments out of a professional desire to serve as intelligence agents. Instead, travel and career enhancement were common motives. For such men the MID course proved little more than a cursory introduction to the intelligence activities in which they were soon immersed.. Lt. Col. Bradford G. Chynoweth epitomized the interwar attaché. An Infantry tank officer, he was selected to become the military attaché to Britain. Upon selection to the post, he admitted his ignorance of the assignment, noting: "I really know nothing of the requirements of the position. I don't know how the attaché spends his time. I have

of the Military Intelligence Division, Department of the Army General Staff: 1775–1941 (Frederick, Md.: University Publications of America, Inc., 1986), pp. 263–64.

[2] Committee no. 12, Suppl no. 2, "Study of Army Translation System," n.d., pp. 1–4, and "Exhibit No. 1, AWC Curricular Archives.

[3] Memo no. 10, Executive Officer (XO), G–2, Maj Vaughn W. Cooper, 30 Jun 27; Lt Col R. H. Williams, Military Attaché and Foreign Liaison Section, G–2, War Department (WD), "Course of Instruction for Newly Appointed Military Attachés," 6 Jun 28; Lt Col R. H. Williams, Mil Attaché and Foreign Liaison Sec, G–2, WD, "Course of Instruction for Newly Appointed Military Attaches," 28 Sep 28; Lincoln, "Military Intelligence Division," 5 Jan 37, p. 5; "Duties and Methods of Military Attachés," n.d.; all in MID Corresp, 1917–1941, Security-Class Corresp and Rpts, Record Group (RG) 165, National Archives and Records Administration (NARA). Bidwell, *History of the Military Intelligence Division*, p. 266.

a foggy idea that there is entertainment to be undertaken (and that it is expensive) but what sort is it?"[4]

Maj. Truman Smith, military attaché to Germany from 1935–1939, and Capt. Ivan Yeaton, appointed attaché to the Soviet Union in 1939, considered the Military Intelligence Division's preparatory course superficial because it focused excessively on codes and ciphers. Both officers attributed the course's inadequacy to the Military Intelligence Division's disorganization.[5] At the War Department's expense, Yeaton completed a three-year program—which included classroom attendance at the University of California, Berkeley, and Columbia University—studying the Russian language and culture. He received minimal guidance regarding the Soviet military and political climate, because MID files concerning the Soviet Union had not been evaluated or organized. Therefore, Soviet publications provided the basis for understanding the Red Army despite their obvious propagandistic nature.[6]

Described as "inadequate and rather hit or miss," the attaché course remained largely unchanged throughout the 1930s due to insufficient funds and personnel. By 1941 dissatisfaction with the method of selecting and training military attachés led Chief of Staff General George C. Marshall to request a critical evaluation of the whole system and corresponding revisions.[7]

For most of the interwar period, however, the Military Intelligence Division selected its military attachés from a list of self-nominated officers. Information on these men included their efficiency rating, language proficiency, military experience, tact and personality, physical appearance and fitness, extent of military schooling, family background, financial status, and eligibility.[8] Such criteria tended to eliminate otherwise capable officers on the basis of socioeconomic status, while an Army-wide shortage of officers further reduced the number of potential attachés actually available for such service.

Of those officers considered for attaché duty, many possessed inadequate language qualifications. It was not uncommon for an officer assigned as a military attaché to have only a limited knowledge of the host country's language.[9] For example, in 1935 appointments for the assistant military attachés for Air to Germany, Italy, and France became vacant. Eight officers appeared as candidates for the posting in Germany, but

---

[4] Ltr, Lt Col Bradford G. Chynoweth to Assistant Chief of Staff (ACS), G–2, Col E. R. W. McCabe, n.d., Bradford G. Chynoweth Papers, MHI Archives.

[5] Truman Smith, "Truman Smith, 1893–1946; The Facts of Life: A Narrative with Documents," pp. 74–75, Truman Smith Papers; Ivan D. Yeaton, "Memoirs of Ivan D. Yeaton, USA (Ret) 1919–1953," pp. 12–13, Ivan D. Yeaton Papers; both in MHI Archives.

[6] Yeaton, "Memoirs," pp. 10–13.

[7] Memo, Lt Col Orlando Ward to ACS, G–2, sub: Training of Military Attachés, 26 Jul 38, Paul M. Robinett Papers, George C. Marshall Library (GCM), Lexington, Va.; Memo, Capt Paul M. Robinett to Chiefs of Intel Br, Public Relations, Finance Sec, Geographic Sec, sub: Training Program for Military Attachés, 27 Jul 38, MID Corresp, 1917–1941, Security-Class Corresp and Rpts, RG 165, NARA; Memo, Orlando Ward to ACS, G–2, sub: Instructions Concerning Military Attachés, 10 Feb 41, Paul M. Robinett Papers, MHI Archives.

[8] Committee no. 12, Suppl no. 1, "Study of Military Attaché System," n.d., pp. 2–3, AWC Curricular Archives.

[9] Ibid., p. 4.

the Military Intelligence Division rated the German-language proficiency of three as fair and the rest only slight. Although eighteen candidates existed for all three vacancies, none spoke Italian and nine had no foreign language ability at all.[10]

The experiences and reports of American officers attending foreign military schools supplemented those of the attachés, but insufficient language proficiency on the part of potential students posed a problem identical to attaché selection. Similarly, lack of language skills did not always prevent an officer's appointment to a foreign school. In 1935 Capt. Albert C. Wedemeyer requested detail to the German *Kriegsakademie* following his graduation from the Command and General Staff School. The Military Intelligence Division, however, did not consider Wedemeyer's two years of high-school German and subsequent tutoring sufficient for a posting to Germany's senior leadership school.[11] Nevertheless, the CGSS commandant supported Wedemeyer's request, reminding the Military Intelligence Division that "Incidentally, Wedemeyer is the son-in-law of General Embick."[12] Wedemeyer obtained the appointment, but a subsequent evaluation by the *Kriegsakademie* commandant attributed difficulties he encountered there to an insufficient knowledge of German.[13]

Aside from language difficulties, the inferior rank of American military attachés compared to those of other nations lowered the prestige accorded the U.S. Army and hindered the ability of American attachés to acquire information. War Department policies stipulated that attachés assigned to England, France, and Japan should be brigadier generals and those assigned to Germany and Italy lieutenant colonels.[14] Truman Smith was only a major and Bradford Chynoweth a lieutenant colonel when appointed military attaché to Germany and Britain, respectively. The small size of the American officer corps and the difficulty of finding eligible officers with the desired qualifications often precluded the appointment of more senior officers.

Consequently, in the numerous diplomatic functions inherent to the assignment of an attaché, American officers found themselves disadvantaged in the presence of foreign officers of superior rank and social status. Moreover, an attaché assignment did not result in a pay increase sufficient to offset the higher cost of living

---

[10] Memo, Col Charles Burnett to Air Liaison Officer, sub: Assistant Military Attachés for Air to Germany, France and Italy, 30 Oct 34, MID Corresp, 1917–1941, Security-Class Corresp and Rpts, RG 165, NARA.

[11] Notice of Capt Albert C. Wedemeyer to The Adjutant General (TAG), sub: Detail to the German War College, 26 Dec 35; Ltr, Col Charles Burnett to Capt Albert C. Wedemeyer, 10 Jan 36; both in MID Corresp, 1917–1941, Security-Class Corresp and Rpts, RG 165, NARA. "Conversations Between General A. C. Wedemeyer and Colonel Anthony Deskis," sec. 1, p. 23, Senior Officers Debriefing Program, 6 Dec 72, MHI Archives (hereafter cited as Wedemeyer/Deskis Conversations).

[12] Ltr, CGSS Commandant Brig Gen H. J. Brees to Col Charles Burnett, 31 Jan 36, MID Corresp, 1917–1941, Security-Class Corresp and Rpts, RG 165, NARA. Maj. Gen. Stanley D. Embick served as deputy chief of staff from May 1936 until September 1938.

[13] Memo, Col F. H. Lincoln to Chief of Staff, G–2, sub: Detail of Officer to German General Staff School, 21 Feb 36; "Report on Captain Wedemeyer, U.S.A.," Aug 37; both in MID Corresp, 1917–1941, Security-Class Corresp and Rpts, RG 165, NARA.

[14] Committee no. 12, Suppl no. 1, "Study of Military Attaché System," p. 3; "Digest of War Department Policies," Policy no. 483, "Selection of Military Attachés at First Class Powers," 15 Feb 24, Robinett Papers, MHI Archives.

abroad. Many American attachés therefore relied on their personal finances to fulfill professional obligations, further elevating the importance of socioeconomic status in attaché selection.[15]

Often American attachés were assigned multiple host nations, because a congressional limit of thirty-two military attachés and assistants worldwide remained in effect until the outbreak of World War II. The dearth of funding and attaché personnel created difficulties for the Military Intelligence Division during international crises. For example, it proved impossible to send a special observer with the Italian Army during its 1935 invasion of Ethiopia. Instead, the Military Intelligence Division relied on the combined efforts of the assistant military attaché to Italy and the military attaché to Ethiopia.[16] An increase in attaché personnel did occur with the outbreak of World War II, but during 1939–1941 the Military Intelligence Division faced another problem: the need to shuffle and relocate its available attachés in Europe in response to German military conquests and the Soviet Union's annexation of the Baltic States.[17]

Upon their return to the United States, military attachés reported to the Military Intelligence Division for temporary duty, which consisted of little more than a short debriefing. No definitive policy existed for exploiting the accumulated knowledge and experience of returning attachés, though some temporarily functioned as translators or acted as observers in military crises involving the armed forces of their previous host country. The Military Intelligence Division retained a listing of previous attachés for potential future use, but until the outbreak of World War II returning attachés remained underutilized sources of military intelligence. Most were reassigned to field commands, ending their affiliation with the Military Intelligence Division.[18] One officer whose intelligence work made him a specialist on French doctrine criticized this trend: "One of the mysteries of the military business is how they do not use the talent available. I am going to Panama to sit around an antiaircraft battalion."[19]

The onset of World War II inspired an effort to reassign returning attachés to positions within the Military Intelligence Division suited to their particular experiences. Upon Truman Smith's return from Germany, he received the title of special consultant on Germany. He became responsible for providing information on German military capabilities and doctrine to the General Staff. Indeed, he considered it his

---

[15] Bidwell, *History of the Military Intelligence Division*, p. 381.

[16] Memo, Col F. H. Lincoln to ACS, G–4, sub: Observer with Italian Army in Ethiopia, 6 Nov 35, MID Corresp, 1917–1941, Security-Class Corresp and Rpts, RG 165, NARA.

[17] For example, see Memos, Maj Lowell M. Riley to ACS, G–2, sub: Status of Military Attaché, 21 Mar 38; Brig Gen Sherman Miles to TAG, sub: Orders, 11 Jun 40; Brig Gen Sherman Miles to CS, G–2, sub: Military Attachés in Europe, 3 Jul 40; all in MID Corresp, 1917–1941, Security-Class Corresp and Rpts, RG 165, NARA.

[18] Memo no. 9, XO, G–2, Maj Vaughn W. Cooper, 30 Jun 27, MID Corresp, 1917–1941, Security-Class Corresp and Rpts, RG 165, NARA; Committee no. 12, Suppl no. 1, "Study of Military Attaché System," p. 5.

[19] Ltr, Thomas R. Phillips to Lt Col Bradford G. Chynoweth, 7 Apr [40], Chynoweth Papers.

personal task "to influence our army to adopt many of the new German innovations with respect to organization and tactics."[20]

Army Intelligence Dissemination

On duty overseas, attachés submitted regular reports detailing military developments in their host nation. Upon receipt of these reports, the Military Intelligence Division sought to corroborate them and incorporate their contents into existing analyses of the military, political, and economic status of foreign powers. These studies were intended for General Staff use and the instruction of new military attachés. When applicable, the Military Intelligence Division also prepared special studies addressing ongoing military actions and any international crises that might trigger military action. These studies then became available to headquarters, branch chiefs, and school commandants.[21]

In 1934 the Military Intelligence Division began to distribute a weekly listing of all military attaché reports received, copies of which were available for ten-day loan. However, the Military Intelligence Division maintained only a small number of such loan copies and severely restricted their duplication and redistribution. Reports of Army-wide interest tended to generate more loan requests than available copies, a problem made worse through the failure of some borrowers to return loaned copies on time. Consequently, during periods of international crisis when interest in attaché reports rose, the actual flow of intelligence from the Military Intelligence Division remained at low ebb. This situation improved only during 1940–1941, when branch chiefs were directed to maintain their own intelligence section and authorized to copy and redistribute attaché reports without consulting the Military Intelligence Division.[22]

The flow of military intelligence to the combat arms therefore proved haphazard during the 1930s, with the Cavalry as an important exception. The Office of the Chief of Cavalry organized and maintained a special intelligence file. It included a variety of information related to foreign mechanized developments drawn from military attaché report excerpts, the Military Intelligence Division's "Intelligence Summary," articles from the civilian press, interviews with returning American attachés and foreign officers, and foreign military publications. The file's contents

[20] Truman Smith, "Facts of Life," pp. 114–15.

[21] Lincoln, "Military Intelligence Division," pp. 6–8; McCabe Discussion Notes, 3 Jan 40, pp. 7–8.

[22] Lincoln, "Military Intelligence Division," p. 8; Memo, TAG to Chiefs of WD Arms and Services, CGs of All Corps Areas and Depts, and Commanding Ofcrs of Exempted Stations, sub: Dissemination of Military Information by the Military Intelligence Division and by Recipients of MID Information, 5 Nov 39, Armored Force Surplus Training Materials, MHI Library; Memo, TAG, sub: Intelligence Sections in the Offices of Chiefs of Arms and Services, 6 Sep 40, Armored Force Surplus Training Materials, MHI Library; Memo, TAG, sub: Dissemination and Reproduction of Information from the Military Intelligence Division, WDGS [War Department General Staff], 30 Sep 40, Armored Force Surplus Training Materials; Memo no. 13, HQ Armd Force, Ofc of the Commanding General, sub: General Policy for the Reproduction and Dissemination of Information Received from the Military Intelligence Division, WDGS, 5 Feb 41, Armored Force Surplus Training Materials; Bidwell, *History of the Military Intelligence Division*, p. 267.

largely addressed organization, doctrine, vehicle development, and weapons. From this data, the Office of the Chief of Cavalry prepared its own summaries of foreign mechanized developments and answered inquiries from Cavalry organizations, including the 7th Cavalry Brigade (Mechanized). These measures heightened the Cavalry's awareness of foreign mechanized developments to a degree unusual among the combat arms.[23]

The Army War College constituted another avenue of access to MID information. Until 1940 MID files were open to officers attending the Army War College. As part of the G–2 course, committees of student officers compiled surveys of the military potential of foreign nations from interviews with MID personnel including returning military attachés, military attaché reports, and MID evaluations intended for General Staff use. The committees also consulted a variety of published foreign and domestic sources. The resultant reports varied in quality depending on the abilities of the committee members, but they did indicate general trends in foreign military developments. Sometimes these reports supplemented the Military Intelligence Division's own analysis. Army War College personnel increasingly participated in General Staff planning and in the compilation of MID intelligence assessments by the late 1930s.[24]

For most officers, however, the Military Intelligence Division's biweekly Intelligence Summary proved the most common form of military intelligence obtainable. Based on military attaché reports, the summary contained articles about the Military Intelligence Division's analysis of international events and military developments, sometimes including a translation of an article appearing in a foreign military journal.[25] In 1928 the security classification of the Intelligence Summary was downgraded, thereby expanding circulation. Duplication of its contents, however, required the approval of the Military Intelligence Division, and its distribution was not universal in the Army.[26]

In 1939 the assistant chief of staff, G–2, Col. E. R. Warner McCabe, discontinued the Intelligence Summary. McCabe considered it a security liability that exposed confidential material. The summary often included copies of attaché reports, resulting in the embarrassment of at least one attaché serving abroad. Although intended for official use, information from the summary became incorporated into speeches delivered to social clubs such as the Kiwanis, Rotary, and Lions. The Intelligence Summary also found its way into the hands of foreign military attachés, who thus learned how the Military Intelligence Division perceived their parent

---

[23] Memo, Lt Col Willis D. Crittenberger to XO, sub: File on Mechanization, 2 Apr 39, Crittenberger Papers. Upon his transfer to the Armored Force shortly after its establishment, Crittenberger also undertook the creation of a similar file for the Armored Force. Subsequent citations within this chapter to military attaché reports from the Crittenberger Papers refer partially to contents within this mechanization file.

[24] Harry P. Ball, *Of Responsible Command: A History of the U.S. Army War College* (Carlisle Barracks, Pa.: Alumni Association of the U.S. Army War College, 1983), pp. 228, 238, 242, 248.

[25] Lincoln, "Military Intelligence Division," 5 Jan 37, p. 8; McCabe Discussion Notes, 4 Jan 38, p. 5.

[26] Bidwell, *History of the Military Intelligence Division*, p. 266.

nations. McCabe also objected to the time and effort the summary's production demanded of an understaffed Military Intelligence Division.[27]

The discontinuance of the Intelligence Summary constituted part of a more general effort by the Military Intelligence Division to eliminate the informal flow of confidential military intelligence that undermined its role as the central processing agency and clearinghouse for military intelligence. McCabe wanted the Military Intelligence Division alone to be responsible for analyzing information from abroad and addressing related inquiries from Army organizations. Moreover, he wanted all such inquiries routed through formal channels.[28] Therefore, McCabe sought to eliminate direct correspondence between military attachés and colleagues serving in various duty assignments. In November 1937 he requested that the secretary of war direct Major Smith, the military attaché to Germany, to comply with standing orders governing correspondence related to official business.[29] Smith had sent information regarding German technical developments directly to a colleague. McCabe also reprimanded Smith, warning him that the incident would: "raise the question of the ability of the Military Intelligence Division properly to evaluate and disseminate information received from its agents outside of Washington; and, what is more serious, it casts a shadow of suspicion as to the loyalty of the officer concerned to the Division of the General Staff under which he is serving."[30]

As a bureau chief, McCabe sought to improve the efficiency of the Military Intelligence Division and eliminate its earlier disorganized and informal operative style. His efforts to tighten the Military Intelligence Division's control and regulation of military intelligence coincided with a dramatic rise in international tension and the outbreak of war in Europe and China. As the Army's general interest in the capabilities of its foreign counterparts rose, so too did its demands for information. The Military Intelligence Division endeavored to answer these inquiries, but such a proliferation of requests followed Germany's invasion of Poland that the Military Intelligence Division directed all branches to submit questionnaires. Upon receipt, the questionnaires were consolidated into a 65-page booklet. Copies were distributed to attachés abroad to instruct them in the type and extent of information each branch desired.[31]

The Military Intelligence Division also acted on a recommendation of Chief of Staff Marshall and in May 1940 began Army-wide dissemination of the Tentative Lessons Bulletin. This publication was intended for instructional purposes. It included excerpts from attaché reports and MID evaluations of the organization, tactics, and battlefield experiences of the belligerent nations. Each issue warned,

---

[27] McCabe Discussion Notes, 3 Jan 40, pp. 2–3.

[28] Ibid.

[29] Memos, Col E. R. Warner McCabe to Maj Truman Smith, sub: Correspondence, 18 Nov 37, and Col E. R. Warner McCabe to TAG, G–2, sub: Correspondence, 20 Nov 37, both in MID Corresp, 1917–1941, Security-Class Corresp and Rpts, RG 165, NARA.

[30] Memo, McCabe to Smith, 18 Nov 37, and 2d End, 12 Jan 38, MID Corresp, 1917–1941, Security-Class Corresp and Rpts, RG 165, NARA.

[31] MID, "Information on Military Operations Abroad Desired by War Department Agencies: A Compilation of Questionnaires Submitted by General Staff Sections, Chiefs of Arms, and Schools," 1 Nov 39, MID Corresp, 1917–1941, Security-Class Corresp and Reports, RG 165, NARA.

British Vickers light tank

"Lessons tentative and not mature studies." Nevertheless, the new bulletin constituted an effort to get current information on combat operations to Army organizations in a timely fashion.[32]

The Confusion of British Mechanization

The British Army held a prominent position in the eyes of many American officers in the 1930s. Its mechanized development since World War I placed it foremost in the field, and its ranks included officers who envisioned a future battlefield radically different from that of World War I. Chief among them was Col. John F. C. Fuller, whose vision of future warfare forecast the tank as the preeminent weapon. Fuller's writings inspired debate and thought among American officers as to the organization and employment of a mechanized combat unit, even if they did not agree with him. Remarking on Fuller's *Lectures on F.S.R. III*, one military attaché found it full of ideas worthy of discussion but warned: "There is a mixture of a great deal that is to the reader either incomprehensible or else entirely unconvincing."[33]

---

[32] Memo, CS to Gen Miles, G–2, 14 May 40, George C. Marshall Papers, Subgp VI, Pentagon Ofc, Selected Corresp, GCM.

[33] Mil Attaché, London, Rpt no. 32613, sub: England (Military): Major General Fuller's Book "Lectures on F.S.R. III" and a Talk with the Author, 11 Aug 32, quote from p. 5, MID Corresp, 1917–1941, Security-Class Corresp and Rpts, RG 165, NARA; J. F. C. Fuller, *Lectures on F.S.R. III* (London: Sifton Praed & Co., Ltd., 1932).

British Morris armored car, ca. 1937

Members of Congress also charted British mechanization and considered it a potential model for the U.S. Army. The impression of the British dramatically modernizing their army through widespread incorporation of motor vehicles inspired the following comment by Mississippi Democrat Ross Collins during budget testimony given by Chief of Staff General Douglas MacArthur in 1934: "The British Army is the most modern of all the armies, as I understand. The fact is, I think it is about the only modern army that we have." General MacArthur replied, "I think the English army would appreciate that remark very much."[34] The British Army's emphasis on motorization and mechanization suggested the influence of a military leadership more progressive than that of the U.S. Army and one willing to exploit technology rather than obstruct its application in favor of personnel retention.[35]

The Military Intelligence Division held a different perception of the British. By 1939 it considered Britain one of several nations deliberately withholding information from American attachés while simultaneously benefiting from the easier access to intelligence in Washington, D.C.[36] One American attaché noted: "To be discreet is to be British. One can commit the rape of a continent, provided one does it with

[34] U.S. Congress, House, Subcommittee of the Committee on Appropriations, *War Department Appropriation Bill for 1934 Military Activities, Hearings*, pt. 1, 72d Cong., 2d Sess., 1933, p. 27.

[35] Ibid., pp. 26–29.

[36] McCabe Discussion Notes, 4 Jan 38, p. 7, and 3 Jan 40, p. 5; Ltr, Lt Col Bradford G. Chynoweth to Brig Gen F. G. Beaumont-Nesbitt, 6 Jul 39, Chynoweth Papers.

Chart 6–British Mobile Division, 1936

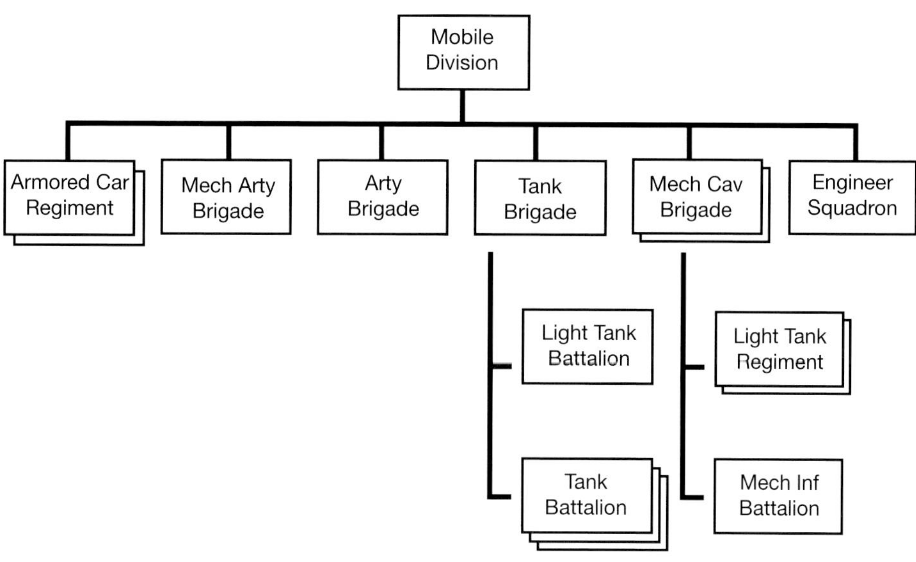

discretion."[37] Such discretion translated into bureaucratic red tape and a clerical inertia that hindered American efforts to acquire military information from the British.[38] Nor did information received by the Military Intelligence Division substantiate the high praise some congressmen gave British Army mechanization efforts, suggesting instead confusion and the absence of a clear goal.

In 1935 the Military Intelligence Division reported Britain's intention to transform all cavalry regiments stationed in the British Isles into mechanized units of light tanks, armored cars, and motorized Infantry. The following year the British resolved to motorize all divisional artillery units and create a division of mechanized and motorized elements. After two years, however, the Military Intelligence Division could discern little progress toward these goals. A mobile division had been organized to undertake powerful, offensive actions; but during maneuvers, the division merely supported friendly forces in a reserve capacity.[39] (*Chart 6*)

The Military Intelligence Division attributed the poor showing to a flawed organization that remained in flux. The mobile division included tanks, mechanized cavalry, infantry, engineers, and signal and service units. The missions of these components did not complement one another. Hence, the large formation

[37] Mil Attaché, London, Rpt no. 40200, sub: Comments on Current Events, 13 Jun 39, p. 3, Chynoweth Papers.

[38] Ltr, Lt Col Bradford G. Chynoweth to Col John A. Crane, 5 May 39, Chynoweth Papers.

[39] MID, WDGS, Intel Sum no. 33, 5 Mar 37, p. 16081; 17 Sep 37, p. 16357; 10 Dec 37, pp. 16531–32; all on Reel 6 of *U.S. Military Intelligence Reports: Biweekly Intelligence Summaries, 1928–1938* (Frederick, Md.: University Publications of America, n.d.).

British motorcycle adapted for military use, 1938

proved unwieldy and difficult to control. In particular, the mechanized cavalry and tanks could not coordinate their actions during maneuvers. The ensuing efforts to restructure the division led to this American evaluation: "Over a decade after the British pioneering in mechanization its army has but one mechanized division, the final form of which is yet to be determined."[40]

The British soon abandoned the mobile division in favor of the armored division. This formation expanded the heterogeneous mix of unit types found in the mobile division through the addition of more motorized infantry and artillery. The armored division, however, failed to resolve the mobile division's command and control problems. Moreover, the armored division's reliance on armored vehicles for rapid, offensive action seemed to contradict the more traditional British emphasis on defensive operations.[41]

One American attaché considered the armored division too large to employ as a single maneuver force yet insufficiently developed for coordinated action by its component units.[42] The Office of the Chief of Cavalry concurred with this assessment, believing the armored division too overburdened with assets for effective control or rapid action. In general, American analysts rejected British efforts to combine different unit types, each with a separate function, within a single formation. Symbolic of the War Department's organizational emphasis on separation by function and homogeneity, they preferred to create smaller units

[40] MID, WDGS, Intel Sum no. 33, 10 Dec 37, pp. 16531–32, quote from p. 16532.

[41] Memo, Lt Col Willis D. Crittenberger to Ch of Cav, 26 Jan 39; Mil Attaché, London, Rpt no. 39856, sub: Great Britain (Combat): British Training—All Arms, Especially Tanks, 6 Jan 39, p. 3; both in Crittenberger Papers.

[42] Mil Attaché, London, Rpt no. 39856, 6 Jan 39, p. 3.

Chart 7–British Armored Division, 1939

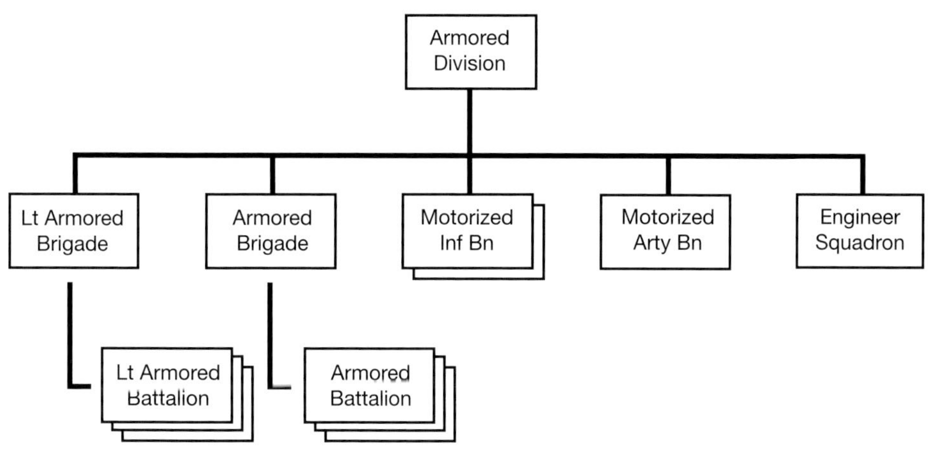

capable of independent action yet capable of combining into larger, temporary groupings.[43]

In March 1939 the British announced the creation of a second armored division and yet another organization change. (*Chart 7*) While some American officers believed these changes resolved earlier problems, the Military Intelligence Division noted that the new divisions were simply smaller. They did possess greater homogeneity, since their principal combat assets consisted of only two tank brigades and two artillery regiments. However, the Military Intelligence Division could find no coherent mechanization trend evident in the new formation. In April an attaché reported that a restudy of mechanization had begun. As late as March 1940 armored division doctrine and organization remained in an experimental state and the subject of lively debate.[44]

---

[43] Memos, Crittenberger to Ch of Cav, 26 Jan 39; Lt Col Willis D. Crittenberger to Col Grimes, 5 Apr 39, pp. 4–5, Crittenberger Papers.

[44] Memo, Crittenberger to Grimes, 5 Apr 39, pp. 3, 5; Asst Mil Attaché, London, Rpt no. 40267, sub: Great Britain (Combat): British Armored Corps Equipment, 19 Jul 39, Crittenberger Papers; Asst Mil Attaché, London, Rpt no. 40493, sub: Great Britain (Combat): Royal Armored Corps and Mechanized Cavalry, 19 Oct 39, pp. 2, 4, Crittenberger Papers; Memo for Ch of Cav, sub: Employment of Mechanized Units in the British Army, 14 Jul 39, p. 2, MID Corresp, 1917–1941, Security-Class Corresp and Rpts, RG 165, NARA; Memo for Gen Herr, sub: 1st Armored Division, British Army, 19 Mar 40, p. 2, Crittenberger Papers. By late 1940 the variety of weapons and units within the formation had actually increased, not decreased as MID believed. The Armoured Division's evolution marked an effort to find a balance of infantry, artillery, armor, antitank, and antiaircraft elements that would be manageable and versatile. The division organizations, however, remained tank-heavy and deficient in their combined-arms ability.

British tank maintenance in the 1930s

Given the turmoil surrounding the armored division's organization, efforts to build an armored corps structure proved moribund.[45]

The British established the Royal Armoured Corps to address manning and training of its tank and mechanized cavalry units. However, inquiries regarding these subdivisional units met with a familiar response: "The Royal Armored Corps is in the process of organization, therefore, tables of organization for mechanized cavalry and tank battalions are not yet available."[46] To the Military Intelligence Division, the Royal Armoured Corps appeared only as a central training organization. Operational control of mechanized units was expected to reside in corps or army command echelons, with separate tank regiments attached to infantry divisions as needed. The British did not appear inclined to concentrate their mechanized units under a single commander during actual operations.[47]

---

[45] Mil Attaché, London, Rpt nos. 40685, sub: Great Britain (Combat): The Corps (Armored), 18 Dec 39, and 40812, sub: Great Britain (Combat): The Corps (Armored), 22 Jan 40; both in MID Corresp, 1917–1941, Security-Class Corresp and Rpts, RG 165, NARA.

[46] Asst Mil Attaché, London, Rpt nos. 40267, 19 Jul 39; 40493, 19 Oct 39, pp. 1–2. Quote from Memo, Lt Col Willis D. Crittenberger to Ch of Cav, 26 Oct 39, Crittenberger Papers.

[47] Memo for Ch of Cav, sub: Employment of Mechanized Units in the British Army, 14 Jul 39. MID assessments of the Royal Armoured Corps were partially correct. Created in April 1939, the corps represented a compromise solution for tank development. The new agency concentrated tank

Matilda I, designed for close infantry support on the battlefield

The Military Intelligence Division succeeded in acquiring considerable information concerning British training and technical developments.[48] However, American officers found little in the British mechanization experience worthy of emulating in their own activities. An attaché visiting the Royal Tank Corps Centre in 1936 found officers there unfamiliar with new tank designs despite a War Office announcement that they would soon be issued these vehicles. He summarized his observations on British tank development with the statement: "It took three years for the Federal Army to learn how to use cavalry in the Civil War and as there is no reason to think that the British have arrived at a sound doctrine of tank employment, the British Tank Corps may be expended in the opening months of the next war."[49] Moreover, the British also appeared to lack the logistical, mechanical, and administrative expertise to sustain a mechanized formation stationed in England, much less overseas.[50]

---

development responsibility and provided uniform mechanized training to personnel from multiple arms of service. It did not, however, command combat units; personal temporarily assigned to it for training retained their affiliation with their parent arm of service. No branch of service dominated the Royal Armoured Corps, and its training influence therefore reflected a mix of concepts. For further elaboration, see Robert H. Larson, *The British Army and the Theory of Armored Warfare, 1918–1940* (Cranbury, N.J.: Associated University Presses, 1984), pp. 219–20.

[48] Mil Attaché, London, Rpt nos. 40480, sub: Great Britain (Combat): Tank Training Center at Aldershot, 18 Oct 39, Crittenberger Papers, and 38095, sub: Great Britain (Combat): Visit to the Royal Tank Corps Centre, 15 Jun 36, Alvan C. Gillem Jr. Papers, MHI Archives.

[49] Mil Attaché, London, Rpt no. 38095, 15 Jun 36, quote from p. 3.

[50] Asst Mil Attaché, London, Rpt no. 40874, sub: Great Britain (Combat): Administration of Armored Divisions, 7 Feb 40, Crittenberger Papers. This report did not fully communicate the lack of preparedness of British armored elements for sustained combat in France and Belgium. Despite the March 1939 announcement of the creation of a second armored division, on the eve of Germany's attack on the Low Countries and France, only one armored division had actually been formed. It was

1937 prototype of the Matilda II, one of the most heavily armored tanks at the start of World War II

Throughout the interwar era, all nations developing mechanized combat units strove to create an effective means of controlling large numbers of vehicles on the battlefield. British tank officers considered the radio too prone to enemy interception or jamming to be an effective means of tactical control. Visual signals were similarly considered unreliable. Therefore, the British endeavored to build tank crews that automatically responded to changing tactical situations in a coordinated manner independent of any visual or electronic communication. American analysis considered this approach unrealistic and viable only against a clear, unchanging objective.[51]

British tanks attracted little positive comment from American observers. British tank design seemed to share the same confusion and uncertainty pervading mechanized doctrine and organization. New tanks crept through the design and development process, ensuring their obsolescence before they could be delivered to combat units. Too many ideas—some contradictory—surrounded each new tank design, which in turn contributed to the general confusion. By 1937 the British had embarked on a new line of tanks based on a chassis purchased from American tank inventor J. Walter Christie.[52]

---

still being trained and reequipped on 10 May 1940. The British Expeditionary Force included only 1 tank brigade, 2 light armored reconnaissance brigades, and 3 cavalry regiments, with a total tank strength of 300. R. H. Barry, "Military Balance," in *History of the Second World War*, 96 parts (n.p.: Marshall Cavendish USA, 1973), 4: 96; Guy Chapman, *Why France Fell: The Defeat of the French Army in 1940* (New York: Holt, Rinehart and Winston, 1968), p. 348.

[51] Mil Attaché, London, Rpt no. 38095, 15 Jun 36.

[52] MID, WDGS, Intel Sum no. 33, 5 Mar 37, p. 16083 and 17 Sep 37, p. 16357; Asst Mil Attaché, London, sub: Great Britain (Combat): Christie Tanks for British Army, 6 Oct 37, Crittenberger Papers; Memo, ACS, G–2, Col E. R. W. McCabe, to Deputy Chief of Staff (DCS), G–2, sub: Christie Type

British tanks during field maneuvers

In addition to tank and mechanized cavalry organizations, the British also established motorized infantry divisions. The Military Intelligence Division noted similarities in the evolutionary path of these mounted formations and the American triangular division. However, unlike the latter, the British divisions possessed sufficient organic transportation to move the entire formation without external support. By 1939 several British motorized infantry divisions existed. Each included a mix of infantry, artillery, antitank weapons, armored cars, and a motorcycle battalion. The inclusion of motorcycles reflected the presence of large numbers of skilled riders and mechanics, as well as politically influential motorcycle clubs in England.[53]

Motorized divisions sent to France with the British Expeditionary Force were expected to support mechanized elements, particularly by securing key objectives. The small size of the motorized divisions, however, led to concerns regarding their capability for sustained combat operations. Despite the perception of limited combat power, the formations still possessed nearly two thousand vehicles that required sixty-six miles of road space when in march formation. The vulnerability of such a mass of vehicles, coupled with logistical and command considerations, led to recommendations that motorized divisions retain only sufficient transport for supply, maintenance, and heavy weapons elements.[54] Such viewpoints indicated that the final organization of the motorized division, like the armored division, had yet to be determined.

Tanks in Russia and Great Britain, 25 Oct 37, MID Corresp, 1917–1941, Security-Class Corresp and Rpts, RG 165, NARA.

[53] Asst Mil Attaché, London, Rpt no. 40680, sub: Great Britain (Combat), Organization—Divisions: The Division (Motor), 18 Dec 39; Mil Attaché, London, Rpt no. 40948, sub: Great Britain (Combat), Training, Organization and Unit, Army: A Territorial Division, Motor, 7 Mar 40; both in MID Corresp, 1917–1941, Security-Class Corresp and Rpts, RG 165, NARA.

[54] Mil Attaché, London, Rpt no. 40948, 7 Mar 40.

French FCM–1936 light tank. While possessing effective armor protection for the era, it had only a one-man turret and carried no radio.

The American perception of British mechanization efforts as erratic and meandering did little to resolve questions concerning the proper direction of U.S. Army mechanization. In 1938 Chief of Cavalry Maj. Gen. John K. Herr used the British example as justification of his own efforts to expand the horse and mechanized cavalries simultaneously. Rather than see horse cavalry superseded by mechanized forces still in a developmental state, he preferred to improve the combat readiness of the former.[55] Conversely, Maj. Gen. Daniel Van Voorhis, previously commander of the 7th Cavalry Brigade (Mechanized) and recently appointed to command the V Corps Area, focused on the British desire to employ mechanized units against enemy weakness, particularly through rapid envelopment. He considered this emphasis a validation of American mechanized cavalry doctrine that stressed the importance of maneuver.[56] Neither officer advocated emulation of British mechanization efforts.

French Mechanized Development

Throughout the interwar period the U.S. Army maintained a high regard for the French military stimulated by the shared combat experiences of World War I.

[55] John K. Herr, "The Cavalry," Lecture at AWC, 19 Sep 38, p. 3, in Army War College Lectures, 1938–1939, pt. 1, AWC Curricular Archives.

[56] Daniel Van Voorhis, "Mechanization," Lecture at AWC, 29 Sep 38, p. 30, in Army War College Lectures, 1938–1939, pt. 1, AWC Curricular Archives.

Company of French Hotchkiss light tanks

French military thought found reflection in American doctrine and training. Until 1935, when American officers began attending the German *Kriegsakademie*, France remained the only major power to allow American officers to attend its senior military school, the *École de Guerre*. Upon graduation, officers joined the CGSS faculty, disseminating French doctrine and the technique of methodical battle to succeeding classes of student officers.[57]

[57] Memos, TAG to ACS, G–2, sub: Attendance of Officers at Foreign Cavalry Schools, 2 Mar 32; CGSS Commandant Brig Gen H. J. Brees to TAG, sub: Detail of Officer for German War School, 17 Dec 35; ACS, G–2, Col F. H. Miles to CS, G–2, sub: Detail of Officers for German School, 26 Dec 35; all in MID Corresp, 1917–1941, Security-Class Corresp and Rpts, RG 165, NARA. Wedemeyer/Deskis Conversations, sec. 3, p. 26.

French Hotchkiss light tanks on parade

French mechanization efforts also attracted attention and analysis. In both production and numbers of combat-ready vehicles, a 1938 American ranking placed France first, followed by Germany and Italy, with Britain a distant fourth. Moreover, the Military Intelligence Division found in French mechanization a clarity of purpose largely absent from parallel British efforts. France appeared to have resolved the doctrinal and organizational issues that surrounded mechanized development in other major military powers. Mechanized cavalry performed traditional cavalry missions, while tank units provided infantry support. This distinction mirrored the division of mechanized responsibility in the U.S. Army.[58]

American analysis, based on information obtained from the *École de Guerre*, found the tactical roles of French and American mechanized cavalry similar. Both were responsible for reconnaissance, envelopment, flank security, screening operations, and limited combat actions. The French stressed the importance of speed

[58] Untitled Doc, 11 Oct 38, Crittenberger Papers. The French Army accepted the use of tanks in traditional infantry and cavalry roles. The views of Col. Charles A. de Gaulle proved a notable exception. He challenged the total war emphasis inherent in French defense planning and advocated the creation of an elite strike force comprising mechanized divisions capable of rapidly responding to any threat to France. He expressed his views openly in the 1930s, but the potential influence of his ideas concerning mechanized divisions was obscured by his views regarding the structure of the French Army. De Gaulle appeared to favor a small, elite force of long-term professional soldiers rather than the mass conscript army incorporated into French military planning throughout the interwar era. His views found little acknowledgment in the United States. For a further understanding of France's interwar military plans and De Gaulle's views, see Robert A. Doughty, *The Seeds of Disaster: The Development of French Army Doctrine, 1919–1939* (Hamden, Conn.: Archon Books, 1985); Don Cook, *Charles De Gaulle: A Biography* (New York: Perigree Books, 1983), pp. 15–57; Charles A. de Gaulle, *The Army of the Future* (London: Hutchinson, n.d.).

and surprise to intensify the effects of these operations, but they believed success depended on coordinating mechanized cavalry with other arms.[59]

American intelligence reported a general increase in the French cavalry's motor-vehicle usage to accomplish these missions. French cavalry regiments relied on armored cars to provide the basis of their mobile firepower.[60] By 1932 several cavalry divisions included both horse and mechanized components. The hybrid nature of these formations provided a high degree of tactical versatility, but they suffered from command complexities related to the coordination of horse and mechanized units. Their strategic mobility also remained poor, limited to the pace of the horse. Conversely, the increased number of vehicles in the division raised questions concerning their vulnerability to air attack.[61]

The Military Intelligence Division chronicled dissatisfaction with the horse-mechanized divisions and their replacement by the *division légère mécanique*, or light mechanized division, by 1936. Based entirely on vehicles, this formation included armored cars, *dragons portés* (motorized Infantry), and artillery. Subsequent modifications included the addition of engineers, an aerial observation squadron, a mechanized brigade, and more artillery. Service and maintenance elements completed the division organization, which also included one thousand one hundred forty motorcycles for both administrative and tactical functions. The French formed a second light mechanized division in 1938 and a third shortly after the outbreak of war.[62] (*See Chart 8.*)

The French acknowledged the influence of British, German, and American ideas on the light mechanized division's employment. Its mission lay in maintaining contact with enemy formations, holding ground, and developing hostile dispositions. When supported by other cavalry units, the light mechanized division also conducted breakthrough operations. Its three thousand five hundred vehicles required a developed road net for sustained action, but they also provided a degree of strategic mobility and combat power superior to the horse mechanized divisions.[63]

American observers considered the light mechanized division a powerful combat formation, but they did not believe the French would permit it to conduct independent operations. The French remained unconvinced of the division's

---

[59] Lt Col H. M. Rayner, "A Conference at the l'Ecole de Guerre: Modern Cavalry," Dec 35, pp. 15–17; "France (Combat)," 1 Oct 39; both in Crittenberger Papers.

[60] "France (Combat)," 1 Oct 39.

[61] Rayner, "Conference at the l'Ecole de Guerre," pp. 9–11; Memo to Col Davis and Maj Gaffey, sub: Germany: Coordination of Horse and Mechanized Cavalry, 20 Apr 38, p. 2, Crittenberger Papers. Despite its title, the latter source contains much information concerning French mechanized cavalry development.

[62] Rayner, "Conference at the l'Ecole de Guerre," Dec 35, pp. 11–12; MID, WDGS, Intel Sum no. 32, 1 May 36, p. 15673, Reel 5 of *U.S. Military Intelligence Reports*; Memo to Davis and Gaffey, 20 Apr 38; Memo, ACS, G–2, Col E. R. Warner McCabe, sub: Mechanized Forces of Foreign Armies, 29 Jul 38, pp. 1–3, Crittenberger Papers; Memo for Ch of Cav, sub: Employment of Mechanized Units in the French Army, 13 Jul 39, pp. 7–8, MID Corresp, 1917–1941, Security-Class Corresp and Rpts, RG 165, NARA.

[63] MID, WDGS, Intel Sum no. 32, 1 May 36, p. 15673; Rayner, "Conference at the l'Ecole de Guerre," pp. 11–12, 14; Memo for Ch of Cav, 13 Jul 39.

Chart 8–French Light Mechanized Division, 1939

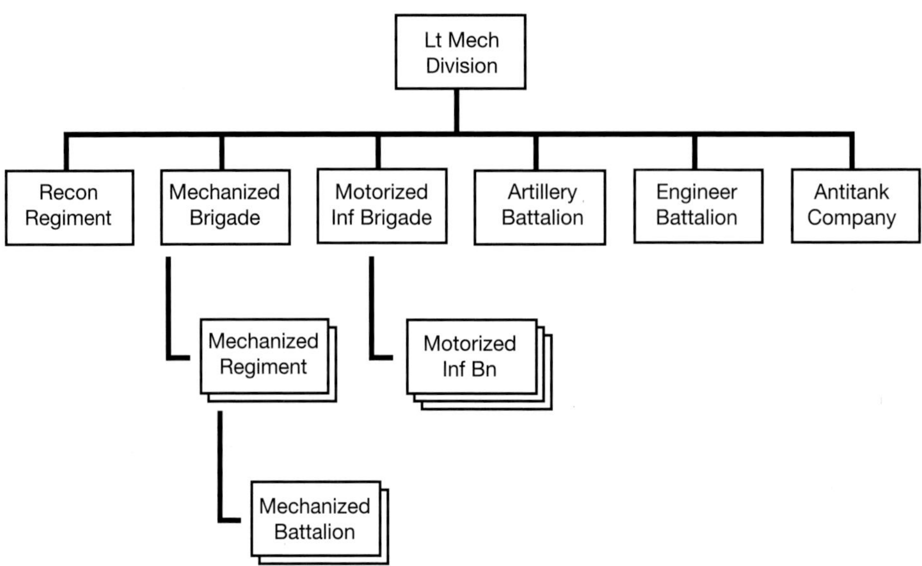

combat power and feared the absence of flank security if employed on its own. Instead, it would support corps, army, or reserve operations. The division's reliance on a mix of radio, wire, and visual communications also suggested its use in close proximity to friendly forces. Organizationally, the division was built to incorporate attachments easily, while its armored car regiment was designed to breakdown into small groupings to conduct screening and reconnaissance operations.[64]

In the light mechanized division, the American Office of the Chief of Cavalry noted a trend among French cavalry units toward greater reliance on motor vehicles and increased firepower and mobility. The assignment of tanks to the mechanized brigade of the light mechanized division seemed to confirm this trend toward combat rather than maneuver. Motorcycle troops in both mechanized and horse cavalry units

[64] Asst Mil Attaché, Paris, Rpt no. 25391–W, sub: France (Combat): Visit to 2d D.L.M., 14 Dec 39, Crittenberger Papers; Memo for Ch of Cav, 13 Jul 39. Instead of constituting a mobile reserve capable of exploiting offensive success or counterattacking enemy breakthroughs—the same missions American mechanized cavalry was expected to perform—the primary mission of the Light Mechanized Division was to precede and screen the advance of French forces into Belgium upon the outbreak of war with Germany and the implementation of plans to link French and British troops with the Dutch Army. See, for example, Robert A. Doughty, "The French Armed Forces, 1918–1940," in *Military Effectiveness*, 3 vols., ed. Allan R. Millett and Williamson Murray (Boston: Allen and Unwin, 1988), 1: 56.

A French Somua tank, designed for use with the light mechanized divisions, transported via truck

supported armored-car action and permitted troops so transported to act as mobile fire reserves, provide flank security, and perform liaison duties.[65]

Despite this embracement of motor vehicles, the Office of the Chief of Cavalry did not consider the French experience sufficient justification to mechanize all American cavalry units. The French Army's reliance on motor vehicles increased maintenance costs and required skilled technical personnel. The French also retained their horse cavalry, suggesting the valuation they placed on both horse and mechanized cavalry. The French example seemed to validate the importance of both types of mounted units, thereby reinforcing the developmental path pursued by successive American chiefs of Cavalry.[66]

French tank units also caught the Military Intelligence Division's attention. Intended to support infantry, only the tank battalion possessed a prescribed table of organization and equipment. The battalion constituted the largest tactical and administrative armor unit in the French Army throughout the 1930s. Initially part of a central reserve, tank units became assigned to army and corps commands as

[65] Memo, Col A. M. Miller to CG, 7th Cav Bde (Mech), and 1st End, sub: French Cavalry Organization and Doctrine of Employment, 17 Apr 37, pp. 7, 10–11; Memo, ACS, G–2, Col E. R. Warner McCabe to Ch of Cav, sub: Motorcycle Units and Armored Cars in the French Army, 17 Apr 39, pp. 2–3, 6; all in Crittenberger Papers. Memo, McCabe, 29 Jul 38, p. 1; Asst Mil Attaché, Paris, Rpt no. 25391–W, 14 Dec 39.

[66] Memo, Miller to CG, 7th Cav Bde (Mech), and 1st End, 17 Apr 37, p. 10; Memo, McCabe, 29 Jul 38, p. 1.

French Char–B tank, one of the most heavily armed and armored tanks at the start of World War II

necessary, the latter in turn subordinating them to infantry division commanders for specific missions.[67]

French plans to employ tanks in small tactical units to support infantry operations paralleled the organization and general doctrine of the American infantry tank force. However, by 1939 the Military Intelligence Division began to note the French Army's efforts to build an armored division. Such formations were expected to help breach strongly organized defenses rather than operate in an independent role.

[67] Memo, McCabe, 29 Jul 38, p. 5; Mil Attaché, Paris, Rpt no. 24728–W, sub: France (Combat): French Field Exercise—Employment of Tanks in an Attack, 3 Jan 39, Crittenberger Papers. The Military Intelligence Division correctly believed the role of these tank units to be direct infantry support similar to that performed in World War I. The Military Intelligence Division was also correct in stressing the French emphasis on the tank battalion as the primary tank organization. The French did plan to organize regiments and larger groupings of tanks, but they considered such organizations temporary measures to address a specific battlefield situation. Therefore, little peacetime preparation was given to the organization and training of tank units larger than battalions. See Robert A. Doughty, "The French Armed Forces," in Millett and Murray, *Military Effectiveness*, 2: 55–56.

Chart 9–French Armored Division, 1940

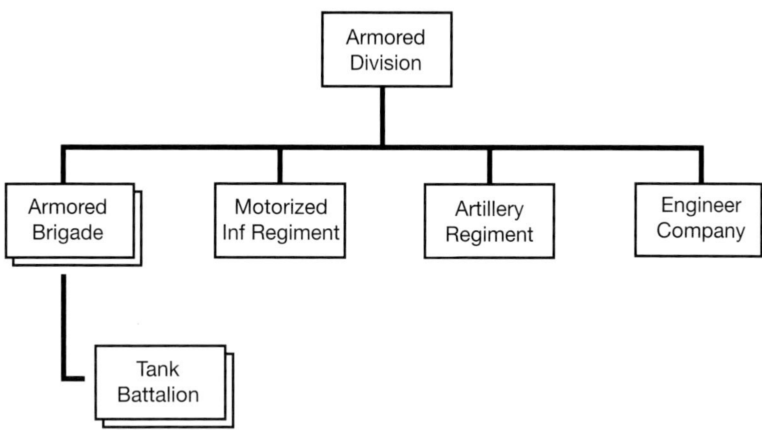

The French also expected to employ these divisions as part of larger mechanized corps.[68]

The *divisions cuirassées* (armored divisions) contained artillery, motorized infantry, antitank guns, a small detachment of engineers, and an aerial observation squadron. (*Chart 9*) Their principal strength reportedly lay in one hundred sixty Hotchkiss H–39 and seventy Char B1–bis tanks. The heavier Char B1–bis tanks were intended to spearhead the division's attack, while the lighter Hotchkiss tanks and motorized infantry would secure objectives in their wake.[69] The division's powerful combination of tanks and artillery led one attaché to note: "The French armored division, from the standpoint of armament and armor, appears to have

[68] Asst Mil Attaché, Paris, Rpt no. 25513–W, sub: Tactical Doctrine of the French Armored Division, 9 Feb 40, Crittenberger Papers; "Notes on Employment of Tanks and Mechanized Units," 1939, Gillem Papers.

[69] Asst Mil Attaché, Paris, Rpt no. 25511–W, sub: France (Combat): Organization of a French Armored Division (Division Cuirassee), 9 Feb 40, Crittenberger Papers; Asst Mil Attaché, Paris, Rpt no. 25513–W, 9 Feb 40.

The French armored divisions suffered from a variety of other problems not identified in American intelligence assessments. They lacked key support assets, including adequate reconnaissance, security, antitank, and antiaircraft elements. Supply and administrative support proved minimal. The mix of tanks resulted from insufficient numbers of Chart B1-bis vehicles rather than intent. In 1940 four armored divisions were created, but they suffered from limited training and poor cohesion when thrown into combat against the Germans. For a greater understanding of the nature of French mechanized development in the interwar era, see Jeffrey J. Clarke, "Military Technology in Republican France: The Evolution of the French Armored Force, 1917–1940," Ph.D. Diss., Duke University, 1969, pp. 206–07, 218, University Microfilms International Order no. 70–2147.

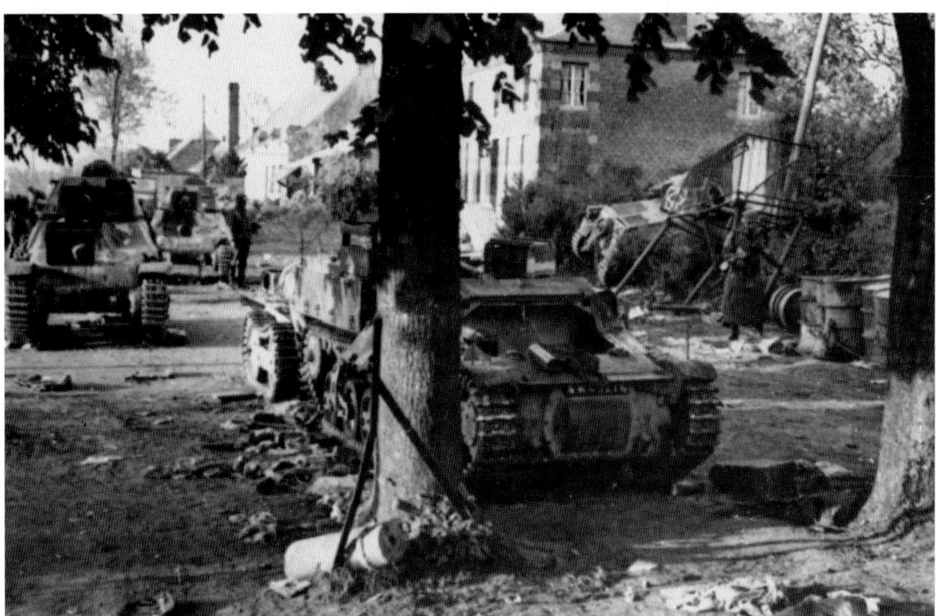

French armored vehicles knocked out or abandoned during the German invasion of France in 1940

greater striking power than the German Panzer Division."[70] The French themselves explained the differences between the *division cuirassée* and the panzer division by relating them to differences in the French Maginot and German Siegfried Lines.[71] Such reports reinforced the tendency of American officers to perceive the mechanized components of European armies as heavy shock units intended to batter a path through the fortified frontiers of their neighbors. European mechanized units seemed determined to assault rather than outmaneuver resistance.[72]

French and American tank tactics proved similar. The French expected to employ their tanks in large numbers attacking in succeeding waves. Maneuver tanks with heavier weapons and armor would precede the assault, neutralizing enemy antitank weapons and machine guns. Waves of lighter accompanying tanks would follow,

[70] Asst Mil Attaché, Paris, Rpt no. 25511–W, 9 Feb 40, p. 8.

[71] Asst Mil Attaché, Paris, Rpt no. 25173–W, sub: France (Combat): Tactical Doctrines of French and German Armored Units, 28 Aug 39, p. 4, Crittenberger Papers.

[72] Daniel Van Voorhis, "Mechanization," Lecture at AWC, 13 Oct 37, p. 14, Army War College Lectures, 1937–1938, AWC Curricular Archives. In the case of France, this conclusion was only partially correct. The French did, as American intelligence reported, intend to use their armored divisions to provide direct support for their corps and armies; but they did not intend to use them as battering rams against German fortifications. They would be held in reserve until attached to an army or corps threatened with a major assault. The French envisioned a counterattack role, and during the German invasion all four divisions endeavored to perform this role. See Clarke, "Military Technology in Republican France," pp. 194, 208–09, and Doughty, "French Armed Forces," p. 56.

directly in advance of the infantry for whom they provided fire support. The action of the tanks coincided with the use of a bounding artillery barrage intended to neutralize enemy antitank weapons. Additional mechanized units followed to exploit breaches in the enemy defenses. Tank operations were coordinated with those of other arms through reconnaissance, planning, and determination of phase lines. Like the Americans, the French considered the tank a support weapon.[73]

The French appeared to rely on the radio to direct the actions of tank units. An American attaché visiting a French tank unit found a simple and effective means of radio communication in use. A signal code permitted transmissions of fewer than ten characters that provided subordinates with directional instructions and map coordinates.[74]

Unlike the American design emphasis on light, fast tanks, the French preferred heavier armor and armament. Their tank designs reflected an appreciation for the growing power of antitank guns reinforced by the demonstrated vulnerability of light tanks during the Spanish Civil War. French tanks were thus designed to operate on a battlefield populated by antitank guns, enemy tanks, and fortified defenses. Survivability in such an environment necessitated more powerful weapons and thicker armor. In these categories, French tanks tended to surpass their European and American counterparts, and French design philosophy anticipated the steady improvements in firepower and protection that would characterize tank development during World War II.[75]

The Char B1–bis tank epitomized this trend. It carried a 75-mm. gun in its hull, a 47-mm. in its turret, two machine guns, and armor reported by the Military Intelligence Division as 1.6 inches thick. The French also planned an even heavier C tank reputed to weigh 70 tons.[76] By 1939 American intelligence reported that French tank production focused on four principal types: the 21-ton Somua, the 15-ton Hotchkiss H–39, the 16.5-ton Renault R–35, and the 32-ton Char B1–bis. The light mechanized divisions used the Somua and the armored divisions the Char

[73] "French Light Tanks," Jun 40, pp. 3–4, Crittenberger Papers; MID, Intel Sum no. 33, 12 Nov 37, p. 16469; Memo, McCabe, 29 Jul 38, pp. 5–6; Mil Attaché, Paris, Rpt no. 24728–W, 3 Jan 39; Asst Mil Attaché, Paris, Rpt no. 25173–W, 28 Aug 39.

[74] Mil Attaché, Paris, Rpt no. 24728–W, 3 Jan 39; Asst Mil Attaché, Paris, sub: France (Combat): Visit to 511th Tank Regiment, Verdun, n.d., Crittenberger Papers. American intelligence greatly exaggerated the French reliance on radio communications to control mechanized elements. The majority of French tanks lacked radios entirely. Those radios that were installed in French tanks tended to be fragile and outdated. See Clarke, "Military Technology in Republican France," pp. 207, 230–31.

[75] MID, WDGS, Intel Sum no. 31, 13 Dec 35, p. 15497, Reel 5 of *U.S. Military Intelligence Reports*; Mil Attaché, Paris, Rpt no. 23451–W, sub: France (Combat): French Tanks, 1 Jun 37, Crittenberger Papers; Memo, McCabe, 29 Jul 38, p. 5; Mil Attaché, Paris, Report 24728–W, sub: France (Combat): French Field Exercise—Employment of Tanks in an Attack, 3 Jan 39.

[76] Memo, McCabe, 29 Jul 38, p. 4; Memo, ACS, G–2, Col E. R. Warner McCabe, to Ch of Cav, sub: Supplementary Information on Mechanized Forces of Foreign Armies, 6 Feb 39, p. 7, Crittenberger Papers. The Char B1–bis actually carried frontal armor over 2 inches (60 millimeters) thick, making it one of the most powerfully armored tanks in the world. The French also undertook development of a 32-ton tank and a 45-ton tank. See Clarke, "Military Technology in Republican France," p. 198.

B1–bis; the Hotchkiss and Renault tanks found employment in both infantry and cavalry mechanized units as accompanying tanks.[77]

Tank engagements fought during the German invasion of France in 1940 convinced one American attaché that the Hotchkiss, Somua, and Char B1–bis tanks were superior to similar German models. He noted the high praise afforded them by the French Army and the confidence tank crews placed in the ability of their vehicles' curved hulls and turrets to deflect antitank projectiles. The supposed superiority of French tank designs encouraged the War Department to pursue an abortive effort to produce the Char B1–bis in the United States.[78]

To assist its mechanized cavalry and tank units in defending the national frontiers until mobilization was completed, the French Army undertook the motorization of several of its infantry divisions and artillery regiments in the mid-1930s. American intelligence noted these plans and charted their progress but concluded that the size of most French infantry divisions—each requiring fifty-seven trains for rail transport—precluded their complete motorization. Nevertheless, the noncombatant and artillery units of seven divisions were motorized. By 1939 motorization extended to the command, supply, and service echelons of most divisions; but the French Army still included large numbers of horses and horse-drawn vehicles.[79]

French motorization and mechanization efforts seemed to confirm existing trends within the U.S. Army. The French example reinforced tactical concepts inherent to *A Manual for the Commanders of Large Units (Provisional)*, providing a model for motor vehicle usage in the event of a sustained war in which continuous frontages and prepared defenses were assumed. However, the French example proved less indicative of how motor vehicles might be used in a war of maneuver more appropriate to the ideas of the 1923 field service regulations. Despite the French doctrinal influence on the U.S. Army, the centralized control and deliberation inherent in French battlefield employment of mechanized and motorized combat formations did not accord with the tactical and command versatility American mechanized

---

[77] Memos, McCabe to Ch of Cav, sub: Supplementary Information on Mechanized Forces of Foreign Armies, 6 Feb 39, pp. 4–5, and Lt Col Willis D. Crittenberger to Ch of Cav, sub: French Tank Production, 25 Mar 40, both in Crittenberger Papers.

[78] Asst Mil Attaché, Paris, Rpt no. 25257–W, sub: France (Combat): Visit to French Front in Vicinity of Verdun, Dalem-Creutzwald, and Maginot Line, 6 Oct 39; Memos, Lt Col Willis D. Crittenberger to Ch of Cav, 3 Jun 40; 4 Jun 40; 5 Jun 40; all in Crittenberger Papers. French tanks also suffered a number of additional problems not immediately clear to American observers. The smaller crew size and one-man turrets of many French tank designs reduced their tactical effectiveness. The weak main armament of the Hotchkiss tanks possessed minimal antitank value against newer models of German tanks. The Char B1–bis proved sluggish and its excessive fuel consumption limited its radius of action while generating supply problems. Its size and weight necessitated special measures for rail transport and battlefield recovery. Nor did the 32-ton Char B1–bis conform to the U.S. Army's preference for lighter tanks easily capable of crossing pontoon bridges and typical highway spans. See Jeffrey A. Gunsberg, "The Battle of the Belgian Plain, 12–14 May 1940: The First Great Tank Battle," *The Journal of Military History* LVI, no. 2 (April 1992): 213; Clarke, "Military Technology in Republican France," pp. 198, 207, 209–10, 231.

[79] MID, WDGS, Intel Sum no. 32, 1 May 36, pp. 15673–74; Intel Br, G–2, "A Study of the French Infantry Division," Jun 39, pp. 5–6, 8, Crittenberger Papers.

cavalry officers preferred. They perceived an affinity between their own doctrinal ideas and those practiced by the Germans.

The Military Intelligence Division and the Panzer Division

Adolf Hitler became chancellor of the German Republic in 1933. He soon began to renounce the restraints on German rearmament that the Versailles Treaty had imposed. In 1935 all semblance of conformance to these restrictions ended, and Germany began a large-scale military buildup that attracted American interest. The Military Intelligence Division assumed the leading role in chronicling the expansion of the German Army. Despite the security consciousness of Hitler's totalitarian regime, the Military Intelligence Division obtained considerable information on German military developments. Colonel McCabe, directing the Military Intelligence Division, commented, "I think all of Europe at the present time is holding out on military information, and I believe the country that gives us more and that we get more out of perhaps than any of the others would be Germany."[80] The German military extended every courtesy to American officers; and while the German press generally disparaged American culture and society, it favorably portrayed the U.S. Army.[81]

The German War Ministry rated foreign military attachés according to diplomatic considerations, the tact of the particular attaché, and the treatment afforded the German military attaché serving in the nation under consideration. Favorably rated attachés received the greatest accessibility to the German Army, including visitation privileges to most military formations and armaments factories. Even experimental projects might be viewed if the corresponding German attaché received similar access. Together with Bulgaria, Hungary, Italy, Japan, Nationalist Spain, Sweden, and Yugoslavia, U.S. military attachés ranked among the highest. Those of the Soviet Union ranked lowest.[82]

American attaché staff, as well as officers fulfilling academic scholarships at German universities and those on leave in Germany, availed themselves of opportunities to visit and serve with German combat units for brief periods. The American attaché assisted in arranging these visits, which included German engineer, antiaircraft, tank, infantry, antitank, and artillery units.[83] The price of German largesse,

---

[80] McCabe Discussion Notes, 4 Jan 38, p. 7.

[81] Memo, Maj Truman Smith to Ch, MID, sub: German Publications, 14 Oct 36, MID Corresp, 1917–1941, Security-Class Corresp and Rpts, RG 165, NARA.

[82] Mil Attaché, Berlin, Rpt no. 15176, sub: Germany (Combat): The G–2 Section of the German General Staff, 3 Mar 37, pp. 6–8, MID Corresp, 1917–1941, Security-Class Corresp and Rpts, RG 165, NARA.

[83] Memo, Maj Truman Smith to Ch, MID, sub: Detail of 2d Lt William M. Connor, 5 Jan 36; Ltr, Maj Truman Smith to Col John B. Coulter, 10 May 37; Mil Attaché, Berlin, Rpt no. 15426, sub: Germany (Combat): The German Light Tank Company; A Unit of the Armored (Panzer) Division (Revision of Report No. 14779), 3 Aug 37, p. 2; Ltr, 1st Lt Paul W. Thompson to Col Warren T. Hannum, 11 Dec 35; Memo, Maj W. F. Heavey to ACS, G–2, 30 Dec 35; Memo, Maj Truman Smith to ACS, G–2, sub: Tour of Duty of Lt Wm. M. Connor in German Infantry Regiment, 21 May 38;

however, was evidenced by the attendance of German officers at U.S. Army schools and their study of American industrial organization and mobilization plans.[84]

In 1935 the American military attaché secured German consent for U.S. Army officers to attend the *Kriegsakademie*, Germany's senior leadership school. The *Kriegsakademie* provided instruction similar to that given at the U.S. Army's War College and the Command and General Staff School. The CGSS commandant supported the arrangement. He desired *Kriegsakademie* graduates for service as instructors. At Fort Leavenworth, their presence would balance the influence of *École de Guerre* graduates and introduce students to current German military thought.[85]

The *Kriegsakademie* exposed American officers to the latest German doctrine and command methods. Field exercises and maneuvers, employing fully equipped, war-strength combat units, allowed students to apply concepts introduced in the classroom. An unparalleled intelligence treasure concerning the German Army's battle technique and organization thus resulted from the experience of American student-officers commanding German combat units and establishing relationships with prospective German staff officers. The German practice of experimenting with new unit organizations at the *Kriegsakademie* before their adoption by the field army, including those like the panzer division otherwise inaccessible to the American attaché, further increased the *Kriegsakademie*'s intelligence value to the Military Intelligence Division.[86]

A regime that prided itself on propaganda and creating false impressions to deceive the world, however, had little compunction concerning the denial of military information to foreign attachés, no matter how courteously received. The German government retained the power to alter at its pleasure the favorable classification granted American attachés. It did not ensure that the Americans would receive information

---

Memo, ACS, G–2, Col E. R. Warner McCabe, to TAG, sub: Cablegram, 27 Jul 39; all in MID Corresp, 1917–1941, Security-Class Corresp and Rpts RG 165, NARA.

[84] Memo, Brig Gen H. H. Knight to CS, sub: Detail of Captain Harlan N. Hartness, Infantry, to German General Staff School, 21 Jun 35, MID Corresp, 1917–1941, Security-Class Corresp and Rpts, RG 165, NARA; Bidwell, *History of the Military Intelligence Division*, pp. 383–84.

[85] Memo, Knight to CS, 21 Jun 35; Bidwell, *History of the Military Intelligence Division*, pp. 268–69, 383; Memo, Brees to TAG, 17 Dec 35.

[86] Acting Mil Attaché, Berlin, Rpt no. 14034, sub: Recent German War College Problems, 16 Apr 35, G–2 Information Digest, Military Attaché Rpts, Germany, vol. 34, AWC Rcds Sec, MHI Archives; Mil Attaché, Berlin, Rpt no. 15260, sub: Germany (Combat): The German General Staff School (Kriegsakademie), 27 Apr 37, MID Corresp, 1917–1941, Security-Class Corresp and Rpts, RG 165, NARA; Mil Attaché, Berlin, Rpt 15999, sub: Germany (Combat): German General Staff School, 11 Jul 38, MID Corresp, 1917–1941, Security-Class Corresp and Rpts, RG 165, NARA; Wedemeyer/Deskis Conversations, sec. 3, pp. 34, 38.

Examples of the types of information gained from service with German combat units and attendance at the *Kriegsakademie* may be found in: Acting Mil Attaché, Berlin, Rpt no. 14116, sub: Report on Field Exercise of War College Class and Signal Troops, 6 Jun 35, G–2 Info Digest, Mil Attaché Rpts, Germany, vol. 34, AWC Rcds Sec, MHI Archives; Memo, Maj Truman Smith to Ch, MID, sub: German Armored Divisions, 27 Dec 35, MID Corresp, 1917–1941, Security-Class Corresp and Rpts, RG 165, NARA; Memo, Maj Truman Smith to Ch, MID, no. D–14510, sub: Evaluation of Reports from M/A, Germany, dated January 16, 1936, 4 Feb 36, MID Corresp, 1917–1941, Security-Class Corresp and Rpts, RG 165, NARA.

Von Schell (*center*) visiting the 7th Cavalry Brigade (Mechanized) in the 1930s

equivalent to their German counterparts in Washington, especially concerning tank and aircraft developments. For example, observing autumn 1935 maneuvers of the German Army, the American attaché believed their primary purpose lay in befuddling foreign attachés because of the absence of tanks and the secrecy surrounding tactical units larger than regiments.[87] American press attacks on Germany following the 1938 Munich settlement also eroded some of the previous courtesy shown U.S. Army officers in Germany.[88]

However, the United States benefited from the excellent services of Maj. Truman Smith. Appointed military attaché to Germany in the critical period 1935–1939, Major Smith was familiar with his host nation as well as the duties of an attaché, unlike many prospective American attachés. A staff officer in the Civil Affairs Office at Koblenz in 1919, Smith became assistant military attaché to Germany from 1920 to 1924, witnessing the rise of Adolf Hitler and the National Socialist German Workers Party. In 1932, at the invitation of the *Reichswehr*, he attended German military

[87] Mil Attaché, Berlin, Rpt no. 14281, sub: Report on Silesian Maneuvers of German Army, Autumn, 1935, 11 Sep 35, pp. 1–2, G–2 Info Digest, Mil Attaché Rpts, Germany, vol. 34, AWC Rcds Sec, MHI Archives.

[88] McCabe Discussion Notes, 4 Jan 39, p. 12. In 1938 German territorial claims on Czechoslovakia led to a diplomatic crisis and the possibility of war. During the Munich conference convened to avert such a conflict, France and Britain agreed to permit Germany to annex the disputed region.

maneuvers in East Prussia. A graduate of the Command and General Staff School and the Army War College, Smith had also taught at the Infantry School.[89]

As attaché, Smith benefited from personal contacts made before 1935 with German officers, many of whom subsequently rose to influential positions in the German Army. These officers included Walther von Reichenau, Walter Warlimont, Werner von Blomberg, Hans Speidel, and Adolf von Schell.[90] Such contacts compensated for Smith's junior rank and negated efforts of the German War Ministry to restrict the exposure of its military personnel to foreign officers. Lacking similar acquaintances, Smith's successor, Col. B. R. Peyton, encountered difficulty acquiring information other than that intended for his consumption.[91]

Assisted by an able staff, Smith's principal value stemmed from his ability to gather and review information from many sources, including American *Kriegsakademie* students. Through Smith the Military Intelligence Division compiled a detailed description of the German Army and its warfighting doctrine. Smith also arranged visits by American officers to German combat units and organized meetings between American and German commanders. He used the occasion of the 1936 Olympic Games in Munich to arrange an inspection tour of German Cavalry for Brig. Gen. Guy V. Henry, leader of the U.S. Olympic Equestrian Team and commandant of the American Cavalry School.[92] In 1937 Smith arranged for Deputy Chief of Staff General Embick to meet with senior officers of the German Army.[93] Confronted with German reticence to reveal technical and operational information concerning military aircraft and production capacity, Smith exploited a German respect for Col. Charles A. Lindbergh as an airman and isolationist by arranging a series of visits by him to *Luftwaffe* bases and aircraft production facilities. Lindbergh actually flew several new German aircraft, and his observations became U.S. Army intelligence.[94]

To penetrate the veil of secrecy initially shrouding German tank development, organization, and doctrine, Smith arranged an agreement between the War Department and the German War Ministry, enabling American tank officers to visit German tank units and production facilities in exchange for similar privileges granted to German officers.[95] Smith also acquired further information on German tank development through his personal friendship with Colonel von Schell, whose

---

[89] Bidwell, *History of the Military Intelligence Division*, pp. 268–70; Truman Smith, "Facts of Life," pp. 54–55, 64.

[90] Katharine Alling Hollister Smith, "My Life: Berlin, August 1935–April 1939," 2 vols., 1: 22, 57–58, 154–55, Truman and Katharine Smith Papers, MHI Archives; Truman Smith, "Facts of Life," p. 105.

[91] K. Smith, "My Life," 1: 261.

[92] Ltr, Col Charles Burnett to Cav Sch Commandant Brig Gen Guy V. Henry, 6 Mar 36, MID Corresp, 1917–1941, Security-Class Corresp and Rpts, RG 165, NARA.

[93] K. Smith, "My Life," 1: 171–72.

[94] Wayne S. Cole, *Charles A. Lindbergh and the Battle Against American Intervention in World War II* (New York: Harcourt Brace Jovanovich, 1974), pp. 31, 33, 36, 39; Bidwell, *History of the Military Intelligence Division*, pp. 269–70.

[95] Ltrs, Col Charles Burnett to Maj Truman Smith, 12 Feb 36; 8 Jun 36; 23 Jun 36; all in MID Corresp, 1917–1941, Security-Class Corresp and Rpts RG 165, NARA.

influence on German motorization and mechanization development grew during Smith's attaché tenure.[96] Von Schell had previously attended the Infantry School at Fort Benning and had met Smith there. The Military Intelligence Division began to question the military value of social visits to Schell, to which Smith responded: "In the case of Colonel von Schell, who is probably the *key-contact* whom I have in the German Army and who possesses absolute power to veto all requests of foreign governments to see German tank units, I have made it my business to be on as intimate personal relationship with him as possible, continuing a friendship begun at Fort Benning."[97]

German mechanization efforts centered on the panzer division. In October 1935 three such formations were established, and German tank units appeared in public during the National Socialist Party Day parade in Nürnberg. Initially, however, the purpose and composition of these tactical organizations remained unclear to both the American attaché and the Military Intelligence Division. German War Ministry statements concerning the panzer divisions indicated a variety of organizations, none of which resembled the paper formations employed in *Kriegsakademie* problems. In 1937 a panzer division participated in the German Army's annual fall maneuvers, but the American attaché was not invited to observe.[98]

Despite these obstacles, Smith compiled a detailed description of the panzer division. He relied on his own attaché staff, his personal contacts with German officers, and information obtained from American officers attending the *Kriegsakademie* or visiting German combat units. Smith's work became the U.S. Army's principal reference on the subject.[99]

According to Smith, the panzer division included a mix of tanks, motorized infantry, motorcycle troops, motorized artillery, antitank assets, and a reconnais-

---

[96] Mil Attaché, Berlin, Rpt nos. 16263, sub: Germany (Combat): Col Adolph von Schell Appointed Czar of German Motor Industry, 20 Nov 38, MID Corresp, 1917–1941, Security-Class Corresp and Rpts, RG 165, NARA; 16264, sub: Germany (Combat): Who's Who: Col. Adolph von Schell, 20 Nov 38, MID Corresp, 1917–1941, Security-Class Corresp and Rpts, RG 165, NARA; 16554, sub: Germany (Economic and Military): German Automobile Show, 1939, 1 Apr 39, Crittenberger Papers.

[97] Memo, Lt Col Truman Smith to ACS, G–2, sub: Circular Letter 112, 22 Aug 38, MID Corresp, 1917–1941, Security-Class Corresp and Rpts, RG 165, NARA.

[98] Mil Attaché, Berlin, Rpt no. 14298, sub: Germany (Political): The German National Socialist Party Day at Nurnberg, 24 Sep 35, p. 22, MID Corresp, 1917–1941, Security-Class Corresp and Rpts, RG 165, NARA; Memo, Truman Smith to Ch, MID, 27 Dec 35; MID, WDGS, Intel Sum no. 33, 23 Jul 37, pp. 16282, 16284, Reel 5 of *U.S. Military Intelligence Reports*; Asst Mil Attaché, Berlin, Rpt no. 15553, sub: Notes on the Employment of Armored Troops in the Mecklenburg Maneuver, 22 Oct 37, p. 1, AWC Rcds Sec, MHI Archives.

[99] Although Smith filed several reports on German armored development, one report in particular is exceptional for its clear depiction and concise evaluation: Mil Attaché, Berlin, Rpt no. 15596, sub: Germany (Combat): The Panzer Division: Revision of Report no. 14406, 24 Nov 37, MID Corresp, 1917–1941, Security-Class Corresp and Rpts, RG 165, NARA. In answering subsequent inquiries from the combat arms, MID repeatedly referenced information contained in this report, as in Memos, Brig Gen George V. Strong to DCS, G–2, sub: Mechanized Forces of the German Army, 1 Jun 38, and XO, G–2, Lt Col C. M. Busbee to Ch of Cav, sub: Employment of Mechanized Units in Foreign Armies, 14 Jul 39, Encl 1, both in MID Corresp, 1917–1941, Security-Class Corresp and Rpts, RG 165, NARA.

Panzerkampfwagen I

sance unit. These assets were distributed between the division's two principal combat components, its panzer brigade and its motorized brigade. The bulk of the division's tank strength lay in the former, while the infantry and supporting arms lay in the latter. Typical attachments to the division included an aerial observation squadron and a chemical unit for smoke delivery.[100] From 1935 to 1937 the division's strength shrank from an unwieldy 9 tank, 6 motorized infantry, and 3 motorcycle battalions to a more manageable 4 tank, 2 motorized infantry, and 1 motorcycle battalion. This reduction marked German efforts to streamline the division and improve command and control.[101]

The development of the panzer division was accompanied by a period of doctrinal confusion, organizational flux, and personality conflicts. Nevertheless, by 1937 clarity of purpose had emerged. German tank units became more frequent participants in field maneuvers and fought in the Spanish Civil War. These experiences provided an opportunity to refine tactics and identify and correct deficiencies. Smith remarked, "The German kindergarten period for playing with tanks is over."[102]

---

[100] Mil Attaché, Berlin, Rpt no. 15596, 24 Nov 37.

[101] MID, Intel Sum no. 33, 23 Jul 37, pp. 16283, 16284; Mil Attaché, Berlin, Rpt no. 15596, 24 Nov 37, pp. 4, 6.

[102] MID, WDGS, Intel Sum no. 33, 23 Jul 37, pp. 16282–84; Mil Attaché, Berlin, Rpt no. 15596, 24 Nov 37, pp. 3–4, quote from p. 4.

From the perspective of American military intelligence, in a two-year period and despite initial confusion, the German Army had formulated the basis of a doctrine for mechanized combat units and begun the physical creation of tank formations without precedent in Europe or the United States. Smith attributed this rapid evolution to Germany's centralization of mechanized and motorized development responsibility within a single organization. The *Inspektion der Kraftfahrkampftruppen* (Motor Combat Corps) included all tank, antitank, motorized infantry, motorcycle, and motorized reconnaissance units. Similarly, a single institute—the *Schnelltruppenschule* (Mobile Combat School) at Wünsdorf—bore responsibility for training the personnel for these units. Smith did not believe the same evolutionary tempo could have been achieved had multiple organizations shared administrative jurisdiction for mechanized and motorized development.[103]

The Military Intelligence Division noted, however, that the high level of centralized administration did not last. Instead, responsibility for motorized infantry and motorcycle troop development was transferred to the Infantry and that for motorized reconnaissance units to the Cavalry. The *Inspektion der Kraftfahrkampftruppen* became the *Inspektion der Panzertruppen* (Armored Corps), retaining responsibility for tank and antitank development, reflecting the German emphasis on the simultaneous crafting of complementary tank and antitank doctrine and equipment. Similarly, the Motor Transport School became the *Panzertruppenschule* (Armored School), responsible for training motorcycle, tank, and antitank personnel.[104]

Within a year, however, the German War Ministry announced additional changes. In December 1938 the Cavalry was dissolved as a separate branch. Smith attributed this action to the unwillingness of the branch to embrace the motorized and mechanized trends within the German Army. Cavalry units now became part of the *Schnelltruppen* (mobile troops), together with tank, antitank, motorized reconnaissance, armored car, motorized infantry, and motorcycle units. American intelligence failed to determine the precise nature of the *Schnelltruppen*'s responsibilities, although the Military Intelligence Division believed it supervised training and doctrine development for panzer and motorized infantry units.[105]

---

[103] Mil Attaché, Berlin, Rpt no. 15426, 3 Aug 37, p. 7; Asst Mil Attaché, Berlin, Rpt no. 15049, sub: Germany (Combat): German Motorized Combat School (Supplementary to M.I.D. Report No. 14, 703), 6 Jan 37, MID Corresp, 1917–1941, Security-Class Corresp and Rpts, RG 165, NARA; Mil Attaché, Berlin, Rpt no. 15466, sub: Germany (Combat): Motor Combat Corps (Major Changes in Organization), 7 Sep 37, MID Corresp, 1917–1941, Security-Class Corresp and Rpts, RG 165, NARA.

[104] Mil Attaché, Berlin, Rpt no. 15156, sub: Germany (Combat): Motor Transport School, School Troops (Supplementary Reports to M.I.D. Reports nos. 14,703 and 15,049), 23 Feb 37, MID Corresp, 1917–1941, Security-Class Corresp and Rpts, RG 165, NARA; Mil Attaché, Berlin, Rpt no. 15466, 7 Sep 37; MID, WDGS, Intel Sum no. 33, 1 Oct 37, p. 16386, Reel 6 of *U.S. Military Intelligence Reports*; Mil Attaché, Berlin, Rpt no. 15587, sub: Germany (Combat): The October 1937 Expansion of the German Army, Annual Preliminary Report, 20 Nov 37, Crittenberger Papers.

[105] Mil Attaché, Berlin, Rpt no. 16316, sub: Germany (Combat): German Cavalry Inspection Abolished, 2 Dec 38, MID Corresp, 1917–1941, Security-Class Corresp and Rpts, RG 165, NARA; Memo, Lt Col Willis D. Crittenberger to Ch of Cav, sub: Information on the German Army, 8 Apr 39, Crittenberger Papers; Memo, XO, G–2, Lt Col C. M. Busbee to Ch of Cav, sub: Employment of

Chart 10–Panzer Division, 1937

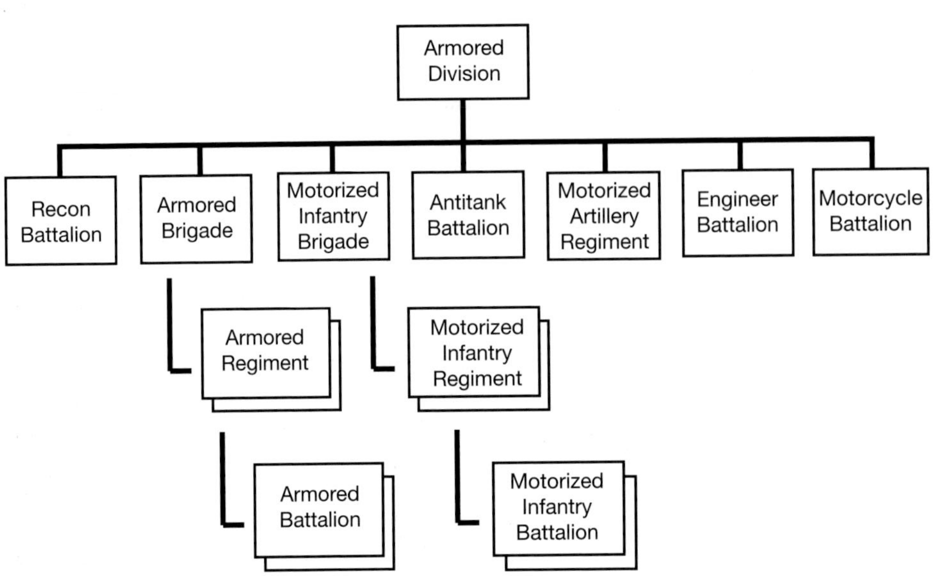

The panzer division continued to undergo modification, but Smith considered these changes consistent with basic organizational and doctrinal principles established by 1937.[106] He did not believe subsequent organizational refinement particularly significant, because "German tables of organization are elastic, and German military thought places little weight on Panzer Divisions for the sake of Panzer Divisions."[107] Instead, the Germans designed combat units as self-contained, combined-arms units capable of attachment or detachment to a parent formation. They preferred doctrinal consistency over organizational rigidity, which they believed stifled tactical versatility.[108] Consequently, while all panzer divisions adhered to the same doctrine, their precise composition varied.[109] (*Chart 10*)

Mechanized Units in Foreign Armies, 14 Jul 39, Encl 1, p. 2; Acting Mil Attaché, Berlin, Rpt no. 16791, sub: Current Events in Germany, No. 25, 17 Jul 39, Crittenberger Papers.

[106] Mil Attaché, Berlin, Rpt no. 15596, 24 Nov 37, p. 4, quote from p. 15.

[107] Ibid.

[108] MID, "Combat Estimate of Germany—Latest Added Revision, December 15, 1939," pp. 3, 5, 7, 10, File 236–D–GE–C2, AWC Rcds Sec; Subcommittee no. 2, Committee no. 5, "Report of Committee No. 5: Survey—Germany," 25 Jan 37, pp. 7–8, File 2–1937–5, AWC Curricular Archives; both in MHI Archives.

[109] In August 1939 the German Army included six panzer divisions. The *1st*, *2d*, and *3d Panzer Divisions* were similar in size and organization. The *4th Panzer Division*, however, had a smaller complement of motorized infantry and antitank units, while the *5th Panzer Division* was the largest formation, due to an unusually large number of motorized infantry and motorcycle troops. The *10th*

German light tanks during winter training maneuvers

Smith listed three likely missions for the panzer division: rapid penetration of the frontiers of a hostile country at the outbreak of war, spearheading a major envelopment aimed at a strategic decision, and operating independently "in a country of great expanse such as Poland and Russia." To accomplish these missions, Smith expected the panzer division to operate as two brigades: one of tanks and the other of the division's motorized assets. This breakdown simplified control of the formation's three thousand vehicles, which included over three hundred tanks.[110]

Smith's analysis of German armored doctrine focused on the ideas of Heinz Guderian. Smith considered him the principal influence on the panzer division's development. He identified him as "Germany's Fuller" in reference to the visionary British officer whose views shaped British Army mechanized efforts in the interwar era.[111] Although acknowledging the vital roles fulfilled by other officers, Guderian's

---

Panzer Division also was in the process of organization. For details on the composition of these formations, see http://www.achtungpanzer.com/articles/pzdiv.htm, last accessed on 10 Jan 06.

[110] Mil Attaché, Berlin, Rpt no. 15596, 24 Nov 37, pp. 2–3, 13, quotes from p. 14. In fact, the panzer divisions were employed in two parts as Smith suggested. During the Polish and French campaigns, the panzer divisions tended to separate their tanks into a tank brigade and concentrate the formation's artillery and infantry in a different support group. Separating the formation's tank and support elements, however, permitted only limited combined-arms action on the battlefield. Tanks required continuous support from infantry and artillery elements that could not be provided when these elements were not integrated with tanks. Consequently, after the French campaign, the practice of separating the tanks and support elements of the panzer divisions was discontinued. Instead combined-arms battle groups known as *Kampfgruppen* were utilized. *Kampfgruppen* that combined tanks and their support elements permitted greater integration of tactical function throughout the division. See F. W. Mellenthin, *Panzer Battles: A Study of the Employment of Armor in the Second World War* (New York: Ballantine Books, 1956), p. 20.

[111] Mil Attaché, Berlin, Rpt no. 15596, 24 Nov 37, p. 3. Heinz Guderian played a key role in the development of the *Panzerwaffe*. As one of the architects of the first panzer formations, he played an

appointment to lead the *Schnelltruppen* appeared to exemplify the continuation of his guidance of tank tactics and doctrine.[112]

Guderian emphasized the concentration of armor on a decisive point to ensure success. Both the panzer division and the panzer corps embodied this concept. The latter combined multiple panzer divisions under a single command and administrative agency. Both formations relied entirely on wheeled or tracked vehicular transport to provide high mobility and permit rapid action.[113] Guderian opposed the creation of separate tank units to support infantry formations, since this practice common in other countries dispersed rather than concentrated available tanks. Moreover, the tank's pace became that of the foot soldier and vulnerability to antitank measures increased.[114] One officer considered the parceling of tanks among infantry formations to be "tank murder."[115] Nevertheless, American observers noted that infantry support constituted the principal function of German tanks during maneuvers and in the Spanish Civil War. Indeed, by 1939 the Military Intelligence Division reported the preparation of several tank battalions specifically for infantry support.[116]

---

influential role in the development of German tank doctrine. In particular he stressed the importance of concentrating tanks in large mobile masses that could attack a single point in an enemy's defense, rupture that defense, and spread chaos and destruction throughout the rear areas. The creation of panzer divisions and corps reflected these views. Guderian also advocated centralized development of all motorized and mechanized combat elements.

Guderian was just one of several German officers responsible for the development of the panzer forces. Yet his writings and influential role made Truman Smith's focus upon his publications and activities appropriate. Smith utilized his personal contact with Schell and read Guderian's writings to compile a description of the nature, purpose, and associated doctrine of the panzer division. His assessment proved essentially correct concerning the basic structure of the panzer division and its intended operation. For information concerning Guderian's influence on the evolution of German tank doctrine and organization, see Heinz Guderian, *Achtung-Panzer!* (Stuttgart: Union Deutsche Verlagsgesellschaft, 1937), and *Panzer Leader* (New York: Dutton, 1952); Kenneth Macksey, *Guderian: Creator of the Blitzkrieg* (New York: Stein and Day, 1976).

[112] Mil Attaché, Berlin, Rpt no. 15760, sub: Germany (Combat): Who's Who: Major General Guderian, 26 Feb 38, MID Corresp, 1917–1941, Security-Class Corresp and Rpts, RG 165, NARA; Mil Attaché, Berlin, Rpt no. 15596, 24 Nov 37, p. 4.

[113] Mil Attaché, Berlin, Rpt nos. 15426, 3 Aug 37, pp. 6–7, and 14994, sub: Germany (Combat): Armored Troops and Their Cooperation with Other Arms, 24 Nov 36, pp. 4, 7, 11–14, MID Corresp, 1917–1941, Security-Class Corresp and Rpts, RG 165, NARA. The second document is Truman Smith's translation of one of Guderian's articles published in German military service journals and thought to represent official German tactical and organizational doctrine for armored elements.

[114] Mil Attaché, Berlin, Rpt no. 14994, 24 Nov 36, pp. 4, 9, 10.

[115] Mil Attaché, Berlin, Rpt no. 14908, sub: Report on German Autumn Maneuvers 1936, 8 Oct 36, p. 27, G–2 Information Digest, Military Attaché Reports, vol. 34, AWC Rcds Sec, MHI Archives.

[116] Mil Attaché, Berlin, Rpt no. 14908, 8 Oct 36, p. 25; Mil Attaché, Berlin, Rpt no. 15062, sub: Germany (Combat): Panzer Divisions, (Revision of Report 14,406), 9 Jan 37, MID Corresp, 1917–1941, Security-Class Corresp and Rpts, RG 165, NARA; Mil Attaché, Berlin, Rpt no. 15426, 3 Aug 37, pp. 7–8; Acting Mil Attaché, Berlin, Rpt no. 16503, sub: Autumn Maneuvers of the German 11th and 21st Divisions (Active Army) 1938, 1 Mar 39, p. 29, "G–2 Information Digest, Military Attaché Reports," vol. 34, AWC Rcds Sec, MHI Archives. The notion that significant tank assets were diverted to special infantry tank support units was incorrect. Throughout the period 1939–1941, German tanks operated principally as components of the panzer divisions. Infantry support tank units were not emphasized or common. Although two tank brigades were created to serve as support units

Guderian's tactical principles dominated the action of the panzer division, the employment of which centered on its tanks. To ensure the success of the panzer division's attack, the Germans sought to achieve a concentration of at least one hundred tanks per kilometer of frontage.[117] They operated in two groups, one responsible for eliminating enemy artillery and antitank weapons and the other for targeting reserves, headquarters, observation posts, and heavy infantry weapons.[118]

The other divisional assets performed supporting roles. Reconnaissance units moved in advance of the tanks, monitoring the disposition of enemy forces and identifying potential march routes for armored vehicles. Pioneers conducted terrain reconnaissance, removed artificial barriers, and assisted the tanks' passage of natural obstacles. Motorized artillery advanced with the tanks to destroy enemy antitank weapons, neutralize hostile artillery, and employ smoke screens. Similarly, divisional antitank guns kept pace with the tanks, ready to engage counterattacks by enemy armor. Motorized infantry sometimes led the tank advance to determine the nature of resistance or to breach defended positions. Once the tanks began to seize objectives, the infantry then secured them.[119]

The principle of infantry support of tanks extended beyond the panzer division. The Germans created motorized infantry divisions to secure and exploit the success of the panzer divisions and corps. These infantry formations included motorized infantry, motorcycle, antitank, artillery, antiaircraft, armored car, signal, pioneer, and service units. They were entirely motorized, providing them a degree of mobility similar to that of the tank formations they routinely supported. Smith believed the presence of motorized infantry divisions eliminated the need for large infantry components in the panzer division, permitting a reduction in the latter's size.[120]

Guderian considered effective reconnaissance critical to the successful employment of the panzer division. Therefore, this formation included a motorized reconnaissance battalion encompassing a signal platoon; two armored car companies; a motorcycle company; and a heavy company composed of an infantry howitzer platoon, an antitank platoon, and an engineer platoon. The motorcycle and heavy companies permitted the creation of smaller combat teams capable of fighting for information or conducting counterreconnaissance. The reconnaissance battalion's signal platoon and the inclusion of radios in half of its armored cars facilitated the rapid transmission of information. The reconnaissance battalion led the panzer division with its armored cars dispersed in small detachments over a broad frontage and reported on

---

attached to army commands, their component tank units already were being incorporated into newly created panzer divisions before the outbreak of war. See Edwards, *Panzer*, p. 31.

[117] Mil Attaché, Berlin, Rpt no. 15426, 3 Aug 37, pp. 31–34.

[118] Mil Attaché, Berlin, Rpt no. 15827, sub: Germany (Combat): The German Armored Division, 7 Apr 38, pp. 39, 40, MID Corresp, 1917–1941, Security-Class Corresp and Rpts, RG 165, NARA.

[119] Mil Attaché, Berlin, Rpt nos. 14994, 24 Nov 36, pp. 9, 11–14; 15596, 24 Nov 37, p. 6; 15827, 7 Apr 38, pp. 36, 38, 39–40.

[120] Mil Attaché, Berlin, Rpt nos. 14278, sub: Germany (Military): Motorization in the German Army, 9 Sep 35, p. 1; 15468, sub: Germany (Combat): Motorization of Four German Divisions, 7 Sep 37; 13904, sub: Germany (Military): The German Motorized Division, 6 Feb 35; 15596, 24 Nov 37, p. 6; all in MID Corresp, 1917–1941, Security-Class Corresp and Rpts, RG 165, NARA.

Panzerkampfwagen II

terrain, road nets, and enemy dispositions. Upon contact with the enemy's main line of resistance, the battalion either continued to report on hostile activity or assumed a flank security role.[121]

The panzer division's motorcycle battalion provided both infantry support and reconnaissance. Its primary roles included screening, flank security, and seizure of key terrain; but its rapid mobility permitted its use as a reconnaissance unit. Equipped with sidecars, American observers noted that these vehicles could attain higher road speeds than trucks. However, the smaller size of these vehicles permitted the unit to disperse faster than motorized infantry and reduced their vulnerability to enemy action. Moreover, sidecar passengers could dismount more quickly than soldiers riding in a truck. If necessary, albeit with some difficulty, motorcycle troops could portage their vehicles over or around obstacles. American intelligence categorized these units as motorized cavalry and recommended the consideration of similar forces for the U.S. Army.[122]

---

[121] Mil Attaché, Berlin, Rpt nos. 14591, sub: Germany (Combat): A German Motorized Reconnaissance Battalion, 17 Mar 36, pp. 3, 10–12, Crittenberger Papers; 14865, sub: Germany (Combat): German Motorized Reconnaissance Battalion, 14 Sep 36, pp. 2, 3–5, 17, 19, Crittenberger Papers; 14994, 24 Nov 36, pp. 2–4; 15286, sub: Germany (Combat): German Motorized Reconnaissance Battalion, 10 May 37, pp. 2, 4, 8–9, 15, 20–21, 24, Crittenberger Papers.

[122] Acting Mil Attaché, Berlin, Rpt no. 14141, sub: Report on German Motorcycles, 17 Jun 35, G–2 Information Digest, Military Attaché Reports, vol. 29, AWC Rcds Sec, MHI Archives; Mil Attaché, Berlin, Rpt no. 15329, sub: Germany (Combat): Motorcycle Battalion, 5 Jun 37, MID Corresp, 1917–1941, Security-Class Corresp and Rpts, RG 165, NARA.

Another reconnaissance organization existed in the form of the light division. In December 1937 the Germans announced the creation of a light brigade, later redesignated as a division. This formation included light tanks; motorized infantry; motorized artillery; and reconnaissance, antitank, antiaircraft, engineer, and signal assets. Smaller than the panzer division, the light division conducted reconnaissance-in-force missions for groupings of motorized or panzer divisions. American analysts believed it would envelop and attack enemy resistance in advance of panzer and motorized infantry divisions, performing the role of "nutcracker." The light division was considered a cavalry formation by American observers, who believed it embodied organizational and doctrinal trends similar to the American 7th Cavalry Brigade (Mechanized).[123]

American intelligence also noted the value placed by the Germans on close cooperation of aircraft with the panzer division. As fast reconnaissance agencies, aircraft scouted the general direction of advance, determining viable march routes and identifying possible obstacles.[124] Maneuver observation also indicated the likelihood of dive-bombers acting in conjunction with the panzer divisions, and experiments were known to have been conducted to determine the viability of controlling tank actions from aircraft.[125]

To coordinate the panzer division's actions, the Germans intended to rely extensively on radio communications. In both the light and panzer divisions—indeed, throughout the German Army—American intelligence noted the increasing prevalence of radios. Brief, fragmentary orders transmitted via radio or in person controlled the actions of the divisional components, written orders being reserved for command echelons above the division.[126] Platoon commanders possessed radios capable of reception and transmission; in controlling tank actions, visual signals and wire communication appeared to supplement radio use. One German officer stressed the value of radio communication: "The successful leading of fast moving armored and mechanized units has been made possible only by the development of this means (radio telephone) of communications,

---

[123] Memo, Lt Col Willis D. Crittenberger to Ch of Cav, sub: German Mechanized Use, 14 Aug 39, Crittenberger Papers. Mil Attaché, Berlin, Rpt nos. 15643, sub: Germany (Combat): 1st Light Brigade, 20 Dec 37; 15741, sub: Germany (Combat): The 1st Light Brigade, 19 Feb 38; 15913, sub: Germany (Combat): 1st Light Division, 19 May 38; 16772, sub: Germany (Combat): Independent Commands, Reorganization of the Light Divisions, 7 Jul 39; all in MID Corresp, 1917–1941, Security-Class Corresp and Rpts, RG 165, NARA. The American perception that the light divisions performed a cavalry function and represented the influence of that arm was essentially correct. In the German Army these formations were intended to perform strategic reconnaissance missions for an army or corps. This concept did not work in practice, and the light divisions were reorganized as panzer divisions following the end of the Polish campaign. See Edwards, *Panzer*, pp. 66, 71; Samuel W. Mitcham Jr., *Hitler's Legions: The German Army Order of Battle, World War II* (New York: Stein and Day, 1985), pp. 23, 354–61.

[124] Mil Attaché, Berlin, Rpt no. 15827, 7 Apr 38, p. 37.

[125] Mil Attaché, Berlin, Rpt nos. 15426, 3 Aug 37, pp. 31–34; 15499, sub: Report on the German Army Autumn Maneuvers, 1937, 27 Sep 37, pp. 33, 44–45, MID Corresp, 1917–1941, Security-Class Corresp and Rpts, RG 165, NARA; Acting Mil Attaché, Berlin, Rpt no. 16503, 1 Mar 39, pp. 1–2.

[126] Mil Attaché, Berlin, Rpt no. 15292, sub: Germany (Combat): German Field Orders, 18 May 37, MID Corresp, 1917–1941, Security-Class Corresp and Rpts, RG 165, NARA.

the initial idea of which was taken from observation of the American police patrol car."[127] The Germans also believed that radio communications would enable attacking tanks to be assigned consecutive objectives without reassembling at preset locations, thereby maintaining the momentum of the tank assault.[128]

General Guderian

Radio usage complemented an existing command emphasis on brevity, simplicity, and clarity.[129] One American *Kriegsakademie* graduate attributed German command efficiency to the quality of the training received by commissioned and noncommissioned officers. He considered the German emphasis on the rapid generation and implementation of commands "the antithesis of our tactical instruction at Leavenworth."[130]

The German command emphasis on rapid, aggressive action required commanders of tank units to lead from the front. There, they coordinated the movements of subordinate elements to sustain an attack's momentum and focus.[131] Tank attacks, however, did not consist of headlong rushes on an objective. They embraced fire and movement principles to overcome resistance. Within each battalion, company, and platoon, some tanks always remained stationary to provide covering fire for the advancing vehicles. Hence, the advance of a German tank unit constituted a continual reversal of roles between those tanks ready to fire and those moving forward.[132]

In the design of tanks to implement these tactics, Smith identified three models: a reconnaissance tank, a light battle tank, and a medium battle tank. American officers personally inspected the *Panzerkampfwagen I* and *II*, which fulfilled the reconnaissance and light battle tank roles. Armament included machine guns and a 20-mm. gun, respectively. Smith also obtained information indicating the development of a second light battle tank and a medium battle tank, both carrying heavier armor and

[127] Asst Mil Attaché, Berlin, Rpt no. 14476, sub: Report on German Short Wave Radio Telephone, 22 Jan 36, p. 5, G–2 Information Digest, Military Attaché Reports, vol. 29, AWC Rcds Sec, MHI Archives.

[128] Mil Attaché, Berlin, Rpt no. 15426, 3 Aug 37, pp. 31–34.

[129] Mil Attaché, Berlin, Rpt no. 15292, 18 May 37.

[130] Wedemeyer/Deskis Conversations, sec. 3, pp. 21, 26.

[131] Mil Attaché, Berlin, Rpt no. 15426, 3 Aug 37, pp. 31–34.

[132] Ibid.; Asst Mil Attaché, Berlin, Rpt no. 15831, sub: Germany (Combat): Minor Tactics of German Light Tank Platoon, 28 Mar 38, Crittenberger Papers.

armament. He believed the medium tank would provide fire support to the more numerous light battle tanks.[133]

Initially, *Panzerkampfwagen I* constituted the bulk of Germany's actual tank strength, despite the reported dissatisfaction of German officers and its ongoing replacement by the *Panzerkampfwagen II*. Contrary statements by the German War Ministry notwithstanding, Smith believed the mass production of the *Panzerkampfwagen I* to have been an error stemming from the initial confusion surrounding the panzer division's organization and purpose. However, he acknowledged the training value and practical experience derived from the production and fielding of an estimated fifteen hundred of these vehicles by late 1937.[134]

From the Military Intelligence Division's perspective, whatever mistakes accompanied German tank production, the Germans did not generate the image of utter confusion suggested by the British mechanization efforts. Instead, the German Army appeared to be implementing a clear program of creating a motorized and mechanized army. As early as 1936, Smith observed: "It is the estimate of both attachés following this parade, that in the matter of motor equipment the German Army is today leading the world by a wide margin and that with the exception of the infantry and its immediate supporting artillery, the motor has everywhere replaced the horse."[135]

The appointment of Colonel von Schell as Germany's motorization czar and the announcement of his implementation of a standardized motor vehicle production plan seemed to confirm this perception, especially as Schell had studied mass production techniques in the United States. Evidence of Germany's intent to adopt standard vehicles occurred during a 1939 Berlin automobile show, which featured the Volkswagen, an inexpensive car intended for general public use throughout Germany.[136]

Militarily, in American eyes the panzer division epitomized German motorization and mechanization efforts. Smith considered the panzer division "the most important development (from an organizational standpoint) of the entire German rearmament program." It had become "a unique organization, without exact or even close parallel in other European countries." Its uniqueness, however, prevented easy resolution of questions concerning its ability to transform German theories of armored warfare into reality.[137]

Germany's 1938 annexation of Austria underscored concerns about the panzer division's effectiveness and the mechanical reliability of its vehicles. *The New York Times* reported the widespread breakdown of German tanks and related traffic jams. The article attributed these problems to Germany's lack of tank experience. Information received by the Military Intelligence Division also included disparaging

---

[133] Mil Attaché, Berlin, Rpt nos. 15426, 3 Aug 37, pp. 9–22, and 15596, 24 Nov 37, pp. 6–8.

[134] Mil Attaché, Berlin, Rpt no. 15596, 24 Nov 37, p. 4.

[135] Mil Attaché, Berlin, Rpt no. 14664, sub: Report on Parade of German Army for Hitler's Birthday, 24 Apr 36, p. 14, G–2 Information Digest, Military Attaché Reports, vol. 34, AWC Rcds Sec, MHI Archives.

[136] Mil Attaché, Berlin, Rpt no. 16554, 1 Apr 39; T. Smith, "Facts of Life," pp. 86–87.

[137] Mil Attaché, Berlin, Rpt no. 15596, 24 Nov 37, p. 3.

appraisals of German organization and the "paper-mache quality of German arms" according to the Czechoslovakian General Staff.[138] Information obtained from the British also indicated a high rate of mechanical failure.[139] These reports suggested that German mechanized combat units were little better than those of rival nations.

The American military attaché to Germany disagreed with these reports. At least one American witness to the *2d Panzer Division*'s crossing of the Austrian border found no evidence of widespread breakdowns. Citing numerous errors, Smith dismissed the article in *The New York Times* as being of a "propagandist nature and so inaccurate that it should be given no weight whatsoever in G–2." He considered the 350-mile march of the German tanks—a distance greater than the operating radius intended for the tanks—a creditable achievement unmarred by the estimated 7 percent breakdown rate. He believed the ability of the *2d Panzer Division* to commence operations rapidly without advance notice indicative of the formation's efficiency and effectiveness. He also noted that the vehicles used in the operation were not afterward withdrawn from service for major overhauls.[140] Subsequent analysis by Hanson W. Baldwin, military and naval correspondent for *The New York Times*, corroborated Smith's conclusions.[141]

Germany's annexation of Austria and the occupation of the Sudetenland and subsequently Czechoslovakia reinforced what American intelligence considered to be the German Army's growing devotion to the motor vehicle. Further validation of this belief occurred with the incorporation of Austrian motorized units into the German Army and the acquisition of the automotive industries of Czechoslovakia—including the tank production plant at Skoda.[142]

World Mechanization

In addition to Britain, France, and Germany, the Military Intelligence Division acquired information concerning mechanized developments in the Soviet Union, Japan, and Italy. Although these nations were major military powers, their use of motor vehicles exerted little influence on the U.S. Army. The extent of Soviet mechanization and the emergence of Soviet Deep Battle concepts in the interwar period remained largely unnoticed by the Military Intelligence Division, primarily because of the difficulty of acquiring reliable information concerning the Red Army and the inferior quality associated with it.

---

138 Memo, XO, G–2, Lt Col C. M. Busbee to Exec, Ofc of the Asst Secretary of War, sub: Efficiency of Tanks in German Occupation of Austria, 13 May 38, Encls 2 and 3, MID Corresp, 1917–1941, Security-Class Corresp and Rpts, RG 165, NARA.

139 Memo, Lt Col Raymond E. Lee to ACS, G–2, no. 39562, sub: Deficiencies of German Tanks, 23 Jul 38, MID Corresp, 1917–1941, Security-Class Corresp and Rpts, RG 165, NARA.

140 1st End, Maj Truman Smith to ACS, G–2, no. D–15941, 31 May 38, MID Corresp, 1917–1941, Security-Class Corresp and Rpts, RG 165, NARA; Memo, Lt Col Willis D. Crittenberger, sub: German Mechanization, 15 Jul 38, Crittenberger Papers.

141 Ltr, Hanson W. Baldwin to Capt G. W. West, 8 Jul 38, Crittenberger Papers.

142 Mil Attaché, Berlin, Rpt nos. 15962, 15 Jun 38, and 16554, 1 Apr 39; T. Smith, "Facts of Life," pp. 86–87.

The assistant chief of staff, G–2, Colonel McCabe, considered the status of military intelligence concerning the Red Army poor and unlikely to improve. He believed foreign military attachés constituted the best information source on Russian military developments. One American military attaché to the Soviet Union found the Swedish, German, Italian, Turkish, and Japanese attachés to be the most reliable.[143] Responding to the suggestion that additional information might be obtained from the Soviet military attaché to the United States, McCabe commented: "Every now and then you can get something. Once in a while a Russian comes in, but he always looks a little jittery to me, after one of those purges and I always size him up that he is a little scared, and I never ask him whether he thought he was going to be shot, but have been almost on the verge of it."[144]

The dearth of reliable information and the skeptical attitude of American officers toward the Red Army ensured the absence of a Soviet influence on U.S. Army mechanized development. The Military Intelligence Division considered the Soviet Union incapable of formulating innovative tank designs and dependent on buying the patent rights to foreign tanks as it had with the Christie tank. The capabilities of Soviet officers were considered inferior to their Western counterparts; after the purges of 1937–1938, the Red Army was considered incapable of sustaining operations beyond either six months or a major defeat.[145]

During the Soviet Union's border conflict with Japan in 1938, one officer, who had recently returned from traveling along the Trans-Siberian Railroad, concluded that the Red Army faced a greater threat from its own supply services than it did from the Imperial Japanese Army. A Soviet pronouncement of its intent to expand motorization and mechanization throughout the Red Army was "to be interpreted as conformity with the present national trend of worship of industry and mechanization rather than as evidence of sound tactical doctrine."[146] Maneuver reports noting French tank officers serving with Soviet tank units, the obsolescence of Soviet tank models, and horse cavalry attacks with sabers against tanks seemed to confirm the image of Red Army ineffectiveness.[147]

---

[143] McCabe Discussion Notes, 4 Jan 38, pp. 5–6, and 4 Jan 39, p. 14; Yeaton, "Memoirs," pp. 17, 25.

[144] McCabe Discussion Notes, 4 Jan 38, p. 7.

[145] MID, Intel Sum no. 33, 24 Dec 37, p. 16589; Committee 3, Rpt Synopsis, sub: Survey—Union of Soviet Socialist Republics, 22 Jan 37, File 2–1937–3, AWC Curricular Archives; Memo, McCabe to Ch of Cav, 29 Jul 38, p. 22; Memo, McCabe to DCS, 25 Oct 37.

[146] Ltr, Lt Col C. M. Busbee to Col Innis P. Swift, 4 Oct 37, quote from p. 4, MID Corresp, 1917–1941, Security-Class Corresp and Rpts, RG 165, NARA; McCabe Discussion Notes, 4 Jan 38, p. 13.

[147] MID, WDGS, Intel Sum no. 33, 24 Dec 37, p. 16589. In "Observing the Soviets: U.S. Army Attachés in Eastern Europe During the 1930s," *The Journal of Military History* LV, no. 2 (April 1991): 153–83, David M. Glantz argues that American military attachés in the Baltic States and the Soviet Union acquired accurate information concerning the Red Army, particularly the development of mechanized doctrine and mechanization throughout the military. While this may actually have been the case, there seems little evidence suggesting that either the Military Intelligence Division or the U.S. Army placed much credence in this information in general. Indeed, while serving in the Soviet Union, Capt. Ivan Yeaton believed that because of the reports he submitted he was "blackballed" by the White House and the British, whose reports contradicted his. Thus the intelligence value of his

The Military Intelligence Division also obtained some information on Japanese tank units but noted the absence of any clearly defined doctrine in their use. Japanese tank tactics appeared to be in an experimental state. In 1937 Japan invaded China, triggering the start of the Second Sino-Japanese War. During the military operations that followed, the absence of effective Chinese antitank measures led American military intelligence to attach little significance to Japanese tank actions. Organized into battalions for detached service with infantry divisions, Japanese tanks appeared incapable of functioning independently, and Japanese mechanized development seemed to lag behind that of the United States.[148]

From the Military Intelligence Division's perspective, Italian mechanization and motorization efforts surpassed those of Japan but did not match those of Britain, France, and Germany. Italian tank organization included independent tank regiments of multiple tank battalions primarily for infantry support and exploitation missions, as well as the inclusion of light tanks within both cavalry and motorized infantry divisions. Large tank formations appeared nonexistent, though the Military Intelligence Division noted the creation of motorized infantry divisions intended for an exploitation role.[149] Like other European armies, however, the Italians made use of motorcycle units. During Italy's occupation of Albania, motorcycle units preceded advancing formations, providing a broad reconnaissance screen that pinpointed resistance for following elements to eliminate.[150]

The Military Intelligence Division did not consider Italy's war in Ethiopia a modern conflict between belligerents possessing similar war capacities. This perception, as well as the rugged terrain of the operational theater, resulted in the conflict's categorization as a special case from which few lessons could be drawn. Yet the Military Intelligence Division did note with interest the Italian use of independently operating motorized columns, the reliance on motor vehicles for supply purposes, and the close cooperation between air and ground elements in attack and pursuit operations. Similarly, it considered worthy of further study the Italian use of aircraft for the sustained supply of combat units.[151]

Italian tanks in Ethiopia merited less consideration. The small, light Fiat tanks proved unsuited to the terrain. Ethiopian soldiers would clamber onto them, bend their machine-gun armament, and burn the tanks. Their poor visibility so interfered

---

information—and that of other American attachés in the Soviet Union—remained limited and did not influence American mechanization efforts. See Yeaton, "Memoirs," p. 2.

[148] Mil Attaché, Tokyo, Rpt no. 9653, sub: Minor Military Operations, Employment of Tanks and Motorized Units," n.d., Crittenberger Papers; Memo, McCabe to Ch of Cav, 29 Jul 38, p. 19.

[149] Van Voorhis, "Mechanization," 29 Sep 38, p. 32; Memo, McCabe to Ch of Cav, 29 Jul 38, p. 16.

[150] Subcommittee no. 1, Committee no. 5, Suppl no. 4 to Rpt of Committee no. 5, sub: Mechanization, Defense Against Mechanization and Against Aviation, 10 Oct 39, p. 7, File 3–1940–5, AWC Curricular Archives.

[151] MID, WDGS, Intel Sum no. 31, 15 Nov 35, p. 15459, Reel 5 of *U.S. Military Intelligence Reports*; MID, WDGS, Intel Sum no. 33, 14 May 37, pp. 16174–16178; Subcommittee no. 1, Committee no. 5, Suppl no. 4 to Rpt of Committee no. 5, 10 Oct 39, p. 7.

Review of Russian armored fighting vehicles used to equip the Republican Populist Army during the Spanish Civil War

with control efforts that commanders of tank units began directing tank operations on foot. High losses among tank commanders resulted.[152]

Nor did Italian mechanized operations in Spain prove an unqualified success. American intelligence noted the Italian reliance on light, fast tanks with limited armor protection and armament. The reported weakness of Italian tank tracks increased the incidence of breakdowns, especially on extended road marches. The failure of these tanks to fulfill expectations in Spain resulted in the disillusionment of some Italian officers, who believed that only equipping them with flamethrowers would redeem their combat value.[153]

Italian doctrine emphasizing the employment of motorized and mechanized units to exploit a breach of the enemy's defenses also came into question following the disaster of Guadalajara in March 1937. Advancing in pursuit of Republican forces, Italian tank and motorized infantry became separated from supporting infantry and artillery. Control of the advance disintegrated. Under sustained Republican counterattacks—especially in the air—the pursuit became a disastrous Italian rout.[154] This defeat discouraged the Italians from employing mobile elements in independent

[152] Memo, McCabe to Ch of Cav, 29 Jul 38, p. 17; MID, Intel Sum no. 33, 14 May 37, p. 16177; Van Voorhis, "Mechanization," 29 Sep 38, p. 32.

[153] Memo, McCabe to Ch of Cav, 29 Jul 38, p. 15; Van Voorhis, "Mechanization," 29 Sep 38, p. 32; Emilio Canevari, "Forecasts from the War in Spain: Lessons Based on Technical and Tactical Experience," *Army Ordnance* XVIII, no. 107 (March-April 1938): 275.

[154] MID, Intel Sum no. 33, 12 Nov 37, p. 16472.

Russian T26B light tank serving with the Populists in the Spanish Civil War

operations. Consequently, Italian tank employment focused predominantly on Infantry support missions.

To the Military Intelligence Division, the Spanish Civil War of 1936–1939 did not represent a viable model for the evaluation of tactical principles for employing mechanized units because of the terrain and the civil nature of the conflict. Poorly trained Spanish tank crews among the Republicans and Nationalists proved undisciplined and prone to attacking heavily defended positions equipped with antitank weapons. Tank attacks occurred with little prior reconnaissance and without coordination with supporting infantry and artillery. Too often tanks made themselves vulnerable to destruction by moving alone through village streets or remaining on roads; and in general the tank tactics appeared incorrect. Aware of these developments, the Military Intelligence Division considered tank operations in the Spanish Civil War a disappointment. They did not appear to prove or disprove any of the existing, conflicting theories regarding the employment of tanks.[155]

[155] Ibid., p. 16472; Memo, McCabe to Ch of Cav, 29 Jul 38, pp. 26–27. In fact, the Military Intelligence Division was not entirely correct. The Spanish Civil War demonstrated the effectiveness of antitank guns. Since no armored divisions or corps were used in this conflict, no conclusions regarding their viability could be offered. However, those tank operations performed clearly indicated the importance of supporting tanks with infantry and artillery. This was the conclusion of the U.S. Infantry and was corroborated by the repeated destruction of groups of tanks that simply charged enemy positions. Isolated and unsupported, these tank units became victims of a variety of antitank means, including Molotov cocktails. Spanish tank crews did, however, prove difficult to train and were not as efficient as those of the major military powers. For information on tank operations in the Spanish Civil War,

The Military Intelligence Division's intelligence assessments of foreign mechanized development, however, permitted the identification of two principal themes concerning the employment of tanks. First, a refinement of concepts introduced in World War I emphasized the use of tanks as infantry support weapons and in the traditional role of cavalry. Second, the concentration of mechanized and motorized combat elements under centralized control for independent operations to enable rapid, strategic decisions. French mechanized development represented the first, while the evolution of the German panzer division symbolized the second trend and epitomized Germany's desire for a rapid war of maneuver. The organizational and tactical ideas inherent in the panzer division, however, remained untested theories. Their departure from more familiar developments in France and Germany's relative lack of experience with tank operations created a degree a skepticism concerning the viability of German mechanized doctrine. Conversely, France's dominant military position throughout much of the interwar period and the clear logic of its national defense policies encouraged greater credence in its mechanized development pattern. By the late 1930s only British mechanized development seemed capable of rivaling that of the French and Germans; but Britain's previous leadership in the field appeared to have dissipated into personality conflicts, administrative confusion, and doctrinal uncertainty.

The diametric opposition of French and German mechanized tactics, organization, and doctrine manifested itself in the files of the Military Intelligence Division. This conceptual divergence found parallel in the doctrinal duality inherent in *A Manual for the Commanders of Large Units (Provisional)* and the field service regulations. This duality also existed in the divergent development trends of the Infantry's tank units and the mechanized cavalry. It epitomized the U.S. Army's uncertainty concerning the appropriate tactical and organizational principles to adopt. Infantry tanks bore a resemblance to French tank units, whereas the tactical versatility and organizational flexibility of the 7th Cavalry Brigade (Mechanized) inspired greater interest in the panzer division. The untested nature of the ideas incorporated in the panzer division's composition and method of operation compared to the twenty years of experience embodied in French mechanized units, however, made evaluation of the relative efficacy of French and German doctrinal principles—and a resolution to the U.S. Army's duality of doctrine—difficult before the outbreak of war.

---

see Charles Messenger, *The Blitzkrieg Story* (New York: Charles Scribner's Sons, 1976), pp. 103–04, 122–23; Kenneth Macksey, *Tank Warfare: A History of Tanks in Battle* (New York: Stein and Day, 1972), pp. 95–96.

6

CAVALRY AT THE CROSSROADS

The years 1936–1939 marked the emergence of the mechanized cavalry into a viable combat force built on increasingly sophisticated organizational and doctrinal concepts. Moreover, these principles reflected less untested theory than experience obtained through maneuvers and tactical exercises. They were also encouraged by analysis of developments in other countries, especially Germany. The evolution of the mechanized cavalry, however, led to its growing divergence from the horse cavalry. By 1939, with tensions building in Europe, the chief of Cavalry proposed a large-scale restructuring of the Cavalry to increase combat readiness and more closely align its mechanized and nonmechanized components. Through this proposal, the chief of Cavalry sought to highlight the problems facing his branch and force a resolution.

Mechanized Cavalry Development, 1936–1939

After the Second Army maneuvers, the 7th Cavalry Brigade (Mechanized) continued its transformation from an untested novelty in the Army's inventory to an organization with discernible form, purpose, and operational technique. In addition to the tactical and organizational principles developed since 1931, the arrival of the 13th Cavalry Regiment (Mechanized) on Fort Knox marked a significant increase in the potential combat power of the 7th Cavalry Brigade. It now included two mechanized cavalry regiments and one mechanized artillery battalion.

In September 1936 the 13th Cavalry Regiment (Mechanized), Col. Charles L. Scott commanding, arrived at Fort Knox. The unit brought an influx of new personnel and their dependants that strained the post's infrastructure and intensified an existing housing shortage. The regiment required its own garages and facilities for maintenance and training, but none of these structures existed. Possessing few funds for new construction, unit personnel opted to build their own facilities. Such initiative, however, could not overcome the lack of equipment and training materials.[1]

Initially, the new regiment also posed challenges for the 7th Cavalry Brigade (Mechanized). The brigade headquarters included only a skeleton staff, initially

[1] Ltrs, Col Charles L. Scott to Maj Robert W. Grow, 12 Sep 36, 23 Sep 36, both in Ofc of the Ch of Cav, Gen Corresp, Record Group (RG) 177, National Archives and Records Administration (NARA).

New construction continued at Fort Knox throughout the 1930s. In this 1938 photograph, the post headquarters is seen in the back right, next to the newly built theater.

activated to provide command oversight for a single regiment. It soon became responsible for post management, new construction, and the supervision of all Civilian Conservation Corps (CCC) activities in the V Corps Area. Headquarters personnel also served on technical boards, participated in training activities, and supervised maintenance work. The arrival of the 13th Cavalry Regiment further involved them in the establishment of the unit's training facilities. Despite this range of responsibilities, recommendations to increase the size of the brigade headquarters remained unfulfilled.[2]

The small size of the brigade headquarters limited the extent to which it could offset officer shortages at the regimental level. This shortfall particularly affected the 13th Cavalry Regiment, since many of its personnel were unfamiliar with mechanized cavalry operations. However, the new regiment benefited from the presence of many graduates of the Motor Transport School and the Signal School. These soldiers constituted a cadre of experienced technicians further augmented by the transfer of radio operators and mechanics from the 1st Cavalry Regiment (Mechanized). Nevertheless, certain technical skills remained in short supply. As late as 1938 combat vehicle crews were being stripped to provide additional radio operators throughout the regiment.[3]

In addition to personnel shortages, Scott encountered difficulty in obtaining equipment for his soldiers. He suspected the 1st Cavalry Regiment (Mechanized)

---

[2] Ltr, Scott to Grow, 12 Sep 36; Ltr, Col Charles L. Scott to Maj Robert W. Grow, 22 Oct 36, Ofc of the Ch of Cav, Gen Corresp, RG 177, NARA.

[3] Ltrs, Scott to Grow, 12 Sep 36, 23 Sep 36, 22 Oct 36; Ltr, Col Charles L. Scott to Maj Robert W. Grow, 3 Feb 38, Ofc of the Ch of Cav, Gen Corresp, RG 177, NARA.

of absorbing equipment intended for both regiments and passing obsolete items to the 13th Cavalry Regiment (Mechanized). He took preventive measures, but he still could not satisfy his equipment needs. Many basic items remained under development, including helmets and goggles for combat car crews.[4]

The 13th Cavalry Regiment also lacked vehicles. Efforts failed to secure sufficient funds to acquire the unit's entire vehicle set within one year and to increase the priority given to combat car deliveries.[5] The shortage of vehicles resulted from the acquisition practices in effect throughout the interwar era. The Army could not afford to mass-produce materiel subsequently considered unsatisfactory or quickly rendered obsolete. Therefore, it sought high-quality prototypes to facilitate mass production in the event of a national emergency. This approach ensured the availability of effective materiel when the nation undertook preparations for war in 1940–1941. However, limited production runs and slow deliveries of new equipment did little for combat readiness in the interim.[6]

Mechanized cavalry scout-car development reflected the impact of Army acquisition policies. The mechanized cavalry and the Ordnance Department worked together to establish desired characteristics for a prototype model that became the subject of extensive testing. The test results then prompted modifications and the construction of a new prototype, followed by another round of tests. This cycle continued until the mechanized cavalry and Ordnance Department deemed the vehicle ready for limited production in 1938. By then eight different scout-car models had been developed.[7]

Congressional legislation mandating the distribution of War Department contracts among multiple manufacturers also slowed this process. Each successive scout-car prototype thus became the responsibility of a different company. To ensure some degree of continuity, mechanized cavalry officers strove to provide each new manufacturer with the latest prototype for use as a guide. However, such action required a series of administrative actions involving the Ordnance Department, the 7th Cavalry Brigade (Mechanized), the chief of Cavalry, and the adjutant general to secure funding and authorization. The complexity of this process reflected the

---

[4] Ltr, Scott to Grow, 12 Sep 36; Ltr, Col Charles L. Scott to Robert W. Grow, 29 Mar 37, Ofc of the Ch of Cav, Gen Corresp, RG 177, NARA.

[5] Ltrs, Scott to Grow, 23 Sep 36, 22 Oct 36; Robert W. Grow, "The Ten Lean Years: From the Mechanized Force to the Armored Force (1940)," p. 67, Robert W. Grow Papers, U.S. Army Military History Institute (MHI) Archives, Carlisle Barracks, Pa.

[6] For example, although John C. Garand began work on designing a semiautomatic rifle for the Army in 1919, not until 1936 did the M1 Garand rifle become standardized, due to the Army's complex development and testing procedures. Constance McLaughlin Green, Harry C. Thomson, and Peter C. Roots, *The Ordnance Department: Planning Munitions for War*, U.S. Army in World War II (Washington, D.C.: Office of the Chief of Military History, 1955), pp. 175–77.

[7] Ltr, Col Charles L. Scott to Maj Robert W. Grow, 1 Mar 37, Ofc of the Ch of Cav, Gen Corresp, RG 177, NARA; Ltr, Scott to Grow, 3 Feb 38; Daniel Van Voorhis, "Mechanization," Lecture at Army War College (AWC), 29 Sep 38, p. 6, in Army War College Lectures, 1938–1939, pt. 1, AWC Curricular Archives, MHI Archives.

Army's efforts to avoid allegations of favoritism in the fulfillment of a War Department contract, but it did not encourage rapid action.[8]

Scout-car development also became influenced by the vehicle's performance compared to the armored car. Both wheeled vehicles possessed similar mobility, but the latter carried greater armor protection due to its intended use in distant reconnaissance missions. The poor experience of Italian tanks with restricted visibility in Ethiopia, however, suggested that the better visibility and field of fire of the open-topped scout car made it more suitable for reconnaissance. The War Department thus supported scout-car development and production, but its enthusiasm led to unsolicited alteration of cavalry tables of organization incorporating the scout car.[9]

Aside from the delays in receiving new vehicles, the mechanized cavalry faced another problem. War Department budgets did not include any provision for vehicle replacement. Consequently, the Army's vehicle fleet gradually deteriorated over time. Lobby efforts by the Cavalry proved only partially successful. The 1939 budget finally included funds to replace worn-out armored cars and halftracks in the 1st Cavalry Regiment (Mechanized), but a similar provision for combat cars was not anticipated until 1941.[10]

Mechanized cavalry trucks proved in far worse shape than combat vehicles. Trucks performed a number of critical support and maintenance functions, but their numbers were insufficient. Moreover, many of those in use were antiquated and parts for them no longer produced, necessitating the dispatch of teams to scour automobile junkyards. The small numbers of trucks available and the difficulty associated with maintaining the obsolescent fleet led the 13th Cavalry Regiment commander to consider his unit unfit for operations beyond the immediate vicinity of Fort Knox.[11]

The gradual cessation of CCC activities released some vehicles for military use. However, mechanized cavalry efforts to secure new vehicles and replace older ones competed with an Army-wide surge in the demand for trucks following the introduction of the triangular division. This formation required far larger numbers of motor vehicles than previous infantry organizations. Hence, the mechanized cavalry proved unable to overcome its truck shortage.[12]

The satisfaction of other equipment needs proved equally frustrating. In 1937 the War Department scheduled tests to determine whether the Thompson submachine gun issued to mechanized cavalry personnel should be replaced with the M1 Garand semiautomatic rifle. Scott considered the Garand unsuitable for combat cars and motorcycles, although he acknowledged its possible use in an open-topped vehicle

---

[8] Ltrs, Maj Robert W. Grow to Col Charles L. Scott, 5 Jan 37, 25 Feb 37, both in Ofc of the Ch of Cav, Gen Corresp, RG 177, NARA; Ltr, Scott to Grow, 1 Mar 37; Daniel R. Beaver, "Politics and Policy: The War Department Motorization and Standardization Program for Wheeled Transport Vehicles, 1920–1940," *Military Affairs* XLVII, 3 (October 1983): 105.

[9] Notes of Discussion Following Lecture of Maj Gen Daniel Van Voorhis at AWC, "Mechanization," 13 Oct 37, p. 2, AWC Curricular Archives (hereafter cited as Van Voorhis Discussion Notes); Grow, "Ten Lean Years," p. 67.

[10] Ltr, Grow to Scott, 25 Feb 37.

[11] Ltr, Scott to Grow, 1 Mar 37.

[12] Ltrs, Grow to Scott, 25 Feb 37, and Scott to Grow, 1 Mar 37.

The gold vault at Fort Knox in 1937

like the scout car. He favored the submachine gun, asserting that the capture of Italian tanks by Ethiopian soldiers could not have occurred had the vehicle crews been equipped with the Thompson.[13]

Similarly, Scott wholeheartedly supported efforts to field the 4.2-inch mortar with the mechanized cavalry. He considered it "*the best smoke and gas weapon we have ever produced.*" His view reflected the general consensus within the 7th Cavalry Brigade (Mechanized). Plans existed to mount the 4.2-inch mortar on a vehicle pending development of a suitable, fully tracked platform.[14] The War Department preferred to equip the mechanized cavalry with the same 81-mm. mortar already in use with the Infantry. Such commonality would reduce the number of different ammunition types in the Army.[15]

Scott characterized the 81-mm. mortar as a "pop gun," but mechanized cavalry officers welcomed a comparative test between the two mortars. They fully expected their preference for the 4.2-inch weapon to be validated because of its greater range and ability to deliver larger smoke concentrations. Throughout 1937 and into the early months of 1938, mortar testing occurred at Fort Knox. In November, however, it was

[13] Ltrs, Grow to Scott, 24 Mar 37, and Scott to Grow, 29 Mar 37.

[14] Ltr, Scott to Grow, 29 Mar 37, quote from p. 2; Ltr, Maj Robert W. Grow to Col Charles L. Scott, 17 Mar 37, p. 1, Ofc of the Ch of Cav, Gen Corresp, RG 177, NARA.

[15] Ltr, Grow to Scott, 17 Mar 37.

the War Department's preference for the 81-mm. mortar that prevailed. After nearly three years of debate the mechanized cavalry finally accepted this weapon.[16]

The mortar's principal role lay in obscuring enemy antitank positions with smoke. A separate weapon was intended to provide general fire support against a broad range of targets. Consequently, mechanized cavalry technical boards devoted considerable energy to the design of a mobile gun. To provide continuous support to the combat cars, this weapon required similar mobility. Therefore, design work embraced a fully tracked, armored chassis and led to efforts to mount a 75-mm. howitzer on an M1 combat car hull. A parallel development included the design of an armored ammunition carrier.[17]

An alternative mount for a mobile gun appeared in the form of the halftrack. This vehicle was already considered for service as an infantry transport. Its mobility surpassed that of a truck, it protected its passengers from small-arms fire, and its open top simplified the engineering required to mount a large-caliber gun. Moreover, the mechanized cavalry was already seeking to replace its truck transports with halftracks. The logic of this solution for a mobile gun, however, could not overcome resistance from the Field Artillery, which considered the development of self-propelled artillery its exclusive responsibility. Lack of funding further hampered halftrack acquisition. Consequently, the development of an effective self-propelled gun and the halftrack became delayed until 1940.[18]

Despite these procurement setbacks, the mechanized cavalry continued to evolve concepts for battlefield maintenance and recovery. In December 1936 representatives from the Office of the Chief of Cavalry, the Signal Corps, the Ordnance Department, and the mechanized cavalry met to discuss maintenance issues. They adopted an echeloned maintenance organization that tiered maintenance responsibility in the mechanized cavalry from the vehicle operators to rear area repair shops. Under this configuration, each successive maintenance echelon to the rear bore responsibility for repairs more comprehensive than its predecessor. Vehicles suffering mechanical difficulty or battle damage were either repaired by the forward echelons or left for the rear echelons to maintain the operational tempo of combat units.[19]

Materiel issues did not prevent training or doctrinal development at Fort Knox. However, in February 1937 the focus of the 7th Cavalry Brigade (Mechanized) temporarily shifted from training to disaster relief. Louisville, Kentucky, suffered extensive damage along its riverfront when the Ohio River flooded. The high waters left much of the city under several feet of water, damaging homes and businesses.

[16] Ibid.; Ltr, Scott to Grow, 29 Mar 37; Grow, "Ten Lean Years," pp. 69–70, 80.

[17] Van Voorhis Discussion Notes, 13 Oct 37, pp. 4, 5–7, and 29 Sep 38, p. 2. Ch of Cav, 3d End, sub: Recommendation for Development of Self-Propelled Artillery, 18 Jan 39, Willis D. Crittenberger Papers, MHI Archives.

[18] Grow, "Ten Lean Years," pp. 68–69; Van Voorhis Discussion Notes, 13 Oct 37, pp. 5–7, 11–12; Green, Thomson, and Roots, *Ordnance Department*, pp. 201–04.

[19] Van Voorhis Discussion Notes, 13 Oct 37, p. 17, and 29 Sep 38, pp. 4–5; Grow, "Ten Lean Years," pp. 68–69.

Downtown Louisville, Kentucky, following severe flooding in 1937

The mechanized cavalry assisted flood victims and prevented looting and in the process received much favorable publicity.[20]

By 1939 the mechanized cavalry had developed an esprit de corps that reflected its growing maturity as a combat organization. It also stimulated rivalry. Mechanized cavalry personnel considered their doctrine and battlefield effectiveness superior to those of infantry tank units. They considered infantry tank organizations too narrowly focused and inferior in both maneuver and communications capabilities. Mechanized cavalry officers believed their tactical organizations superior and the result of greater experience in the actual operation of a mechanized unit.[21]

These views reflected the growing competition between the Infantry and Cavalry in the area of mechanization. The Infantry's development of the partially motorized triangular division greatly increased its need for funding, new equipment, and vehicles at the same time the Cavalry sought additional monies to acquire combat vehicles and equipment for its mechanized component. The personal dimension of this rivalry manifested itself in the eagerness with which mechanized cavalry officers sought to confront infantry tank units in a maneuver setting, convinced that such an event would demonstrate the superiority of the tactics and doctrine developed at Fort Knox.[22]

Mechanized Cavalry Maneuvers, 1937–1938

In July 1937 a series of tactical exercises at Fort Knox pitted horse and mechanized cavalry units against each other in a contest for control of a single crossing site on the Salt River. The mechanized cavalry force included the 1st Cavalry Regiment (Mechanized) and a combat-car squadron from the 13th Cavalry Regiment (Mechanized). The horse cavalry consisted of a National Guard cavalry brigade of two regiments. Each side also included a flight of observation aircraft and attachments from the 68th Field Artillery Regiment (Mechanized). The horse cavalry received scout cars, more radios, and machine guns—additions that soon became standard issue for all horse cavalry regiments. To boost antitank

[20] Grow, "Ten Lean Years," p. 68.

[21] Ltr, Grow to Scott, 5 Jan 37.

[22] Ltr, Brig Gen Adna R. Chaffee to Lt Col Willis D. Crittenberger, 29 Apr 39; Memo, Lt Col Willis D. Crittenberger to Ch of Cav, sub: Extract of Lieutenant Colonel McQuillen's Letter, 20 Jun 39; Inquiry from Ofc of Commandant of Inf Sch Rtd Through Adjutant General's Ofc to Commanding General (CG), 7th Cav Bde (Mech), sub: Use of Prearranged Message Codes, 18 Dec 39, and Handwritten Comment, Lt Col Willis D. Crittenberger; all in Crittenberger Papers.

capability, all .30-caliber machine guns in the horse regiments were treated as .50-caliber weapons.[23]

Reconnaissance units and aircraft led the advance of each force. Anticipating ambushes, the mechanized cavalry integrated its combat-car and machine-gun elements. The latter possessed a dismounted capability and better visibility in the close, wooded terrain. Conversely, the horse cavalry used its scout cars to locate and track the movement of the hostile combat cars and adjusted its dispositions to counter likely actions of the mechanized cavalry.[24]

The horse cavalry reached the crossing site first and prepared a defensive perimeter. In response the mechanized cavalry launched a series of coordinated attacks, relying on smoke to blind enemy antitank positions and observation points. The execution of these attacks required time. When the maneuver terminated, the mechanized cavalry remained over two miles from the crossing site and faced a difficult fight through rugged terrain.[25]

This outcome owed much to Brig. Gen. Newell C. Bolton, commanding the National Guard cavalry. In preparation for the maneuvers, he had issued special instructions to counter the combat cars of the mechanized cavalry. He formed antitank teams around his .50-caliber machine guns and tasked them with harrying and obstructing combat-car operations. Horse cavalry units were directed to exploit terrain and natural cover to avoid detection until they were poised to strike against the unarmored elements of the mechanized cavalry. Consequently, the horse cavalry remained in wooded terrain and ravines throughout the maneuvers. Only once did mechanized cavalry overrun horse cavalry. Most of the horse cavalry remained concealed in woods near the crossing site, their presence unreported by the mechanized cavalry.[26]

Bolton's tactics reflected the horse cavalry's ability to adapt to changing battlefield conditions. However, its effectiveness at Fort Knox obscured the horse cavalry's growing dependence on favorable terrain in which to operate against mechanized units. Bolton's antitank scheme similarly depended on antitank weapons easily concealed and moveable. The .50-caliber machine gun suited this role and did not compromise the horse's tactical mobility. In 1937 the Army considered the .50-caliber machine gun capable of defeating most combat vehicles it was likely to encounter. The horse cavalry faced a challenge if a heavier, less easily transported antitank weapon became necessary.

The 7th Cavalry Brigade was criticized for possessing too many radios and relying too much on this medium of communication. However, the mechanized cavalry found the radio an effective means of battlefield coordination. It saved time

[23] Willis D. Crittenberger, "Cavalry Maneuvers at Fort Knox," *Cavalry Journal* XLVI, no. 5 (September-October 1937): 420.

[24] Ibid., p. 421.

[25] Ibid., pp. 421–24.

[26] Ibid., pp. 423–24. It is possible that these instructions reflected the influence of Colonel Scott, who acted as adviser to General Bolton. Scott's previous experience commanding the 2d Cavalry Regiment stationed at Fort Riley prior to assuming command of the 13th Cavalry (Mechanized) would have made such a contribution logical.

otherwise spent writing and distributing orders, and it permitted the rapid movement of separated combat elements toward a common objective. Consequently, the mechanized cavalry sustained a steady momentum throughout the maneuvers, despite the rugged terrain, innovative antitank tactics, and the horse cavalry's efforts to remain concealed. Through its combination of firepower, mobility, and effective command and control, the mechanized cavalry forced a change in horse cavalry tactics, represented by General Bolton's pre-maneuver instructions.[27]

Mechanized cavalry officers also derived satisfaction from the comments of Col. Adolf von Schell, who visited Fort Knox in July. Schell, a German officer who would later direct his nation's motorization efforts, noted similarities between the tactics applied by the mechanized cavalry and German tank units to overcome antitank positions. He also expressed praise for the latest combat car models.[28]

While German doctrine did not rule out the use of tanks in an antitank role, mechanized cavalry doctrine discouraged such activity. Commanding the 7th Cavalry Brigade (Mechanized) during the maneuver, Col. Bruce Palmer identified the battlefield priorities of the combat car as "primarily purposed to destroy or hamper the movements of hostile personnel (including the crews of anti-tank weapons), and secondarily, to resist or overcome opposing mechanization."[29] Subsequent descriptions of the combat car's purpose stressed antipersonnel rather than antitank capability. Brig. Gen. Daniel Van Voorhis, the normal 7th Cavalry Brigade (Mechanized) commander, rejected suggestions to increase combat-car armor and armament. He believed that only misuse of the vehicle in noncavalry roles would necessitate such changes.[30]

The cavalry mission did not include sustained engagements with hostile tanks. In command post and field exercises the mechanized cavalry secured its most significant results against rear area and nonmechanized forces. This employment became embedded in the doctrine governing combat-car action. The defeat of enemy tanks received little attention, despite their likely use in a counterattack role against the mechanized cavalry.

In May 1938 the 7th Cavalry Brigade (Mechanized) embarked on a tactical march to and from Fort Oglethorpe, Georgia, to test new materiel and marching techniques. The mechanized cavalry formed into two columns moving on parallel routes through Kentucky, Tennessee, and Georgia. Reconnaissance elements preceded the advance and screened the flanks of the columns while radio assisted communications between the marching columns. From an aircraft, General Van Voorhis observed and controlled the movements of the brigade in the first incidence of aerial leadership of the 7th Cavalry Brigade. Air-ground communication occurred through radio and airdropped messages recovered by motorcycle couriers.[31]

---

[27] Van Voorhis Discussion Notes, 13 Oct 37, pp. 8, 9–11.

[28] Memo, Lt Col Willis D. Crittenberger to CG, Fort Knox, 30 Jul 37, Crittenberger Papers.

[29] Crittenberger, "Cavalry Maneuvers at Fort Knox," p. 425.

[30] Van Voorhis, "Mechanization," 13 Oct 37, p. 8; Van Voorhis Discussion Notes, 13 Oct 37, p. 14.

[31] Van Voorhis, "Mechanization," 29 Sep 38, p. 19; "The Mechanized Cavalry Takes the Field," *Cavalry Journal* XLVII, no. 4 (July-August 1938): 291, 296.

General Van Voorhis (*third from left*) assumes command of the 7th Cavalry Brigade (Mechanized).

Mechanized cavalry organizations expected to operate as a collection of dispersed tactical columns. The attachment of observation aircraft, therefore, offered a number of advantages. During the road march, aircraft monitored and coordinated ground movements, and they identified potential obstacles in advance of the columns. These uses were considered an ideal form of air-ground liaison. Communication between the aircraft and ground units occurred via a combination of radio, air-dropped messages, and visual signals. Observers appreciated the ability to transmit information without relying exclusively on radios, which proved mechanically frail and prone to interception.[32]

However, radios were widely used throughout the road march. During the return to Kentucky, aircraft and ground reconnaissance vehicles sent a steady stream of information via radio to the 7th Cavalry Brigade (Mechanized) headquarters. This information permitted the latter to plan en route a mock assault on the 10th Infantry Brigade at Fort Knox. The mechanized cavalry then conducted a 150-mile night march onto the installation, concentrated, and executed a morning attack on the infantry. In the process, the mechanized cavalry demonstrated its ability to conduct continuous operations and to transition quickly from a road

[32] Anon, "Mechanized Cavalry Takes the Field," pp. 291, 296–97, 299, 300.

march to combat operations. The ensuing battle ended with the mechanized cavalry converging in the infantry rear area poised for further attacks.[33]

These operations underscored the importance of vehicle maintenance. Despite the long hours of vehicle use and the high roundtrip mileage, only two vehicles failed to complete the entire road march to and from Fort Oglethorpe.[34] American officers favorably contrasted their own experience with that of the German Army in Austria by asserting that "it is doubted that the mechanized elements, engaged on an advance of less than half the distance of the march to Fort Oglethorpe and return, bettered the record of the 7th Cavalry Brigade of reaching the final objective with 99.97 percent of the vehicular strength with which the march was started."[35]

In October 1938 the 7th Cavalry Brigade marched to Fort Riley, Kansas, where it supported Cavalry School instruction and participated in combined maneuvers with horse cavalry. During the latter, tactical scenarios included combat-car reinforcement of a horse cavalry attack, separate night marches by mechanized and horse cavalry followed by a coordinated daylight attack, and delaying actions against infantry and motorized units. Aircraft also participated, conducting ground attacks in conjunction with both mechanized and horse cavalries.[36]

These maneuvers demonstrated the difficulty of coordinating horse and mechanized cavalries. In addition to the mobility difference between each cavalry type, radio communications proved problematic. Technical failures and inadequate radio support in the horse cavalry hindered the smooth flow of information and command guidance. Frustration made some horse cavalry officers critical of the radio-based communications network advocated by the mechanized cavalry.[37]

Only one scenario pitted the two cavalry types against each other. The final maneuver, set at night, required the horse cavalry to conduct delaying operations against the mechanized cavalry while retreating. In this action, the mechanized cavalry proved unable to track the horse units at night. The latter escaped, established a new defensive position, and placed demolitions on bridges the mechanized cavalry would have to cross.[38]

Analysis of the maneuver experience highlighted the difficulties encountered in the coordination of horse and mechanized cavalries. The chief of Cavalry used these results to strengthen arguments for the permanent stationing of mechanized cavalry at Fort Riley. Through editorial comments published in the *Cavalry Journal*, the chief of Cavalry attributed the coordination difficulties to the inability of both cavalry types to train together. He also recommended further study of branch-wide

---

[33] Ibid., pp. 292–94; Van Voorhis, "Mechanization," 29 Sep 38, p. 19.

[34] Van Voorhis, "Mechanization," 29 Sep 38, pp. 19–20.

[35] "Mechanized Cavalry Takes the Field," p. 295.

[36] Vennard Wilson, "Combined Cavalry Maneuvers," *Cavalry Journal* XLVIII, no. 1 (January-February 1939): 41–51.

[37] Ibid.

[38] Ibid.

command and control techniques to simplify them and reduce the time necessary to transmit and implement orders.[39]

Within the mechanized cavalry, analysis focused on desired organizational changes. These included the addition of a third combat-car squadron within each regiment and a brigade reconnaissance unit to reinforce regimental reconnaissance or serve as the brigade reserve. Additional motorcycles, particularly sidecars, were also considered essential for command and liaison purposes.[40]

However, Brig. Gen. Adna R. Chaffee Jr., the 7th Cavalry Brigade (Mechanized) commander, disagreed with efforts to more closely align horse and mechanized cavalries. In correspondence with Deputy Chief of Staff Brig. Gen. George C. Marshall, Chaffee wrote:

> The period of maneuvers wherein the mechanized Brigade operated in part or in whole in cooperation with the reinforced regiment of horse cavalry was valuable, but it brought out nothing particularly new to us, since we have always felt and known that we can cooperate with horse cavalry if and when we find ourselves in contiguous positions on the battlefield at the same time, but it only served as a further demonstration of the fact that any consideration of brigading or divisioning horse and mechanized elements is faulty organization. You can just as well put a yoke around the tortoise and the hare and expect them to race as a team.[41]

The Cavalry Field Manual of 1938

Maneuver participation by the 7th Cavalry Brigade (Mechanized) demonstrated tactical concepts developed since its creation. These principles found expression in the January 1938 Cavalry field manual, which for the first time in a War Department publication offered detailed doctrinal guidance for the mechanized cavalry.[42] The manual signaled the mechanized cavalry's transition from an experimental organization into one with a clear purpose and method of operation. The unique nature of the vehicle-based mechanized cavalry, however, made its operation significantly different from that of horse units. The manual acknowledged these differences by including separate mechanized and horse sections for every subject addressed. In effect it constituted two manuals, one for each cavalry type.

The mechanized cavalry regiment represented the smallest tactical unit that included combat cars, armored cars, machine gunners, and mortars. (*See Chart 11.*) For

---

[39] Ibid. Editorial comments included in *Cavalry Journal* articles represented the views of the Office of the Chief of Cavalry.

[40] "Report of the March of the Seventh Cavalry Brigade (Mechanized) to and from Fort Riley, Kansas, and Participation in Demonstrations and Maneuvers at Fort Riley, October 3, 1938 to November 5, 1938," pp. 10–11, Ofc of the Ch of Cav, Gen Corresp, RG 177, NARA.

[41] Ltr, Brig Gen Adna R. Chaffee to Deputy Chief of Staff (DCS) Brig Gen George C. Marshall, 17 Nov 38, George C. Marshall Papers, George C. Marshall Library (GCM), Lexington, Va.

[42] War Department (WD), *Cavalry Field Manual*, 3 vols., 1938.

Front, left to right: Chief of Cavalry Maj. Gen. Leon B. Kromer, General Van Voorhis, and Lt. Col. Willis D. Crittenberger

administrative purposes, each of these assets constituted a separate troop or squadron. For tactical operations they merged to form one or more combined-arms teams, each possessing a core of combat cars supported by mortars and a machine-gun unit. The precise composition of each team varied to suit the overall regimental mission and the specific tactical situation. Hence, no prescribed structure for these teams existed. The ability of the regimental headquarters to detach smaller command components facilitated control over them.[43] The combined-arms nature of the mechanized cavalry permitted this organizational flexibility and marked a fundamental break with the Army's emphasis on structuring units by a single function or capability.

The Cavalry field manual described the mechanized cavalry regiment as a combat unit designed to conduct offensive missions. The combat car squadrons symbolized this nature, and their employment constituted the central focus of regimental operations. The combat cars strove to envelop or penetrate enemy positions, and, if successful, conduct an aggressive, relentless pursuit to ensure maximum destruction and disruption of retreating enemy forces. The regiment's combination of combat power and mobility made it suitable for other missions, including flank security,

[43] Ibid., 2: 92–93. See pages 19–20 for discussion of the intended operation of the mechanized cavalry as multiple columns with detachable headquarters elements.

Chart 11–Mechanized Cavalry Regiment, 1938

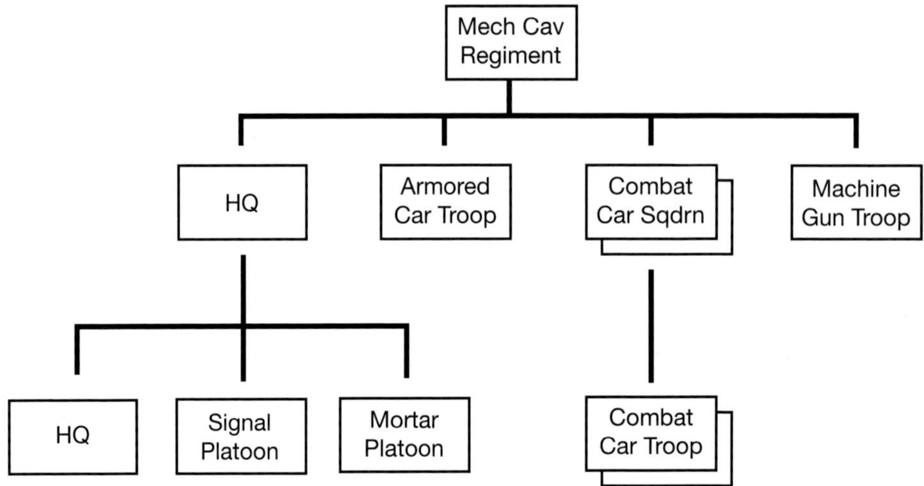

rearguard, and raids against communication and supply lines. The manual also acknowledged the mechanized cavalry's value in defensive operations, particularly counterattacks, although such employment was considered exceptional.[44]

The action of the combat cars predominated in all mechanized cavalry operations. The other regimental assets supported the combat-car squadrons, which represented the unit's principal offensive capability. Combat cars were expected to "crush and smother resistance by their speed, weight, and fire power." Their principal role lay in attacking, but secondary missions included reinforcement of reconnaissance units, rearguard, advance guard, and counterattack. In whatever role, combat cars were expected to work closely with other regimental assets.[45]

In all combat-car activities, the manual stressed the importance of brevity and flexibility in the formulation and implementation of plans of action unlike the careful deliberation taught infantry tank commanders. Combat-car battle formations consisted primarily of echelon, line, and waves, the last reserved for attacks upon positions that could not be outflanked. In combat, dispersal was discouraged, because control derived "through observation of the leader by subordinate commanders."[46]

The armored-car troop provided the information necessary to plan the combat car's action. Generally, this troop operated as a collection of platoons moving in advance of the regiment along parallel routes. These platoons remained separated

[44] WD, *Cavalry Field Manual*, 3: 41, 43, 80–82, 109–10, 133–35.

[45] WD, *Cavalry Field Manual*, 2: 106–12; quote from 3: 80.

[46] Ibid., 2: 107–11.

An M1 combat car of the 1st Cavalry Regiment (Mechanized) in 1938

from the parent regiment by up to one hundred miles, necessitating radio communications and liaison with any supporting aircraft. When contact with enemy units became imminent, the armored cars withdrew to the regiment's flanks and continued to report on enemy actions while simultaneously providing flank security. Secondary roles included interdicting enemy movement, seizing critical terrain in advance of the regiment, and screening friendly actions. The wheeled armored cars, however, generally required a satisfactory road net to achieve maximum effectiveness.[47]

The machine-gun troop and the mortar platoon provided direct support to the combat cars. The former provided fire support, protected exposed flanks, and covered terrain unsuitable for combat-car movement. When the combat cars overran an objective, the machine-gun troop secured it. Defensively, this unit deployed to provide interlocking fires that also provided protection against mechanized attacks. The mortar platoon supported the combat cars with smoke barrages that blinded enemy antitank positions or screened friendly movement. The regiment's tendency to operate as a collection of columns resulted in a mortar unit organized to function either as a single platoon or in sections supporting each combat car squadron.[48]

All action by the mechanized cavalry regiment required effective communications, particularly since the unit was expected to operate as a collection of columns

---

[47] WD, *Cavalry Field Manual*, 2: 94–106; 3: 20, 22, 82.

[48] WD, *Cavalry Field Manual*, 3: 122–23, 129.

over a broad frontage. The strategic mobility of the motor vehicle further increased the potential geographic dispersion of the unit. To sustain communications, the regiment included a communications platoon. The Cavalry field manual also acknowledged the link between sound communications and mission success, but it offered only general guidelines rather than clearly defined operating procedures for the communications platoon. No precise method had yet emerged to coordinate the movement of large numbers of vehicles over a broad area toward common goals. Related foreign developments either proved unsatisfactory or as in the case of Germany were veiled in secrecy.

The mechanized cavalry employed a variety of communication mediums. The use of handheld flags proved the most useful at the platoon level, because only the platoon leader's vehicle possessed a radio. Air-ground communication included the use of colored panels by ground units and messages dropped from aircraft. Other methods, including aircraft-wing signals, pyrotechnics, lights, sound, and semaphores, were all tested. Their dependence on unpredictable atmospheric and weather conditions made them unreliable. Wire communication also proved impractical due to the speed and distances associated with mechanized cavalry operations.[49]

Consequently, the radio, supplemented by motorcycle courier, served as the primary communication medium: "Radio is the means of signal communication which most closely approximates fulfillment of the need of mechanized units for a reliable and flexible agency. It is very fast and is independent of road conditions. The radiotelephone enables commanders to hold personal conversation with their subordinates and superiors."[50]

In the 1930s the radio offered the best means of relaying information quickly over long distances. However, its use was subject to atmospheric interference. The sets themselves were not very robust and prone to damage or breakdown. Moreover, each transmission was considered subject to jamming or interception. These limitations, coupled with the dispersed, fast-paced nature of mechanized cavalry operations, encouraged the adoption of a more flexible and decentralized command style than that taught in Army schools or described in doctrine.

To achieve the fastest rate of information transfer, mechanized cavalry leaders relied on messages transmitted in the clear. They believed the benefits of timely information outweighed the risks associated with enemy interception.[51] Radio transmissions were restricted to short, cryptic messages. To be understood, they had to be placed in the broader context of the regiment's mission and that of each subordinate team.

All commanders in the mechanized cavalry regiment received a detailed briefing outlining the unit's overall mission and the role to be played by each subordinate element.[52] Armed with an understanding of the regiment's objectives and their own specific mission, subordinates were left to determine the best means of accomplishing their tasks: "Since mobility of all elements may result in considerable dispersion,

[49] WD, *Cavalry Field Manual*, 2: 131–33.
[50] Ibid., pp. 133, 143, quote from p. 133.
[51] Ibid., pp. 139, 144–45.
[52] Ibid., p. 134.

Armored car of the 13th Cavalry Regiment (Mechanized)

the greatest possible latitude is given subordinates to accomplish their missions in their own manner under the general plan. This plan must not only be simple, but must be thoroughly understood by all."[53]

The cryptic messages received once operations began made sense against the backdrop of the pre-mission briefing. Without this context, a hostile force that intercepted these messages had to build the situational framework from scratch, a time-consuming process dependent on effective intelligence. However, mechanized cavalry operations emphasized the importance of rapid, continuous action. By moving faster than an enemy could react, the mechanized cavalry sought to disrupt defensive responses. Rapid action also reduced the risk posed by intercepted radio traffic. By the time the meaning of intercepted messages became clear to the enemy, the tactical situation would have changed, making obsolete the information gained.

These measures constituted a command method that decentralized control, exploited the mechanized cavalry's organizational flexibility, and permitted a high operational tempo. Subordinate commanders were expected to rely on their own initiative to accomplish their missions, adjusting their plans as the brief radio updates

---

[53] WD, *Cavalry Field Manual*, 3: 82.

warranted. In this manner, the combined-arms teams, operating under loose regimental control, moved rapidly and independently toward a common objective.

To ensure the timely and continuous flow of information throughout the fast-moving columns, the mechanized cavalry developed a flexible and extensive communications organization. Radio nets, or collections of radios operating on the same frequency, were its basic components. (*Chart 12*) Each net corresponded to a specific tactical organization or headquarters function. A net control station, corresponding to the set of a subunit commander or headquarters staff officer, regulated and monitored radio traffic within each net. The regimental command net included the service and support elements of the regiment and designated sets within the armored car troop and combat-car squadrons. Thus it served as a communications nexus for the regiment. The regimental commander monitored the various nets within his command, interjecting as necessary to provide critical information or guidance. Additional nets were created to communicate with attached aircraft or higher headquarters when the regiment operated as part of a mechanized cavalry brigade.[54]

The net organization developed by the mechanized cavalry mirrored the organizational flexibility of the regiment. As the regiment organized and reorganized subordinate combat teams in response to tactical developments, it similarly altered its net structure.[55] The regiment created additional nets to communicate with attached aircraft or its parent headquarters when employed as part of a brigade. This robust and flexible communications design required large numbers of radio sets that sometimes attracted criticism from other Army organizations. The mechanized cavalry, however, understood the direct correlation between effective communications and mission success. It also emphasized strict radio discipline to prevent the airspace from becoming jammed with simultaneous friendly transmissions.[56]

The mechanized cavalry's reliance on radios to share information and permit decentralized command led it to break with Army regulations governing military communications. These regulations emphasized security and recordkeeping at the expense of rapid information flow. Radio operators, for example, were required to maintain a detailed written record of all incoming and outgoing message traffic. They also had to ensure delivery of their message, relying on couriers if the recipient could not be raised via radio. These messages also required multiple copies to be generated and retained.[57]

Such an orderly procedure ensured complete records of all communications, but no guarantee existed that effective bookkeeping methods would survive initial contact with an enemy. Without providing a solution, the cavalry field manual noted, "Operators are instructed to copy the voice transmission of officers in their logs, but due to the swaying and pitching of the vehicles and the tendency

[54] WD, *Cavalry Field Manual*, 2: 136–39.
[55] Ibid., p. 137.
[56] Van Voorhis, "Mechanization," 13 Oct 37, p. 9; WD, *Cavalry Field Manual*, 2: 137.
[57] WD, *Cavalry Field Manual*, 2: 140–43.

Chart 12—Mechanized Cavalry Regiment Tactical Radio Nets

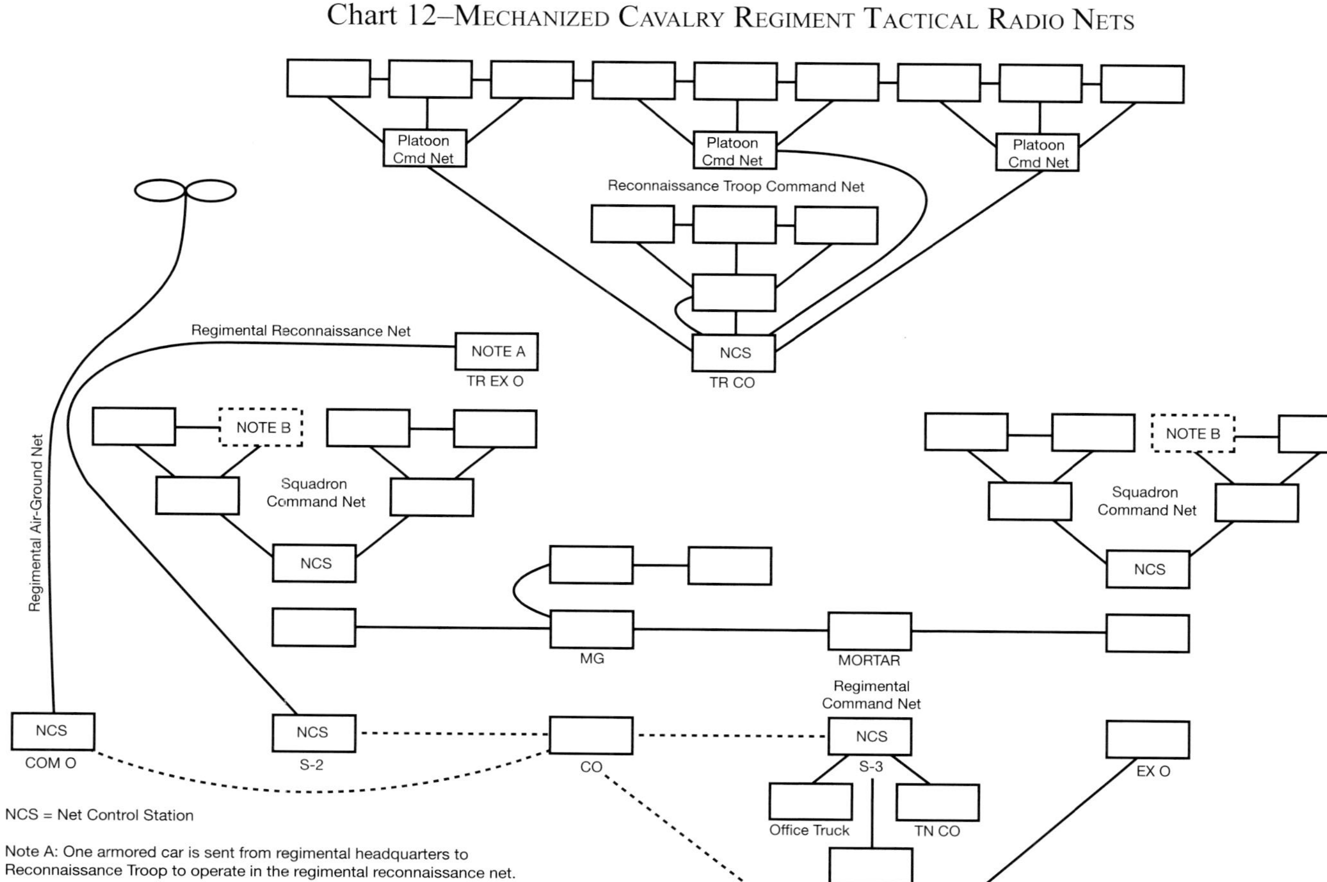

NCS = Net Control Station

Note A: One armored car is sent from regimental headquarters to Reconnaissance Troop to operate in the regimental reconnaissance net.

Note B: Under the present tables of basic allowances, squadron nets can be operated only by taking one platoon car (radio equipped) from one of the troops in each of the squadrons. Otherwise, all squadron, troop, and platoon cars of combat car units operate in the regimental command net.

Source: War Department, *Cavalry Field Manual*, 3 vols., 1938, 2: 139.

of some officers to talk faster than the radio operator can copy, it is difficult to comply with these instructions."[58] The observed difficulty reflected the ongoing transition from traditional written orders and coded messages to oral orders and direct voice communications.

The War Department and Mechanization

In the autumn of 1937 the War Department undertook a review of its mechanization policy. Information provided by Maj. Truman Smith, the military attaché to Germany, prompted this action. He relayed the critical view of American mechanization held by a prominent German officer. The latter considered American tank design unbalanced in favor of speed rather than armor and armament. He also deemed the organization of American mechanization "the very worst possible. Dividing tank responsibility between the Cavalry and the Infantry has led to a wide variety of technical ideas and no clear cut policy of development. He thinks our tank tactics of attaching small numbers of tanks to the Infantry or Cavalry childish." The unnamed German officer recommended consolidation of all tank and antitank units in a single tank corps or the assignment of tank development responsibility to the Cavalry.[59]

Although the Army's bureau system made such a concentration of responsibility unlikely, Chief of Staff General Malin Craig recommended a General Staff study of mechanization.[60] Between October 1937 and April 1938, the G–3 (Operations and Training) Division of the War Department General Staff conducted this study and worked closely with Army organizations to draft a new mechanization directive. During the course of this study, several viewpoints regarding the future development of mechanization were recommended, including the creation of a separate mechanized arm.[61]

Predictably, this proposal was rejected. It posed the same threat to funding, personnel, and stature as the earlier Mechanized Force. Without an increase to the Army's overall budget and size, creation of a central mechanized organization would occur at the expense of the existing branches already laboring under personnel shortfalls, limited budgets, and readiness issues. In 1938 there appeared no pressing need to consolidate mechanized activity.

Yet General Staff members did begin to question the wisdom of decentralized mechanized development. Early drafts of a new War Department directive included the observation: "In endeavoring to apply mechanization to the Army as a whole under this policy, there has resulted a duplication of effort and a misunderstanding of the proper tactical role of the arms equipped with mechanized vehicles."[62] The

[58] Ibid., p. 140.

[59] Memo, Chief of Staff (CS) to Assistant Chief of Staff (ACS), G–3, sub: Tanks, 14 Oct 37, Item 4961, Reel 315, National Archives Project, GCM.

[60] Ibid.

[61] Grow, "Ten Lean Years," p. 71.

[62] Memo, ACS, G–3, Brig Gen George P. Tyner, sub: Policies and Tactical Doctrine on Mechanization," 14 Feb 38, p. 1, Item 4961, Reel 315, National Archives Project, GCM.

General Chaffee (*left*) and Chief of Cavalry Maj. Gen. John K. Herr (*second from left*) at Fort Knox in 1939

removal of this statement from the final version reflected the consensus-building nature of the bureau system.

In April 1938 the War Department issued a new directive to guide subsequent mechanized development. In an effort to reduce duplication of effort, the Infantry and Cavalry Branches were identified as the principal leaders for future mechanized development. However, even this limited centralization of responsibility carried the cautionary note: "This will not be construed as excluding further development of other mechanized materiel needed as an organic part of larger mechanized units."[63] Any expansion of the mechanized cavalry into a division would require the development of mechanized engineer, artillery, and chemical warfare units whose responsibility lay with those branches.

The directive's doctrinal guidance reflected principles already demonstrated in maneuvers and incorporated into the cavalry field manual. It defined the principal influences on mechanized cavalry employment as movement, surprise, and objective. It characterized mechanized cavalry as an offensive weapon, largely unsuited to defensive actions beyond delay missions due to its inability to hold ground once seized. Roles considered appropriate for mechanized cavalry included

[63] Memo, The Adjutant General (TAG), sub: Policies Governing Mechanization, and the Tactical Employment of Mechanized Units, 6 Apr 38, p. 1, Crittenberger Papers.

distant reconnaissance, pursuit, envelopment, and exploitation. In such actions, all mechanized cavalry assets supported the action of the combat car through reconnaissance, fire support, and the seizure of terrain favorable for combat-car attack. As the offensive operations developed, these same assets secured objectives gained and prepared to support the next assault.[64]

In 1935 the War Department's policy statement on mechanization transferred responsibility for mechanized cavalry development from the Cavalry to the V Corps Area commander and referred to the 7th Cavalry Brigade (Mechanized) and attached 68th Field Artillery Regiment (Mechanized) as the Mechanized Force.[65] These actions encouraged the fissure between horse and mechanized cavalries. The new directive did not address administrative responsibility for mechanized cavalry development, thus giving de facto endorsement to the quasi-independent status of the 7th Cavalry Brigade and complicating the chief of Cavalry's efforts to provide centralized direction to the Army's mounted branch.

The Case for Horse Cavalry

In March 1938 Maj. Gen. John K. Herr became the last chief of Cavalry. He assumed leadership of a branch gradually dissolving into its mechanized and nonmechanized components. The absence of mechanized cavalry at Fort Riley, the inability of the Cavalry School to address mechanized training, and the growing influence of the 7th Cavalry Brigade (Mechanized) on its own materiel development underscored the divergent tendencies of the horse and mechanized cavalries. Moreover, the proliferation of mechanized combat units abroad seemed to augur the demise of horse cavalry.

Herr undertook the challenge of unifying the Cavalry under centralized leadership. He also sought to preserve the status of the horse cavalry while promoting expansion of the mechanized cavalry. He waged a tireless information campaign that highlighted the historical relevance of cavalry and leveraged military intelligence assessments to identify foreign mechanized developments with cavalry missions. The association of mechanization with cavalry was considered vital by at least one officer serving in the Office of the Chief of Cavalry:

> If we create mechanized units to carry out cavalry missions but fail to properly designate them, it will only be a question of time when the Cavalry will lose them. I fully expect the next war to bring about a separate Tank Corps in spite of the efforts now being made by the Infantry. Such a Tank Corps would be almost certain to absorb any loose "mechanized" units. The retention of mechanized cavalry units as Cavalry is vital to the future of our Arm. I am frightened at the thought of a "Mechanized Force" or a

---

[64] Ibid., p. 2. See chapter 4 for an analysis of how this directive applied to the Infantry.

[65] Maj Gen James F. McKinley, "War Department Policies for Mechanization," 5 Apr 35, Crittenberger Papers.

M1A1 combat car, showing equipment and ammunition

"Mechanized Division" and what could happen to Cavalry as a result of such organizations.[66]

The *Cavalry Journal* nevertheless promoted Herr's views. Articles appearing there were carefully screened to make sure they did not further encourage the split between horse and mechanized cavalries. Thus, in April 1939 the Office of the Chief of Cavalry viewed with disfavor an article submission that criticized the mechanized cavalry and depicted it as undesired by the Cavalry.[67]

Herr also attacked the administrative obstacles that barred his effective influence on the mechanized cavalry. He somewhat successfully sought to reestablish the chief of Cavalry as the principal factor in mechanized cavalry development. In June 1938 the War Department restored responsibility for mechanized cavalry development to the chief of Cavalry, although administrative and operational control remained with the V Corps Area commander. The following month, direct communication between the chief of Cavalry and the mechanized cavalry was authorized.[68]

---

[66] Memo, Maj Robert W. Grow to Col A. M. Miller Jr., sub: Thought for the Day, 10 Jan 37, Ofc of the Ch of Cav, Gen Corresp, RG 177, NARA.

[67] Memo, Lt Col Willis D. Crittenberger to Ch of Cav, sub: Comments on Proposed Article of Brigadier General H. S. Hawkins, 1 Apr 39, Crittenberger Papers.

[68] Grow, "Ten Lean Years," p. 77.

These gains were offset by leadership changes in the mechanized cavalry. In October General Van Voorhis became the V Corps Area commander and General Chaffee replaced him as commander of the 7th Cavalry Brigade (Mechanized). Van Voorhis' influence on mechanized development had grown since his command of the Mechanized Force in 1930. Within the War Department, he had become an oft-consulted expert on mechanization. As the V Corps Area commander, he continued to exert a direct influence on the mechanized cavalry independent of the chief of Cavalry. The appointment of Chaffee to command the 7th Cavalry Brigade (Mechanized) placed another strong mechanization advocate in charge of the Army's only combined-arms brigade. Chaffee also had influence within the War Department through prior General Staff service and association with mechanized development since the late 1920s.

These leadership changes formed the backdrop against which horse and mechanized cavalry development occurred. While Chaffee and Van Voorhis encouraged development of the 7th Cavalry Brigade (Mechanized) independent of horse cavalry, Herr worked to align both cavalry types more closely and to restore branch unity. He considered horse and mechanized cavalry natural complements. The mechanized cavalry possessed greater strategic mobility and firepower than the horse cavalry; but it depended on fixed supply lines, suffered from high-terrain sensitivity, and appeared brittle as a combat organization.[69] The tactical mobility of horse cavalry was considered superior to all other combat organizations. Moreover, its strategic mobility could be enhanced through rail or motor transport and it possessed the ability to sustain forced marches of 150 miles within a 48-hour period.[70]

The vulnerabilities of mechanized cavalry led Herr to envision its use in close conjunction with horse cavalry, especially if employed in the varied terrain of the Western Hemisphere.[71] He did not believe the mechanized cavalry to have "reached a position in which it can be relied on to displace horse cavalry. For a considerable period of time it is bound to play an important but minor role while the horse cavalry plays the major role so far as our country is concerned."[72] In particular, he considered the reconnaissance and security capabilities of the mechanized cavalry too weak. Therefore, horse cavalry would precede it to ensure its proper employment in favorable tactical conditions. Once enemy defenses had been penetrated or ruptured, the mechanized cavalry would exploit the breakthrough.[73]

---

[69] John K. Herr, "The Cavalry," Lecture at AWC, 19 Sep 38, p. 6, in Army War College Lectures, 1938–1939, pt. 1, AWC Curricular Archives.

[70] Memo, Ch of Cav Maj Gen John K. Herr to TAG, sub: Cavalry Requirements for the United States Army, 16 Aug 38, p. 4, Ofc of the Ch of Cav, Gen Corresp, RG 177, NARA; John K. Herr, "What of the Future," *Cavalry Journal* XLVIII, no. 1 (January-February 1939): 5.

[71] Memo, Herr to CS, 17 Oct 38; Memo, Ch of Cav Maj Gen John K. Herr to TAG, sub: Regular Army Cavalry Requirements for National Defense, 1 Dec 38, p. 2, Item 4851, Reel 313, National Archives Project, GCM.

[72] Memo, Ch of Cav Maj Gen John K. Herr to CS, 17 Oct 38, Ofc of the Ch of Cav, Gen Corresp, RG 177, NARA.

[73] Notes of Discussion Following Lecture of John K. Herr at AWC, "The Cavalry," 19 Sep 38, p. 3, File G–3, #4, 1939, AWC Curricular Archives (hereafter cited as Herr Discussion Notes); Memo,

Mechanized cavalry scout car, ca. 1938

Some Command and General Staff School graduates agreed with Herr's views. In tactical problems they noted the deployment of mechanized cavalry behind a screen of horse cavalry, where it awaited a favorable combat opportunity.[74] Other officers found Herr's assertions of mechanized Cavalry vulnerability in conformance with their own maneuver experience, citing incidents in which combat cars had blundered unaware onto antitank gun positions.[75] Mechanized cavalry vulnerability did not necessarily result in support for more horse cavalry. The Army War College commandant, for example, considered the attachment of motorized infantry a viable means of supporting mechanized cavalry without sacrificing the latter's strategic mobility.[76]

Abroad, most major military powers expanded their motorized and mechanized components at the expense of horse cavalry. Herr noted that the same nations nevertheless retained higher proportions of horse cavalry than did the United States. He noted a study underway at the *École de Guerre*, France's senior leadership school,

Ch of Cav Maj Gen John K. Herr to TAG, 1 Dec 38, p. 2; Ltr, John K. Herr to Maj Gen Leon B. Kromer, 12 May 39, Leon B. Kromer Papers, MHI Archives.

[74] Notes of Discussion Following Lecture of George A. Lynch at AWC, "The Infantry," 20 Sep 38, p. 2, File G–3, #5, 1939, AWC Curricular Archives (hereafter cited as Lynch Discussion Notes).

[75] Herr Discussion Notes, 19 Sep 39, pp. 12–13.

[76] Ibid., pp. 6–7.

concerning the employment of a mixed corps of horse and mechanized cavalry. Reports of combat operations in the Spanish Civil War included references to the valuable contributions of horse cavalry to Nationalist and Republican forces. These examples suggested the need for both cavalry types.[77]

In general, however, Herr considered the European gravitation away from horse cavalry the result of special circumstances, including fortified frontiers, declining horse populations, and population density. He did not believe Europe offered a viable model for American cavalry: "It is high time we cease aping those European thinkers who seek chiefly some panacea to break well nigh impregnable defense systems. We should shun this intellectual whirlpool and do our own thinking in terms of our probable needs."[78]

The chief of Cavalry considered the Western Hemisphere the U.S. Army's most likely theater of operations. The combination of mixed terrain and open expanses without significant road nets made it ideal for horse cavalry operations. Indeed, when the Military Intelligence Division ranked foreign armies according to their proportion of horse cavalry, Mexico topped the list, followed by Canada.[79] With a horse population estimated at 12 million, the United States also possessed the animals necessary to sustain a large body of horse cavalry.[80] These figures seemed to confirm the value of horse cavalry on the American continent.

The Future of Cavalry

Herr believed horse cavalry should constitute the bulk of the mounted force while the mechanized cavalry continued to develop. However, the status of the horse cavalry was worrisome. Between 1901 and 1938 the number of Army cavalry troops fell from 180 to 40. Scattered across the nation, these units labored under significant personnel and materiel shortfalls. Combat readiness suffered, but the dispersed nature of the cavalry undermined efforts to provide uniform and effective

---

[77] Note with Encl, Lt Col C. M. Busbee to Col Innis P. Swift, G–2, 4 Oct 37; Memo, ACS, G–2, Col E. R. W. McCabe to TAG, sub: Radiogram, 5 Oct 37; both in MID Corresp, 1917–1941, Security-Class Corresp and Rpts, RG 165, NARA. Herr, "Cavalry," 19 Sep 38, p. 5; Herr Discussion Notes, 19 Sep 39, pp. 12–13.

[78] Herr, "Cavalry," 19 Sep 38, p. 5, quote from p. 9; Herr Discussion Notes, 19 Sep 39, pp. 12–13.

[79] Memo for ACS, War Plans Division (WPD), sub: Cavalry Component of the Armies of Canada, France, Germany, Great Britain, Italy, Japan, Mexico, and Russia, 20 Apr 38, pp. 1, 5–6, MID Corresp, 1917–1941, Security-Class Corresp and Rpts, RG 165, NARA. According to this study, the cavalry comprised 42.7 percent of the Mexican Army, 10.4 of the Canadian, 6.7 of the French, 5.64 of the Russian, 5.4 of the British, 4.7 of the Japanese, 1.6 of the Italian, and .64 of the German.

[80] Memo, Herr to CS, 17 Oct 38; Memo, Ch of Cav Maj Gen John K. Herr to TAG, sub: Regular Army Cavalry Requirements for National Defense, 1 Dec 38, p. 2, Item 4851, Reel 313, National Archives Project, GCM.

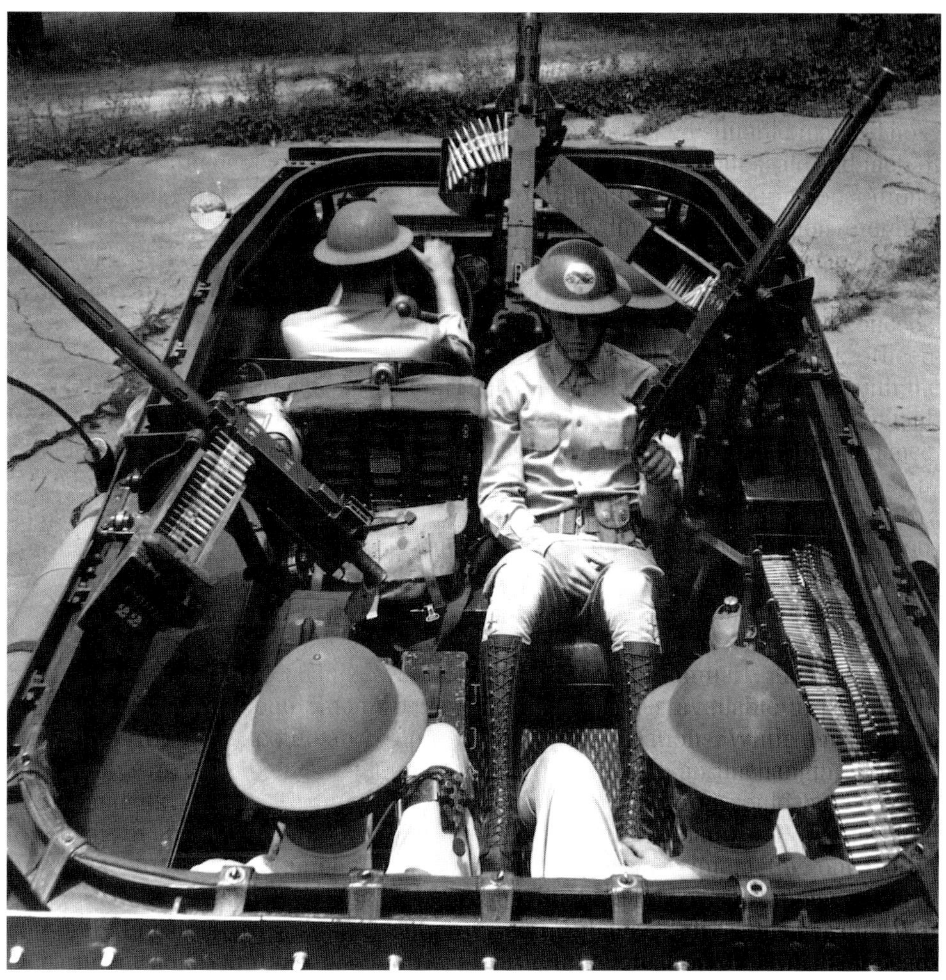

Mechanized cavalry scout car with crew in position

training.[81] National Guard cavalry was even less prepared and considered incapable of combat missions without several months of sustained preparation.[82]

To provide uniform and effective training to all Cavalry components, Herr proposed the creation of a large-scale training center. This center would become the branch's center of gravity, capable of supporting division- and corps-level maneuvers. It would also include the Cavalry School, the Cavalry Board, and the bulk of the Army's horse and mechanized cavalry. Herr's proposal concentrated the branch

[81] Herr, "Cavalry," 19 Sep 38, pp. 8–9; Herr Discussion Notes, 19 Sep 38, pp. 5–7.

[82] Memo, ACS, G–4, Brig Gen George P. Tyner, to ACS, G–3, sub: Equipment for Mechanized Cavalry, 5 Jun 39, pp. 2–3, Ofc of the Ch of Cav, Gen Corresp, RG 177, NARA; Herr Discussion Notes, 19 Sep 39, pp. 6–7.

leadership with its training, technical, and doctrine development components. It thus offered the prospect of ending the internal fissure threatening the Cavalry.[83]

Analysis of potential sites identified the Fort Bliss region as most suitable for the proposed training center. The climate permitted year-round training and ensured the presence of a large mounted force capable of rapid deployment in the event of a crisis with Mexico. Considerable acreage existed in federal domain and was due for transfer to the War Department. Additional land was available and affordable at the rate of three cents per acre. Fort Bliss already housed elements of the 1st Cavalry Division, simplifying the number of cavalry units that would need to relocate to Texas.[84]

Herr proved an outspoken advocate of combat training and unit readiness. He did not believe cavalry organizations could be created on an ad hoc basis. They required sustained peacetime development and stable personnel assignments.[85] He criticized the historical failure of the U.S. Army to prepare soldiers adequately for combat before the outbreak of war, stating, "All we think about is mobilizing the citizen army to be shot."[86]

The proposed training center provided an important foundation for improving the Cavalry's battlefield capabilities. However, simply collocating cavalry regiments would not generate the type of results Herr desired. Each regiment suffered from a serious deficiency in personnel. On paper, a regiment's wartime strength numbered 1,673 enlisted men and its peacetime strength 779. The actual average strength of a regiment, however, was only 662. Herr sought to remove these discrepancies, which he considered detrimental to training and unit cohesion.[87]

Consequently, Herr wanted Cavalry personnel relieved from administrative and post duties and released for combat training. He considered the former tasks of little utility and thus made no provision for continuing the summer training of reservists and civilian military camps. Critical of the Army's emphasis on providing military training to interested civilian organizations, he summarized his viewpoint: "I think it is high time we quit sending all our officers around the country teaching high school students and reserve officers, teaching correspondence courses and how to fight a correspondence war."[88]

Simply returning all Cavalry soldiers to their units did not satisfy Herr's personnel requirements. He anticipated an increase in the Army's end strength as tensions in Europe mounted. He recommended additional personnel for the cavalry units, reminding the War Department that the existing strength of the Cavalry constituted only half of what

---

[83] Herr, "Cavalry," 19 Sep 38, pp. 10–11; Herr, "What of the Future," pp. 5–6; Herr, "Cavalry," 19 Sep 39, pp. 4–5; Memo, Ch of Cav Maj Gen John K. Herr to CS, sub: Increase in Personnel with Certain Other Related Matters, 7 Aug 39, Ofc of the Ch of Cav, Gen Corresp, RG 177, NARA.

[84] Herr, "Cavalry," 19 Sep 38, pp. 10–11; Herr, "What of the Future," pp. 5–6; Herr, "Cavalry," 19 Sep 39, pp. 4–5; Memo, Ch of Cav to CS, 7 Aug 39.

[85] Memo, Herr to TAG, 1 Dec 38, p. 5.

[86] Herr Discussion Notes, 19 Sep 39, p. 12.

[87] Memo, Ch of Cav to CS, 7 Aug 39, Ofc of the Ch of Cav, Gen Corresp, RG 177, NARA; Herr, "Cavalry," 19 Sep 38, p. 10.

[88] Herr Discussion Notes, 19 Sep 39, pp. 21–22.

the National Defense Act of 1920 had prescribed. In building up the branch's personnel level, he sought to make Cavalry between 15 and 25 percent of the entire Army.[89]

The need for additional personnel was driven in part by Herr's desire to establish a permanent cavalry corps structure. Such a formation had been the subject of study by the Cavalry since 1936. The corps suited Herr's belief that massed cavalry could play a decisive role in any future conflict characterized by maneuver. His organization included an armored car squadron, three horse cavalry divisions, and one mechanized cavalry division. The entire corps would be partially motorized, reflecting the growing number of motor vehicles included in horse cavalry organizations. The proposed training center provided the means by which the corps structure could be tested and its components trained and provided with suitable doctrine.[90] By October 1939 Herr was recommending a cavalry corps for each of the four field armies, a proposal that gained at least some General Staff support.[91]

An increase in Cavalry personnel also permitted the creation of additional units. In particular, Herr wanted to remedy the lack of reconnaissance organizations in nonmotorized infantry divisions through the attachment of horse cavalry—a development he noted the Germans had already implemented.[92] He also desired the creation of special horse-mechanized regiments to provide reconnaissance for corps and divisions conducting independent operations. Previous Cavalry studies had also recommended this idea.[93] This expansion of horse cavalry into noncavalry formations spurred further suggestions to station horse cavalry at Fort Benning, Georgia, for combined training with infantry formations and to assign horse cavalry to the Panama Canal Zone. The National Guard was to organize its separate horse cavalry units into divisions and corps that would activate upon mobilization.[94]

Herr's strong advocacy of horse cavalry did not blind him to the growing value of mechanization. He believed both forms of cavalry had important roles to play, and he sought to improve each under the chief of Cavalry's banner. Hence, his plans for the branch's future also included expansion of the 7th Cavalry Brigade (Mechanized) into a division and the establishment of a combat-car squadron at Fort Riley. Similarly, proposals to increase principal cavalry installations included Fort Knox.[95]

By August 1939 Herr's plans for developing the cavalry focused on five primary objectives:

---

[89] Memos, Herr to TAG, 16 Aug 38, p. 5; Herr to CS, 17 Oct 38; Herr to TAG, 1 Dec 38, pp. 1, 6.

[90] Memo, Ch of Cav to CG, 1st Cav Div, sub: Organization of the Corps and Army, 10 Nov 36, Ofc of the Ch of Cav, Gen Corresp, RG 177, NARA; "Report of Committee on Reorganization of the Corps and Army," 16 Dec 36, Ofc of the Ch of Cav, Gen Corresp, RG 177, NARA; Memo, Herr to TAG, 1 Dec 38, pp. 3, 5; Herr, "What of the Future," pp. 3–5.

[91] Memos, Ch of Cav Maj Gen John K. Herr to CS, 13 Oct 39, Item 4893, Reel 314; Ch of Cav Maj Gen John K. Herr to CS, sub: Cavalry Requirements, 18 Oct 39, Item 4851, Reel 313; both in National Archives Project, GCM.

[92] Memo, Ch of Cav to CS, 20 Apr 39, Item 4851, Reel 313, National Archives Project, GCM.

[93] Memo, Herr to TAG, 1 Dec 38, p. 4; Memo, Ch of Cav to CG, 1st Cav Div, sub: Organization of the Corps and Army, 10 Nov 36; "Report of Committee on Reorganization," 16 Dec 36.

[94] Memos, Herr to TAG, 1 Dec 38, p. 3, and 16 Aug 38, pp. 21–23.

[95] Memo, Herr to TAG, 16 Aug 38, pp. 21–23; John K. Herr, Remarks re Conference with ACS, G–3, 10 Oct 38, Ofc of the Ch of Cav, Gen Corresp, RG 177, NARA.

1. increasing the strength of eight cavalry regiments and collocating them at a new training center in the Southwest;
2. creating a combat-car unit at Fort Riley;
3. expanding the 7th Cavalry Brigade (Mechanized) into a mechanized division;
4. establishing two new regiments as mixed horse-mechanized cavalry for reconnaissance;
5. activating the inactive elements of the 2d Cavalry Regiment.[96]

The outbreak of war in Europe in September resulted in only minor changes to these objectives. Following President Franklin D. Roosevelt's declaration of a limited national emergency, activation of the 2d Cavalry Regiment was given precedence over expansion of the mechanized cavalry.[97] Symbolic of the racial prejudice of the era and despite Herr's desire for additional manpower, not until after the German invasion of Poland did he suggest releasing the two African American cavalry regiments from their menial assignments to participate in combat training.[98]

Herr developed a comprehensive plan that provided a means of resolving many of the difficulties facing the Cavalry in the 1930s. Many of his specific proposals found support within the War Department. The War Plans Division of the General Staff, for example, concurred with Herr's relative emphasis on horse and mechanized cavalry and his desire for horse-mechanized reconnaissance units. However, implementation of the full range of actions advocated by Herr proved too controversial and dependent on nonexistent personnel and financial resources. Though the War Plans Division supported the concept of special reconnaissance units, it refused to increase the strength of cavalry units without an increase in the overall size of the Army. As to the training center, it was considered "outside the realm of reasonable possibility."[99]

Herr's recommendations blatantly violated General Staff instructions to assist in preparing "a detailed program for decreasing the existing military establishment, designed to absorb a reduction of funds with a minimum disturbance to the balance of national defense requirements."[100] While the Army sought to balance mission requirements against available resources, Herr sought an unprecedented expansion of a single branch—even at the expense of other Army organizations. During his annual address to Army War College students, he suggested that funds be diverted

[96] Memo, Ch of Cav to CS, 7 Aug 39, Ofc of the Ch of Cav, Gen Corresp, RG 177, NARA; Herr, "Cavalry," 19 Sep 38, p. 10.

[97] Memo, Ch of Cav Maj Gen John K. Herr to CS, sub: Increase in Personnel with Certain Other Related Matters, 5 Sep 39, Ofc of the Ch of Cav, Gen Corresp, RG 177, NARA.

[98] Herr, "Cavalry," 19 Sep 39, p. 3.

[99] Memo, ACS, WPD, Brig Gen George V. Strong, to ACS, G–3, sub: Regular Army Cavalry Requirements for National Defense, 5 Jan 39, Item 4851, Reel 313, National Archives Project, GCM.

[100] Memo, Acting ACS, WPD, Col F. S. Clark, to Ch of Cav, sub: Special Study on a Balanced War Department Objective, 28 Jul 39, Ofc of the Ch of Cav, Gen Corresp, RG 177, NARA.

Mechanized cavalry training maneuver

from aircraft and warship production to the cavalry, much to the chagrin of the naval and Air Corps officers present.[101]

The G–3 Division of the General Staff offered little support to Herr's proposals. Sympathetic to the desire to eliminate the discrepancy between wartime and peacetime regimental strengths, the G–3 simply recommended the paper solution of lowering the former to match the latter. With the adjutant general's backing the G–3 also restructured the relative importance of Herr's objectives for Cavalry development. Mechanized cavalry expansion received a higher priority.[102]

In building a comprehensive plan to improve the overall effectiveness of the cavalry and resolve multiple internal issues, Herr acted as a responsible branch chief. The resources required to implement his plan underscored the serious readiness issues facing the Cavalry—as he intended. His outspoken demands for better combat training and the resolution of manning discrepancies in field units resonated throughout the other branches.

The consensus-driven nature of the War Department's decision-making process, however, ensured the failure of Herr's efforts. His planned restructuring of the Cavalry required widespread support throughout the War Department and congressional acquiescence that was problematic at best. The General Staff considered his

[101] Herr Discussion Notes, 19 Sep 38, p. 4, and 19 Sep 39, p. 12.

[102] Memo, ACS, G–3, Brig Gen F. M. Andrews to CS, sub: Memo, the Chief of Cavalry, re: Increase of Personnel with Certain Other Related Matters, 21 Oct 39, Item 4882, Reel 313, National Archives Project, GCM; Memo, TAG to Ch of Cav, sub: Increase in Personnel with Certain Other Related Matters, 17 Nov 39, Ofc of the Ch of Cav, Gen Corresp, RG 177, NARA.

proposals unrealistic in their entirety. The other branch chiefs faced training and resource concerns of their own. They anticipated an increase in the Army's budget and end strength as a result of rising international tension and were as determined as Herr to improve the status of their respective branches. The Cavalry's rejection of the triangular division and the organizational principles it represented further distanced the branch from the rest of the Army. By retaining the square division, the Cavalry encouraged the view that it constituted the least progressive branch of the Army.[103] Herr's outspoken views on the provision of military training to the Army's civilian components had a similar effect.

By September 1939 the Army's focus lay on motor vehicle usage, epitomized by the triangular division, and expansion of the Air Corps. The proliferation of mechanized forces throughout the world and the attribution of Germany's success in Poland to its panzer divisions did not encourage War Department support for the large-scale increase in horse cavalry Herr demanded. German military success more clearly demonstrated Van Voorhis' expectation that mechanized development would encompass a broader range of activities than those represented by the 7th Cavalry Brigade (Mechanized).[104]

The outbreak of war in Europe led President Roosevelt to declare a limited national emergency. Intended to accelerate Army modernization efforts, it also further discouraged the War Department from undertaking the type of large-scale reorganization that Herr's proposals necessitated. Such changes required altering existing mobilization plans at a time when the Army was beginning to prepare for war in earnest.

However, Herr and the War Department concurred on the need to expand the 7th Cavalry Brigade (Mechanized). Poland's collapse after being overrun by German panzer divisions encouraged this action. Despite his efforts on behalf of horse cavalry, Herr also advocated a major increase in mechanized cavalry. The creation of a mechanized cavalry division would secure War Department commitment for one of Herr's principal objectives and preempt the creation of an independent mechanized force likely to absorb the mechanized cavalry. Such a loss would constitute a serious blow to the Cavalry. Consequently, the course of future branch developments hinged on the ability to secure War Department approval for a mechanized cavalry division.

---

[103] "Report of Board of Review on Field Service Tests of the Proposed Cavalry Division Conducted by the 1st Cavalry Division U.S. Army, 1938," 4 vols., vol. 1, MHI Library.

[104] Van Voorhis, "Mechanization," 13 Oct 37, pp. 13–15, and 29 Sep 38, pp. 17–18.

7

A NEW BEGINNING: THE ARMORED FORCE

Starting in 1937, the Cavalry sought to expand the 7th Cavalry Brigade (Mechanized) into a division. The War Department, however, hesitated to create a formation that would impact multiple branches. Lacking a clear vision of the extent, pace, and course of future mechanized development, it repeatedly deferred decisions regarding mechanization. Maneuver experiences in 1939 and 1940, coupled with Germany's high-profile use of panzer divisions in the opening campaigns of World War II, finally provided the impetus to centralize mechanized development. In place of the separate Infantry and Cavalry mechanization programs, the War Department established the Armored Force.

Building a Mechanized Cavalry Division

By 1937 the 7th Cavalry Brigade (Mechanized) had grown to two mechanized cavalry regiments plus an attached artillery battalion. It possessed a flexible organization and communications architecture that could be tailored to fit changing tactical situations. These developments encouraged the brigade's leadership to press for a larger organization. In the summer of 1937 Chief of Cavalry Maj. Gen. Leon B. Kromer proposed to the War Department that the mechanized cavalry be expanded into a division.[1]

Maj. Gen. John K. Herr also supported this recommendation when he succeeded Kromer in March 1938. Herr's plan for modernizing the mounted branch included expansion of the mechanized cavalry in general and building a mechanized division in particular. He envisioned a powerful cavalry force organized into corps that included horse and mechanized cavalry. To realize this goal, Herr sought additional personnel and funding for the entire branch. To him, the mechanized cavalry division represented only one part of a broader objective. Consequently, Herr requested that personnel increases for the mechanized cavalry be matched with similar additions to horse cavalry.[2]

---

[1] Ltr, Lt Col Willis D. Crittenberger to Lt Col Raymond E. McQuillen, 30 Jan 39, Willis D. Crittenberger Papers, U.S. Army Military History Institute (MHI) Archives, Carlisle Barracks, Pa.

[2] John K. Herr, "Remarks Re Conference with Assistant Chief of Staff, G–3," 10 Oct 38, Ofc of the Ch of Cav, Gen Corresp, Record Group (RG) 177, National Archives and Records Administration (NARA); Memo, Lt Col Willis D. Crittenberger to Ch of Cav, sub: Why Not To Tie the Creation of a Mechanized Division to an Increase in Horse Cavalry Personnel, 22 Nov 38, Crittenberger Papers.

Chief of Cavalry General Herr (*left*) with Brig. Gen. Adna R. Chaffee Jr. in 1939

Not all cavalry officers agreed with this caveat. Lt. Col. Willis D. Crittenberger, who worked in the Office of the Chief of Cavalry from 1938–1940, advised Herr that associating the creation of a mechanized cavalry division with increases in horse cavalry personnel might undermine War Department support for the former. Instead, he recommended emphasizing an expansion of the mechanized cavalry to exploit favorable public sentiment. Approval seemed likely, and he considered it possible to secure additional personnel without detriment to the horse cavalry. Establishing the mechanized cavalry division would also lay the foundation for Herr's cavalry corps concept.[3]

Crittenberger's views highlighted the problem facing cavalry modernization. Horse cavalry effectiveness required an influx of personnel and materiel, but public opinion consistently favored mechanized cavalry. The latter's reliance on motor vehicles made it appear modern and progressive, while the horse cavalry seemed a relic of the past. From the chief of Cavalry's perspective, pursuing the expansion of the mechanized cavalry without a parallel effort to address horse cavalry needs risked the permanent neglect of the latter. Subsequent attempts to secure personnel and funds for horse cavalry risked rejection as unprogressive and antimodern.

---

[3] Memo, Crittenberger to Ch of Cav, 22 Nov 38.

Herr's reservations made sense in the absence of a clear War Department statement regarding mechanized development objectives. Nevertheless, he accepted Crittenberger's advice and recommended a mechanized cavalry division organization to the War Department in the spring of 1938. This formation included three mechanized cavalry regiments whose configuration reflected the prior analytical efforts of a board of mechanized cavalry officers convened from November 1937 until January 1938.[4]

The board focused on improving combat effectiveness. Its final report recommended additional vehicles, more personnel, increased automatic weapons, and the restructuring of the brigade headquarters troop. Scout cars were to replace unarmored vehicles assigned to administrative and maintenance tasks to provide protection to crew and passengers. The board also proposed increasing regimental combat power through the addition of more combat cars. Together these recommendations boosted the mechanized cavalry brigade by 45 more scout cars and 66 combat cars for a total of 178. The report also provided for additional officers and technical personnel. These modifications improved combat capability without significant increases in overhead, but they still cost an estimated $1 million.[5]

War Department minimization tendencies soon reduced the size of the proposed mechanized cavalry formation. In June 1938 Herr was directed by the G–3 Division (Operations and Training) of the War Department General Staff to redesign the formation as a two-regiment division. Following the mechanized cavalry's participation in the October maneuvers, the revised division organization was submitted for War Department review with approval again considered likely.[6] (*See Chart 13.*) The proposed mechanized cavalry division now included a divisional headquarters, a headquarters troop, a rifle troop, two mechanized cavalry regiments, and an artillery regiment. A reconnaissance and support squadron was included to address organizational flaws identified in the brigade. Its missions included reconnaissance and security, holding ground, and serving as the brigade reserve. Signal, engineer, chemical, ordnance, medical, and quartermaster units supported the combat elements, and a flight of observation aircraft provided a means of aerial reconnaissance. Despite the smaller size of the revised division organization, it included several new units that had to be established, manned, and equipped. The new additions drove the cost of the division to $4 million.[7]

The proposed division reflected a mixture of influences. War Department guidance and the cumulative experience of the 7th Cavalry Brigade (Mechanized) constituted the

---

[4] Memo, Brig Gen Daniel Van Voorhis to Ch of Cav, sub: Tables of Organization for Mechanized Cavalry, 30 Jan 38, RG 177, NARA; Ltr, Crittenberger to McQuillen, 30 Jan 39.

[5] "Proceedings of a Board of Officers for Tables of Organization, 7th Cavalry Brigade (Mecz)," 29 Jan 38, RG 177, NARA; Memo, Van Voorhis to Ch of Cav, 30 Jan 38, p. 3.

[6] Ltr, Crittenberger to McQuillen, 30 Jan 39.

[7] Memo, Lt Col Willis D. Crittenberger to Lt Col W. M. Grimes, sub: Informal Submission of Tables of Organization and Equipment Recommended and Reference Information, 13 Jan 39, Crittenberger Papers; Ltr, Maj Gen Daniel Van Voorhis to Chief of Staff (CS) Gen Malin Craig, 17 May 39, Item 4962, Reel 315, National Archives Project, George C. Marshall Library (GCM), Lexington, Va.; Memo to Ch of Cav, Extract, sub: Mechanized Cavalry Division, 2 May 39, RG 177, NARA.

Chart 13—PROPOSED MECHANIZED CAVALRY DIVISION, 1938

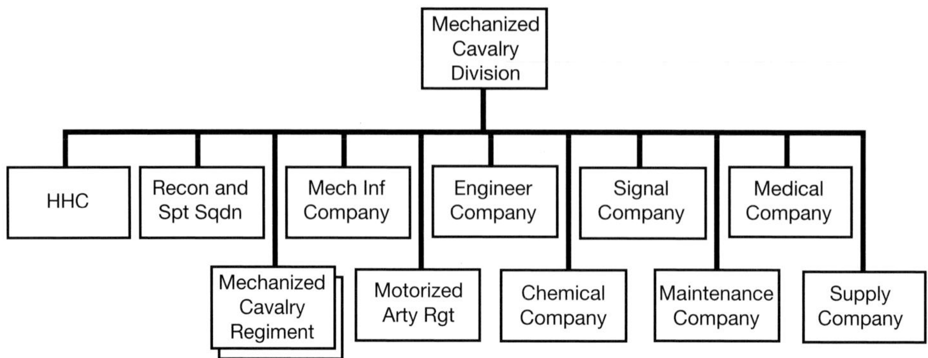

HHC = Headquarters and Headquarters Company

dominant shaping factors. Yet it was also influenced by American awareness of the German panzer division. Through the intelligence-gathering efforts of military attaché Maj. Truman Smith and the interest of successive chiefs of Cavalry in foreign mechanized developments, considerable information about the panzer division was available. This formation incorporated organizational qualities similar to those developed by the mechanized cavalry, and it became the comparison standard for the mechanized division.[8]

The mechanized cavalry division represented a significant commitment of personnel and funding, which in the interwar years ensured an extended period of debate and analysis within the War Department. Moreover, the new formation forced the Army to reassess its mechanization effort and determine its related impact on strategic and mobilization planning. In the absence of a strong central executive authority, the War Department could not readily resolve these issues. Therefore, the creation of a mechanized cavalry division and its impact became the subject of discussion among nearly every organization represented within the War Department.

The widespread attention garnered by the proposed formation led to unsolicited organization changes. Many of these modifications were not grounded in practical experience. This development prompted Col. Charles L. Scott, commander of the 13th Cavalry Regiment (Mechanized), to remark: "The old expression, 'A little learning is a dangerous thing,' is typified by some of the proposals I've heard for the detailed organization and operation of a mechanized Division."[9]

Herr responded by pressing the War Department for rapid approval of the proposed division organization in its original form. He reminded General Staff members that the organization represented two years of study by the Cavalry and incorporated War Department guidance, maneuver experiences, and input from

[8] Memo, Lt Col Willis D. Crittenberger to Lt Col W. M. Grimes, sub: Informal Submission of Tables of Organization and Equipment Recommended and Reference Information, 16 Jan 40, Crittenberger Papers.

[9] Ltr, Col Charles L. Scott to Lt Col Willis D. Crittenberger, 20 Feb 39, Crittenberger Papers.

Mechanized cavalry combat cars during the First Army maneuvers of August 1939

the Command and General Staff School. Given the time and expertise applied in building the proposed division, Herr saw little need for further War Department analysis and modification, particularly when other nations had already fielded larger mechanized formations.[10]

Herr's reference to foreign mechanization struck a resonant chord. By 1939 the prospect of a new war in Europe had risen and with it the possibility of U.S. involvement. The proliferation of mechanized units in Britain, France, Germany, and Italy ensured their presence on the next battlefield, but the U.S. Army possessed only a single mechanized cavalry brigade and a handful of infantry tank units. This situation drove Assistant Chief of Staff, G–3, Maj. Gen. Robert M. Beck Jr., to support the mechanized cavalry division. He believed "that the War Department cannot afford to appear to the public to be reticent or backward in developing mechanization along the lines of the Mechanized Cavalry unit for it is this unit that most readily compares with the mechanized divisions of foreign countries, such as those of Germany." Indeed, Beck acknowledged the desire to present an American equivalent to foreign mechanized formations as his principal reason for designating an augmented 7th Cavalry Brigade (Mechanized) as a mechanized division.[11]

Support for the proposed mechanized division did not always equate to endorsement of the organizational and doctrinal principles it represented. General Beck felt impelled to support the mechanized cavalry division proposed, but he preferred a simpler and smaller augmentation of the 7th Cavalry Brigade (Mechanized).[12] Similarly, Maj. Gen. Daniel Van Voorhis urged acceptance of the proposed formation, but he believed it represented the maximum force that could be effectively controlled.

---

[10] Draft Memo to Assistant Chief of Staff (ACS), G–3, 3d End, 29 Mar 39, Crittenberger Papers.

[11] Memo, ACS, G–3, Maj Gen Robert M. Beck Jr., to CS, G–3, sub: General Van Voorhis' Letter on Mechanization, 24 May 39, Item 4962, Reel 315, National Archives Project, GCM.

[12] Ibid.

He considered a smaller formation, created by adding a reconnaissance and support squadron to the mechanized cavalry brigade, sufficient.[13] Assistant Chief of Staff, G–4 (Supply) Brig. Gen. George P. Tyner also questioned the ability of one man to command a large mechanized formation. He preferred augmentation of the existing brigade components rather than the creation of a new division.[14]

Nevertheless, approval for the mechanized cavalry division appeared likely. Budget and Army augmentation plans began to incorporate a larger mechanized cavalry force that included a division. A congressional bill to enlarge military reservations included Fort Knox, reinforcing expectations of War Department endorsement of mechanized Cavalry expansion.[15]

Stepping Back: The Mechanized Cavalry Division Rejected

Therefore, in May 1939 Chief of Staff General Malin Craig caused a stir when he disapproved the mechanized cavalry division proposed by Herr. Instead, Craig recommended the creation of a second mechanized Cavalry brigade.[16] In a letter to Van Voorhis, Craig explained his decision: "Personally, I feel that our mechanized tactical doctrine should be completely re-studied. I question whether we have not over-emphasized the employment of mechanical elements on detached and independent missions at the actual expense of main battle missions. By this I mean direct participation as a decisive attack element".[17]

The chief of staff's action underscored the uncertainty surrounding the direction of mechanized development. He hesitated to commit the Army to supporting a formation that did not have universal War Department support and appeared only tangentially to support the action of the traditional infantry-artillery team. No demonstrated need existed for the proposed mechanized cavalry division. While some General Staff members favored such a formation, their motive lay in proving that U.S. Army mechanization did not lag behind that of other nations.

The decision surprised supporters of the mechanized cavalry division, who had considered its approval secured. Faced with this defeat, Herr worked to salvage the funds set aside to meet the now defunct division's materiel needs. He wanted them reallocated to strengthening the 7th Cavalry Brigade and establishing a second mechanized cavalry brigade at Fort Riley, Kansas, or Fort Bliss, Texas. The presence of mechanized cavalry at either of these posts would promote greater integra-

---

[13] Ltr, Van Voorhis to Craig, 17 May 39.

[14] Memo, ACS, G–4, Brig Gen George P. Tyner, to CS, G–4, sub: Comments on General Van Voorhis' Letter of May 17, 1939, on Mechanization, 10 Jun 39, Item 4962, Reel 315, National Archives Project, GCM.

[15] Ltrs, Lt Col Willis D. Crittenberger to Maj Hugh J. Gaffey, 31 Jan 39, and Lt Col Willis D. Crittenberger to Brig Gen Adna R. Chaffee, 24 Apr 39; both in Crittenberger Papers.

[16] Memo, General Staff Secretary Lt Col H. R. Bull to ACS, G–3, sub: Mechanized Cavalry Division, 12 May 39, Ofc of the Ch of Cav, Gen Corresp, RG 177, NARA.

[17] Ltr, CS Gen Malin Craig to Maj Gen Daniel Van Voorhis, 28 Jun 39, Item 4962, Reel 315, National Archives Project, GCM.

The 7th Cavalry Brigade (Mechanized) on the parade ground at the U.S. Military Academy in 1939 after the First Army maneuvers

tion of horse and mechanized cavalry training. It would also break the mechanized cavalry's exclusive association with Fort Knox.[18]

Herr's new recommendations proved less controversial than the mechanized cavalry division. He gained the support of General Tyner, who shared Herr's desire not to expand mechanization at the expense of the horse cavalry. Tyner further requested that the War Department restate its guidance on mechanized cavalry development.[19] Brig. Gen. Adna R. Chaffee's chief concern now lay in securing additional personnel and materiel for the 7th Cavalry Brigade (Mechanized), which now appeared likely. He supported the mechanized cavalry division, and he did not want "younger fellows who are enthusiastic and visionary" to develop a sense of loss as a result of the chief of staff's decision.[20]

In June Herr informed Chaffee that the chief of staff favored redirecting funds from the defunct mechanized cavalry division to the 7th Cavalry Brigade. Herr suggested a

[18] Memo, ACS, G–3, Maj Gen Robert M. Beck Jr., to Ch of Cav, sub: Chief of Staff's Disapproval of the Expansion of the Mechanized Brigade, 16 May 39, and 1st End, 20 May 39, both in Ofc of the Ch of Cav, Gen Corresp, RG 177, NARA; Ltr, Lt Col Willis D. Crittenberger to Maj Gen Daniel Van Voorhis, 6 Jun 39, Crittenberger Papers.

[19] Memo, Lt Col Willis D. Crittenberger to Ch of Cav, sub: Mechanized Cavalry Status, 9 Jun 39, Crittenberger Papers.

[20] Ltr, Brig Gen Adna R. Chaffee to Lt Col Willis D. Crittenberger, 1 Jun 39, Crittenberger Papers.

number of changes to the brigade organization, including the addition of motorcycles. He considered the mechanized cavalry a "great field for the exploitation of the motorcycle, both solo and tricycle."[21] Accordingly, the Office of the Chief of Cavalry drafted a motorcycle troop organization for inclusion in the mechanized cavalry brigade.[22]

Chaffee proved less than enthusiastic. He agreed to accept the motorcycle troop on an experimental basis, but he preferred additional personnel in armored vehicles. He acknowledged the utility of the motorcycle for liaison and some scouting functions, but he did not accept it as the basis for a combat unit.[23] Herr, inspired by reports of motorcycle units in European armies and their employment for reconnaissance and security, continued to press for further development of the motorcycle troop. He directed the mechanized cavalry to build a formal table of organization and conduct the corresponding field tests. Despite these urgings, Chaffee offered little additional input and largely ignored the chief of Cavalry's requests for action.[24]

Motorcycle units, however, proved a sideshow to the more pressing issue of the mechanized cavalry's future status. In the weeks following the rejection of the mechanized cavalry division, the 7th Cavalry Brigade began to receive funding for more combat vehicles. Eliminating organizational deficiencies assumed precedence over earlier plans to create additional mechanized cavalry units.[25] In June Herr informed Chaffee: "There is some talk, unofficially, about the desirability of organizing a mechanized force. Whether such a project would absorb our mechanized cavalry into a general force somewhat similar to those of foreign armies has not yet been indicated."[26]

Indeed, throughout the summer, mechanization continued to attract Army-wide attention. Although the Munich Conference of 29–30 September 1938 averted a European war, War Department planners considered the outbreak of such a conflict probable in the near future. Consequently, plans to improve the state of the Army received renewed emphasis.[27] Widespread support existed for additional mechanized units, but finding the personnel for these forces remained an insurmountable problem.

---

[21] Ltr, Ch of Cav Maj Gen John K. Herr to Brig Gen Adna R. Chaffee, 1 Jun 39, Ofc of the Ch of Cav, Gen Corresp, RG 177, NARA.

[22] Memo, Ch of Cav Maj Gen John K. Herr to Commanding General (CG), 7th Cav Bde, sub: Recommendations on Motorcycle Troop, 5 Jun 39, Ofc of the Ch of Cav, Gen Corresp, RG 177, NARA.

[23] Memo, Ch of Cav Maj Gen John K. Herr to CG, 7th Cav Bde, sub: Recommendations on Motorcycle Troop, 5 Jun 39, and 1st End, 23 Jun 39, both in Ofc of the Ch of Cav, Gen Corresp, RG 177, NARA.

[24] Radiogram, Ch of Cav Maj Gen John K. Herr to CG, 7th Cav Bde, 18 Sep 39; Memo, Ch of Cav to CG, 7th Cav Bde, 5 Jun 39, and 1st End, 23 Jun 39; Memo, Ch of Cav Maj Gen John K. Herr to CG, 7th Cav Bde, sub: Utilization of Motorcycles with Mechanized Cavalry for Reconnaissance Purposes, 30 Jun 39; all in Ofc of the Ch of Cav, Gen Corresp, RG 177, NARA.

[25] Memo, Lt Col Willis D. Crittenberger to Ch of Cav, 23 May 39, Crittenberger Papers; Ltr, Crittenberger to Van Voorhis, 6 Jun 39.

[26] Ltr, Herr to Chaffee, 1 Jun 39.

[27] Mark Skinner Watson, *Chief of Staff: Prewar Plans and Preparations*, U.S. Army in World War II (Washington, D.C.: Department of the Army, 1950), pp. 152–56.

Neither the chief of Infantry nor the chief of Cavalry was willing to expand mechanization at the expense of nonmechanized components.

However, on 1 July the Army establishment increased to two hundred ten thousand. General Craig began terminal leave, and his duties were assumed by Deputy Chief of Staff Brig. Gen. George C. Marshall.[28] The increased manpower and leadership change spurred hopes that the mechanized cavalry division might be resurrected. In the words of Colonel Crittenberger, still assigned to the Office of the Chief of Cavalry, "Things are now moving to a show-down."[29] Amid the heightened speculation surrounding the future course of mechanized development, the 7th Cavalry Brigade (Mechanized) participated in the First Army maneuvers and Germany invaded Poland.

First Army Maneuvers, 1939

In August 1939 the 7th Cavalry Brigade (Mechanized) joined the First Army for maneuvers near Plattsburg, New York. This event served as part of the Army's overall effort to improve combat readiness. The scenario assumed that an invading force, dubbed the Black Army, had invaded the United States and had reached Lake Champlain. There it lay poised for a further advance westward. The invaders included four infantry divisions, a National Guard horse cavalry regiment, two artillery regiments, and an Infantry tank battalion. A defending force, designated the Blue Army, deployed to stop the invaders. Its components included an infantry division, an infantry brigade, and the mechanized cavalry.[30]

The maneuvers offered an opportunity for the 7th Cavalry Brigade (Mechanized) to demonstrate the value of independent mechanized action even on a rolling landscape of wooded areas, mountainous regions, and river valleys. Chaffee commanded the brigade, but his first challenge lay in reaching the maneuver area. Original notions of conducting a road march from Kentucky to New York foundered on the high cost to do so. The cost for the brigade to move only one mile totaled $94.69, and few funds were available for gasoline and oil. Therefore, the 7th Cavalry Brigade arrived in New York via much cheaper rail transportation.[31]

There, it undertook demonstrations and unit training exercises from 8–22 August. On 23 August the maneuvers began. To disrupt and stop the advance of the invading Black Army, the mechanized cavalry attacked its left flank. Simulated demolitions and Black delaying actions amid defile-studded terrain, however, limited the gains of

---

[28] *The War Reports of General of the Army George C. Marshall, General of the Army H. H. Arnold, and Fleet Admiral Ernest J. King* (Philadelphia: J. B. Lippincott Co., 1947), p. 16; Watson, *Chief of Staff*, p. 155.

[29] Ltr, Crittenberger to Van Voorhis, 6 Jun 39.

[30] Adna R. Chaffee, "The Seventh Cavalry Brigade in the First Army Maneuvers," *Cavalry Journal* XLVIII, no. 6 (November-December 1939): 451–52.

[31] Ibid.; Adna R. Chaffee, "Mechanized Cavalry," Lecture at Army War College (AWC), p. 6, 29 Sep 39, in Army War College Lectures, 1939–1940, pt. 2; Chaffee, "Seventh Cavalry Brigade," p. 450.

the mechanized cavalry. The day ended with Chaffee preparing for further attacks in the same area while his brigade pulled back to resupply and conduct maintenance.[32]

New orders interrupted these tasks and sent the brigade on a sixty-mile night march via narrow, mountainous roads under blackout conditions. It traversed the Blue rear area and prepared for a daylight assault on the Black Army's right flank. The 13th Cavalry Regiment (Mechanized) spearheaded the attack, but a strong defensive position atop a dominant hill soon stopped its advance. The 1st Cavalry Regiment (Mechanized) responded by enveloping the position and neutralizing the defenders. Its freedom of maneuver restored, the mechanized cavalry thrust into the Black rear area and reached the town of Plattsburg. The ensuing chaos resulted in midday orders directing the brigade into bivouac for rest and refueling. This action acknowledged the fatigue of the unit's personnel, particularly drivers who had had little sleep, but it also prevented the mechanized cavalry's successful flank attack from necessitating an early termination to the maneuvers.[33]

The 7th Cavalry Brigade (Mechanized) took no further action until the next morning. Then it again penetrated into the Black Army rear area, overrunning headquarters installations and surprising a tank company. The brigade continued to attack targets of opportunity and disrupt hostile operations until the maneuver's end. Chaffee kept the brigade concentrated, employing it as a single, powerful maneuver force that roved throughout the Black rear area largely with impunity. The presence of the mechanized cavalry alone triggered the diversion of large numbers of Black 75-mm. artillery pieces from fire support to antitank operations. However, the pieces deployed in isolated, unsupported positions; the mechanized cavalry dispatched them with a combination of artillery fire and envelopment.[34]

After the maneuvers ended, Chaffee gained publicity and visibility for the mechanized cavalry by marching it across New York State. The brigade visited the U.S. Military Academy at West Point before traveling to New York City. There it participated in the World Fair and paraded through the city before returning to Fort Knox on 8 September.[35]

Chaffee considered the maneuvers a vindication of the mechanized cavalry's doctrine and its ability to achieve decisive battlefield results. His views received added emphasis from the initial reports concerning Germany's September invasion of Poland. Early combat successes against the Polish Army were attributed to the panzer divisions, formations that appeared to employ tactics similar to those of the mechanized cavalry.[36] Hence, the maneuver success of the mechanized cavalry, followed within days by reports of German panzer divisions and corps overrunning Poland, offered a powerful argument for sustaining the course of mechanized development the 7th Cavalry Brigade (Mechanized) had begun.

---

[32] Chaffee, "Seventh Cavalry Brigade."

[33] Ibid.

[34] Ibid.

[35] Ibid.

[36] Mildred H. Gillie, *Forging the Thunderbolt: A History of the Development of the Armored Force* (Harrisburg, Pa.: Military Service Publishing Co., 1947), p. 130; Chaffee, "Seventh Cavalry Brigade in the First Army Maneuvers"; Chaffee, "Mechanized Cavalry," 29 Sep 39, p. 31.

The 7th Cavalry Brigade (Mechanized) at the World Fair in New York City in 1939

The momentum created by these two events led Chaffee to press for organizational improvements. In particular, he sought an increase in the brigade headquarters staff and the addition of a reconnaissance and support unit. The former enhanced overall command and control of the brigade. The reconnaissance and support unit provided additional reconnaissance, served as the brigade reserve, or conducted security missions as necessary. The value of effective, timely reconnaissance was demonstrated by the mechanized cavalry's ability to avoid obstacles and eliminate antitank positions throughout the maneuvers. Conversely, the absence of reconnaissance and support elements in infantry tank units made them more susceptible to such dangers and at a disadvantage when confronting mechanized cavalry.[37]

Chaffee also requested the permanent assignment to Fort Knox of additional support units for the 7th Cavalry Brigade (Mechanized). To him, the successful application of mechanized cavalry tactics depended on the ability of all mechanized cavalry assets to train and operate as a team instead of a collection of attachments thrown together in the midst of battle. Through combined training, Chaffee sought to realize peak unit efficiency before combat. Moreover, his belief in the importance of organizing mechanized cavalry and support assets together led him to recommend creation of a mechanized cavalry division.[38]

Not every observer of the Plattsburg maneuver considered the mechanized cavalry's actions an unqualified success. One officer recollected, "From all I saw of the cavalry armored forces at Plattsburg and in Georgia, their principal function seemed to be racing up and down the roads, offering more of a traffic problem than a tactical one."[39]

---

[37] Chaffee, "Seventh Cavalry Brigade"; Chaffee, "Mechanized Cavalry," 29 Sep 39, pp. 11–13, 17–18.

[38] Chaffee, "Seventh Cavalry Brigade," p. 460, and "Mechanized Cavalry," 29 Sep 39, pp. 31–33.

[39] Raymond E. Lee, "Journal of Raymond E. Lee," 4 vols., 2: 362, Raymond E. Lee Papers, MHI Archives.

The Mechanized Cavalry Division Revisited

On 15 September Chaffee submitted to the War Department a formal proposal to expand the 7th Cavalry Brigade (Mechanized) into a division. He believed that German panzer operations in Austria, Czechoslovakia, and Poland demonstrated the value of large mechanized formations, writing, "It can no longer be said—'It might be done in maneuvers but how about war?'" He now sought approval of the previously developed mechanized cavalry division organization, rapid procurement of the corresponding materiel, and improvements to Fort Knox to house the formation.[40]

The proposed division required additional manpower. Chaffee wanted its full complement and a 50 percent surplus to provide a trained cadre for additional mechanized units upon mobilization. He preferred to cover these personnel needs through an increase in the Army's establishment; but as an alternative he recommended transferring officers and enlisted men from horse cavalry, infantry, and nonmechanized artillery units. Moreover, because of the greater technical demands of the mechanized cavalry, he requested that Regular Army soldiers constitute the bulk of the new division's strength, leaving National Guard and reservists as the principal manpower source for the horse cavalry and infantry units.[41]

Chaffee's proposal represented a deliberate effort to assert the primacy of mechanized cavalry. He saw little utility for horse cavalry: "It is my belief also, based on maneuvers and the war reports, that in any important war involving armies, and fought in a terrain where important wars are fought, mechanized cavalry is a vastly more powerful, mobile and decisive force than an equal or greater force of horse cavalry. I believe that a nucleus of horse cavalry should be kept for mountain, desert or tropical expeditions."[42]

Implicit in Chaffee's recommendations lay a clear preference for an independent branch. His desire to collocate personnel from multiple branches, subordinate their training to mechanized cavalry needs, and expand Fort Knox to accommodate them all indicate his unwillingness to subordinate mechanized cavalry interests to those of the Cavalry Branch. Already gaining influence on materiel developments through technical boards convened at Fort Knox, Chaffee's proposals would also give him de facto authority over doctrine development, personnel, and training—responsibilities normally held by a branch chief.

Chaffee also routed his recommendations to the War Department through Van Voorhis, the V Corps Area commander, rather than through Herr, the chief of Cavalry. The latter learned of Chaffee's actions only after the adjutant general disseminated copies of his memorandum for comment. While Van Voorhis supported the proposals, they constituted a complete break with Herr's plans for branch mod-

[40] Memo, Brig Gen Adna R. Chaffee to The Adjutant General (TAG), sub: Some Observations and Recommendations Pertinent to Any Future Expansion and Development of Mechanized Cavalry Which May Be Contemplated by the War Department, 15 Sep 39, quote from p. 1, Ofc of the Ch of Cav, Gen Corresp, RG 177, NARA.

[41] Ibid.

[42] Ibid., quote from p. 2.

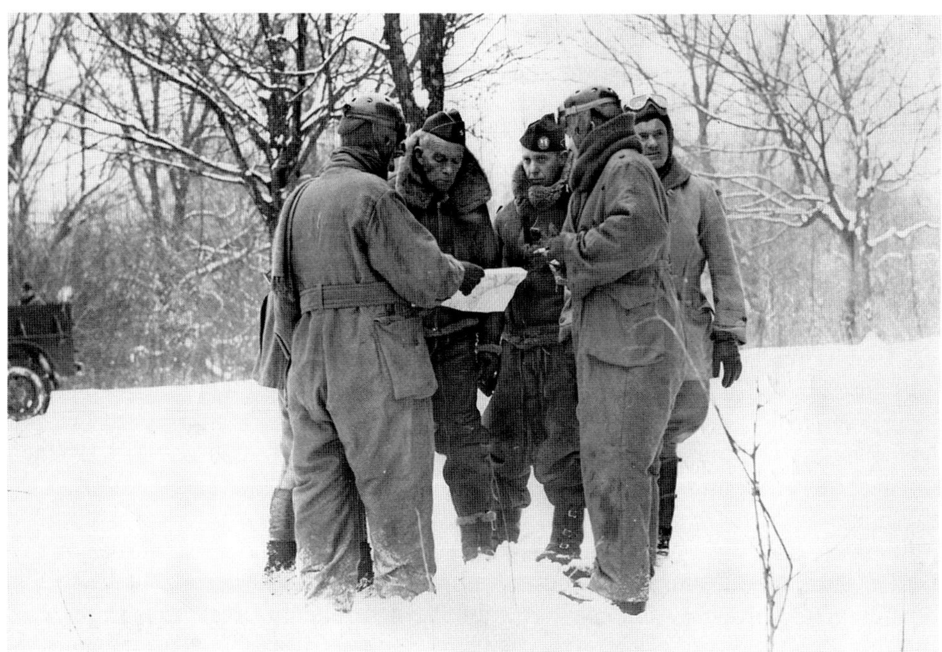

General Chaffee (*second from left*) consulting with officers during winter training

ernization, and, indeed, from the branch chief altogether.[43] Chaffee's rejection of horse cavalry in favor of a greatly expanded mechanized cavalry force ruptured the relationship between the mechanized cavalry commander and the chief of Cavalry. It also threatened to destroy the unity of the mounted branch.

Herr reacted with his own set of proposals to the War Department. He used the similarity between German armored operations in Poland and mechanized cavalry concepts to justify continued American mechanization efforts under Cavalry leadership. He reminded the War Department of the prior support rendered to expansion of the mechanized cavalry by successive chiefs of Cavalry and proposed a new division organization. Given the disparity between Germany's ten mechanized divisions and the U.S. Army's single mechanized brigade and assorted tank units, he believed that public sentiment favored increasing the Cavalry's mechanized component. In fact, with 450 combat cars and tanks in service, the U.S. Army's mechanized assets proved inferior to the nearly 1,100 armored vehicles in Poland's preinvasion inventory.[44]

Therefore, on 3 October, in lieu of the earlier two-regiment configuration, Herr proposed a larger mechanized cavalry division. He boosted combat-car strength

[43] Memo, Chaffee to TAG, 15 Sep 39, 1st End, 18 Sep 39, and 2d End, AG, 3 Oct 39.

[44] Memo, Chaffee to TAG, 15 Sep 39, and 3d End, 9 Oct 39; Memo, Lt Col Willis D. Crittenberger to Ch of Cav, sub: Tanks and Combat Cars in Army, 10 Oct 39, Crittenberger Papers; Steven J. Zaloga and Victor Madej, *The Polish Campaign, 1939* (New York: Hippocrene Books, Inc., 1985), p. 88.

from 112 to 500 and included a motorized infantry regiment.[45] Like Chaffee, Herr recommended that supporting motorcycle, antitank, engineer, signal, and medical units be stationed at Fort Knox. Although he did not envision the Kentucky post's becoming the permanent center of mechanized development, he did seek to make it an important training point for mechanized cavalry. Consequently, he also worked to expedite equipment deliveries to the 7th Cavalry Brigade (Mechanized).[46]

The proposed division organization continued to change. In general, organization planners sought to create an American panzer division. The formation grew to include a tank brigade and a holding brigade built around a motorized infantry regiment. Emulation of the Germans resulted in organizational changes that lacked meaning. For example, a divisional antitank unit was initially included, but "then, in order to make our proposed division comparable with the German Panzer Division, the antitank unit was taken out of the divisional troops and put in the holding brigade." Similarly, "we had our hands forced somewhat when a signal battalion and signal and engineer squadron were included. Once again the injection of these two sizeable elements was somewhat due to the German influence." The large number of motorcycles reflected the German usage and Herr's interest in motorcycle troops—an enthusiasm one assistant described as his being "motorcycle-minded."[47] Generally, these changes increased the size of the formation, but they received consistent support from the assistant chief of staff, G–3.[48]

Simultaneous with the design of a new mechanized division, the chief of Cavalry sought to preserve the mounted branch and defend the utility of its preponderance of horse cavalry. To Herr, "the equipment, training, and methods of employment of American horse cavalry in every way fit it to perform a necessary role in the army which no expansion of mechanization, in its present state of development, can hope to replace." Rather than strip already understrength horse regiments to meet mechanized cavalry needs for skilled soldiers, Herr recommended withdrawing Regular Army personnel from civilian component training assignments, replacing them with reservists and retirees. Similarly, he did not want Fort Knox to receive exclusive responsibility for mechanized cavalry training. While he supported efforts

---

[45] Robert W. Grow, "The Ten Lean Years: From the Mechanized Force to the Armored Force (1940)," p. 86, Robert W. Grow Papers, MHI Archives; Ltr, John K. Herr to Maj Gen Robert W. Grow, 7 Jun 45, Grow Papers; Draft Memo, Ch of Cav Maj Gen John K. Herr to CS, sub: Expansion of Mechanized Cavalry, 30 Sep 39, Crittenberger Papers. This document is the draft for the 3 October Memo and indicates the principal views expressed in the latter.

[46] Memo, ACS, G–3 Brig Gen Frank M. Andrews to CS, G–3, sub: 7th Cavalry Brigade (Mechanized), 11 Oct 39, National Archives Project, GCM; Draft Memo, Herr to CS, 30 Sep 39.

[47] Ltrs, Lt Col Raymond E. McQuillen to Lt Col Willis D. Crittenberger, 17 Oct 39, and Lt Col Willis D. Crittenberger to Lt Col Raymond E. McQuillen, 20 Oct 39, both in Crittenberger Papers.

[48] Memo, ACS, G–3, Brig Gen Frank M. Andrews, to CS, G–3, sub: 7th Cavalry Brigade (Mechanized), 11 Oct 39. "American Panzer Division" became a common expression in War Department memorandums following the Polish invasion, suggesting the impact of Germany's successes with armored units on War Department thinking.

German tanks advancing into Poland, 1939

to acquire more land at Fort Knox, he reminded the War Department of his broader plan to create a cavalry training complex near Fort Bliss.[49]

Herr also asserted his role as the principal Army adviser on Cavalry matters. As a bureau chief, he considered it his prerogative to suggest modifications to cavalry mechanization. In a thinly veiled reference to Chaffee's proposals, he wrote, "I cannot refrain from adding that recommendations as to methods to be employed in any expansion of cavalry units are within the province of the Chief of Cavalry, rather than that of a commander of any individual unit in the field."[50]

Chaffee in turn asserted the right of a field commander to present his views directly to the War Department. Van Voorhis supported him, and the War Department found itself barraged with competing proposals for mechanized cavalry expansion from the chief of Cavalry and the 7th Cavalry Brigade (Mechanized).[51] With each round of correspondence the rift between Chaffee and Herr widened. Each considered his own views superior and came to perceive the other as an obstruction to implementation of his proposed courses of action. Ultimately, however, Herr's efforts to coordinate Cavalry modernization under his own leadership failed. Lacking direct control over the 7th Cavalry Brigade (Mechanized) or the V Corps Area, he could not prevent Chaffee—with Van Voorhis' support—from recommending actions at variance with those of the chief of Cavalry.

---

[49] Memo, Chaffee to TAG, 15 Sep 39, and 3d End, 9 Oct 39.

[50] Ibid.

[51] Memo, Chaffee to TAG, 15 Sep 39, 6th End, 12 Dec 39, and 7th End, AG, 14 Dec 39, all in Item 4886, Reel 314, National Archives Project, GCM.

The G–3 Division of the War Department General Staff favored plans to build a mechanized division similar to the panzer division. It generally supported the proposals of Herr and Chaffee. Germany's conquest of Poland and a military intelligence report identifying the panzer division as the criterion for determining an army's modernity or obsolescence fueled this support. The report further considered the German Army, with its mechanized divisions and air support, easily capable of defeating any army not similarly equipped.[52]

The War Department faced a dilemma. The desire to create a combined-arms mechanized division did not accord with the bureau system's emphasis on organizational separation by function. The Army eschewed the creation and collocation of combined-arms formations for training purposes throughout the 1920s and 1930s. Instead, it encouraged the branches to develop separately according to mutually exclusive missions. Such a precedent could not easily be overturned.

Manning a mechanized division also posed a problem. No branch chief wished to transfer personnel to the new formation. Each feared the transfer would become a permanent loss, undermining his own modernization efforts. A similar fear had contributed to the earlier demise of the Mechanized Force. The larger size of the mechanized division and the likely need for more of these formations in the future threatened a much greater personnel loss. Despite the onset of war in Europe, Congress could not be relied on to provide sufficient additional soldiers. It had indeed raised the Army's strength—but only by seventeen thousand. The transformation of square to triangular divisions quickly absorbed this small increase.[53]

Centralized leadership might have overridden branch considerations and simply directed the transfer of personnel. The Army's command structure in 1939, however, still reflected the decentralized, horizontal organization of the interwar years. Its decision-making process lacked decisiveness and rapidity. Indeed, the acceleration of war-readiness measures threatened to overwhelm the leadership altogether. The combination of intensified strategic and mobilization planning, increased training activities and field maneuvers, and Air Corps expansion resulted in a rising tide of administrative minutiae. Related correspondence created endless paperwork for all War Department agencies, but especially for the Office of the Chief of Staff.

In August 1936 the chief of staff became the field army's commander in time of peace and war until replaced by an officer designated by the president. These responsibilities added to the chief of staff's existing duties of presiding over preparations for future conflict and supervising implementation of actions approved by the secretary of war. Collectively, these changes increased the authority of the chief of staff. Moreover, President Franklin D. Roosevelt's willingness to consult directly with Chief of Staff General George C. Marshall further enhanced the chief of staff's influence on military affairs, particularly the course of Army modernization.[54]

---

[52] Memo to ACS, G–3, Brig Gen Frank M. Andrews, sub: Mechanization, 1 Dec 39; Ltr, Col Charles L. Scott to Brig Gen Adna R. Chaffee, 13 Dec 39; both in Crittenberger Papers.

[53] *War Reports*, p. 18.

[54] Watson, *Chief of Staff*, pp. 64, 66; James E. Hewes Jr., *From Root to McNamara: Army Organization and Administration, 1900–1963*, Special Studies (Washington, D.C.: U.S. Army Center of Military History, 1975), pp. 58–60.

An exponential increase in administrative responsibilities charged exclusively to the chief of staff paralleled the increased authority. Consequently, nearly every War Department organization and field army (some sixty different offices by 1941) reported directly to the chief of staff. These responsibilities undermined the chief's ability to focus on broad policy measures, even with the support of a deputy. Worse, the failure to separate policy from implementation threatened the War Department with a breakdown of its administrative machinery similar to that experienced at the start of the Spanish-American War and World War I.[55]

Consequently, 1940 began with no War Department action on the mechanized division. Not until February, five months after submission, was Chaffee notified that his division proposal had been received and taken under consideration.[56] The competitive relation developing between the 7th Cavalry Brigade (Mechanized) and the Office of the Chief of Cavalry further complicated the determination of how to create a combat formation now generally considered necessary. The General Staff continued to study the issue, but the time-consuming nature of formal analysis generated further delay. In the interim, mobilization plans included only one mechanized cavalry brigade per field army, although funds were budgeted to enlarge Fort Knox and procure additional materiel for mechanization. Finally, the War Department opted to delay action on the mechanized cavalry division until after the Third Army maneuvers scheduled to occur in May.[57]

Third Army Maneuver Preparations

The continuing war in Europe prompted Congress to provide additional funds for military training. This money permitted the Army to plan a series of maneuvers in 1940 to improve overall combat readiness. Chief of Staff General Marshall considered these maneuvers vital for preparing the Army for war. He was particularly concerned about the discrepancy between the Army's doctrinal emphasis on corps operations and its actual battalion orientation. The small scale of most Army training activities precluded the combined-arms training and development of division and corps cohesion, which he considered vital to battlefield success. Therefore, the planned maneuvers would permit divisions and corps to operate against one another. He intended to use lessons learned from the maneuvers to influence changes to the Army's training and educational system.[58]

---

[55] Hewes, *Root to McNamara*, pp. 62–63.

[56] Memo, TAG to CG, Fifth Corps Area, sub: Some Observations and Recommendations Pertinent to Any Future Expansion and Development of Mechanized Cavalry Which May Be Contemplated by the War Department, 7 Feb 40, Item 4886, Reel 314, National Archives Project, GCM.

[57] Memos, ACS, G–3, Brig Gen Frank M. Andrews, to CS, G–3, sub: Ltr, Commanding General, 7th Cavalry Brigade (Mecz), 23 Jan 40, Item 4886, Reel 314, and CS Gen George C. Marshall to Deputy Chief of Staff (DCS), 6 Apr 40, Item 4851, Reel 313, both in National Archives Project, GCM.

[58] Note, CS Gen George C. Marshall to Col Burns, 23 Feb 40, Gen Corresp, George C. Marshall Papers, GCM; Christopher R. Gabel, "The 1940 Maneuvers: Prelude to Mobilization": http://www.crt.state.la.us/tourism/lawwii/maneuvers/1940_Maneuvers.htm last accessed 15 Feb 06.

German tanks in Poland

The Third Army maneuvers were scheduled to begin in May and constituted the first corps-versus-corps training event in Army history. Third Army's principal objective lay in the accumulation of field experience for all ranks. However, this event included the mechanized cavalry and most of the Army's tank units in an unprecedented concentration. The maneuvers also served as a field test for experimental organizations, including the corps reconnaissance regiment and an ad hoc mechanized division. The Cavalry further planned to use the maneuver experience to explore the viability of combined operations by horse and mechanized units.[59]

In preparation, the Cavalry planned a series of training activities for the 1st Cavalry Division. Chosen to participate in the maneuvers, this formation was to demonstrate the effectiveness of American horse cavalry on a battlefield populated with mechanized forces. Its success would bolster the chief of Cavalry's case for the creation of combined horse and mechanized formations, which so far the War Department had not embraced. Indeed, formal action on Herr's repeated requests for a cavalry corps and greater integration of horse and mechanized cavalry was deferred until after the Third Army maneuvers.[60]

---

[59] Memo, ACS, G–3, Brig Gen Frank M. Andrews, to CS, G–3, sub: Cavalry Requirements, 6 Mar 40, p. 3, Item 4851, Reel 313, National Archives Project, GCM; Gabel, "1940 Maneuvers."

[60] Memos, Andrews to CS, G–3, 6 Mar 40, p. 3, and Acting DCS Brig Gen Lorenzo D. Gasser to Ch of Cav, 8 Apr 40, Item 4851, Reel 313, National Archives Project, GCM.

The 1st Cavalry Division began to concentrate near Fort Bliss in October 1939. There it undertook divisional training exercises that soon revealed a number of deficiencies. Reconnaissance and security missions received insufficient emphasis. Too many subordinate commanders continued to rely on mounted charges against mortars and machine guns, while others avoided the exercise of initiative. Animal care also received inadequate attention, despite the importance of the mounts to all cavalry operations. These problems reflected the dispersed, undermanned nature of the division's subordinate regiments. They were not insurmountable and were symptomatic of a division whose components did not routinely train together. Therefore, the Cavalry planned to continue divisional training until the start of the Third Army maneuvers.[61]

Political and economic considerations disrupted these plans. While the formation conducted training, its component units had been temporarily withdrawn from their home stations along the Texas-Mexico border. Communities there feared the economic impact of a prolonged absence of military personnel, believing it might presage the permanent closing of Army posts. These fears triggered political action and led to the War Department's premature termination of the 1st Cavalry Division field exercises. The formation's regiments were ordered to return to home station by 31 January 1940.[62]

The assistant chief of staff, G–3, in vain recommended against this action, warning: "The breaking up of this Division before the completion of the field training in June, 1940, simply to provide an Army payroll for the communities in the vicinity of the permanent stations of the troops, appears unjustifiable. Further, if the precedent is established, pressure might be brought to do likewise concerning the various infantry division concentrations."[63]

The early return of 1st Cavalry Division elements disrupted the formation's training and impaired its effectiveness in the upcoming maneuvers. The largest exercises and those that focused on building division cohesion, scheduled for February, were now cancelled. Similarly, organizational changes recommended by the War Department could not be field tested. Instead, the division's regiments dispersed to their home stations. They would not concentrate or work as a team again until the Third Army maneuvers in May.[64]

The Cavalry fared better with its corps reconnaissance regiment. This unit included a mix of mechanized and horse cavalry assets. It was intended for

---

[61] E. E. Schwien, "Cavalry Division Maneuvers, October, 1939," *Cavalry Journal* XLVIII, no. 6 (November-December 1939): 467–68.

[62] Ltr, Maj Gen Herbert J. Brees to Gen George C. Marshall, 11 Dec 39, National Archives Project, GCM; Memo, ACS, G–3, Brig Gen Frank M. Andrews, to CS, sub: Temporary Absence of Border Cavalry Regiments from Garrisons During Concentration and Intensive Training, 19 Dec 39, National Archives Project, GCM; Ltr, Gen George C. Marshall to Maj Gen Herbert J. Brees, 24 Jan 40, National Archives Project, GCM.

[63] Memo, ACS, G–3, to CS, G–3, 19 Dec 39, p. 3.

[64] Memo, ACS, G–3, Brig Gen Frank M. Andrews, to CS, G–3, sub: Covering Memo for G–3/29400–40, December 19, 1939, "Temporary Absence of Border Cavalry Regiments from Garrisons During Concentration and Intensive Training," 26 Dec 39, National Archives Project, GCM.

attachment to infantry divisions, which lacked their own reconnaissance organization. To ensure uniform mobility, the horse cavalry components were to be transported by vehicles when not tactically employed. Herr had argued for such a unit since 1938, and now one was to be formed and field tested during the Third Army maneuvers.

In December 1939 the 6th Cavalry Regiment began to transition into a corps reconnaissance regiment. Stationed at Fort Oglethorpe, Georgia, its proximity to Fort Benning encouraged input from the Infantry School and facilitated its employment with infantry formations. The regiment's increased vehicle requirements were met through the use of older models scheduled for replacement in other cavalry units and the diversion of new vehicle deliveries from other Regular Army and National Guard organizations. However, other materiel needs could not be entirely satisfied, particularly the radios considered vital to the regiment's operation. Personnel needs similarly proved difficult to realize, especially after rejection of a proposal to transfer soldiers from other branches to the 6th Cavalry Regiment.[65]

Despite these difficulties, the regiment's transition and training in its new configuration continued. It served as a corps reconnaissance asset designed to operate as a single force or as a collection of detachments supporting those divisions assigned to corps headquarters. The regiment's unique mix of horse and mechanized cavalry permitted reconnaissance operations over most terrain types. Herr intended this capability to be available to every supported division simultaneously. Therefore, he designed the regiment to subdivide into identical squadrons. Each one included a horse rifle troop, a scout-car troop, a motorcycle platoon, a 37-mm. antitank section, and a pioneer and demolitions section.[66] This organization reflects Herr's appreciation of the German regiment, also a corps reconnaissance unit. Although larger and possessing more horses than the 6th Cavalry Regiment, the German organization was also intended to function as multiple, combined-arms teams attached to infantry divisions.[67]

The War Department did not concur with Herr's attempt to build organizational flexibility and tactical versatility into the 6th Cavalry Regiment's configuration. The detachable teams envisioned by the chief of Cavalry contradicted War Department organizational principles based on separating rather than merging tactical functions.

---

[65] Memo, Ofc of the Ch of Cav Acting Exec Lt Col Karl S. Bradford to TAG, sub: Corps Reconnaissance Regiment, 9 Sep 39, Ofc of the Ch of Cav, Gen Corresp, RG 177, NARA. Memo, Lt Col G. Keyes to ACS, G–4, Brig Gen George P. Tyner, sub: Cavalry Regiment (Corps Reconnaissance), 28 Sep 39; Memo, Gen Staff Secretary Lt Col Orlando Ward to ACS, G–3, sub: Corps Reconnaissance Regiments, 18 Dec 39; Memo, ACS, G–1, Brig Gen William E. Shedd, to ACS, G–3, sub: Corps Reconnaissance Regiment, 5 Dec 39; Memo, ACS, G–4, Brig Gen George P. Tyner, to ACS, G–3, sub: Corps Reconnaissance Regiments, 6 Dec 39; Memo, ACS, War Plans Division (WPD), Brig Gen George V. Strong, to ACS, G–3, sub: Corps Reconnaissance Regiment, 9 Dec 39; all in Item 4887, Reel 314, National Archives Project, GCM.

[66] Memo, Ch of Cav Maj Gen John K. Herr to ACS, G–3, sub: Corps Reconnaissance Regiment, 16 Jan 40, Ofc of the Ch of Cav, Gen Corresp, RG 177, NARA.

[67] Military Attaché, Berlin, Rpt no. 15307, sub: Germany (Combat): The German "Cavalry" (Reconnaissance) Regiment, 26 May 37; Ltr, Lt Col Willis D. Crittenberger to Capt William S. Biddle, 11 Mar 40; both in Crittenberger Papers.

Consequently, Herr's regimental configuration was rejected in favor of a more traditional one. The 6th Cavalry Regiment thus included a headquarters troop, service troop, horse squadron, and mechanized squadron. It also included fewer support units and headquarters personnel, thereby reducing its cost.[68]

Compared to horse cavalry preparations, the 7th Cavalry Brigade (Mechanized) encountered fewer obstacles in its preparations for the Third Army maneuvers. Training activities occurred without interruption, and Chaffee successfully lobbied the War Department for the attachment of motorized infantry to the mechanized cavalry for the maneuver period. Accordingly, the 6th Infantry Regiment was motorized and temporarily assigned to the mechanized cavalry.[69]

Mechanized cavalry officers, however, continued to view Infantry mechanization with a mixture of disparagement and suspicion. Col. Charles L. Scott, commander of the 13th Cavalry Regiment (Mechanized), wrote:

> I note a concentration of infantry tanks down South. Unless I miss my guess, there isn't anyone I know of in the infantry sufficiently up to date to handle a large unit of this kind effectively. I'd like to take our brigade and work against them. I think I could show the value of large unit training and the value of fire and movement on appropriate occasions (which the infantry won't listen to nor practice). I don't believe you can throw a large of unit of tanks together quickly, organize a staff and select a commander who will do it justice without considerable reorganization and training.[70]

Scott referred to the Infantry's maneuver preparations. In December 1939 infantry tank units concentrated at Fort Benning. There, the three battalions of the 66th Infantry Regiment; the 2d Battalion, 67th Infantry Regiment; the 1st and 2d Battalions, 68th Infantry Regiment; and the regimental headquarters company of the 66th Infantry Regiment were formed into the Provisional Tank Brigade, commanded by Brig. Gen. Bruce Magruder. The new unit reflected the Infantry's interest in massing its tanks on the battlefield. A ten-week training period provided the brigade's components an opportunity to develop unit cohesion and to determine basic principles of employment. Afterward, they participated in IV Corps maneuvers also held at Fort Benning.[71]

---

[68] Memo, ACS, G–3, Brig Gen Frank M. Andrews, to TAG, G–3, sub: Corps Reconnaissance Regiment, 17 Jan 40, Item 4887, Reel 314, National Archives Project, GCM; Memo, TAG to Ch of Cav, sub: Corps Reconnaissance Regiment, 22 Jan 40, Ofc of the Ch of Cav, Gen Corresp, RG 177, NARA.

[69] Hist Sec, Army Ground Forces, Study no. 27, "The Armored Force, Command and Center," Washington, D.C., U.S. Army Center of Military History, 1946, pp. 6–7.

[70] Ltr, Col Charles L. Scott to Lt Col Willis D. Crittenberger, 20 Dec 39, Crittenberger Papers.

[71] Component list taken from reception units of Memo, Provisional Tank Bde Comdr Brig Gen Bruce Magruder dtd 24 Mar 40, Alvan C. Gillem Jr. Papers, MHI Archives; Col Alvan C. Gillem, "Lessons Drawn from a Concentration of the Provisional Tank Brigade, Fort Benning, Georgia, January 10, 1940 to [illegible]," 7 Oct 40, pp. 2, 4–5, Gillem Papers; Hist Sec, "Armored Force Command and Center," p. 6.

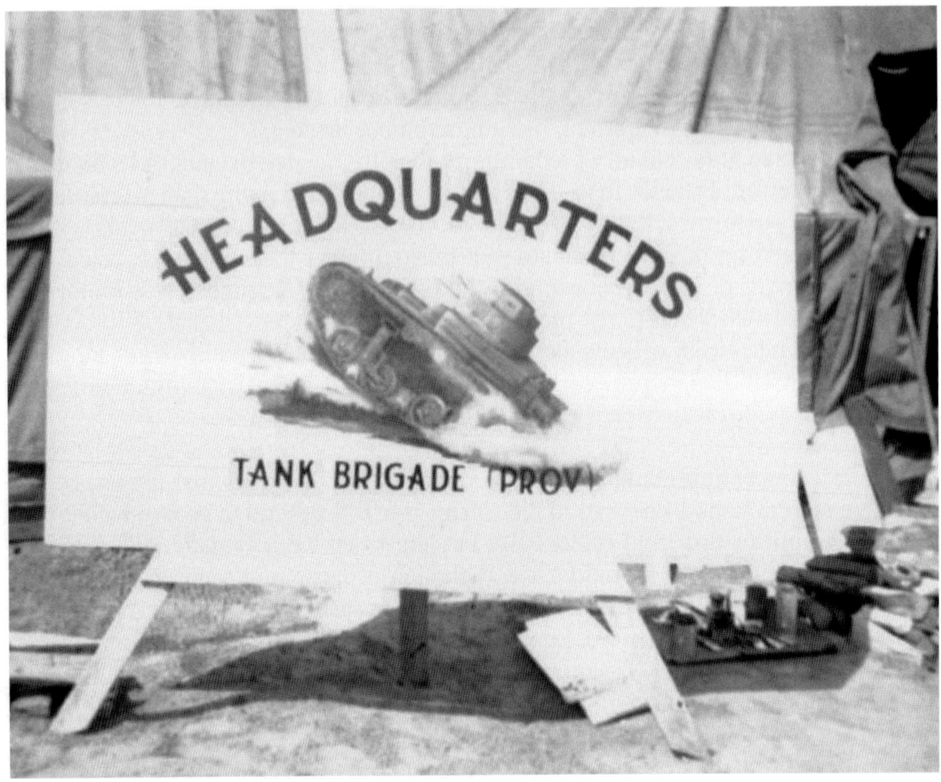

Signpost for the Provisional Tank Brigade, formed from infantry tank units in 1940

The Provisional Tank Brigade was not built upon a preexisting brigade organization. It needed maintenance, supply, and headquarters assets more than those available to individual tank regiments and battalions. The necessary personnel were provided by stripping them from already understrength subordinate tank units. Such measures could not alleviate a shortage of materiel and spare parts made worse by the variety of vehicles within the brigade. Even with the support of the Ordnance Department, adequate maintenance equipment was not received before May 1940.[72]

Communications within the Provisional Tank Brigade proved much less developed than in the mechanized cavalry. The tank force included only a small number of widely diverse radios with equally variegated capabilities. Many sets proved fragile, resulting in a high breakdown rate. Some repairs could be affected only at the Brooklyn Signal Depot, requiring the sets to be shipped to and from New York even during training and maneuvers. Although the brigade secured two

72 Gillem, "Lessons Drawn," pp. 2, 7–8.

radio-equipped scout cars for reconnaissance, it proved less successful in obtaining radio trucks, command vehicles, or its full complement of trucks.[73]

The Provisional Tank Brigade permitted the Infantry to experiment with the use of a large tank grouping. Throughout much of the interwar period, dispersed stationing precluded all but small-unit maneuvers by tank units. The Infantry welcomed the opportunity to employ a large tank group, but it lacked experience in large-scale tank operations. The War Department deliberately abstained from issuing doctrinal guidelines to allow the Provisional Tank Brigade's officers to develop their own tactical methods. This new flexibility contrasted sharply with the previous twenty years' emphasis on employing tanks strictly in an infantry support role.[74] It reflected the War Department's desire for expansion of mechanization and the influence of General Marshall, underscored by events in Europe.

Nevertheless, the brigade leadership soon established standard operating procedures based on doctrinal concepts developed by the Infantry School Tank Section. These ideas had also been incorporated into a field manual still awaiting War Department approval.[75] Generally, the Provisional Tank Brigade would perform infantry support, either as a single mass or as a collection of battalions attached to separate infantry divisions. Where possible, night marches were to be conducted to preserve secrecy and obtain surprise.[76]

The emerging tactical guidelines, however, placed a much greater emphasis on radio communications than prior Infantry tank instructions had. Couriers, flag signals, and direct liaison provided supplementary communication mediums; but radio nets governed the flow of information within the brigade. Like earlier mechanized cavalry developments, increased radio use stimulated changes in command technique. Fragmentary and oral orders also took precedence over written ones in an attempt to accelerate the tempo of operations.[77]

The new flexibility in command and control measures led to further experimentation at the battalion level. The 1st Battalion, 66th Infantry Regiment, for example, relied on prearranged signals. By transmitting a single word or phrase, a commander could cause his command to react in a precise and predictable fashion. The use of terms such as "huddle," "scrimmage," and "play one-two" indicate the football stadium influence on these experimental measures.[78]

The Crucible of Mechanization: Third Army Maneuvers, 1940

The Third Army maneuvers followed a period of extensive preparation by most of the participating corps, divisions, and smaller units. The maneuvers constituted one of the largest peacetime training events, but they also served to test several new organizations and concepts under simulated combat conditions.

[73] Memo, Magruder, 24 Mar 40.
[74] Gillem, "Lessons Drawn," p. 3.
[75] Inf Sch, "Tank Combat Principles (Tentative)," 1939–1940, Gillem Papers.
[76] Brig Gen Bruce Magruder, Training Memo no. 29, 4 Apr 40, Gillem Papers.
[77] Ibid.
[78] Notice to Members of 1st Bn, 66th Inf, 10 Feb 40, Bradford G. Chynoweth Papers, MHI Archives.

Tanks of the 66th Infantry Regiment advance while bombers fly over them at Fort Benning in 1940.

In particular, they provided an opportunity to gain experience in the operation of corps and triangular divisions.[79]

The maneuvers also provided a chance to explore concepts central to the future course of mechanized development. They represented the first simultaneous employment of nearly every mechanized unit in the Army's inventory with the principal exception of tank units in the National Guard. For the Cavalry, the maneuvers offered an opportunity to demonstrate the relative value of horse cavalry, symbolized by the presence of the 1st Cavalry Division and the 6th Cavalry Regiment. The chief of Cavalry also saw the maneuvers as a means to justify creation of a mechanized cavalry division and expand the entire mounted branch.

The principal maneuver participants were the IV and IX Corps. The former included the 1st, 5th, and 6th Infantry Divisions—all recently converted to triangular divisions. The IV Corps also included the Provisional Tank Brigade. This corps' forty-one thousand soldiers reached the maneuver area near Alexandria, Louisiana, via a 600-mile road march spanning six days. The 2d Infantry Division and 1st Cavalry Division constituted the opposing IX Corps, which also included the 7th Cavalry Brigade (Mechanized).[80] Despite expectations to the contrary, the

---

[79] Gabel, "1940 Maneuvers."

[80] *War Reports,* p. 40; Gabel, "1940 Maneuvers."

latter organization did not play a central role in the maneuvers. It conducted both offensive and defensive missions, but the maneuvers gave more attention to the newly created Provisional Tank Brigade.

On 9 May the maneuvers began. They included four scenarios, each lasting about three days. In the first scenario, IV Corps defended a river line against repeated IX Corps attacks. The Provisional Tank Brigade participated, but this action began before the entire tank force had reached the maneuver area. Hence, the brigade entered the maneuvers with only two battalions that lacked maintenance assets, support vehicles, and many of their officers. Skeleton crews manned the tanks. In this condition, the battalions provided direct support to infantry attacks.[81]

The second scenario reversed the roles of the two corps. The IV Corps attacked, launching a double envelopment of IX Corps. During this phase of the maneuvers, the 7th Cavalry Brigade (Mechanized) with the attached 6th Infantry Regiment joined the Provisional Tank Brigade together with antitank and engineer assets to form the Provisional Mechanized Force.[82] This force tested the viability of creating an ad hoc mechanized division. Maneuver planners allowed only forty-eight hours to establish the Provisional Mechanized Force. Starting from dispersed locations, its component units had to effect a concentration, execute a 175-mile flank march into the IX Corps rear area, and prepare for counterattacks. With an overwhelming mass of 382 tanks, the improvised mechanized formation proved difficult to stop.[83]

In the final two scenarios, the mechanized cavalry and Provisional Tank Brigade resumed separate operations. The former largely provided direct support to infantry attacks. In the third scenario, the IV Corps continued offensive operations into the IX Corps positions. In the fourth, the Provisional Tank Brigade executed a mass tank attack with air, artillery, and infantry support. Despite heavy rains, it attacked on schedule, but the terrain over which it advanced had become a muddy morass. Possessing high ground pressure and narrow tracks, 75 percent of the tanks became mired, and the attack collapsed.[84]

Analysis of the maneuver experience began after the conclusion of the last scenario. All participating units received criticism for remaining too close to roads, although this partially reflected maneuver restrictions intended to protect private property. Traffic jams and intermixed units resulted, generating recommendations for military police to regulate vehicle movements. Tactical engagements resulted from road-bound columns launching frontal assaults against blocking forces. Behind the attacking columns, additional units waited while soldiers remained in or near

---

[81] Brig Gen Bruce Magruder, "Report of the Tank Brigade (Provisional) Based on the Tank Concentration, Fort Benning, Georgia, January 10–April 12, 1940; IV Corps Maneuvers, Fort Benning, Georgia, April 13–30, 1940; 3rd Army Maneuvers, Louisiana, May 1–27, 1940," n.d., p. 24, Gillem Papers. This source is a compilation of responses to questionnaires issued to officers in the Provisional Tank Brigade.

[82] Ibid., p. 28.

[83] Gillem, "Lessons Drawn," p. 15; Magruder, "Report of the Tank Brigade (Provisional)," p. 28; Hist Sec, "Armored Force Command and Center," p. 7; Gabel, "1940 Maneuvers."

[84] Gillem, "Lessons Drawn," p. 14; Magruder, "Report of the Tank Brigade (Provisional)," pp. 14, 23, 24.

Tank maintenance on medium tank during the Third Army maneuvers of 1940

their vehicles without attempting to outflank the resistance. The general absence of aircraft in these maneuvers precluded the Air Corps elements' demonstrating the vulnerability of these stationary formations.[85]

Reconnaissance measures proved inadequate or nonexistent. Too many battles resulted from columns simply blundering into one another. Poor reconnaissance led to uncertainty regarding the status of important bridges and the selection of advance routes without knowledge of road conditions or trafficability. Commanders remained equally ignorant of enemy dispositions.[86]

The resultant confusion undermined tactical effectiveness. During one phase of the maneuvers, the 1st Infantry Division wandered about the battle area, wasted time and energy assaulting unoccupied positions, and frequently lost its momentum

---

[85] Magruder, Training Memo no. 29; Magruder, "Report of the Tank Brigade (Provisional)," pp. 25–26; Gillem, "Lessons Drawn," p. 10; Memo, Col George S. Patton Jr. to Ch Control Ofcr, 16 May 40, National Archives Project, GCM; Personal Memo, ACS, G–3, Brig Gen Frank M. Andrews, to Gen George C. Marshall, 18 May 40, National Archives Project, GCM; Memo, Lt Col John S. Wood to CG, Third Army, sub: Comments, Third Army Maneuvers, May 1940, 22 Jun 40, p. 1, Crittenberger Papers.

[86] Memo, Brig Gen Lesley J. McNair to TAG, sub: Report of Observers on Spring Maneuvers, 31 May 40; Brig Gen Lesley J. McNair, "Notes on Third Army Maneuvers, Leesville, May 13, 14, 15, 1940"; both in RG 337, NARA.

when advancing columns encountered unreported bridge demolitions. Division components often lost touch with one another and never contacted enemy forces.[87]

Materiel and personnel shortfalls undermined an already deficient reconnaissance ability in the Provisional Tank Brigade. It also lacked suitable maps. Those used proved little better than commercial road maps. Their small scale and lack of topographical features made them ill-suited for planning and executing operations. Onto these maps, tank commanders marked grid coordinates and common reference points. These items changed depending on the unit's location, but the map did not. Worse, no uniformity of maps existed in the brigade.[88]

Nevertheless, the maneuver experience stimulated new organizational concepts for tank units. The most important constituted a proposal by infantry tank officers for a permanent tank brigade structure. This unit reflected their experience with the Provisional Tank Brigade. The proposed brigade included a variable number of tank battalions with headquarters, signal, reconnaissance, engineer, medical, maintenance, and supply echelons. Such an organization, they believed, addressed problems encountered during the maneuvers and offered a more versatile unit. Engineers were considered particularly important because of their ability to help tanks traverse obstacles. The brigade headquarters guided and coordinated the tank battalions, providing them with service support as necessary. This organization eliminated the regiment, since it served no role.[89]

The Provisional Mechanized Force did not evoke a similarly favorable consensus. It lacked the equipment, personnel, and vehicles available to permanent formations for proper command, control, and communications. While it performed adequately, its effectiveness stemmed from adherence to an unchanging plan of action and its Regular Army composition. Neither condition could be expected to prevail in an actual war. Moreover, the Provisional Mechanized Force suffered from a lack of cohesion among component units that began interacting only forty-eight hours before starting tactical operations. Such ad hoc organizations were not considered desirable. In the event improvised mechanized divisions became War Department policy, Infantry tank officers desired the creation of permanent headquarters trained to accept and support unit attachments on short notice.[90]

Similarly, greater uniformity was sought among tank units. Infantry tank officers expressed an interest in concentrating tank units for training and development purposes and creating a Tank Board separate from the Infantry Board.[91] They also preferred permanent organizations possessing the appropriate equipment and staff rather than

---

[87] Memo, McNair to TAG, 31 May 40; Brig Gen Lesley J. McNair, "Notes on Third Army Maneuvers."

[88] Magruder, "Report of the Tank Brigade (Provisional)," p. 16; Lt Col Bradford G. Chynoweth, "Streamlines," pp. 7–8, n.d., Chynoweth Papers.

[89] Gillem, "Lessons Drawn," pp. 2, 10, 12–13; Magruder, "Report of the Tank Brigade (Provisional)," pp. 7–9, 11.

[90] Magruder, "Report of the Tank Brigade (Provisional)," pp. 28–29.

[91] "Report on Maneuvers of the 1st Battalion, 66th Infantry (Light Tanks)," 27 May 40, Chynoweth Papers.

ad hoc formations such as the Provisional Mechanized Force. These views paralleled sentiments espoused by mechanized cavalry officers.

Command and control of tank units of all sizes throughout the maneuvers benefited from a much greater reliance on radio communications. Pre-maneuver fears that atmospheric interference and jamming from too many friendly transmissions would generate a communications blackout were found to be unsubstantiated.[92] Therefore, Infantry officers urged the addition of more radios in every tank unit and the inclusion of a radio maintenance unit in their proposed brigade. This new confidence in radio communications, however, did not trigger immediate changes in net organization. Infantry tank radio nets used in the maneuvers proved too inflexible for rapidly changing developments on the battlefield. Coupled with the Infantry's continued emphasis on encrypted signals, this inflexibility undermined command responsiveness, particularly in comparison with the mechanized cavalry.[93]

The maneuvers also tended to increase Infantry support for the medium tank. Few participated in the maneuvers, but those present performed a variety of actions. Initially intended to lead infantry attacks, they also served as mobile roadblocks, provided flank security, attacked strongly defended enemy obstacles, and supported light tanks. This employment marked the Infantry's evolution toward a battle tank capable of many tactical functions, including nullification of enemy mechanization. Although the maneuvers provided few opportunities for infantry tank units to confront mechanized cavalry, Infantry officers planned to exploit the superior armor and armament of their medium tanks to overcome the Cavalry's lighter combat cars.[94]

The maneuvers did not trigger significant changes to infantry tank doctrine. Infantry tank officers considered the principles developed by the Infantry School Tank Section adequate and validated. Defensive operations, however, received heightened visibility, because tank units had repeatedly launched successful counterattacks. Tank units also performed missions similar to those of the mechanized cavalry, but Infantry tank officers considered these assignments exceptional.[95]

The experience of cavalry units in the maneuvers similarly did not raise doctrinal questions. However, several issues surrounded the organization and employment of the 6th Cavalry Regiment in its debut as a corps reconnaissance unit. The maneuvers constituted a field test for the regiment's unique horse-mechanized cavalry mix, but equipment deficiencies made a definitive assessment impossible. Insufficient motorized transport for the horses made road marches by the entire regiment impossible due to the mobility differential between its horse and mechanized components. Despite its information-gathering mission, it lacked sufficient numbers of modern radios with the range and power to sustain communications with corps headquarters.

---

[92] Chynoweth, "Streamlines," pp. 18–20, 21.

[93] Ibid., p. 6; Magruder, "Report of the Tank Brigade (Provisional)," pp. 18–20.

[94] Magruder, "Report of the Tank Brigade (Provisional)," p. 25; Gillem, "Lessons Drawn," p. 15.

[95] Gillem, "Lessons Drawn," p. 14; Magruder, "Report of the Tank Brigade (Provisional)," pp. 25–26.

Laundry, bedding, and personal gear adorn this tank of the 68th Infantry Regiment during the Third Army maneuvers, 1940.

The mechanized component also suffered from the inexperience of its personnel, whose backgrounds lay in horse cavalry operations.[96]

Nevertheless, Col. John Millikin, the 6th Cavalry Regiment commander, used the maneuvers to determine how to improve the regiment's effectiveness. He recommended the addition of scout cars armed with antitank weapons and observation aircraft. Additional motorcycles were also desired for reconnaissance and liaison, inspired by reports of foreign motorcycle usage provided by the Office of the Chief of Cavalry. Unfortunately, the Harley-Davidson bikes then in Army use proved too frail and unable to cope with sand, mud, rough terrain, or poor roads. They also overheated during sustained operation at low speeds.[97]

Millikin also believed the regiment should focus exclusively on reconnaissance missions to prevent its dissipation in unnecessary combat operations. He considered

---

[96] Memos, Col John Millikin to Ch of Cav, sub: Report on Operations of the 6th Cavalry in Maneuvers of IV Corps at Fort Benning, Georgia, 2 May 40, and Col John Millikin to CG, IV Corps, sub: Final Report of Third Army Maneuvers, May 1940, 25 May 40, both in Ofc of the Ch of Cav, Gen Corresp, RG 177, NARA.

[97] Ltrs, Lt Col Clyde Pickett to Maj Paul M. Robinett, 2 Jan 40, Paul M. Robinett Papers, GCM, and Maj Paul M. Robinett to Lt Col Clyde Pickett, 4 Jan 40, Robinett Papers; Memo, Millikin to Ch of Cav, 2 May 40; Magruder, "Report of the Tank Brigade (Provisional)," p. 15; George A. Lynch, "Final Report of Major General George A. Lynch: A Summary of Infantry Developments During His Term of Office," pp. 31–32; app. vi, pp. 9–13, 30 Apr 41, MHI Library.

the regiment a corps asset that should remain under corps control and not be dispersed among subordinate divisions. However, a final determination of the unit's organization and purpose depended on rectification of the regiment's equipment deficiencies.[98]

The performance of the 1st Cavalry Division similarly proved less than impressive. Maneuver restrictions prevented any demonstration of superior cross-country mobility, and the division was often observed moving concentrations of mounted troops too close to known enemy positions.[99] Herr believed the complementary qualities of horse and mechanized cavalry justified a mixed corps, but the maneuver experience did not validate this belief. One observer noted: "The operations of the cavalry division in combination with and against mechanized and motorized forces showed no advantages for a combination of such arms. They demonstrated, however, the inability of cavalry to meet the wide spread thrusts made possible by the use of motors."[100]

In general, divisions operated as collections of combat teams operating independently against separate objectives. These teams included at least one infantry regiment and one artillery battalion. However, neither the corps nor the division possessed the necessary support assets to sustain the simultaneous operations of these teams, triggering renewed discussion of the desired strength and composition of both formations.[101] These views reflected the particular qualities of the triangular division. It possessed great mobility, but it lacked the means to sustain operations as a collection of regimental combat teams without augmentation. Without such reinforcement, these teams lacked sufficient combat power, particularly when compared with the firepower available to comparable German organizations.

Recommendations for a corps organization included self-contained mechanized units "rapidly supported by motorized divisions of infantry and artillery—all manned by personnel trained for quick action on their own initiative and responsibility." Self-propelled artillery and aircraft would provide additional fire support.[102] In effect, a corps would comprise a combined-arms grouping designed for operations as a collection of fast-moving teams. This view reflected a growing awareness of organizational principles based on integrating rather than separating tactical functions, but they did not yet have universal acceptance within the Army.

The Armored Force and the Centralization of Mechanized Development

The Third Army maneuvers prompted open discussion of organizational and employment concepts related to mechanization. Similar discussion had followed the activities of the Experimental Mechanized Force in 1928, but subsequent mechanized

---

[98] George A. Lynch, "Final Report," pp. 31–32; app. 6, pp. 9–13; Memo, Millikin to CG, IV Corps, 25 May 40.

[99] Memo, Patton to Ch Control Ofcr, 16 May 40; Personal Memo, Andrews to Marshall, 18 May 40.

[100] Memo, Wood to CG, Third Army, 22 Jun 40, p. 1.

[101] Ibid.

[102] Ibid.

development had remained mired in controversy and uncertainty. In the immediate aftermath of the Third Army maneuvers, however, the War Department resolved to create a separate mechanized force; consolidate within it responsibility for related materiel, doctrinal, and training development; and establish several mechanized divisions.

After years of paper analysis and deferred decisions, the War Department acted in 1940 with astonishing speed to fundamentally change the nature and direction of Army mechanization. This upheaval of interwar inertia stemmed from a confluence of developments that triggered change in an unusually decisive manner. The escalation of the war in Europe, the increased authority of the chief of staff, a less stringent budgetary environment, and the impact of key individuals all contributed to a reshaping of Army mechanization.

The Third Army maneuvers occurred against the backdrop of war in Europe. The collapse of Poland had been followed by several weeks of relative inactivity, a period known as the Phoney War. On 10 May, however, Germany invaded France and the Low Countries. In ten days, German spearheads swept through the Ardennes and reached the Channel Coast, effectively splitting the Allied forces. As the Third Army maneuvers ended in Louisiana, the British were evacuating France at Dunkirk. France surrendered at the end of June. The French Army had served as a model for the American military throughout the interwar period; thus, its rapid defeat underscored the importance of modernization in the United States, particularly in the area of mechanization. German panzer and motorized infantry formations figured prominently in France's collapse, but the unsatisfactory Provisional Mechanized Division constituted the extent of American experience with similar organizations.

The creation of additional mechanized units, however, no longer seemed problematic in 1940. The war in Europe and the danger it posed to American interests encouraged increased military spending and the related production of war materiel. The changed budgetary climate stemmed from a common interest between Congress and the military in the rapid improvement of the nation's defenses. The greater availability of resources served to ease branch rivalry, a welcome development after years of competition over scarce dollars.

The international situation and improved funding alone did not transform the War Department's decision-making ability. They did, however, contribute to a centralization of Army executive authority in the chief of staff. The previous decade witnessed the emergence of the chief of staff as a key influence upon the success or failure of branch proposals, including, for example, expansion of the mechanized cavalry. Further expansion of the chief's authority occurred when General Marshall assumed this position. He benefited from President Franklin D. Roosevelt's direct support and served him as his principal military adviser. Although further changes would occur in the nature and function of the War Department, Marshall's central role did not.[103]

[103] Hewes, *Root to McNamara*, pp. 58–60, 64, 67.

Marshall demonstrated his authority early in his tenure when he secured the appointment of Brig. Gen. Frank M. Andrews as assistant chief of staff, G–3. Andrews' aviation background and outspoken support of long-range bomber development generated criticism of his ability to oversee ground-force training and readiness. However, from 1935–1939 he had commanded the General Headquarters (GHQ) Air Force, which concentrated tactical control over all operational air units, effectively creating a powerful aerial strike force. As G–3, Andrews actively promoted policies intended to improve the effectiveness of air power with Marshall's support.[104]

Andrews attended the Third Army maneuvers and upon their conclusion on 25 May convened a meeting of officers from the 7th Cavalry Brigade (Mechanized) and the Infantry's Provisional Tank Brigade. The informal gathering in a Louisiana schoolhouse provided a forum for discussion of future mechanized development. A consensus emerged among those present to concentrate mechanization responsibility in an organization separate from the existing branches.[105] Andrews endorsed this intent in a proposal to the War Department for the creation of a separate armored corps that would include all mechanized units. This recommendation immediately received Marshall's support, and implementation planning began.[106]

On 10 June a mechanization conference convened in Washington, D.C., to address the establishment of the new mechanized force and the related creation of mechanized divisions. Attendees included representatives from the General Staff divisions, the branch chiefs, and senior mechanization leaders that included Chaffee, Magruder, Scott, and Lt. Col. Sereno E. Brett. During the three-day event, the emerging plan for a separate mechanized force was presented and the details of its execution discussed.[107] All tank units and the 7th Cavalry Brigade (Mechanized) were to be grouped into two identical mechanized divisions: one stationed at Fort Knox, the other at Fort Benning. Infantry light tank units would restructure to emulate the organization of the mechanized cavalry regiments. Infantry and mechanized cavalry personnel would be distributed between the two divisions, but mechanized cavalry officers and tactics were expected to constitute the dominant influence in the new armored corps.[108]

---

[104] H. O. Malone, "The Influence of Frank Andrews," *Air Force Magazine* 85, no. 2 (February 2002): 2–7, internet article last accessed on 9 Jul 07: http://www.afa.org/magazine/Feb2002/0202andrews_print.html; DeWitt S. Copp, "Frank M. Andrews: Marshall's Airman," Air Force History and Museums Program, 2003, internet article last accessed 9 Jul 07: http://permanent.access.gpo.gov/airforcehistory/www.airforcehistory.hq.af.mil/Publications/fulltext/FrankMAndrews.pdf.

[105] Gillie, *Forging the Thunderbolt*, p. 163; Hist Sec, "Armored Force Command and Center," p. 7. Significant participants included Brig. Gen. Adna R. Chaffee Jr., Brig. Gen. Bruce Magruder, Col. Alvan C. Gillem, and Col. George S. Patton Jr.

[106] Ltr, Lt Col Willis D. Crittenberger to Maj Gen Daniel Van Voorhis, 20 Jun 40, Crittenberger Papers.

[107] John B. Wilson, *Maneuver and Firepower: The Evolution of Divisions and Separate Brigades* (Washington, D.C.: U.S. Army Center of Military History, 1998), pp. 149–50.

[108] Ibid.

Within days of the mechanization conference, a technical board formed to address the materiel requirements of the new divisions. From the mechanized cavalry, the board's members included Chaffee and Scott. They were joined by Colonel Brett from the Infantry Branch and Col. Gladeon M. Barnes from the Ordnance Department. Within a day the board submitted its first report outlining the principal needs of the new armored corps. All tanks were to carry a 37-mm. main gun in a powered turret and to possess increased armor protection. Other development priorities included medium tanks with 75-mm. guns, halftracks for multiple applications, and self-propelled artillery. Diesel engines were to equip all new armored vehicles. To support mechanized action, the board also identified the need for a stronger pontoon bridge, improved radio sets, tank-mounted flamethrowers, and better air-ground communications.[109]

Responsibility for developing the projects identified by the technical board was distributed among the branches. The prospective armored organization initially received responsibility only for tactical matters.[110] Such an arrangement merely balanced the advantages of centralized tactical development against the bottleneck of decentralized technical development. It threatened a recrudescence of the problems that had plagued American tank manufacturing in World War I.

Mobilization planning paralleled the pace of organizational development and materiel requirements determination. Although a formal decision regarding the new force had not yet been made, the War Plans Division of the General Staff began to alter mobilization plans to include armored divisions. This action symbolized the sense of urgency that surrounded the creation of the new force.[111]

On 10 July 1940, the adjutant general ended the speculation surrounding further mechanized development by authorizing the establishment of the Armored Force. He followed this watershed decision with a second ruling on 16 July that assigned to the Armored Force all responsibility for tactical and technical developments for mechanized units.[112] The creation of the Armored Force Board replaced the earlier technical board.

The Armored Force included the I Armored Corps, consisting of the 1st and 2d Armored Divisions, and the 70th Tank Battalion (Medium). The divisions constituted combined-arms formations built around an armored brigade and an infantry regiment. (*See Chart 14.*) Reconnaissance, artillery, engineer, maintenance, and service elements supported these combat organizations.[113]

Chaffee became chief of the Armored Force and commander of the I Armored Corps. His responsibilities included "the development of tactical and training

---

[109] Memo for ACS, G–4, sub: Report of Board of Officers on Development of Equipment for Armored Divisions, 15 Jun 40, Item 1479, Reel 36, National Archives Project, GCM.

[110] Ibid.

[111] Memo, ACS, WPD, Brig Gen George V. Strong, to ACS, G–3, sub: Priority in the Organization of Tank Units, 3 Jul 40, Item 1479, Reel 36, National Archives Project, GCM.

[112] Memos, TAG, sub: Organization of Armored Force, 10 Jul 40, and TAG to Chiefs of All Arms and Services, sub: Report of Board of Officers on Development of Equipment for Armored Divisions, 16 Jul 40, both in Item 1479, Reel 36, National Archives Project, GCM.

[113] Memo, TAG, 10 Jul 40, p. 2.

Chart 14–Armored Division, July 1940

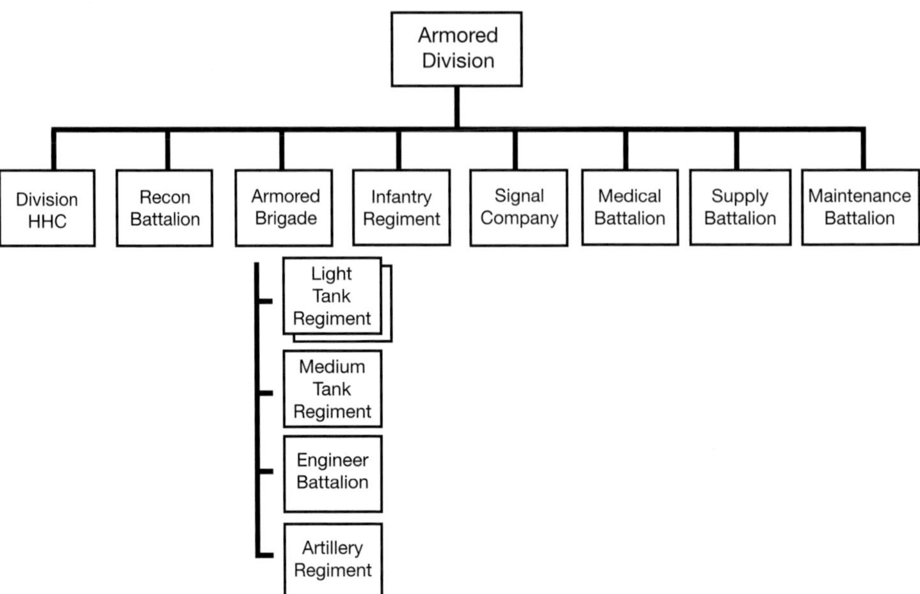

HHC = Headquarters and Headquarters Company

doctrine for all units of the Armored Force, and research and advisory functions pertaining to development and procurement of all special transportation, armament and equipment used primarily by armored units." Consequently, he became responsible for training, fiscal planning, and maintaining liaison officers on technical committees outside the Armored Force. In effect, Chaffee became a branch chief; but unlike the existing combat arm chiefs, in his capacity as I Armored Corps commander he also commanded all units assigned to the Armored Force regardless of their branch of origin. The War Department also exempted the new organization from corps area control.[114] No other branch chief received such an exemption. Indeed, corps area interference had obstructed previous Cavalry efforts to coordinate mechanized and horse cavalry development.

With the exception of the 4th and 6th Cavalry Regiments, all Regular Army mechanized units became Armored Force organizations. All Infantry and Cavalry units so absorbed were redesignated to eliminate prior branch affiliations. The 1st Cavalry Regiment (Mechanized) and the 66th Infantry Regiment, for example, became the 1st Armored Regiment (Light) and the 66th Armored Regiment (Light), respectively. Infantry and Cavalry personnel in these units were considered assigned to the Armored Force and represented a permanent loss to

[114] Ibid., pp. 1, 10.

their parent branches. The Infantry and Cavalry were also required to provide additional officers to staff the Armored Force.[115]

Symbolic of the mechanized cavalry influence on the new organization, Fort Knox became the Armored Force's center of gravity. It became the home station for the I Armored Corps and the 1st Armored Division in addition to being the site of choice for an Armored Force School. Fort Benning became home to the 2d Armored Division, while the 70th Tank Battalion (Medium) was organized at Fort George G. Meade, Maryland.[116]

The directive establishing the Armored Force classified the action as a service test.[117] This categorization permitted the War Department to create the organization unilaterally without securing legislative approval or incurring any delay related to congressional debate. The absence of legislative authority in its creation, however, meant that the structure and composition of the Armored Force remained flexible and subject to change by the War Department.

Nevertheless, the establishment of the Armored Force resolved the uncertainty concerning the course of future mechanized development. The divergence of mechanized cavalry development from its parent branch, coupled with the difficulty of creating a mechanized division that did not transgress branch interests, suggests that mechanized development had reached a crossroads by 1940. The desire for a combined-arms mechanized division contradicted the decentralization path of mechanized development adopted in 1931. The 7th Cavalry Brigade (Mechanized) represented the Army's only combined-arms unit, yet it was the focal point of controversy between Chaffee and Herr. After the Third Army maneuvers, the War Department opted with uncharacteristic speed to centralize mechanized development in an independent organization.

The composition of the Armored Force owed much to the influence of General Andrews. An airman who spent the 1930s promoting military aviation, he had no particular interest in advancing either Infantry or Cavalry concerns. Faced with the problem of how to achieve the centralized development desired by mechanized cavalry and infantry tank leaders, Andrews followed the model of the GHQ Air Force that he had been instrumental in creating. In doing so, he benefited from Marshall's support and the War Department's desire for swift action. Andrews' work in establishing the Armored Force framework provided Chaffee the opportunity to break with the Cavalry and apply himself to developing the new organization on a solid foundation.

Andrews' role in establishing the Armored Force was never widely acknowledged. His own focus as G–3 lay in promoting an effective air arm, for which he is well remembered. Yet, as a representative of Marshall, he constituted the senior leadership involvement that had been lacking from mechanized development in the previous decade.

---

[115] Ibid., pp. 8, 9.
[116] Ibid., pp. 1–8.
[117] Ibid., p. 1.

Column of M2 medium tanks of the 67th Infantry Regiment during the Third Army maneuvers of 1940

Predictably, the chiefs of Infantry and Cavalry opposed the Armored Force. Planning for the Armored Force did not include their input. Although present during the Third Army maneuvers, they were deliberately not invited to the 25 May meeting of mechanized leaders that set in motion the events leading to the Armored Force's establishment. When the branch chiefs were finally consulted, they were presented with a fait accompli. The June mechanized conference had little to do with whether to create the Armored Force. Rather, its intent lay in communicating the decision to do so and determining the manner in which it would occur.

The branch chiefs were expected to support the Armored Force, not debate its creation. Just as the earlier development of the 1939 field service regulations had short-circuited branch chief involvement, so too did the decision to create the Armored Force. By the summer of 1940, the War Department—under Marshall's guidance—possessed the will and authority to subordinate branch interests to Army needs.

Neither the chief of Infantry nor the chief of Cavalry believed that the new organization would meet the needs of his branch. Chief of Infantry Maj. Gen. George A. Lynch believed the tank had become a universal weapon and therefore should be available to all combat arms rather than restricted to one. Lynch expected the development of tank units for infantry support to be neglected by what he considered a mechanized cavalry organization unfamiliar with and uninterested in such missions. He noted that all except one infantry tank unit had been absorbed into the armored divisions. The lone tank battalion ranked last in the fielding priority for new tanks. Lynch feared that the dominance of mechanized cavalry personnel in the Armored Force would result in the development of tanks unsuited for infantry support and a decline in training between tanks and riflemen.[118] Events would prove him correct.

The creation of the Armored Force also effectively ended Herr's plans for expanding the Cavalry. His vision of masses of both horse and mechanized cavalry dominating the battlefield could not be realized by horse units alone—especially if understrength and under equipped. Efforts to better coordinate training between the two cavalry types also ended with the incorporation into the Armored Force of the combat car unit only recently approved for establishment at Fort Riley.[119] Herr retained responsibility for horse cavalry development and the experimental corps reconnaissance regiments, but the Cavalry faced extinction. In creating the Armored Force the War Department had irrevocably shifted away from horse cavalry, and many of the tasks previously assigned to it were assumed by the new mechanized organization.

Herr faced the specter of supervising a combat arm without a mission. He had sought to improve Cavalry efficiency and expand its combat responsibilities. The creation of the Armored Force negated these efforts, reduced the Cavalry's size, and nearly extinguished its growth potential. In response, Herr personalized the events culminating in the Armored Force's creation, perceiving a conspiracy by Chaffee, Van Voorhis, and several mechanized cavalry officers aimed at creating a separate arm to realize personal ambitions.[120]

Certainly, Chaffee and Van Voorhis used their personal contacts and War Department influence to advance a view of mechanized development divergent from Herr's, but all three officers shared a keen professional interest in improving the Army's effectiveness. As a branch chief, Herr sought to improve the Cavalry. As independent field commanders, Chaffee and Van Voorhis focused on improving the 7th Cavalry Brigade (Mechanized) and gave little heed to the branch interests and concerns that governed Herr's actions. The same obstacles that prevented Herr from exercising greater control over mechanized cavalry development encouraged Chaffee's experimentation with new ideas that would now find expression in the Armored Force.

---

[118] Lynch, "Final Report," pp. 50–54.

[119] Memo, TAG, sub: Reorganization and Movement of Certain Cavalry Units, 22 Apr 40, p. 1, Ofc of the Ch of Cav, Gen Corresp, RG 177, NARA.

[120] Ltr, Herr to Grow, 7 Jun 45.

8

ARMORED FORCE DEVELOPMENT, 1940–1941

The creation of the Armored Force ended the Army's bifurcated mechanized development. The new organization owed much to the continued success of German panzer formations abroad. Forging an American equivalent to the panzer division was the Armored Force's primary purpose. This objective drove efforts to build training facilities, establish doctrine, train armored soldiers, and refine tactical organizations. These activities in turn stimulated further plans to expand the Armored Force into an autonomous organization and build permanent armored corps. While these measures seemed to reflect developments in the German Army, they led to debate within the War Department. At issue was the type of Army the United States would take to war: one that embraced the primacy of the tank and the aircraft, or one that relied on a more traditional combination of infantry and artillery.

Building the Training Base

The Armored Force centralized development responsibility for mechanization within the Army. Although charged with creating armored formations similar to the German panzer division, the U.S. Army's experience with mechanization extended only to a brigade. The training, doctrine, and support facilities necessary for mechanized divisions did not exist. Moreover, the panzer division's combined-arms nature found little reflection in the U.S. Army outside the experience of the 7th Cavalry Brigade (Mechanized) and some experimentation with regimental combat teams.

The 1st and 2d Armored Divisions initially represented little more than a motley collection of assets that lacked cohesion. Nevertheless, the Armored Force determined to make these formations operational by 1 October 1940, less than three months after their creation. Each division also became responsible for training the nucleus of a new armored formation within the same timeframe.[1]

The limited time available resulted in a simplified training program focused on leadership fundamentals, physical fitness, and rudimentary soldier skills. Unit activities

---

[1] Hist Sec, Army Ground Forces (AGF), Study no. 27, "The Armored Force Command and Center," 1946, pp. 12, 50, U.S. Army Center of Military History, Washington, D.C.; Brig Gen Bruce Magruder, Training Memo no. 8: Training Directive 1st Armored Division, 1940–41, 10 Aug 40, p. 1, Willis D. Crittenberger Papers, U.S. Army Military History Institute (MHI) Archives, Carlisle Barracks, Pa.

New construction at Fort Knox during World War II

emphasized combined-arms operations, fire and maneuver, and air-ground coordination; but the need to master basic skills led to deemphasis of tank gunnery and fire support. After the October deadline passed, training focused on improving individual soldier and small-unit skills. By January 1941 training stressed regiment, brigade, and division operations in preparation for spring maneuvers. Headquarters operations, combined-arms actions, and air-ground coordination received special attention.[2]

At first, units bore responsibility for developing the internal cohesion necessary for combat while simultaneously training new armored soldiers. In the 1st and 2d Armored Divisions, improvements in tactical proficiency were offset by the periodic loss of trained soldiers to support the establishment of new armored formations and training facilities. Conversely, the readiness of National Guard tank units often benefited from greater personnel stability. In 1940 the National Guard tank companies were inducted into federal service. Reorganized into tank battalions, they became part of the Armored Force. When the War Department opted to reinforce

[2] Magruder, Training Memo no. 8, 10 Aug 40, pp. 2–3; Brig Gen Henry W. Baird, Training Memo no. 61, 28 Oct 40, Crittenberger Papers; Hist Sec, "Armored Force Command and Center," pp. 50–51.

the Philippines with tanks, it selected two of these battalions, the 192d and 194th, because they were the most combat ready.[3]

Unit training burdens gradually eased. New soldier training became the responsibility of the Armored Force Replacement Training Center in 1941. Similarly, the loss of trained cadres to support new armored units ended in 1942. The Armored Force School, however, became the principal training facility for armored soldiers, and its mission paralleled that of existing branch schools. To organize and direct the new facility, Brig. Gen. Adna R. Chaffee Jr., the Armored Force commander, selected Lt. Col. Stephen G. Henry, an Infantry officer with experience as a tank instructor. Henry's administrative ability and teaching technique made him a logical choice for establishing the new school. On 25 July 1940, he was formally appointed commandant of the Armored Force School and charged with its planning, organization, and operation. Chaffee selected Maj. Robert G. Howie, also from the Infantry School, to serve as the new school's executive officer.[4]

Henry's initial focus lay in expanding Fort Knox's training capabilities. However, pending the construction of new buildings and the acquisition of trained instructor personnel, he intended to rely on civilian trade schools and colleges to provide necessary technical expertise. These institutions trained mechanics, electricians, welders, radio operators, and related specialist functions. In so doing they performed a vital service that the Armored Force at first could not. As the Armored School began to train its own personnel, attendance at these schools declined.[5]

In November 1940 the first classes began at the Armored School amid ongoing building construction. Some 200 officers and 2,000 enlisted men attended instruction in eight major subject areas: tanks, wheeled vehicles, motorcycles, communications, tactics, gunnery, field engineering, and clerical. This initial student load, however, quickly grew to accommodate Armored Force expansion plans. Lacking sufficient time to build new facilities, the Armored Force School began to operate in two shifts. Despite the increased scale and tempo of activity, the basic style of instruction remained unchanged. Each class included a lecture, followed by discussion, demonstrations, and practical exercises. Wherever possible, students received instruction in small groups.[6]

---

[3] Memo, Armd Force Liaison Ofcr Lt Col G. X. Cheves to War Plans Division (WPD), 13 Sep 41, Item 1732, Reel 50, National Archives Project, George C. Marshall Library (GCM), Lexington, Va.; Memo, Acting Assistant Chief of Staff (ACS) Brig Gen L. T. Gerow to Chief of Staff (CS), WPD, sub: Additional Tank Battalion for U.S. Army Forces in the Far East, 16 Sep 41, Item 1732, Reel 50, National Archives Project, GCM; Oral History of Gen John K. Waters, pp. 130–31, 136–37, Senior Officers Oral History Program, MHI Archives, 1980 (hereafter cited as Waters Oral History); Bruce Jacobs, "The Evolution of Tank Units in the Pre–WWII National Guard and the Defense of Bataan," *Military Collector and Historian* XXXVIII, no. 3 (Fall 1986): 125; Hist Sec, "Armored Force Command and Center," p. 50.

[4] Hist Sec, "Armored Force Command and Center," pp. 50–51, 61. Chaffee was promoted to major general in October 1940.

[5] Ibid., p. 62; Ltr, Brig Gen Adna R. Chaffee to CS Gen George C. Marshall, 27 Jul 40, George C. Marshall Papers, GCM; C. H. Unger, "Organization of Armored Force," 25 Feb 41, p. 3, Crittenberger Papers.

[6] Hist Sec, "Armored Force Command and Center," p. 62.

The initial student groups largely constituted quotas provided by armored units. Unit commanders used the opportunity to rid themselves of troublesome soldiers. Consequently, to ensure a basic skill level, the Armored Force School established requirements that all incoming students would have to meet or exceed. A personal letter from the Armored Force chief, which every unit commander received, explained the purpose of these requirements. A noticeable improvement in the quality of incoming students followed.[7]

Plans for the Armored Force School initially included a replacement center responsible for replacing casualties among armored units with trained soldiers. This function became a separate operation on 1 October 1940 with the establishment of the Armored Force Replacement Training Center. Brig. Gen. Jack W. Heard, its first commanding officer, became immersed in the challenge of creating a replacement program from scratch. The initial training cadre included officers and noncommissioned officers from the 1st and 2d Armored Divisions, as well as reservists. In January 1941 the armored formations provided an additional 1,000 soldiers and 60 officers, mostly captains.[8]

This influx permitted the replacement center to start training in February. Arriving soldiers were assigned to one of thirty-six companies. Each company assumed responsibility for training up to 220 soldiers the skills associated with a particular tactical organization, such as medium tanks, reconnaissance, field artillery, or armored infantry. The combined-arms nature of the armored divisions resulted in soldiers from all branches receiving instruction from the Armored Force Replacement Training Center. However, in the summer of 1941 the War Department restricted replacement responsibility at Fort Knox to soldiers intended for tank and armored reconnaissance units.[9]

The first replacement training courses lasted twelve weeks, extended subsequently to seventeen weeks. Upon completion of this course, most trainees went to units to assume their duties. However, those soldiers being trained as specialists received additional instruction at the Armored Force School. Some trainees who demonstrated particular aptitude and competency were retained in the replacement center as instructors, while others immediately entered officer candidate school.[10]

The rapid growth of the Armored Force resulted in large numbers of officers arriving at Fort Knox without familiarity with armored operations. To prepare these leaders in the fundamentals of armored doctrine and tactics, they were first placed in a special familiarization course run by the replacement center. This course was designed and directed by Lt. Col. Henry C. Newton. Designated the Officers' Orientation School, it became better known as Newton's College.[11]

Both the Armored Force School and the Replacement Training Center initially lacked sufficient training literature and related teaching aids. At first the Armored

---

[7] Ibid., p. 66.
[8] Ibid., p. 71.
[9] Ibid., pp. 71–73.
[10] Hist Sec, "Armored Force Command and Center," p. 72.
[11] Ibid., p. 73.

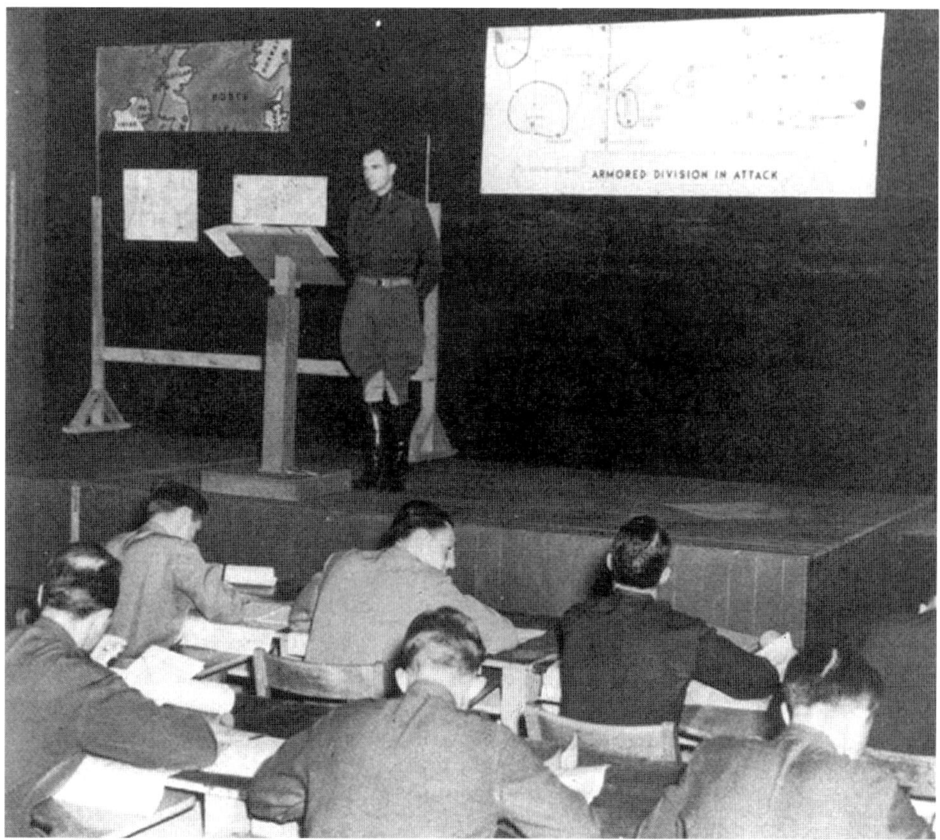

Tactics instruction at the Armored Force School

Force Board had responsibility for developing training literature. It relied on doctrinal publications for the mechanized cavalry and infantry tanks, intelligence reports, input from former Cavalry School instructors, and a familiarization briefing on armored organization and tactics that General Chaffee delivered in September 1940. Later, responsibility for training literature shifted to the Armored Force School. By March 1943 a special department within the school was drafting literature and staffing it throughout the War Department and the armored community before publication.[12]

Materiel shortfalls also plagued the Armored Force from its inception throughout 1941. The creation and rapid expansion of the new organization generated large-scale requirements for equipment and vehicles that competed with the needs of other Army branches. While American industrial mobilization proved much less chaotic than in World War I, it still required time for factories to begin mass production of war materiel, particularly when—as in the case of armored vehicles—new production

[12] Ibid., pp. 56, 73.

lines had to be established. Army needs further suffered from the higher priority given to the production of air and naval assets.[13]

Consequently, the Armored Force lacked combat vehicles in numbers sufficient to equip new units and support training. The replacement center was authorized 100 light and 32 medium tanks, but had received only 27 light tanks by July 1941. The units upon which the first armored organizations were built included some 400 largely obsolescent tanks and a variety of armored personnel carriers. Each armored division required 3,243 vehicles, including 1,140 combat vehicles. Production lines for tanks and halftracks took time to establish, particularly since the design of these vehicles continued to evolve. To expedite production, changes to the M2A4 and M3 light-tank designs were stopped.[14]

Light-tank deliveries increased slowly in 1941, but medium tanks remained in short supply. Although production rose sharply toward a goal of one thousand medium tanks per month by April 1942, most of the new vehicles were not delivered to the Armored Force. Instead, many were diverted to support British operations in North Africa. Indeed, the War Department assigned a higher priority to meeting British requests for medium tanks than it did those of the Armored Force.[15]

The supply of American tanks to foreign powers rose throughout 1941, especially after the Soviet Union became eligible for Lend-Lease aid. At first the War Department opted to withhold new tanks from Lend-Lease programs to meet Armored Force needs. However, the diversion of American tanks abroad soon resumed. Between October and December, 874 tanks were scheduled for shipment to Britain and 673 to the Soviet Union.[16]

In personnel matters, the Armored Force fared better. It initially included 530 officers and 9,329 men, representing the various units restructured as the 1st and 2d Armored Divisions and the 70th Tank Battalion. However, more soldiers were needed to fully staff the divisions and training organizations and to build the cadres for additional armored units. These manpower requirements were met through the mandatory transfer of officers from the Infantry and Cavalry Branches, the appointment of reservists to the Armored Force, and implementation of the September 1940 Selective Service Act.[17]

---

[13] Memos, Acting ACS Brig Gen L. T. Gerow to CS, General Headquarters (GHQ), sub: Priority of Equipment for Armored Force Divisions, 21 Jul 41, Item 1479, Reel 36; Deputy Chief of Staff (DCS) Brig Gen Harry J. Malony to ACS, WPD, sub: Priority of Equipment for the Armored Force, 24 Jul 41, Item 1479, Reel 36; Secretary of War Henry L. Stimson to the President, sub: Tank Production, 26 Jul 41, Xerox 1519; all in National Archives Project, GCM.

[14] Ltr, Brig Gen Adna R. Chaffee to CS Gen George C. Marshall, 27 Jul 40, Marshall Papers; Hist Sec, "Armored Force Command and Center," pp. 73, 12.

[15] Memo, Acting ACS Brig Gen L. T. Gerow to DCS Maj Gen Richard C. Moore, 11 Jun 41, Item 1590, Reel 40, National Archives Project, GCM; Memo, Stimson to President, 26 Jul 41.

[16] Memos, Acting ACS Brig Gen L. T. Gerow to DCS Maj Gen Richard C. Moore, sub: Priority of Equipment for Armored Divisions, 21 Aug 41, Item 1479, Reel 36, and DCS Maj Gen Richard C. Moore to Ch of Ord, sub: Transfers of Tanks for Defense Aid Purposes, 7 Nov 41, Xerox 1520; both in National Archives Project, GCM.

[17] Hist Sec, "Armored Force Command and Center," pp. 9, 12; Ltr, Maj Gen Adna R. Chaffee to CS Gen Marshall, 4 Apr 41, Marshall Papers. Chaffee was promoted in October 1940.

These measures alleviated basic manpower needs, but armored organizations continued to lack personnel with mechanized experience. The shortage of experienced leaders particularly affected the 1st Armored Division, which had to provide officers to staff the Armored Force's school and replacement center, operate divisional schools, train Army reservists, and supervise weekly deliveries of gold to the U.S. Gold Depository.[18]

Initially, the Armored Force possessed few of the facilities necessary to house and train the influx of men and vehicles that accompanied its creation. Fort Knox in particular required a multitude of new structures to support training activities. A massive building program began and resulted in the construction of 160 buildings a month at its zenith. In July 1940 the post encompassed 864 buildings. By August 1943 this number had risen to 3,820. The post itself grew from 30,000 acres in 1940 to 106,861 in 1943. This growth, however, did not prevent a number of inconveniences for the installation's military population, including periodic water shortages. In addition, the sudden deluge of people at the post created traffic congestion that temporarily made the Fort Knox vicinity one of the most hazardous in the country for travel.[19]

Command Climate

Armored Force command effectiveness at first suffered from the combination of too many responsibilities and insufficient staff. Chaffee served simultaneously as the chief of the Armored Force, commander of the I Armored Corps, and commander of Fort Knox. The I Armored Corps functioned not only as a tactical headquarters but also as the staff for the Armored Force. In August 1940 some relief occurred through the creation of a separate post commander and staff. Not until May 1941, however, did the I Armored Corps and Armored Force separate through the appointment of a commander for the former and a headquarters company for the latter.[20]

These positive developments were offset by feuding between Infantry and Cavalry personnel now assigned to the Armored Force. Questions concerning the role, organization, and tactics of armored units too often triggered arguments and divided the Armored Force into two camps. In February 1941 the acting assistant chief of staff, G–3, Col. Harry L. Twaddle, noted, "Unofficial information indicates that bickering and petty branch jealousies exist at present in the cavalry and infantry elements of the Armored Divisions."[21]

---

[18] Ltr, Chaffee to Marshall, 4 Apr 41; Unger, "Organization of the Armored Force," p. 4; Lucian K. Truscott Jr., *The Twilight of the U.S. Cavalry: Life in the Old Army, 1917–1942* (Lawrence: University of Kansas Press, 1989), pp. 162–65.

[19] Ltr, Lt Col Willis D. Crittenberger to Lt Gen Daniel Van Voorhis, 2 Dec 40, pp. 2–3, Crittenberger Papers; Ltr, Chaffee to Marshall, 4 Apr 41; Hist Sec, "Armored Force Command and Center," p. 11; Truscott, *Twilight of the U.S. Cavalry*, pp. 160–61.

[20] Hist Sec, "Armored Force Command and Center," pp. 10–11.

[21] Memo, Acting ACS Col Harry L. Twaddle to CS, G–3, sub: The Establishment of the Armored Force as a Separate Arm, 27 Feb 41, HQ AGF, GHQ, Record Group (RG) 337, National Archives and Records Administration (NARA).

General Chaffee (*left*) inspecting rail loading of M2 medium tanks at Fort Knox

Officers associated with the development of the mechanized cavalry believed that the Armored Force should represent the application of mechanized assets to cavalry roles, considering Infantry conceptions of tank operations conservative.[22] The 1st Armored Division's chief of staff, Lt. Col. Willis D. Crittenberger, sought "to help in a modest way to hold [the Armored Force] to cavalry missions and executions, but I am having a very difficult time even in my own limited sphere. The tendency on many sides seems to be to pretend that we started all of this Armored Force business in July of 1940, and that nothing which transpired before that time was of value or importance."[23]

Cavalry officers outside the Armored Force considered it a Cavalry organization. One of Crittenberger's colleagues serving in the Office of the Chief of Cavalry wrote: "If you feel that the Cavalry quality and nature of the instrument is in

[22] Draft Ltr, Lt Col Willis D. Crittenberger to Maj Gen Daniel Van Voorhis, n.d., Crittenberger Papers.

[23] Ltr, Lt Col Willis D. Crittenberger to Lt Col Charles S. Kilburn, 7 Feb 41, p. 2, Crittenberger Papers.

jeopardy, you might care to advise me as to what course of action should be taken in Washington."[24]

The sense of superiority Cavalry officers felt in relation to their Infantry counterparts carried into the Armored Force, contributing to the rivalry within the new organization. The former feared that the new armored division would devolve "into the old GHQ tank battalion practices."[25] Chaffee noted to Army Chief of Staff General George C. Marshall: "Ever since the earliest experiences with the old Infantry Tank Board, when it was under [Brig. Gen. Samuel D.] Rockenbach and I used to see them standing around arguing about the size of a bolt hole to the point where they never got any tanks and never thought about tactics, I have dreaded the same thing happening in any force that I had anything to do with."[26]

The Armored Force also faced criticism from Col. Bruce Palmer, who had once commanded the 7th Cavalry Brigade (Mechanized). He found fault with the armored division's organization, accused the leadership of neglecting antitank measures, and denounced training practices. These failures he attributed to the leaders of the Armored Force, who, he asserted, neglected the tactical concepts developed by the mechanized cavalry. Palmer's unprofessional personal criticisms and assertions of his own superior abilities as a mechanized adviser to the War Department alienated support. Moreover, his attacks on the armored division's organization received little credence, because the formation had been closely modeled on the successful panzer division.[27]

Continuing War Department debates concerning the future status of the Armored Force did not assuage internal rivalries. The new organization had no legal basis and lacked permanency. In its role as a field laboratory for the operation of armored formations, however, it did possess a freedom to experiment similar to that given the mechanized cavalry. Chaffee sought to preserve this independence by keeping the Armored Force headquarters at Fort Knox. He successfully resisted War Department pressure to transfer it to Washington and reduce the chief of the Armored Force's responsibilities.[28]

The close proximity of the Armored Force headquarters to its field components tightened Chaffee's personal control over Armored Force development. However, in December 1940 Chaffee was diagnosed with cancer. In the months following, he frequently required hospitalization. Chaffee's deteriorating health prevented him

---

[24] Ltr, Lt Col Charles S. Kilburn to Lt Col Willis D. Crittenberger, 11 Feb 41, Crittenberger Papers.

[25] Draft Ltr, Crittenberger to Van Voorhis, n.d.

[26] Ltr, Chaffee to Marshall, 4 Apr 41.

[27] Ltr, Col Bruce Palmer to CS Gen George C. Marshall, 20 Jul 40, Item 1005, Reel 27, National Archives Project, GCM; Ltr, Brig Gen Adna R. Chaffee to CS Gen George C. Marshall, 26 Jul 40, Marshall Papers; Memo, ACS Brig Gen F. M. Andrews to CS, G–3, 1 Aug 40, Item 1005, Reel 27, National Archives Project, GCM.

[28] Draft Ltr, Crittenberger to Van Voorhis, n.d.; Ltr, Lt Col Willis D. Crittenberger to Lt Gen Daniel Van Voorhis, 2 Dec 40, p. 2, Crittenberger Papers; Memo, Acting ACS Col Harry L. Twaddle to CS, G–3, sub: Organization of the Armored Force To Meet Proposed Expansion, 13 Mar 41, HQ AGF, GHQ, RG 337, NARA.

from continuing to exercise strong leadership over the Armored Force. His command responsibilities devolved on Maj. Gen. Charles L. Scott, who commanded in succession the 2d Armored Division and the I Armored Corps. Nevertheless, Chaffee's illness left a leadership void. Scott could not match Chaffee's aggressive and intelligent representation of the Armored Force to Washington. Nor did he possess Chaffee's network of influential friends in the War Department.[29]

Conditions at Fort Knox continued to deteriorate. In the absence of strong leadership, friction between Infantry and Cavalry personnel continued unabated to the detriment of morale. By July 1941 it had become clear that Chaffee was dying and unable to continue his duties as chief of the Armored Force. Therefore Army Chief of Staff General Marshall appointed Maj. Gen. Jacob L. Devers as Chaffee's replacement. Devers assumed command of the Armored Force shortly before Chaffee's death on 22 August.[30]

Devers graduated from the U.S. Military Academy in 1909 and spent his early career in the Field Artillery. Although he did not see combat in World War I, he was preparing an artillery unit for deployment when hostilities ended. In the 1920s he held several training appointments at the Field Artillery School, where he developed advanced fire-support techniques that found widespread employment during World War II. In 1939 Devers served in the Panama Canal Department under Maj. Gen. Daniel Van Voorhis, whom he favorably impressed. Devers' abilities came to the attention of Marshall, who promoted him to brigadier general in May 1940.[31] Marshall then appointed Devers to command at Fort Bragg, North Carolina, where he was directed to resolve several problems. Devers' success there earned him a reputation as a troubleshooter.[32]

Devers' leadership abilities, troubleshooting skills, and artillery background contributed to his appointment to the Armored Force. Throughout the interwar period, he remained an advocate of mechanized artillery and monitored Army mechanization efforts. Indeed, he had been responsible for the inclusion of qualified artillerists in the earlier Mechanized Force. Devers' artillery credentials also ensured his neutrality in the rivalry between Infantry and Cavalry personnel within the Armored Force, while his troubleshooting ability provided him the means to end

[29] Ltrs, Crittenberger to Van Voorhis, 2 Dec 40; Brig Gen Willis D. Crittenberger to Lt Gen Daniel Van Voorhis, 16 Jul 41, Crittenberger Papers.

[30] Transcription Extract from Interv with Gen Anthony C. McAuliffe, tape 3, side 1, pp. 4–6 (hereafter cited as McAuliffe Interv); War Department (WD), Special Orders no. 165 Extract, 17 Jul 41; HQ Armd Force, General Orders no. 20, 4 Aug 41; Gen Jacob L. Devers, "Inspect, Command and Develop Armored Force," Transcript, tape 4, 15 Jul 68, pp. 1–3; all in Jacob L. Devers Papers, York County Historical Society, York, Pa.

[31] At the time of his promotion, Devers was fifty-two years old and the youngest general officer in the Army. The reductions in rank that followed World War I, coupled with the slow rates of promotion of the interwar era, had resulted in an officer corps relatively advanced in years.

[32] Bio Sketch in Rededication Program for Jacob L. Devers Elementary School, York, Pa., 25 Sep 87, Devers Papers; McAuliffe Interv, pp. 4–9.

M2A4 light tanks of the 1st Armored Division training at Fort Knox in 1940

this dissension. He also had the support of General Marshall, who wanted Devers to report directly to him.[33]

At Fort Knox, Devers found disarray. The Armored Force staff suffered from the absence of a personnel officer. Its chief of staff was considered a capable tanker but also a heavy drinker.[34] The adjutant general appeared to be the dominant influence. Disputes between Cavalry and Infantry officers quickly found their way to the new commander in the form of anonymous letters. Devers recognized a need for new leadership, noting "There were quite a few discards in officers throughout the organization."[35]

Devers' solution to the leadership problem lay in the creation of a new staff. He surrounded himself with officers with whom he was familiar and who generally shared his Field Artillery background. These men assumed key positions on the Armored Force staff and shared Devers' vision of reshaping the Armored Force into an effective organization. Devers, however, sought to find the most capable

---

[33] Devers, "Inspect, Command and Develop Armored Force," tape 4, 15 Jul 68, p. 2; Transcript Extract, Interv with Gen Jacob L. Devers, tape 38, side 1, pp. 13–15; Transcription Extract, Interv with Gen Jacob L. Devers, tape 32, side 2, pp. 119–21; all in Devers Papers.

[34] The chief of staff at this time was Lt. Col. Sereno E. Brett. He had served in the Tank Corps in World War I and received the Distinguished Service Cross for valor during the St. Mihiel offensive. After the war, he continued to serve in infantry tank units until they were absorbed by the Armored Force. He earned a reputation as a tank expert and continued to contribute to armored development after Devers' arrival at Fort Knox.

[35] Devers, "Inspect, Command and Develop Armored Force," tape 4, 15 Jul 68, pp. 1–2.

individuals for specific assignments, regardless of their branch background. Thus, while Col. Edward H. Brooks, an artillerist, became responsible for overseeing artillery support in the Armored Force, Colonel Henry remained commandant of the Armored Force School in recognition of the school's organization and effectiveness. Command of the replacement center was given to General Scott, who expanded training activities and made them more realistic. Similar attention to individual capabilities characterized Devers' selection of command and staff appointments within the armored divisions.[36]

Through these measures, the last months of 1941 witnessed a steady improvement in the leadership and effectiveness of the Armored Force. Devers then turned his attention to improvements in training and materiel. He oversaw the establishment of the Desert Training Center to prepare armored soldiers for combat in desert conditions, and he became a principal factor in the rapid development of the M4 medium tank.[37] Devers built his own network of War Department support that began with the chief of staff and proved an intelligent advocate of armored organizations and their needs.

A New Doctrinal Base

In the absence of established doctrine for an armored division, Armored Force personnel at first improvised. Officers in the 1st and 2d Armored Divisions used multiple sources to establish basic principles of employment, including extracts from existing field manuals, training memorandums, and senior leader briefings. This mix, however, reflected divergent ideas not universally acceptable. The predominantly Infantry leadership in the 2d Armored Division, for example, refused to apply extracts from a mechanized cavalry field manual without widespread changes.[38]

In September 1940 the War Department issued Training Circular no. 4 to guide Armored Force doctrine development. The circular defined the armored division as "a self-sustaining unit of specially equipped elements of the combined arms and services. It has great offensive power and mobility but only a limited and temporary capacity for the defense." The division's primary purpose lay in attacks on enemy rear areas or open flanks. In such operations, tanks provided the principal offensive force. Aircraft supported its forward movement, while motorized infantry or cavalry consolidated its successes.[39]

By January 1941 a tentative field manual for the armored division had emerged. It stressed the offensive nature of the formation. Principal missions included critical-objective seizure, envelopment, exploitation, and pursuit. In all such activities the focus of the armored division lay "*deep in the hostile rear.*" There it would work to spread destruction, confusion, and demoralization among enemy forces, thereby compromising the latter's ability to conduct

[36] McAuliffe Interv, pp. 4–9; Devers, "Inspect, Command and Develop Armored Force," tape 4, 15 Jul 68, pp. 2–5, 22.

[37] McAuliffe Interv, pp. 4–9; Devers, "Inspect, Command and Develop Armored Force," tape 4, 15 Jul 68, pp. 3–4, 13.

[38] Ltr, Lt Col Willis D. Crittenberger to Col Geoffrey Keyes, 9 Dec 40, Crittenberger Papers.

[39] Secretary of War, Training Circular no. 4, 27 Sep 40, p. 1, Crittenberger Papers.

a coherent defense. The goal of armored action lay in achieving decisive results capable of influencing the outcome of a battle.[40] This emphasis derived partly from analysis of German combat operations and partly from mechanized cavalry officers whose experiences fostered confidence in the ability of a mechanized arm to do more than simply assist the advance of friendly forces.

The manual identified two primary combat situations: operations against a known, prepared defense and those characterized by uncertainty about enemy dispositions. In the former case, the armored division was to conduct a deliberate attack, planning its actions carefully in advance and maximizing the degree of support from all arms. In the latter case, commanders were exhorted to take the initiative and attack without detailed preparations, lest the division lose momentum.[41] Indeed, inactivity was denounced as the most "ineffective and inexcusable" form of tank employment that contradicted the Armored Force emphasis on bold and aggressive action.[42]

Teamwork, flexibility, and initiative were considered vital to all armored operations. Subordinate commanders were to aggressively pursue their own unit objective and the broader division mission without awaiting detailed orders. They bore responsibility for determining the best tactics and formations to employ. Inspiration for this decentralized command style came from the mechanized cavalry experience and analysis of German operations. Panzer division components reportedly operated independently of one another but in accordance with broad divisional guidance.[43]

To facilitate rapid, coordinated action by armored units in response to unforeseen developments, the Armored Force developed a "play" system. Units learned a series of tactical movements and firing patterns. To activate one of these battle drills, a commander simply called the play over the radio.[44] Infantry tank officers had recommended similar measures during the Third Army maneuvers. The concept also found support from General Marshall: "I have held the view for some time that if we trained our tactical units more as football teams, with plays which can be called by signals rather than detailed and voluminous orders, that we can expedite entry into action tremendously."[45] Moreover, the use of plays simplified the training of new Armored Force personnel unfamiliar with mechanized combat units.

Play usage complemented the Armored Force's emphasis on the radio as the most efficient means of transmitting information. Only at the company and platoon level were visual signals to supplant radio as the primary mode of communication.

---

[40] Field Manual (FM) 100–5 (Tentative), "The Armored Division," 24 Jan 41, Alvan C. Gillem Jr. Papers, MHI Archives; Bruce Magruder, "The Armored Division," 4 Mar 41, 1st Armd Div Ofcrs Sch Conf, p. 1, Crittenberger Papers.

[41] G. A. Hadsell, "Notes on 'Employment of the Armored Division,'" 3 Nov 40, p. 6, Gillem Papers.

[42] Brig Gen Charles L. Scott, "Tactical Principles of the Battalion—Company—Platoon," 20 Aug 40, Gillem Papers.

[43] Scott, "Tactical Principles"; Magruder, "Armored Division."

[44] Hadsell, "Notes on 'Employment of the Armored Division,'" p. 6; Col Alvan C. Gillem Jr., Training Memo no. 6: Tank Company Exercise in Attack, 13 Feb 41, Gillem Papers.

[45] Draft Memo, CS Gen George C. Marshall to ACS, G–3, n.d., Orlando W. Ward Papers, MHI Archives.

Fort Knox cantonment area in 1941. The parade ground is visible at the top, flanked by barracks buildings to the right.

Some question remained, however, whether radio transmissions should follow the mechanized cavalry pattern of short, voice messages sent in the clear or rely on codes and ciphers. Infantry tank officers favored the latter, since infantry tank units had used a system of numbers and letters to control basic troop movements.[46]

On the battlefield, Armored Force doctrine encouraged the use of fire and movement techniques. Companies and platoons were expected to maximize the use of covered positions and "leapfrog" their way forward.[47] Attacks consisted of "a combination of position fire and movement to reduce opposition in much the same manner as small dismounted units of cavalry and infantry use fire and movement to reduce a machine gun emplacement."[48] However, engagements with hostile mechanized forces were discouraged. Training routinely emphasized the importance of maneuver over tank gunnery despite the objections of Infantry tank officers.[49]

Armored division maintenance support expanded the echeloned system developed by the mechanized cavalry. Forward echelons conducted minor repairs and service, while those to the rear bore responsibility for comprehensive and time-consuming maintenance. In combat, vehicles that could not be repaired quickly were left for rear maintenance elements to recover and restore to service. Maintenance personnel

---

[46] Scott, "Tactical Principles"; "Training Notes for Armored Force," 6 Feb 41, Crittenberger Papers.

[47] Scott, "Tactical Principles"; Hadsell, "Notes on 'Employment of the Armored Division,'" p. 2.

[48] Scott, "Tactical Principles."

[49] Scott, "Tactical Principles"; Hadsell, "Notes on 'Employment of the Armored Division,'" p. 8; FM 100–5 (Tentative); Hist Sec, "Armored Force Command and Center," p. 17.

proved insufficient at the regimental and battalion levels, partially because forward maintenance teams preferred to do their own service work rather than permit vehicles to be removed to the rear.[50]

The successful support given to German panzer divisions by dive bombers ensured a consensus of Armored Force opinion in support of close cooperation between aircraft and armored units. Early Armored Force doctrine thus assumed the presence of friendly close air support.[51] These expectations, however, found no parallel within the General Headquarters (GHQ) Air Force, which considered close air support missions a waste of resources. Instead, it intended to focus aircraft against enemy lines of supply and communication to isolate the battlefield.[52]

On 20 June 1941, the War Department reorganized aerial assets into the Army Air Forces and gave them greater autonomy from the ground forces. Close air support development suffered as a result. Although exercises involving aircraft and the 4th Motorized and 2d Armored Divisions provided valuable lessons, they also revealed the inefficacy of American tactical air support. Air-ground communication relied on colored panels displayed by ground troops and aircraft motions, both highly subject to misinterpretation. Coordination of air support remained a complex and time-consuming process inadequate to Armored Force needs.[53]

Early Training Activities

Armored Force training activities began in 1940 simultaneously with the establishment of instructional facilities and the development of basic tactical principles. Field exercises constituted an important aspect of unit training, but these underscored the training challenge facing the Armored Force. During the attack, tanks failed to coordinate their efforts, instead racing toward their objectives and treating phase lines as finish lines. Armored units proved incapable of mounting effective counterattacks against hostile mechanized forces. Reconnaissance tended to focus

---

[50] Maj Gen Bruce Magruder, Memo no. 12: Maintenance Procedure in Combat, 3 Feb 41; Paul Steele, "Training Notes for Armored Force—*Maintenance*," 3 Mar 41, pp. 4–5, 7; both in Crittenberger Papers.

[51] Secretary of War, Training Circular no. 4, 27 Sep 40; FM 100–5 (Tentative), 24 Jan 41; Magruder, "Armored Division"; Memo, Maj L. C. Jaynes to CS, 15 Apr 41, Crittenberger Papers; Memo, Ch of Inf Maj Gen Courtney H. Hodges to CS, sub: Evaluation of Modern Battle Forces, 6 Jun 41, Xerox 698, National Archives Project, GCM.

[52] Memo, Lt Gen Delos C. Emmons to CS, sub: Evaluation of Modern Battle Forces, 2 Apr 41, Xerox 694, National Archives Project, GCM.

[53] Memo, Lt Col V. E. Prichard to ACS, G–3, sub: Air Ground School, n.d., Crittenberger Papers; Maj Gen Bruce Magruder, "Signal Operation Instructions, Identification Panel Code No. 1," 15 Dec 40, p. 1, Crittenberger Papers; Kent Roberts Greenfield and Robert R. Palmer, "Origins of the Army Ground Forces: General Headquarters, United States Army, 1940–42," in *The Army Ground Forces: The Organization of Ground Combat Troops*, ed. Kent Roberts Greenfield, Robert R. Palmer, and Bell I. Wiley, U.S. Army in World War II (Washington, D.C.: U.S. Army Center of Military History, 1947), pp. 102–07.

Training demonstration with an M2A4 light tank

on near objectives rather than conducting the distant reconnoitering necessary for rapid, long-distance movements by the armored divisions.[54]

Tactical planning proved no more effective. One exercise included a river-crossing operation similar to those conducted by the German Army in the opening days of the French campaign. The American effort, however, suffered from "glossed over" preparations, loss of surprise, and the concentration of vital materiel within easy range of enemy weapons.[55] A separate river-crossing exercise netted no better results. A detachment sent to locate a viable crossing site that would permit an envelopment of hostile forces failed to carry the necessary bridging equipment.[56]

Armored personnel were warned against employing tanks in frontal attacks on prepared positions. Such action contradicted the doctrinal emphasis on seeking the enemy's rear area through maneuver. It also exposed armored units to potentially high losses for little gain. However, the lesson was not always clear. During one

---

[54] Brig Gen George S. Patton, Training Memo no. 21, 24 Oct 40; Col Alvan C. Gillem Jr., "Notes on Conference," 6 Jan 41, p. 3; Brig Gen Alvan C. Gillem Jr., "Brief Summaries of Several Exercises Held by Armored Regiments of the 2nd Armored Brigade," 4 Apr 41; all in Gillem Papers. Maj Gen Charles L. Scott, "Comments on Tactical Inspection of 1st Armored Division," 31 May 41, pp. 2–3, Crittenberger Papers.

[55] 1941 Daybook of Col Alvan C. Gillem Jr., 66th Armd Rgt, Fort Benning, 10 Mar 41, Gillem Papers.

[56] Gillem, "Brief Summaries."

demonstration intended to illustrate the defensive strength of infantry positions supported by antitank guns and artillery, a tank ran over a machine-gun emplacement manned by dummies.[57]

Battlefield communication lacked uniformity. Signal flags and short, two-letter radio transmissions continued to compete with voice messages sent in the clear. Despite the success of the radio-based command and control process pioneered by the 7th Cavalry Brigade (Mechanized), many Armored Force organizations failed to apply it. This reluctance reflected the Infantry's preference for coded messages and the War Department's encouragement of wire to supplement radio communications.[58]

Poor march discipline became a chronic problem. Command-directed changes in direction or formation too often went unnoticed. Vehicle drivers routinely ignored traffic regulations, particularly speed limits. During the course of one field maneuver, military police arrested up to a hundred soldiers per day for speeding.[59] New tank crews relished the idea of running over obstacles despite the exhortations of unit commanders that "tanks need not knock down every tree they see."[60] Vehicles also tended to remain bunched, despite their vulnerability to aircraft and the criticism of British observers who had experienced real air attacks.[61]

Similar problems existed in the separate tank battalions. These units were intended to support infantry and cavalry formations.[62] Armored Force officers recognized that only nomenclature differentiated the separate battalions from previous infantry tank units. The same deficiencies that had plagued the latter remained. According to one Armor officer:

> Another development here is the realization that the G.H.Q. tank battalions without reconnaissance, fire support, and adequate radio are nothing more than a herd of elephants, and blind at that! In the Tennessee maneuvers an attempt was made by the various high commanders to use them as mechanized troops, on mechanized missions, and it simply didn't work. The tanks, lumbering down the road without any reconnaissance in front, would run into one anti-tank gun, and there die on the spot.[63]

Armored training encouraged envelopment by large tank masses. Single and double envelopments found repeated expression in tactical demonstrations and exercises. Indeed, the basic tactical principle guiding all armored operations in contact with the enemy called for the establishment of a base of fire while a second

---

57 Lt Col Willis D. Crittenberger, Training Memo no. 25, 30 Sep 40, Crittenberger Papers.

58 Gillem, "Brief Summaries"; Secretary of War, Training Circ no. 4, 27 Sep 40, p. 2.

59 Scott, "Tactical Principles"; "Comments by the Army Commander on Second Army Field Training, June 28, 1941," 28 Jun 41, pp. 4–5, Crittenberger Papers.

60 Patton, Training Memo no. 21, 24 Oct 40.

61 "Informal Conference by Maj. W. E. H. Grylls, British Army, Before the Staff of the 1st Armored Division, July 9, 1941," p. 1, Crittenberger Papers.

62 Secretary of War, Training Circ no. 4, 27 Sep 40, pp. 2–3.

63 Ltr, Crittenberger to Van Voorhis, 16 Jul 41.

A column of M3 light tanks from the 13th Armored Regiment
moving down a road on Fort Knox, 1941

force conducted a flanking movement to either destroy the enemy force or cause its retreat. The simplicity of this concept made it especially suitable for teaching new Armored Force personnel and ensured a fundamental uniformity of doctrine with the other combat arms.[64]

The 1st and 2d Armored Divisions made their maneuver debuts in the summer of 1941. In Tennessee, the 2d Armored Division acted in concert with the VII Corps. Employed as a collection of task forces, the 2d Armored Division repeatedly undertook envelopment operations and progressively improved in effectiveness. Indeed, the division caused the early termination of every scenario in which it participated because of the speed with which it achieved all of its objectives.[65] Both the 1st and 2d Armored Divisions received high praise for their maneuver activities.

Yet despite the public acclaim given the 2d Armored Division by the press, the maneuvers indicated several deficiencies. The division's tank and infantry components failed to coordinate their actions, resulting in large numbers of armored vehicles "destroyed" by enemy antitank weapons. In the first exercise alone, the division lost 135 tanks and numerous other vehicles. Reconnaissance organizations too often failed to discover or eliminate antitank positions. Divisional columns operated in a disjointed and uncoordinated fashion.[66] Such problems underscored the Armored Force's training challenge and the mediocre readiness state of the nation's armored formations.

The Armored Force and Foreign Experiences

In formulating tactical concepts, Armored Force leaders sought to identify lessons from the early campaigns of World War II. Following France's defeat, however, analysis of the Polish campaign diminished. In retrospect, the Polish defeat seemed a foregone conclusion given the avalanche of German forces from the west and Soviet intervention from the east. The training value of the Polish campaign was further eroded by the negative view of Polish leadership within the Armored Force. In a lecture given at Fort Knox, Brig. Gen. George S. Patton Jr. compared the Polish leadership to that of the Romans at the Battle of Cannae in 216 BC: "There is an old Latin saw to the effect that, 'To have a Cannae, you must have a Varro.' Varro as you probably remember, was the Roman commander of that ill-fated day, and the idea meant to be conveyed by the saying, is that in order to win a great victory, you must have a dumb enemy commander. From what we know at the moment, the

---

[64] Brig Gen Charles L. Scott, Training Memo no. 16, 24 Sep 40, Crittenberger Papers; Maj Gen Charles L. Scott, "Orientation Talk to Regular Officers Class of the 1st Armored Division School, February 13, 1941," p. 4, Crittenberger Papers; Gillem, "Brief Summaries."

[65] Donald E. Houston, "The Second Armored Division's Formative Era," Ph.D. Diss., Oklahoma State University, 1974, pp. 132, 135, 137, 139, University Microfilms International Order no. 75–8795.

[66] "Comments by the Army Commander on Second Army Field Training, June 28, 1941," pp. 6, 8–9; Houston, "Second Armored Division's Formative Era," pp. 139, 142.

Poles qualified with such a high command."[67] Patton transferred to the Armored Force in 1940 and commanded a brigade in the 2d Armored Division.

Similarly, French and British armored operations in May and June 1940 offered few positive lessons. American analysis attributed the defeat of French mechanized units to their use of outmoded tactics and reluctance to create tank divisions until too late. British armor lacked air and artillery support, and tank operations suffered from communication failures and insufficient numbers. Long before British tanks entered combat, mechanical breakdowns associated with extended road marches and German air attacks attritted their strength.[68] American observers also discounted the counterattack at Arras as little more than "a reconnaissance in force that developed into a series of small, piecemeal, uncoordinated attacks against enemy positions and formations wherever encountered."[69] While the British disparaged German antitank measures in this action, American analysts noted that only twenty of eighty-six tanks remained operational after the first day.[70]

Nevertheless, British combat operations provided the Armored Force a wealth of data regarding the battlefield employment of mechanized units. Britain's need for American assistance ensured the steady flow of lessons learned from combat in France and North Africa. This information was supplemented through the work of a group of American officers sent to Britain specifically to study armored organization, doctrine, tactics, equipment, and training methods.[71]

The British experience tended to confirm existing trends in American armored development. The British Army's prewar disbelief in the combat utility of radio communications ended with the French campaign. Tank training subsequently stressed maximum radio usage as an effective command tool. Combat operations led the British to reorganize engineer units attached to armored units to perform combat and construction/demolition missions, a practice already adopted by the Americans and Germans. Operations in North Africa led the British to abandon easily distinguishable vehicle markings in favor of camouflage that might conceal them from enemy fire.[72]

Despite its combat experience, however, British armor continued to suffer from organizational flaws. American observers noted the absence of effective support

---

[67] George S. Patton Jr., "Training Notes for Armored Force Units," Lecture at Fort Knox, 6 Feb 41, p. 3, Crittenberger Papers.

[68] Ltr, Henry Cabot Lodge to Lt Col Willis D. Crittenberger, 15 Aug 40, Crittenberger Papers; Brig Gen Pratt, "Offensive Operations Carried Out South of Arras on 21 May 1940," p. 13, n.d., Xerox 1521, National Archives Project, GCM; Percy G. Black, "The Armored Force and Its Development," *Cavalry Journal* XLIX, no. 6 (November-December 1940): 485–88; J. A. Pickering, "Training Notes for Armored Force Units: Armored Units in Belgium and France," Officers Conf, 9 Mar 41, p. 1, Crittenberger Papers.

[69] Memo, Acting ACS Lt Col W. M. Grimes to CS, G–3, sub: Operations Carried Out North of Arras on 22*nd* and 23*rd* May, 1940, 7 Aug 40, Xerox 1521, National Archives Project, GCM.

[70] Pratt, "Offensive Operations Carried Out South of Arras," pp. 12–15; Memo, Grimes to CS, G–3, 7 Aug 40.

[71] Bruce C. Clarke, "Observations in Great Britain," Lecture at Fort Knox, 18 Mar 41, p. 1, Crittenberger Papers.

[72] Ltr, Lodge to Crittenberger, 15 Aug 40; Clarke, "Observations in Great Britain," pp. 8, 10.

units, particularly reconnaissance elements, bridging assets, and self-propelled artillery.[73] British armored divisions remained tank heavy. The 1941 armored division, for example, included 1 armored car regiment, 6 tank regiments, 2 motorized infantry battalions, and 1 artillery regiment. In contrast, American and German armored formations sought to balance tank and infantry components.[74]

While the Armored Force benefited from analysis of British combat experiences, British tank design received insufficient attention. The British stressed the importance of power traverse for turrets, vehicle compasses, and heavier armor. They found the light tanks of the interwar era increasingly inadequate on the battlefield.[75] General Motors Corporation sent a representative to England to study British tanks. Noticing the lack of an Ordnance Department presence, he asked for:

> [General Gladeon M.] Barnes, the head of the American Ordnance Tank Section to come over and have a look around, and he points out what is precisely true, which is that the American Ordnance Department is so swollen up with pride that they will not admit that anybody else has any good ideas. We have authority to have all sorts of Observers over here, but in a country which is manufacturing an immense amount of war material and which is actually using it in battle against steel bullets, not rubber ones, the Ordnance has never shown any interest.[76]

Despite the value of British experiences, the Armored Force had greater interest in German panzer operations. Previous military attaché staff members and *Kriegsakademie* students represented an invaluable intelligence resource. However, while their written reports became available through established Army channels, further efforts to exploit their expertise on the German Army proved less fruitful.

Maj. Truman Smith, attaché to Germany from 1935–1939, returned to the United States only to find himself under investigation by the Army's inspector general and facing a court-martial. His loyalty was questioned because of his personal friendship with Charles A. Lindbergh and his praise of the German Army. The press accused him of disparaging the president and serving as a ghost writer for the America First Party. These allegations eliminated Smith's potential intelligence value throughout much of 1940 and 1941. Eventually, he was exonerated and became an effective intelligence specialist on Germany.[77]

---

[73] Ltr, Lodge to Crittenberger, 15 Aug 40; Clarke, "Observations in Great Britain," pp. 3–4; Grylls, "Informal Conference," p. 6.

[74] Grylls, "Informal Conference," p. 6; Clarke, "Observations in Great Britain," p. 12.

[75] Ltr, Lodge to Crittenberger, 15 Aug 40.

[76] Raymond E. Lee, "Journal of Raymond E. Lee," vol. 3, 8 Apr 41 to 1 Jul 41, quote from 23 Apr 41, Lee Papers.

[77] Truman Smith, "Truman Smith: 1893–1946: The Facts of Life; A Narrative with Documents," n.d., pp. 116, 117–19, 122–24, Truman Smith Papers, MHI Archives. The America First Party sought to keep the United States out of the war in Europe and to focus on the nation's domestic needs. The

Maj. Percy Black served as Smith's assistant and later replaced him as attaché. Black accompanied German troops into Poland and observed them in combat. Considered an expert on German military affairs, he was scheduled to visit American mechanized units upon his return to the United States.[78] However, this plan ended after comments Black made to the press resulted in "a violent Jewish reaction."[79] His subsequent assignment as the G–2 to the I Armored Corps generated further controversy.[80] He sought to publish an article denouncing the other Army branches as obstructions to Armored Force development. The article, described by one officer as "Billy Mitchell stuff," required drastic editing by the assistant G–2 to the Armored Force, whose principal duty became characterized as "keeping Percy Black in line, both in the protocol and publicity field."[81]

Rail transport of M3 tanks of the 1st Armored Division

Capt. Harlan N. Hartness, the first American officer to attend the *Kriegsakademie*, became an instructor at the Infantry School upon his return from Germany. He was ostracized after criticizing American military practices and unfavorably comparing the U.S. and German Armies. Disenchanted, Hartness advised his replacement at the *Kriegsakademie*, Capt. Albert C. Wedemeyer, to avoid Army school assignments. Wedemeyer followed this advice but found himself subsequently under investigation by the Federal Bureau of Investigation for allegedly leaking to the press details of the Victory Plan, America's blueprint for mobilizing and organizing the resources necessary for a

party favored a strong military for defense, but its isolationist emphasis placed it at odds with the Roosevelt administration's interventionist policies.

[78] Ltr, Brig Gen Adna R. Chaffee to CS Gen George C. Marshall, 11 Dec 39, Marshall Papers.

[79] Ltr, CS Gen George C. Marshall to Brig Gen Adna R. Chaffee, 20 Dec 39, Marshall Papers.

[80] Ltrs, Col Geoffrey Keyes to Maj Paul Robinett, 5 Sep 40, and Maj Paul M. Robinett to Col Geoffrey Keyes, 10 Sep 40, both in Paul M. Robinett Papers, GCM.

[81] Ltr, Crittenberger to Van Voorhis, 2 Dec 40. General William Mitchell was an outspoken advocate of air power in the 1920s and early 1930s. He waged a continuous campaign to demonstrate the power of aircraft, including the highly publicized sinking of a battleship. Prescient and tireless in his efforts to promote air power, Mitchell routinely criticized senior military leaders with whom he disagreed. When after the crash of a dirigible he denounced the Army and Navy leadership as incompetent, he was court-martialed for insubordination, effectively ending his military career.

global conflict. These charges were dropped, but the investigation temporarily nullified Wedemeyer's intelligence value.[82]

Despite these difficulties, information concerning German tank forces did become available to the Armored Force. Throughout 1940 and 1941 the panzer division remained a powerful combined-arms formation intended to initiate and sustain ground offensives. Combat operations in Yugoslavia revealed no significant change in the formation's use and tactics. It continued to function as a collection of fast-moving groups that included tanks, infantry, artillery, reconnaissance, antitank, engineers, antiaircraft, and communications elements.[83]

The organization of the panzer division, however, underwent a number of changes. American intelligence noted: "It is doubtful if a fixed table of organization for such a division has actually been prescribed by the German General Staff. Moreover, it is doubtful if two panzer divisions exist with identical organizations."[84] Expansion of the panzer arm resulted in further diversity as existing divisions formed the cadres for new formations and materiel deficiencies appeared. Consequently, a variety of organizations represented the panzer division, including a smaller formation with added antitank assets for use in North Africa. It became part of the famous Africa Corps, but American intelligence dubbed it a Colonial Cooperation Division.[85]

While the size and precise configuration of panzer divisions varied, their principal components did not. Each appeared to retain a tank brigade, rifle brigade, artillery regiment, reconnaissance battalion, and engineer battalion supplemented by self-propelled antitank weapons and aircraft. The most important change lay in a balancing of infantry and tank assets. In 1941 the panzer division generally included two tank and two infantry regiments, a proportion most German commanders were believed to support.[86]

In fact, the panzer division had undergone a significant reduction by 1941. The new division establishment increased the infantry component to four battalions arrayed in two regiments, while it reduced the tank element to just two battalions. Between the Polish campaign and Germany's invasion of the Soviet Union, formation tank strength fell from 324 to 196. In the same period, the number of panzer divisions grew from ten to twenty-one, generating large-scale demands for additional combat and support vehicles. German production could not meet this

---

[82] Oral History of Gen Thomas T. Handy, pp. 2–3, Senior Officers Oral History Program, 1974, MHI Archives.

[83] Mil Attaché, Berlin, Rpt no. 17418, sub: The Principles of Employment of Armored Units (Tanks)—Germany, 29 Jul 40, Military Intelligence Division (MID) Corresp, 1917–1941, RG 165, NARA; Memo, Lt Col Louis J. Fortier to ACS, G–2, sub: Replies to Questionnaire Submitted by London War Office, 7 Jul 41, MID Corresp, 1917–1941, RG 165, NARA; James C. Crockett, "Some Fundamentals of German Military Operations," 6 May 41, p. 3, 1st Armd Div Offcrs Sch Conf, Crittenberger Papers.

[84] Mil Attaché, Berlin, Rpt no. 18031, sub: Organization of German Armored (Panzer) Division, 3 Mar 41, MID Corresp, 1917–1941, RG 165, NARA.

[85] Mil Attaché, Belgrade, Rpt no. 5072, sub: German Colonial Cooperation Divisions, 2 Mar 41; Mil Attaché, Berlin, Rpt no. 18258, sub: German Armored (Panzer) Division Organization, 12 Mar 41; both in MID Corresp, 1917–1941, RG 165, NARA.

[86] Mil Attaché, Berlin, Rpt nos. 18031, 3 Mar 41, and 18258, 12 Mar 41.

requirement. Consequently, commandeered civilian and captured vehicles began to equip panzer divisions. The practice helped satisfy transport requirements, but the great variety of vehicles greatly complicated maintenance and supply within the divisions so equipped.[87]

American intelligence noted the German use of combined-arms task forces crafted for a particular mission. Task force commanders generally received great latitude in their operations, but their actions were also intended to contribute to the accomplishment of their parent formation's mission.[88] Describing the relationship between task force and parent formation missions, one analyst found it to "be more of the football idea where all players know the location of the goal and dash forward to assist the progress of the ball."[89]

American attachés in Germany attributed the organizational and operational flexibility of the panzer division to the uniform training given to all personnel in the formation. Such training aimed to make "each armored unit a smooth working organization rather than a collection of individual experts."[90] The Germans trained the components of each new panzer division as a team before committing it to combat, a concept also favored by the Armored Force.[91]

Some aspects of German armored operations remained unknown. One Armored Force staff officer noted: "There is practically no information available covering such subjects as: (1) standard operation procedure; (2) the detailed employment of small units; (3) how coordination is assured between all arms; (4) how the artillery supports the attack; (5) security on the march and in bivouac."[92]

Some clarification came from Lt. Col. James C. Crockett, an officer who had served with Major Smith in Germany and later became the assistant chief of staff, G–2, for the Armored Force. Crockett passed along his personal experience of the German Army to Armored Force personnel through officer conferences and special studies.[93] He also provided the Armored Force with a translated copy of a German tank platoon manual. Heavily illustrated to show correct and incorrect actions, it also included lessons learned from the French campaign and a forward written by Heinz Guderian, one of Germany's leading armored commanders and an architect of the panzer division. These features made this manual an excellent training tool for an organization that lacked training literature of its own yet was responsible for

[87] Roger Edwards, *Panzer: A Revolution in Warfare, 1939–1945* (London: Arms and Armour Press, 1989), pp. 64, 71; Kenneth Macksey, *Guderian: Creator of the Blitzkrieg* (New York: Stein and Day, 1976), pp. 127–28; H. P. Willmott, *The Great Crusade: A New Complete History of the Second World War* (London: Michael Joseph, 1989), pp. 217–18, 420.

[88] Mil Attaché, Berlin, Rpt no. 17825, sub: German Command and Tactical Employment, 20 Dec 40, MID Corresp, RG 165, NARA.

[89] Memo, Fortier to ACS, G–2, 7 Jul 41, p. 2.

[90] Mil Attaché, Berlin, Rpt no. 17610, sub: Visit to the German Armored (Panzer) Troop School at Wünsdorf, October 4, 1940, 11 Oct 40, p. 17, MID Corresp, RG 165, NARA.

[91] Mil Attaché, Berlin, Rpt no. 17355, sub: Principles of Employment of Armored Units (Tanks)—German, 22 Jun 40, p. 5, MID Corresp, RG 165, NARA.

[92] Pickering, "Training Notes," pp. 8, 9 (quote from p. 8).

[93] See for example Crockett, "Some Fundamentals."

instructing new platoon leaders unfamiliar with armored operations. The translated manual was therefore reprinted and issued as an Armored Force publication.[94]

Armored Division Development

The initial purpose of the Armored Force lay in the development of mechanized formations similar to the panzer division. The resulting armored division organization was described as self-sustaining and capable of independent operations similar to those conducted by German panzer divisions in Poland.[95] This characterization suited an Army sensitive about its ability to match the capabilities of Germany's combat-proven mechanized forces. By November 1940 the initial armored division organization had changed since its creation in July. The formation's principal offensive force lay in its armored brigade, which included two light- and one medium-tank regiment. (*See Chart 15.*) The light regiments bore the brunt of offensive operations, since: "due to its organization and equipment, [it] is the most mobile, self-contained combat element of the armored division.... Its main role, as part of the armored brigade, is to furnish the striking power necessary for the conduct of highly mobile ground warfare against strategical or tactical objectives deep in the hostile rear."[96] The medium-tank regiment reinforced the light regiments as necessary. However, the medium units could not be employed independently, since they lacked reconnaissance and support elements.[97]

The medium tanks possessed heavier armor and firepower. They were intended to provide additional firepower to light-tank units confronting enemy mechanization or antitank weapons. They also performed the role of artillery when required. Initially, the obsolescent M2 medium tank equipped these regiments until replaced by the more powerful M3, which entered production in 1941. This 30-ton vehicle carried a 37-mm. antitank gun in its turret; a hull-mounted 75-mm. gun capable of firing smoke, shrapnel, and high explosive rounds; and three machine guns.[98]

The other divisional components supported the armored brigade. The reconnaissance battalion operated in advance of the armored division, scouting enemy positions and road conditions. Engineers assisted the tank advance either by eliminating

---

[94] Kurt Kauffmann, *Panzerkampfwagenbuch* (*The German Tank Platoon: Its Training and Employment in Battle*) (Berlin: Offene Worte, 1939); Ltr, Lt Col James C. Crockett to CS Gen George C. Marshall, 22 Sep 41, Marshall Papers; Hist Sec, "Armored Force Command and Center," p. 56.

[95] Percy Black, "The Armored Force," *Cavalry Journal* XLIX, no. 6 (November-December 1940): 485–88.

[96] WD, Draft Armored Force Field Manual, "Tactics and Technique," 7 Jul 41, ch. 7: "The Regiment (Tank) Light and Medium," p. 2, Crittenberger Papers. This chapter was intended for inclusion in FM 17–10 and prior to the latter's publication was used as a guide for Armored Force training.

[97] WD, "Tactics and Technique," ch. 5: "The Armored Company (Tank) and the Armored Battalion, Regiment, Light and Medium," 17 Jun 41, p. 34, and ch. 7, pp. 14–15. Like chapter 7, chapter 5 was intended for inclusion in Field Manual 17–10 and prior to the latter's publication was used as a guide for Armored Force training.

[98] WD, "Tactics and Technique," ch. 7, pp. 14–15; Hadsell, "Notes on 'Employment of the Armored Division,'" pp. 1–2; J. K. Christmas, "Our New Medium Tank: A Fast, Heavily Armored Vehicle of Great Fire Power," *Army Ordnance* XXII, no. 127 (July-August 1941): 27–29.

Chart 15–Armored Division, November 1940

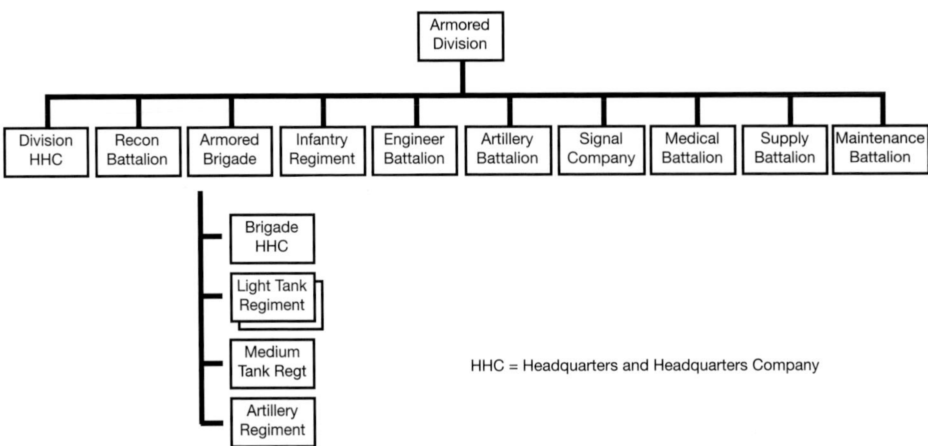

obstacles or through mobility assistance, particularly bridge construction. Artillery provided smokescreens and general fire support, while the infantry disrupted enemy defenses prior to a tank attack and secured captured objectives afterward.[99]

These basic functions did not change, but the armored division organization underwent continuous refinement throughout 1941. Most proposed changes included increases in vehicles or personnel. Foreign tendencies toward more heavily armed and armored tanks encouraged modification of the armored brigade to include two medium-tank regiments and only one light regiment. All tank units were to possess organic reconnaissance and support elements.[100] Related improvements were proposed for the infantry regiment and supply echelons. These alterations aimed at a single purpose: "Our Armored Division should be organized and equipped to be at least the equal of, but preferably, superior to, the German Armored Division."[101]

Another aim of armored division modifications lay in decreasing the variety of vehicle types in use, thus simplifying movement and maintenance. General Scott described the problem: "We now have what I call too many 'road lice' in various elements of the division."[102] The multiplicity of vehicle types resulted in recom-

[99] "Employment of the Armored Artillery of the Armored Division (Tentative)," 8 Oct 40, p. 8, Gillem Papers; WD, "Armored Force Field Manual, Tactics and Technique," ch. 8: "The Reconnaissance Battalion, Armored," 26 May 41, Crittenberger Papers; Thomas H. Stanley, "The Armored Engineer Battalion,"1st Armd Div Ofcrs Sch Conf, 20 May 41, Crittenberger Papers; Memo, Lt Col Willis D. Crittenberger to Divisional Commander, 22 Apr 41, Crittenberger Papers.

[100] Memo, Brig Gen Alvan C. Gillem Jr. to Ch of Armd Force, sub: Report on Reorganization of Armored Division, 3 Jun 41, app. B, Gillem Papers; Memo, Maj Gen Bruce Magruder to Col Unger, sub: Reorganization of the Armored Division, 7 Jun 41, Crittenberger Papers.

[101] Memo, Gillem to Ch of Armd Force, 3 Jun 41.

[102] Memo, Maj Gen Charles L. Scott to Maj Gen Adna R. Chaffee, 26 Apr 41, Gillem Papers.

icture was taken circa 1941.
Tank Regiment had just received
new tanks and some of its new equipment.
This picture was to develop a uniform
method of display in the regiment.

Ammunition and equipment load with crew of M3 light tank, 1941

mendations to substantially increase the division's ordnance and quartermaster elements to ensure adequate supplies of spare parts and vehicles.[103]

The appearance of the jeep addressed the need for a general-purpose light vehicle. Despite continued interest in motorcycles and sidecars, those in use proved too fragile and prone to mechanical breakdown. Similar problems reportedly had afflicted the Germans in Poland. Consequently, the Army sponsored development of a small 4-wheel-drive vehicle to replace its motorcycles and sidecars, resulting in the jeep issued to Army units in 1941 for extensive field testing. In Germany, too, military intelligence noted the development of a similar vehicle by Volkswagen.[104]

---

[103] Hadsell, "Notes on 'Employment of the Armored Division,'" pp. 2–3.

[104] "Statement by Maj. Percy G. Black, Field Artillery, Who Recently Returned from Germany Where He Has Been on Duty as Assistant Military Attaché," 5 Dec 39, p. 6, Crittenberger Papers; Memo, Liaison Br Ch Lt Col A. R. Harris, to Military Attaché, Berlin, Germany, sub: Motorcycles in the German Army, 18 Feb 41, and 1st End, Col B. R. Peyton, 18 Mar 41, MID Corresp, RG 165, NARA; William B. Fraser, "Motorcycle Maintenance Problems," *Cavalry Journal* XLIX, no. 5 (September-October 1940): 453; Anonymous, "Quarter-ton Trucks To Be Distributed to Army for Field Service Tests," *The Quartermaster Review* XX, no. 5 (March-April 1941): 47; E. P. Hogan, "The Army 'Bug': New Quarter-ton Command Reconnaissance Car," *The Quartermaster Review* XX, no. 5 (March-April 1941): 29.

Tank gunnery on a subcaliber firing range, 1941

To minimize delays in settling organizational questions, Chaffee convened conferences of the senior Armored Force officers. These conferences did not always facilitate decisions. In describing them, Scott wrote: "We frequently have these meetings without any concrete ideas and with everyone with a definite idea and the final result is that we get nothing but a lot of differences of opinion."[105] The divisional table of organization remained a work in progress on the eve of the autumn 1941 maneuvers.

An Armored Corps?

In October 1940 Chaffee proposed the creation of the II Armored Corps to incorporate the 3d and 4th Armored Divisions. These divisions were scheduled for activation in 1941.[106] War Department guidance emphasized the importance of employing armored formations as a "decisive mass." Therefore, Chaffee sought to create a permanent organization to function in the same manner as a German panzer corps. He intended corps assets to include military police, signal, artillery, medical, ordnance, quartermaster, antiaircraft, antitank, engineer, and air units. All of these units were to be organized and trained by the Armored Force.[107]

War Department reaction was mixed. Support came from General Headquarters Chief of Staff Maj. Gen. Lesley J. McNair and War Plans Division Chief Brig. Gen. Leonard T. Gerow, who noted: "The role of the armored division and armored corps in large scale modern warfare is now definitely defined as a result of German operations in Poland and France, and cannot be confined to the former restricted

[105] Ltr, Maj Gen Charles L. Scott to Brig Gen Alvan C. Gillem, 29 May 41, Gillem Papers.

[106] Greenfield and Palmer, "Origins of the Army Ground Forces," p. 61.

[107] Secretary of War, Training Circ no. 4, 27 Sep 40; Greenfield and Palmer, "Origins of the Army Ground Forces," p. 61.

roles assigned to infantry tanks and mechanized cavalry."[108] The assistant chiefs of staff, G–1 (Personnel), G–2 (Intelligence), and G–3 (Operations and Training), together with the chiefs of Infantry and Cavalry opposed Chaffee's corps proposal. General Marshall offered neither support nor opposition. Instead, in January 1941, he directed a restudy of Armored Force organization.[109]

Discussion of a corps organization led to debate over whether the Armored Force should become a permanent, legally constituted branch of the Army. This action also found only limited War Department support. Opponents noted the already large number of combat and service arms that made "prompt unity of W.D. [War Department] effort difficult." In fact, the War Department supervised fourteen combat, service, and administrative organizations; General Headquarters; the Army commands; the Corps Areas; the National Guard Bureau; and the overseas garrisons. Advocates of a separate Armored Force who argued that one more agency would not unduly complicate the existing bureaucratic arrangement were correct.[110] However, such allusions to the War Department's already complex structure did not constitute an effective justification for adding another permanent organization.

Chaffee considered the legal status of the Armored Force secondary to its organizational effectiveness. He did not want the chief of the Armored Force to be reduced to an adviser like the traditional branch chiefs. Instead, he wanted the Armored Force to become a separate field force that controlled multiple armored divisions grouped into corps. In this arrangement, the chief of the Armored Force would possess his own staff and preside over the doctrinal, organizational, training, and materiel development of armored formations. In effect, the Armored Force chief would merge the functions of a combat-arm chief and senior field commander.[111] This command structure served to build "an armored army capable of being employed in whole or in part as the Germans have organized and used it."[112] Modeled on the GHQ Air Force, this concept reflected the influence of Brig. Gen. Frank M. Andrews during his tenure as assistant chief of staff, G–3.

Chaffee's views were not widely accepted within the War Department, and he thus focused his energies on overcoming opposition to the armored corps and

---

[108] Memo, Col J. W. Anderson to Gen Gerow, sub: Advantages and Disadvantages of Organizing the Armored Force as a Separate Arm, Dec 40, p. 2, Item 1479, Reel 36, National Archives Project, GCM.

[109] Ltr, GHQ CS Maj Gen Lesley J. McNair to Maj Gen Charles L. Scott, 24 Jan 41; Memo, Gen Staff Sec Col Orlando Ward to ACS, G–3, sub: Organization of the Armored Force, 21 Jan 41; both in HQ AGF, Gen Corresp, RG 337, NARA. Greenfield and Palmer, "Origins of the Army Ground Forces," pp. 62–63.

[110] "Comments on Draft Written by General Gerow—Subject: Organization of the Armored Force," n.d., Item 1479, Reel 36, National Archives Project, GCM.

[111] Memo, Ch of the Armd Force Maj. Gen. Adna R. Chaffee to The Adjutant General (TAG), sub: Organization of the Armored Force To Meet Proposed Expansion, 22 Feb 41, HQ AGF, Gen Corresp, RG 337, NARA; Ltr, Chaffee to McNair, 18 Mar 41; Ltr, Brig Gen Adna R. Chaffee to CS Gen George C. Marshall, 1 Mar 41, Marshall Papers; Ltr, Maj Gen Adna R. Chaffee to GHQ CS Maj Gen Lesley J. McNair, 18 Mar 41, HQ AGF, Gen Corresp, RG 337, NARA; Memo, Twaddle to CS, 13 Mar 41; Greenfield and Palmer, "Origins of the Army Ground Forces," p. 64.

[112] Ltr, Chaffee to Marshall, 1 Mar 41.

developing a sound organization for this formation. The demonstrated success of the German panzer corps justified this emphasis, but he did not believe such a formation could be improvised on short notice. A study conducted at Fort Knox, "Organization for Command of Large Armored Units in European Armies," found that of the European belligerents only the Germans had trained and organized in peace the corps headquarters necessary to direct mobile formations.[113]

The French did create armored corps, but these failed to achieve significant results, "because of faulty organization and insufficient time to train in the employment of large armored units in battle." Similar problems, compounded by doctrinal confusion and materiel failure, resulted in the destruction of British armor in Flanders.[114] The lesson implied in the study was simple: decentralized peacetime development of armored units coupled with the absence of corps-level training and preparation before the onset of hostilities meant ruin for a nation's mechanized assets. To avoid suffering the same fate, the United States had to organize and train in peace at least one armored corps.

On paper, the I Armored Corps included a corps headquarters and the 1st and 2d Armored Divisions. In fact, it possessed none of the signal and support assets considered necessary for the control of mobile formations and its headquarters personnel also served as the Armored Force staff. Yet the Armored Force leadership failed to secure the War Department support necessary to develop the I Armored Corps into an effective tactical command and activate a second corps headquarters. Deputy Chief of Staff Maj. Gen. William Bryden considered armored corps unnecessary and opposed plans to create them. He thus eliminated the II Armored Corps from the Army's 1942 expansion plans.[115]

General Marshall reinforced his deputy's stand by deferring indefinitely the activation of any additional armored corps. Contrary to Chaffee's intentions, he limited the authority of the Armored Force chief to that of other branch chiefs. Moreover, instead of allowing the expansion of armored formations to continue under Armored Force direction, the 3d and 4th Armored Divisions were to be organized and trained under GHQ supervision before assignment to separate armies. Similarly, GHQ would assume responsibility for separate tank battalion development. These measures marked a major reduction in the influence of the Armored Force, effectively ending efforts to secure greater autonomy. They also constituted a step backward from the centralized mechanized development once considered vital to the nation's interests.[116]

---

[113] Armd Force HQ, "Organization for Command of Large Armored Units in European Armies, 18 Jan 41, HQ AGF, Gen Corresp, RG 337, NARA; Ltr, Chaffee to McNair, 18 Mar 41; Hist Sec, "Armored Force Command and Center," p. 14.

[114] Armd Force HQ, "Organization for Command," pp. 2–6, quote from p. 9.

[115] Memo, TAG, sub: Organization of Armored Force, 10 Jul 40, Item 1479, Reel 36, National Archives Project, GCM. Memo, Armd Force Liaison Ofcr Lt Col F. R. Waltz to Ch of the Armd Force, 5 March 41; Ltr, GHQ CS Maj Gen Lesley J. McNair to Maj Gen Charles L. Scott, 10 Mar 41; both in HQ AGF, Gen Corresp, RG 337, NARA.

[116] Greenfield and Palmer, "Origins of the Army Ground Forces," p. 66.

The face of the Armored Force in its first years

Fortunately for the Armored Force, these limiting instructions were largely revoked after Chaffee personally intervened with Marshall. Instead, in April 1941 the War Department directed the creation of an Armored Force staff, thereby relieving the I Armored Corps of this responsibility. The Armored Force also retained responsibility for organizing and training the 3d and 4th Armored Divisions. However, these formations were to be established as separate divisions. Activation of a second armored corps was not authorized; and, while the Armored Force chief remained the controlling authority over the separate tank battalions, he was required to consult with the chief of Infantry on their development.[117]

The April directive reduced but did not eliminate the autonomy of the Armored Force. Nor did it clarify War Department policy regarding either armored corps development or permanent branch status. Consequently, the Armored Force leadership continued to seek additional corps, as well as authority over mechanization. However, by summer, armored formations were no longer considered the only means of countering the threat posed by the German Army. The 1st Armored Division's Chief of Staff commented: "During the past few months the Armored Force has been somewhat crowded out of the picture by the anti-tank weapon group first, and then more recently by the mechanization-of-triangular-divisions crowd. Both are sure

[117] Memo, TAG, sub: Armored Force, 3 Apr 41, Item 1479, Reel 36, National Archives Project, GCM; Greenfield and Palmer, "Origins of the Army Ground Forces," p. 67.

fire projects and are popular in the War Department because they can be offered as tangible evidence of what is being accomplished in the 'wholesale mechanization of the army.'"[118] The mechanized triangular division was inspired by the emergence of German panzer grenadier divisions, which included small numbers of tanks and relied on armored halftracks for infantry transport.

The motorized division also received War Department attention as a means of combating a highly mobile enemy. Unlike the triangular divisions, which possessed transport sufficient only for their heavier support weapons, all components of the motorized division had their own vehicle transport. Motorized divisions also included additional support units to sustain independent operations in conjunction with armored divisions.[119]

In June 1940 the War Department had activated the 4th Motorized Division at Fort Benning. This formation developed motorized tactics, techniques, and procedures under the chief of Infantry's guidance. It was inspired and modeled on the German motorized divisions that accompanied the panzer formations in Poland and France. However, motorized divisions generated little interest in the American armored community, whose leaders preferred an expansion of the Armored Force. Although motorized and armored divisions were intended to work together, they did not share a uniform doctrine. Therefore, Chaffee recommended placing responsibility for the motorized division with the Armored Force, where it could be integrated into an armored corps of two armored and one motorized division. No such consolidation occurred.[120]

The War Department's Army

The German Army's continued successes in the Balkans, North Africa, and the Soviet Union posed a dilemma for the War Department. Germany appeared to rely on tanks and aircraft to achieve victory, whereas the U.S. Army remained primarily an infantry-artillery force. The War Department had to decide whether to rely on this traditional combination, supplemented with air and mechanized assets, or restructure the Army around the tank-air team. The latter seemed to represent the future of warfare, but mobilization needs favored the familiarity of traditional means.

Military intelligence analysis of military operations in France, the Balkans, and North Africa led the assistant chief of staff, G–2, to conclude that armies composed chiefly of infantry and artillery offered little match against mechanization and aircraft. He cited Germany's growth in panzer divisions and related augmentation of

---

[118] Ltr, Crittenberger to Van Voorhis, 16 Jul 41.

[119] Shelby L. Stanton, *Order of Battle: U.S. Army, World War II* (Novato, Calif.: Presidio Press, 1984), pp. 9, 11.

[120] Memo, Maj Gen Adna R. Chaffee to CS, sub: Comments on G–2 Memo 2016–1297, dated March 1, 1941, subject: Evaluation of Modern Battle Forces, 5 Apr 41, Item 1233, Reel 30, National Archives Project, GCM; Memo, GHQ CS Maj Gen Lesley J. McNair to ACS, WPD, sub: Evaluation of Modern Battle Forces, 9 May 41, Item 1233, Reel 30, National Archives Project, GCM; Ltr, Crittenberger to Van Voorhis, 16 Jul 41; *The Fourth Motorized Division* (n.p.: Special Service Office, 1942), pp. 12–15.

its motorized infantry as evidence that the German Army understood this lesson. The G–2 concluded that the U.S. Army's doctrinal base, organization, tactics, and equipment had to be redesigned to reflect developments abroad.[121] His view reflected a widely held belief in the predominance of mechanization and motorization in the German Army. Journalists, including William L. Shirer, whose subsequent book caught the chief of staff's attention, further reinforced this belief.[122]

In fact, Germany's partially mobilized industrial base could not provide the vehicles necessary for an entirely mechanized army. Before the war, Germany began to standardize vehicle production, but these efforts never came to fruition. In 1938, for example, the German Army still used over 300 different models of trucks, automobiles, and motorcycles. This variation increased exponentially at war's start when the army resorted to the requisition of civilian vehicles to meet its transportation requirements. Combat operations generated irreplaceable vehicle losses. Consequently, the German Army began to de-motorize on the eve of its invasion of France. Horses replaced vehicles in infantry divisions to provide sufficient vehicles for the panzer and motorized division spearheads. After the French campaign, motorized infantry formations underwent a strength reduction and few new ones were created.[123]

Although the reality of Germany's vehicle status remained largely unknown to the U.S. War Department, little support existed for redesigning the U.S. Army. Additional armored and air assets were desired, together with more motorized infantry divisions, antitank weapons, and antiaircraft guns. But the triangular infantry division remained the principal component of the ground forces.[124]

GHQ Chief of Staff McNair became an outspoken opponent of efforts to increase the primacy of armored and air forces. He believed that the G–2's assessment of combat operations abroad exaggerated the tank's value while neglecting the vital contributions of infantry. Instead, McNair considered the general absence of effective antitank measures a key factor in the success of Germany's panzers. Therefore, the U.S. Army needed to enhance the traditional infantry-artillery team with sufficient

---

[121] Memos, Acting ACS Brig Gen Sherman Miles to CS, G–2, sub: Evaluation of Modern Battle Forces, 1 Mar 41; Acting ACS Brig Gen Sherman Miles to CS, G–2, sub: Evaluation of Modern Battle Forces—The German Motorized Infantry Division, 24 Apr 41; Acting ACS Brig Gen Sherman Miles to ACS, WPD, sub: Evaluation of Modern Battle Forces, 9 May 41; all in Item 1233, Reel 30, National Archives Project, GCM.

[122] Memo, Gen Staff Sec Col Orlando Ward to CS, 4 Mar 41, Ward Papers; William L. Shirer, *Berlin Diary: The Journal of a Foreign Correspondent, 1934–1941* (Boston: Little, Brown and Co., 1941); Memo, Acting ACS Brig Gen Leonard T. Gerow to CS, sub: Evaluation of Modern Combat Forces, n.d., p. 4, Item 1233, Reel 30, National Archives Project, GCM.

[123] Franz Halder, "The Halder Diaries," English Trans, 23 Jan 40, Franz Halder Diaries, Manuscript Collection no. 59, GCM; Len Deighton, *Blitzkrieg: From the Rise of Hitler to the Fall of Dunkirk* (London: Jonathan Cape Ltd., 1979), pp. 171–73.

[124] Memos, Acting ACS Col General Harry L. Twaddle to CS, G–3, sub: Evaluation of Modern Battle Forces, 11 Mar 41, Item 1233, Reel 30; Acting ACS Col J. W. Anderson to CS, WPD, sub: Preliminary Comment on "Evaluation of Modern Battle Forces," 13 Mar 41, Item 1233, Reel 30; Chaffee to CS, 5 Apr 41; ACS Brig Gen Harry L. Twaddle to CS, G–3, sub: Evaluation of Modern Battle Forces, 13 Jan 42, Xerox 700; all in National Archives Project, GCM.

antitank means rather than replace it.[125] As the head of the organization responsible for Army combat readiness, McNair focused on preventing enemy tanks from interfering with American battlefield activities. To him, the tank was a threat to be nullified rather than a weapon to revolutionize warfare. He therefore supported the creation of special units intended solely to counter mass tank attacks.

Leading the War Plans Division, General Gerow stressed the importance of structuring the Army for the exclusive purpose of defeating Germany. To do so, he urged integrating the missions of the combat arms. Instead of an air-tank or infantry-artillery team, he proposed an air-ground combination in which all ground and air elements played an equally important tactical role. He supported efforts to expand armored and air forces but only as part of a balanced Army in which no single arm predominated. He criticized ongoing efforts to create an independent air force: "The prevailing campaign for 'a separate air force' nullifies progress in this direction. Continued argument and disagreement on this topic can lead only to doubt and suspicion. A military organization imbued with such attributes does not wage successful war."[126]

The debates concerning Army force structure necessarily involved the Armored Force. Upon their resolution depended the latter's future status, including the establishment of a permanent armored corps. In 1941 such debates did not lead to definitive action. Instead, many of the most pressing issues, including the future development of the Armored Force, were deferred until the conclusion of the autumn maneuvers. These maneuvers would also test new antitank tactics and provide the Cavalry a final opportunity to demonstrate its battlefield relevance.

---

[125] Memo, Maj Gen Lesley J. McNair to CS, sub: Evaluation of Modern Battle Forces, 12 Mar 41, Item 1233, Reel 30, National Archives Project, GCM.

[126] Draft Memo, Acting ACS Brig Gen Leonard T. Gerow to CS, sub: Evaluation of Modern Combat Forces, n.d., pp. 5–6, Item 1233, Reel 30, National Archives Project, GCM.

9

CREATING AN ARMORED FORCE NEMESIS

The armored division was designed as an American equivalent to the panzer division. However, the Armored Force did not intend the armored division to fight its German counterpart. The onset of World War II therefore found the U.S. Army facing a highly mechanized threat against which it had little defense. Between 1939 and 1941 the War Department belatedly struggled to generate an antitank capability. It failed, however, to reconcile antitank operations with the existing branch missions; and controversy clouded questions of doctrine, organization, and materiel. The War Department's answer to the antitank question lay in the creation of another de facto branch solely responsible for antitank development. The resultant antitank force served to provide a necessary capability, but it also perpetuated the War Department's organizational emphasis on functional separation.

Antitank Development in the 1930s

For much of the interwar era, the U.S. Army devoted little attention to antitank development. The Infantry and Field Artillery shared responsibility for antitank measures, but these competed unfavorably with the other concerns of each branch. As late as 1941 the principal Field Artillery gunnery manual devoted just six pages to antitank action. Similarly, corps and army headquarters bore responsibility for antitank training but did not actively encourage it.[1]

Army ambivalence to antitank development reflected the lack of effective War Department guidance. In 1934 a policy letter for defending against mechanized forces included a general description of armored fighting vehicles and antitank weapons yet offered few organizational or tactical recommendations. The letter described how a tank attack might develop, but the information reflected World War I attacks on trenches. In the absence of antitank guns, soldiers were encouraged to engage vehicles with small arms as soon as possible. Even though no armor penetration would occur, the resultant "bullet splash" was considered effective in interfering with the vehicle's action. Snipers were to fire at vulnerable points on vehicles; as

[1] Christopher R. Gabel, *The U.S. Army GHQ Maneuvers of 1941* (Washington, D.C.: U.S. Army Center of Military History, 1991), pp. 31–32.

a last resort soldiers were to immobilize enemy armored vehicles by "thrusting a rifle barrel into the moving track mechanism."[2]

In 1938 the War Department issued a second, more effective policy statement that included antitank doctrine and training guidance for regiments and divisions. Hostile mechanized attacks were expected to begin with small numbers of vehicles supporting an infantry assault. As the nature of the defenses became clear, waves of massed tanks would attack. This depiction mirrored the French doctrinal emphasis on the gradual escalation of offensives through the steady insertion of fresh forces.[3]

To defend against such an attack the War Department emphasized the coordinated use of all available antitank measures to channel the attacking tanks into narrow, easily defended corridors. Using terrain and map analyses, defensive positions were to be established in a manner that exploited the terrain sensitivity of armored vehicles. Buildings, fortifications, artificial barriers, and mines all constituted means of channeling mechanized attackers into areas covered by antitank weapons.[4]

The emphasis on mines, barriers, and natural obstacles reflected the findings of an Army War College analysis of German barrier tactics. The Germans believed that the deployment of mines and obstacles in sufficient width and depth could make large areas of the battlefield impassable to vehicles. Antitank guns could then be concentrated on those avenues of attack deliberately left open. The War College study found the essence of the German idea worthy of further consideration but questioned its applicability in the vast, open areas of the United States.[5]

During the 1934 Cavalry maneuvers at Fort Riley, Kansas, the horse cavalry relied on attached engineers to simulate widespread bridge demolitions. This defensive measure forced the attacking mechanized cavalry to conduct a 500-mile detour through Nebraska to reach its objective.[6] Despite this success, the use of mines, obstacles, and demolitions to thwart mechanized operations continued to receive little Army-wide emphasis. The Army War College study noted that published doctrine treated "the subject as an appendix to the general subject of defense and is considered somewhat as an afterthought."[7]

War Department guidance left the details of antitank development to the individual branches. In the Cavalry, early antitank measures stemmed from a desire to sustain the combat effectiveness of horse regiments in the presence

[2] Memo, The Adjutant General (TAG), sub: Defense Against Mechanized Units, 10 Oct 34, Alvan C. Gillem Jr. Papers, U.S. Army Military History Institute (MHI) Archives, Carlisle Barracks, Pa.

[3] Memo, TAG, sub: Defense Against Mechanized Units, 15 Mar 38, p. 2, Item 4959, Reel 315, National Archives Project, George C. Marshall Library (GCM), Lexington, Va.

[4] Ibid., pp. 2–6.

[5] J. M. Young, "Obstacles To Impede and Stop the Movement of Mechanized Forces," 17 Apr 37, pp. 17, 20, 21, quote from p. 20, U.S. Army War College (AWC) Curricular Archives, MHI Archives.

[6] Ibid., p. 26.

[7] Ibid., p. 27.

of hostile mechanization. By the 1930s the proliferation of mechanized units among the major military powers increased the branch's attention to antitank operations. Discussion of antitank measures began to permeate Cavalry School training literature.[8]

The Cavalry believed a mechanized force capable of impeding the action of any unit insufficiently equipped with antitank weapons. In response, the Cavalry emphasized tracking hostile mechanized units and deploying antitank assets to favorable positions in a timely manner. The Cavalry School embraced the use of mobile antitank teams, each one built around a single antitank weapon. The teams deployed in depth to mutually supporting locations with predetermined alternate firing positions. Once a mechanized attack began, they moved from one position to another, relying on mobility and firepower to outmaneuver and destroy enemy vehicles. During offensive operations, the Cavalry School intended antitank teams to screen friendly columns from mechanized threats.[9]

Antitank teams were used to good effect during the combined horse and mechanized cavalry maneuvers at Fort Knox, Kentucky, in 1937. There National Guard horse cavalry, commanded by Brig. Gen. Newell C. Bolton, relied on antitank teams to counteract the mechanized cavalry. Each horse-mounted team included a .50-caliber machine gun and several troopers for security and local reconnaissance. These teams deployed in depth throughout the battle area, seeking favorable opportunities to attack the combat cars of the mechanized cavalry. Bypassed teams sought to engage the mechanized cavalry from the flanks and rear. While the antitank teams blocked the action of the combat cars, the remainder of the horse cavalry sought out the mechanized cavalry's supporting units.[10]

Bolton's tactics reflected an awareness of the combat car's dependence on combined-arms support. They also foreshadowed the later tank-destroyer concept in their emphasis on mobility, firepower, and tactical aggressiveness. However, antitank team effectiveness depended on the ability to locate and track the fast-moving combat cars. Attached scout cars performed this role, delivering timely information that permitted the horse cavalry and its antitank teams to respond to mechanized cavalry actions.[11]

In contrast to the mobile tactics favored by the Cavalry, the Infantry tended toward the static employment of antitank weapons. Nevertheless, in May 1938, during combined maneuvers with the mechanized cavalry at Fort Knox, the 10th Infantry Brigade captured Army attention through application of an "accordion defense."

---

[8] J. M. Young, "Obstacles," p. 26.

[9] Memos, Cav Sch Asst Commandant Col Bruce Palmer to Cav Sch Commandant, sub: Comments on Proposed Experimental 1933 Tables of Organization, 2d Cavalry, 19 Apr 33, p. 4, and Col Selwyn D. Smith to Ch of Cav, sub: Experimental Organization, 5th Quarterly Report, 20 Apr 33, pp. 5–8; both in Ofc of the Ch of Cav, Gen Corresp, Record Group (RG) 177, National Archives and Records Administration (NARA).

[10] Willis D. Crittenberger, "Cavalry Maneuvers at Fort Knox," *Cavalry Journal* XLVI, no. 5 (September-October 1937): 424–25.

[11] Ibid.

The brigade's commander, Brig. Gen. William K. Naylor, applied antitank measures employed in the ongoing Spanish Civil War.[12]

The accordion consisted of three lines of antitank positions arranged in checkerboard fashion, supported by a mobile reserve of antitank guns and a tank platoon. Further support came from artillery barrages placed on likely attack routes and radio-equipped observation teams to provide early warning of mechanized action. The accordion relied on firepower to sap the mechanized cavalry's combat power as it passed through each line of antitank guns. Naylor's mobile reserve attacked the survivors.[13]

The accordion defense lacked sufficient numbers of modern antitank weapons. Most of the guns used were small caliber, machine guns, or the brigade's artillery diverted from its primary fire-support role. The antitank reserve included only four .50-caliber machine guns. Despite these limitations, the Army considered Naylor's tactics worthy of further study. Like those adopted by the Cavalry a year earlier, they suggested a method of eroding an attacker's strength.[14]

In 1939 the First Army maneuvers held near Plattsburg, New York, provided an opportunity to test antitank measures on a larger scale. However, the mechanized cavalry still managed to envelop the opposing force and conduct destructive operations throughout its rear area. Antitank weapons proved too few, and infantry panicked when confronted by combat cars intent on overrunning them. Efforts to divert artillery from fire support to an antitank role similarly failed, because the artillery deployed in isolated positions. Effective reconnaissance permitted the mechanized cavalry to identify and destroy each gun position piecemeal without losing its momentum.[15]

These results led the mechanized cavalry commander, Brig. Gen. Adna R. Chaffee Jr., to recommend the creation of mobile antitank units for division, corps, and army assignment. Equipped with 37-mm. antitank guns, these units would provide rear-area security, reinforce positions threatened with a tank attack, or

---

[12] Memo, Brig Gen W. K. Naylor to Commanding General (CG), V Corps Area, sub: Tactical Inspection of 10th Infantry Brigade and Attached Units, 8 Jun 38, included as Exhibit 1 of Memo, Col John F. Goodman to Chairman, Subcommittee no. 1 of Committee no. 5, sub: Mechanization: Defense Against Mechanization and Against Aviation, 10 Oct 39, p. 3, AWC Curricular Archives.

[13] Memo, Naylor to CG, V Corps Area, 8 Jun 38, p. 2; "The Mechanized Cavalry Takes the Field," *Cavalry Journal* XLVII, no. 4 (July-August 1938): 293–94; Notes of Discussion Following Lecture of Maj Gen John K. Herr at AWC, "The Cavalry," 19 Sep 39, p. 5, in Army War College Lectures, 1939–1940, pt. 2, AWC Curricular Archives (hereafter cited as Herr Discussion Notes); Notes of Discussion Following Lecture of Maj Gen Daniel Van Voorhis at AWC, "Mechanization," 29 Sep 38, p. 3, in Army War College Lectures, 1938–1939, pt. 1, AWC Curricular Archives (hereafter cited as Van Voorhis Discussion Notes).

[14] Herr Discussion Notes, 19 Sep 39, p. 5.

[15] Memo, Brig Gen Adna R. Chaffee to TAG, sub: Some Observations and Recommendations Pertinent to Any Future Expansion and Development of Mechanized Cavalry Which May Be Contemplated by the War Department, 15 Sep 39, p. 2, Ofc of the Ch of Cav, Gen Corresp, RG 177, NARA; Notes of Discussion Following the Lecture of Brig Gen Adna R. Chaffee at AWC, "Mechanized Cavalry," 29 Sep 39, pp. 9–10, in Army War College Lectures, 1939–1940, pt. 2 (hereafter cited as Chaffee Discussion Notes); Adna R. Chaffee, "The Seventh Cavalry Brigade in the First Army Maneuvers," *Cavalry Journal* XLVIII, no. 6 (November-December 1939): 461.

support the mechanized cavalry when confronted by enemy armor.[16] Chaffee believed that antitank weapons "should be organized not to drop down at particular places in advance in a passive defense but should be held mobile and ready to go to a threatened area and should be accompanied by reconnaissance for that purpose."[17] As a mobile antitank reserve, they would advance to predetermined positions once warned by reconnaissance organizations.[18]

Chaffee's preference for centrally controlled, mobile antitank units to counter hostile mechanized attacks found support in an antitank study conducted at the Army War College. This study concluded that "since terrain determines the location of the mass attack of tanks, the allocation of anti-tank weapons to all echelons must be such that they can be concentrated where needed, as contrasted to being spread uniformly among units."[19]

Critics noted that a force inadequately equipped with effective antitank guns—no matter how organized—generally suffered defeat when attacked by a powerful mechanized force. They attributed the success of the mechanized cavalry in the First Army maneuvers and the German panzers in Poland to the absence of effective antitank measures. A recommended solution included the attachment of early warning teams to infantry divisions. These teams identified enemy mechanized threats to which an army or corps headquarters responded with mobile antitank units. In this manner, infantry divisions would not be encumbered with an accretion of antitank weapons: "There is no need whatever for any unit to surround itself with antitank guns and thus become like a porcupine with its quills all out and its legs folded underneath in an attitude of immobility."[20]

The maneuver experiences and debates that followed helped the Army to develop antitank concepts, but it still lacked a comprehensive doctrine. The War Department had not approved any field manual to govern antitank operations, and the only antitank units in existence were companies assigned to infantry regiments.

Building an Antitank Unit

The War Department's 1938 policy letter envisioned the incorporation of antitank units at the regiment and division levels. The regimental antitank company served to provide immediate security to its parent unit. The divisional antitank unit constituted a central reserve to reinforce any regiment threatened with a large-scale tank attack. This two-tiered antitank organization combined

---

[16] Chaffee Discussion Notes, 29 Sep 39, pp. 10–11.

[17] Ibid., p. 11.

[18] Brig Gen Adna R. Chaffee, "Mechanized Cavalry," Lecture at AWC, 29 Sep 39, p. 27, in Army War College Lectures, 1939–1940, pt. 2.

[19] Memo, Capt Verne D. Mudge to Chairman, Subcommittee no. 1 of Committee no. 5, Suppl no. 4, sub: Mechanization: Defense Against Mechanization and Against Aviation, 10 Oct 39, p. 11, AWC Curricular Archives.

[20] Hamilton S. Hawkins, "General Hawkins Notes: Conclusions Drawn from First Army Maneuvers," *Cavalry Journal* XLIX, no. 2 (March-April 1940): 163–65, quote from p. 163.

the benefits of decentralization among the regiments and centralization of effort at the division level.[21]

However, in 1938 antitank units existed largely on paper. Equipment plans for the following year included the assignment of six 37-mm. antitank guns to each infantry regimental antitank company and two .50-caliber machine guns to each battalion. Cavalry regiments were to receive twenty-three .50-caliber machine guns. This branch rejected heavier weapons, which it considered unnecessary for normal cavalry operations and a restraint on mobility.[22]

In 1939 Chief of Infantry Maj. Gen. George A. Lynch proposed increasing the regimental antitank company strength from six to twelve guns. The change reflected awareness of the larger size of foreign antitank companies, and it received War Department support. Symptomatic of the interwar decision-making process, however, the expense associated with the measure led to deferment and restudy. A final cost assessment led the assistant chief of staff, G–3, to recommend only a paper increase in the company's strength.[23] He considered the six-gun company sufficient for operations in the Western Hemisphere but had concerns: "If we were to base our needs in antitank defense for operation in the Central European theater of war and against one of the powers which has an exceptionally large quantity of mechanized vehicles, the active defense represented by our present organization might prove entirely inadequate."[24] The destruction of the French Army in 1940 ended the debate over regimental antitank strength in favor of an actual strength of twelve guns per regiment.[25]

Divisional antitank units proved more controversial. In 1937 the Army began testing a new organization known as the Proposed Infantry Division. This formation became the basis for the later triangular division. The test formation included an antitank battalion and regimental antitank companies. The battalion, however, remained idle throughout much of the testing period; and the final report on the Proposed Infantry Division recommended the unit's removal from the division organization. Observers recommended that antitank battalions be assigned to corps and General Headquarters control to reinforce threatened areas. The infantry divi-

[21] Memo, TAG, 15 Mar 38, pp. 3, 7–8.

[22] Memo, Lt Col George E. Stratemeyer to AWC Asst Commandant, sub: Anti-tank Defense, 25 Feb 39, p. 2, AWC Curricular Archives.

[23] Memos, Assistant Chief of Staff (ACS), G–3, Brig Gen F. M. Andrews, to Chief of Staff (CS), G–3, sub: Type Army, 1 Dec 39, p. 4, Item 4892, Reel 314; General Staff Sec Lt Col Orlando Ward to ACS, G–3, sub: Increase in Number of 37mm Antitank Guns and Browning Automatic Rifles in the Infantry Regiment, 22 Dec 39, Item 4876, Reel 313; ACS, G–3, Brig Gen F. M. Andrews, to CS, G–3, sub: Antitank Defense, 30 Mar 40, Item 4876, Reel 313; all in National Archives Project, GCM.

[24] Memo, ACS, G–3, Brig Gen F. M. Andrews, to CS, G–3, sub: Antitank Defense, 23 Jan 40, p. 4, Item 4876, Reel 313, National Archives Project, GCM.

[25] Memo, ACS, G–3, Brig Gen F. M. Andrews, to TAG, G–3, sub: Antitank Defense, 26 Jul 40, Reel 313, Item 4876, National Archives Project, GCM; General Headquarters (GHQ) CS Maj Gen Lesley J. McNair to Deputy Chief of Staff (DCS), sub: Antitank Defense, 30 Dec 40, HQ Army Ground Forces (AGF), GHQ, RG 337, NARA.

sion would thus not be burdened with a unit considered unnecessary to its normal operations.[26]

Development of an antitank battalion lagged until 1939. In January the War Department ordered extended field tests to determine the organization, armament, training, and communication methods of such antitank units.[27] The growing prevalence of tank and antitank forces in foreign armies, their employment in the Spanish Civil War, and the trend in tank design toward heavier armor and armament stimulated this interest. Assistant Chief of Staff, G–3, Maj. Gen. R. M. Beck Jr., argued: "The United States Army is the only army of any major power that does not include anti-mechanized units in addition to organic regimental anti-tank weapons. We do not even have a paper organization for them."[28]

The question of branch responsibility for the antitank battalion soon emerged. The Infantry and Field Artillery both claimed proponency. Analysis of foreign antitank organizations provided little resolution, since antitank responsibility varied by nation. At the chief of staff's direction, each branch began a separate unit design effort.[29] Finally, in September the Infantry received proponency for the antitank battalion, reflecting that branch's familiarity with tanks and tactical developments associated with the 37-mm. antitank gun. The Infantry's proposed organization included a headquarters and three antitank companies, each equipped with twelve 37-mm. guns. The first antitank battalion was to be formed at Fort Benning, Georgia, in November, later delayed until January 1940. The unit cobbled together materiel, personnel, and transport from existing combat units.[30]

Design work on the new unit did not end the debate over how it should be assigned. General Lynch desired the inclusion of antitank battalions within each infantry division to supplement the regimental antitank companies. Brig. Gen. Lesley J. McNair, then the Command and General Staff School (CGSS) commandant, supported this view. He believed each division should possess a reserve of antitank weapons to support any threatened regiment and defeat massed tank attacks with concentrated antitank firepower.[31]

---

[26] Memo, ACS, G–3, Maj Gen R. M. Beck Jr., to CS, G–3, sub: Infantry Battalion, Anti-Mechanized, 9 May 39, p. 6, Item 4854, Reel 313, National Archives Project, GCM; Memo, Andrews to CS, G–3, 23 Jan 40, pp. 2–4.

[27] Memo, Stratemeyer to AWC Asst Commandant, 25 Feb 39, pp. 2–3.

[28] Memo, Beck to CS, G–3, 9 May 39, pp. 1–2, quote from p. 2.

[29] Memos, Ofc of the Ch of Field Arty Exec Col R. E. D. Hoyle to Col John Magruder, 16 Mar 39, Military Intelligence Division (MID) Corresp, 1917–1941, Security-Class Corresp and Rpts, RG 165, NARA; XO, G–2, Lt Col C. M. Busbee, to Ch of Field Arty, G–2, sub: Antitank Gun Units in Major Foreign Armies, 21 Mar 39, MID Corresp, Security-Class Corresp and Rpts, RG 165, NARA; Beck to CS, G–3, 9 May 39, pp. 2–4; General Staff Asst Sec Maj S. R. Mickelsen to ACS, G–3, sub: Infantry Battalion, Anti-Mechanized, 29 May 39, Item 4854, Reel 313, National Archives Project, GCM.

[30] 2d End to Memo, TAG to Ch of Inf, 27 Sep 39, Item 4854, Reel 313, National Archives Project, GCM. Memos, Beck to CS, 9 May 39, pp. 4–5; ACS, G–3, Brig Gen F. M. Andrews to CS, G–3, sub: Organization of Anti-tank Battalion, 20 Sep 39, p. 1, Item 4854, Reel 313, National Archives Project, GCM; Andrews to CS, G–3, 9 Oct 39; ACS, G–3, Brig Gen F. M. Andrews, to CS, G–3, sub: Organization of 4th Antitank Battalion, 4 Nov 39, Item 4854, Reel 313, National Archives Project, GCM.

[31] Memo, Beck to CS, G–3, 9 May 39, p. 6; Gabel, *GHQ Maneuvers*, pp. 31–32.

Two views of the German 37-mm. antitank gun that became the model for the U.S. antitank weapon of the same caliber

However, some within the War Department considered the new antitank unit a corps asset. The only data available on such a unit derived from the Proposed Infantry Division tests, and these had not favored permanent divisional antitank battalions. General support was given to extending the assignment of antitank units to army as well as corps headquarters, thereby creating several tiers of antitank support. Only at the division level did uncertainty remain as the Army worked to build an effective antitank force.[32]

Antitank Weapons

The .50-caliber machine gun served as the Army's principal antitank weapon for much of the 1930s. Most of these weapons were found in cavalry formations, while infantry divisions were expected to rely on their artillery for antitank defense. The firepower and mobility of the .50-caliber machine gun made it ideal for cavalry operations. Considered capable of destroying any lightly armored vehicle and highly effective against unarmored targets, it became the mounted arm's weapon of choice. Easily concealed and carried via packhorse, it possessed the same high level of cross-country mobility as horse cavalry.[33] The .50-caliber machine gun also posed a threat to the light tanks that predominated in most armies in the interwar era. Indeed, the threat posed by this weapon to combat cars encouraged the mechanized cavalry to develop mobile fire-support techniques to neutralize it.[34]

By 1937 analysis of foreign trends in tank development indicated the need for a heavier weapon capable of greater armor penetration. Development of a new antitank gun, however, experienced the same budgetary constraints and prolonged acquisition cycle as tank designs. Therefore, instead of building a new weapon, the Army opted to purchase a proven, foreign antitank gun already in production.[35] It selected the German 37-mm. gun built by Rheinmetall-Borsig Company and used by the German Army. The military attaché in Germany, Maj. Truman Smith, arranged the purchase of several guns. After extensive testing and minor modification, an American-built version was accepted for service with the U.S. Army.[36]

---

[32] Memos, Beck to CS, G–3, 9 May 39, p. 6, and Andrews to CS, G–3, 9 Oct 39; Memoranda Brief of Operations and Training Division, G–3, 23 Jan 40, Item 4876, Reel 313, National Archives Project, GCM.

[33] Memos, Palmer to Cav Sch Commandant, 19 Apr 33, pp. 4–5, and Smith to Ch of Cav, 20 Apr 33, p. 3; Crittenberger, "Cavalry Maneuvers at Fort Knox," pp. 424–25.

[34] Memo, Smith to Ch of Cav, 20 Apr 33, p. 2; Col Bruce Palmer, "The Cavalry," Lecture at AWC, 12 Oct 36, pp. 2, 6, 7, in Army War College Lectures, 1936–1937, AWC Curricular Archives; Bruce Palmer, "Mechanized Cavalry in the Second Army Maneuvers," *Cavalry Journal* XLV, no. 6 (November-December 1936): 476; Brig Gen Daniel Van Voorhis, "Mechanization," Lecture at AWC, 13 Oct 37, p. 8, Army War College Lectures, 1937–1938, AWC Curricular Archives; Van Voorhis Discussion Notes, 13 Oct 37, p. 14.

[35] Notes of Conversation Between Mark Skinner Watson and Maj Gen Stanley D. Embick, 18 May 47, Mark Skinner Watson Notes, 1942–1947, GCM; Constance McLaughlin Green, Harry C. Thomson, and Peter C. Roots, *The Ordnance Department: Planning Munitions for War*, U.S. Army in World War II (Washington, D.C.: U.S. Army Center of Military History, 1955), pp. 204–07.

[36] Memo, Col J. E. Munroe to Military Attaché to Germany, sub: 37-mm. Anti-Tank Gun, Etc., Rheinmetall-Borsig Co., Germany, 20 Apr 36, MID Corresp, Security-Class Corresp and Rpts, RG 165, NARA; Memo, Stratemeyer to AWC Asst Commandant, 25 Feb 39, pp. 2–3; George A. Lynch, "Final Report of Major General George A. Lynch: A Summary of Infantry Developments During His Term of Office," 30 Apr 41, app. 1, pp. 11–12, MHI Library; Grow, "The Ten Lean Years: From the Mechanized Force to the Armored Force (1940)," p. 70; Gabel, *GHQ Maneuvers*, p. 31.

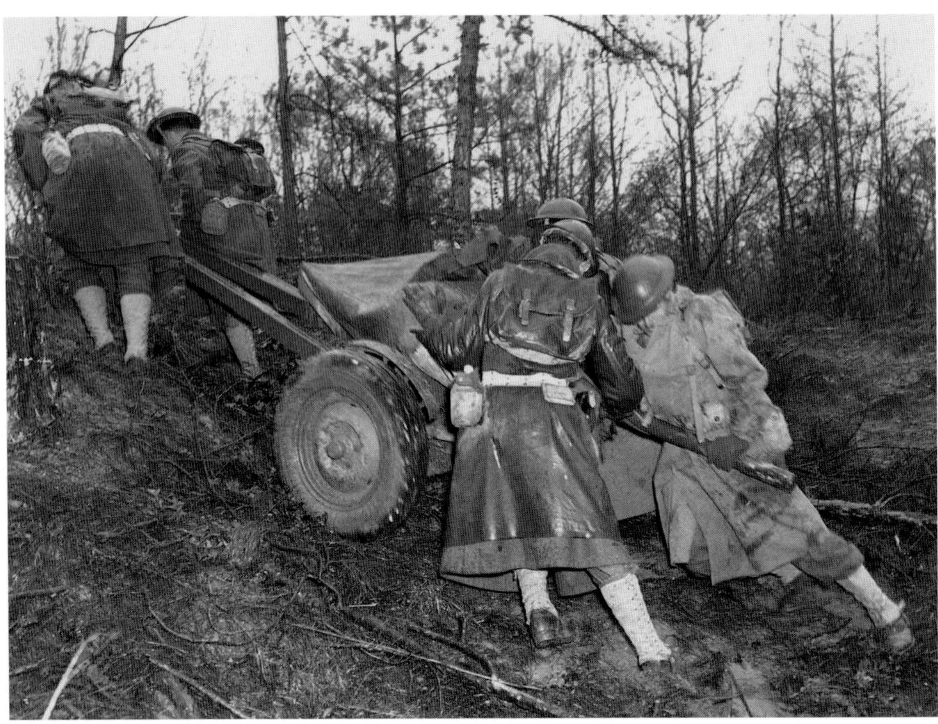

Manhandling a 37-mm. antitank gun through wooded terrain

Designated the M3 37-mm. antitank gun, the new weapon entered production in November 1939; deliveries to field units began in early 1940.[37]

Responsibility for developing tactics for the new gun became subject to the same branch dispute between the Infantry and Field Artillery that surrounded the antitank battalion. In 1938 the adjutant general ruled in favor of the Infantry, but the Field Artillery retained responsibility for developing the doctrine for antitank weapons larger than 37-mm.[38] This compromise offered a short-term solution, but it did not provide for centralized antitank development.

Nevertheless, the addition of the 37-mm. antitank gun marked a significant improvement in the antitank capabilities of infantry regiments. Such units received six of the guns in addition to their existing six .50-caliber machine guns. Thus equipped, an American infantry division possessed eighteen .50-caliber machine guns and eighteen 37-mm. antitank guns. One Army War College student noted: "When these guns are compared with the 72 37-mm. guns in each German division

[37] "37 MM Anti-Tank Gun, M3," http://www.robertsarmory.com/37mm.htm, last accessed 7 May 06; Steven Zaloga, *U.S. Anti-tank Artillery, 1941–45* (New York: Osprey Publishing, 2005), pp. 4–7, 21.

[38] Notes of Discussion Following the Lecture of Maj Gen George A. Lynch at AWC, "The Infantry," 30 Sep 38, p. 4, in Army War College Lectures, 1938–1939, pt. 1, AWC Curricular Archives; Lynch, "Final Report," app. 1, p. 12.

American 37-mm. antitank gun moved via jeep

the advantage is decidedly with them."[39] Worse, by late 1939 Ordnance Department testing had found the .50-caliber machine gun largely ineffective against the latest combat cars.[40]

The Cavalry, however, proved reluctant to adopt the 37-mm. antitank gun. Both the horse and mechanized cavalry feared that the adoption of the gun would reduce mobility. Use of a heavier weapon also meant that it could not be transported via packhorse. Towed guns, however, lacked the cross-country mobility of the horse cavalry, although ongoing efforts to improve the organization of the cavalry division did include an antitank unit equipped with the 37-mm. gun. For the cavalry regiments, however, the .50-caliber machine gun was still considered effective against the light armor and soft targets likely to be encountered.[41]

Similarly, the mechanized cavalry preferred to retain the .50-caliber machine gun as the main armament of its combat cars. Heavier weapons simply increased the weight of the vehicle, created space problems in the turret, and required more room

---

[39] Memo, Goodman to Chairman, Subcommittee no. 1 of Committee no. 5, Suppl no. 5, 10 Oct 39, pp. 10–11, quote from p. 11.

[40] Chaffee, "Mechanized Cavalry," 29 Sep 39, p. 4.

[41] Maj Gen John K. Herr, "The Cavalry," Lecture at AWC, 19 Sep 39, p. 3, in Army War College Lectures, 1939–1940, pt. 2, AWC Curricular Archives.

for ammunition stowage. Accurate firing required the vehicle to stop, whereas the .50-caliber machine gun's higher rate of fire offset the loss of accuracy associated with moving fire and increased the chance of hitting a vital spot.[42]

The prominent role German tanks played in Poland led the Cavalry to reverse its ambivalence toward the 37-mm. antitank gun. The branch accelerated design of a divisional antitank unit based on this weapon, but it lacked the guns to actually create such an organization. Previous reluctance to adopt the 37-mm. gun resulted in production orders that did not include cavalry units. The branch therefore endured lengthy delays while belatedly securing sufficient numbers of this weapon to provide an improved antitank capability. The Infantry loaned one 37-mm. gun to the Cavalry School, while subsequent deliveries permitted the mixed horse and mechanized 4th and 6th Cavalry Regiments each to organize an antitank company of six guns.[43]

Unfortunately, by the time the Army began fielding the 37-mm. antitank gun, larger caliber weapons were eclipsing it. Germany had begun developing a successor to the 37-mm. gun in 1937. Two years later American intelligence found that all major powers were developing larger antitank weapons and the Italians had already fielded 47-mm. guns. In February 1939 Secretary of War Harry H. Woodring directed the Field Artillery to study the question of whether the U.S. Army required a larger antitank gun.[44]

German military operations in Poland and France convinced the Army of the need for a more powerful weapon. In June 1940 Chief of Staff General George C. Marshall recommended the necessary development in response to reports of the 37-mm. gun's ineffectiveness against heavier tanks.[45] These allegations found support from Maj. James C. Crockett, who had previously served on the military attaché staff in Germany. He believed: "The caliber of the AT [antitank] Gun (except the AT rifles in the hands of Infantry Companies) should be greater than 37-mm. The present 37-mm. Gun is on the border of obsolescence."[46]

Information on foreign antitank use, however, offered little guidance for American efforts. Contradictory reports from the fighting in France indicated both the

---

[42] Van Voorhis, "Mechanization," 13 Oct 37, p. 8, 29 Sep 39, pp. 22–23.

[43] Memo, Brig Gen Robert C. Richardson to Ch of Cav, sub: 37-mm Antitank Gun, 16 Oct 39, and 1st End, Lt Col Karl S. Bradford to TAG, 20 Oct 39; Memo, Brig Gen Robert C. Richardson to Ch of Cav, sub: 37-mm Antitank Gun, 16 Oct 39, and 3d End, Brig Gen Earl McFarland to TAG, 28 Oct 39; Memo, ACS, G–4, Brig Gen George P. Tyner, sub: Loan of 37 mm Gun, M3, and Carriage, M4, 20 Nov 39; Memo, Office of the Ch of Inf Exec Lt Col E. W. Fales to TAG, sub: Distribution of Gun, 37 mm, M3 and Carriage, M4, 16 Dec 39, and 1st End, TAG to Ch of Ord, 10 Jan 40; all in Item 4953, Reel 315, National Archives Project, GCM.

[44] Memo, Stratemeyer to AWC Asst Commandant, 25 Feb 39, pp. 2–3; Memo, ACS, G–2, Col E. R. W. McCabe, to CS, G–2, sub: Antitank Weapons in Various Armies, 28 Oct 39, pp. 1–2, Item 4876, Reel 313, National Archives Project, GCM; Green, Thomson, and Roots, *Ordnance Department*, pp. 210–11.

[45] Memo, CS Gen George C. Marshall to ACS, G–4, 3 Jun 40, Reel 27, Item 1055, National Archives Project, GCM.

[46] Ltr, James C. Crockett to Asst Commandant Col K. B. Edmunds, 20 Jul 40, HQ AGF, Gen Corresp, RG 337, NARA.

ability of the French 25-mm. gun to destroy most German tanks and the inability of weapons smaller than 47-mm. to knock out tanks. The French themselves came to prefer a self-propelled 47-mm. gun with a minimum muzzle velocity of 850 feet per second. The British considered a 47-mm. gun with a muzzle velocity of 2,500 feet per second the minimal requirement. At the same time, they undertook development of a 57-mm. gun and continued to use a 40-mm. weapon. Persistent rumors of German heavy tanks impervious to most existing antitank guns added still further confusion to American efforts to determine the optimum caliber size.[47]

In the United States, the Ordnance Department considered the 37-mm. antitank gun an ideal balance between weight and firepower. Ordnance personnel wanted to continue its production while developing an armor-piercing round to transform the venerable 75-mm. gun into an antitank weapon. They rejected development of an intermediate caliber weapon, since it would complicate the production and supply of ammunition. Ironically, however, the British had already placed contracts in the United States for the production of a 57-mm. antitank gun. Nevertheless, the Ordnance Department rejected the adoption of this weapon by the U.S. Army, preferring to await the arrival of the special 75-mm. ammunition.[48]

Command and General Staff School Commandant McNair opposed the Ordnance position. An artillery officer who had participated in the development of the American 37-mm. gun, McNair considered this weapon inadequate by 1940.[49] He also believed that the 75-mm. gun's low muzzle velocity and curved trajectory made it unsuitable for an antitank role. He criticized efforts to develop antitank ammunition for this gun, because it "will create a general impression that we are prepared against tanks when in reality we are not."[50] Instead, McNair sought a weapon with high muzzle velocity, a flat trajectory, and maximum armor penetration. He considered the German 88-mm. antiaircraft gun the embodiment of these features when used in an antitank role.[51]

Despite the mounting evidence abroad of the 37-mm. antitank gun's ineffectiveness, its production in the United States continued throughout 1941. In the absence of any alternative, the War Department opted to continue production of the weapon until a heavier antitank gun became available. In the interim the presence

---

[47] "Paraphrase of Code Cablegram Received at the War Department 8:54 a.m., May 31, 1940," Item 4338, Reel 289, National Archives Project, GCM; Military Intelligence Division, G–2, Tentative Lessons Bull no. 3, sub: Tentative Lessons from the Recent Active Campaign in Europe, 31 May 40, Item 4338, Reel 289, National Archives Project, GCM; Memo, ACS, G–3, to CS, G–3, sub: Antitank Defense, 18 Nov 40, p. 1, HQ AGF, GHQ, Gen Corresp, RG 337, NARA.

[48] Memo, Ch of Ord Maj Gen C. M. Wesson to ACS, G–4, sub: Employment of Antitank Artillery and Antiaircraft Artillery in Antimechanization Defense, 7 Jun 40, Item 4338, Reel 289, National Archives Project, GCM; "Notes on G–3, Anti-Tank Conference, July 14–20, 1941, War College, Washington, D.C.," pp. 48, 50, Andrew D. Bruce Papers, MHI Archives.

[49] Ltr, Command and General Staff School (CGSS) Commandant Brig Gen Lesley J. McNair to Lt Col Earl W. Bacon, 20 Jun 40, p. 1, HQ AGF, GHQ, Gen Corresp, RG 337, NARA.

[50] Ltr, McNair to Bacon, 20 Jun 40, p. 2.

[51] Ibid.; Memo, GHQ CS Lt Gen Lesley J. McNair to CS, sub: Use of Antiaircraft Artillery Against Tanks, 10 Jul 41, HQ AGF, GHQ, Gen Corresp, RG 337, NARA.

The ubiquitous German 88-mm. antiaircraft gun. During the Spanish Civil War, this weapon was used effectively for the first time as an antitank weapon. It later became the bane of Allied tanks in all theaters in which it was deployed.

of large numbers of 37-mm. guns was believed sufficient to stop or at least contain a hostile tank attack.[52]

The Army also encouraged the use of other means of destroying or disabling enemy armored vehicles. Mines were encouraged by the War Department's 1938 policy letter and again by General Marshall. The Army, however, lacked mines. The M1 antitank mine became available in October 1940, but it carried only half the charge of its German counterpart. Nevertheless, the American mine was considered sufficient: it could immobilize a tank by breaking its tracks. Its continued usefulness declined as enemy tanks became larger and more heavily armored, but no substantial replacement emerged until September 1944.[53]

Antitank rifles also received Army attention, especially after the Germans began issuing them to their infantry companies following the Polish campaign. Several foreign models were tested in the United States with special attention given to weight, armor-piercing ability, tracking ability, rate of fire, and recoil. A German antitank rifle offered the most promise, but the cost of acquiring sufficient quantities of the weapons for extended field tests proved prohibitive. Nevertheless, War Department

[52] Memo, Acting ACS, G–3, Col Harry L. Twaddle, to CS, G–3, sub: Antitank Defense, 18 Nov 40, p. 2, HQ AGF, GHQ, Gen Corresp, RG 337, NARA; Lt Col Andrew D. Bruce, "Notes for Conference with General Twaddle," 28 May 41, p. 2, Bruce Papers; Green, Thomson, and Roots, *Ordnance Department*, p. 211.

[53] Memo, CS Gen George C. Marshall to ACS, G–3, sub: Antitank Mines, 13 Jan 41, Selected Corresp, George C. Marshall Papers, GCM; "Notes on G–3, Anti-Tank Conference," pp. 40–41; Green, Thomson, and Roots, *Ordnance Department*, pp. 382, 384, 387.

support resulted in continuous development of an antitank rifle throughout 1941 with the intent of issuing it to infantry companies.[54]

Other antitank measures considered by the Army included aircraft, small-arms fire, and artillery fire. During emergencies aircraft were expected to bomb enemy mechanized units. However, such attacks could not have been of much value in the absence of a suitable bombsight or aircraft designed for ground attack. Small-arms fire and grenade attacks at least provided ground troops without antitank weapons some chance of damaging vehicle optics or wounding crew members. Molotov cocktails and antitank trenches also constituted cheap antitank measures. Artillery sought to disrupt tank attacks through the delivery of barrages against assembly points and along likely attack avenues.[55]

Self-propelled Antitank Weapons

The outbreak of war in Europe stimulated Army-wide interest in self-propelled antitank guns. Earlier efforts to design self-propelled artillery provided a modicum of technical familiarity with the difficulties inherent to self-propelled ordnance. The basic concept included an antitank gun mounted on a lightly armored, tracked carriage to achieve the desired result of mobility and firepower. Not all ideas proved realistic, including one proposal for a vehicle with a 105-mm. gun capable of penetrating ten inches of armor. Against this unrealizable objective, the Armored Force proved willing to use older guns on trucks or obsolete chassis until a better weapon could be designed.[56]

In July 1940 the Ordnance Department accelerated its development of a self-propelled 75-mm. gun for use with the armored divisions. The resultant vehicle matched a gun with a light-tank chassis. It possessed no overhead cover for the crew and little space for the gun's operation. The Armored Force rejected the vehicle.[57]

Despite this setback, the Ordnance Department remained convinced that either a 75-mm. gun or a 3-inch antiaircraft gun could be mounted effectively on a vehicle. Instead of a tank chassis, a new design based on a halftrack emerged. This vehicle

---

[54] Asst Mil Attaché, Paris, Rpt no. 25367–W, sub: German Armament—Anti-tank Rifle, 4 Dec 39, Willis D. Crittenberger Papers, MHI Archives; Memo, Ch of Opns Branch Lt Col Edward S. Ott to ACS, G–3, sub: Antitank Defense, 19 Jul 41, Bruce Papers; "Notes on G–3, Anti-Tank Conference," p. 11.

[55] Memo, TAG, 15 Mar 38, pp. 3–4; "Notes on G–3, Anti-Tank Conference," p. 51.

[56] Memo, Marshall to ACS, G–4, 3 Jun 40; Memo for CS, 15 Mar 41, Xerox 692, National Archives Project, GCM; Memo, Lt Col Allen F. Kingman to GHQ CS, sub: War Department Conference on Antitank Defense, 15 April, 1941, 17 Apr 41, HQ AGF, GHQ, Gen Corresp, RG 337, NARA; Memo, Lt Col Allen F. Kingman to GHQ CS, sub: Report on Meeting Called by General Bryden on Branch Responsibility for Antitank Defense, 10 May 41, HQ AGF, GHQ, Gen Corresp, RG 337, NARA; Bruce, "Conference with General Twaddle," p. 3; Memo, Maj Gen Charles L. Scott to Ch of the Armd Force, sub: New Means and Methods to Combat Armored Units, 5 Jul 41, p. 3, Orlando W. Ward Papers, MHI Archives; "Notes on G–3, Anti-Tank Conference," pp. 43–44.

[57] Memo, Wesson to ACS, G–4, sub: Employment of Antitank Artillery and Antiaircraft Artillery in Antimechanization Defense, 7 Jun 40; Memo, Lt Col Allen F. Kingman to GHQ CS, sub: Mechanized Antitank Organization, 13 Jan 41, HQ AGF, GHQ, Gen Corresp, RG 337, NARA.

proved more effective, and the Ordnance Department ordered thirty-six for testing during the autumn 1941 maneuvers. This weapon was considered only a temporary measure until a superior self-propelled antitank weapon could be developed.[58]

Similar energy was expended to build a mobile 37-mm. gun platform. Yet by July 1941 one observer admitted: "We haven't got very much beyond putting the 37-mm. on a small automobile."[59] The 1st Cavalry Division's Provisional Antitank Squadron received 37-mm. guns mounted on ¾-ton trucks. In August the unit participated in maneuvers and achieved success by surprising hostile armor. Through the use of concealment, constant movement, and stealth, it repeatedly attacked the vulnerable flanks and rear of tank units.[60]

Consequently, the 1st Cavalry Division commander considered the self-propelled antitank gun the optimal weapon for offensive operations against mechanized forces. Towed weapons proved much slower to maneuver and bring into action. The availability and low production cost of the truck-mounted 37-mm. led to its production and fielding for training purposes. However, the Provisional Antitank Squadron's exploits notwithstanding, this vehicle was considered too vulnerable for actual combat operations; thus work began on a better design.[61]

The self-propelled antitank gun did not receive universal support. General McNair considered such weapons suitable only for armored divisions and not likely to be available for widespread use because of their design complexity. In his view, "we cannot have a high velocity rapid fire weapon which has the characteristics of moderate weight, of facility for concealment, of strategical and reasonable cross-country mobility, and mechanical simplicity, which are believed essential for an antitank weapon."[62] He believed the self-propelled antitank gun's size, difficulty of concealment, and unstable firing platform limited its utility. Moreover, he noted that damage to either gun or mount rendered the weapon inoperative.[63]

McNair's influence increased in July 1940, when he became the General Headquarters chief of staff with responsibility for Army training and readiness. To counter growing support for self-propelled antitank guns, he insisted that they undergo extensive comparison testing against towed weapons. The Army chief of staff's intervention, however, preempted this delaying measure. General Marshall believed that the combat experiences of other nations provided sufficient data on the pros and cons of towed and self-propelled antitank guns.[64]

---

[58] Memo, Kingman to GHQ CS, 13 Jan 41; "Notes on G–3, Anti-Tank Conference," pp. 29, 77.

[59] "Notes on G–3, Anti-Tank Conference," p. 32.

[60] Ltr, Maj Don E. Carleton to Ch of Cav Maj Gen John K. Herr, 29 Aug 41, Ofc of the Ch of Cav, Gen Corresp, RG 177, NARA.

[61] Ltr, Innis P. Swift to Ch of Cav Maj Gen John K. Herr, 30 Aug 41, Ofc of the Ch of Cav, Gen Corresp, RG 177, NARA; Charles M. Baily, *Faint Praise: American Tanks and Tank Destroyers During World War II* (Hamden, Conn.: Archon Books, 1983), p. 40.

[62] Note of Gen Staff Sec Col Orlando W. Ward, 2 Jul 40, Xerox 3474, National Archives Project, GCM; quote from Memo, Kingman to GHQ CS, 13 Jan 41.

[63] Baily, *Faint Praise*, p. 22.

[64] Memo, GHQ CS Maj Gen Lesley J. McNair to ACS, G–3, sub: Defense Against Armored Forces, 3 Jun 41, HQ AGF, GHQ, Gen Corresp, RG 337, NARA; Brig Gen Harry L. Twaddle, "Con-

Indeed, the recently concluded French campaign offered ample evidence of self-propelled antitank gun usage by the French and Germans. The former considered such weapons necessary to defeat mechanized forces. They improvised mobile antitank guns by mounting guns on available vehicles. Organized into ad hoc units, these weapons entered combat shortly before France's surrender.[65]

The Germans experimented with self-propelled weapons before the war. As early as 1936 they demonstrated a keen interest in using mobile, lightly armored antitank guns to destroy enemy armor. Their speed, cross-country mobility, and ability to respond rapidly to mechanized threats made them appear ideal as antitank weapons. In 1940 they employed both light tank destroyers with 47-mm. antitank guns and assault guns for infantry support. The latter were turret-less vehicles that carried a 75-mm. gun on a tank chassis. By early 1941 German panzer divisions included both weapons. Antiaircraft weapons mounted on armored halftracks and capable of a dual antitank role also began to appear in increasing quantities.[66]

Foreign Antitank Developments

The U.S. Army closely tracked antitank developments among the major military powers. Through analysis of foreign experience, it sought insights with which to resolve the organizational, doctrinal, and materiel issues associated with antitank development. However, antitank measures abroad followed no discernible pattern. Each nation pursued its own distinct method of countering mechanized attacks with similarly varied organizations and weapons. Until the outbreak of war, American intelligence could not offer a qualitative assessment of the different practices.[67]

The Spanish Civil War, 1936–1939, demonstrated the value of antitank guns. This conflict featured the first widespread employment of tanks and antitank guns among belligerents. Analysis of combat operations found that, after mechanical breakdowns, antitank guns accounted for the most tank losses. While Molotov

---

sideration of Non-concurrences," in Memo, ACS, G–3, Brig Gen Harry L. Twaddle, to CS, G–3, sub: Organization of Antitank Units in the Army, 18 Aug 41, Bruce Papers; Memo, Lt Gen Lesley J. McNair to ACS, G–3, sub: Organization of Antitank Units in the Army, 2 Sep 41, Bruce Papers.

[65] Memo, Miles to ACS, G–3, sub: Mechanized Antitank Organization, 17 Jan 41.

[66] Memo, Acting ACS, G–2, Brig Gen Sherman Miles, to ACS, G–3, sub: Mechanized Antitank Organization, 17 Jan 41, MID Corresp, Security-Class Corresp and Rpts, RG 165, NARA; Mil Attaché, Berlin, Rpt no. 18031, sub: Organization of German Armored (Panzer) Division, 3 Mar 41, p. 21, Crittenberger Papers; Walter Nehring, "Antitank Defense," pp. 16–17, CGSS Translation of 1936 German Article by Walter Nehring, MHI Library; "Tanks or Tank-Chasers," 18 Sep, 4 Oct 36, AWC Translation of Article in *Militär Wochenblatt*, MHI Library.

[67] For examples, see Memos, ACS, G–2, Col E. R. W. McCabe, to CS, G–2, sub: Antitank Weapons in Various Armies, 28 Oct 39, Item 4876, Reel 313, National Archives Project, GCM; Busbee to Ch of Field Arty, G–2, sub: Antitank Gun Units in Major Foreign Armies, 21 Mar 39, pp. 4–5; ACS, G–2, Col E. R. W. McCabe, to ACS, G–3, sub: Antitank Units in Armies of Germany, France, Great Britain, and Italy, 6 Apr 39, Item 4854, Reel 313, National Archives Project, GCM.

cocktails, mines, and artificial obstacles also destroyed tanks, they did so with far less frequency than antitank guns.[68]

Germany's employment of panzer divisions and corps to quickly overrun Poland in 1939 highlighted the need for large numbers of antitank guns. Military intelligence attributed the Polish defeat in part to inadequate and insufficient antitank weapons. Although the Poles possessed several modern antitank guns and planned to create antitank units for each infantry division, these efforts were incomplete when the Germans attacked. Nevertheless, when German tanks encountered modern antitank defenses—as at Mlawa and Warsaw—they suffered heavy losses. These instances suggested that armored formations were not invincible.[69]

Similarly, during the Winter War of 1939–1940, Finnish soldiers achieved notable successes against Soviet tank units. The Finns used antitank guns, Molotov cocktails, antitank rifles, and artillery pieces. They also resorted to assaulting the vehicles. However, American intelligence assessments attributed Finnish success to the faulty employment of poorly crafted tanks crewed by low-caliber Russian soldiers. The Winter War, like the Spanish Civil War and the Polish campaign, was viewed as a special case from which few valid conclusions regarding tank and antitank doctrine could be drawn.[70]

The fighting in France could not be so discounted. There too, however, insufficient antitank measures contributed to the German success. Officers from the defeated French and Polish Armies drew on their experiences to recommend to the U.S. Army more effective antitank tactics. In their view, defeat of German panzer formations required the deployment of combined-arms teams echeloned in depth with a concentrated, mobile reserve available to counterattack deep penetrations by hostile tanks. Polish officers also advocated the aggressive use of aircraft against enemy mechanized units.[71]

---

[68] Basil H. Liddell Hart, "Lessons of the Spanish War: An Estimate of the Military Factors: Men and Matériel," *Army Ordnance* XVIII, no. 106 (January-February 1938): 201–03; Emilio Canevari, "Forecasts from the War in Spain: Lessons Based on Technical and Tactical Experience, *Army Ordnance* XVIII, no. 107 (March-April 1938): 273–80; J. F. C. Fuller, "The Tank in Spain: Tactics Still Fail To Keep Pace With Technics," *Army Ordnance* XIX, no. 109 (July-August 1938): 24–27; Henry J. Reilly, "Proving Ground in Spain: Armament Trends as Revealed by the Civil War," *Army Ordnance* XIX, no. 114 (May-June 1939): 333–36; Mil Attaché, Barcelona, Rpt no. 6862, Spain (Military), G–4, sub: Analysis of Tank Casualties—Spain, 25 Jul 38, Crittenberger Papers; Voorhis, "Mechanization," 29 Sep 38, p. 25.

[69] Memo, Mudge to Chairman, Subcommittee no. 1 of Committee no. 5, Suppl no. 4, 10 Oct 39, p. 10; Maj Percy G. Black, "Employment of German Mechanization in the Polish Campaign," 5 Dec 39, pp. 7, 9, Crittenberger Papers; Memo, McCabe to CS, G–2, 28 Oct 39, pp. 2–3; Mil Attaché, Berlin, Germany (Combat), sub: Visit to Polish Theater of Operations, 22 Sep 39, p. 12, Crittenberger Papers.

[70] Memo, Mudge to Chairman, Subcommittee no. 1 of Committee no. 5, Suppl no. 4, 10 Oct 39, p. 10; Mil Attaché, Paris, Rpt no. 25307–W, France (Combat), sub: Employment and Organization of German Armored Division During Polish Operations, 2 Nov 39, quote from p. 5, Crittenberger Papers; ACS, G–2, Special Bull no. 2, sub: Soviet-Finnish War: Operations From November 30, 1939, to January 7, 1940, 10 Jan 40, pp. 132–34, in *Selected Readings in Military History: Soviet Military History* (Fort Leavenworth, Kans.: U.S. Army Command and General Staff College, 1984), vol. 1.

[71] Mil Attaché, Paris, Rpt no. 25307–W, 2 Nov 39, pp. 3–4; Memo, Miles to ACS, G–3, 17 Jan 41.

By 1941 American intelligence could find no instance in which antitank measures had stopped a major offensive spearheaded by armored formations, despite isolated incidents of small numbers of tanks being defeated. Analysis of antitank measures among the principal military powers identified those of Germany as the strongest and those of the United States as the weakest.[72] This finding stimulated further interest in German antitank doctrine and organization, particularly because the Army's principal intelligence officer, Col. E. R. W. McCabe, believed that "German antitank strength is undoubtedly calculated on the basis of what they themselves consider necessary to stop the attacks of their own Panzer divisions."[73]

In building an antitank capability, the Germans assumed they would encounter enemies who possessed large numbers of tanks and employed them in a manner similar to German panzers. Therefore, antitank development sought to defeat parallel organizations in foreign armies. The Germans integrated armored and antitank actions by consolidating development responsibility for both in a single organization.[74]

American efforts to understand and apply German antitank principles benefited from prewar intelligence efforts. The German government permitted American personnel access to most military units. The American military attaché staff therefore visited antitank organizations and observed them during maneuvers. While attending the *Kriegsakademie*, Germany's senior training institute for officers, Capt. Albert C. Wedemeyer actually served with an antitank unit for several weeks. His subsequent report provided a detailed depiction of German antitank organization and tactics. American Attaché Maj. Truman Smith highlighted the report's potential value: "I believe that any American officer given the job of training an antitank battalion or company might well take this manuscript as a guide."[75] In fact, the report guided the operations of the Proposed Infantry Division's antitank battalion during testing of that formation.[76]

In addition to Wedemeyer's report, the Army also purchased instructional materials from the Germans, including charts that showed "the German method of instructing anti-tank gunners how to attack the list of tanks of France, England, Russia, Italy, Poland, Czechoslovakia and Sweden with the various German antitank guns."[77] From attaché reports, Wedemeyer's experience, and these training

[72] Memo, McCabe to CS, G–2, 28 Oct 39.

[73] Ibid., p. 3.

[74] Memo, Goodman to Chairman, Subcommittee no. 1 of Committee no. 5, 10 Oct 39, p. 6; Asst Mil Attaché, Berlin, Rpt no. 15049, sub: Germany (Combat): German Motorized Combat School (Supplementary to M.I.D. Report 14,703), 6 Jan 37, MID Corresp, Security-Class Corresp and Rpts, RG 165, NARA; Mil Attaché, Berlin, Rpt no. 15466, sub: Germany (Combat): Motor Combat Corps (Major Changes in Organization), 7 Sep 37, MID Corresp, Security-Class Corresp and Rpts, RG 165, NARA.

[75] Memo, Goodman to Chairman, Subcommittee no. 1 of Committee no. 5, 10 Oct 39, p. 6.

[76] Memo, Mil Attaché Maj Truman Smith to Ch, MID, Report no. D–15544, sub: Copy of Report no. 15,511 to Experimental Division, Fort Sam Houston, Texas, 27 Oct 37, MID Corresp, Security-Class Corresp and Rpts, RG 165, NARA.

[77] Memo, Ordnance Dept XO Lt Col Charles A. Walker to ACS, G–2, sub: German Chart for Anti-Tank Instruction, 2 Nov 36, and 2d End, Acting Mil Attaché Capt James C. Crockett to Ch, MID, 12 Nov 36, both in MID Corresp, Security-Class Corresp and Rpts, RG 165, NARA.

aids, the U.S. Army possessed a wealth of information concerning the nature of German antitank tactics.

In 1941 this information was being disseminated and studied as part of the Army's quest for a viable antitank capability. Wedemeyer's report and related intelligence was accessible to the War Department General Staff and the branches. In an article published in the *Field Artillery Journal*, Wedemeyer outlined a plan for American antitank tactics that borrowed heavily from German methods.[78] Truman Smith also compiled a report on German antitank measures for General Marshall and frequently discussed the topic with General Staff Secretary Col. Orlando W. Ward.[79]

The Germans relied on a combination of antitank guns and obstacles to stop mechanized attacks. Each infantry division included an antitank battalion with thirty-six 37-mm. antitank guns and three regimental companies of twelve 37-mm. guns apiece. Corps and army formations included additional antitank battalions. Mines and obstacles served to deny enemy tanks access to areas of the battlefield, while the antitank guns deployed in depth to cover likely avenues of advance. In penetrating German defenses, attacking mechanized elements had to negotiate a succession of antitank barriers that grew in depth and firepower as an attacker advanced.[80]

These concepts found parallel in the antitank measures employed during maneuvers at Fort Knox in 1937 and 1938. However, German antitank operations possessed a degree of sophistication lacking in the more tentative American approach. The Germans employed real antitank units, while similar American organizations existed largely on paper. German doctrine emphasized the importance of fire discipline, concealment, and careful positioning of antitank guns to increase the likelihood of short-range flank shots at enemy tanks. In contrast, American antitank crews deployed their weapons along military crests and at the head of terrain corridors—positions easily anticipated and vulnerable to enemy artillery.[81]

The Problem of Antitank Doctrine, 1940–1941

France's defeat intensified American efforts to develop an antitank capability. However, the Atlantic Ocean would remain the nation's best antitank defense until the Army could eliminate the confusion surrounding antitank doctrine, organization, and armament. Despite general agreement on the need for antitank measures, the

---

[78] A. C. Wedemeyer, "Antitank Defense," *Field Artillery Journal* XXXI, no. 5 (May 1941): 258–72.

[79] Memo, Col Orlando Ward to General George C. Marshall, OCS, 1 Nov [year unspecified], Item 4876, Reel 313, National Archives Project, GCM.

[80] Memos, Stratemeyer to AWC Asst Commandant, 25 Feb 39, pp. 1–2, and Goodman to Chairman, Subcommittee no. 1 of Committee no. 5, 10 Oct 39, pp. 6–7; MID, "Tentative Lessons No. 16: Tactics of Antitank Units in the German Army," 16 Jul 40, p. 4, AWC Rcds Section, MHI Archives; "Notes on German Antimechanized Defense 1937–1938," n.d., Alvan C. Gillem Jr. Papers, MHI Archives.

[81] Asst Mil Attaché, Berlin, Rpt no. 17665, sub: German Tactical Disposition of Antimechanized Forces, 30 Oct 40, Crittenberger Papers.

details of antitank operations remained the subject of dispute between the chief of Infantry, the War Department, and General Headquarters.

In July 1940 Chief of Infantry General Lynch became an outspoken advocate of the use of tanks in an antitank role. He attributed the French defeat to the lack of mobile weapons with which to counteract armored breakthroughs. Lynch acknowledged the value of antitank guns, but he considered them insufficiently mobile and too vulnerable when in motion to combat rapidly moving combined-arms teams. He therefore rejected plans to withhold antitank guns in a central reserve because the tempo of mechanized action might easily preempt their deployment. Hence, all antitank guns needed to be in place before the enemy attacked.[82]

Lynch believed that only tanks possessed the firepower, mobility, and protection necessary for antitank action. Tank units should therefore constitute the backbone of any antitank defense and counterattack enemy mechanized forces that penetrated friendly lines. The antitank role constituted an expansion of the tank's existing roles. Lynch also recommended a large-scale expansion of the Army's tank fleet. He considered ten thousand tanks a moderate estimate of the Army's wartime needs.[83]

Lynch's ideas found support among the CGSS faculty. The latter agreed that armored units constituted the key to antitank defense, but they also felt that antitank guns had an important role to play. Building on Lynch's concept, the faculty envisioned the distribution of antitank guns throughout all command echelons supported by tanks.[84]

In September 1940 the War Department issued a training circular for antitank operations that at least in part acknowledged the tank's antitank role. The circular also reflected the influence of the previous year's First Army maneuvers and the war in Europe. It ignored Lynch's criticisms of antitank guns and did not consider the tank the primary means of antitank defense. Instead:

> Employment of antitank guns is based on a minimum of guns in position initially to cover obstacles and as a first echelon of antimechanized defense, and a maximum of guns as mobile reserves. Based on information of hostile mechanized forces, reserve guns are moved rapidly and disposed so as to permit timely and powerful reinforcement of threatened or actual points of hostile mechanized attack, and to provide a pivot of maneuver for the counterattack. The hostile attack is met by the maximum fire. Available tanks or armored units maneuver to deliver a surprise blow against flanks and rear of hostile mechanized units. Certain mobile antimechanized units are held for maneuver against hostile mechanized vehicles which succeed in breaking through.[85]

---

[82] Memo, Ch of Inf Maj Gen George A. Lynch to ACS, G–3, sub: Antitank Doctrine and Development, 3 Jul 40, HQ AGF, GHQ, Gen Corresp, RG 337, NARA.

[83] Ibid.

[84] Ltr, Crockett to Edmunds, 20 Jul 40; Memo, Asst Commandant Col K. B. Edmunds to Commandant, 22 Jul 40, HQ AGF, GHQ, Gen Corresp, RG 337, NARA.

[85] CS Gen George C. Marshall, Training Circ no. 3, 23 Sep 40, p. 2, Crittenberger Papers.

Artillery barrages, bombing, strafing, and aerial chemical attacks were to support antitank operations.[86]

In War Department thinking mechanized attacks no longer constituted unsupported masses of tanks. Instead, they included combined-arms forces moving behind ground reconnaissance forces under an aerial umbrella. Such a threat could carefully select the point at which to attack, concentrating on a narrow frontage. To combat this threat, the War Department intended a tiered defense in depth, with each tier corresponding to a higher command echelon. Regimental antitank companies occupied the foremost positions. Behind them lay the division's antitank reserve. Successively to the rear lay corps and army antitank units. At the division, corps, and army levels, antitank units were initially held in reserve until the strength and direction of the mechanized attack became clear. Only then would they move forward to engage the threat with concentrated firepower.[87]

This concept of operations envisioned antitank units' wearing down armored attackers with an intensity of fire that increased the deeper they advanced. Therefore, most antitank guns were held as mobile reserves ready to reinforce a threatened point. The objective of these mobile antitank tactics lay in funneling attackers into narrow channels of advance where they could be counterattacked by friendly tanks supported with antitank guns. Each division, corps, and army also received an antitank officer who served as an adviser to ensure effective antitank employment.[88]

Implementation of the War Department's echelon defense required a massive expansion of antitank units. By 1941, however, only regimental antitank companies existed. New organizations would have to be created for army, corps, and division assignment despite prior rejection of divisional antitank battalions. The Camp Forrest, Tennessee, maneuvers in June therefore witnessed the employment of improvised divisional antitank units that also included attached engineers for laying mines. Plans for higher echelon antitank units favored organizations with a mix of antitank, reconnaissance, communications, antiaircraft, engineer, and security elements. Such self-contained units possessed considerable combat power and the ability to operate on their own. The design attracted the attention of General Marshall, who directed the preparation of such units for testing during the autumn maneuvers.[89]

Despite these measures, the War Department's antitank guidance was not universally accepted. Lynch continued to advocate a much stronger reliance on tanks

---

[86] Ibid., pp. 3–4.

[87] Memo, Twaddle to CS, G–3, sub: Antitank Defense, 18 Nov 40, pp. 3–4; "Notes on G–3, Anti-Tank Conference," pp. 17–18.

[88] Memo, ACS Brig Gen Harry L. Twaddle to CS, G–3, sub: Defense Against Armored Forces, 28 May 41, Bruce Papers; "Notes on G–3, Anti-Tank Conference," pp. 17–20, 23, 33.

[89] Memos, Twaddle to CS, G–3, 18 Nov 40, pp. 2–4; Gen Staff Sec Col Orlando Ward to ACS, G–3, sub: Creation of Additional Antitank-Antiaircraft Units, 14 Mar 41, Bruce Papers; Acting ACS, G–3, Brig Gen Harry L. Twaddle, to CS, G–3, sub: Creation of Additional Antitank-Antiaircraft Units, 19 Mar [Apr] 41, Bruce Papers; Opns and Trng Div Exec Lt Col W. E. Chambers to Ch, Planning Br, G–3, sub: Provisional Antitank Battalion, 19 May 41, HQ AGF, Gen Corresp, RG 337, NARA; Twaddle to CS, G–3, 28 May 41, pp. 2–3; ACS, G–3, Brig Gen Harry L. Twaddle to TAG, G–3, sub: Organization of Provisional Division and GHQ Antitank Battalions for Use in Current Maneuvers, 19 Jun 41, Bruce Papers.

rather than antitank guns. McNair constituted a more influential opponent, having come from a Field Artillery background. In World War I, he had trained artillery units for combat. He played an active role in the branch throughout the interwar years and demonstrated an interest in antitank operations. By 1939 he held the confidence of General Marshall, who appointed him commandant of the Command and General Staff School. In this position, McNair began to formulate a set of ideas for antitank operations. In July 1940 he became chief of staff for the newly activated General Headquarters responsible for the Army's combat readiness.[90]

Antitank operations constituted one of McNair's key priorities. The Army faced the likelihood of war with Germany in the near future, but it lacked the means with which to defeat the panzer formations that had overrun much of Europe. McNair sought to remedy this deficiency by implementing his own concept of antitank operations. The basis for his ideas lay in the perception of mechanized attacks as principally massed tank assaults on a narrow frontage. Defeating this concentration of armor therefore required the concentration of an equivalent mass of antitank guns. By pooling available antitank guns in a central reserve that moved behind friendly lines opposite enemy tanks, the latter's attack would be met by "something that they cannot survive."[91]

McNair rejected the War Department's preference for deploying antitank guns in deep echelons. Such deployment dispersed antitank assets and prevented their concentration into a decisive mass at a critical point. He believed that the ability of attacking tanks to focus on a narrow front would permit them to avoid most of the antitank guns in each echelon. The attacker would have great superiority wherever he attacked, while many of the defending antitank weapons sat idle in positions far removed from the actual penetration point.[92] Pooling antitank guns theoretically ensured that wherever a mechanized force attacked it would be met with a maximum of antitank strength.

Similarly, McNair criticized the War Department's intent to build antitank units for divisions, corps, and armies. These assignments institutionalized the very dissipation of antitank strength that McNair sought to avoid. Instead, he wanted antitank units—other than regimental companies whose value to local defense he acknowledged—assigned to General Headquarters either for attachment to any formation or for massed employment anywhere on the battlefield. He proposed the creation of a GHQ antitank force to train and organize these units.[93]

---

[90] Ltr, Brig Gen George C. Marshall to Brig Gen Lesley J. McNair, 23 Feb 39; Memo, Brig Gen George C. Marshall to Brig Gen Lesley J. McNair, 9 Mar 39; Ltrs, Brig Gen George C. Marshall to Brig Gen Lesley J. McNair, 3 May, 7 Aug 39; all in Selected Corresp, Marshall Papers. Kent Roberts Greenfield and Robert R. Palmer, "Origins of the Army Ground Forces: General Headquarters United States Army, 1940–1942," in *The Army Ground Forces: The Organization of Ground Combat Troops*, ed. Kent Roberts Greenfield, Robert R. Palmer and Bell I. Wiley, U.S. Army in World War II (Washington, D.C.: U.S. Army Center of Military History, 1947), pp. 4, 6; Baily, *Faint Praise*, pp. 8–9.

[91] Ltr, McNair to Bacon, 20 Jun 40; Gabel, *GHQ Maneuvers*, pp. 31–32.

[92] Ltr, McNair to Bacon, 20 Jun 40.

[93] Memo, Lynch to ACS, G–3, sub: Antitank Doctrine and Development, 3 Jul 40, and 2d End, CGSS Commandant Brig Gen Lesley J. McNair to TAG, 29 Jul 40, pp. 8, 10; Memo, GHQ CS Maj

McNair believed that the use of massed antitank weapons against enemy armor freed American tanks to pursue their own objectives. He did not agree with Lynch's assertion of the tank's value as an antitank weapon. He criticized Germany's use of panzer units to defeat Soviet tanks as uneconomical and driven by the absence of a powerful antitank reserve.[94] In his view, it was "poor economy to use a $35,000 medium tank to destroy another tank when the job can be done by a gun costing a fraction as much."[95] Moreover, McNair considered the towed antitank gun superior to the tank in firepower: "The struggle [between tanks and antitank guns] is analogous to that between ships and shore guns, and there is no question that the shore guns are superior—so much so that ships do not accept such a contest. The Chief of Infantry in effect asserts that ships are superior to shore guns."[96]

Broader differences than antitank operations characterized the relationship between Lynch and McNair. Both had supported their respective branches during the prior disputes between the Infantry and Artillery over antitank development responsibility. McNair subsequently played a leading role in refining the Army's field service regulations after their publication in tentative form in 1939. In this capacity, he ensured that the resultant doctrine reflected his preference for concentrating antitank weapons in a central, mobile reserve. Lynch, however, considered the field service regulations deficient and deliberately devoid of branch input. While McNair had overseen the entire development process, Lynch had had little input. The two men did not share a common sense of the doctrinal, organizational, and materiel changes necessary to make the U.S. Army battle ready. This difference shaped their discourse on antitank matters.[97]

However, critics of McNair's antitank concept echoed Lynch's concerns about its viability. They considered the employment of massed antitank guns a one-time possibility. McNair's preference for towed guns and their vulnerability during movement meant that once committed they became a collection of essentially immobile weapons. Their effectiveness therefore depended on the ability to continuously track enemy tank movements and assume firing positions before an attack began. McNair was convinced such action was viable, particularly if it relied on an early warning system extended at least twenty miles forward of friendly lines. During the testing of the Proposed Infantry Division in 1937 and again during the Camp Forrest maneuvers of 1941, defending forces had successfully tracked hostile tanks.[98]

Gen Lesley J. McNair to DCS, sub: Antitank Defense, 30 Dec 40; all in HQ AGF, Gen Corresp, RG 337, NARA.

[94] Memo, Lynch to ACS, G–3, sub: Antitank Doctrine and Development, 3 Jul 40, and 2d End, McNair to TAG, 29 Jul 40, p. 8; Draft Memo, GHQ CS, Lt Gen Lesley J. McNair, to ACS, G–3, sub: Organization of Antitank Units in the Army, 21 Aug 41, p. 2, HQ AGF, Gen Corresp, RG 337, NARA.

[95] "Notes on G–3, Anti-Tank Conference," p. 83.

[96] Memo, Lynch to ACS, G–3, 3 Jul 40, and 2d End, McNair to TAG, 29 Jul 40, pp. 6–7.

[97] Lynch, "Final Report," pp. 68–75; "Notes on G–3, Anti-Tank Conference," p. 80.

[98] Memo, Lt Col Allen F. Kingman to GHQ CS, sub: Report on Meeting Called by General Bryden on Branch Responsibility for Antitank Defense, 10 May 41, HQ AGF, GHQ, RG 337, NARA; Ltr, McNair to Bacon, 20 Jun 40, p. 2; Memo, Lynch to ACS, G–3, sub: Antitank Doctrine and Develop-

Unfortunately, maneuver experiences also seemed to confirm some of the critics' fears. Too often, commanders deployed antitank guns in static positions at the start of a maneuver where they remained until the exercise terminated. According to McNair, "There is no more certain method than this of ensuring the triumph of armored forces in maneuvers—to say nothing of more serious consequences in battle."[99] The 2d Armored Division achieved success during the Camp Forrest maneuvers due in part to insufficient antitank guns and the makeshift nature of antitank units.[100]

Nevertheless, McNair looked to the ongoing war for justification of his pooling concept and for lessons applicable to the U.S. Army. In the opening campaigns, however, he found little of positive value. Antitank defenses appeared to be inadequate and lacked sufficient antitank guns. The French compounded these problems by dispersing the few antitank assets available.[101] These deficiencies also plagued the Italians in North Africa. Following their crushing defeat by a much smaller British mechanized force, McNair observed: "Our present organization will place us in little better condition than France and Italy. We are building a great armored force, but are doing little to defeat such a force in the hands of an enemy."[102]

In June 1941 the British in turn suffered defeat by the Germans while trying to relieve Tobruk. In three days of fighting, the British lost an estimated two hundred tanks. German 88-mm. antitank weapons played a prominent role at Halfaya Pass, where a "tank-proof" locality was reportedly created. Although the Germans relied on a combination of mines, antitank guns, and tank counterattacks, American analysis considered this battle the first instance in which antitank guns defeated an armored offensive. To McNair, it validated his emphasis on concentrating antitank weapons and relying on high-velocity, towed antitank weapons. He would not be able to field test his concept until the autumn maneuvers.[103]

Antitank the American Way

By mid-1941 the dilemma surrounding American antitank operations remained unresolved. Three separate concepts had emerged, but none had been implemented. Lynch's emphasis on tanks did not conform to the Armored Force's emphasis on using armor against nonmechanized forces in the enemy's rear areas. McNair's preference for pooling antitank assets suited the minimization tendency evident

ment, 3 Jul 40, and 2d End, McNair to TAG, 29 Jul 40, p. 6; Ltr, GHQ CS Lt Gen Lesley J. McNair to Col J. A. Considine, 7 Jul 41, HQ AGF, GHQ, RG 337, NARA.

99 Memo, GHQ CS Maj Gen Lesley J. McNair sub: Antitank Defense, 15 May 41, HQ AGF, Gen Corresp, RG 337, NARA.

100 "Comments by the Army Commander on Second Army Field Training, June 28, 1941," p. 12, 28 Jun 41, Crittenberger Papers.

101 Ltr, McNair to Bacon, 20 Jun 40, p. 3; Memo, Lynch to ACS, G–3, 3 Jul 40, and 2d End, McNair to TAG, 29 Jul 40, p. 9.

102 Memo, McNair to DCS, 30 Dec 40, p. 1.

103 Memos, Kingman to GHQ CS, 10 May 41; Acting ACS, G–2, Col C. H. Mason, to CS, G–2, sub: Use of Antiaircraft Artillery Against Tanks, 26 Jun 41, Item 1233, Reel 30, National Archives Project, GCM.

in the triangular division's organization. These formations would not lose their mobility through acquisition of permanent antitank units, but the entire concept remained unproven. Conversely, maneuver experience and foreign doctrine favored an echeloned antitank defense but insufficient antitank weapons precluded such an option for the entire Army.

To help resolve this dilemma, Marshall directed the Operations and Training Division of the General Staff: "You should organize in your division a small planning and exploring branch, composed of visionary officers, with nothing else to do but think about improvements in methods of warfare, study developments abroad and tackle such unsolved problems as measures against armored force action, night bombardment, march protection and the like."[104] The establishment of the Planning Branch in May 1941 resulted. Its first chief responsibility lay in analysis of the antitank problem.[105]

The steady growth of Germany's mechanized strength made resolution of this issue imperative for the U.S. Army. While American antitank units remained in a provisional state without uniform organization or doctrine, intelligence estimates of Germany's mechanized strength in 1941 ranged from twenty to twenty-seven panzer divisions with a growth rate of one division per month.[106] In fact, Germany possessed twenty-one panzer divisions and one light division with a reduced complement of tanks. This number marked an increase of ten panzer and one light division from 1940. However, in 1942 the Germans added only three new panzer divisions and one light division. Subsequent additions in 1943 and 1944 reflected the conversion of motorized infantry divisions into panzer formations, but most of these new divisions lacked the tank strength of the early war organizations.[107]

The War Department finally determined to solve its antitank problem through the mass proliferation of antitank units. It opted to organize no fewer than two hundred twenty antitank battalions. Each of the fifty-five infantry divisions planned would receive one battalion. In addition, corps headquarters would receive forty-five and army commands ten battalions. The remaining one hundred ten battalions were intended for General Headquarters control. In effect the Army intended to provide sufficient antitank units to permit both an echeloned defense and McNair's pooling concept.[108]

---

[104] Memo, CS Gen George C. Marshall to ACS, G–3, sub: Defense Against Armored Force, 14 May 41, Selected Corresp, Marshall Papers.

[105] Memo, Lt Col W. E. Chambers, sub: Planning Br, 15 May 41, HQ AGF, Gen Corresp, RG 337, NARA.

[106] Memo, ACS, G–3, Brig Gen Harry L. Twaddle, to CS, G–3, sub: Organization of Antitank Units in the Army, 18 Aug 41, p. 2, HQ AGF, GHQ, RG 337, NARA.

[107] Roger Edwards, *Panzer: A Revolution in Warfare, 1939–1945* (London: Arms and Armour Press, 1989), pp. 70–71.

[108] Memos, Lt Col Andrew D. Bruce to ACS, G–3, sub: Additional Antitank Units, 10 Jul 41, p. 1, Bruce Papers; ACS, G–3, Brig Gen Harry L. Twaddle, to CS, G–3, sub: Organization of Antitank Units in the Army, 11 Aug 41, pp. 2–4, Bruce Papers; ACS, G–3, Brig Gen Harry L. Twaddle, to CS, G–3, sub: Organization of Antitank Units in the Army, 18 Aug 41, p. 2, HQ AGF, GHQ, RG 337, NARA; ACS, G–3, Brig Gen Harry L. Twaddle, to CS, G–3, sub: Antitank and Antiaircraft Defense, Field Forces, 9 Sep 41, pp. 1–2, Item 1479, Reel 36, National Archives Project, GCM; Asst Gen Staff

Initially, the General Staff planned to divide responsibility for the organization and training of these units among the existing combat arms. This plan utilized extant training facilities and raised the visibility of antitank operations throughout the Army. However, each installation responsible for antitank training would have to purchase additional land for the establishment of firing ranges. Decentralized development and duplication of effort would also complicate the establishment of uniform doctrine.[109]

The General Staff also considered assignment of antitank responsibility to a single branch, but it found none entirely suited to the task. The Infantry already played a central role in the training of regimental antitank companies equipped with 37-mm. antitank guns, but its ongoing expansion and the likelihood that larger caliber weapons might become necessary reduced its viability.[110] Similarly, the Field Artillery's expansion and emphasis on indirect fire made its ability to take over antitank development problematic. While the branch possessed much of the necessary equipment for antitank operations, artillery units lacked the high mobility desired for the antitank weapons.[111]

The Cavalry possessed the offensive doctrine and mobility considered vital to antitank operations. Despite the branch's late acquisition of 37-mm. antitank guns, when these weapons did become available, they were organized into provisional units and used during maneuvers.[112] Using jeeps to tow them, the 6th Cavalry Regiment commander found the 37-mm. guns mobile and able to enter combat in under ten seconds. The 1st Cavalry Division's Provisional Antitank Squadron employed 37-mm. guns mounted on ¾-ton trucks. In operations against the 2d Armored Division, the squadron received credit for the elimination of ninety-nine tanks, numerous other

Sec Lt Col John R. Deane to CS, sub: Organization of Antitank Units in the Army, 26 Sep 41, tab A, p. 3, Bruce Papers.

[109] Memo, Gen Staff Sec Col Orlando Ward to ACS, G–3, sub: Creation of Additional Antitank-Antiaircraft Units, 29 Apr 41, p. 5, tab E in Memo, Twaddle to CS, G–3, 19 Mar [Apr] 41; Memo, ACS, G–3, Harry L. Twaddle, to CS, G–3, sub: Organization of Antitank Units in the Army, 11 Aug 41, Bruce Papers; "Agency or Agencies for the Creation, Development and Replacement Training of Division, Army Corps and Army and GHQ Antitank and Tank Destroyer Units," p. 3, tab C of Memo, ACS, G–3, Brig Gen Harry L. Twaddle, to CS, G–3, sub: Organization of Antitank Units in the Army, 18 Aug 41, Bruce Papers.

[110] "Summary of Discussion at War Department Conference on Antitank Defense, April 15, 1941," p. 3, Encl in Memo, Kingman to GHQ CS, 17 Apr 41; Memo, Twaddle to CS, G–3, 19 Mar [Apr] 41, pp. 1–2; Memo, Mobilization Br Ch Lt Col C. H. Karlstad to Planning Branch Ch, G–3, sub: Additional Antitank Units, 18 Jul 41, Bruce Papers; Memo, Twaddle to CS, G–3, 11 Aug 41, tab C; Ltr, Maj Gen Andrew D. Bruce to Brig Gen Earnest J. Dawley, 13 Jun 44, p. 2, Bruce Papers.

[111] "Agency or Agencies for the Creation," pp. 1, 6; Memo, Kingman to GHQ CS, 17 Apr 41; Ltr, Bruce to Dawley, 13 Jun 44, p. 2; Memo, Karlstad to Planning Br Ch, G–3, 18 Jul 41; Memo, Opns Br Ch Lt Col Edward S. Ott to ACS, G–3, Harry L. Twaddle, sub: Antitank Defense, 19 Jul 41, Bruce Papers; Memo, ACS, G–3, Brig Gen Harry L. Twaddle, sub: Antitank Organization in Field Forces, 22 Jul 41, Bruce Papers; Memo, Twaddle to CS, G–3, 18 Aug 41, p. 4.

[112] Memo, Col B. Q. Jones, sub: Bantam Regiment: A Proposed Antimechanized Reconnaissance Force, 22 Jul 41, Item 4327, Reel 287, National Archives Project, GCM; "Plan I: Agency or Agencies for Creation, Development and Replacement Training of Antitank Units Other than Organic Divisional Units," tab C of Memo, Twaddle to CS, G–3, 11 Aug 41; Memo, Col B. Q. Jones to Planning Br Ch, sub: Bantam Regiment, 20 Aug 41, Item 4327, Reel 287, National Archives Project, GCM.

vehicles, and over four hundred men with minimal friendly losses. This success encouraged further Cavalry experimentation with mobile antitank weapons. Moreover, the Cavalry was the only combat arm largely unaffected by Army expansion, permitting the devotion of time and personnel to antitank development.[113]

For these reasons, the Planning Branch recommended that the Cavalry receive responsibility for antitank development. However, Chief of Cavalry Maj. Gen. John K. Herr refused to build antitank units by converting horse cavalry. His uncompromising stance effectively removed the Cavalry from any significant role in antitank development. Worse, the antitank requirements of the branch were given a low priority and the General Staff began deliberations on whether to transfer Cavalry antitank weapons to other branches.[114] Herr's efforts to sustain horse cavalry while the Army struggled to counter the armored threat represented by Germany's panzer divisions hardened General Staff sentiment against him. Planning Branch Chief Lt. Col. Andrew D. Bruce, who initially proposed giving antitank responsibility to the Cavalry, summarized this feeling: "The Chief of Cavalry, who was very much horse-minded, said he would like to have the Tank Destroyers very much but he wouldn't give up a single horse. Of course he, in my opinion, should have been relieved."[115] The mounted arm was considered too dependent on horse cavalry and characterized as having "almost completely divorced itself from the use of track vehicles."[116]

This separation occurred as a direct result of the Armored Force's creation. That organization had subsumed the Cavalry's entire mechanized component. The Cavalry retained control over the 4th and 6th Cavalry Regiments only because they included a mixture of horse and mechanized elements. Even so, the assistant chief of staff, G–3, considered them unfit to locate and track hostile armor and recommended the removal of the horse component. Herr rejected these criticisms, noting severe unit equipment shortages and the success of the 6th Cavalry Regiment's antitank element during maneuvers.[117] However, by the summer of 1941 the chief of Cavalry had become an isolated figure who presided over a branch many considered obsolete.

The Armored Force was the only other branch seriously considered to assume responsibility for antitank development. The complementary combat roles of tank and antitank units made centralized training and development a logical step and

---

[113] Memo, Kingman to GHQ CS, 17 Apr 41; Ltr, Bruce to Dawley, 13 Jun 44, p. 2; Ltr, Col J. A. Considine to GHQ CS Lt Gen Lesley J. McNair, 3 Jul 41, HQ AGF, Gen Corresp, RG 337, NARA; Memo, Twaddle to CS, G–4, 11 Aug 41, tab C; Ltr, Carleton to Herr, 29 Aug 41; "Discussion of Questions Involved in the Creation of a Tank Destroyer Force," p. 2, tab A of Memo, Asst Gen Staff Sec Lt Col John R. Deane to CS, sub: Organization of Antitank Units in the Army, 26 Sep 41, Bruce Papers; Ltr, Maj Gen Andrew D. Bruce to Brig Gen A. O. Gorder, 8 Feb 45, p. 2, Bruce Papers.

[114] Memo, Bruce to ACS, G–3, sub: Additional Antitank Units, 10 Jul 41, p. 2; Memo, Twaddle to CS, G–4, 11 Aug 41, tab C; "General Plan: Improvement of Antitank Measures in the Army," pp. 2–3, tab B of Memo, Twaddle to CS, G–3, 11 Aug 41.

[115] Ltr, Bruce to Gorder, 8 Feb 45, p. 2.

[116] "General Plan"; Quote from "Discussion of Questions," p. 2.

[117] Memo, Ott to Twaddle, G–3, 19 Jul 41; "General Plan," pp. 2–3; Memo, Ch of Cav Maj Gen John K. Herr to ACS, G–3, 3 Sep 41, Item 4327, Reel 287, National Archives Project, GCM.

mirrored an earlier, similar development in the German Army.[118] The Armored Force, however, was already experiencing difficulty in organizing and training new armored units. Potentially overburdened, some General Staff members questioned the wisdom of assigning it another major mission.[119] Chaffee flatly rejected any association of the Armored Force and antitank development. His position raised fears that the latter would be neglected if assigned to the Armored Force.[120]

The failure to determine branch responsibility for antitank development led the General Staff to consider creating a separate force. Freed from the other concerns that absorbed each branch, antitank development would benefit from focused, centralized development. A separate force offered the prospect of rapid evolution, administrative simplicity, and uniformity—important considerations for an Army struggling to build an antitank capability quickly. It also required only one land purchase instead of the several originally considered to establish firing ranges.[121]

General Marshall supported the separate antitank force and directed the Operations and Training Division to assume responsibility for antitank development.[122] The chief of staff's intervention moved antitank development from endless discussion of branch responsibility to the establishment of an actual organization to address and resolve the issues surrounding antitank doctrine, materiel, and organization. The General Staff secretary offered: "The problem seems to me to be almost exactly like the problem of machine gun training in the last war. No one knew anything about machine guns and everyone had to use them. The M.G. [machine gun] training center was the answer."[123] The Machine Gun Center had provided instruction in machine-gun tactics and usage to personnel from all arms. Once familiarity with the weapon became universal, the Machine Gun Center disbanded.[124] This experience served as the model for establishing an antitank force under the G–3.

The War Department Planning Branch arrived at the same conclusion, following its own independent analysis of antitank development. Colonel Bruce's staff studied Army organizations in World War I to find useful parallels: "Looking in the far future, our committee thought that the analogy of tank destroyer and machine guns were very great; that one of the biggest threats of the battlefield was tanks

---

[118] Memo, Maj Gen Charles L. Scott to Armd Force Ch, sub: New Means and Methods to Combat Armored Units, 5 Jul 41, Ward Papers; Memo, Twaddle to CS, G–4, 11 Aug 41, tab C; "Agency or Agencies for the Creation," p. 4; Memo, Deane to CS, 26 Sep 41, tab A, pp. 3–5.

[119] Memo, Twaddle to CS, G–3, 19 Mar [Apr] 41, pp. 1–2, tab D; Memo, Twaddle to CS, G–4, 11 Aug 41, tab C; "Agency or Agencies for the Creation," p. 4; Memo, Gen Staff Sec Col Walter B. Smith to CS, sub: Antitank Organization, 7 Oct 41, Bruce Papers.

[120] "Views on Branch Responsibility," tab D of Memo, Twaddle to CS, G–3, 19 Mar [Apr] 41; Ltr, Lt Col Townsend Heard to GHQ CS Maj Gen Lesley J. McNair, 8 Apr 41, HQ AGF, Gen Corresp, RG 337, NARA; "Agency or Agencies for the Creation," p. 4; Memo, Smith to CS, 7 Oct 41; Ltr, Bruce to Dawley, 13 Jun 44, p. 2.

[121] Memo, Marshall to ACS, G–3, 14 May 41; "Agency or Agencies for the Creation," pp. 2–3.

[122] For the discussion surrounding this decision, see Memos, Twaddle to CS, G–3, 19 Mar [Apr] 41, p. 3; Marshall to ACS, G–3, 14 May 41; Lt Col Andrew D. Bruce to ACS, G–3, sub: Antitank Organization in Field Forces, 22 Jul 41, Bruce Papers; Twaddle to CS, G–3, 18 Aug 41, p. 3.

[123] Memo, Smith to CS, 7 Oct 41.

[124] Ltrs, Bruce to Dawley, 13 Jun 44, p. 2, and Bruce to Gorder, 8 Feb 45, p. 2.

M6 Gun Motor Carriage modified through the addition of an awkwardly mounted antiaircraft machine gun

and as a consequence everyone would have to have some sort of anti-tank defense. The Machine Gun Center thus became the model for the proposed Antitank Force."[125] Bruce's own World War I duty with a machine-gun battalion also probably fostered the use of the Machine Gun Center as a model for antitank development.[126] The Planning Branch envisioned an organization that incorporated personnel from all branches to form and train antitank units. These in turn would be distributed throughout the Army. However, once antitank organization, doctrine, and materiel became universal throughout the Army, the force would dissolve.[127]

In many respects the prospective antitank force resembled the Armored Force. Both bore responsibility for providing the Army with a specific capability not easily incorporated into the existing branches. Both managed responsibilities similar to those of the combat arms, but neither possessed a legal foundation. However, the antitank force was deliberately separated from the Armored Force to foster a rivalry between them that paralleled the battlefield rivalry between tanks and antitank weapons and aircraft and antiaircraft weapons. Although armor and antitank units might train together, the Armored Force was not to influence antitank development.[128]

General Marshall supported this plan. On 8 October he authorized the creation of the Tank Destroyer Tactical and Firing Center directly subordinate to the War Department, commanded by an officer he would select. The commander's responsibilities included training, developing doctrine, and recommending materiel requirements. The adjutant general issued more detailed orders on 27 November.[129] The term *tank destroyer* emerged from the War Department's desire for antitank units capable of attacking tanks rather than passively awaiting their action. The ideal tank destroyer

---

[125] Ltr, Bruce to Gorder, 8 Feb 45, p. 2.

[126] Baily, *Faint Praise*, p. 17.

[127] "Agency or Agencies for the Creation," p. 2; Ltr, Bruce to Dawley, 13 Jun 44, p. 2; Ltr, Bruce to Gorder, 8 Feb 45, pp. 2–3.

[128] Ltr, Heard to McNair, 8 Apr 41; Memo, McNair to ACS, G–3, 2 Sep 41.

[129] Memo, DCS Maj Gen Richard C. Moore to CS, sub: Organization of Antitank Units in the Army, 16 Sep 41, Bruce Papers; Memo, Gen Staff Sec Col Walter B. Smith to ACS, G–3, sub: Organization of Antitank Units in the Army, 8 Oct 41, Bruce Papers; Memo, Adjutant General's Office to Commanding Ofcr, Tank Destroyer Tactical and Firing Ctr, sub: Organization of Tank Destroyer Tactical and Firing Center, 27 Nov 41, Bruce Papers.

stalked and hunted its prey. The term was used to describe all nondivisional antitank units and to encourage in them an offensive spirit.[130]

Unfortunately, the change in nomenclature from antitank to tank destroyer proved no replacement for effective doctrine, training, and organization. The name generated confusion concerning the weapon itself as well as its purpose. Both towed and self-propelled antitank weapons became known as tank destroyers. Tank destroyers alternatively implied "tank-chasers" or weapons that destroyed enemy tanks with firepower from previously assumed positions. Nevertheless, field testing of the tank-destroyer concept occurred during the autumn maneuvers concurrent with the establishment of the Tank Destroyer Tactical and Firing Center.

---

[130] ACS, G–3, Brig Gen Harry L. Twaddle, "Consideration of Non-Concurrences," p. 12, attached to Memo, Twaddle to CS, G–3, 11 Aug 41.

10

THE ART OF MANEUVER, 1941

In 1941 the Army conducted its largest peacetime maneuvers. These events would become the forums for testing the relative capabilities of armored formations and antitank organizations. In a series of maneuvers in Louisiana and the Carolinas, the Army found its armored divisions unable to replicate the combat successes of similarly organized German panzer divisions. Instead, American armor was handicapped by inexperienced commanders, novice soldiers, and scenario designs that prevented their use in a decisive manner. Conversely, antitank operations benefited from General Headquarters (GHQ) support and from maneuver rules that unrealistically boosted their effectiveness against tanks. Consequently, the War Department began to establish a separate antitank force even before the conclusion of the maneuvers. The Cavalry, however, failed to remove the stigma of obsolescence, despite the effectiveness of cavalry organizations throughout the maneuvers. Upon their conclusion, the Cavalry's status continued to decline while armored and antitank organizations expanded.

Louisiana Maneuvers

Throughout 1941 the Army prepared for war. Primary responsibility for ensuring combat readiness lay with GHQ Chief of Staff Lt. Gen. Lesley J. McNair. Charged with overseeing Army training, General Headquarters prepared and implemented a rigorous training program. It included a sequence of successively larger field maneuvers beginning with regiments and battalions. Division and corps maneuvers followed in the spring and summer months. These events built unit cohesion and prepared participating formations for the capstone autumn maneuvers.[1]

These training events included three army maneuvers planned and supervised by General Headquarters. They involved over seven hundred forty thousand soldiers from the Regular Army and National Guard. The magnitude of these maneuvers mandated extraordinary preparations, including leasing vast tracts of land and securing

[1] Kent Roberts Greenfield and Robert R. Palmer, "Origins of the Army Ground Forces: General Headquarters United States Army, 1940–1942," in *The Army Ground Forces: The Organization of Ground Combat Troops*, ed. Kent Roberts Greenfield, Robert R. Palmer, and Bell I. Wiley, U.S. Army in World War II (Washington, D.C.: U.S. Army Center of Military History, 1947), pp. 38–41; Christopher R. Gabel, *The U.S. Army GHQ Maneuvers of 1941* (Washington, D.C.: U.S. Army Center of Military History, 1991), pp. 44–45.

trespassing rights. For the first time the Army would use large-scale training areas free from the constraints of private property restrictions that had kept prior maneuvers road bound. To further enhance realism, the army commanders were free to conduct operations as they desired without mandatory interruptions.[2]

The Armored Force participated in two of the three army maneuvers. In September the 1st and 2d Armored Divisions and several independent tank battalions joined the Second Army versus Third Army maneuvers in Louisiana. In November the armored divisions fought against First Army in the Carolinas.

The Louisiana phase of the GHQ maneuvers consisted of two scenarios enacted in a large rectangular area in western Louisiana bounded by the Sabine River in the west, the Red River in the east, the city of Shreveport in the north, and an imaginary line in the south between the towns of De Ridder and Oakdale. The topography included woods, streams, ridges, and marshland. Deploying to the northeast of the Red River, the Red Second Army included 5 infantry divisions; 1 cavalry division; and the I Armored Corps, which controlled the 1st and 2d Armored Divisions. Compared to the opposing Blue Third Army's 9 infantry divisions, 1 cavalry division, 1 tank group, and 3 provisional antitank groups, the Red Army possessed fewer soldiers but superior mobility. Both armies relied on aerial assets numbering about three hundred fighter and bomber aircraft.[3]

The first scenario began on 15 September with both armies conducting offensive missions. While the Red Army moved across the Red River, Blue forces moved northward on a broad front between the Sabine and Red Rivers (*see Map 2*). Providing flank protection for Blue's western flank, the 1st Cavalry Division crossed the Sabine River into Texas. Contact between the two armies resulted in both deploying along a line running east to west between the two rivers with the Kisatchie National Forest in the center. The I Armored Corps occupied the Red western flank and was poised to move south. Over the next two days both armies launched mutual attacks along this front. In these operations, the Red left flank, held by only a single infantry division, retreated under pressure from four Blue divisions.[4]

On 18 September the Red Army launched an offensive employing the I Armored Corps to breach the Blue lines to the south and bolster Red's sagging eastern flank. (*See Map 3.*) The 1st Armored Division attacked in an easterly direction before pivoting to the southwest to support the 2d Armored Division advancing along a southeasterly axis. The latter's attack bogged down in a series of unproductive frontal assaults against strong Blue positions buttressed with antitank guns.[5]

The 1st Armored Division formed three groupings for its attack: the 69th Armored Regiment, the 1st Armored Regiment, and the 1st Armored Brigade. Brig. Gen. Orlando W. Ward commanded the last organization, which included the

---

[2] Gabel, *GHQ Maneuvers*, pp. 50, 59, 127; Greenfield and Palmer, "Origins of the Army Ground Forces," pp. 40, 43.

[3] Brig Gen Mark W. Clark, "Critique of 1st Phase, GHQ-directed Maneuvers, Camp Polk, La., September 14–19, 1941," p. 1, Headquarters Army Ground Forces (HQ AGF), GHQ Gen Staff, G–1 Section, Record Group (RG) 337, National Archives and Records Administration (NARA).

[4] Clark, "Critique of 1st Phase," pp. 3–8.

[5] Ibid., p. 8; Gabel, *GHQ Maneuvers*, pp. 77, 79–80, 82.

M2A4 light tank of the 1st Armored Division during the autumn maneuvers of 1941. The band around the turret identifies it as part of the Red Army.

13th Armored Regiment, one medium tank battalion, and the divisional infantry, artillery, and engineers. The 69th Armored Regiment moved into the Kisatchie National Forest and lost its way in the wooded, swampy terrain for most of the day. The 1st Armored Regiment attacked Blue forces to the east and spent itself in costly assaults on antitank positions. The 1st Armored Brigade also attacked to the east. It defeated several Blue forces before pivoting to the southwest and advancing into the Kisatchie National Forest. Poor route reconnaissance resulted in the unit moving move deeper into the forest over muddy lanes. Its tanks became mired amid the swampy woodland. They proved easy targets for the Blue infantry and antitank guns that massed around the stranded armored unit. Estimated losses for the armored divisions on this day included 115 tanks and 98 other vehicles in the 2d Armored Division and 62 tanks in the 1st Armored Division.[6]

On 19 September heavy losses forced the Red Army to retreat, closely pursued by Blue forces. The Blue 1st Cavalry Division interdicted the 2d Armored Division's withdrawal, destroying numerous rear-area elements before the maneuver's termination

[6] Note, Lt Col Clarence C. Benson to Lt Col Allen F. Kingman, 19 Sep 41, and Handwritten Note, Anon, "Tank Losses 18 September," both in HQ AGF, GHQ, RG 337, NARA. Gabel, *GHQ Maneuvers*, p. 82.

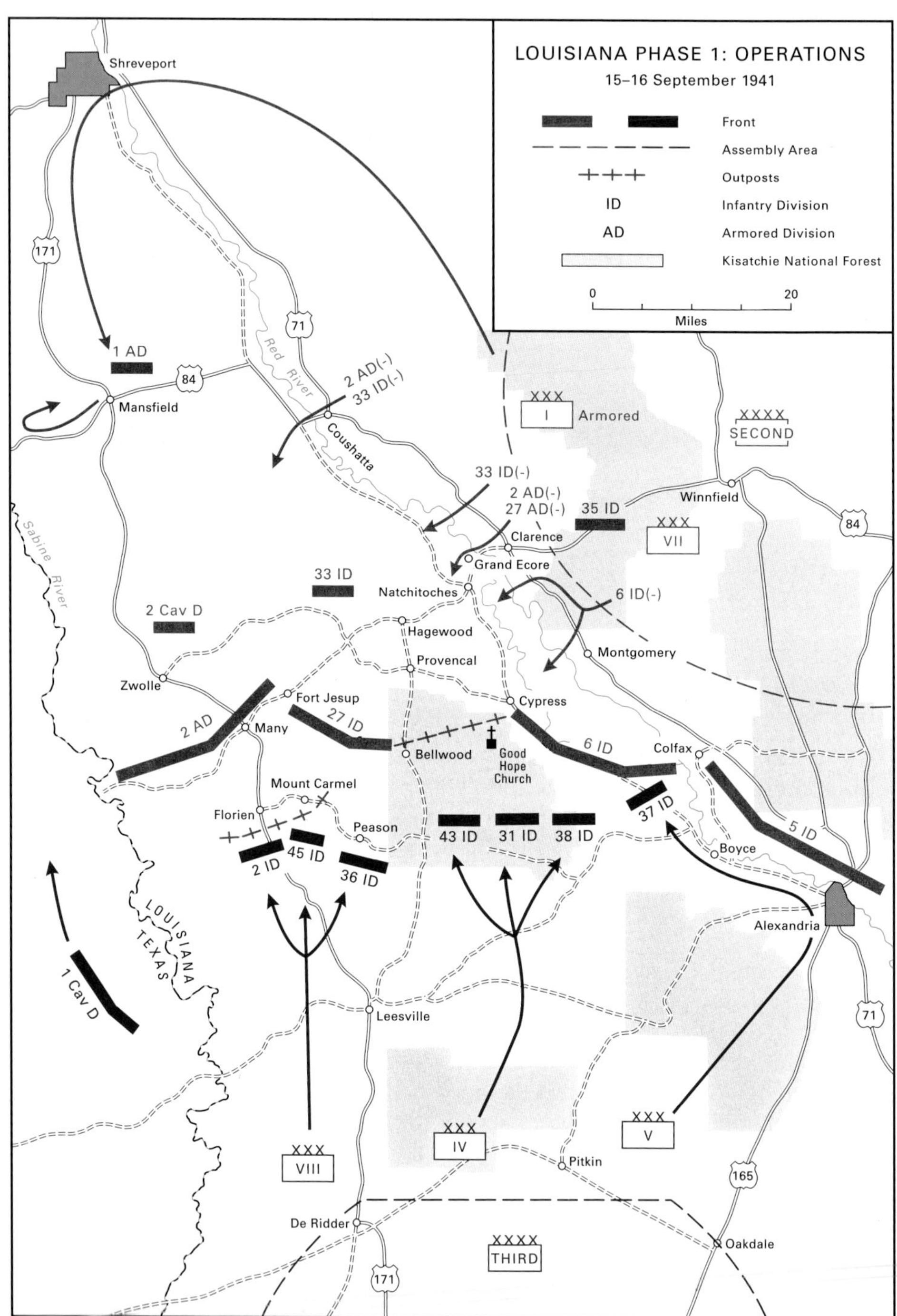
LOUISIANA PHASE 1: OPERATIONS
15–16 September 1941
Front
Assembly Area
Outposts
ID
Infantry Division
AD
Armored Division
Kisatchie National Forest
0
20
Miles
Shreveport
171
71
Red River
1 AD
84
Mansfield
2 AD(-)
33 ID(-)
Coushatta
XXX
I
Armored
XXXX
SECOND
33 ID(-)
2 AD(-)
27 AD(-)
35 ID
Winnfield
XXX
VII
84
Clarence
Grand Ecore
Sabine River
33 ID
Natchitoches
6 ID(-)
2 Cav D
Hagewood
Montgomery
Provencal
Zwolle
Fort Jesup
Cypress
2 AD
Many
27 ID
6 ID
Colfax
Bellwood
Good Hope Church
Mount Carmel
37 ID
Florien
5 ID
Peason
43 ID
31 ID
38 ID
45 ID
Boyce
2 ID
36 ID
Alexandria
LOUISIANA
TEXAS
1 Cav D
71
Leesville
XXX
V
XXX
IV
XXX
VIII
Pitkin
165
De Ridder
Oakdale
XXXX
THIRD
171

Map 2

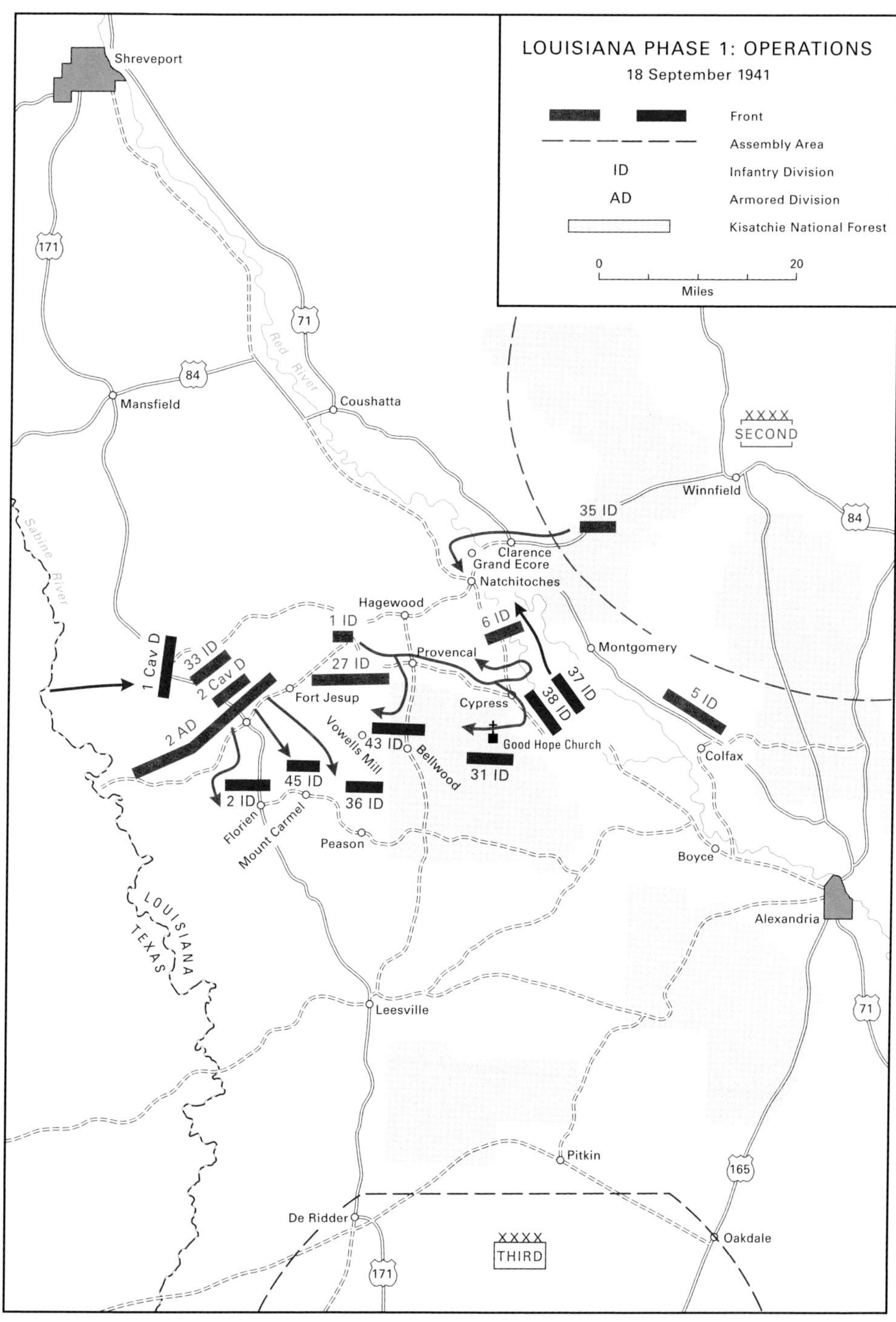
LOUISIANA PHASE 1: OPERATIONS
18 September 1941
Front
Assembly Area
ID
Infantry Division
AD
Armored Division
Kisatchie National Forest
0
20
Miles
Shreveport
Mansfield
Coushatta
Red River
Sabine River
SECOND
Winnfield
35 ID
Clarence
Grand Ecore
Natchitoches
Hagewood
1 ID
6 ID
Provencal
27 ID
Montgomery
37 ID
38 ID
1 Cav D
33 ID
2 Cav D
Fort Jesup
Cypress
5 ID
2 AD
Vowells Mill
43 ID
Bellwood
Good Hope Church
Colfax
45 ID
31 ID
2 ID
36 ID
Florien
Mount Carmel
Peason
Boyce
Alexandria
LOUISIANA
TEXAS
Leesville
Pitkin
De Ridder
Oakdale
THIRD
171
71
84
165

Map 3

the same day. The 1st Armored Division also suffered losses estimated at 138 tanks, 166 other vehicles, and 1,264 officers and men.[7]

Faulty employment of the armored formations partially accounted for the high losses. Both divisions attempted to hold the Red western flank instead of seeking critical targets deep in the Blue rear. Difficult terrain and insufficient information concerning Blue antitank dispositions further limited the effectiveness of the Red Army's 18 September attack. The 2d Armored Division also had a breakdown of radio communications between its reconnaissance battalion and divisional headquarters at the maneuver's outset.[8]

Blue antitank assets contributed to the destruction of Red armor. Divisional antitank battalions, regimental antitank companies, and divisional artillery employed in a static defensive role provided effective defense against Red tanks. For example, the 45th Infantry Division alone received credit for eliminating 151 tanks and 152 other vehicles of the 2d Armored Division. The antitank companies of the 31st and 38th Infantry Divisions engaged the 1st Armored Division in and around the Kisatchie National Forest, blocking the armored thrust and cutting its supply flow.[9]

Blue forces also included three Provisional Antitank Groups (*Chart 16*). Each group had three antitank battalions equipped with a mix of 37-mm. and 75-mm. antitank guns. Support components for each group included command, reconnaissance, intelligence, signal, infantry, and engineer elements. These groups represented an effort to test the viability of concentrating antitank assets for use in aggressive offensive operations against enemy tanks. However, the antitank groups remained in reserve too long and conducted no offensive operations against hostile armor. Their efforts were poorly coordinated with the antitank elements of the infantry divisions, and only one antitank battalion from these groups actually entered combat. Nevertheless, General McNair praised the efforts of these groups. He considered their actions positive examples of the potential efficacy of concentrations of antitank guns.[10]

The 1st Cavalry Division performed the most aggressive antitank operations. It employed an excellent warning system that incorporated a variety of reconnaissance

---

[7] Clark, "Critique of 1st Phase," p. 9; Lt Col Clarence C. Benson, "Estimate of 1st Armored Division Losses During Period September 14–19, 1941," HQ AGF, GHQ, RG 337, NARA.

[8] Lt Col John A. Smith Jr., "Comments Concerning Maneuver Operations of 2d Armored Division," 10 Sep 41, HQ AGF, GHQ, RG 337, NARA.

[9] Lt Col Cabell C. Cornish, Rpt of Antitank Activities of 45th Inf Div, 21 Sep 41; Maj Claude F. Clayton, Rpt of Antitank Activities of 31st Inf Div, 26 Sep 41; Maj Charles J. Cronan, Rpt of Antitank Activities of 38th Inf Div, 26 Sep 41; all in HQ AGF, GHQ, RG 337, NARA.

[10] Memo, Lt Col Clyde L. Hyssong to CG, Third Army, sub: GHQ Antitank Units in GHQ-directed Maneuvers, 8 Aug 41, HQ AGF, GHQ, RG 337, NARA; Memo for Record (MFR), Maj C. W. Stewart Jr., sub: Summary of 1st and 3d Provisional TD Group Reports, 12 Nov 41, pp. 1–2, Item 4327, Reel 287, National Archives Project, George C. Marshall Library (GCM), Lexington, Va.; Maj Douglas C. McNair, "Check List on Antitank Units," 5 Sep 41, pp. 1, 5, HQ AGF, GHQ, RG 337, NARA; Memo, Maj Douglas C. McNair to Lt Col Allen F. Kingman, sub: Antitank Action in First Phase, 20 Sep 41, p. 2, HQ AGF, GHQ, RG 337, NARA; GHQ Chief of Staff (CS) Lt Gen Lesley J. McNair, G.S.C., "Comments, 1st Phase, GHQ-directed Maneuvers, Camp Polk, La., September 14–19, 1941," n.d., p. 10, HQ AGF, CG, RG 337, NARA.

Chart 16–Provisional Antitank Group, Louisiana Maneuvers, 1941

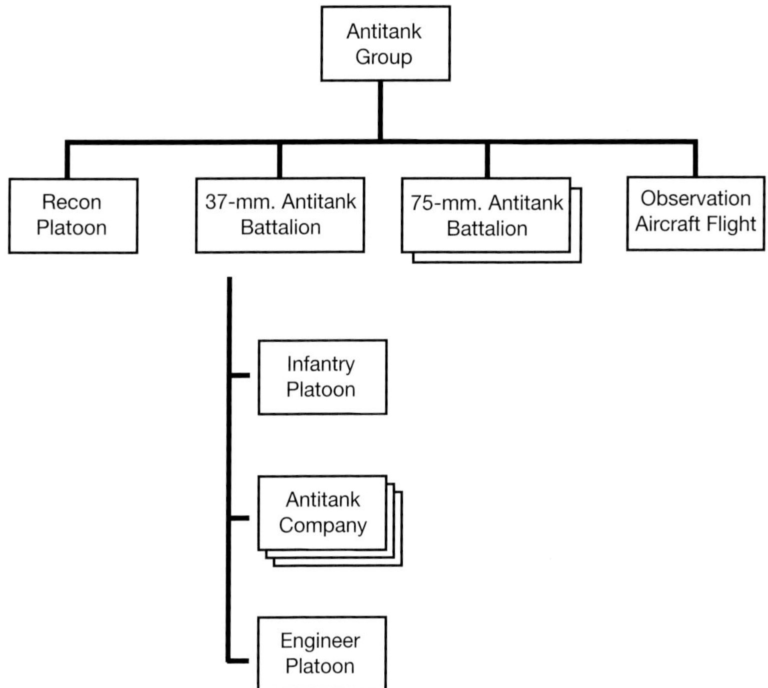

and communication mediums to locate and track enemy armored elements. The formation's towed 37-mm. antitank guns and the divisional artillery successfully repulsed 2d Armored Division tank attacks in open terrain. The 1st Cavalry Division also included the Provisional Antitank Squadron. Equipped with truck-mounted 37-mm. antitank guns, this unit blocked the movement of Red armor and attacked the 2d Armored Division's flank and rear. When the Red Army began to retreat, the Provisional Antitank Squadron moved astride the armored division's path, overran rear-echelon elements, and interdicted supplies.[11]

The Provisional Antitank Squadron represented the offensive style intended for tank destroyers, but general criticisms aimed at the 1st Cavalry Division obscured these accomplishments. McNair praised the 1st Cavalry Division for avoiding detection throughout much of the maneuver, fording the Sabine River, and conducting attacks skillfully. Yet the formation received criticism for inadequate reconnaissance,

[11] Memo, Maj Don E. Carleton to GHQ Antitank Dir Lt Col Allen F. Kingman, sub: Anti-Tank Action, 21 Sep 41, HQ AGF, GHQ, RG 337, NARA.

A tank column of the 67th Armored Regiment during the autumn 1941 maneuvers

as well as risking air attack while moving along roads in daylight and transmitting too much information via radio.[12]

McNair's criticisms were not entirely justified. The Cavalry traditionally operated in dispersed battle groups that relied on rapid transmission of information via voice radio messages without resort to the complicated security measures mandated by Army regulations. Faulty reconnaissance and unnecessary exposure to air attack proved errors common to all participating combat units; but given the Cavalry's ebbing popularity, they reinforced perceptions of that arm's obsolescence.

The second scenario in Louisiana required the Red Second Army to conduct defensive operations against the Blue Third Army. The Red Army was reconfigured to include five infantry divisions, a cavalry division, the 1st Armored Division, and two provisional antitank groups. The larger Blue Army included eight infantry divisions, a cavalry division, a tank group, and a provisional antitank group. It also controlled the I Armored Corps, reorganized to include the 2d Armored Division

[12] L. McNair, "Comments," p. 9; Lt Col M. J. Conway, "Comments on Second and Third Army Maneuver, 1941," n.d., p. 4, HQ AGF, GHQ, RG 337, NARA.

and an infantry division motorized through the attachment of additional trucks. Only in aircraft were the two armies of similar strength.[13]

The Blue Army's mission lay in advancing northward and seizing Shreveport. To contest this movement, the Red Army deployed in a zone to the south of Shreveport between the Red and Sabine Rivers. Using tactics previously applied during corps maneuvers in the same area, the Red Army planned a staged withdrawal through predetermined defensive lines. Large-scale demolitions and motorized, combined-arms teams were to cover the retrograde movement and slow the Blue Army's pursuit. Planning also anticipated the arrival of poor weather to interfere with air operations. In preparation for their retreat, Red forces simulated the demolition of over nine hundred bridges and culverts.[14]

Operations began amid heavy rains on 24 September. Red Army forces withdrew while the Blue Army struggled forward in its wake slowed by the time-consuming necessity of rebuilding bridges. On 27 September the Red forces temporarily ceased withdrawing and prepared to give battle. The Blue Army responded with an envelopment attempt, sending the I Armored Corps and the 1st Cavalry Division into Texas around the Red Army's western flank. A smaller column consisting of motorized infantry, engineers, reconnaissance, and artillery from the 2d Armored Division marched west into Texas and north to attack Shreveport in the Red Army's rear. (*See Map 4.*) This column overcame limited resistance and moved over two hundred miles in preparation for an attack on Shreveport from the north. The column secured fuel sufficient for its deep thrust through purchases from local gas stations.[15]

The scenario terminated on 28 September, before the Blue Army's flying column could attack Shreveport. Blue Army personnel claimed a victory nevertheless. Other observers were less sure. While the 2d Armored Division column possessed a tenuous supply line and lay beyond effective support from friendly forces, the Red Army still held the entire 1st Armored Division in reserve, ready to counterattack. Red commanders also held the advantage of knowing the exact location of the Blue I Armored Corps. Red reconnaissance easily tracked its movements, since this formation made little attempt to conceal its activities or conduct night marches. It moved openly through areas subjected to extensive demolitions that slowed its advance.[16]

During this scenario the three provisional antitank groups played only a minor role because little combat occurred. The Red Army endeavored to deploy its antitank groups in response to armored threats. Unfortunately, hostile tank reports often proved false, resulting in continuous redeployment of antitank weapons that did not engage the enemy. Organizationally, the provisional antitank groups were

---

[13] Brig Gen Mark W. Clark, "Comments, 2d Phase, GHQ-directed Maneuvers, Camp Polk, La., September 24–28, 1941," n.d., p. 1, HQ AGF, GHQ, RG 337, NARA.

[14] Clark, "Comments," pp. 2–4; Gabel, *GHQ Maneuvers*, pp. 100–102; Maj Gen Robert Richardson, "Critique of the Army Phase," 10 Sep 41, U.S. Army Military History Institute (MHI) Archives, Carlisle Barracks, Pa.

[15] Clark, "Comments," pp. 4–7; Gabel, *GHQ Maneuvers*, pp. 103, 110.

[16] Clark, "Comments," pp. 7–8; Memo, GHQ CS Lt Gen Lesley J. McNair to CG, Third Army, sub: Comments on Second Versus Third Army Maneuvers, September 15–30, 1941, 10 Oct 41, pp. 5–6, HQ AGF, GHQ, RG 337, NARA.

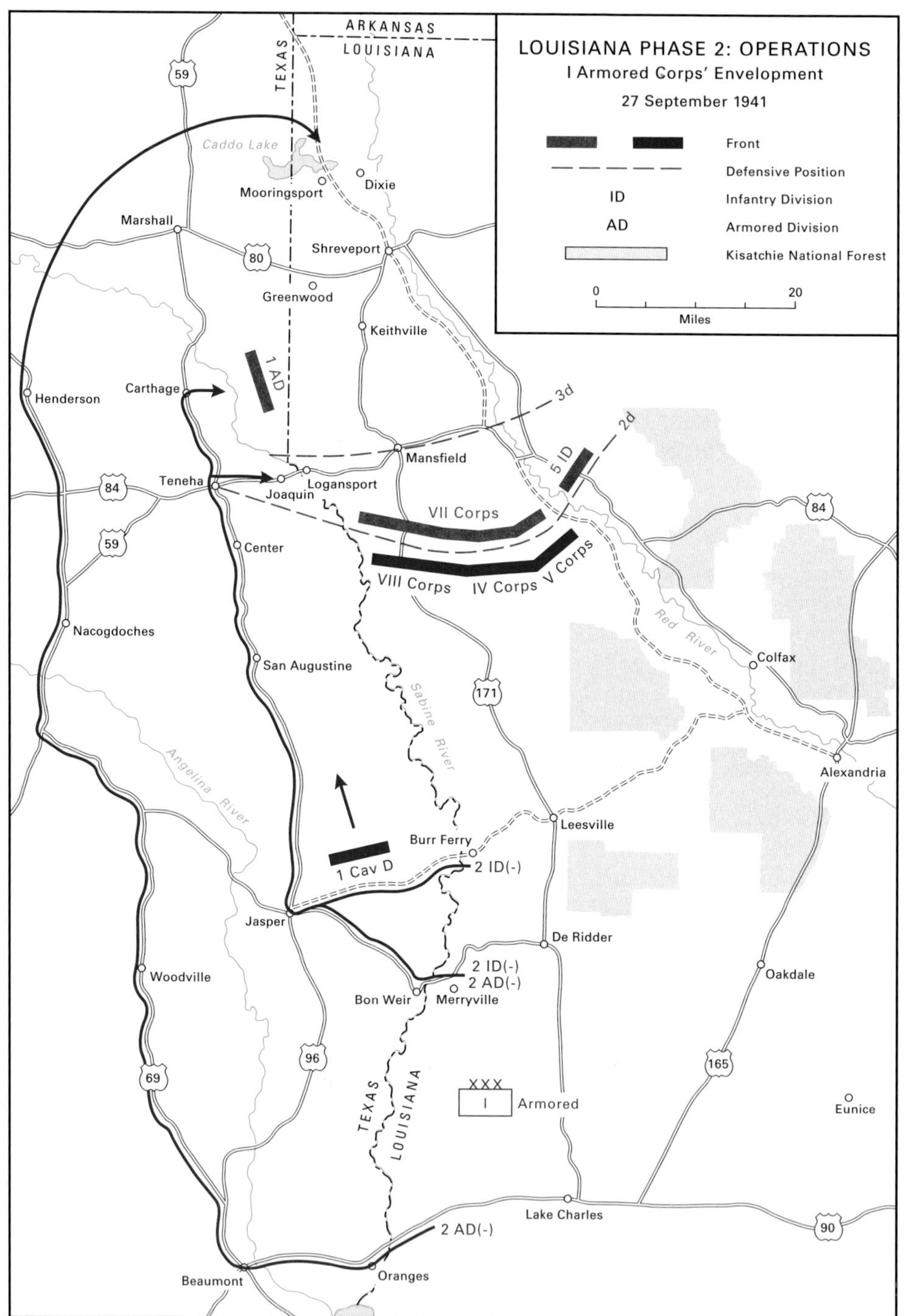

LOUISIANA PHASE 2: OPERATIONS
I Armored Corps' Envelopment
27 September 1941
Front
Defensive Position
ID
Infantry Division
AD
Armored Division
Kisatchie National Forest
0
20
Miles
ARKANSAS
LOUISIANA
TEXAS
Caddo Lake
Mooringsport
Dixie
Marshall
Shreveport
Greenwood
Keithville
1 AD
Henderson
Carthage
3d
2d
Mansfield
5 ID
Teneha
Joaquin
Logansport
VII Corps
Center
VIII Corps
IV Corps
V Corps
Nacogdoches
Red River
Colfax
San Augustine
Sabine River
Angelina River
Alexandria
Leesville
Burr Ferry
1 Cav D
2 ID(-)
Jasper
De Ridder
Woodville
2 ID(-)
2 AD(-)
Bon Weir
Merryville
Oakdale
TEXAS
LOUISIANA
XXX
I
Armored
Eunice
Lake Charles
2 AD(-)
Beaumont
Oranges
59
80
84
59
171
84
96
69
165
90

Map 4

not structured for offensive operations. Therefore, their use in any role other than static defense was considered a "criminal blunder." Most recommendations sought to transform the antitank groups into mobile combined-arms teams with antitank, antiaircraft, chemical warfare, rifle, engineer, reconnaissance, and aerial observation components.[17]

Carolina Maneuvers

In November armored and antitank forces participated in maneuvers that pitted the First Army against the IV Corps and I Armored Corps. The maneuver area encompassed parts of North and South Carolina. It formed a quadrangle bounded in the west by the Wateree River, in the east by the Pee Dee River, in the north by the line Van Wyck–Albemarle, and in the south by the line Camden-Cheraw.

The first scenario tested an army's ability to rely on superior mobility to offset numerical deficiency. The Red Army's one hundred thousand men included the IV Corps and I Armored Corps. The former included the 43d and 31st Infantry Divisions and the 4th Motorized Division. The 1st and 2d Armored Divisions constituted the latter. The IV Corps headquarters also served as a de facto army command, directing the actions of the Red Army. The larger Blue First Army numbered one hundred ninety-five thousand soldiers in 8 infantry divisions organized into 3 corps, 1 tank group, 6 antitank units, and 1 anti-airborne unit. In the air, the Red Army's 366 aircraft possessed a slight superiority over the Blue Army's 320.[18]

In preparation, I Armored Corps Commander Maj. Gen. Charles L. Scott issued special instructions incorporating lessons learned from the Louisiana maneuvers. He described the nature of expected antitank defenses to allow armored commanders to devise appropriate countermeasures. He did not want armor to charge headlong into antitank positions or suffer unnecessary delays from a single demolition or roadblock. Combined-arms teams of reconnaissance, artillery, infantry, and engineer troops would lead armored columns, securing advance routes for tank units. The latter were to avoid commitment to battle until they were able to strike critical targets in the hostile rear area in accordance with Armored Force doctrine. The use of extended columns of vehicles on roads was discouraged, lest they become victims of enemy air attacks.[19]

The Blue First Army organized three Tank Attacker Groups, designated TA–1, TA–2, and TA–3, to supplement its existing antitank forces. The first two units included a combined-arms mix. TA–1 included a light tank company, an antitank battalion equipped with 75-mm. guns mounted on halftracks, a 37-mm. antitank company, an engineer company, a motorized infantry battalion, artillery, and

---

[17] Maj Douglas C. McNair, "Report of Second Maneuver Phase: 3rd AT Group," 28 Sep 41, HQ AGF, GHQ, RG 337, NARA; Memo, Lt Col Ben M. Sawbridge to Lt Col Allen F. Kingman, sub: Report on Second Phase—Second–Third Army Maneuver, 1st and 2d AT Gps., 29 Sep 41, HQ AGF, GHQ, RG 337, NARA.

[18] Gabel, *GHQ Maneuvers*, pp. 125, 127–28.

[19] Memo, Maj Gen Charles L. Scott to CG, 1st Armd Div, sub: Tactical Procedure and Operation of Armored Units, 8 Nov 41, HQ AGF, GHQ, RG 337, NARA.

Horse cavalry on the attack during maneuvers in the Carolinas in 1941

reconnaissance elements. The principal components of TA–2 included three antitank battalions and a tank company. Artillery charged with the static defense of rear-area installations constituted the bulk of TA–3. The Blue Army also included the antitank groups from the Louisiana maneuvers, redesignated GHQ–X, GHQ–Y, and GHQ–Z.[20]

The attention given to antitank measures and the special mission given to TA–3 reflected the experience of the Blue Army's commander, Lt. Gen. Hugh A. Drum. He had also commanded the First Army during the Plattsburg maneuvers of 1939, during which the 7th Cavalry Brigade (Mechanized) had run amok in the First Army rear area. Drum determined to prevent the I Armored Corps from performing similar feats. Although faced with a much greater armored threat than in 1939, First Army possessed 4,321 antitank and artillery guns distributed among its antitank groups and infantry divisions.[21]

Operations began on 16 November. The Blue Army crossed the Pee Dee River and advanced westward to attack Red forces. (*Map 5*) The Red Army's mission lay in attacking hostile bridgeheads on the Pee Dee River. First, however, the army had

---

[20] MFR, Lt Col J. H. Phillips, G–3, sub: Brief of Report on First Army Tank Attacker Group, 29 Dec 41, Item 4327, Reel 287, National Archives Project, GCM; Gabel, *GHQ Maneuvers*, p. 125.

[21] Lt Gen Lesley J. McNair, "Critique of the First Phase, GHQ-directed Maneuvers, Carolina Area, November 16th to 21st, 1941," n.d., pp. 2–3, HQ AGF, CG, Gen Corresp, RG 337, NARA.

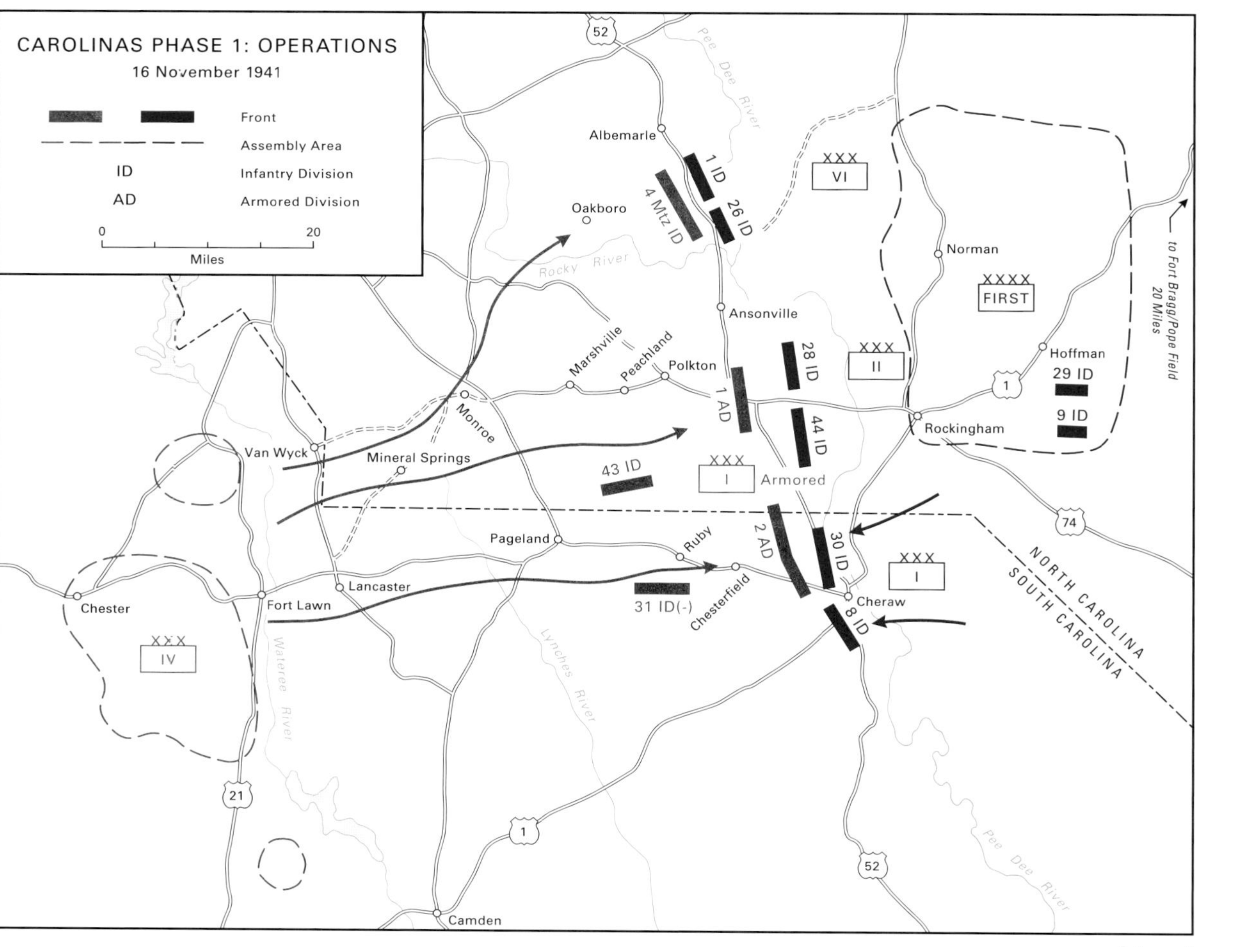

CAROLINAS PHASE 1: OPERATIONS
16 November 1941
Front
Assembly Area
ID Infantry Division
AD Armored Division
0 20
Miles
Albemarle
Oakboro
Rocky River
Pee Dee River
1 ID
26 ID
4 Mtz ID
VI
Ansonville
Marshville
Peachland
Polkton
28 ID
1 AD
44 ID
II
Norman
FIRST
Hoffman
29 ID
9 ID
Rockingham
to Fort Bragg/Pope Field 20 Miles
Monroe
Van Wyck
Mineral Springs
43 ID
I Armored
2 AD
30 ID
I
Cheraw
8 ID
74
NORTH CAROLINA
SOUTH CAROLINA
Pageland
Ruby
Chesterfield
31 ID(-)
Lancaster
Fort Lawn
Chester
IV
Wateree River
Lynches River
21
1
52
Camden

Map 5

to cross the Wateree River and advance seventy-five miles eastward. The Red Army had a one-hour head start, but Blue forces negated this lead by violating deployment and movement restrictions.[22]

Each Blue corps therefore secured a bridgehead over the Pee Dee River before the arrival of Red forces. The I Armored Corps raced to contain these crossings, but its forces became dispersed in the process. The Red Army failed to launch a coordinated strike against the bridgeheads; its operations devolved into a series of small, disjointed attacks on just two of the Blue crossing points. The 1st and 2d Armored Divisions prevented further Blue advances, but they became engaged in combat operations that precluded further maneuver. The 2d Armored Division, for example, captured the city of Cheraw after a protracted struggle. However, it suffered heavy losses in uncoordinated frontal assaults on antitank positions. Resistance ended only after a small column moved cross country to enter the city.[23]

Red armor remained in place on 17 November, conducting holding operations while awaiting relief by slower-moving infantry. North of the I Armored Corps, the 4th Motorized Division retreated before the onslaught of the entire Blue VI Corps. This development placed the Red Army's left flank in jeopardy. In response, the 1st Armored Division moved behind the 4th Motorized Infantry Regiment to attack the VI Corps' northern flank on 18 November. (*Map 6*) This operation was marred by the short notice given to the armored formation and the resultant rushed planning and execution.[24] Bad tactics further eroded the effectiveness of the attack. The armored division attacked in three columns, two of which quickly lost their combat power in unsupported frontal assaults on antitank guns. The third column reached the VI Corps rear area by nightfall, but it lacked infantry to secure its gains. Inadequate security permitted Blue antitank assets to surround it during the night.[25]

The morning of 19 November found the 1st Armored Division broken into three pieces, beset by attacking antitank units, and unable to sustain a supply flow. It spent the day vainly trying to improve its position and was defeated the next day. Reduced

---

[22] L. McNair, "Critique of the First Phase," pp. 1–2; Gabel, *GHQ Maneuvers*, p. 133.

[23] Maj B. P. Purdue, "Report of Antitank Action of Units Opposite 2nd Armored Division from 12:00 Noon, November 17 to 6:00 p.m., November 18, 1941," n.d., HQ AGF, GHQ, RG 337, NARA; Memo, Maj B. P. Purdue to Lt Col Allen F. Kingman, sub: Summary of Antimechanized Action, Cheraw and Vicinity, from 10:00 a.m., Nov 17, to Midnight, Nov 17–18, 1941, n.d., HQ AGF, GHQ, RG 337, NARA; Maj B. P. Purdue, "Report on Antitank Activities," 18 Nov 41, HQ AGF, GHQ, RG 337, NARA; Gabel, *GHQ Maneuvers*, pp. 136–38.

[24] Lt Col Riley F. Ennis, "Report of Assistant Armored Force and Antitank Director Concerning Armored Operations in First Carolina Maneuver," n.d., pp. 1, 3, HQ AGF, GHQ, RG 337, NARA; Gabel, *GHQ Maneuvers*, pp. 140–41.

[25] GHQ CS Lt Gen Lesley J. McNair, "Notes of Action by I Armored Corps, First Phase, First Army Versus IV Army Corps, November 16–21, 1941," 21 Nov 41, HQ AGF, GHQ, RG 337, NARA; Ennis, "Report Concerning Armored Operations in First Carolina Maneuver," pp. 1–2; Lt Col Robert W. Hasbrouck, "Report Concerning 2d Armored Division Actions," n.d., p. 3, HQ AGF, GHQ, RG 337, NARA; Gabel, *GHQ Maneuvers*, pp. 140–41.

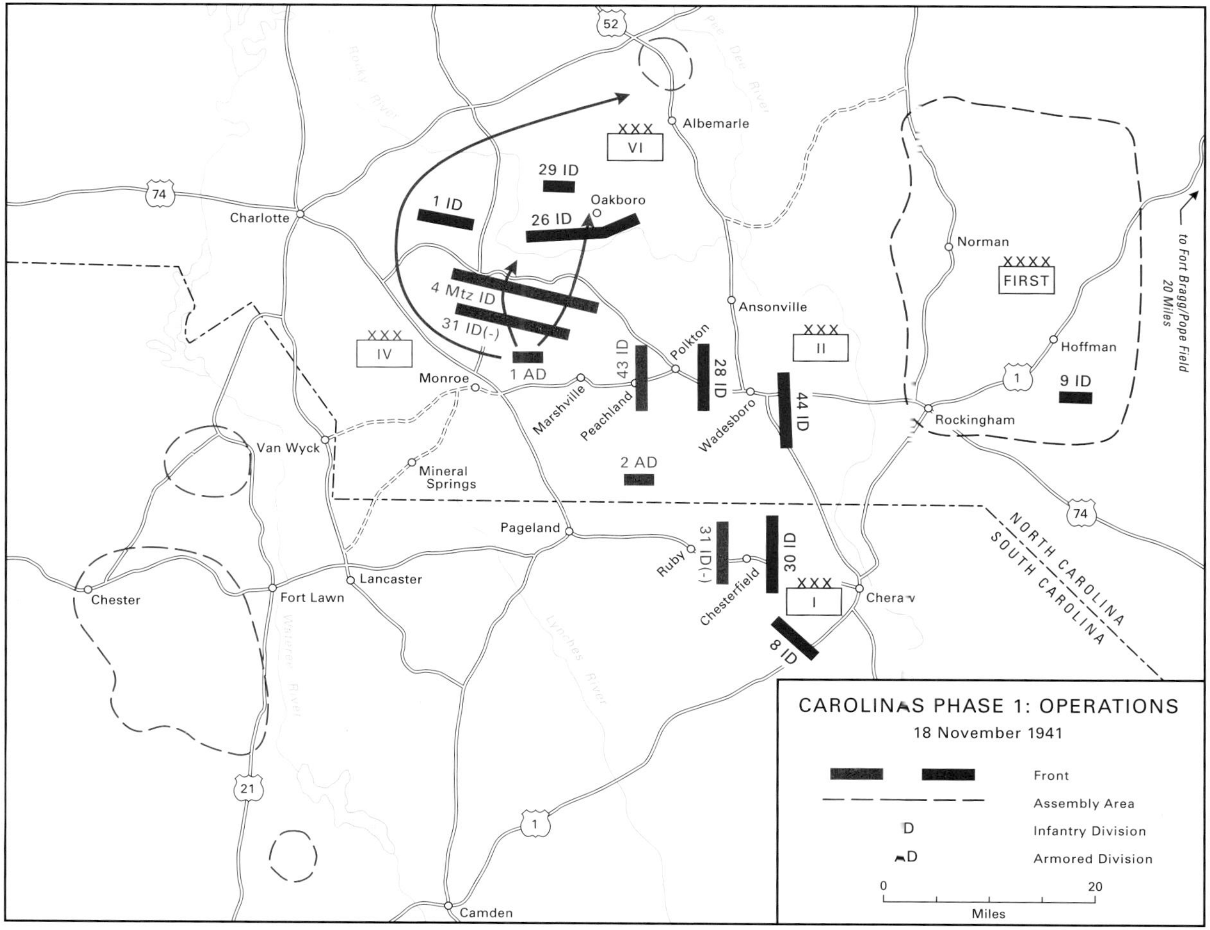

CAROLINAS PHASE 1: OPERATIONS

18 November 1941

Front

Assembly Area

Infantry Division

Armored Division

0 20

Miles

to Fort Bragg/Pope Field
20 Miles

FIRST
VI
II
IV
I

29 ID
1 ID
26 ID
4 Mtz ID
31 ID(-)
1 AD
43 ID
28 ID
44 ID
9 ID
2 AD
31 ID(-)
30 ID
8 ID

Charlotte
Albemarle
Oakboro
Norman
Hoffman
Rockingham
Ansonville
Polkton
Wadesboro
Peachland
Marshville
Monroe
Van Wyck
Mineral Springs
Pageland
Ruby
Chesterfield
Cheraw
Chester
Fort Lawn
Lancaster
Camden

NORTH CAROLINA
SOUTH CAROLINA

Rocky River
Pee Dee River
Lynches River
Wateree River

74
52
1
74
21
1

Map 6

to a collection of isolated pockets, the division survived only because the maneuver rules permitted "destroyed" vehicles to return to action the following day.[26]

The 2d Armored and 4th Motorized Divisions launched a relief attack into the center of the Blue VI Corps. Despite early progress, the mobile formations could not secure their flanks and faced envelopment. They withdrew, leaving the stranded 1st Armored Division to its fate. When the fighting terminated on 21 November, the Red Army possessed little remaining combat power and faced complete annihilation. The successful surprise attack on the 1st Armored Division survivors by a Blue tank battalion underscored the extent of the Red Army's defeat.[27]

Most Red tank losses, however, occurred during attacks on antitank weapons passively employed. Only the 93d Antitank Battalion maneuvered in response to armor sightings and attacked when possible. GHQ–Y spent the entire battle continuously redeploying to avoid being overrun. Most Blue antitank units, however, occupied positions and simply awaited the possible arrival of hostile armor.[28]

Both armies employed corps cavalry regiments possessing both horse and mechanized elements. These units performed a variety of reconnaissance and security missions; but senior commanders undermined their efficiency by stripping their mechanized elements, radio equipment, and horse trailers over the objections of their commanders. The Red Army reorganized the 107th and 6th Cavalry Regiments, reassigning the mechanized elements of both to the 6th Cavalry Regiment and the horse elements to the 107th Cavalry Regiment and thereby preventing analysis of the tactical effectiveness of the original corps cavalry regiment. Chief of Cavalry Maj. Gen. John K. Herr attempted to prevent this reconfiguration, but General George C. Marshall overruled him.[29]

Nevertheless, cavalry units performed well. Blue cavalry primarily gathered information concerning Red Army movements and dispositions. In this capacity it proved especially successful, capturing the operational plans of the 1st and 2d Armored Divisions. A mixed task force of antitank, cavalry, and engineer elements also screened and protected the Blue Army's northern flank. Red Army cavalry similarly performed flank security and maintained contact between infantry divisions. The end of the fighting found the Red 3d Cavalry Regiment waging a successful delaying action against superior Blue forces.[30]

---

[26] Memo, Lt Col Robert W. Hasbrouck to Armd Force Dir Lt Col Allen F. Kingman, sub: Activities of 1st Armored Division on 20 November 1941, 20 Nov 41, HQ AGF, GHQ, RG 337, NARA; L. McNair, "Notes of Action by I Armored Corps."

[27] Hasbrouck, "Report Concerning 1st Armored Division Actions," p. 2; Gabel, *GHQ Maneuvers*, pp. 141, 143.

[28] Hasbrouck, "Report Concerning 1st Armored Division Actions," p. 2; Maj B. P. Purdue, "GHQ Y," n.d., HQ AGF, GHQ, RG 337, NARA.

[29] Memo, Cav Dir Lt Col Wayland B. Augur to GHQ G–3 Dir, sub: Report of Cavalry Operations, First Phase Carolina Maneuvers, November 16–21, 1941, 22 Nov 41, pp. 1–3, HQ AGF, GHQ, RG 337, NARA; Gabel, *GHQ Maneuvers*, pp. 127–28.

[30] Memo, Augur to GHQ G–3 Dir, 22 Nov 41, pp. 1–3.

In preparation for the next scenario, each army reorganized. The Red Army received the 1st Tank Group headquarters, including one brigadier general and two aides. The Blue Army motorized two of its infantry divisions through the attachment of truck companies and placed these formations in reserve to exploit successes. Both armies received equivalent air strength through the transfer of aircraft from the Red to the Blue Army.[31]

In the second scenario, the Red Army defended Camden against Blue forces advancing south across the Pee Dee and Rocky Rivers. Operations began on 25 November with three Blue corps advancing on a broad front on that day and the next. (*See Map 7.*) The Red I Armored Corps conducted local counterattacks to delay the Blue forces and inflict casualties, while cavalry protected the Red Army's flanks.[32]

The Red commander intended to withdraw the armored divisions into the fortified locale being built around Camden. During the night of 26–27 November, however, a miscommunication led the 1st and 2d Armored Divisions to prematurely withdraw in the wrong direction. Their departure left an eighteen-mile strip of Red lines weakly defended.[33] Worse, a Blue scouting team captured a copy of the Red Army's plans. On 27 November Blue forces lunged forward. They seized the town of Lancaster, threatened to disrupt the retrograde movement of the I Armored Corps, and prepared to advance on Camden itself. The I Armored Corps responded with a succession of tank attacks that contained the Blue threat in Lancaster and forced the commitment of Blue reserves. These operations cost the Red Army 219 tanks. Nevertheless, Red attacks continued on 28 November, effectively halting the Blue Army's advance. When the fighting ended, the Red Army was ensconced behind prepared defenses north of Camden.[34]

The Red Army could claim victory, but its armor sustained heavy losses in action against Blue antitank guns. The latter were credited with the destruction of 462 tanks, a significant part of the I Armored Corps' offensive capability. However, the ability of Blue antitank units to respond to reports of hostile armor proved less than ideal. The I Armored Corps was criticized for squandering its strength in multiple, local attacks rather than preserving itself for a decisive blow against the Blue Army flank. Nevertheless, armored units performed more effectively against Blue antitank units through better reconnaissance and the prior dissemination of detailed information on antitank organizations and tactics.[35]

[31] Brig Gen Mark W. Clark, "Critique of the Second Phase, GHQ Directed Maneuvers, Carolina Area, November 25th to 28th, 1941," p. 1, MHI Archives; Gabel, *GHQ Maneuvers*, pp. 156, 158.

[32] Clark, "Critique of the Second Phase," pp. 1–4; Gabel, *GHQ Maneuvers*, pp. 155–59.

[33] Memo, Lt Gen Lesley J. McNair to CG, IV Army Corps, sub: Comments on First Army Versus IV Army Corps Maneuvers, November 16–30, 1941, 7 Jan 42, p. 7, HQ AGF, GHQ, RG 337, NARA; Clark, "Critique of the Second Phase," p. 4.

[34] Clark, "Critique of the Second Phase," pp. 4–6; Lt Col Allen F. Kingman, Rpt of Tank Losses Assessed by Umpires During Period Nov. 25–28, 1941, n.d., HQ AGF, GHQ, RG 337, NARA.

[35] Memo, Lt Gen Lesley J. McNair to CG, First Army, sub: Comments on First Army Versus IV Army Corps Maneuvers, November 16–30, 1941, 22 Dec 41, p. 6, HQ AGF, GHQ, RG 337, NARA; Kingman, Rpt of Tank Losses; Memo, L. McNair to CG, IV Army Corps, 7 Jan 42, pp. 2, 4–5.

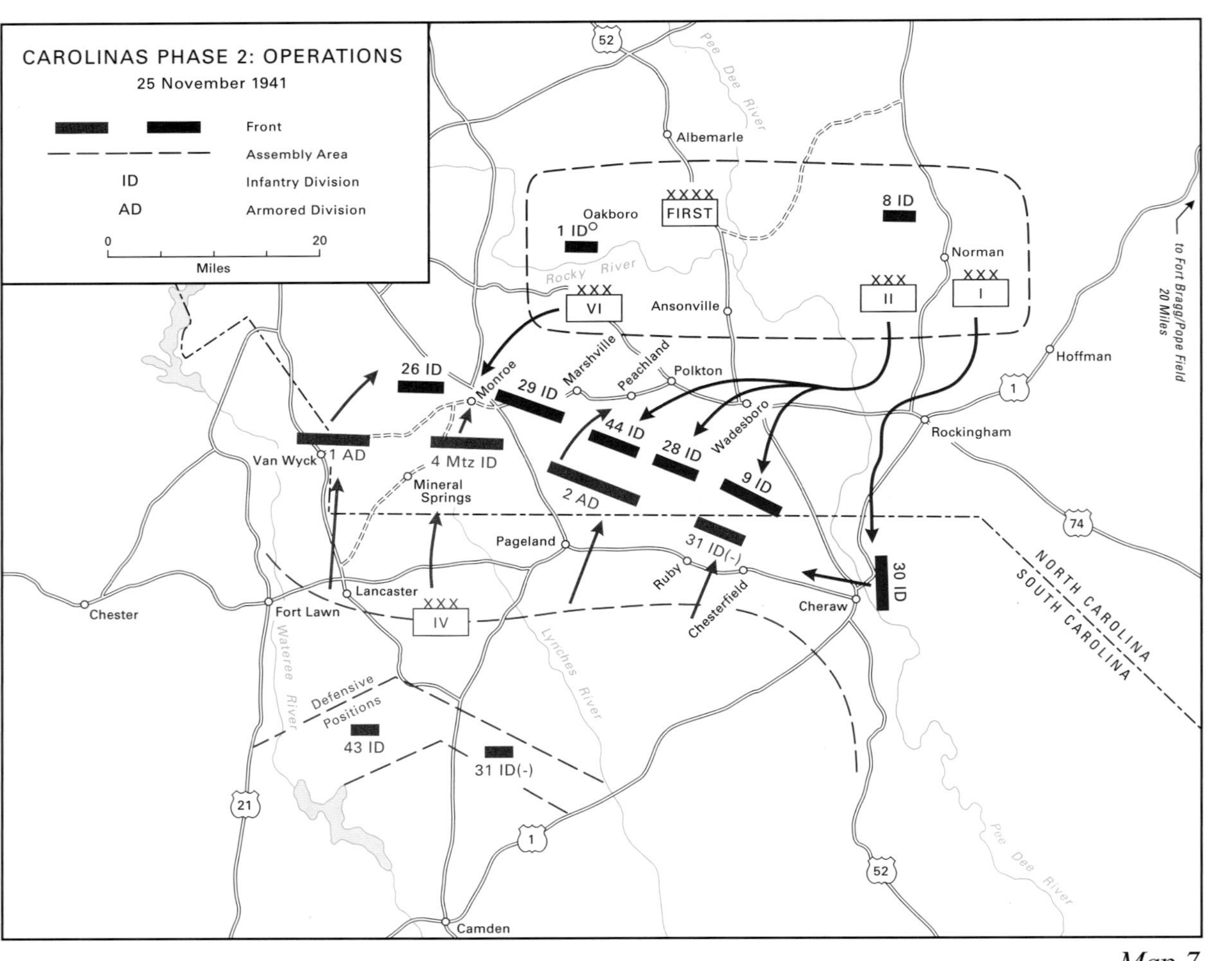
CAROLINAS PHASE 2: OPERATIONS
25 November 1941
Front
Assembly Area
ID Infantry Division
AD Armored Division
0
20
Miles
to Fort Bragg/Pope Field 20 Miles
Albemarle
Oakboro
1 ID
XXXX FIRST
8 ID
Norman
XXX II
XXX I
XXX VI
Rocky River
Pee Dee River
Ansonville
Hoffman
Polkton
Peachland
Marshville
Monroe
Wadesboro
Rockingham
26 ID
29 ID
44 ID
28 ID
9 ID
2 AD
4 Mtz ID
1 AD
Van Wyck
Mineral Springs
Pageland
31 ID(-)
30 ID
Ruby
Chesterfield
Cheraw
NORTH CAROLINA
SOUTH CAROLINA
Chester
Fort Lawn
Lancaster
XXX IV
Wateree River
Lynches River
Defensive Positions
43 ID
31 ID(-)
Camden
52
1
74
21

Map 7

Assessing Mobile Operations

As the Carolina operations ended, so did the autumn maneuvers. With justification General Marshall claimed, "The troops have performed a particularly important service in convincing the majority of our people that a powerful and highly trained army is developing with amazing speed."[36] While the maneuvers proved reassuring to a public concerned about national security, they also revealed serious deficiencies in combat readiness that required attention.

Armored operations constituted one such focus area. Armored corps and division staffs generally included officers experienced in mechanized operations; but brigade, regiment, and battalion leadership proved less capable. Leadership ability tended to decline with command echelon, because the lower levels absorbed most of the officers new to the Armored Force. These novice commanders often failed to supervise the implementation of their orders or coordinate the efforts of subordinate commanders.[37]

General Ward served as the General Staff secretary until transferred to the Armored Force in August 1941. He assumed command of the 1st Armored Brigade of the 1st Armored Division on the eve of the maneuvers. In a note to a colleague, he admitted his incomprehension of armored doctrine: "A tank is a far cry from a horse, but I am going to the Armored Force. I am totally ignorant on the subject, so will have plenty to do and plenty of incentive to learn."[38] The 1st Armored Brigade received a severe mauling during maneuver operations in Louisiana and the Carolinas.

Despite the Army's emphasis on combined-arms action, the maneuvers revealed the general inability of subordinate commanders to comprehend the purpose and value of combined-arms task forces whose composition changed in relation to tactical developments. Too many commanders preferred the retention of regimental integrity and abstained from violating the precedent of functional separation that constituted the Army's traditional organizational credo.[39]

Armored Force doctrine embraced the task force concept, but the maneuver experience indicated the need for additional task force training and familiarization. Multi-arm task forces too often degenerated into random collections of dispersed units that failed to coordinate their actions before attacking enemy positions. Armor officers consistently failed to integrate tanks, infantry, and artillery within these groups. Tactical engagements therefore occurred in which friendly units either

---

[36] Telg, Gen George C. Marshall to Lt Gen Lesley J. McNair, 29 Nov 41, George C. Marshall Papers, GCM.

[37] Hasbrouck, "Report Concerning 2d Armored Division Actions," pp. 1, 4; Conway, "Comments on Second and Third Army Maneuver," p. 2.

[38] Note, Brig Gen Orlando W. Ward to Lt Col Henry D. Jay, 23 Aug 41, Orlando W. Ward Papers, MHI Archives.

[39] Memo, Hasbrouck to Armd Force Dir, 20 Nov 41; First Army CS Brig Gen Kenneth P. Lord, Training Memo no. 2, sub: Analysis of 1941 Training and Maneuvers, 26 Jan 42, pp. 2, 5, HQ AGF, GHQ, RG 337, NARA.

attacked while supporting artillery remained idle or failed to apply the principles of fire and movement to pin and envelop enemy forces.[40]

Armored Force failures during the maneuvers, however, did not stem exclusively from internal factors. In three of four maneuvers, the I Armored Corps constituted part of an outnumbered army that lacked support elements. These conditions led to the use of armored divisions simply to hold portions of the front in a defensive posture. Such employment contradicted the intended purpose of these special formations.[41]

None of the participating army commanders possessed significant experience with armored operations. Maj. Gen. Oscar W. Griswold, for example, became IV Corps commander in October 1941. After one month, he assumed command of the Red Army, which included the I Armored Corps, for the Carolina maneuvers. Although he previously commanded the 4th Motorized Division, he possessed no direct experience in leading armored formations. His staff officers possessed similar credentials. This inexperience detracted from the effectiveness of the army headquarters.[42]

Maj. Gen. Charles L. Scott commanded the I Armored Corps throughout the maneuvers. He considered higher headquarters' inexperience with armored doctrine a major constraint on his formation's activities. Subjected to continuous guidance from higher headquarters, the I Armored Corps achieved little operational independence throughout the maneuvers. Moreover, orders received often left little time for planning and preparation and tended to ignore the status and conditions of available roads. These problems resulted in the employment of the armored corps without regard for its special purpose and ability. Perceived as glorified GHQ tank battalions, armored divisions were either employed as small detachments for infantry support or left in reserve. These practices misused the armored divisions and marginalized the command and control capability of the I Armored Corps.[43]

These problems hampered armored operations, especially during the Carolina maneuvers. Red Army headquarters issued attack orders without regard for the preparation time necessary for their implementation. These instructions also generally arrived at night and interfered with the routine maintenance functions conducted during the hours of darkness. In one instance, the I Armored Corps received orders to conduct a dawn attack. This operation required the armored divisions to first refuel and execute a night march, but the divisions did not receive the orders until nearly midnight.[44] These and similar problems led the senior Armored Force umpire to conclude:

---

[40] Lord, Training Memo no. 2, 26 Jan 42, pp. 2, 5, 13; Memo, Hasbrouck to Armd Force Dir, 20 Nov 41.

[41] Lt Col Riley F. Ennis, "Report Concerning Armored Action in Both Phases of Carolina Maneuver," n.d., p. 3, HQ AGF, GHQ, RG 337, NARA.

[42] Memo, L. McNair to CG, IV Army Corps, 7 Jan 42, p. 3; Gabel, *GHQ Maneuvers*, p. 128.

[43] Memo, Maj Gen Charles L. Scott to Ch of the Armd Force, sub: Report on GHQ Exercises in Which Armored Force Participated, 10 Dec 41, pp. 1–2, Henry C. Newton Papers, MHI Archives.

[44] Ennis, "Report Concerning Armored Action in Both Phases," p. 2.

Symbolic of the changing times, a light tank of the 67th Armored Regiment passes a horse cavalry column during the autumn 1941 maneuvers.

> I believe the Red high command erred in employing tanks in driblets at different parts of the front. The Armored Corps Commander should be given a mission and then allowed to work out the details of its execution. Decisions as to employment should be reached in time to allow the planning of proper coordination. Otherwise all the "blitz" is in the planning and none in the execution.[45]

Critics of I Armored Corps operations in the Carolina maneuvers noted its failure to attack en masse to obtain decisive results, instead dissipating its strength in a series of small-scale engagements. Armored formations were believed incapable of sustaining more than three days' continuous combat. Therefore, commanders needed to avoid the piecemeal commitment to battle that actually occurred during the maneuvers, instead preserving the mass of armor for a decisive strike.[46] At the conclusion of the second phase of the Carolina maneuvers, Griswold compounded

---

[45] Hasbrouck, "Report Concerning 1st Armored Division Actions," p. 6.

[46] Memo, L. McNair to CG, IV Army Corps, 7 Jan 42, pp. 1–2; Ennis, "Report Concerning Armored Operations in First Carolina Maneuver," p. 1; Ennis, "Report Concerning Armored Action in Both Phases," p. 1.

these errors by separating the tank and support elements of the armored divisions. He deployed their infantry and artillery in static defensive positions near Camden and placed the tank units in reserve, ignoring the importance of divisional integrity and the value of combined action by all three components.[47]

Command and staff functions within the armored elements depended on rapid communication of information between commanders, but many officers employed radios as telephones. They sent long voice messages that compromised security rather than the short, coded transmissions prescribed in Army regulations.[48] Criticism of radio usage by armored units, however, tended to overlook Armored Force emphasis on uncoded voice transmissions to facilitate rapid communication. The Armored Force inherited this practice from the 7th Cavalry Brigade (Mechanized), whose leaders considered the speed of transmission more important than security.

Communication mediums had a variety of technical problems. The radios possessed insufficient range. The short range limited the effectiveness of antitank groups that relied on distant early warning of enemy armor for timely and concentrated deployment. Frustration with the unreliability of wire and radio communications during the maneuvers prompted consideration by antitank commanders of messenger pigeons to maintain communications among small units in fast-moving tactical situations.[49]

Inadequate reconnaissance further hampered armored operations. Attached observation aircraft failed to provide advance warning of hostile antitank positions, whereas ground reconnaissance units did not aggressively seek enemy weak points for subsequent exploitation by tank elements. Reconnaissance assets too often remained road bound and failed to perform route reconnaissance or identify alternate paths of advance. Armored columns therefore remained unaware of nearby enemy units, blundered into obstacles and ambushes, and suffered unnecessary casualties and delays. These columns also invited aerial attack by standing idle awaiting the clearance of minor obstacles on roads.[50]

While reconnaissance operations suffered from lack of aggressiveness, tank units proved overzealous in their efforts to close with the enemy. This combination resulted in headlong frontal assaults against prepared antitank positions that left large numbers of tanks ruled destroyed. Frequently, tanks simply charged the nearest enemy force without using terrain for cover or applying fire and movement

---

[47] Clark, "Critique of the Second Phase," p. 6; Gabel, *GHQ Maneuvers*, p. 164.

[48] Maj Gen Robert C. Richardson Jr., "Report of VII Army Corps Field Exercises and Maneuvers in Southwestern Arkansas—August 17–28 and Participation of VII Army Corps in Second Army and GHQ Maneuvers August 29–September 30, 1941," 29 Oct 41, p. 7, MHI Archives; L. McNair, "Critique of the First Phase," p. 5; Memo, L. McNair to CG, First Army, 22 Dec 41, pp. 8–9.

[49] Richardson, "Report of VII Army Corps Field Exercises and Maneuvers, 29 Oct 41," p. 7; D. McNair, "Check List on Antitank Units," 5 Sep 41, p. 5; Conway, "Comments on Second and Third Army Maneuver," p. 9.

[50] Smith, "Comments Concerning Maneuver Operations"; L. McNair, "Comments," p. 6; Ennis, "Report Concerning Armored Operations in First Carolina Maneuver," p. 1; Ennis, "Report Concerning Armored Action in Both Phases," pp. 1, 3; Memo, L. McNair to CG, Third Army, 10 Oct 41, p. 5; Lord, Training Memo no. 2, 26 Jan 42, p. 6.

Horse cavalry during a pause in the autumn 1941 maneuvers. Note the firearms and truck, which reflect the increases in motorization and firepower that occurred in cavalry organizations throughout the interwar period.

principles. They also attacked towns rather than bypass them, advancing into narrow streets without infantry support.[51]

Armored commanders violated their own doctrine by not integrating the action of infantry, artillery, and tanks. The preferred method of attacking an antitank position entailed its suppression by artillery fire, followed by a tank attack that neutralized the surviving antitank guns and their infantry protection. Friendly infantry then destroyed remaining resistance and secured the position while the tanks continued their advance. Few commanders followed this procedure. Nor did they delegate the task of eliminating small pockets of resistance to following infantry elements. Instead, they assumed this responsibility themselves despite

[51] Smith, "Comments Concerning Maneuver Operations"; "Comments on First Phase, 22 Nov 41," p. 9; Memo, L. McNair to CG, First Army, 22 Dec 41, p. 6; Memo, L. McNair to CG, IV Army Corps, 7 Jan 42, p. 4; Maj F. T. Searcy, "Report Concerning Actions of 13th Armored Regiment During First Phase of Carolina Maneuver," 21 Nov 41, p. 2, HQ AGF, GHQ, RG 337, NARA.

the associated loss of forward momentum.[52] Armored division infantry relied on halftracks to achieve mobility comparable to tanks. The halftracks also possessed light armor that protected passengers from small-arms fire. Unfortunately, armored infantry commanders tended to employ tactics similar to the tanks, blindly charging opposition without disembarking. Not intended for such employment, the halftracks and their passengers suffered extensive losses.[53]

Traffic control problems plagued armored operations throughout the maneuvers. McNair consistently exhorted commanders to learn how to move large amounts of men and equipment via vehicles without confusion and chaos, asserting "there can be no excuse for another Guadalajara."[54] Such skills eluded the U.S. Army in 1941. Vehicular columns of supply and combat elements failed to exploit secondary roads. They crowded onto major highways instead but neglected antiaircraft measures. In one instance, three hundred vehicles moved as one mass while another column moving via highway measured five miles in length. Poor traffic and antiaircraft discipline characterized these columns. Efforts to coordinate their movements largely failed, resulting in traffic jams of staggering proportions throughout the maneuvers.[55]

Overuse and misuse of trucks contributed to the vehicular mayhem dominating the maneuver area road nets. The desire to increase the mobility of combat troops resulted in supply, medical, and artillery elements' being stripped of their transport. Consequently, artillery became incapable of intervening in tactical engagements and necessary supplies failed to arrive at their destinations.[56]

Misallocation of trucks and faulty coordination of motorized columns resulted in mobile operations' becoming stalled for want of gasoline. Armored units sought to overcome this problem by following the German example of attaching five- and ten-gallon gasoline cans to tanks, but this practice incurred the criticism of maneuver umpires. They believed it increased the combat vulnerability of the vehicle and undermined the training of supply officers responsible for ensuring adequate provision of fuel.[57]

All motor vehicle operations, moreover, suffered from a general neglect of preventive maintenance. Too many units simply ignored maintenance consider-

[52] Conway, "Comments on Second and Third Army Maneuver," p. 5; Memo, Hasbrouck to Armd Force Dir, 20 Nov 41; Smith, "Comments Concerning Maneuver Operations"; Ennis, "Report Concerning Armored Operations in First Carolina Maneuver," pp. 1–2, and "Report Concerning Armored Action in Both Phases," p. 2.

[53] L. McNair, "Critique of the First Phase," p. 6.

[54] L. McNair, "Comments," p. 9. During the Spanish Civil War, Nationalist motorized and mechanized elements exploiting a victory near Guadalajara in March 1937 overextended themselves. Inclement weather and incessant Republican air attacks turned their exploitation into a disastrous rout.

[55] Memo, L. McNair to CG, Third Army, 10 Oct 41, p. 3; Lt Col N. L. Simonds, "Annex No. 1 to G–4 Report: Report of Quartermaster Activities for August–September Maneuvers," 8 Oct 41, pp. 4–5, in Richardson, "Report of VII Army Corps Field Exercises and Maneuvers"; L. McNair, "Comments," p. 11; Conway, "Comments on Second and Third Army Maneuver," pp. 6, 8–9; Comments on First Phase," p. 3; L. McNair, "Critique of the First Phase," p. 3.

[56] Conway, "Comments on Second and Third Army Maneuver," pp. 3, 8; Memo, L. McNair to CG, Third Army, 10 Oct 41, pp. 4, 12.

[57] Simonds, "Annex No. 1," p. 3; Memo, L. McNair to CG, IV Army Corps, 7 Jan 42, p. 9.

ations until the cessation of each maneuver scenario, thereby increasing the rate of mechanical failure. The most common problems stemmed from damage to transmissions, failure to check lubricants, neglect of tire wear and pressure, and unnecessary collisions.[58] A Third Army inspection of 2,127 vehicles from three divisions revealed an average of ten mechanical deficiencies per vehicle. These deficiencies included dry batteries, broken or missing mirrors, loose wheel bearings, leaking radiators, bent fenders, axle damage, cracked windshields, broken instruments, and a host of other problems related to rough usage.[59]

These maintenance concerns could not be readily addressed without sufficient quantities of spare parts on hand. Such supplies were not maintained. Combat units responded by stripping vehicles tagged for rear-echelon maintenance. This practice disrupted the normal repair procedure, resulting in vehicles' arriving in the rear-area shops in need of much more extensive and time-consuming overhauls than anticipated.[60]

Air support for armored elements proved no more effective than efforts to integrate engineer, reconnaissance, artillery, and infantry actions with tanks. Throughout 1941 the Army sought a viable method of air-ground cooperation that ensured adequate support of ground troops without precluding air attacks on targets of strategic significance. This desire resulted in an air-support procedure that required cumbersome collaboration between ground- and air-unit commands. A request for air support had to be channeled from the headquarters of origin to the controlling corps command. At each interim command echelon, discussion ensued between ground and air officers concerning the viability of the request. If the request reached the corps command, an Army Air Forces liaison officer and the corps staff considered it along with all other requests for air support. After prioritizing these requests according to their suitability for aerial operations, the air officers might dispatch available aircraft.[61]

This process did not provide rapid responsiveness to the needs of battalion and company commanders. During the Louisiana maneuvers, for example, the average time lag between the initiating request and the arrival of aircraft over the target was nearly one-and-a-half hours. The uncertainty surrounding fulfillment of a request and the time lapse between request and response led some armored formation commanders to ignore air support altogether during operational planning.[62]

Air support missions actually flown lacked proper air-ground communications. They also demonstrated the preference of the Army Air Forces for interdicting

---

[58] Simonds, "Annex No. 1," p. 4; Memo, L. McNair to CG, Third Army, 10 Oct 41, p. 3; Memo, IV Army Corps CS Col Raymond O. Barton, sub: Maneuver Instructions Number 19: Operation and Maintenance of Motor Vehicles, 23 Oct 41, Willis D. Crittenberger Papers, MHI Archives.

[59] Memo, Capt Alan W. Hall, sub: Motor Maintenance [list of mechanical deficiencies included], 17 Nov 41, HQ AGF, GHQ Ground Adjutant General, RG 337, NARA.

[60] Simonds, "Annex No. 1," p. 3; Memo, Barton, 23 Oct 41.

[61] Gabel, *GHQ Maneuvers*, pp. 56–57.

[62] Conway, "Comments on Second and Third Army Maneuver," p. 6; Greenfield and Palmer, "Origins of the Army Ground Forces," p. 111.

M2A2 light tanks of an independent tank battalion during maneuvers in 1941

enemy rear-area movements, attacking enemy air bases, and destroying hostile air strength through aerial combat. Consequently, aircraft did not constitute an important battlefield presence. During the first phase of the Louisiana maneuvers, umpires ruled 501 aircraft from both armies destroyed. Of these losses, 64 percent occurred in aerial combat, 22 percent in attacks on air bases, and 11 percent from antiaircraft fire. During the first phase of the Carolina maneuvers, the Red Army exhausted its aerial assets in costly attacks on heavily defended bridges.[63]

Antitank Operations

The high numbers of tanks ruled destroyed during the maneuvers suggested the effectiveness of the antitank units and tactics employed. Antitank units appeared capable of blunting tank attacks. However, the misuse and faulty employment of

[63] Lt Col Carlos L. Reavis, "Annex No. 8 to G–3 Report: Aviation Section Report of Corps Phase of Maneuvers August 17 to 29, 1941," 9 Oct 41, p. 1, in Richardson, "Report of VII Army Corps Field Exercises and Maneuvers"; L. McNair, "Comments," p. 8, and "Critique of the First Phase," p. 4.

participating armored units helped to create an environment favorable to antitank action and to obscure deficiencies in antitank operations.

The antitank units struggled due to faulty reconnaissance. Aerial observers tended to report every vehicle as a tank. They provided a steady stream of misinformation concerning the movements of hostile armored units that ensured frequent redeployments of antitank weapons and interfered with efforts to hold them in a central reserve for massed employment. Aerial and ground reconnaissance organizations also failed to coordinate their efforts. This resulted in antitank units' receiving a confusing intelligence picture. In some instances, antitank guns were aware of distant armored movements but ignorant of nearby enemy tanks.[64]

The haphazard flow of inaccurate information resulted in uncoordinated antitank deployments and the commitment of antitank organizations against unsubstantiated or erroneous tank sightings. During the Carolina maneuvers the 93d Antitank Battalion, equipped with self-propelled 75-mm. guns, raced from one road junction to another, blindly seeking enemy armor without benefit of accurate intelligence or support from other antitank units.[65]

The tank attacker and GHQ antitank groups did not function as massed concentrations of antitank weapons as the Army had intended. Their large size precluded rapid movement and deployment. Their commanders further reduced their responsiveness by requiring all administrative and supply assets to accompany each tactical movement, whether needed or not. To compensate for their increased mass and slower speed, these antitank units often deployed without awaiting the most favorable opportunity to punish attacking tanks. The effect of concentrated combat power might have offset the impact of premature deployment, but the components of these special units were often dispersed.[66]

Antitank operations demonstrated the same need for additional training as their armored counterparts. The selection of gun positions showed little cognizance of fields of fire or the avenues of approach likely to be used by hostile vehicles. Antitank weapons emplaced near crossroads, buildings, and small clusters of trees generally lacked concealment. Easy to anticipate, they became prime artillery targets. Gun crews further increased their vulnerability to artillery fire by deploying their weapons in tight clusters.[67]

General McNair envisioned highly mobile antitank units moving in response to and attacking enemy tanks. In fact, most antitank guns deployed rapidly in

[64] Lt Col Ben M. Sawbridge, "Comments with Respect to 1st AT Group," 20 Sep 41, HQ AGF, GHQ, RG 337, NARA; Memo, Sawbridge to Kingman, 29 Sep 41; Conway, "Comments on Second and Third Army Maneuver," p. 6; D. McNair, "Check List on Antitank Units," 5 Sep 41, p. 2; Maj F. T. Searcy, "Report of TA1 and GHQ Y," 19 Nov 41, p. 2, HQ AGF, GHQ, RG 337, NARA.

[65] D. McNair, "Check List on Antitank Units," p. 5; Purdue, "Report on Antitank Activities," p. 6; Memo, L. McNair to CG, First Army, 22 Dec 41, p. 6; Ennis, "Report Concerning Armored Action in Both Phases," p. 1.

[66] Memo, D. McNair to Kingman, 20 Sep 41, p. 2; Conway, "Comments on Second and Third Army Maneuver," p. 6; Memo, L. McNair to CG, Third Army, 10 Oct 41, p. 2.

[67] D. McNair, "Check List on Antitank Units," p. 4; Anon, "Comments on First Phase," p. 10; Purdue, "Report on Antitank Action of Units," p. 3; Purdue, "Report Concerning Actions of GHQ Y," n.d., p. 1.

response to reports of hostile armor, but they then remained in place for hours or even days waiting for an attack that might not occur. Infantry divisions similarly employed their artillery in a static antitank role. In both cases, gun crews adopted the dubious practice of relying on willing civilians to provide early warning of hostile tanks.[68]

In addition to antitank guns and artillery, the maneuvers also witnessed the use of other countermeasures. General Headquarters encouraged soldiers to stalk tanks and attack them when circumstances permitted. Flour sacks that soldiers could throw at vehicles represented grenades, which General Headquarters believed capable of destroying or disabling armored vehicles. The flour bags tended to be underused due to the absence of plans for their supply and distribution.[69]

Soldiers often devised other means of attacking tanks. Armored vehicle crews found themselves the targets of rock-filled sacks, bottles of acid, and 75-mm. blank ammunition fired at pointblank range.[70] Acid attacks proved the most common throughout the maneuvers: "The soldier could not harm the tank so his psychological reaction was to throw whatever he had at an individual in the tank."[71] Such incidents violated the maneuver umpire rules and encouraged the crews of armored vehicles to emulate an armored car driver who tried to run over a machine-gun crew.[72]

Overall, antitank operations during the maneuvers did not reflect the mobile, aggressive antitank tactics McNair advocated. Ironically, it was a cavalry organization—the Provisional Antitank Squadron—that most closely approximated the tank destroyer concept. Most antitank guns, however, tended to be dispersed and deployed in passive defensive roles, awaiting rather than seeking enemy armor. The failure of antitank organizations to apply McNair's tank destroyer tactics meant that the maneuvers neither validated nor invalidated the new antitank concept. If anything, the maneuvers demonstrated the feasibility of the echelon defense many Army commanders favored.

McNair, however, interpreted the large number of tanks ruled destroyed and the inability of armored formations to achieve major success as vindication of the tank destroyer concept. Without awaiting the conclusion of maneuvers, he began to press for the establishment of a tank destroyer force. General Marshall supported him by directing the creation of the Tank Destroyer Tactical and Firing Center under direct War Department authority before the start of the Carolina maneuvers. Within days of their conclusion, on 27 November, the adjutant general formally charged

---

[68] D. McNair, "Check List on Antitank Units," p. 4; Memo, D. McNair to Kingman, 20 Sep 41, p. 1; Memo, L. McNair to CG, First Army, 22 Dec 41, p. 6; Conway, "Comments on Second and Third Army Maneuver," p. 5; Lord, Training Memo no. 2, 26 Jan 42, p. 13.

[69] Memo, Lt Col Allen F. Kingman to Deputy Dir, sub: Flour Bag Grenades, 22 Nov 41, HQ AGF, GHQ, RG 337, NARA; Gabel, *GHQ Maneuvers*, p. 125.

[70] L. McNair, "Comments," p. 13, and "Critique of the First Phase," p. 7; Memo, Lt Col John M. Lentz to Brig Gen Mark W. Clark, 20 Nov 41, HQ AGF, GHQ, RG 337, NARA.

[71] Memo, Kingman to Deputy Dir, 22 Nov 41.

[72] Memo, Lentz to Clark, 20 Nov 41.

the Tank Destroyer Tactical and Firing Center with the organization and training of tank destroyer units for the entire Army.[73]

These actions fundamentally changed the nature of antitank development and doctrine in the U.S. Army on the basis of unproven theory. The Tank Destroyer Tactical and Firing Center embodied McNair's views on antitank operations. Although never subjected to extensive field testing, these ideas now became the essence of a de facto branch, which did, however, consolidate responsibility for antitank development.

Maneuver Management

In preparation for the autumn maneuvers, General McNair supervised the crafting by General Headquarters of a comprehensive umpire manual to govern operations. Completed in February 1941, it marked a major improvement in maneuver management, particularly in its emphasis on small-unit actions. It encouraged the employment of task forces and combat teams, because the actions of these groups determined the ability of their parent formations to accomplish their missions.[74]

Similarly, the umpire manual stressed the importance of establishing firepower superiority. The outcome of each simulated engagement rested largely on a firepower comparison between opposing forces. Combat occurred whenever opposing forces came into physical contact with one another. Umpires raised colored flags to notify each side of the other's presence. All activities halted while the umpires conferred to assess combat results using firepower and casualty ratings outlined in the manual. The manual's emphasis on small-unit actions, however, mandated a large umpire staff to permit the assignment of umpires to each command level down to the company.[75]

The umpire manual reflected McNair's belief in the superiority of the towed antitank gun over the tank. Whereas Armored Force doctrine encouraged the use of moving fire by advancing tanks to suppress their target, the umpire manual ruled such fire ineffective beyond three hundred yards. This limitation tended to reduce vehicular combat to close-range affairs with consequent high losses. The manual considered weapons fired from stationary vehicles equivalent in effect to similar dismounted armament; but whether moving or stationary, vehicle-mounted weapons could not attack antitank guns. The presence of a tank nullified the combat potential of all infantry within one hundred yards, yet tanks could not destroy antitank guns except by overrunning them. Armored units confronted by an antitank position

[73] Memo, General Staff Secretary Col Walter B. Smith to Asst Ch of Staff, G–3, sub: Organization of Antitank Units in the Army, 8 Oct 41, Andrew D. Bruce Papers, MHI Archives; Memo, Adjutant General's Office to Commanding Ofcr, Tank Destroyer Tactical and Firing Ctr, sub: Organization of Tank Destroyer Tactical and Firing Center, 27 Nov 41, Bruce Papers, MHI Archives.

[74] GHQ, U.S. Army, "Umpire Manual," Feb 41, pp. 15–16, Armored Force Surplus Training Material, MHI Library.

[75] Ibid., pp. 7–8, 15–16, 18–19.

Watering horses after the maneuvers in Louisiana

could either wait for supporting units to act or suffer high losses by charging the guns themselves.[76]

Armored Force doctrine stressed the importance of fire and maneuver tactics. When attacking forces encountered an enemy position, they organized one force to fire on the hostile force. A second grouping simultaneously maneuvered to envelop the position. The umpire manual prevented application of this basic principle by requiring all activity to cease when two opposing forces came into contact, including flanking or unseen elements. Only the firepower ratings of those units in direct physical contact counted for determining an engagement's victor. Together with the prohibition against vehicles firing at antitank guns, these restrictions made it difficult to outflank antitank positions and costly to charge them.[77]

Only two factors determined the effect of antitank fire at armored vehicles: range and number of guns firing. The umpire manual ignored crew proficiency, the target's armor protection, and how well the gun was positioned. It also overrated the lethality of antitank weapons. Both the 75-mm. and 37-mm. guns were permitted to destroy any vehicle within one thousand yards. The manual also allowed the .50-caliber machine gun used by infantry and horse cavalry units to destroy light tanks at one thousand yards. Light tanks constituted the bulk of those used in the maneuvers. Many carried a .50-caliber machine gun, but this vehicular armament was declared ineffective against tanks at any range. These rulings exceeded the

[76] L. McNair, "Critique of the First Phase," p. 6; GHQ, "Umpire Manual," pp. 7, 10, 19; Memo, Lt. Col. Clyde L. Hyssong to CGs, All Armies and Gen HQ Air Force, and Ch of the Armd Force, sub: Changes, GHQ Umpire Manual, 10 Jun 41, HQ AGF, GHQ, RG 337, NARA.

[77] Memo for Lt Col Allen F. Kingman, sub: Draft of Proposed Changes to Umpire Manual, 24 Nov 41, pp. 5–6, HQ AGF, GHQ, RG 337, NARA; Memo, Scott to Ch of the Armd Force, 10 Dec 41, p. 5.

actual antitank capabilities of these weapons and artificially boosted the lethality of antitank fire throughout the maneuvers.[78]

The capabilities of other antitank weapons were similarly exaggerated. The manual ruled that tanks hit with grenades or contacting a mine were destroyed. However, in actual combat, grenades had not proved capable of halting tank attacks. Mine usage abroad also did not warrant this ruling. Foreign armies using antitank mines had thus far achieved only limited success against armored attacks. Moreover, American antitank mines were few in number and possessed only a fraction of the explosive charge found in German mines.[79]

The representation of artillery fire and assessment of its impact remained a problem throughout the maneuvers. Soldiers and umpires were not always aware of the presence of artillery fire. The problematic influence of artillery support was discouraging to those armored commanders seeking to coordinate tanks and fire support. In frustration, many units simply left their artillery in road columns to the rear during attacks rather than employ them to no effect.[80]

Combat resolution forced frequent interruptions of tactical operations while umpires compared the firepower ratings of the units involved. These pauses, however, contradicted the Armored Force emphasis on rapid, continuous action. Umpire rulings tended to generate disputes and further delays to the resumption of operations. Soldiers crowded around the umpires to voice their opinions, and brawls sometimes resulted. The subjective rulings of partisan umpires also led to disagreements that hindered the speedy determination of a battle's outcome. The inadequate provision of umpires for antitank units further reinforced the tendency for argument, because participating unit commanders assumed umpire responsibility. Disputes also surrounded attempts by senior officers to use their rank to overrule or ignore adverse decisions.[81]

---

[78] GHQ, "Umpire Manual," p. 10; Memo, Scott to Ch of the Armd Force, 10 Dec 41, p. 5; Memo, Hyssong to CGs, All Armies and Gen HQ Air Force, and Ch of the Armd Force, 10 Jun 41; Memo, Lt Col Clyde L. Hyssong to the CGs, All Armies and GHQ Air Force, and Ch of the Armd Force, sub: Changes, GHQ Umpire Manual, 15 Jul 41, HQ AGF, GHQ, RG 337, NARA.

[79] GHQ, "Umpire Manual," p. 10; Constance McLaughlin Green, Harry C. Thomson, and Peter C. Roots, *The Technical Services: The Ordnance Department: Planning Munitions for War*, U.S. Army in World War II (Washington, D.C.: U.S. Army Center of Military History, 1955), pp. 382, 384, 387.

[80] Richardson, "Report of VII Army Corps Field Exercises and Maneuvers," p. 5; Lord, Training Memo no. 2, 26 Jan 42, p. 3; Smith, "Comments Concerning Maneuver Operations"; Ennis, "Report Concerning Armored Operations in First Carolina Maneuver," p. 1; Purdue, "Report on Antitank Activities," p. 5.

[81] D. McNair, "Check List on Antitank Units," 5 Sep 41, p. 6; Memo, D. McNair to Kingman, 20 Sep 41, p. 1; Maj B. P. Purdue, "Report of Operations of GHQ Z and TA 2, Second Army, November 19–20, 1941," n.d., pp. 1, 5, HQ AGF, GHQ, RG 37, NARA; Purdue, "Report Concerning Actions of GHQ Y," p. 6; Purdue, "Report of Antitank Action," p. 1; Searcy, "Report of TA1 and GHQ Y," pp. 1, 5; Searcy, "Report Concerning Actions of 13th Armored Regiment During First Phase," p. 1; L. McNair, "Comments," pp. 4–5; Conway, "Comments on Second and Third Army Maneuver," p. 1; Anon, "Comments on First Phase," p. 1; Memo, Hasbrouck to Armd Force Dir, 20 Nov 41, p. 1; Smith, "Comments Concerning Maneuver Operations"; Hasbrouck, "Report Concerning 2d Armored Division Actions," p. 1; Anon, "Comments on First Phase," p. 4.

Determination of tank-antitank gun combat often led to controversial interpretations of the umpire manual. Armored Force umpires claimed the exclusive right to rule a tank destroyed. In their absence, tank commanders frequently ignored loss assessments and argued that the presence of a tank neutralized all infantry and antitank guns within one hundred yards.[82] Such activities led the antitank director for the maneuvers to conclude: "No wonder they [the Armored Force] have been so successful previously."[83] Another participant predicted: "Until we get rid of the 'prima donna' aura now surrounding the tanker we can expect trouble with tank umpiring."[84]

But antitank umpires exhibited similar shortcomings. Some refused to rule antitank guns neutralized under any circumstance and did not modify tank destruction rates to account for the time necessary to move and deploy an antitank gun. When umpires signaled the cessation of activity to determine combat results, many antitank guns continued to advance, thereby increasing the firepower rating in their favor.[85]

The paucity of equipment resulted in the use of guidons to represent antitank guns, which in turn enabled antitank guns to achieve unrealistic levels of mobility. The unlimbering procedure devolved into throwing the guidon from a truck. One gun crew threw its guidon off the transport and raced through heavy underbrush to attack a tank. The crew claimed the tank's destruction, although it could not have moved an actual antitank gun with the same speed and agility.[86]

Tank crews responded by exploiting the cross-country mobility of their vehicles to creep through heavy brush in the blind zone of antitank guns and surprise them. Such action, however, did not provide a quick combat resolution. Tank and antitank gun crews could not be entirely sure when they were fired on or when they had been spotted. More arguments ensued.[87]

The maneuvers ended with calls for more realistic representation of tank-antitank engagements. Recommendations included better representation and computation of antitank fire and the inclusion of fire and movement principles in assessments of tactical engagements. In addition, stationary vehicles were to be permitted to destroy antitank guns by fire while the ostensible lethality of .50-caliber machine guns, Molotov cocktails, and hand grenades was to be reduced.[88]

Some analysts warned against hasty conclusions regarding the efficacy of antitank units based on the maneuver experience. They noted the deficient training

[82] Memo, D. McNair to Kingman, 20 Sep 41, p. 1; Sawbridge, "Comments with Respect to 1st AT Group," p. 1.

[83] Memo, D. McNair to Kingman, 20 Sep 41, p. 4.

[84] Sawbridge, "Comments with Respect to 1st AT Group," p. 2.

[85] Conway, "Comments on Second and Third Army Maneuver," p. 1; Memo, Hasbrouck to Armd Force Dir, 20 Nov 41, p. 5; Handwritten Memo, Col John B. Thompson to Dir Armd Force, sub: Final Report for Possible Inclusion in General McNair's Report—1st Armored Division, 28 Nov 41, HQ AGF, GHQ, RG 337, NARA.

[86] Memo, D. McNair to Kingman, 20 Sep 41, p. 5.

[87] Ibid., p. 4; Searcy, "Report Concerning Actions of 13th Armored Regiment," p. 5.

[88] Ennis, "Report Concerning Armored Action in Both Phases," p. 3; Memo for Kingman, 24 Nov 41.

status of participating armored and antitank units and the paucity of equipment. None were considered ready for combat. The confining terrain of the maneuver areas also provided opportunities for antitank action not necessarily available in an actual combat theater. This cautious approach to maneuver analysis did not prevent or slow the establishment of the Tank Destroyer Tactical and Firing Center.[89]

Cavalry: A Maneuver Casualty

For the Cavalry the maneuvers represented a final opportunity to demonstrate battlefield usefulness and secure War Department support for the large-scale expansion and training program General Herr envisioned. The key to achieving these goals lay in creating a favorable impression on General Headquarters, the organization responsible for overseeing the Army's combat training. The Cavalry did not possess a strong proponent in the GHQ Chief of Staff, and Herr's emphasis on the horse cavalry's relevance had already precluded the Cavalry's receiving responsibility for tank destroyer development.

The Cavalry appeared antiprogressive in its continued advocacy of horse cavalry, and Herr reinforced this perception by refusing to allow the further conversion of horse cavalry into mechanized units. Yet the continued use of horses contradicted the Army's growing reliance on motor vehicles, raising questions concerning the Cavalry's ability to conduct mobile operations on battlefields dominated by tanks, aircraft, and motorized infantry.

During the maneuvers, the fully motorized 91st Reconnaissance Squadron and the Provisional Antitank Squadron of the 1st Cavalry Division demonstrated their ability to locate, track, and destroy hostile mechanized forces. All cavalry units conducted themselves satisfactorily and employed their cross-country mobility to advantage, departing from the road-bound nature of earlier maneuvers; but such performance fell short of impressing critical observers and reversing the misperceptions haunting the Cavalry.[90]

Moreover, cavalry units committed a number of tactical errors common to most Army units and symptomatic of their lack of combat experience. Reconnaissance ability proved deficient in some operations, security missions were neglected, and radio usage did not conform to Army regulations. Horse cavalry units needlessly exposed themselves to aerial attack despite the vulnerability of columns of horses. Too many scout cars tried to emulate tank tactics by charging

---

[89] Searcy, "Report of TA1 and GHQ Y," p. 5; Purdue, Report of Operations of GHQ Z and TA 2," p. 5; Ennis, "Report Concerning Armored Action in Both Phases," p. 3; Hasbrouck, "Report Concerning 2d Armored Division Actions," p. 5; Memo, Hasbrouck to Armd Force Dir, 20 Nov 41, p. 5; Maj Clark L. Ruffner, Ann. no. 5 to G–3 Rpt: Rpt of Antitank Officer VII Army Corps, August–September Maneuvers in Arkansas and Louisiana, 11 Oct 41, p. 1, in Richardson, "Report of VII Army Corps Field Exercises and Maneuvers."

[90] Gen Robert W. Porter Jr., Oral History, pp. 183, 187, Senior Officers Oral History Program, 1981, MHI Archives; Memo, Augur to G–3, 22 Nov 41, p. 2; Memo, L. McNair to CG, First Army, 22 Dec 41, p. 8.

hostile positions, resulting in heavy scout car losses. Although Cavalry doctrine required the dispersal of combat elements in small groups throughout the battle area, the 1st Cavalry Division received criticism for not coordinating the efforts of its component elements.[91]

Similar problems afflicted the operations of all participating combat troops, but their impact on cavalry development was amplified by preexisting questions concerning the value of horse cavalry on a modern battlefield. Despite tactical mistakes by their participating combat units, the maneuvers did not threaten the existence of the Armored Force, Infantry, or Field Artillery. Together with the Army Air Forces these arms constituted the backbone of the Army, and the maneuvers simply highlighted areas requiring further training. For the Cavalry, however, the maneuvers tended to confirm preconceptions of the Cavalry and to accelerate its dissolution. It already faced the prospect of subsumption by the Armored Force and languished under personnel and funding reductions.

The corps reconnaissance regiments, including horse and mechanized components, lacked sufficient forage and radio equipment, mandating the use of relay stations. Rapid strategic movement of the horses depended on specially designed trucks; but these proved difficult to maneuver even on roads, and units had received inadequate numbers. Equipment shortages made fulfillment of the units' intended purpose difficult, but senior officers made it impossible by splitting the regiments and employing the horse and mechanized elements separately.[92]

After the maneuvers the Cavalry continued to diminish in size, especially through personnel transfers to the Armored Force. By March 1942 only two active cavalry divisions of eleven thousand men existed, but their small size and square organization contradicted the Army's embracement of larger, triangular formations. In May the War Department opted to retain these cavalry divisions with their horse components for possible use in difficult terrain, but it did not activate a cavalry corps. Nor did these formations operate with their horses. Limited transport space precluded shipping the personnel along with horses and fodder. Consequently, the 1st Cavalry Division served in the Asiatic-Pacific Theater as a modified infantry formation. In 1944 the 2d Cavalry Division was sent to North Africa, where it was inactivated.[93]

Following the maneuvers, development of the corps reconnaissance regiments did not continue. The bulk of Cavalry development thus centered on provision of mechanized reconnaissance units for infantry and armored divisions, a mission the War Department had reserved for the Cavalry in initial orders establishing

---

91 Conway, "Comments on Second and Third Army Maneuver," p. 4; Memo, Augur to G–3, 22 Nov 41, pp. 2–5; Anon, "Comments on First Phase," p. 8; Memo, L. McNair to CG, First Army, 22 Dec 41, p. 8.

92 Lt Col A. R. Reeves, App. no. 2, G–2 Rpt, [29 Oct 41], pp. 3, 6, in Richardson, "Report of VII Army Corps Field Exercises and Maneuvers"; Lt Col John R. Hodge, App. no. 3, G–3 Rpt, 20 Oct 41, p. 13, in Richardson, "Report of VII Army Corps Field Exercises and Maneuvers."

93 Robert R. Palmer, "Reorganization of Ground Troops for Combat," in Greenfield, Palmer, and Wiley, *Army Ground Forces*, pp. 278–79.

the Armored Force. These units became the principal cavalry force to see combat throughout World War II.[94]

Administratively, the Cavalry's influence within the War Department steadily declined. In March 1942, the Army underwent a reorganization that abolished the branch chiefs. Without a chief of Cavalry, the Cavalry Board and School came under the control of Army Ground Forces headquarters. Unable to compete with other combat arms to justify continued investments of men and materiel, or to prevent much of its traditional mission from being assumed by the Armored Force, the Cavalry lost its identity and ability to influence Army development.[95]

---

[94] Ibid., p. 278.

[95] Robert R. Palmer, "Organization and Training of New Ground Combat Elements," in Greenfield, Palmer, and Wiley, *Army Ground Forces*, chart, pp. 406–07.

11

FROM ARMORED FORCE TO ARMORED CENTER

The period 1942–1943 witnessed a watershed in American armored development. During this timeframe the Armored Force underwent its greatest expansion, experienced combat, and adopted a unique division organization. Training began to reflect firsthand combat experience and to incorporate greater realism. However, the role and status of the Armored Force remained uncertain until after the conclusion of combat operations in North Africa. Then, its quasi-independent status was ended and many of the functions of the Armored Force removed, underscoring the clear subordination of the Armored Force to Army Ground Forces (AGF). Consequently, the latter's influence predominated over doctrine, training, and materiel developments and the armored community became less a special force than a small collection of specialists.

Armored Force Expansion and Personnel Shortfall

A rapid expansion of the Army occurred in the months following the autumn 1941 maneuvers, particularly after the Japanese attack on Pearl Harbor. Germany's subsequent declaration of war on the United States ensured the likelihood of facing German mechanized formations in battle and accelerated Armored Force expansion. War Department planning envisioned a massive armored buildup culminating in forty-six armored divisions. This figure later dropped to just sixteen, including the five formed before the end of 1941. The Army activated nine more armored divisions in 1942, making that year the most significant in terms of Armored Force growth. (*See Table.*) The last two divisions organized in 1943. The number of armored corps similarly rose from one in 1941 to four in 1942.[1]

The rapid expansion of the Armored Force generated requirements for new training sites and facilities. Despite efforts to geographically disperse new armored divisions, construction and development of cantonments became a growth industry that could not always keep pace with unit activation rates. The II Armored Corps

[1] Robert R. Palmer, "Ground Forces in the Army, December 1941–April 1945, A Statistical Study," in *The Army Ground Forces: The Organization of Ground Combat Troops*, ed. Kent Roberts Greenfield, Robert R. Palmer, and Bell I. Wiley, U.S. Army in World War II (Washington, D.C.: U.S. Army Center of Military History, 1947), table "Ground Forces in the Army, December 1941–April 1945"; Army Ground Forces (AGF) Hist Sec, Study no. 27, "The Armored Force Command and Center," 1946, p. 147, U.S. Army Center of Military History, Washington, D.C.

Table—Armored Division and Corps Activation, 1940–1943

Formation	Activation Date
Armored Divisions	
1st & 2d	15 July 1940
3d & 4th	15 April 1941
5th	1 October 1941
6th	15 February 1942
7th	1 March 1942
8th	1 April 1942
9th & 10th	15 July 1942
11th	15 August 1942
12th	15 September 1942
13th & 14th	15 November 1942
20th	15 March 1943
16th	15 July 1943
Armored Corps	
I	15 July 1940
II	17 January 1942
III	20 August 1942
IV	5 September 1942

formed in January 1942 at Camp Polk, Louisiana. The post, however, lacked the infrastructure to support the corps headquarters let alone the 3d and 7th Armored Divisions also stationed there. Therefore, training began simultaneously with the construction of housing and training facilities. Similar circumstances surrounded the organization of other armored formations.[2]

The global nature of World War II forced Army leaders to consider how to prepare for combat in a variety of terrain and climate conditions. The ongoing battle for North Africa and its mobile nature spurred development of a site to prepare armored units for desert warfare. In April the Desert Training Center was organized at Camp Young, California, for this purpose. The new center encompassed a large desert landmass, considered ideal for the maneuver of armored divisions.[3]

---

[2] Memo, Maj Gen Alvan C. Gillem Jr. to Ch of the Armd Force, 23 Jan 42, Jacob L. Devers Papers, York County Historical Society, York, Pa.

[3] Hist Sec, Study no. 15, "The Desert Training Center and C–AMA," 1946, prefatory note, pp. 1–3, CMH; Rod Crossley, "The Desert Training Center in World War II," *La Posta: A Journal of American Postal History* 28, no. 5 (November 1997), article accessed on line on 22 May 06, http://www.la-posta.com/Online%20Reprints/Desert%20Training%20Center.pdf.

Key leaders of the Armored Force, *left to right*: Maj. Gen. Jacob L. Devers, Maj. Gen. George S. Patton Jr., Maj. Gen. Alvan C. Gillem Jr., Maj. Gen. Willis D. Crittenberger, Maj. Gen. Walton H. Walker, and Maj. Gen. John S. Wood

Establishment of the Desert Training Center fell to the I Armored Corps and its commander, Maj. Gen. George S. Patton Jr. The corps headquarters provided the leadership and administrative support necessary for large-scale training activities. Patton opted to focus the center's attention on training rather than administrative tasks. Hence, Camp Young remained a spartan installation with few buildings beyond those required for health and sanitation. However, Patton's leadership resulted in a comprehensive training program that began to include corps and division maneuvers starting in August 1942. By then Patton and the I Armored Corps had been replaced by Maj. Gen. Alvan C. Gillem Jr. and the II Armored Corps headquarters.[4]

The Desert Training Center's early association with the Armored Force continued through the IV Armored Corps' assumption of maneuver responsibility in November. This relationship diminished as the center's administration, organization, and operation grew.[5] After the surrender of Axis forces in North Africa in May 1943, the desert no longer constituted a likely battlefield for American soldiers;

---

[4] Hist Sec, "Desert Training Center and C–AMA," prefatory note, pp. 13–18, 31–34; Crossley, "Desert Training Center in World War II."

[5] On 20 October 1943, the Desert Training Center became the California-Arizona Maneuver Area, denoting its changing scope and nature.

the following December the Army opted to close the center. By then the Desert Training Center had trained many of the new armored organizations formed in 1942 and 1943.[6]

Preparation for maneuvers at the Desert Training Center sometimes overtaxed organizations suffering from personnel and materiel shortfalls and manned with inexperienced soldiers. The 5th Armored Division, for example, lacked its full complement of vehicles and compressed unit and individual soldier training to meet its maneuver timeline. The division also had an officer shortage unrelieved by mandatory umpire assignments at the training center. The division's commander, Maj. Gen. Jack W. Heard, reported to Chief of the Armored Force Maj. Gen. Jacob L. Devers that "I can lead a second-to-none skeletonized Division of about half strength into full scale maneuvers or into actual combat."[7]

The personnel status of the 5th Armored Division was not unique. Most armored divisions experienced similar deficiencies. The rapid expansion of the Armored Force caused it to outstrip available manpower pools and posed manning problems for new formations. The 7th Armored Division activated in March 1942 with just 62 officers and 8,766 soldiers, most of whom lacked prior military training. Stationed at Camp Polk with the 3d Armored Division, the two formations together mustered fewer officers than those mandated for a single division. This leader shortage resulted in a prolonged basic training period and less effective instruction. Similar personnel shortages in the Armored Force headquarters and school prevented Fort Knox, Kentucky, from providing assistance and lowered the quality of training.[8]

Devers looked to the newly established Armored Force officer candidate school for relief. As officers became available, he planned to overfill each tank battalion. The excess leaders would train with their unit and provide a pool of experienced commanders ready for assignment to newly activated armored organizations. At Patton's urging, Devers also considered inducing Cavalry officers assigned to horse cavalry divisions to request transfers to the Armored Force.[9]

The dearth of experienced officers affected the Armored Force's visibility and influence within the War Department. There, proposed Armored Force actions often triggered debate that delayed or blocked implementation. The Armored Force liaison officer noted the absence of powerful armored advocates: "I look around for people who are thinking, who know, or who are sympathetic to Armored Forces and I don't

---

[6] Hist Sec, "Desert Training Center and C–AMA," prefatory note; Crossley, "Desert Training Center in World War II." Armored units trained at the Desert Training Center in 1942 and 1943 included the 2d, 3d, 6th, 9th, and 10th Tank Groups; the 3d, 4th, 5th, 6th, 7th, 9th, and 11th Armored Divisions; the 11th Cavalry Group; and the 4th, 15th, and 107th Cavalry Regiments.

[7] Ltr, Maj Gen Jack W. Heard to Ch of the Armd Force, 21 Jul 42, Devers Papers.

[8] Memos, Col Sereno E. Brett to Maj Gen Henry W. Baird, 19 Sep 41; Maj Gen Alvan C. Gillem Jr. to Commanding General (CG), Armd Force, 16 Mar 42; Maj Gen Alvan C. Gillem Jr. to CG, Armd Force, 3 Apr 42, 1st End to Memo, Maj Gen Lindsay McD. Silvester, sub: Report of Progress, 7th Armored Division, n.d.; all in Devers Papers.

[9] Ltrs, Maj Gen Jacob L. Devers to Lt Col Severne S. MacLaughlin, 21 Mar 42; Maj Gen George S. Patton Jr. to Maj Gen Jacob L. Devers, 16 Apr 42; Maj Gen Jacob L. Devers to Maj Gen George S. Patton Jr., 22 Apr 42; all in Devers Papers.

see them."[10] He recommended emulation of the Army Air Forces, which maintained a large-scale presence in the War Department and proved much more effective at sustaining support and visibility. Devers shared these concerns, but he preferred to appoint the few experienced officers of high rank to command positions in new armored divisions rather than to liaison duties in Washington, D.C.[11]

Training Challenges and Accomplishments

The activation of new formations kept Armored Force training focused on basic training, small-unit operations, and physical conditioning throughout 1942. Unit training emphasized small-unit tactics to correct deficiencies identified during maneuvers. The implementation of proficiency tests provided a more effective gauge of unit readiness. Yet new divisions were still expected to achieve a base level of combat readiness within three months of formation. Adherence to this timeline proved difficult, especially after the Armored Force began to channel Selective Servicemen directly into armored organizations without prior training. This action provided a steady flow of new soldiers, but it also meant that new formations included a mass of inexperienced personnel unfamiliar with the rigors of military life—let alone armored operations.[12]

In February the command groups of the I and II Armored Corps met to coordinate training. They proposed a more active training role for each corps headquarters and recommended the transfer of select training responsibilities from Fort Knox to each corps. This action would have eliminated the need for new combat units to disrupt training while their personnel traveled to the Armored Force School for instruction. The corps commanders felt that with appropriate training literature units could perform this instruction at home stations. Devers preferred to keep specialized training concentrated in the Armored Force School to ensure uniformity throughout the force. He wanted graduates of Armored Force School courses to disseminate within their units the knowledge gained at Fort Knox.[13]

The process of creating new formations did change. Initially, cadres from existing formations became the nuclei for new divisions. This method stripped experienced soldiers from units just as they began to develop cohesion and effectiveness. Moreover, new divisions struggling with masses of untrained Selective Servicemen could ill afford to part with a core of trained leaders and soldiers. Therefore, when the 6th Armored Division activated at Fort Knox in February 1942, it was formed

---

[10] Ltr, Col R. P. Shugg to Maj Gen Jacob L. Devers, 18 Mar 42, Devers Papers.

[11] Ltrs, Shugg to Devers, 18 Mar 42; Maj Gen Jacob L. Devers to Col R .P. Shugg, 21 Mar 42, Devers Papers.

[12] Memo, Chief of Staff (CS) General George C. Marshall to Maj Gen William Bryden, 4 Dec 41, Selected Corresp, George C. Marshall Papers, George C. Marshall Library (GCM), Lexington, Va.; Col C. M. Daly, Training Memo no. 7, sub: Training Directive, Period January 1–March 31, 1942, 14 Jan 42, Thomas J. Camp Papers, U.S. Army Military History (MHI) Archives, Carlisle Barracks, Pa.

[13] Ltrs, Maj Gens. Alvan C. Gillem Jr. and George S. Patton Jr. to CG, Armd Force, 27 Feb 42, and Maj Gen Jacob L. Devers to Maj Gen Alvan C. Gillem Jr., 11 Mar 42, both in Devers Papers.

from a cadre provided by the seasoned 2d Armored Division rather than a more recently established formation.[14]

In March the 7th Armored Division was activated at Camp Polk, where it benefited from the mentoring of the 3d Armored Division. The latter formation assumed responsibility for the 7th Armored Division's individual and small-unit training, passing on its experience. In effect the 3d Armored Division became host to the new formation, its members "working and living side by side" with the 7th Armored Division personnel. In this manner the 3d Armored Division nurtured the latter until it could assume responsibility for its own training and further development. In the process, however, the training requirements and combat readiness of the 3d Armored Division tended to suffer—a situation prolonged by the shortage of officers at Camp Polk.[15]

A better solution to the training of new formations emerged with the activation of the 8th Armored Division at Fort Knox in April. This formation received the exclusive responsibility of training and organizing cadres for new armored divisions. It relieved existing formations of this function and left them free to focus on combat readiness. After completing its own training, the 8th Armored Division prepared cadres for the 9th through 14th Armored Divisions between June 1942 and January 1943. Afterward, the 8th Armored Division transitioned to a combat organization; cadre preparation became the responsibility of the 20th Armored Division in March 1943.[16]

Use of cadre divisions did not solve the Armored Force's shortage of experienced junior officers and noncommissioned officers. Therefore, inexperienced leaders assumed training responsibilities in the Armored Force Replacement Training Center. Struggling themselves to comprehend the nuances of armored warfare, these instructors were not permitted to specialize. Each became responsible for training thirty-two different subject areas to a single student body. Quality of instruction suffered.[17]

Maj. Gen. Charles L. Scott assumed command of the Replacement Training Center in July 1942. He devoted himself to improving training effectiveness and identified the absence of specialization among instructors as a problem: "The Army is the only educational institution where a student 'goes to school' under one instructor who is supposed to train him in all subjects. The entire system of American education is based on specialized instruction from highly trained instructors whose field of activity is limited to their specialty."[18] Scott recommended permitting instructors to focus on select subject areas. A team system resulted in which trainees received

---

[14] Shelby L. Stanton, *Order of Battle, U.S. Army, World War II* (Novato, Calif.: Presidio Press, 1984), inside cover.

[15] Memo, Gillem to CG, Armd Force, 3 Apr 42; quote from Ltr, Maj Gen Alvan C. Gillem Jr. to Maj Gen Jacob L. Devers, 4 Apr 42, Devers Papers.

[16] Hist Sec, "Armored Force Command and Center," p. 51; Charles R. Leach, *In Tornado's Wake* (Chicago: Argus Press, 1956).

[17] Lt Col T. E. Boudinot, "Estimate of the Training Situation (Officer's Schools)," 3 Oct 41; Memo, Maj Gen Charles L. Scott to Ch of Armd Force, sub: Centralized Training under Group Command in Armored Force Replacement Training Center, 23 Sep 42; both in Henry C. Newton Papers, MHI Archives.

[18] Memo, Scott to Ch of Armd Force, 23 Sep 42, p. 1.

The 66th Armored Regiment during training at Fort Benning, February 1942

instruction from a set of individuals, each an expert in select topics. This change enhanced training quality and permitted instructors to become more effective in a shorter time because they had fewer subjects to master.[19]

Similar efficiencies also began to emerge within the armored divisions. For example, the 3d Armored Division developed a "golf course" to simultaneously train newly formed companies. It included eighteen different tactical problems that addressed the various skills associated with armored company operations. The golf course permitted eighteen tank companies, or two armored regiments, to train simultaneously. Upon completion of each problem, the companies rotated. The success of this method led to its adoption throughout the Armored Force.[20]

Training also emphasized greater realism through the use of simulated combat sounds and the creation of environments that more closely resembled a battlefield with its related physical and psychological stresses. Early in 1942 the 2d Armored Division began to apply training techniques adapted from British commando training that emphasized close-combat skills for the individual soldier. The Armored Force School then adopted this training approach. By January 1943 the school began training for urban combat and attacks on fortified positions. The following month armored battalion training cycles ended with a period of operations under simulated battlefield conditions. For armored divisions the training program lengthened to thirty-eight weeks in which the final eleven consisted of training exercises involving the entire formation. Afterward, it participated in corps maneuvers.[21]

---

[19] Hist Sec, "Armored Force Command and Center," pp. 75–76.

[20] Memo, HQ Armd Force, sub: Tactical Training Aid No. 2: The Tactical "Golf Course," 15 Jul 42, Camp Papers.

[21] Memo, Brig Gen Henry C. Newton to CG, Armd Force Replacement Trng Ctr, sub: Battle Training, 6 Feb 43, p. 1, Newton Papers; Hist Sec, "Armored Force Command and Center," pp. 53–54, 65–66.

Realism in training reflected the availability of accurate intelligence concerning ongoing combat operations. In 1942 General Scott visited armored divisions throughout the United States, as well as British armored forces in North Africa. His observations helped to refine American armored training through the infusion of lessons the British had learned. He particularly stressed the importance of combined-arms operations and organizational flexibility. "All commanders of units in an Armored Division must know and be trained in the employment of not only their own units, but in the proper use of any other elements of the division which may be attached."[22]

A steady stream of information on German mobile operations also became available to armored organizations. The Armored Force G–2 (Intelligence) regularly compiled publications describing German mechanized forces, combat activities, and related tactics. Distinctive by their use of clear language, pictures, and common-sense interpretations, these publications were well received by Armored Force components.[23]

Devers maintained a personal notebook that included a translated German manual outlining how the different components of the panzer division should integrate their actions. It emphasized flexibility in tactics and organization and reinforced Devers' own preference for teamwork.[24] In leaders, he sought mental and tactical agility: "Combat commanders should be trained so that they have sufficient flexibility to command any tactical grouping. Commanders must learn to use the tools furnished them. The elasticity of the formation will produce elasticity of the mind."[25]

Generating leaders imbued with this spirit and necessary tactical competency required time. Observed training mistakes paralleled errors noted during maneuvers in 1941. They included the premature commitment of tanks without prior reconnaissance, assaulting antitank guns with tanks rather than relying on artillery, employing tanks in rough terrain without first performing a terrain analysis, and using excessive force for minor resistance. Tanks tended to move as a dense mass rather than disperse in the face of hostile fire, blindly following the leading vehicle without providing covering fire. At the crew level, Devers identified tank gunnery and driving as skills in need of improvement.[26] Tank drivers tended to "change speed in final assault, cross ditches at excessive speed, drive recklessly through tree lanes or hedge rows, etc., all of which detracts from the tank commander's and gunner's efficiency when they are attempting to engage a target."[27]

---

[22] Memo, Maj Gen Charles L. Scott to Ch of Armd Force, sub: Maintenance of Depth, Value of Sustained Action and Use of Combined Arms in Armored Units, 1 Sep 42, Devers Papers.

[23] Ltrs, Maj Gen George S. Patton Jr. to Maj Gen Jacob L. Devers, 16 Apr 42, and Maj Gen Jacob L. Devers to Maj Gen George S. Patton Jr., 22 Apr 42, both in Devers Papers.

[24] Lt Gen Jacob L. Devers, Personal Notebook, Devers Papers (hereafter cited as Devers Notebook).

[25] Devers Notebook, "Organization of the Present Armored Division," 2 Nov 42.

[26] Memo, M. R., sub: U.S. Medium Tanks on Maneuver, n.d. [addresses maneuver of 21 Feb 42], Willis D. Crittenberger Papers, MHI Archives; Devers Notebook; Memo, Scott to Ch of the Armd Force, 1 Sep 42.

[27] Brig Gen Henry C. Newton, "Tactical Notes," 31 Aug 43, quote from p. 8, Newton Papers.

These problems resulted from rushed training programs and the high percentage of inexperienced personnel in new armored divisions. Veteran formations, however, also remained prone to a variety of tactical errors. During one exercise, distances of six miles separated tank companies belonging to a regiment of the 2d Armored Division. March discipline and vehicle security proved lax, and subordinate commanders failed to prevent their units from becoming mixed. Nearly a year after the 12th Armored Division's creation, a critique of its training noted what had become common errors: inadequate reconnaissance, radio messages notorious for their verbosity, and the inability of the formation's components to coordinate their actions on the battlefield.[28]

The Question of Separate Branch Status

The acknowledged importance of armored combat units and the rapid growth in armored divisions did not change the Armored Force's status. It remained a de facto branch without a legal basis, officially described as a service test. Devers sought the permanent establishment of the Armored Force as a combat arm and an expansion of its headquarters. Following the precedent of the Army Air Forces, he sought an organization that possessed both developmental and tactical authority.[29]

Devers believed that armored units' combination of firepower and mobility made them superior to all other ground troops. He noted the leading role played by tank forces abroad and concluded, "This is an air-gun-tank war."[30] He challenged the preeminent status afforded the triangular infantry division: "The triangular division has its place in the scheme of affairs to protect lines of communication, to hold ground, to assist the armored units in supply and in the crossing of obstacles, such as rivers, defiles, etc. They do not carry the spearhead of the fight and never will when tanks or guns are present."[31]

Devers considered tank destroyers, self-propelled artillery, and tanks merely variations on the theme of mobile, armored firepower, seeing little reason for their separate development. He sought to consolidate responsibility for all mechanized development in an expanded Armored Force headquarters, incorporating not only tank destroyers but the mechanized cavalry as well.[32]

These proposals led to discussion and debate but little change in the Armored Force's status. Moreover, they were overshadowed by the Army's March 1942

---

[28] Anon, "Day by Day Maneuver Notes for General Crittenberger," n.d. [addresses divisional exercise in Apr 42], Crittenberger Papers; Brig Gen Henry C. Newton, "Tactical Notes," 31 Aug 43, quote from p. 8, Newton Papers.

[29] Ltr, Maj Gen Jacob L. Devers to General George C. Marshall, 1 Feb 42, Selected Corresp, Marshall Papers.

[30] Ltrs, Maj Gen Jacob L. Devers to Lt Gen Lesley J. McNair, 18 Dec 41, and Maj Gen Jacob L. Devers to Lt Gen Lesley J. McNair, 18 Jul 42, both in HQ AGF, CG Gen Corresp, Record Group (RG) 337, National Archives and Records Administration (NARA).

[31] Ltr, Devers to McNair, 19 Jul 42, p. 1.

[32] Ltrs, Lt Gen Lesley J. McNair to Maj Gen Jacob L. Devers, 9 May 42, HQ AGF, CG Gen Corresp, RG 337, NARA; Devers to McNair, 18 Jul 42, p. 1.

Light tank platoon of the 2d Armored Division during training in March 1942

reorganization of its command structure. The chiefs of the combat and service arms were eliminated. The functions previously performed by these offices were apportioned among the Army Air Forces and the newly created Army Ground Forces and Army Service Forces. The War Department General Staff's authority also increased within the Army. The chief of staff established the broad policies governing the Army's strategic employment and development in accord with guidelines set by the president and the secretary of war. The General Staff divisions implemented these policies.[33]

In effect, this reorganization replaced the horizontal command structure of the prewar bureau system with a vertical one that consolidated executive authority in the General Staff. It provided a more effective and efficient mechanism for conducting the war effort along a functional rather than a consensus basis. It also paralleled similar changes made during World War I.

Lt. Gen. Lesley J. McNair assumed command of the Army Ground Forces, charged with training, equipping, and mobilizing soldiers. His authority included the combat and service arms, which became subject to his organizational preference for minimizing specialization and pooling support assets at the corps and army levels.[34]

---

[33] Kent Roberts Greenfield and Robert R. Palmer, "Origins of the Army Ground Forces: General Headquarters, United States Army, 1940–1942," in Greenfield, Palmer, and Wiley, *Army Ground Forces*, p. 152; James E. Hewes Jr., *From Root to McNamara: Army Organization and Administration, 1900–1963* (Washington, D.C.: U.S. Army Center of Military History, 1975), pp. 67–70, 74–76.

[34] Robert R. Palmer, "Reorganization of Ground Troops for Combat," in Greenfield, Palmer, and Wiley, *Army Ground Forces*, pp. 268, 273–74.

These changes at first seemed to have little effect on the Armored Force. Despite the elimination of the combat- and service-arm chiefs, Devers retained his title as chief of the Armored Force. In September he was promoted to lieutenant general, the same rank McNair held. The Armored Force continued to train its own personnel, develop its own doctrine, control personnel appointments in armored units, and influence the distribution of tanks within the Army. It played a central role in the development of new armored materiel, and it stamped its influence on the Desert Training Center. Devers also commanded those armored organizations not yet assigned to field commands, including the armored corps, several armored divisions, and the independent tank battalions. He became responsible for the inspection of all armored units to ensure uniformity in doctrine and training standards.[35]

Devers, therefore, continued to press for an expansion of Armored Force authority. He succeeded in gaining General Staff support for increasing the size of the Armored Force headquarters, but McNair blocked his efforts to consolidate mechanized development. The AGF commander believed that the Cavalry School provided a degree of focused development for mechanized cavalry greater than that possible as an Armored Force component.[36] Similarly, he believed that "tanks and [tank] destroyers should be rivals, not partners, although they are associated closely in operations." Such rivalry could best be instilled by the separation of tank and tank destroyer development.[37]

McNair did not share Devers' faith in the superiority of armored formations and instead emphasized the importance of teamwork among the combat arms. Hence, while still General Headquarters chief of staff, McNair had tied the pace of Armored Force expansion to that of the other Army components to guarantee a balanced force structure. Triangular infantry divisions, not armored formations, constituted the principal gauge of the Army's buildup for war.[38]

Demise of the Armored Corps

In 1941 Armored Force efforts to establish a special armored corps organization met with opposition within the War Department. However, the employment of the I Armored Corps in maneuvers prompted renewed efforts to secure support for such a formation. McNair permitted experimentation with various armored corps concepts to determine the most effective, but he saw little need for rapid action. He considered small-unit training and combat readiness throughout the Army a

---

[35] Robert R. Palmer, "Organization and Training of New Ground Combat Elements," in Greenfield, Palmer, and Wiley, *Army Ground Forces*, pp. 397, 408.

[36] Memo, Lt Gen Lesley J. McNair to Assistant Chief of Staff (ACS), G–3, sub: Table of Organization, Headquarters, Armored Force, 23 Jan 42; Ltr, Lt Gen Lesley J. McNair to Maj Gen Jacob L. Devers, 9 May 42; both in HQ AGF, CG Gen Corresp, RG 337, NARA.

[37] Ltr, McNair to Devers, 9 May 42.

[38] Memo, Lt Gen Lesley J. McNair to Deputy Chief of Staff (DCS) Richard C. Moore, sub: Command Set-up of Armored Units, 23 Dec 41, Item 6034, Reel 655, National Archives Project, GCM; Draft Reply, Lt Gen Lesley J. McNair to Ltr, Maj Gen Jacob L. Devers, 18 Jul 42, HQ AGF, CG Gen Corresp, RG 337, NARA.

M3 medium tank and crew of the 1st Armored Division
in North Africa in November 1942

higher priority. Therefore, he did not seek formal War Department approval of the armored corps.[39]

In the absence of a definitive policy, the Armored Force continued its advocacy of the armored corps and proposed an organization that included two armored divisions; one motorized division; and the permanent assignment of signal, medical, engineer, military police, and maintenance elements.[40] This structure's specialized nature contradicted McNair's preference for more generic organizations to which other forces could be attached as necessary. He considered an armored corps of two armored divisions and a headquarters sufficient. Additional forces—like the motorized division and corps troops included in the Armored Force proposal—would be attached when required and pooled in a central Army reserve until then.[41]

---

[39] Memo, Lt Gen Lesley J. McNair to ACS, sub: Proposed Organization of Armored Corps, 22 Jan 42, HQ AGF, CG Gen Corresp, RG 337, NARA.

[40] Ltr, Maj Gen Jacob L. Devers to General George C. Marshall, 4 Oct 41, Marshall Papers; Palmer, "Origins of the Army Ground Forces," p. 70.

[41] Memos, McNair to ACS, G–3, sub: Proposed Organization of Armored Corps, 22 Jan 42; Lt Gen Lesley J. McNair to ACS, G–3, sub: Supporting Elements for Armored Divisions and Corps, and Organization of an Armored Corps, 4 Feb 42, HQ AGF, CG Gen Corresp, RG 337, NARA.

Devers did not think such a minimal corps sufficient, but he urged its rapid approval and the activation of additional corps headquarters to permit training. The War Department responded in 1942 with the activation of the II, III, and IV Armored Corps. The Armored Force quickly recommended troop assignments to the I and II Armored Corps, which it obtained albeit with some modifications. However, both corps found their ability to develop as armored combat formations interrupted by assignments to the Desert Training Center, where they served as the command agencies directing training maneuvers. The III and IV Armored Corps also activated in 1942, but neither ever received any permanent troop assignments.[42]

In September the question of armored corps organization ended with the War Department's acceptance of a generic corps concept proposed by McNair. McNair's preference for organizational flexibility and interchangeable ground combat forces encouraged the adoption of a corps structure that possessed no permanent forces other than a headquarters and a signal unit. All administrative functions were removed from the corps. They became exclusively tactical commands whose combat potential stemmed from the attachment of forces by army and theater commanders. Such attachments derived from available forces and a corps mission that could be continually altered.[43]

The new corps structure eliminated the need for a specialized armored corps. Upon completion of training, armored divisions were assigned to various corps headquarters, enabling corps commanders to accumulate experience handling armored formations, a goal long desired by Army Chief of Staff General George C. Marshall. The War Department abolished the armored corps table of organization in August 1943, although the formation's demise in effect had already occurred. None of the activated armored corps functioned in its intended role in a combat theater. The I Armored Corps was deactivated in July 1943; in October the II, III, and IV Armored Corps became the XVIII, XIX, and XX Corps, respectively.[44]

Evolution of the Armored Division

The uncertainty surrounding the armored corps did not afflict the armored division. The need for such a formation remained unquestioned and indeed had justified the creation of the Armored Force. However, the division's organization remained a work in progress throughout 1942 (*see Chart 17*). In March the table of organization and equipment for the armored division included a division headquarters; two

[42] Memo, Harmon to McNair, 23 Dec 41; Memo, The Adjutant General (TAG) to Ch of the Armd Force, sub: Organization of the I and II Armored Corps, 20 Feb 42; 1st End, Maj C. M. Wells to TAG, sub: Organization of the I and II Armored Corps, 24 Feb 42; 2d End, Col Clyde L. Hyssong to Ch of Armd Force, sub: Organization of the I and II Armored Corps, 12 Mar 42. Memo, Col Clyde L. Hyssong to Ch of the Armd Force, sub: Assignment of 3d and 7th Armored Divisions, 16 Mar 42; all in U.S. Army War College (AWC) Curricular Archives, MHI Archives. Stanton, *Order of Battle*, p. 6.

[43] Palmer, "Reorganization of Ground Troops," pp. 355, 370.

[44] Memo, McNair to Moore, 23 Dec 41; Palmer, "Reorganization of Ground Troops," pp. 355, 364, 370; Stanton, *Order of Battle*, p. 6.

Chart 17–Armored Division, 1942

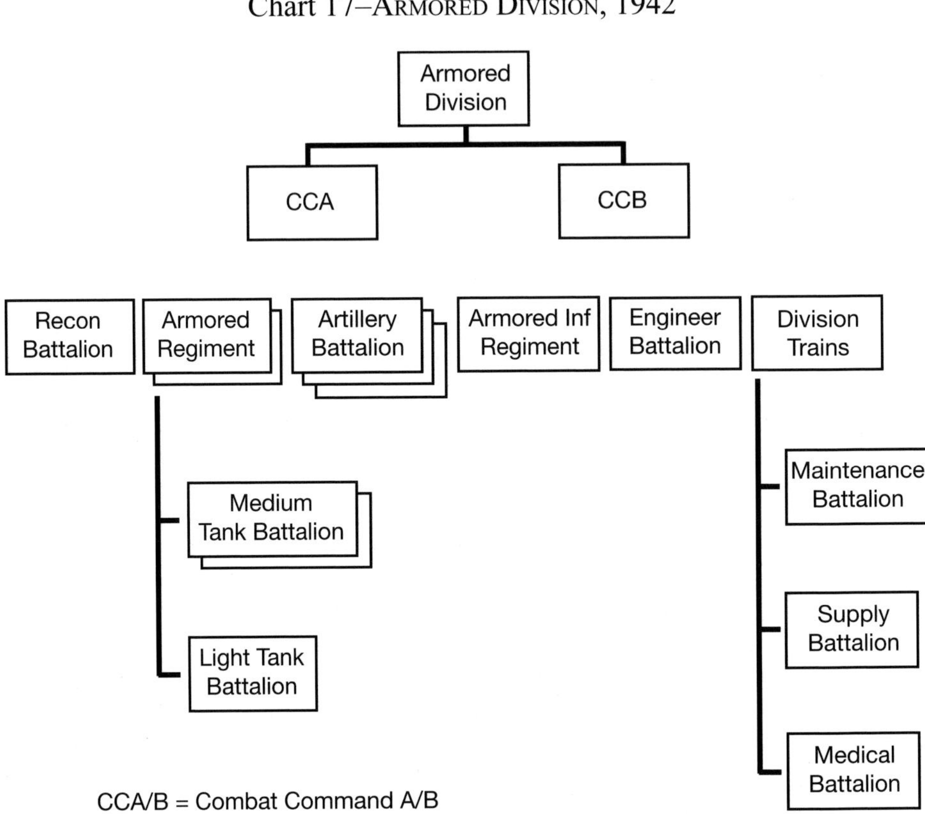

combat commands; two armored regiments; an armored infantry regiment; three artillery battalions; and reconnaissance, engineers, and support services.[45]

This structure reflected the interwar influence of the mechanized cavalry and the guidance of Devers. The 7th Cavalry Brigade (Mechanized) had operated as a collection of self-sufficient combat teams coordinated by a brigade headquarters designed to subdivide into two command cells. This organizational flexibility encouraged an emphasis on combined-arms teams, which became a central facet of Armored Force doctrine. Maneuver experiences in 1940 and 1941 simply reinforced the need for integrating the action of tanks, infantry, and artillery. According to one armored officer, "The tank battalion (light or medium), alone and unsupported, is incapable of successfully waging combat under modern conditions."[46]

---

[45] Hist Sec, "Armored Force Command and Center," p. 31.

[46] Memo, Brig Gen William M. Grimes to CG, 4th Armd Div, sub: The Organization and Employment of a Combat Team, 19 Dec 41, p. 3, Crittenberger Papers.

Devers sought to encourage combined-arms action by developing a divisional structure that facilitated the integration of tactical functions. In December 1941 the 4th Armored Division undertook the necessary experimentation, reorganizing itself into a collection of combat teams. The division transformed its brigade headquarters into two command agencies known as combat commands. A tank regiment, supplemented with infantry, artillery, engineer, and reconnaissance elements, formed the backbone of each combat command. The division commander, who maintained a small reserve force, could assign additional signal, service, and reconnaissance units. The other armored divisions soon began to follow the pattern established by the 4th Armored Division and fashioned their own combat commands. The precise configuration of each combat command varied, but each generally included a combined-arms mix organized around a tank regiment.[47]

The combat commands were little more than subordinate headquarters. From the assets assigned to them they fashioned smaller combined-arms task forces. Normally, each such task force included a tank battalion reinforced with combat and service elements. The division commander assigned missions to each combat command. The latter then determined the composition, objective, and operational boundaries of its task forces. Successful accomplishment of the combat command's objective rested on the collective efforts of these independently operating task forces. Therefore, task force commanders were expected to exercise initiative and determine how best to employ the units assigned to them.[48]

This decentralized command structure provided an unprecedented degree of tactical agility. The combat commands provided the means to track the multiple, fast-moving task forces, which in turn could react quickly to tactical developments. With the emergence of task forces, the armored division had evolved into a collection of combined-arms teams and could redistribute its resources to capitalize on the success of any of them. It constituted "a self-contained unit of the several arms and services organized tactically and administratively for independent action."[49]

The division's emerging command structure pushed decision-making responsibility down to task force commanders. To maximize the utility of the formation's organizational flexibility, these leaders needed to possess an understanding of combined-arms operations and to accept the continuous task-force reconfiguration necessary to exploit tactical opportunities. In 1942, however, most armored officers had not yet reached this level of professional development. At both the combat-command and task-force levels, too many leaders preferred functional separation in lieu of combined-arms teams. A common organizational recommendation separated tanks and their supporting infantry and artillery into different combat commands.

---

[47] Ibid., pp. 3–4, diagram showing division organization; Maj Gen Willis D. Crittenberger, "Unit Commanders' Meeting," 11 Apr 42, p. 2, Crittenberger Papers.

[48] Memo, Grimes to CG, 4th Armd Div, 19 Dec 41, pp. 3–4, diagram showing division organization; Crittenberger, "Unit Commanders' Meeting," p. 2; Brig Gen William M. Grimes, "Notes on Combat Team Organization—Technique," n.d. [ca. Jun 42], pp. 2–6, Camp Papers.

[49] Anon, "Armored Troops in the Exploitation of a Break-through," 4 Jun 42, pp. 1–2, 6, Crittenberger Papers.

This practice had been discredited during maneuvers in 1941; the Germans had abandoned it in 1940.[50]

To provide a basic understanding of combined-arms principles, the Armored Force used rigid combined-arms organizations in training. New tank-battalion commanders also received charts indicating common tactical situations and suitable responses. These training aids assisted officers unfamiliar with armored units.[51] The measures helped ground new commanders in the fundamentals of armored operations. However, they also established precedents for combat based on fixed organizations and templated responses. They did not prepare commanders to rely on organizational flexibility and innovative thinking to achieve tactical success.

The anomalous role of the regiment further complicated leader development. Since the Army's foundation the regiment had constituted the primary tactical and administrative unit. In the new armored division structure, the regiment possessed no tactical authority. The regimental commander subordinated himself to his parent combat command, but he did not influence task-force composition or activity. Conversely, the combat commands lacked the means to provide supply and administrative support to their subordinate task forces. The regimental headquarters therefore served as a supply conduit between its component battalions and division headquarters. These battalions, however, generally served with different task forces possibly separated by great distances. The regiment thus had to track and supply multiple units operating independent of each other and assigned to organizations over which it had no authority.[52]

The role of the regiment in the armored division's command structure remained unresolved as the formation's organization continued to change. Army Ground Forces also assumed a more active role in determining the optimal composition of the division. General McNair desired a leaner formation more easily controlled by a generic corps headquarters. He worked to reduce the armored division to the smallest size commensurate with its mission. He sought to eliminate from the division those components that then could be temporarily attached from higher commands as needed, and he blocked efforts to incorporate antiaircraft and tank destroyer battalions in the division.[53]

Devers opposed McNair's reduction efforts, and he succeeded in delaying any downsizing of the armored division until after the accumulation of combat experience. Nevertheless, debate over potential changes continued. Devers and McNair

---

[50] Crittenberger, "Unit Commanders' Meeting," p. 3; F. W. von Mellenthin, *Panzer Battles: A Study of the Employment of Armor in the Second World War* (New York: Ballantine Books, 1956), p. 20; Horst Ohrloff, "XXXIX Motorized Corps Operations," in *The Initial Period of War on the Eastern Front, 22 June–August 1941*, ed. David M. Glantz (London: Frank Cass and Co., 1993), p. 168.

[51] For example, see HQ Armd Force, "Tactical Training Aid No. 5: Troop Leading—Separate Tank Battalion," 15 Apr 42, Camp Papers.

[52] Memo, Brig Gen William M. Grimes to CG, 4th Armd Div, sub: Supply Problems, Combat Command, 7 Mar 42, pp. 1–2, Camp Papers; Grimes, "Notes on Combat Team Organization—Technique," pp. 4–5.

[53] Memo, Maj Gen Ernest N. Harmon to Maj Gen Harold R. Bull, Apr 43, Ernest N. Harmon Papers, MHI Archives; Draft Reply, McNair to Devers, 18 Jul 42, p. 5; Palmer, "Reorganization of Ground Troops," pp. 273, 295.

Tunisian terrain

both desired an increase in the ratio of infantry to tanks. McNair preferred to follow German trends by reducing the armored division's tank strength and providing it more riflemen. Devers wanted to expand the motorized divisions, designed to be grouped with armored divisions in armored corps. However, the demise of the armored corps also eliminated support for the motorized division. This formation lacked the combat power of an armored division, but it required the same shipping space for overseas deployment. Hence, those motorized divisions actually formed were reorganized into conventional infantry formations. The latter required less transport tonnage and could attain comparable mobility through the attachment of truck companies.[54]

Combat Operations in North Africa

Before Japan's attack on Pearl Harbor, the U.S. Army deployed the 192d and 194th National Guard Tank Battalions to the Philippines. These battalions fielded 108 M3 Stuart light tanks crewed by a mix of National Guardsmen, reservists, and draftees. Grouped together to form the Provisional Tank Group, they became the first American tank units to enter combat. Following the Japanese invasion of the Philippines, they conducted a series of free-wheeling counterattacks against Japanese tanks and infantry to cover the American withdrawal to Bataan. After destroying their remaining vehicles, the Provisional Tank Group survivors surrendered in April 1942.[55]

---

[54] Palmer, "Reorganization of Ground Troops," pp. 324–26, 337–38; Stanton, *Order of Battle*, p. 11.

[55] Bruce Jacobs, "The Evolution of Tank Units in the Pre-WWII National Guard and the Defense of Bataan," *Military Collector and Historian* XXXVIII, no. 3 (Fall 1986): 126–32.

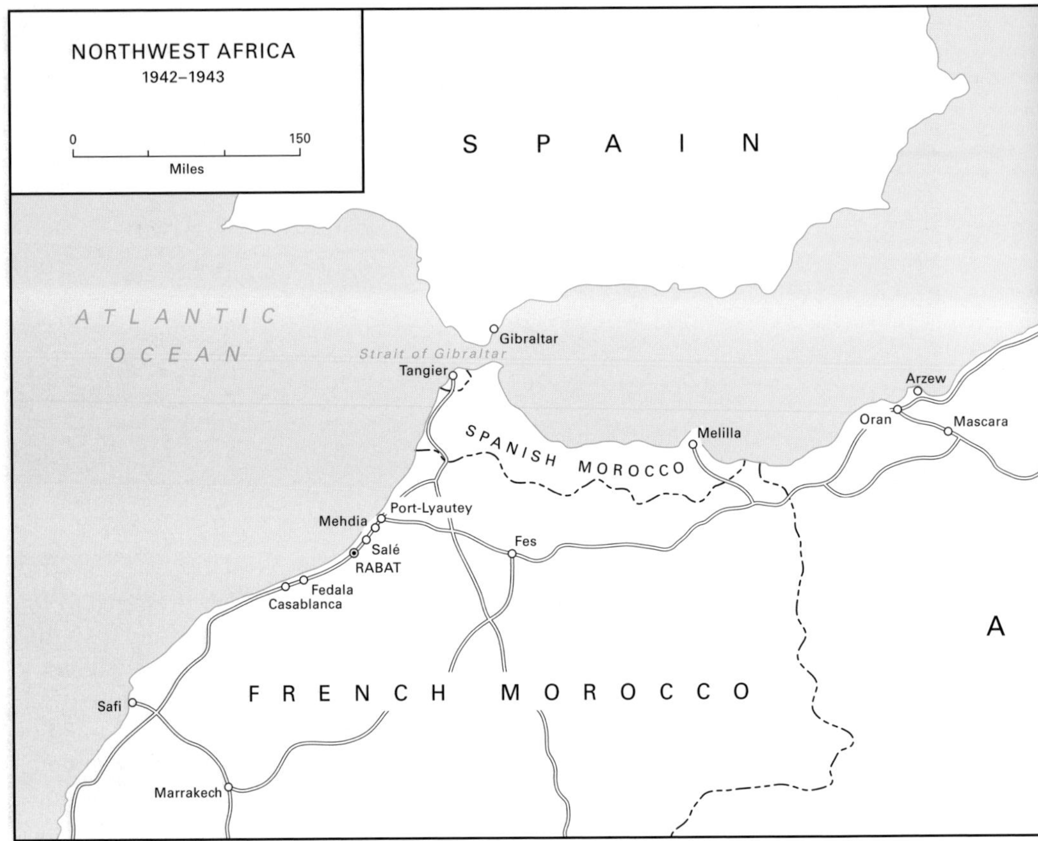

Map 8

The dramatic exploits of the Provisional Tank Group had little influence on Armored Force development, which remained focused on the activation and training of new organizations. The armored divisions did not enter combat until November 1942, when the 1st and 2d Armored Divisions participated in Operation TORCH, the Allied invasion of northwest Africa. After the initial landings, these formations engaged Vichy French forces defending Morocco and Algeria and fought Axis formations in Tunisia. (*Map 8*) The latter fighting pitted American armor against German panzers for the first time.

For much of the campaign the 2d Armored Division played only a limited role, although a detachment from the 67th Armored Regiment served with the British 78th Division. The detachment largely provided vehicle and personnel replacements to the 1st Armored Division, which bore the brunt of the fighting. Ironically, the 1st Armored Division was one of the few armored divisions that had not attended the Desert Training Center. In April 1942 it went to Ireland for use in a possible cross-channel invasion of the European continent. There, its training was limited to small-unit activities on roads. Without any tactical or

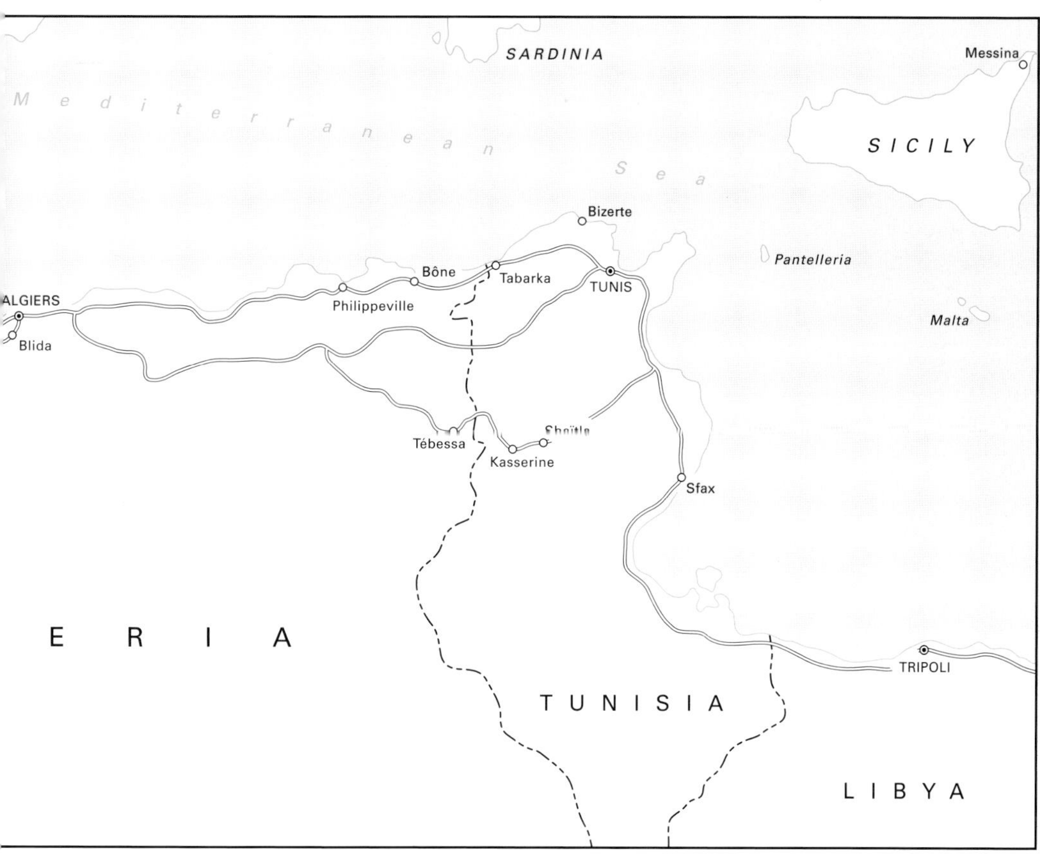

physical acclimation, the 1st Armored Division arrived in North Africa equipped with woolen clothing intended for a European winter.[56]

Landing in Morocco, the division engaged Vichy French forces, including armored units that proved no match for American tanks. The formation moved overland through Morocco and Algeria into Tunisia. By December some elements withdrew to Oran for rehabilitation. The division joined the II Corps, participated in the fighting around Kasserine Pass, and remained at the front until the final surrender of Axis forces in May.[57]

---

[56] "Remarks and Opinions of 1st Armored Division Chief of Staff Col Clarence C. Benson Concerning Operations in North Africa," 28 Dec 42, pp. 6, 8, Item 5611, Reel 375, National Archives Project, GCM (hereafter cited as Benson Remarks); "Conversations Between General Hamilton Howze and Lieutenant Colonel Robert Reed," sec. 2, pp. 45, 47, 52, Senior Officers Debriefing Program, 1972–1973, MHI Archives (hereafter cited as Howze/Reed Conversations); George F. Howe, *Northwest Africa: Seizing the Initiative in the West*, U.S. Army in World War II (Washington, D.C.: U.S. Army Center of Military History, 1957), pp. 332, 546, 576.

[57] Interv with Lt Col John K. Waters, Commanding 1st Bn, 1st Armd Rgt, 1st Armd Div, and Lt Col Hyman Bruss, Commanding 2d Bn, 13th Armd Rgt, 1st Armd Div, 29 Dec 42, pp. 1–2, Item

Throughout these operations, the 1st Armored Division's performance was unspectacular. Continuous corps interference marginalized the role of the division commander and resulted in the formation's dispersal. The division suffered several setbacks at the hands of more-experienced German units. The 1st Armored Division did not spearhead a decisive offensive or seize critical objectives in the enemy's rear area as Armored Force doctrine mandated. Its singular use in an exploitation role occurred only after the Axis defeat became unavoidable. Nevertheless, its combat experience made it the subject of scrutiny in the ongoing debate over the optimal armored division organization.[58]

At first, few changes were recommended. Commanders of both the 1st and 2d Armored Divisions preferred their tank-heavy structures. They believed the British and Germans had weakened their armored formations by reducing the ratio of tanks to infantry. The Armored Force expected the superior number of tanks to assure victory in engagements between American and German armored divisions. Attachments by higher headquarters would provide additional infantry if necessary.[59]

However, the armored division's size posed problems for deployment and tactical operations. It required considerable scarce tonnage to transport overseas. Once in theater, it proved difficult to quickly move overland due to the lack of developed road and rail nets. The formation's prodigious fuel, ammunition, and maintenance requirements necessitated the attachment of additional service units, which in turn further complicated movement.[60]

Each move required careful planning that nevertheless failed to avert large-scale traffic-control problems. These difficulties encouraged recommendations for greater self-sufficiency within the division. The inclusion of a supply battalion offered independence from attached service units, while the addition of military police to the division organization offered a means of preventing traffic jams.[61] Recommended increases in combat power included additional infantry, antiaircraft weapons, and tank destroyers. Commanders considered the related strength requirements to be offset by the division's greater capacity for independent operations.[62]

5611, Reel 375, National Archives Project, GCM (hereafter cited as Waters/Bruss Interv); Howe, *Seizing the Initiative*, p. 576.

[58] Ltr, Maj Gen Ernest N. Harmon to Lt Gen Lesley J. McNair, 23 Mar 44, p. 4, Harmon Papers.

[59] Memo, Harmon to Bull, Apr 43, pp. 1–2.

[60] Benson Remarks, 28 Dec 42, p. 7; Waters/Bruss Interv, 29 Dec 42, p. 8.

[61] Benson Remarks, 28 Dec 42, p. 7; Maj Gen Alvan C. Gillem Jr., "Report of Observations at European Theater of Operations and North African Theater of Operations," 1 Aug 43, pp. 4, 8–9, Xerox no. 2300, National Archives Project, GCM.

[62] Waters/Bruss Interv, 29 Dec 42, p. 2; Interv, Col Robert T. Maraist, 29 Dec 42, p. 2, Item 5611, Reel 375, National Archives Project, GCM; Memo, Col Stanley J. Grogan to Mr. McCloy, sub: Report on Matters Other than Public Relations During North African Trip, February 10–March 17, 1943, 20 Mar 43, p. 9, Item 5612, Reel 375, National Archives Project, GCM; Benson Remarks, 28 Dec 42, p. 7; "Conclusions and Recommendations of Gen. Devers in His Report on His Observations Abroad—December 14, 1942 to January 25, 1943," p. 1, in Ltr, Lt Gen Lesley J. McNair to Maj Gen Andrew D. Bruce, 19 Feb 43, Xerox 2363, National Archives Project, GCM; Gillem, "Report of Observations," 1 Aug 43, p. 4.

Devers supported the recommended changes to the armored division's organization, but they contradicted AGF reduction efforts. Opinion in North Africa favored Devers, who attempted to use this support to influence McNair's view during the latter's visit to the combat zone. Devers instructed the 1st Armored Division commander: "You and your officers should have a great influence when McNair visits you and I hope that you can convince him that he is on the wrong track when he cuts men and vehicles so thin that the units cannot operate. This is a peacetime trend. We should base all our changes on wartime experience and you all have had that."[63]

While the organizational debate continued, combat operations also revealed command and control problems in the armored division. The creation and employment of combined-arms teams did not suffice. Indiscriminate attachments to regiments and battalions prevailed, leaving some task force commanders with resources insufficient to complete combat missions.[64] The 1st Armored Division blurred the distinction between task force and combat command by creating and deploying five different combat commands. The division's chief of staff observed that "None of the action reported to date have employed Combat Command 'B' as a Combat Command or even in coordinated teamwork between small components of the Combat Command."[65]

The presence of both combat commands and regimental headquarters complicated divisional command. Orders were supposed to be routed through the combat command headquarters and regimental commander, although the latter had no tactical function. In practice the division commander short-circuited the command chain by communicating directly with battalion commanders. The 1st Armored Division's chief of staff concluded, "It would appear desirable to eliminate either the regimental echelon or the combat command echelon to secure increased speed and execution of orders."[66]

The regiment, however, provided administrative and supply services not easily replicated by the combat commands. The latter did not possess the staff, communications, or resources to perform these functions for attached units. The dispersed nature of the 1st Armored Division's operations, however, forced the combat commands to periodically assume these roles. They did so by diverting personnel and resources from other division components—including the regimental headquarters—and attached units. The effectiveness of the losing organizations suffered, yet the resultant combat-command supply conduit proved fragile and easily overwhelmed by unforeseen situations. During the initial advance into Tunisia, for example, Combat Command B found itself responsible for the supply of all American troops temporarily attached to the British First Army. The immensity of the task required British assistance.[67]

---

[63] Ltr, Lt Gen Jacob L. Devers to Maj Gen Ernest N. Harmon, 16 Apr 43, Harmon Papers.

[64] Col Richard J. Werner, Lt Col Randall R. Wilson, M Sgt Marvin J. Bennett, S Sgt Robert D. Dieterle, S Sgt Roy J. Jefferds Jr., "Observers' Report to the Commanding General, Army Ground Forces, Washington, D.C.," p. 8, in Memo, Lt Col James D. Tanner, sub: Observer Report, 29 Mar 43, Item 5612, Reel 375, National Archives Project, GCM.

[65] Benson Remarks, 28 Dec 42, pp. 4, 7.

[66] Ibid., p. 7.

[67] Ibid., pp. 1, 7; Waters/Bruss Interv, 29 Dec 42, p. 8.

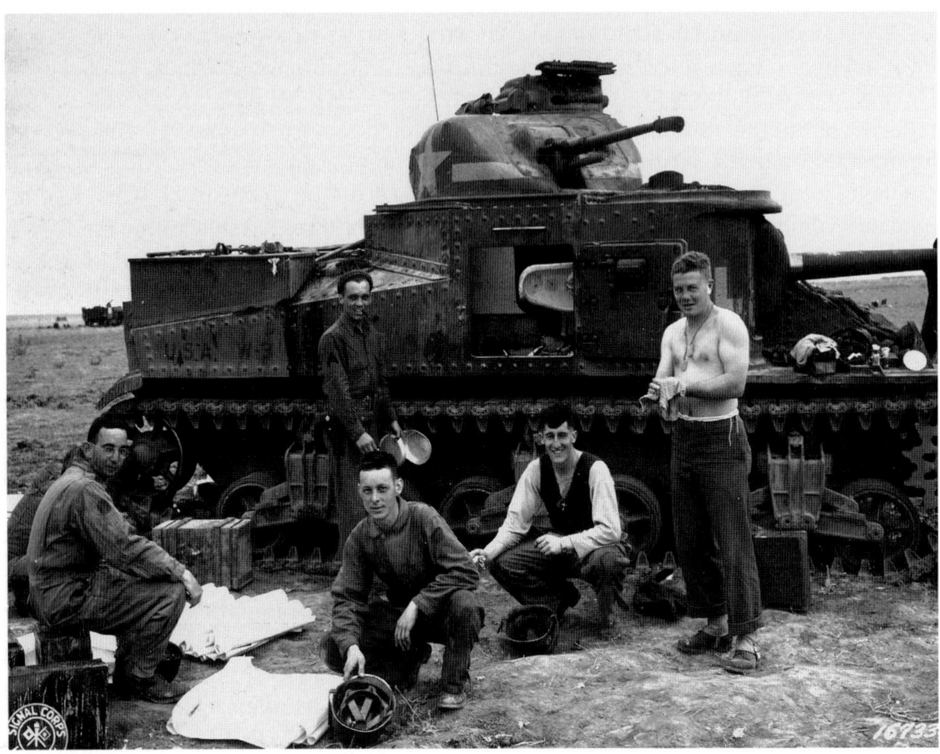

M3 medium tank and crew during pause in operations in North Africa

These problems led armored commanders to propose the battalion as the principal administrative and tactical unit in the division. Tank and infantry battalions often formed the basis of each task force. Providing each battalion with its own supply, maintenance, and reconnaissance elements improved combat effectiveness and transferred responsibility for supply and maintenance considerations from the regiment to the battalion. This self-sufficiency at the battalion level allowed the combat commands to retain their tactical orientation and obviated the need for a regimental command echelon.[68]

The Armored Division's New Look

Combat operations did not end McNair's determination to downsize the armored division. He disagreed with the permanent increases to the division recommended

[68] Lt Col William B. Kern, Capt Thomas W. Hoban, and Capt Walter R. Geyer, "Proceedings of a Board of Officers for Recommendations for Changes and Improvements in Organization, Tactics, and Equipment," 21 Dec 42, pp. 4–5, in P. M. Robinett, "CCB, 1st Armored Division: North African Operations," Paul M. Robinett Collection, Manuscript Collection no. 28, Box 12, GCM; Benson Remarks, 28 Dec 42, p. 5; Memo, Harmon to Bull, Apr 43, p. 2.

by the Armored Force. Instead, he preferred temporary attachments from higher headquarters, despite concerns over the lack of cohesion between organic and temporarily assigned units.[69]

The Armored Force found itself subjected to a two-pronged reduction effort by McNair and the Reduction Board that threatened to emasculate the armored division. The Reduction Board convened between November 1942 and June 1943. Its mission lay in paring the vehicle, equipment, and personnel complements of all Army formations to facilitate overseas deployment and minimize transport requirements. McNair supported the board's efforts, criticizing the accumulation of too many motorized vehicles in the triangular infantry divisions. Indeed, both McNair and General Marshall considered the Army "over-motorized."[70]

Devers managed to delay the formal reorganization of the armored division until after the conclusion of the North African campaign. Then a separate board of officers convened in the North African Theater of Operations to address the armored division's organization. It recommended a further delay, and no reorganization occurred until September 1943.[71] (*See Chart 18.*)

In that month the War Department approved a new armored division organization. The new structure embraced the combat command concept and the recommendations of armored commanders for self-sufficient battalions. The regiment disappeared, resulting in a chain of command that led from the division headquarters to the combat commands to battalions parceled out among task forces. Three Combat Commands existed: A, B, and R. The last had a skeleton staff intended to control only those forces not assigned to Combat Command A or B. In effect, the armored division now included a collection of battalions that could be attached to combat commands to suit changing tactical situations.[72] Aptly described as a "federation of thirteen battalions led by a major general," it consisted of 1 engineer, 1 reconnaissance, 1 maintenance, 1 medical, 3 armored, 3 armored infantry, and 3 field artillery battalions.[73]

The overall size and composition of the armored division largely reflected the minimizing efforts of McNair and the Reduction Board. The personnel strength of the new division fell from 14,620 to 10,936. Similarly, the formation's tank strength fell from six battalions to three and from 390 to 263 tanks. Each tank battalion reconfigured into three medium tank companies, a light tank company, and an assault-gun platoon of six tanks armed with 105-mm. guns. (*See Chart 19.*) The light tanks provided reconnaissance and security, and the assault guns offered direct

---

[69] Memo, Maj Gen Ernest N. Harmon, sub: Notes on Combat Experience During the Tunisian and African Campaigns, n.d., p. 11, Harmon Papers.

[70] Memo, Lt Gen Lesley J. McNair to Lt Gen [Brehon B.] Somervell, sub: Transportation for Motor Maintenance, 21 Apr 42, Item 4769, Reel 310, National Archives Project, GCM; Memo, General George C. Marshall to Lt Gen Lesley J. McNair, 28 Sep 42, Verifax no. 3628, National Archives Project, GCM; Palmer, "Reorganization of Ground Troops," pp. 288–89, 297–99.

[71] Palmer, "Reorganization of Ground Troops," p. 326.

[72] Ltr, Maj Gen Robert W. Grow to Col Barrows, 12 Sep 45, p. 2, Robert W. Grow Papers, MHI Archives.

[73] Palmer, "Reorganization of Ground Troops," pp. 326, 331, 333.

Chart 18–Armored Division, 1943

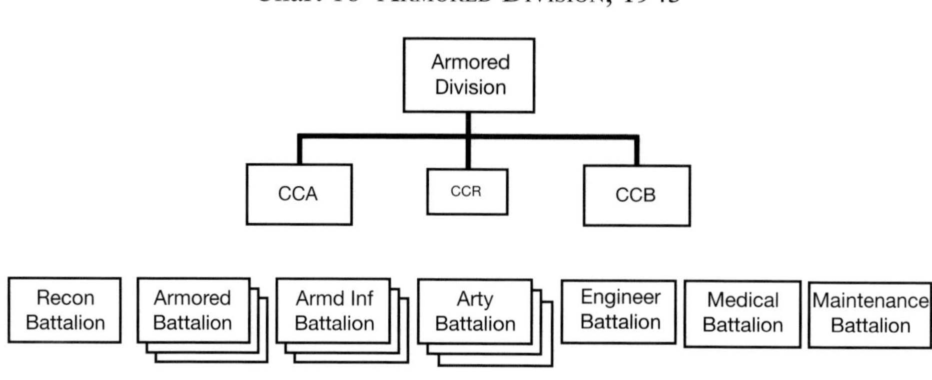

fire support. However, the new armored division included no tank destroyers, no antiaircraft units, and no supply battalion. The engineer battalion also lost its treadway bridge company, and the division's combat service support capability shrank. These special functions were expected to be attached as needed by a controlling corps or army headquarters.[74]

To ensure sufficient corps assets, McNair worked to create a reserve of tank, armored infantry, engineer, armored artillery, and ordnance units. He intended these to either reinforce the armored divisions or provide a replacement pool. However, the Army's available manpower pool proved insufficient to support these extra units, and the concept was abandoned. Several independent armored infantry battalions actually formed, but all but one inactivated in 1943. The pool of independent tank units continued to grow, but their continuous attachments to infantry formations precluded their availability for attachment to armored divisions.[75]

The new armored division organization provided a high degree of flexibility. Its smaller size facilitated deployment, movement, and tactical control. It constituted a radical departure from tradition in its abandonment of the regiment and in its existence as a malleable collection of combat resources. The division possessed the ability to continuously reconfigure itself in response to changing tactical situations. These characteristics suited a vision of mobile warfare in which chaos reigned and front lines remained in flux, but they contradicted the Army's traditional preference for rigid organizations. Moreover, the smaller size of the armored division found little support among armored officers. Devers, for example, considered the new design an exercise in reducing firepower and increasing overhead. He preferred the larger division structure, which he

[74] Ibid.; Stanton, *Order of Battle,* pp. 17–19.
[75] Palmer, "Reorganization of Ground Troops," pp. 324–28.

Chart 19—Armored Division Tank Battalion, 1943

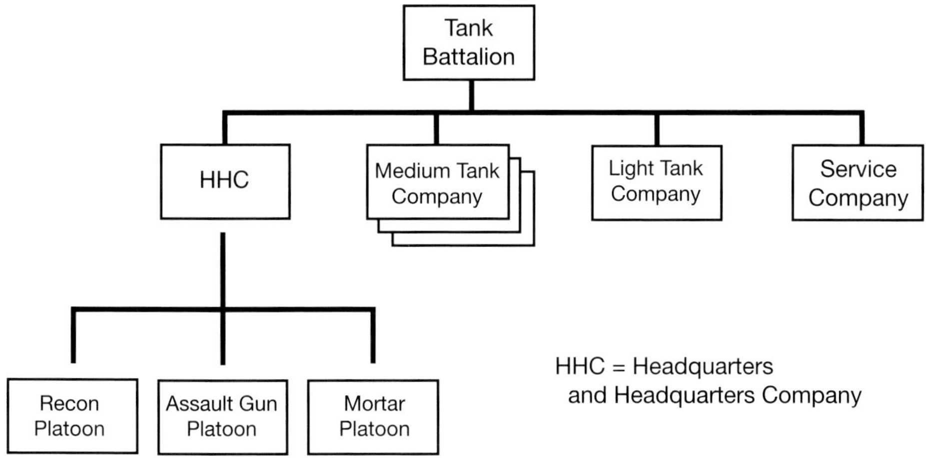

believed superior to any foreign mechanized formation and the equivalent of two of the new armored divisions.[76]

Applying Lessons Learned in North Africa

The Armored Force made a deliberate effort to obtain information about ongoing combat and to apply lessons learned in its own training and doctrine development efforts. Before Operation Torch, the Armored Force benefited from the experiences of officers sent to observe the British Eighth Army in North Africa. These officers disseminated their findings in lectures, reports, and instructional tasks. The Armored Force also sent a team of officers and enlisted men to serve with British tank units in North Africa and obtain firsthand combat experience. Upon their return to the United States the mission members assumed training responsibilities at Fort Knox.[77]

Operation Torch subsequently provided a wealth of combat experience that the Army mined to identify deficiencies and improve training. The most prevalent criticism of American troops fighting in North Africa concerned leadership problems and tactical errors. The latter were attributed to inexperience and the brevity of training programs. One Army Ground Forces observer considered it "impossible to train

[76] Devers Notebook, 2 Nov 42.

[77] Ltr, Maj Gen Jacob L. Devers to General of the Army George C. Marshall, 27 Jun 42, Marshall Papers; G–2 Sec, Armd Force, "G–2 Notes No. 29: Consolidated Reports by American Personnel in Combat in the Middle East," 5 Nov 42, pp. 1–3, Armored Force G–2 Bulls, vol. 2, Tactics and Operations, 1941–1943, MHI Archives; George B. Jarrett, "Middle East 1942," n.d., p. 140, George B. Jarrett Papers, MHI Archives.

German armored column on the move in North Africa

troops adequately for combat in eight months, especially such highly complicated branches as tank destroyers or armored units."[78]

Leadership problems further reduced the operational effectiveness of the armored divisions. The II Corps and 1st Armored Division commanders lacked experience controlling armored formations, particularly within the new corps structure. Consequently, the 1st Armored Division received orders that disregarded time and space considerations. Mismanagement of the 1st Armored Division resulted, and the formation found itself operating less as a division than as a collection of smaller units. Combat leadership improved with the appointment of Maj. Gen. Ernest N. Harmon and Lt. Gen. George S. Patton Jr. to command the 1st Armored Division and its parent II Corps.[79]

Within the armored divisions, inexperienced unit commanders struggled to lead their men under fire. Prior to Operation Torch, Armored Force observers of British operations concluded that American commissioned and noncommissioned officers lacked sufficient practice in solving tactical problems and leading troops. In Tunisia, they often needed additional planning time to rehearse their roles in upcoming

[78] Maj Allerton Cushman, Obsvr Rpt, p. 1, attached to Memo, Lt Col James D. Tanner, sub: Observer Report, 29 Mar 43, Item 5612, Reel 375, National Archives Project, GCM.

[79] Memo, Grogan to McCloy, 20 Mar 43, p. 3; Werner et al., "Observers' Report to the Commanding General, Army Ground Forces," p. 9; Gillem, "Report of Observations at European Theater of Operations and North African Theater of Operations," 1 Aug 43, p. 3. Previously, Maj. Gen. Lloyd R. Fredendall had commanded the II Corps and Maj. Gen. Orlando Ward the 1st Armored Division.

operations, but senior leaders ignored this need. The inexperience of many noncommissioned officers made them ill equipped to assume command responsibility in an emergency. Consequently, Devers began rotating combat-experienced personnel to the Armored Force School and Replacement Training Center as instructors.[80]

Inexperience led to numerous tactical mistakes, but most observers considered Armored Force doctrine sound. Unfortunately, American troops often failed to read their field manuals and apply the tactical principles learned stateside. Instead, they relearned the same principles in combat through trial and error and at a cost in lives and materiel.[81]

Errors made during maneuvers recurred in battle. Armored units ignored the use of concealment and deception. They routinely conducted frontal assaults rather than employ flanking maneuvers. They also failed to effectively coordinate the action of infantry, artillery, and tanks. Tank crews demonstrated a propensity for rapid, wild fire that rapidly exhausted ammunition and gave away their location with little effect on the enemy.[82] Neglect of fire and movement principles led one 1st Armored Division officer to conclude: "These matters have been drilled into our troops repeatedly for 2 years but apparently it takes enemy bullets to make this lesson stick."[83] The absence of effective combined-arms action continued to plague armored forces during subsequent fighting in Sicily and Italy.[84]

Too often armored units routinely employed the same templated attack plans practiced in training. Repeated use of the same tactics ensured their comprehension by the Germans. They responded with double envelopment counterattacks that disrupted the advance of American troops and overtaxed local reserves.[85]

Ineffective reconnaissance also undermined tactical effectiveness. Failure to identify enemy dispositions, probe for weaknesses, and reconnoiter march routes mirrored similar mistakes made during maneuvers in 1941. Armored units advanced blindly until they encountered the enemy. Other tactical movements occurred with a similar absence of information and situational awareness. For example, in December

---

[80] G–2 Sec, Armd Force, "G–2 Notes No. 29," 5 Nov 42, pp. 1–3; Ltr, Lt Gen Jacob L. Devers to Gen George C. Marshall, 1 Mar 43, Item 4679, Verifax no. 3353, National Archives Project, GCM; Conf with Maj Gen Orlando W. Ward, 1 Mar 43, in Memo, Brig Gen Lowell W. Rooks to War Department (WD) Opns Div, 21 Mar 43, Item 5612, Reel 375, National Archives Project, GCM; Conf with 1st Lt Herbert F. Hillenmeyer, 1 Mar 43, p. 7, in Memo, Rooks to WD Opns Div, 21 Mar 43 (hereafter cited as Hillenmeyer Conf); Obsvr Rpt of Maj Gen C. P. Hall, p. 8, in Memo, Capt R. J. Delacroix, sub: Report of Visit to the North African Theatre of Operations, 7 May 43, Item 5612, Reel 375, National Archives Project, GCM.

[81] Benson Remarks, 28 Dec 42, pp. 5–6; Maraist Interv, 29 Dec 42, p. 1; Werner et al., "Observers' Report to the Commanding General, Army Ground Forces," p. 8; Hall, Obsvr Rpt, p. 7; Cushman, Obsvr Rpt, p. 3; Ltr, Maj Gen Omar N. Bradley to General of the Army George C. Marshall, 29 May 43, Marshall Papers; Gillem, "Report of Observations at European Theater of Operations and North African Theater of Operations," 1 Aug 43, p. 3; Ltr, Harmon to McNair, 23 Mar 44.

[82] Waters/Bruss Interv, 29 Dec 42, p. 4; Memo, Lt Col J. R. Dryden, sub: Notes on Recent Fighting in Tunisia, 27 Jan 43, Camp Papers, MHI Archives; Memo, Capt Joseph B. Cohn to Brig Gen Thomas J. Camp, sub: Tunisian Campaign Observations, 23 Aug 43, p. 1, Camp Papers.

[83] Benson Remarks, 28 Dec 42, p. 6.

[84] Memo, Harmon, n.d., p. 3.

[85] Hillenmeyer Conf, 1 Mar 43, p. 8.

1942 Combat Command B endeavored to retreat from fighting near Medjez el Bab without first surveying its withdrawal route. The force became mired in mud and lost 18 tanks, 132 other vehicles, and 41 guns.[86]

Reconnaissance failures derived in part from the lack of combat power and survivability associated with maneuver battalion reconnaissance platoons. Armored battalions relied on a platoon configuration that on paper included 22 men, 1 halftrack, 4 jeeps, and 2 motorcycles. Actual organizations in the field sometimes differed. In the 1st Armored Division, the reconnaissance platoon of the 1st Battalion, 1st Armored Regiment, for example, possessed only four jeeps and four motorcycles. Whatever the platoon's actual composition, jeep-mounted scouts constituted the core of the parent battalion's reconnaissance capability. They did not possess the ability to fight for information and proved vulnerable to nearly every weapon on the battlefield. Lacking significant armament, they were expected to rely on stealth for survivability; but they fared badly when confronted by German combined-arms counterreconnaissance teams. The attachment of tanks to recon teams improved their survivability but at the expense of the parent armored battalion's combat power. The redesign of the armored division altered the reconnaissance platoon through the removal of its motorcycles and the addition of another jeep. This change provided no significant improvement to the platoon's combat power or survivability.[87]

Without effective reconnaissance screens, armored units blundered into contact with enemy forces. Too often they did so at high speed, eager to enter combat. Such blind charges proved even less successful in North Africa than they had in maneuvers. Massive dust clouds heralded the presence and intent of all rapidly moving vehicles. Moreover, the combination of inadequate reconnaissance and overeager tank units increased American armor's vulnerability to German antitank traps. The Germans routinely deployed antitank guns in carefully concealed weapons pits that left only their gun barrels exposed. The crossfire from these emplacements created a killing zone for American tanks. Such positions often included an 88-mm. gun, considered capable of disrupting an attack if undiscovered and the equal of any four tanks.[88]

The Germans also employed decoy vehicles to tempt American tanks into pursuit. Too often they succeeded. Expecting an easy victory, the pursuing tanks suddenly found themselves drawn into an ambush. Engaged from multiple directions at short range by antitank guns, the American tanks also discovered previously

---

[86] Lt Col William S. Myrick Jr., Obsvr Rpt, 27 Jan 43, p. 20, AGF, Obsvr Board, Report of Observers, Mediterranean Theater of Operations, MHI Archives; Howe, *Seizing the Initiative*, p. 332.

[87] Waters/Bruss Interv, 29 Dec 42, p. 6; Gillem, "Report of Observations at European Theater of Operations and North African Theater of Operations," 1 Aug 43, p. 5; Maj Craig S. Harju, "White Paper—A Study of the Maneuver Battalion Reconnaissance or Scout Platoon," Fort Knox, Ky., U.S. Army Armor School, 1989, pp. 6–8, Rpt no. AD–A214 798, Defense Technical Information Center.

[88] Hillenmeyer Conf, 1 Mar 43, p. 6; Conf with Lt Col Louis V. Hightower, 1 Mar 43, p. 2, in Memo, Rooks to WD Opns Div, 21 Mar 43 (hereafter cited as Hightower Conf); Second Conf with Lt Col Louis V. Hightower, 1 Mar 43, p. 2, in Memo, Rooks to WD Opns Div, 21 Mar 43 (hereafter cited as Second Hightower Conf); Memo, Cohn to Camp, 23 Aug 43, p. 1.

unseen German armor advancing on their flanks. These encounters normally resulted in the loss of American tanks and crews.[89]

Awareness of similar tactics employed previously against the British did not diminish their efficacy against Americans. The Armored Force generally disparaged British armored tactics and ignored the lessons of their ally's accumulated combat experience. American officers considered their British counterparts inferior in ability, a viewpoint also reflected in Army-wide criticism of the British Army and its doctrine. Consequently, American soldiers failed to benefit fully from British combat experiences gained since 1940.[90]

Tank and crew of the 1st Armored Division in North Africa

The British, for example, learned to keep unarmored, wheeled service vehicles away from the front lines and did not allow them to move in dense masses in the rear areas. American forces ignored these basic protective measures. Kitchen trucks endeavored to deliver hot meals to forward combat positions despite their vulnerability and the likelihood of drawing fire. Similarly, combat personnel tended to disembark from transport trucks within full view and small-arms range of German positions. In the rear, long columns of trucks moved along the few available roads in daylight, inviting aerial attack. Similar practices had been condemned in the 1941 maneuvers by observers who prophesied the unnecessary loss of life and vehicles that actually resulted in North Africa.[91]

The repetition of tactical errors led Maj. Gen. Omar N. Bradley, who assumed command of the II Corps in April 1943, to attribute them to a maneuver-induced mindset. Bradley observed a wide cross section of American troops, concluding:

> It seems to me that our large scale maneuvers are partially responsible for creating one frame of mind which must be corrected by special methods. In maneuvers, when two forces meet, the umpires invariably decide that the smaller force must withdraw, or if greatly outnumbered, it must surrender. And while the umpires deliberate, the men simply stand or sit about idly. No means are provided for giving proportionate weight to the many intangibles of warfare, such as morale, training, leadership, conditioning. There have

[89] Hightower Conf, 1 Mar 43, p. 2.

[90] Ibid.; Memo, Grogan to McCloy, 20 Mar 43, p. 13; Maj Gen Willis D. Crittenberger, "Notes on Unit Commanders' Meeting," 16 May 42, p. 12, Crittenberger Papers; Ltr, Maj Gen Ernest N. Harmon to Lt Gen Lesley J. McNair, 23 Mar 44.

[91] Memo, Dryden, sub: Notes on Recent Fighting in Tunisia, 27 Jan 43.

been cases here where, in my opinion, forces have surrendered unnecessarily. According to the umpire rules, they were probably justified.[92]

Nevertheless, the accumulation of combat experience did lead to improvements in the training and efficiency of American troops. The perils of the battlefield improved the discipline of men who had been ambivalent toward stateside training exercises.[93] The first encounters with German forces demonstrated the tactical deficiencies of American troops, but most officers shared the conclusion that "Our troops will fight better in the future, as a result of the beating they took initially."[94]

Combat did yield useful lessons. A new method of coordination between tanks and artillery emerged in which the latter placed air bursts above enemy positions on which the tanks were advancing. Night operations by armored units were no longer discouraged. Instead, they were considered a viable means of achieving surprise, and training guidelines were developed for use stateside. Combat experience also encouraged efforts to improve the reality of logistical considerations in training exercises by introducing conditions that deliberately fouled the normal flow of supplies and necessitated improvisation.[95]

Armored Materiel

Despite shortcomings in tactical ability, American armored personnel participating in Operation TORCH universally expressed confidence in their tanks.[96] The light companies of the 1st and 2d Armored Divisions were equipped with the M3 Stuart light tank. This vehicle first entered combat with the British Eighth Army in November 1941. The British praised its reliability and maintenance simplicity, unofficially dubbing it Honey. Its engine could be replaced much faster than those of British-built tanks, and the use of rubber track blocks greatly extended track life.[97]

American crews disliked the M3's small main armament and high silhouette. Its 37-mm. gun proved only marginally effective against German armor. Consequently, tank crews employed hit-and-run tactics for flank and rear shots against the more heavily armored German tanks. By March 1943 the better-protected M5 light tank replaced the M3. However, light tank usage had passed its zenith.[98]

---

[92] Ltr, Bradley to Marshall, 29 May 43.

[93] Werner et al., "Observers' Report to the Commanding General, Army Ground Forces," p. 8.

[94] Memo, Grogan to McCloy, 20 Mar 43, p. 3.

[95] Hillenmeyer Conf, 1 Mar 43, p. 7; Hall, Obsvr Rpt, p. 6; Gillem, "Report of Observations at European Theater of Operations and North African Theater of Operations," 1 Aug 43, p. 5.

[96] Memo, Grogan to McCloy, 20 Mar 43, p. 2.

[97] George B. Jarrett, "Ordnance: The Theme Song of Military History," p. 49, Jarrett Papers.

[98] Benson Remarks, 28 Dec 42, p. 4; Waters/Bruss Interv, 29 Dec 42, p. 2; Memo, Grogan to McCloy, 20 Mar 43, p. 9.

The 1st and 2d Armored Divisions both fielded the M3 Lee medium tank.[99] It first entered service with the British Eighth Army, but its combat debut featured the absence of appropriate fuses for its 75-mm. ammunition and the tendency of its engines to overheat after only twenty-five hours. Correction of these problems occurred before the tank entered combat with American armored formations. The vehicle's radio, however, remained unreliable. Frequency shifts followed the discharge of the 75-mm. gun or whenever the tank sustained a hit. The difficulty of charging batteries and securing spare parts further stymied crews trying to maintain radio operability. Nevertheless, American crews expressed confidence in the vehicle until they realized its obsolescence in comparison with other tanks.[100]

The M3's principal armament included a turret-mounted 37-mm. antitank gun and a 75-mm. gun mounted in the hull. The latter constituted a secondary weapon for supporting fire. It possessed a low muzzle velocity and short range; its slow, limited traverse made engagement of moving targets nearly impossible. Nevertheless, crews often tried to use it as an antitank weapon due to the poor armor penetration of the 37-mm. gun. An Ordnance Department team in Egypt found the 75-mm. gun capable of penetrating the frontal armor of most tanks encountered but at a maximum range of only four hundred yards. In combat, German tanks had destroyed M3s at ranges up to eleven hundred yards.[101]

The condition of the M3 tanks in the 1st Armored Division aggravated the problems. These vehicles suffered from extensive wear before Operation TORCH, and combat operations quickly eroded the pool of operational M3s. By May 1943 Harmon, the division commander, wanted to restrict their use to training, serving as gunnery targets, or clearing minefields. He considered it "criminal to send an armored division into battle where it will be heavily engaged against anti-tank guns and tanks with the M-3 tank." The morale of M3-equipped tank units was not helped by awareness that British units were outfitted with newer, American-built tanks.[102]

The M3, however, constituted a stopgap vehicle pending development and fielding of a new tank with a turret-mounted 75-mm. gun. This platform emerged as the M4 Sherman medium tank. The M4 began to reach combat units before Operation TORCH and gradually replaced the M3 in the North African Theater of Operations. The M4's 75-mm. gun fired armor-piercing, high-explosive, or smoke ammunition. In September 1942 the tank received its baptism of fire with British forces, but the issuance of the wrong fuses for its high-explosive ammunition marred its debut. In American service the tank provided reliability and high mobility and carried heavier armor than the M3. Crews considered it one of the best tanks on the battlefield.[103]

---

[99] In British service, the M3 medium tank was known as the Grant and distinguishable from the Lee by its reduced turret height.

[100] Waters/Bruss Interv, 29 Dec 42, pp. 5–6; Jarrett, "Middle East 1942," pp. 55–56, 90.

[101] Memo, Maj Gen Ernest N. Harmon to CG, Allied Force, sub: Modern Equipment for the 1st Armored Division, 21 May 43, Harmon Papers; Jarrett, "Middle East 1942," p. 62.

[102] Memo, Harmon to CG, Allied Force, 21 May 43.

[103] "Conclusions and Recommendations of Gen. Devers in His Report on His Observations Abroad—December 14, 1942 to January 25, 1943," in Ltr, McNair to Bruce, 19 Feb 43; Memo,

Elements of the 10th Armored Division during training in 1943

It was not without problems, however. Its height generated a high silhouette, made ship transport difficult, and precluded negotiation of railroad tunnels. Initial models suffered from defective turret armor unusually susceptible to penetration. The most serious criticism concerned the tank's tendency to burst into flames when hit. Crews attributed this flammability to the gasoline engines, which they believed more prone to fire than diesel.[104] Testing at Fort Knox traced the cause to German antitank munitions fused to explode after armor penetration. In many cases the round struck the turret, penetrated, and exploded inside where most of the tank's ammunition was stored. The resultant explosion killed the crew and left a burned-out wreck with no salvage value.[105]

American tank optics also proved inferior to those of the Germans. The latter were able to engage targets more accurately at longer ranges. A number of American tanks in North Africa, however, were equipped with gyrostabilizers, devices intended to improve target acquisition and the accuracy of main-gun fire while

Grogan to McCloy, 20 Mar 43, p. 9; Second Hightower Conf, 1 Mar 43, p. 2; Jarrett, "Middle East 1942," pp. 167–69.

[104] Second Hightower Conf, 1 Mar 43, p. 2; Memo, Grogan to McCloy, 20 Mar 43, p. 9; "Recap of Pertinent Issues from Interviews with Personnel of the 1st Armored Division, March 1, 1943," in Memo, Rooks to WD Opns Div, 21 Mar 43; Conf with Sgt Baskem Bennett, p. 9, in Memo, Rooks to WD Opns Div, 21 Mar 43; Ltr, Lt Gen Jacob L. Devers to Maj Gen Ernest N. Harmon, 16 Apr 43, Harmon Papers.

[105] Gillem, "Report of Observations at European Theater of Operations and North African Theater of Operations," 1 Aug 43, p. 8; Jarrett, "Middle East 1942," p. 195.

moving. The potential value of this capability was offset by the lack of training in the device's operation. Crews exhibited little faith in the gyrostabilizer and disliked the additional maintenance associated with it. They continued to stop moving before engaging targets.[106]

Among the other combat vehicles in the armored divisions, the self-propelled artillery platforms proved the most popular. American troops employed a 75-mm. howitzer mounted on a halftrack and a 105-mm. gun carried on a fully tracked mount. Devers considered the latter the best light artillery available; and the ability of both weapons to keep pace with tanks and provide rapid, indirect fire on demand made them highly valuable.[107]

The halftrack became the most controversial combat vehicle. Designed as an armored troop carrier, it came to be used in many other roles. In Tunisia, it was found to lack sufficient mobility in mountainous regions. It frequently threw its tracks and became immobilized. Its armor provided only minimal protection but gave its passengers a false sense of security. Devers considered it ineffective as a troop carrier.[108] When it was used as an ambulance, enemy gunners could not distinguish it from combat versions and it garnered the reputation as a "man killer on the road."[109]

Sustaining Combat Capability

To retain combat effectiveness American armored units relied on the constant flow of parts, replacement vehicles, and maintenance services from rear-area installations to the battle zone. The forward thrust of this system sought to prevent maintenance from interfering with combat operations. Combat units performed only minor repairs, leaving more seriously damaged vehicles for rear-echelon maintenance crews.

The greater reliability of American vehicles over their British counterparts aided implementation of this scheme, but it did not eliminate the need for large reserves of spare parts, tools, and replacement vehicles. In North Africa and Italy, shortages of critical parts resulted in additional vehicle losses. Combat units reacted by cannibalizing damaged tanks before resigning them to rear-echelon maintenance. These vehicles then required extensive rebuilding and repair that greatly prolonged their absence from active operations.[110]

---

[106] Benson Remarks, 28 Dec 42, p. 5; Waters/Bruss Interv, 29 Dec 42, p. 5; Hillenmeyer Conf, 1 Mar 43, p. 7; Second Hightower Conf, 1 Mar 43, p. 1; Jarrett, "Middle East 1942," pp. 170–71; Constance McLaughlin Green, Harry C. Thomson, and Peter C. Roots, *The Ordnance Department: Planning Munitions for War*, U.S. Army in World War II (Washington, D.C.: U.S. Army Center of Military History, 1955), pp. 342–43.

[107] Benson Remarks, 28 Dec 42, p. 8; "Conclusions and Recommendations of Gen. Devers," p. 1; Second Hightower Conf, 1 Mar 43, pp. 2, 4; Cushman, Obsvr Rpt, p. 3.

[108] Kern, Hoban, and Geyer, "Proceedings of a Board of Officers," 21 Dec 42, p. 3; Hillenmeyer Conf, 1 Mar 43, p. 8; Ltr, Devers to Marshall, 1 Mar 43; Second Hightower Conf, 1 Mar 43, p. 4.

[109] Ltr, Harmon to McNair, 23 Mar 44.

[110] Memo, Maj Gen Ernest N. Harmon to CG, Allied Forces HQ, 23 Jul 43, Harmon Papers; Gillem, "Report of Observations at European Theater of Operations and North African Theater of

Replacement parts, tools, and vehicles for units serving in North Africa had to be shipped from the United States. Unfortunately, the defeat at Kasserine Pass in February 1943 damaged the credibility of armored elements as war-winning instruments and resulted in a presidential order lowering the priority given Armored Force equipment deliveries.[111]

The decline in armored materiel availability in the United States and existing deficiencies in the North African Theater of Operations mandated employing the 2d Armored Division as a replacement pool for the spare parts, vehicle, and personnel needs of the 1st Armored Division. When the 2d Armored Division subsequently participated in the invasion of Sicily, the 1st Armored Division became its vehicle and personnel pool. The inability to simultaneously employ both formations in combat prompted Maj. Gen. Ernest N. Harmon, who commanded the 2d and 1st Armored Divisions in succession, to complain:

> We are having a helluva time over here to put one armored division into battle. It seems it takes two armored divisions to keep one of them going in battle. When the 1st Armored Division was at the front the 2nd Armored Division was required to send replacements for vehicles and all sorts of specialists to help out, and now that the 2nd Armored Division is about to engage and we are in a rest area, we are being bled to death to help the 2nd Armored Division out. I wish the time would soon come when sufficient equipment and personnel would be available in Africa so that both divisions could operate independently without the other as it is very hard to train a division with people and equipment continually being sent away and not knowing when they will get back.[112]

Equipment shortages increased the importance of preventive maintenance by tank crews. The crews found that active operations generated unprecedented repair work but left little time for such tasks. After participating in the initial assault on Oran, the 1st Armored Division marched seven hundred fifty miles because of inadequate rail transport before engaging Axis forces in Tunisia. The overland movement resulted in an additional five hundred hours of engine usage and extensive track wear, necessitating extraordinary maintenance efforts before combat. In Tunisia, divisional elements engaged in continuous operations for up to three hundred hours at a time, suffering losses from enemy action, bogging down, and engine burnout that necessitated a subsequent rehabilitation period.[113]

Operations," 1 Aug 43, p. 8; Student Paper, "Maintenance of Armor in World War II," Armd Sch, Fort Knox, 1950, p. 72; Jarrett, "Middle East 1942," p. 82.

[111] Mildred H. Gillie, *Forging the Thunderbolt: A History of the Development of the Armored Force* (Harrisburg, Pa.: Military Service Publishing Co., 1947), p. 245.

[112] Note, Maj Gen Ernest N. Harmon to Maj Gen Alvan C. Gillem Jr., 14 Jun 43, Harmon Papers.

[113] Benson Remarks, 28 Dec 42, p. 3; Waters/Bruss Interv, 29 Dec 42, p. 8; Myrick, Obsvr Rpt, 27 Jan 43, p. 20.

M4 medium tank landing on Sicily in July 1943

Replacement vehicles became notable for their absence. The 1st Armored Division, following its departure from the United States, received no further vehicle deliveries before Operation TORCH. The division began operations without its full complement of vehicles and secured only limited replacements. Its tanks had been with the division since before its departure from the United States and began to deteriorate before entering combat. Those replacement tanks received lacked vital equipment, necessitating the diversion of scarce spare parts and maintenance personnel to prepare them for active use.[114]

These difficulties increased the importance of recovering disabled tanks from the battlefield. This aspect of armored operations had received little emphasis in Armored Force training. At Operation TORCH's start, American forces possessed no tank transporters or tank recovery vehicles and relied on the unsatisfactory practice of using one or more 10-ton wreckers to tow disabled tanks. Early disparagement of German willingness to recover wrecked tanks during combat changed to emulation as the value of rapid tank recovery became clear to American forces. Recommendations for suitable vehicular equipment soon emerged from North Africa. The 1st Armored Division eventually developed its own method of coordinating the efforts of combat and maintenance personnel to regain damaged tanks at the earliest moment regardless of enemy fire. The practice did not become Armored Force doctrine because critics disagreed with the principle of risking personnel and vehicles to recover a disabled tank.[115]

In addition to the readiness of its vehicles, the combat value of an armored unit derived from its personnel. Although replacement troops proved more accessible than vehicles, they received training as individuals and lacked the cohesion of complete tactical units. The replacement center at Fort Knox trained replacement personnel for the tank and reconnaissance units of the armored divisions. Despite their specialization, these soldiers received unrelated unit assignments. In a visit to North Africa, Chief of the Armored Force General Gillem noted:

> As a result several thousand men who have received specialized training as tanker replacements have been assigned to infantry elements (both foot and

[114] Benson Remarks, 28 Dec 42, pp. 1–2; Myrick, Obsvr Rpt, 27 Jan 43, p. 20.

[115] Benson Remarks, 28 Dec 42, p. 8; Maraist Interv, 29 Dec 42, p. 1; Memo, Col W. T. Sexton to Lt Gen Lesley J. McNair, 12 Feb 43, Item 4795, Verifax no. 3698, National Archives Project, GCM; Memo, Cohn to Camp, 23 Aug 43; Committee no. 26, "Maintenance of Armor in World War II," p. 28.

> armored), to artillery, to motor transport units and to the various services. As a result of this practice, there have been frequent assignments of non-armored trained personnel to tank units although in excess of 20,000 tanker trained replacements were present in the theater. During a visit to the 2d Replacement Depot (Casablanca) it was found that all the armored trained personnel in the depot (1,435 EM [enlisted men]) were set up as armored infantry replacements. None of these had ever received any infantry training.[116]

Air Support

Above the advance of American armored divisions, the Armored Force envisioned large numbers of friendly aircraft providing close support in a manner similar to that of the German *Luftwaffe*, but such coordination proved chimerical in North Africa. In April 1942 the War Department published Field Manual 31–35, *Aviation in Support of Ground Forces*.[117] This manual described the method of tactical air support that had been tested during the autumn 1941 maneuvers. A training memorandum issued in February 1943 provided refinements and together with the field manual constituted the Army's tactical air support doctrine.[118]

An Air Support Command assigned to each field army controlled the operations of all air assets designated by the theater air commander to assist that army. It determined whether and how air support requests should be met. Subordinate to the Air Support Command, an Air Support Control advised divisional or corps-level headquarters concerning air support capabilities, maintained liaison with the aircraft units in question, and operated multiple Air Support Parties. The latter constituted mobile groups of officers who provided the necessary communications for requesting air support and communicating directly with aircraft in the sky. In the armored divisions the combat commands and the reconnaissance battalion normally received an Air Support Party. In addition, an officer designated S–3 (Operations staff officer) Air accompanied each combat headquarters down to the battalion level, coordinating with the divisional staff information regarding air support needs and ongoing missions.[119]

> A combat unit requesting air support followed these steps, though the request might be rejected at any point:
>
> 1. Unit commander initiates request.
> 2. S–3 Air fills out necessary form.
> 3. S–3 Air submits request form to Air Support Party.

[116] Gillem, "Report of Observations," 1 Aug 43, p. 4.

[117] WD, Field Manual (FM) 31–35, *Aviation in Support of Ground Forces*, 1942.

[118] Brig Gen David G. Barr, Training Memo no. 4, sub: Air-Ground Support, 1 Feb 43, Camp Papers; Christopher R. Gabel, *The U.S. Army GHQ Maneuvers of 1941* (Washington, D.C.: U.S. Army Center of Military History, 1991), pp. 180–81.

[119] Barr, Training Memo no. 4, 1 Feb 43, pp. 1–2.

4. Air Support Party passes request to Air Support Control.
5. Air Support Control seeks approval from Air Support Command.
6. Air Support Command determines aerial missions.
7. Orders issued to aircraft formations.[120]

This process permitted the assignment of aerial strength on the basis of prioritized targets. Reflecting the emphasis of the Army Air Forces upon the centralized control of aircraft masses, the process in theory permitted maximum effort to be applied against those targets most important to the ground forces. While safeguarding against the dispersion of aircraft on missions of little yield, it failed to provide air support capable of responding to rapidly changing tactical situations.

The exceptional time lag between request and response led ground troops to consider air support ineffective. Requests for air support too often ignited time-consuming debates concerning their merits. In North Africa and Sicily, two to three hours often elapsed before available aircraft received mission instructions. The flight time to the target exacerbated this delay. Hence, aircraft frequently arrived after their target had departed. In contrast, the Americans observed that German aircraft generally arrived within thirty minutes of contact between opposing ground forces. Continual requests for air support generated few actual missions, reinforcing the sense of abandonment ground troops felt toward their air force.[121]

The tendency of American aircraft to attack their own troops further discouraged faith in air support. Methods of target identification included using an observation plane, contacting friendly ground troops directly by radio, using ground panels, referencing prominent landmarks, firing smoke or high-explosive shells, and even arranging friendly vehicles in a giant arrow pointing at the target. Nevertheless, friendly aircraft appeared unable to distinguish between American and Axis vehicles. In one extreme case, a flight of P–38s nearly destroyed a company of the 701st Tank Destroyer Battalion.[122]

Tank crews proved reluctant to use signal flags and pyrotechnics because they attracted the attention of German antitank guns. Some tank crews preferred not to reveal their position to friendly aircraft lest they become targets. Similarly, poor aircraft identification skills encouraged American units to withhold antiaircraft fire unless attacked. They feared exposing their position and suffering a German aerial attack.[123]

---

[120] Ibid., p. 3.

[121] Waters/Bruss Interv, 29 Dec 42, p. 7; Hillenmeyer Conf, 1 Mar 43, p. 6; Hightower Conf, 1 Mar 43, pp. 2–3; Memo, Brig Gen Albert C. Wedemeyer to CS, sub: Observer's Report, 24 Aug 43, pp. 1–2, Item 4734, Verifax no. 4011, National Archives Project, GCM.

[122] Waters/Bruss Interv, 29 Dec 42, p. 6; Barr, Training Memo no. 4, 1 Feb 43, p. 4; Maj Allerton Cushman, "Final Report to Commanding General, Army Ground Forces on Tank Destroyer Operations in North Africa," 15 Apr 43, pp. 16–18, in Memo, Lt Col J. R. Dryden, sub: Observer Report, 3 May 43, Item 5612, Reel 375, National Archives Project, GCM; Howe, *Seizing the Initiative*, p. 302.

[123] Waters/Bruss Interv, 29 Dec 42, p. 6; Hillenmeyer Conf, 1 Mar 43, p. 8; Hightower Conf, 1 Mar 43, p. 5; "Recap of Pertinent Issues."

Other ground forces preferred to fire at anything that flew.[124] The 1st Armored Division chief of staff observed: "Our vehicles have been attacked by our own planes and our planes have been shot down by our own vehicles. It is extremely difficult under favorable conditions and frequently impossible to identify planes. Our supply company commander has ordered all his men to shoot anything flying overhead the size of a goose."[125]

Aerial reconnaissance was no more effective than tactical air support.[126] This dual failure seemed to confirm the fears of the ground forces that increased administrative autonomy for the Army Air Forces sacrificed their aerial umbrella. Certainly, the North African experience demonstrated the Army's inability to coordinate ground-attack aircraft and armored action. Such affinity could be achieved only by allowing armored divisions at least temporary control over tactical support aircraft. Such control, however, contradicted the Army Air Forces' preference for autonomy and strategic bombing.

Branch Status Resolution

The end of combat operations in North Africa coincided with several changes to the Armored Force. In May 1943 General Devers became commander of the European Theater of Operations responsible for preparing for a cross-channel invasion. General Gillem replaced him as chief of the Armored Force. Devers left an Armored Force that performed many of the functions and responsibilities associated with a separate branch. Alone among the combat arms, its commander retained the designation of chief and commanded all armored units not assigned to field commands. Moreover, Devers' direct communications with the chief of staff and equivalent rank with the Army Ground Forces commander gave him considerable autonomy. An effective public relations office ensured that armored developments and exploits remained highly visible and generated public interest. In addition, the Armored Force maintained a grassroots network throughout the Army via the personnel of other branches assigned to armored formations.[127]

The Armored Force had proven especially effective in rapidly expanding the number of armored divisions available for combat operations. However, as these formations completed their initial training, they were assigned to corps and army commands for further combat preparation. These assignments removed them from Armored Force control. By mid-1943 the number of armored units thus assigned outnumbered those still subordinated to the Armored Force chief. With only one more armored division to be activated, the importance of the Armored Force's tactical control of combat organizations diminished.[128]

---

124 Waters/Bruss Interv, 29 Dec 42, p. 6.
125 Benson Remarks, 28 Dec 42, p. 4.
126 Hightower Conf, 1 Mar 43, p. 2; Cushman, "Final Report," 15 Apr 43, pp. 16–18.
127 Hist Sec, "Armored Force Command and Center," pp. 19, 109.
128 Ibid., p. 109.

M8 howitzer motor carriage training in 1943

In the reorganized Army structure, the Armored Force was an anomaly. Its confusing name suggested parity with the Army Ground Forces, Supply Services, and Air Forces. Consequently, in July the Armored Force was more clearly subordinated to the Army Ground Forces through its redesignation as the Armored Command. Similarly, the chief of the Armored Force became the commanding general of the Armored Command. These nomenclature changes clarified the subordinate status of the armored organization and paralleled the similar establishment of the Antiaircraft, Airborne, and Tank Destroyer Commands.[129]

These changes were more than cosmetic. General Gillem found his influence on armored development limited. Unlike his predecessors, he did not have direct access to General Marshall and therefore could not appeal AGF directives to a higher headquarters as both Chaffee and Devers had repeatedly done. Gillem maintained direct liaison with Army Ground Forces, but the junior status of the Armored Command gave it little influence on decision making. Hence, Gillem's headquarters became smaller and armored training programs underwent modification to make them resemble in structure and organization those provided by other AGF components.[130]

---

[129] Ibid., pp. 108–09; Palmer, "Organization and Training of New Ground Combat Elements," pp. 408–09.

[130] Charles M. Baily, *Faint Praise: American Tanks and Tank Destroyers During World War II* (Hamden, Conn.: Archon Books, 1983), pp. 28–29; Palmer, "Reorganization of Ground Troops," p. 269, and "Organization and Training of New Ground Combat Elements," pp. 408–09.

Similarly, the diminished influence of the Armored Command became evident in organizational and materiel developments. In July the armored corps disappeared in favor of the generic corps concept recommended by Army Ground Forces. In September the AGF-backed reorganization of the armored division occurred, despite widespread opposition from armored commanders. The Army Ground Forces also became the dominant influence on armored materiel development. It provided the Ordnance Department with the requirements for new vehicles and equipment, accepting Armored Command input as mere suggestions.[131]

Tank development suffered as a consequence. Both Devers and Gillem favored tanks carrying heavier armor and armament in lieu of the early war light-tank emphasis. This shift in view reflected battlefield reports and the personal emphasis of both leaders on the importance of tank gunnery. Gillem in particular wanted to mount a 90-mm. gun in a redesigned turret for the M4 medium tank.[132]

McNair opposed these efforts because they derived from a desire to employ American tanks against their German counterparts rather than in an exploitation role. Tank destroyers, not tanks, were expected to engage hostile armor. Therefore tanks did not require additional armor and armament. McNair also preferred to continue mass production of the M4 medium tank rather than incur the production disruption and reduced output associated with a new design. When the Ordnance Department nevertheless undertook the independent development of a heavy tank, McNair tried to block the work. In January 1944 only the intervention of General Marshall allowed the Ordnance Department to continue its efforts. The M26 Pershing heavy tank resulted and entered combat during the war's closing weeks. Significantly, the salvation of this tank program reflected the influence of the Army chief of staff, not the Armored Command.[133]

In February 1944 the Armored Command became the Armored Center, which had even less influence on armored developments. The Armored Center headquarters shrank to a cell of thirty officers within the Replacement and School Command, itself subordinate to Army Ground Forces. The Armored Center principally functioned to inspect armored units, review training literature, and recommend changes in armored tactics, doctrine, and training literature through channels to AGF headquarters. Largely an advisory body, the Armored Center did not control personnel appointments or materiel development or retain any tactical command responsibilities.[134]

Nor did the Armored Center possess any significant training role. It did not administer the Armored School and Replacement Training Center. McNair intended these organizations to be administered by the Armored Center under the Replacement and School Command, but this command chain did not work in practice. The school and replacement training center bypassed the Armored Center, instead reporting

[131] Baily, *Faint Praise*, pp. 29, 76; Palmer, "Reorganization of Ground Troops," p. 268, and "Organization and Training of New Ground Combat Elements," p. 409.

[132] Baily, *Faint Praise*, p. 86; Palmer, "Reorganization of Ground Troops," p. 325.

[133] Green, Thomson, and Roots, *Planning Munitions for War*, pp. 236–37, 284; Baily, *Faint Praise*, pp. 81, 86, 94, 98; Palmer, "Reorganization of Ground Troops," p. 325.

[134] Palmer, "Organization and Training of New Ground Combat Elements," pp. 409–11.

directly to the Replacement and School Command. The Armored Center provided advice and guidance when queried by the training organizations, but it no longer played any dominant role in determining the nature and structure of armored training—even after a change in the flow of correspondence required all reports from the school and replacement training center to pass through the Armored Center.[135]

The diminished role of the Armored Command/Center reflected less a deliberate paring of its influence than the effects of broader organizational changes within the Army Ground Forces. With the support of General Marshall, McNair centralized his authority within the Army Ground Forces and integrated Army doctrine, organization, training, and materiel development within it. The AGF G–3 (Operations and Training) and Requirements Sections symbolized this change. Doctrinal concepts nurtured by the G–3 drove requirements for new materiel, while another AGF component, the Replacement and School Command, bore responsibility for disseminating the doctrine through Army training programs. Similarly, the work of the Requirements Section stemmed from doctrine.[136]

These changes made the Army Ground Forces a central influence on the Army's battlefield effectiveness. Significantly, its actions guided the work of the subordinate commands and centers rather than the reverse. The commands and centers focused expertise and energy into particular areas considered vital to the Army Ground Forces. They tested new weapons, studied emerging organizational concepts, and analyzed doctrine; but they had no controlling authority over these activities. The top-down, centrally guided nature of AGF functions left no room for independent organizations. Hence the subordinate organizations, including the Armored Command/Center, served in a junior capacity that prevented their actions from duplicating or interfering with those of AGF headquarters.

The change from Armored Force to Armored Command and finally to Armored Center eliminated all prospects of an independent armored organization. Instead, armored development and training became streamlined and administered in the same fashion as those of the other combat arms. Following the large-scale expansion of 1942, armored development became more firmly under the direct control of Army Ground Forces. Henceforth, organization, doctrine, and materiel developments bore the imprint of McNair, whose focus lay on streamlined organizations and a balanced force structure. The leveling influence of the administrative reorganizations eliminated the aspirations of the Armored Force and allowed the capabilities of armored elements to be harnessed to those of infantry and artillery.[137]

Evaluating the Armored Wartime Experience

No established mechanism for gathering, evaluating, and applying information on American armor in battle existed at war's start. However, Army Chief of Staff Marshall strongly advocated learning through experience, which included peacetime

---

[135] Hist Sec, "Armored Force Command and Center," pp. 109–10.

[136] Hewes, *Root to McNamara*, pp. 80–82.

[137] Palmer, "Organization and Training of New Ground Combat Elements," pp. 411–17.

training maneuvers. With his encouragement, after-action reports—normally required only for combat actions—began to follow each maneuver. The contents of these reports influenced the field manuals published in 1940–1942. Simultaneously, Marshall supported analysis of foreign combat experiences and incorporation of appropriate lessons into American doctrine. The most tangible evidence of this support was the *Tentative Lessons Bulletin*, later renamed *Information Bulletin*. These publications included information obtained through military intelligence channels and were broadly disseminated throughout the Army.[138]

The March 1942 Army reorganization made the Army Ground Forces responsible for managing and developing the nascent lessons-learned process. Under McNair's leadership, this management remained largely decentralized. The AGF headquarters received data from combat theaters and forwarded it to the subordinate commands and centers for evaluation and application.[139]

To secure the raw data from which to extract lessons, Army Ground Forces relied on observers who deployed either individually or in small teams to every theater and command. In most cases observers were field-grade officers, although general officers were not uncommon. Before leaving the United States, observers were briefed on the developments within the deployment area and current Army concerns. The observers then spent several weeks in theater meeting with commanders and soldiers to gather data on a broad range of activities.[140]

Observers reported their findings directly to AGF headquarters, to which they also submitted after-action reports, command guidance, and training memorandums generated by the formations they visited. Upon completion of their mission, observers imparted their firsthand impressions directly to training organizations. In effect they served as a "nexus between classroom and battlefield, doctrine and experience."[141]

The Operations Division of the War Department General Staff also relied on its own observers. This division served as the principal planning and coordinating agency for the war effort. Its observers, however, tended to interact directly with headquarters and staff elements in combat theaters. Their principal source of information was battle reports compiled by units in the field. These reports also included lessons learned and tactical guidance issued by division, corps, and army headquarters. The Operations Division reviewed this data and disseminated key information in two publications: the *Operations Division Information Bulletin*, which targeted corps and division commanders, and *Combat Lessons*, which provided useful tips to the front-line soldier. Broad dissemination of these publications ensured that their contents were generally available to all headquarters.[142]

In the combat theaters, formation headquarters leveraged their own battle experiences to generate guidance for subordinate commands. This guidance often emerged

[138] Dennis J. Vetock, *Lessons Learned: A History of U.S. Army Lesson Learning* (Carlisle Barracks, Pa.: U.S. Army Military History Institute, 1988), pp. 56–57.

[139] Ibid., pp. 58–59.

[140] Ibid., p. 60.

[141] Ibid.

[142] Ibid., pp. 61–63.

in memorandums and training notes, and it influenced how soldiers fought.[143] This type of field instruction became more prevalent as the war progressed, and its influence reached not only soldiers in subordinate commands, but—through transmission to Army Ground Forces—stateside training facilities as well. In this manner the battlefield experience as understood by the combatants themselves shaped training and doctrine development. Shortly after the war in Europe concluded, a general board convened in Germany to assess the significance of the recently concluded combat operations. The board's purpose lay in conducting a "factual analysis of the strategy, tactics, and administration employed by the United States forces in the European Theater."[144] A series of reports emerged based on the war experience that included recommendations for postwar developments. The board's findings addressed the full spectrum of battle, including armored and mechanized cavalry activities. These findings formed the basis for recommendations on postwar developments.

While the war continued, the Armored Command/Center and the Cavalry School digested and assessed observer data concerning mounted units. They provided recommendations for combat units and directed the application of lessons learned from combat theaters to training, doctrine, and materiel developments. Indeed, the reduction in personnel that accompanied the change from Armored Command to Armored Center left the latter with little capacity to conduct any other type of analysis.

Lessons learned from analysis of combat experiences triggered changes in armored and cavalry organizations, tactics, and training. They replaced the earlier dominant influence of German activities on American armor development. Increasingly, American armored leaders became less interested in how the Germans conducted mounted, mobile warfare and more focused on how to improve the combat effectiveness of their own formations. Consequently, self-analysis of American armor in battle eclipsed the attention previously given to German organization and doctrine, a shift encouraged by the decline of German armor into a largely defensive role.

---

[143] See, for example, HQ 34th Inf Div, "Lessons Learned in Combat, November 7–8, 1942," Sep 44, in "Army Ground Forces Observer Board, Mediterranean Theater of Operations," vol. 4, A–M 89; HQ 2d Armd Div, "Training Notes," 23 Dec 43, in "Army Ground Forces Observer Reports, European Theater of Operations," vol. 1, C–62; HQ First U.S. Army, Memo no. 1, sub: Armored Notes: Lessons from Combat in Normandy, 19 Jun 44, in "Army Ground Forces Observer Reports, European Theater of Operations," vol. 2, C–110; all at MHI Library.

[144] General Board, Study no. 48: "Organization, Equipment, and Tactical Employment of the Armored Division," title page, CMH. The format and organization of this report is typical for the entire range of reports.

12

TANK DESTROYER DEVELOPMENT

Army combat preparations anticipated the battlefield presence of large German armored formations similar to those used to overrun much of Europe and Russia. Therefore, the War Department established a tank destroyer force to nullify the German tank threat. Tank destroyers represented a new concept, and responsibility for their development was thus deliberately separated from the existing combat arms. Unfortunately, the mission and doctrine of the tank destroyer developed largely in isolation from other combat organizations, resulting in misuse and heavy casualties in North Africa. Criticism of the tank destroyer concept followed, but efforts to educate Army leaders and to clarify doctrine only partially succeeded. The diminished size of German tank forces further obscured the tank destroyer's value and spurred efforts to use the weapon for missions other than antitank. By 1944 the tank destroyer force had shrunk, and its continued development was no longer an Army priority.

Building a Tank Destroyer Force, 1941–1942

In November 1941 Col. Andrew D. Bruce, previously head of the War Department Planning Branch and a key figure in the development of the tank destroyer concept, became commander of the new antitank force. He became responsible for the establishment of a tank destroyer tactical and firing center, school, board, and related headquarters. Symbolic of the importance attached to tank destroyers, Bruce reported directly to the War Department. His responsibilities also included the development of tank destroyer doctrine and materiel. The War Department, however, controlled personnel assignments to tank destroyer units through transfers from other branches of service.[1]

Pending selection of a permanent site, Fort George G. Meade, Maryland, became home to the Tank Destroyer Tactical and Firing Center in December. There, Bruce assembled a small staff from the handful of officers and civilians assigned by the

[1] Memorandum, The Adjutant General's Office (TAGO) to Commanding Officer (CO), Tank Destroyer Tactical and Firing Center, sub: Organization of Tank Destroyer Tactical and Firing Center, 27 Nov 41, pp. 2–4, Andrew D. Bruce Papers, U.S. Army Military History Institute (MHI) Archives, Carlisle Barracks, Pa.; Hist Sec, Army Ground Forces (AGF), Study no. 29, "The Tank Destroyer History," 1946, p. 6, U.S. Army Center of Military History, Washington, D.C. (CMH).

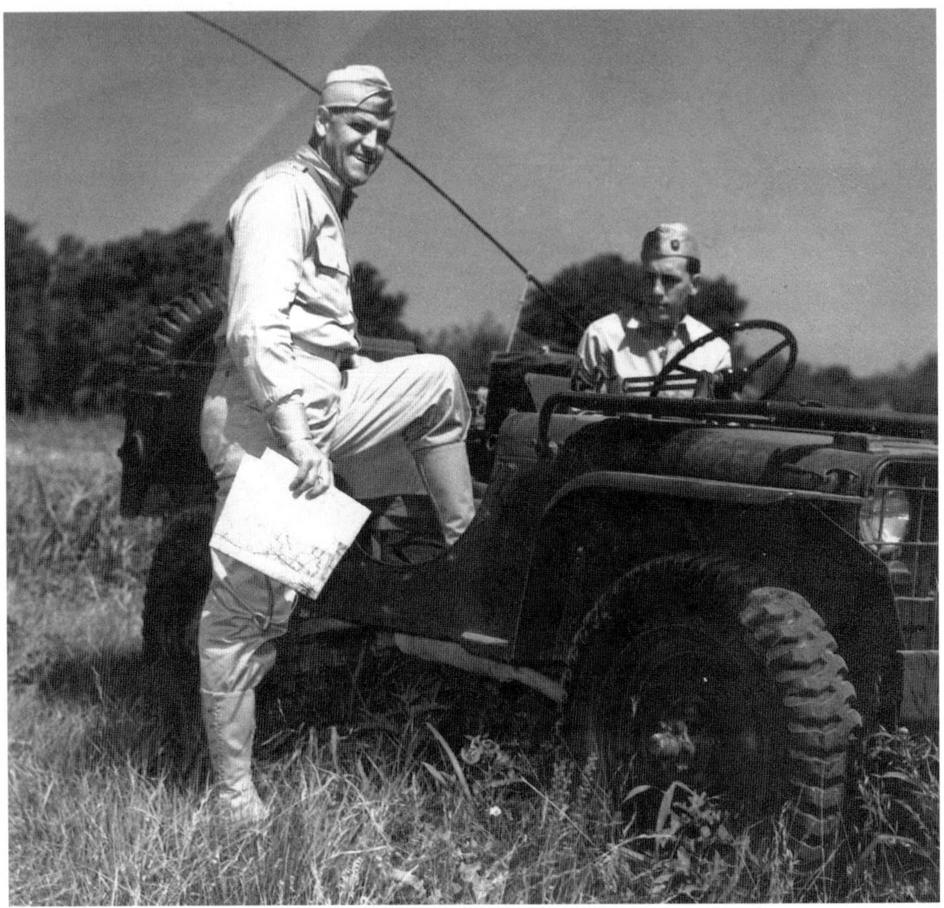

Colonel Bruce

War Department. His initial focus lay in the organization and administration of the new force. He also began development of doctrinal concepts to guide tank destroyer activities and sought to establish liaisons with the Armored Force, Infantry, and Field Artillery. Bruce studied the methods of instruction and doctrinal development used by these arms for application to tank destroyers.[2]

The War Department's initial activation of forty-four tank destroyer battalions underscored the importance of Bruce's preparations. These units were formed primarily from existing antitank units in armored, infantry, cavalry, and field artillery organizations. Starting in January 1942, the tank destroyer force began to receive officers and enlisted personnel. Some two hundred and fifty were

[2] Ltr, Brig Gen Andrew D. Bruce to Brig Gen Mark W. Clark, 3 Mar 42, Bruce Papers; Hist Sec, "Tank Destroyer History," pp. 6–7.

redirected to existing branch schools for additional training as instructors before joining the Tank Destroyer School.[3]

Amid efforts to build a framework for the tank destroyer force, Bruce also sought a permanent location with sufficient space for maneuver and gunnery. He secured War Department approval and funding to establish a new tank destroyer home near Killeen, Texas. The new installation was named Camp Hood to commemorate Civil War Confederate General John Bell Hood and promote positive relations with the local community. The name also associated tank destroyers with the aggressive fighting spirit believed typical of that officer. At first, however, Camp Hood only amounted to open land. The extensive construction and development necessary to house the tank destroyers prevented its occupation for several months.[4]

The tank destroyer force assumed temporary quarters in Temple, Texas, between February and August. During these months the administrative underpinnings of Bruce's command became firmly established. Bruce was promoted to brigadier general in February. In March the reorganization of the Army triggered changes in the status of the tank destroyer force. It became subordinated to Army Ground Forces (AGF) and redesignated the Tank Destroyer Command. The name change paralleled similar developments in armored and antiaircraft development, but the Tank Destroyer Command did not possess any tactical authority. It functioned largely as a training organization. Consequently, in July it became the Tank Destroyer Center aligned under the Replacement and School Command together with the schools of the traditional combat arms.[5]

By then the tank destroyer force included a school and a unit-training center, the latter responsible for preparing individual soldiers and tank destroyer units for combat. An officer candidate school came into existence, and demonstration and service units were assigned to support training activities. The Tank Destroyer Board, informally convened in 1941, was also formally activated, and Bruce's own headquarters rapidly expanded.[6] The continued interest of AGF Commander Lt. Gen. Lesley J. McNair in tank destroyer development provided Bruce with a powerful War Department patron. McNair instructed Bruce to "feel at liberty to phone me or, of course, anyone else here at any time you are perplexed. I personally will give my time without stint if there is anything I can do, since the Tank Destroyer command is very, very high in my scale of priorities."[7]

McNair's partiality toward tank destroyers ensured that their development remained an Army priority. By May 1942 Army Ground Forces included fifty-three

---

[3] Hist Sec, "Tank Destroyer History," pp. 7–8.

[4] Ltr, Maj Gen Andrew D. Bruce to Brig Gen A. O. Gorder, 8 Feb 45, p. 1, Bruce Papers; Charles M. Baily, *Faint Praise: American Tanks and Tank Destroyers During World War II* (Hamden, Conn.: Archon Books, 1983), pp. 16, 18; Hist Sec, "Tank Destroyer History," pp. 10–11.

[5] Robert R. Palmer, "Organization and Training of New Ground Combat Elements," in *The Army Ground Forces: The Organization of Ground Combat Troops*, ed. Kent Roberts Greenfield, Robert R. Palmer, and Bell I. Wiley, U.S. Army in World War II (Washington, D.C.: Department of the Army, Historical Section, 1947), pp. 402–04; Hist Sec, "Tank Destroyer History," p. 13.

[6] Hist Sec, "Tank Destroyer History," pp. 14–16, 20.

[7] Ltr, Lt Gen Lesley J. McNair to Brig Gen Andrew D. Bruce, 10 Jul 42, Bruce Papers.

tank destroyer battalions. However, only one was assigned to the tank destroyer force.[8] The rest remained scattered among various field commands. Most derived from the provisional antitank units created in 1941. They lacked equipment, a central doctrine, and uniform organization; and they reflected the influences of multiple combat arms. This chaotic state of development underscored the importance of the Tank Destroyer Center and its related training program and facilities. Bruce later received the authority to inspect tank destroyer organizations to ensure a degree of uniformity in training, doctrine, and materiel.[9]

The training program for Camp Hood anticipated all tank destroyer units' undergoing training there for two or three months, depending on their initial proficiency. Later a three-month training program became standard. It included 5 weeks of gunnery, 1 week of battle conditioning, and 6 weeks of tactical maneuver and instruction. During this program a unit progressed from mastery of crew skills to unit actions. Tactical exercises focused on those aspects of antitank operations proven deficient in prior maneuvers, including the tracking of enemy armor and the movement of tank destroyers in response to tank threats.[10]

Doctrine and Organization

In June the first tank destroyer battalions began to arrive in Texas for training. By then considerable progress had been made in doctrinal development as well. The debates over antitank operations in 1940–1941 and the maneuvers of 1941 provided the baseline for a codified approach to tank destroyer employment in 1942. The tank destroyers possessed a singular mission: the destruction of enemy tanks. In accomplishing their mission, tank destroyers permitted friendly armor to concentrate on lucrative targets in the enemy's rear area.[11] Bruce used a football analogy to describe the tank destroyer's purpose to an audience of armored soldiers: "Tank destroyers will often run interference and block out the enemy tanks so you can carry the ball."[12]

---

[8] The unit assigned to the tank destroyer force was the 893d Tank Destroyer Battalion. Assigned as a school unit, this battalion previously had been the 93d Antitank Battalion and participated in the 1941 maneuvers. It represented a physical link between the tank destroyers and the maneuver experience and related lessons learned.

[9] Palmer, "Organization and Training of New Ground Combat Elements," pp. 400, 403–04.

[10] "Comments by Lt. Gen. L. J. McNair, G.S.C., 1st Phase, GHQ-directed Maneuvers, Camp Polk, La., September 14–19, 1941," p. 10, HQ AGF, Commanding General (CG), Gen Decimal File, 1940–1944, Record Group (RG) 337, National Archives and Records Administration (NARA); Maj Gen Robert C. Richardson, "Report of VII Army Corps Field Exercises and Maneuvers in Southwestern Arkansas—August 17–28 and Participation of VII Army Corps in Second Army and GHQ Maneuvers August 29–September 30, 1941," p. 4, MHI Archives; Hist Sec, "Tank Destroyer History," pp. 17, 28.

[11] Brig Gen Andrew D. Bruce, "The Tank Destroyer Command," May 42, pp. 7–8, 16, Bruce Papers.

[12] Brig Gen Andrew D. Bruce, Address to 753d Tank Battalion upon the First Anniversary of the Unit's Organization, 1 Jun 42, Bruce Papers.

M6 Gun Motor Carriage

This concept of operations and the related principles of employment found expression in Field Manual 18–5, *Tank Destroyer Field Manual, Organization and Tactics of Tank Destroyer Units*, published in June 1942. This manual was the first effort to describe how tank destroyers operated, and its contents shaped the training program developed for new tank destroyer units. The principal target of all tank destroyer operations lay in the destruction of enemy armor, described as masses of tanks supported by distinct echelons of artillery and infantry. The manual focused tank destroyer action on enemy tanks, mirroring McNair's earlier depictions of the armored threat. However, it offered less clear guidance on how tank destroyers should counter the threat posed by the combined-arms teams routinely employed by the Germans.[13]

Nevertheless, tank destroyer doctrine focused on aggressive operations guided by easily comprehensible principles. Initially deployed behind the front lines, tank destroyer battalions relied on friendly forces and their own reconnaissance companies to identify and track enemy armor. Once the latter committed to an attack, the tank destroyers advanced to preselected firing positions and destroyed the tanks with massed gunfire. The tank destroyers exploited their mobility to respond quickly to tank threats and relocate from one firing position to another once engaged. In this manner they avoided set-piece engagements and reduced their vulnerability to enemy counterfire.[14]

---

[13] U.S. War Department (WD), Field Manual (FM) 18–5, *Tank Destroyer Field Manual, Organization and Tactics of Tank Destroyer Units*, 1942, pp. 1–15; Christopher R. Gabel, *Seek, Strike, and Destroy: U.S. Army Tank Destroyer Doctrine in World War II*, Leavenworth Papers no. 12 (Fort Leavenworth, Kans.: Combat Studies Institute, 1985), pp. 24–25.

[14] WD, FM 18–5, 1942, pp. 7–8, 19–22; Gabel, *Seek, Strike, and Destroy*, p. 25.

Prototype of self-propelled 75-mm. gun, 1941

The success of this concept depended on the ability of tank destroyers to track enemy armor and to displace forward quickly. These conditions in turn depended on the degree of cooperation between tank destroyers and other friendly forces, particularly with respect to communication nets and road space. Bruce sought to maximize cooperation by making tank destroyer battalions a permanent component of each division. This proposal contradicted McNair's preference for pooling specialized assets: it was not implemented. Tank destroyers operated among friendly forces in a quasi-independent status. They included their own reconnaissance and antitank weapons, but they needed support from other units with whom they did not routinely interact.[15]

Worse, tank destroyer doctrine developed largely in isolation. In 1942 tank destroyer units rarely trained with other combat organizations. Nor were the emerging employment principles disseminated throughout the Army. The multiple actions necessary to establish the tank destroyer force focused Bruce's attention inward. Not until November 1942 did the Tank Destroyer Center begin orientation classes at Camp Hood for field commanders and staff officers—too late for those

[15] Gabel, *Seek, Strike, and Destroy*, pp. 26, 30.

units and commanders participating in Operation Torch.[16] Hence the important strides in tank destroyer doctrine and training development remained largely unknown to the rest of the Army.

Bruce approved the tank destroyer motto, "Seek, Strike, Destroy," because it emphasized the importance of locating enemy armor and destroying it by offensive action. Unfortunately, the motto created a false impression of tank destroyer action. Instead of suggesting massed tank destroyers in favorable positions destroying enemy armor through concentrated gunfire, the motto suggested that tank destroyers stalked tanks and engaged them in a melee. Overemphasis on an aggressive fighting spirit, exemplified in the tank destroyer emblem that showed a panther devouring a tank, encouraged such "tank-chasing." Racing about the battlefield seeking enemy armor, however, was not the desired method of tank destroyer employment.[17]

To implement tank destroyer doctrine, unit organization became more streamlined. In December 1941 three types of tank destroyer battalions existed: heavy, self-propelled; light, towed; and light, self-propelled. The heavy battalion included a mix of 75-mm. and 37-mm. antitank guns together with 37-mm. antiaircraft guns. The light battalions both included 37-mm. antitank guns and antiaircraft machine guns. By June 1942 these three organizations had been replaced by a single standard battalion structure (*see Chart 20*). Patterned on the heavy, self-propelled unit, it included a headquarters and headquarters company, a reconnaissance company, three tank destroyer companies, and a medical company. Each tank destroyer company included three platoons of four tank destroyers, a security element, and two mobile antiaircraft guns.[18]

The battalion organization embodied lessons learned since the 1941 maneuvers. Designed as a self-sufficient organization, it incorporated engineering, reconnaissance, supply, and maintenance functions. The security details in each platoon reflected maneuver recommendations to use infantry to protect antitank weapons once deployed. Reliance on self-propelled rather than towed tank destroyers reflected Bruce's desire for high mobility. However, while many post-maneuver recommendations found expression in the tank destroyer organization, efforts to secure aircraft for liaison and reconnaissance failed. Nevertheless, the tank destroyer battalion represented a balanced, self-sufficient organization optimized for its principal role.[19]

The formal adoption of a single battalion organization, coupled with the publication of Field Manual 18–5 and the development of a unit-training program,

---

[16] Hist Sec, "Tank Destroyer History," p. 26.

[17] Ltr, Maj Gen Andrew D. Bruce to Brig Gen Earnest J. Dawley, 13 Jun 44, p. 3, Bruce Papers.

[18] Hist Sec, "Tank Destroyer History," pp. 7, 9–10; Gabel, *Seek, Strike, and Destroy*, pp. 20–21.

[19] Maj Douglas C. McNair, "Check List on Antitank Units; First Phase September 14–19, 1941," 5 Sep 41, p. 5, HQ AGF, General Headquarters (GHQ) G–3 Section; Lt Col Ben M. Sawbridge, "Comments with Respect to 1st AT Group," 20 Sep 41, HQ AGF, GHQ G–3 Section; Lt Col M. J. Conway, "Comments on Second and Third Army Maneuver, 1941, n.d., p. 6, HQ AGF, GHQ G–1 Section; First Army Chief of Staff (CS) Brig Gen Kenneth P. Lord, Training Memo no. 2, sub: Analysis of 1941 Training and Maneuvers, 26 Jan 42, pp. 13–14, HQ AGF, GHQ G–3 Section; all in RG 337, NARA.

Chart 20–Tank Destroyer Battalion, June 1942

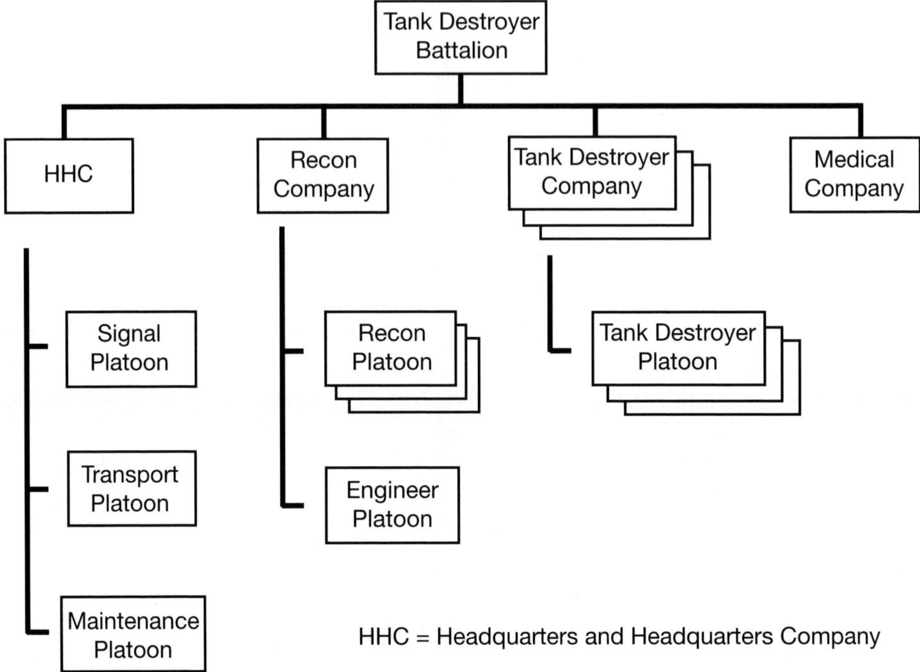

facilitated the rapid expansion of the tank destroyer force. The orders establishing the Tank Destroyer Tactical and Firing Center in November 1941 anticipated the activation of fifty-three tank destroyer battalions. A year later this number had risen to seventy-four, but it remained far short of the over two hundred the Army desired. For each division activated, planners intended to field four tank destroyer battalions apportioned among division, corps, army, and General Headquarters.[20]

The First Tank Destroyers

Implementation of tank destroyer doctrine required a viable tank destroyer. Bruce desired a simple, inexpensive vehicle that mounted a 3-inch gun, possessed high mobility, proved lightweight, and could be easily mass produced. Designing and building such a weapon required time. In the interim the tank destroyer force utilized available expedients, including the M6 and M3 Gun Motor Carriages.

[20] Memo, TAGO to CO, Tank Destroyer Tactical and Firing Ctr, 27 Nov 41, p. 1; Memo, Col Andrew D. Bruce to Assistant Chief of Staff (ACS), G–3, sub: Report on the Maneuver Experiences of Provisional Antitank Battalions (First Army), 21 Jan 42, Item 4327, Reel 287, National Archives Project, George C. Marshall Library (GCM), Lexington, Va.; Ltr, McNair to Bruce, 10 Jul 42.

A 37-mm. antitank gun of the 894th Tank Destroyer Battalion

The former constituted a 37-mm. antitank gun mounted on a ¾-ton truck. Its light armament, lack of armor protection, and limited cross-country mobility adversely affected its combat value. The M3, however, mounted a 75-mm. gun on a halftrack, and it began to equip tank destroyer units in 1942.[21]

Efforts to procure a more effective tank destroyer languished under longstanding friction between General Bruce and Ordnance Department officials. When Bruce became director of the War Department Planning Branch in 1941, the press incorrectly reported his responsibilities to include new-weapons development, a function traditionally performed by the Ordnance Department. Ordnance personnel believed Bruce sought to subvert their materiel development role. Consequently, relations between the two organizations soured. The resultant distrust directly affected tank destroyer development, which remained a primary focus of the Planning Branch until creation of the tank destroyer force. Bruce's successive leadership of each organization ensured that Ordnance distrust of the Planning Branch also extended to the tank destroyer force.[22]

Although Bruce could rely on McNair's support, the Army Ground Forces could not impose its will on the Ordnance Department. The latter's continued development of tanks whose principal characteristics contradicted those established by McNair exemplified its independent nature and led to a growing dispute with Army Ground Forces. Nor did the Ordnance Department prove any more

[21] Hist Sec, "Tank Destroyer History," p. 9; Gabel, *Seek, Strike, and Destroy*, p. 27.
[22] Ltr, Andrew D. Bruce to Wendell Westover, n.d., pp. 1, 3, Bruce Papers.

submissive in the development of tank destroyers. It designed and built prototype models without consulting the Tank Destroyer Center or AGF headquarters. Such a disjointed development process resulted in the construction of weapons—some of which entered mass production—that the Tank Destroyer Center neither desired nor planned.[23]

For example, the Ordnance Department undertook development of a self-propelled 3-inch antiaircraft gun adapted to an antitank role. Mounted on a tractor built by the Cleveland Tractor Company, the weapon became dubbed the Cletrac. Before field-testing the pilot model, the Ordnance Department began building the factories to mass-produce the new weapon. After poor test results, however, the War Department rejected the Cletrac. Those organizations responsible for its development refused to accept the vehicles already produced. McNair sought in vain a command willing to use the Cletracs and in frustration concluded that they would become a dead loss to the Army unless they could be shipped abroad via Lend-Lease.[24]

The Cletrac fiasco did not dissuade the Ordnance Department from continuing development of a self-propelled 3-inch gun. It mounted the gun on a tank chassis and presented the result to the Tank Destroyer Center for evaluation. Bruce's command played little role in the vehicle's design, and it therefore recommended numerous improvements considered necessary by tank destroyer personnel before the vehicle entered mass production. Nevertheless, Bruce supported the production of a small number for test purposes. The Ordnance Department dismissed the Tank Destroyer Center recommendations as too numerous to incorporate. Ordnance personnel considered the existing design satisfactory and implemented its mass production without Bruce's consent.[25]

Known as the M10 Gun Motor Carriage, the resultant vehicle mounted a 3-inch gun in an open-topped turret. The gun's weight resulted in an unbalanced turret that made operation of its manual traverse difficult in sloped terrain. The addition of deadweights to the turret rear alleviated this problem and gave the M10 a distinctive silhouette. The vehicle proved less mobile and too slow to meet Bruce's requirements for a tank destroyer. Nevertheless, it began to equip tank destroyer battalions in the latter half of 1942 and entered combat in March 1943.[26]

Combat Debut

Operation TORCH provided tank destroyers their first combat opportunities. The initial landings in French Morocco and Algeria pitted American and British forces

---

[23] Ibid., p. 5; Ltr, Maj Gen Andrew D. Bruce to Wendell Westover, 24 Nov 43, p. 3, Bruce Papers; Baily, *Faint Praise*, pp. 23–27.

[24] Ltrs, Bruce to Westover, n.d., p. 4, and McNair to Bruce, 10 Jul 42.

[25] Ltr, Bruce to Westover, n.d., pp. 4–5; Baily, *Faint Praise*, pp. 42–44.

[26] Maj Allerton Cushman, "Final Report to Commanding General, Army Ground Forces, on Tank Destroyer Operations in North Africa," 15 Apr 43, p. 19, in Memo, Lt Col J. R. Dryden, sub: Observer Report, 3 May 43, Item 5612, Reel 375, National Archives Project, GCM; George Forty, *United States Tanks of World War II* (New York: Sterling Publishing Co., 1983), pp. 143–45; Steven J. Zaloga, *M10 and M36 Tank Destroyers, 1942–53* (Oxford, U.K.: Osprey Publishing, 2002), pp. 8–11.

against Vichy French defenders. The latter attempted to use their few armored assets in counterattacks on Allied landing areas. At Oran, a platoon of tank destroyers from the 701st Tank Destroyer Battalion helped elements of the 1st Armored Division repel one such effort. Generally, though, combat against the Vichy French offered few opportunities for the tank destroyers to engage hostile armor. Not until they entered Tunisia did they begin to encounter the German panzers that had engendered them. Ironically, however, the first significant mission given to a tank destroyer unit in Tunisia required it to assault a town without infantry or artillery support. Subsequently, tank destroyers earned the praise of those combat units with which they served, resulting in requests for additional tank destroyer units.[27]

Between November 1942 and February 1943, however, only the 601st and 701st Tank Destroyer Battalions actually entered combat. Both units supported the 1st Armored Division, attached to Combat Command B. The 701st Tank Destroyer Battalion bore a special relation to the 1st Armored Division. Personnel from the division formed the original cadre for the tank destroyer battalion. After the latter's activation in December 1941 it had been attached to the 1st Armored Division, which struggled to retain control of the tank destroyer unit throughout the North African campaign. This effort reflected the Armored Force preference for the permanent assignment of tank destroyers to armored divisions.[28]

Tank destroyer units participated in all major engagements with Axis forces in Tunisia, including Kasserine Pass. During this battle the 805th and 894th Tank Destroyer Battalions entered combat, although the latter saw only limited action before withdrawing. The companies of the 805th Tank Destroyer Battalion were dispersed over a broad frontage in violation of tank destroyer doctrine. Unable to mass their fires, the companies suffered defeat in detail and the collective loss of twenty-four self-propelled guns.[29]

In March 1943 tank destroyers supported the American II Corps thrusts toward Gafsa, Maknassy, and El Guettar. During these operations the first units to be trained entirely at Camp Hood and equipped with the M10 Gun Motor Carriage—the 776th and 899th Tank Destroyer Battalions—made their combat debut. At El Guettar, however, the 601st Tank Destroyer Battalion distinguished itself by blunting a German armored attack and destroying thirty tanks. The engagement was characterized as one of the "most magnificent and bloody fights" because the unit lost twenty of its twenty-eight tank destroyers. Nevertheless, the battle represented the first instance in which an entire tank destroyer battalion had been permitted to occupy favorable positions and concentrate its fire on enemy armor. Despite the losses, this action was considered a successful application of tank destroyer doctrine.[30]

---

[27] Remarks of 1st Armd Div CS Col Clarence C. Benson, 28 Dec 42, pp. 2–3, Item 5611, Reel 375, National Archives Project, GCM.

[28] Ibid., p. 2.

[29] Memo, Col William P. Ennis Jr. to ACS, G–1, Brig Gen Ben M. Sawbridge, sub: 805th Tank Destroyer Battalion, 17 Mar 43, Bruce Papers; Cushman, "Final Report," 15 Apr 43, p. 19; George F. Howe, *Northwest Africa: Seizing the Initiative in the West*, U.S. Army in World War II (Washington, D.C.: U.S. Army Center of Military History, 1957), pp. 453–55.

[30] Cushman, "Final Report," pp. 1, 7, 19.

Gun Motor Carriages at Camp Hood

Such successful employment could not disguise the more general chronic misuse that characterized tank destroyer operations in North Africa and violated the tactical principles taught at Camp Hood. Commanders routinely broke attached tank destroyer battalions into independent companies and platoons and scattered them over wide frontages. This dispersion greatly complicated the battalion's supply, administration, and maintenance concerns and exposed each component to isolated destruction.[31]

Members of the separated tank destroyer organizations also found themselves continuously reassigned to support different units. This reshuffling lacked consistency and purpose, and it encouraged the perception that tank destroyer battalions were simply collections of antitank guns to be employed however a commander saw fit. The special mission of the tank destroyers and the importance of integrating their action with that of other ground forces became obscured. Because division

[31] Maj Allerton Cushman, Preliminary Rpt, p. 1, attached to Memo, Lt Col James D. Tanner, sub: Observer Report, 29 Mar 43, Item 5612, Reel 375, National Archives Project, GCM; Ltr, Col H. J. McChrystal to Maj Gen Andrew D. Bruce, 30 Oct 43, p. 3, Bruce Papers.

Maj. Gen. Andrew D. Bruce

and corps staffs did not include tank destroyer liaison officers, this misuse proved difficult to correct.[32]

Although the combination of tank destroyer battalions into groups for corps attachment and brigades for army use had been envisioned, the North African experience effectively ended such planning. The American II Corps included the 1st Tank Destroyer Group, a collection of seven tank destroyer battalions. Introduced into combat during the fighting around El Guettar in March 1943, this unit never functioned as a single tank destroyer mass as intended. Instead, its component battalions received orders that scattered them among II Corps elements.[33]

Consequently, the group commander became an unnecessary link in the corps command chain, serving as a superfluous intermediary between the corps and individual tank destroyer battalions. The appointment of special officers to coordinate corps antitank measures also precluded the group commander from assuming this role. Nor did the concentration of tank destroyer battalions under a special command facilitate greater integration of action with other ground combat forces. No apparent need existed for the organization of tank destroyer groups or the even larger brigade concentrations.[34]

Field commanders, however, employed tank destroyers in a variety of roles never intended. These included use as infantry support weapons, rear area security, and bridge defense. The 1st Armored Division assigned tank destroyer platoons equipped with the 37-mm. gun to defend its supply trains. Division and corps headquarters employed the reconnaissance companies of attached tank destroyer battalions in independent reconnoitering missions, although the companies did not possess the appropriate training or organization. This practice impaired the ability of the affected tank destroyer battalions to locate and track enemy armor.[35]

The use of tank destroyers to provide artillery support, however, succeeded. Battlefield expediency revealed the tank destroyer's ability to perform indirect-fire

[32] Cushman, Preliminary Rpt, p. 1; Ltr, McChrystal to Bruce, 30 Oct 43, p. 3.

[33] Howe, *Seizing the Initiative*, p. 546.

[34] Cushman, "Final Report," p. 15.

[35] Interv with Lt Col John K. Waters, Commanding 1st Bn, 1st Armd Rgt, 1st Armd Div, and Lt Col Hyman Bruss, Commanding 2d Bn, 13th Armd Rgt, 1st Armd Div, 29 Dec 42, pp. 1–2, Item 5611, Reel 375, National Archives Project, GCM (hereafter cited as Waters/Bruss Interv); Cushman, "Final Report," pp. 2, 19.

missions. When forced to perform artillery missions without preparation, the 776th Tank Destroyer Battalion obtained excellent results, although the unit's high percentage of Field Artillery personnel largely accounted for this success. Requests soon emerged from the combat theater for all tank destroyer personnel to receive training in indirect-fire methods and artillery observation. Similarly, all tank destroyers were to be fitted with necessary ranging devices and sights.[36]

Tank Destroyer Criticism

Combat operations in North Africa triggered widespread criticism of tank destroyers. When Army Chief of Staff General George C. Marshall visited North Africa, he gave the discipline and training of the 899th Tank Destroyer Battalion a poor assessment, judging the unit unfit for combat. He reprimanded the commanders of the Tank Destroyer Center and Army Ground Forces, resulting in McNair's recommending to Bruce numerous training improvements.[37]

While many combat units received similar criticisms reflective of their unseasoned nature, the entire concept of the tank destroyer became the subject of controversy. Maj. Gen. Omar N. Bradley, special representative to Allied Forces Commander General Dwight D. Eisenhower, believed tank destroyers suited only for defensive missions. He considered the tank a more versatile weapon and preferred a greater allocation of scarce transport tonnage to armored rather than tank destroyer units. His distaste for the tank destroyer further manifested itself in an undisguised preference for towed antitank guns with low silhouettes.[38]

Senior field commanders tended to share Bradley's views. Lt. Gen. George S. Patton Jr., who commanded the II Corps in the final weeks of fighting in Tunisia, considered the celebrated action of the 601st Tank Destroyer Battalion at El Guettar a failure because of the heavy losses the unit incurred. Patton's preference for tanks rather than tank destroyers reflected the sentiment of most field commanders following operations in North Africa.[39] Self-propelled tank destroyers were considered helpless against tanks because of their light armor. They could not "slug it out" with German tanks, and their large size precluded the easy concealment available to towed antitank guns.[40]

Following a visit to North Africa, Chief of the Armored Force Lt. Gen. Jacob L. Devers criticized the separate status given the Tank Destroyer Center and questioned the validity of the entire tank destroyer concept:

---

[36] Cushman, "Final Report," p. 3, and Preliminary Rpt, p. 4.

[37] Ltrs, General George C. Marshall to Maj Gen Andrew D. Bruce, 30 Jan 43, and Lt Gen Lesley J. McNair to Maj Gen Andrew D. Bruce, 2 Feb 43, both in Bruce Papers.

[38] Ltr, Maj Gen Omar N. Bradley to General George C. Marshall, 29 May 43, George C. Marshall Papers, GCM.

[39] Ltr, Lt Gen Lesley J. McNair to Maj Gen Andrew D. Bruce, 12 Apr 43, HQ AGF, CG Gen Decimal File, RG 337, NARA; Baily, *Faint Praise*, pp. 57–58.

[40] Maj Gen J. P. Lucas, "Extract from Report on Sicilian Campaign," 8 Sep 43, Bruce Papers.

Headquarters of the Tank Destroyer Center

> The separate tank destroyer arm is not a practical concept on the battlefield. Defensive antitank weapons are essentially artillery. Offensively the weapon to beat a tank is a better tank. Sooner or later the issue between ground forces is settled in an armored battle—tank against tank. The concept of tank destroyer groups and brigades attempting to overcome equal numbers of hostile tanks is faulty unless the tank destroyers are actually better tanks than those of the enemy.[41]

Devers believed enemy armor should be defeated by a combination of offensive tank tactics supported by antitank weapons employed in a defensive posture. Therefore, he considered Camp Hood's primary function the training of personnel to operate weapons of 75-mm. or larger in artillery and antitank roles. Devers further encouraged a defensive perception of tank destroyers with his recommendations to equip self-propelled guns to infantry battalions and employ 37-mm. antitank weapons in passive security missions.[42]

He questioned the wisdom of separating the Tank Destroyer Center from the Armored Force and advocated the subordination of tank destroyers to the latter. He also sought the permanent inclusion of a tank destroyer battalion in each armored

[41] "Conclusions and Recommendations of Gen. Devers in His Report on His Observations Abroad—December 14, 1942 to January 25, 1943," in Ltr, Lt Gen Lesley J. McNair to Maj Gen Andrew D. Bruce, 19 Feb 43, Xerox 2363, GCM.

[42] Ibid.

General Ward

division. Following the replacement of Bruce by Maj. Gen. Orlando W. Ward in May 1943, Devers anticipated an increased influence on the Tank Destroyer Center. An armored officer who had risen to command the 1st Armored Division in North Africa, Ward was also a personal friend of Devers. Learning of Ward's appointment to the Tank Destroyer Center, Devers informed him: "All of us who have been overseas and know what's required have a very definite idea about them [tank destroyers]. You will find at Hood everything but tank destroyers and a good doctrine."[43]

This criticism of the tank destroyers attracted attention throughout the Army's administration. The secretary of war expressed interest and appreciation for Devers' views, and the War Department General Council convened to discuss them. After visiting North Africa, even the assistant secretary of war echoed Devers' ideas by advocating an increase in artillery units for mass action against enemy tanks.[44]

Nevertheless, the widespread discussion did not result in War Department endorsement of Devers' agenda. The latter included the incorporation of antiaircraft and tank destroyer units in the armored division and the Armored Force's annexation of the Tank Destroyer Center.[45] McNair's authority as AGF commander protected the Tank Destroyer Center from being reorganized in response to the storm of tank destroyer criticism. He did not believe the North African experience alone should determine the tank destroyer's future. He apprised Bruce of ongoing discussions within the War Department and assured him that the Tank Destroyer Center would remain the principal influence on tank destroyer development. Privately, McNair believed that more tank destroyer units in lieu

[43] Ltr, Lt Gen Jacob L. Devers to Maj Gen Orlando W. Ward, 23 Apr 43, Orlando W. Ward Papers, MHI Archives.

[44] Ltr, Lt Gen Lesley J. McNair to Maj Gen Andrew D. Bruce, 19 Feb 43, Xerox 2363, National Archives Project, GCM; Memo Slip Concerning Comments on Devers' Report by RQT 1, R.C.M., Submitted to General Staff Secretary, 15 Feb 43, Xerox 2363, National Archives Project, GCM; Memo, Col Stanley L. Grogan to Mr. McCloy, sub: Report on Matters, Other than Public Relations, During North African Trip, February 10–March 17, 1943, 20 Mar 43, p. 11, Item 5612, Reel 375, National Archives Project, GCM.

[45] Memo Slip Concerning Comments on Devers' Report, 15 Feb 43.

of the 1st Armored Division would have prevented the heavy losses inflicted by German armored action.[46]

Much of the tank destroyer criticism reflected a general ignorance of the weapon's purpose. Bruce accepted responsibility for not aggressively disseminating information concerning tank destroyer operations. Amid the effort to build Camp Hood, develop doctrine, and establish a training program in 1942, Bruce had not established a link with the Desert Training Center—the principal facility responsible for preparing combat troops for operations in the desert. In the absence of tank destroyer information, the Desert Training Center, directed by a succession of armored corps headquarters, reflected the Armored Force's view of the primacy of armored formations. Patton established the center and its training program without any knowledge of tank destroyer operations. Bruce believed this ignorance led to Patton's subsequent condemnation of tank destroyers.[47]

Tank Destroyer Doctrine and Training Revisited

As criticism of tank destroyer operations began to emerge in North Africa, General Eisenhower acted to clarify their role and use. In March 1943 his headquarters issued "Employment of Tank Destroyer Units," a training memorandum summarizing tank destroyer doctrine. It sought to improve tank destroyer effectiveness by educating subordinate commands in the basic principles of tank destroyer doctrine.[48] Tank destroyer personnel supported the action. They shared the views of the 776th Tank Destroyer Battalion commander: "If this paper is followed perhaps we will be allowed at some time to utilize our mass of fire and ability to move as contemplated rather than being used as the point of the advance guard for movement into action."[49]

Eisenhower also requested that Army Ground Forces send tank destroyer officers to North Africa for assignment as antitank advisers to army, corps, and division staffs. McNair obliged the request but opposed it in principle because this advisory role was the responsibility of the tank destroyer battalion commanders already in the theater of operations. However, senior leaders generally ignored them, directing tank destroyer movements without consulting the affected unit commanders.[50]

At Camp Hood, Bruce acknowledged the criticism of tank destroyer training, organization, and combat effectiveness; but he did not consider tank destroyer doctrine unsound. Instead he attributed the problems encountered in North Africa to the absence of accurate information describing the tank destroyer's purpose and method

---

[46] Ltrs, McNair to Bruce, 19 Feb 43; Lt Gen Lesley J. McNair to Maj Gen Andrew D. Bruce, 11 Jun 43, Bruce Papers.

[47] Ltr, Bruce to Dawley, 13 Jun 44, p. 3.

[48] Allied Force HQ, Training Memo no. 23, sub: Employment of Tank Destroyer Units, 21 Mar 43, in Cushman, "Final Report," 15 Apr 43, p. 2.

[49] Ltr, Lt Col James P. Barney Jr. to Maj Gen Andrew D. Bruce, 1 Apr 43, Bruce Papers.

[50] Ltrs, Brig Gen Ben M. Sawbridge to Maj Gen Andrew D. Bruce, 19 Mar 43, and Lt Gen Lesley J. McNair to Maj Gen Andrew D. Bruce, 20 Mar 43, both in Bruce Papers.

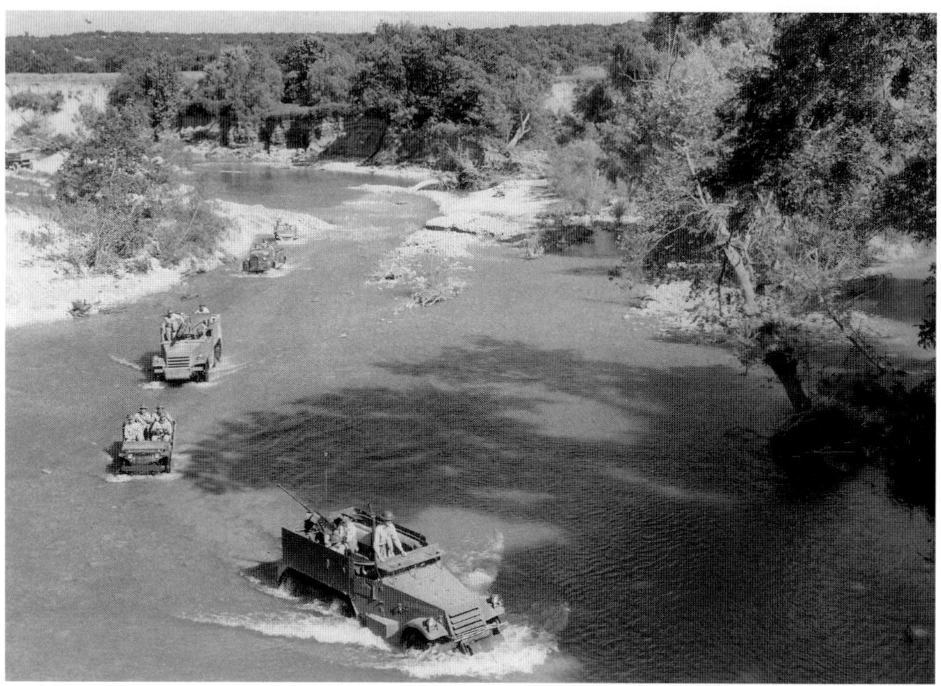

Tank destroyer column moving along Cow House Creek, Camp Hood

of operation. Unfamiliar with its doctrine, commanders based their understanding of the tank destroyer from the publicity that surrounded its development. This source created a false impression of tank destroyer tactics. For example, one advertisement announced, "Armed with armor-piercing guns, the half-track in a tank melee can dart in from rear or quarter—and away—like a terrier harrying a bear."[51]

Similar statements gave credence to reports from North Africa that tank destroyers with inferior armor protection chased more heavily armored enemy tanks, engaged them in battle, and consequently suffered heavy losses. Tank chasing contradicted the Tank Destroyer Center's emphasis on destroying hostile tanks through massed fire from secure firing positions, and Bruce believed these reports greatly exaggerated. Nor did analysis of tank destroyer unit records confirm them. In fact, further study showed the battlefield conduct of tank destroyers in North Africa to be satisfactory though initially plagued by problems typical of new units: poor discipline and insufficient training.[52]

Eliminating the misconceptions surrounding tank destroyer operations thus became Bruce's primary objective. The expanded authority granted the Tank Destroyer Center in 1942 permitted him to establish inspection teams to visit every stateside tank destroyer

---

[51] Maj Gen Andrew D. Bruce, "Notice to Tank Destroyers," 19 May 43, Bruce Papers.

[52] Ltrs, Maj Gen Andrew D. Bruce to Lt Gen Lesley J. McNair, 5 Jun 43, Bruce Papers; Sawbridge to Bruce, 19 Mar 43; McChrystal to Bruce, 30 Oct 43, p. 3.

battalion and to brief tank destroyer doctrine to military audiences. At Camp Hood, Bruce personally briefed all instructors to ensure an educational focus that instilled tank destroyer doctrine in new personnel. The course entitled "Training for Tank Hunting" became "Battle Conditioning." The name change reflected a deliberate effort to eliminate all reference to tank chasing and the course's expansion to include new combat skills for tank destroyer crews.[53]

Bruce also created a special board of officers to investigate criticisms of tank destroyers and compile a training circular to correct deficiencies in tactical instruction. He instructed the board to emphasize massed gunnery over tank chasing and to address the negative views expressed by senior commanders. The circular also sought to present tank destroyer doctrine in simple terminology to facilitate its comprehension and dissemination throughout the Army.[54]

To ensure the circular's clarity and effectiveness, Bruce consulted the Command and General Staff School faculty. The response proved less than helpful, despite that institute's responsibility for developing Army doctrine and tactics. One instructor noted his ignorance of tank destroyers and inability to offer a constructive critique. However, he epitomized the Army's confusion concerning tank destroyers:

> Sometimes I think we are somewhat screwy in our thinking. Our tanks are made with thick armor but their prime mission is to destroy personnel. When a slugging match is evident we endeavor to let them slide out and let antitank guns take over. But the tank destroyer built to destroy tanks is comparatively thin skinned with only its agility to protect it. However, we all agree that a high velocity hit against a tank or tank destroyer will penetrate, so armor in many cases is somewhat valueless.[55]

Despite such lackluster input, the completed training circular constituted a clear and effective description of tank destroyer operations. It denounced tank chasing and focused on the lessons learned from combat in North Africa, particularly emphasizing the importance of tank destroyer concentrations. Tank destroyer battalions were to be employed as complete units rather than broken into component elements and scattered across the battlefield. The circular also denounced the use of the reconnaissance company for any purpose other than supporting its parent battalion. However, the tank destroyer's versatility found expression in the identification of suitable missions other than antitank. These included fire support for infantry and tank units, indirect fire, and destruction of enemy fortifications.[56]

The circular affirmed the desirability of attaching a tank destroyer battalion to each division. Other battalions were to be concentrated under corps or army control

---

[53] Bruce, "Notice to Tank Destroyers"; Ltr, Bruce to McNair, 5 Jun 43, pp. 1–2.

[54] Ltr, Maj Gen Lloyd R. Fredendall to Maj Gen Andrew D. Bruce, 10 May 43, Bruce Papers; Bruce, "Notice to Tank Destroyers"; Ltr, Maj Gen Andrew D. Bruce to Maj Gen Lloyd R. Fredendall, 15 May 43, Bruce Papers.

[55] Ltr, Roberts to Maj Gen Andrew D. Bruce, 7 Apr 43, Bruce Papers.

[56] HQ, Tank Destroyer Ctr, "Suggested Training Circular Concerning the Employment of Tank Destroyer Units," 15 May 43, Bruce Papers.

Gun crew, 1942

for massed employment against enemy armor. To improve coordination of tank destroyer battalions with other forces, tank destroyer battalion commanders were to serve as antitank advisers in the formations to which the battalions were attached. This guidance reflected both the desire for improved antitank strength within the divisions and McNair's emphasis on pooling special assets at the corps and higher levels. Tank destroyer groups and brigades, however, received little attention, since the North African experience largely discredited their value.[57]

Bruce also began revising the tank destroyer field manual in response to McNair's request to do so. Bruce sought to clarify its content and explain the operation of tank destroyer units from the perspective of division, corps, and army commanders. These changes included ideas similar to those expressed in the training circular, but Bruce disliked the frenzied atmosphere in which the manual's revision occurred. He preferred a more deliberate pace and approach to ensure that the manual did not increase the existing doctrinal confusion surrounding tank destroyers. The subsequent addition of towed tank destroyer battalions and the need to include comments from other arms led to a more graduated pace of

---

[57] Ibid.

development under the supervision of Bruce's successors in the Tank Destroyer Center. The final revision was not published until July 1944.[58]

The North African experience also triggered training improvements. Inexperience and insufficient preparation had plagued initial tank destroyer operations. Inadequate map reading and navigation skills resulted in surprise encounters with German forces and unnecessary losses. Like other ground combat troops, tank destroyer personnel demonstrated only a marginal ability to perform night operations or remove mines. Too many vehicle crews preferred to apply paint schemes reflective of individual artistic taste rather than appreciation of the surrounding terrain.[59]

To improve tank destroyer efficiency, unit commanders in North Africa recommended training exercises more reflective of the battlefield and exhorted vehicle crews to await enemy tanks from secure firing positions rather than hunt them. They also stressed the importance of thorough terrain reconnaissance, because neglect of this function resulted in tactical embarrassments similar to those experienced by tank units. The M10 Gun Motor Carriage's versatility and the employment of tank destroyers in roles not initially intended for them further encouraged the preparation of tank destroyer personnel for action against a variety of targets in addition to tanks.[60]

In May 1943 Bruce's replacement by General Ward brought to Camp Hood a commander with recent combat experience. Tank destroyer training activities soon reflected the lessons learned in North Africa. Ward emphasized gunnery and battle drills to assist tank destroyer units' response to tactical situations. Battle conditioning of tank destroyer crews also received greater emphasis, including such skills as night operations, medical evacuation, and grenade use. Maneuver areas on Camp Hood soon became dotted with signs indicating good and bad firing positions to assist new crews. In addition, tank destroyers increased training activities with other unit types, particularly after the 51st Armored Infantry Regiment joined the school units already assigned to the Tank Destroyer School.[61]

The collective result of remedial measures in North Africa and the United States lay in the improved efficiency of tank destroyer battalions. Greater appreciation of tank destroyer doctrine helped to eliminate many of the impediments to effective tank destroyer action present during the initial fighting in Tunisia. The quality of tank destroyer units and personnel also steadily improved. Disciplinary problems observed in overseas tank destroyer battalions gradually disappeared, and in June 1943 McNair could congratulate Bruce on the excellent performance of a tank destroyer battalion during maneuvers against the 5th Armored Division.[62]

---

[58] Ltr, Bruce to Fredendall, 15 May 43; Ltr, Bruce to McNair, 5 Jun 43; WD, FM 18–5, *Tactical Employment, Tank Destroyer Unit*, 1944; Robert R. Palmer, "Organization and Training of New Ground Combat Elements," in Greenfield, Palmer, and Wiley, *Army Ground Forces*, pp. 426–27.

[59] Cushman, "Final Report," pp. 12–14.

[60] Ibid., p. 7.

[61] Hist Sec, "Tank Destroyer History," pp. 31–32.

[62] Memo, Col William P. Ennis Jr. to ACS, G–1, General Sawbridge, sub: 805th Tank Destroyer Battalion, 17 Mar 43; Ltr, Lt Gen Lesley J. McNair to Maj Gen Andrew D. Bruce, 11 Jun 43; both in Bruce Papers.

M10 Gun Motor Carriage

Unfortunately, these measures did not remove the stigma attached to the tank destroyers. Criticism of their value continued to surround their employment, and many senior commanders continued to condemn the weapon throughout the war. Although significant steps had been taken to educate the Army in tank destroyer principles, these very principles continued to be contentious.[63]

Organizational and Materiel Development

Combat operations led to recommended changes in the organization of the tank destroyer battalion. They included the replacement of all M3 and M6 platforms with the M10. Additional firepower was to be provided by adding a platoon of self-propelled 105-mm. guns to each tank destroyer company. These weapons were to provide artillery support and offset the emergence of heavier German tanks, particularly the *Panzerkampfwagen VI* (Tiger I), considered to be a "super Tank Destroyer."[64]

Tank destroyer reconnaissance companies also became the target of suggested improvements. These units included three reconnaissance platoons, each of two sections, equipped with an armored car and two jeeps. Responsible for locating and tracking enemy armor, these scout organizations proved vulnerable to German light tanks performing counterreconnaissance. To ensure the survivability of the tank destroyer scouts, they had to be reinforced with light tanks diverted from tank

[63] Ltr, Barney to Bruce, 1 Apr 43.
[64] Cushman, Preliminary Rpt, pp. 3–4.

battalions. Consequently, proposed improvements to the reconnaissance company included increases to its combat power.[65]

None of these proposals came into effect, although M10s became much more common in tank destroyer units. Instead, reorganization of the tank destroyer battalion occurred through the efforts of the Reduction Board. This body convened in October 1942 to reduce the vehicular and personnel strengths of combat units. The actions of the board resulted in changes to the tank destroyer battalions that became effective in January 1943. These alterations included the elimination of all antiaircraft sections and the loss of administrative and support personnel. Battalion size shrank from 898 to 673 soldiers, but the unit retained its full complement of thirty-six self-propelled tank destroyers.[66]

Combat operations did not trigger changes to the organization of tank destroyer battalions, but they did reopen a controversy over the relative merits of towed versus self-propelled weapons. Bruce favored self-propelled mounts, whose combination of mobility and firepower more closely suited his intent for the tank destroyer. Prewar maneuver experience suggested that towed guns were more likely to be deployed and left in place because of their vulnerability during transport. Tank destroyer personnel favored the more versatile self-propelled weapons. Yet they feared that senior leaders critical of the tank destroyer concept would encourage the replacement of self-propelled weapons with conventional towed ones.[67]

In fact, criticism of the tank destroyers in North Africa did lead to the creation of towed tank destroyer battalions. The British and Germans used towed weapons successfully in the desert, partially because they proved easier to conceal than the self-propelled tank destroyer. The M3 also proved vulnerable. Consequently, in January 1943 McNair directed the Tank Destroyer Center to begin developing a towed tank destroyer battalion. In March fifteen battalions then in training were ordered to convert to a towed configuration. Several months later Army Ground Forces resolved to make half of all tank destroyer battalions towed.[68]

By May an organization for the towed units had been approved. It resembled the self-propelled battalions in basic structure, but it possessed fewer reconnaissance assets. The reconnaissance company was eliminated and replaced by two reconnaissance platoons attached to the battalion headquarters. The towed companies each included twelve 3-inch guns towed by halftracks. However, despite their similarities to self-propelled units, the towed tank destroyer battalions proved sufficiently different to warrant separate training procedures and the publication of a unique

---

[65] Cushman, "Final Report," pp. 5–6, 12–14; WD, FM 18–5, 1942, pp. 58, 62, 67.

[66] Robert R. Palmer, "Reorganization of Ground Troops for Combat," in Greenfield, Palmer, and Wiley, *Army Ground Forces*, pp. 297–99; Gabel, *Seek, Strike, and Destroy*, p. 45.

[67] Ltr, Maj Gen John H. Hester to Maj Gen Andrew D. Bruce, 15 Nov 43, Bruce Papers.

[68] General Board, U.S. Forces, European Theater, Study no. 60, "Report on Study of Organization, Equipment, and Tactical Employment of Tank Destroyer Units," p. 10, 1945, CMH; Hist Sec, "Tank Destroyer History," p. 27; Gabel, *Seek, Strike, and Destroy*, pp. 46–47; Palmer, "Organization and Training of New Ground Combat Elements," p. 427.

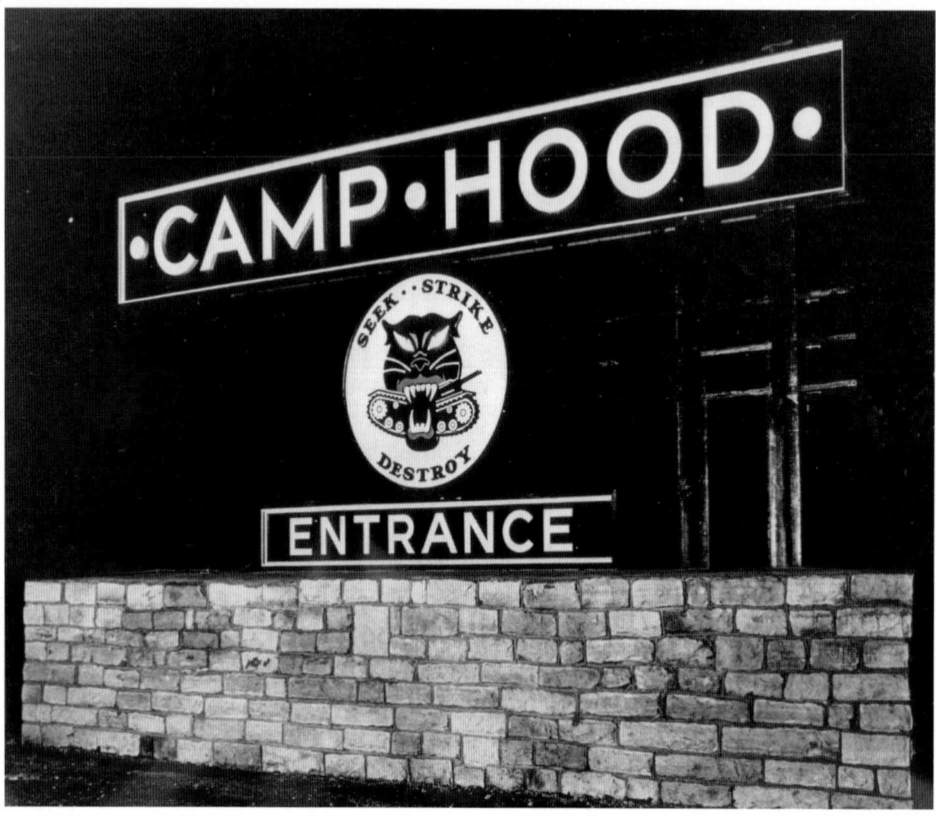

The entrance to Camp Hood, ca. 1943, showing the insignia of the Tank Destroyers

platoon manual. The latter required time to develop and contributed to the delayed revision of Field Manual 18–5, the overarching manual for tank destroyers.[69]

The development of both towed and self-propelled tank destroyers reflected the views of commanders in North Africa and McNair's own preference for towed weapons. Their use together seemed to offer the best means of providing antitank protection. The towed battalions were to supplement division antitank assets, while the self-propelled units constituted the pool of mobile weapons ready to react to enemy armored thrusts.[70]

Tank Destroyers

The tank destroyer battalions entered combat in North Africa equipped with M6 and M3 Gun Motor Carriages. The former was intended only for training purposes.[71]

---

[69] Gabel, *Seek, Strike, and Destroy*, pp. 47, 50.
[70] Cushman, "Final Report," 15 Apr 43, p. 20.
[71] Waters/Bruss Interv, 29 Dec 42, p. 7; Memo, Grogan to McCloy, 20 Mar 43, p. 9.

One Army Ground Forces observer concluded that "the sending of such a patently inadequate destroyer into combat can at best be termed a tragic mistake."[72] With a 75-mm. gun, some armor protection, and reasonable mobility, the M3 proved more effective. Though the weapon initially was popular among tank destroyer crews, satisfaction with it evaporated after engagements with better-armed and armored German tanks. Following these encounters, the M3 became known as the Purple Heart Wagon.[73]

The M10 Gun Motor Carriage replaced the self-propelled 75-mm. The M10 featured a more powerful turret-mounted 3-inch gun and a fully tracked chassis that provided better cross-country mobility. The main armament's gun sight and armor penetration ability surpassed that of the M4 Sherman medium tank, but the longer range of the 3-inch gun encouraged crews to exaggerate its performance. Initially, they commenced firing far beyond the weapon's effective range. Moreover, the M10 did not possess the ability to engage enemy tanks on even terms. Failure to heed this principle invariably resulted in its destruction.[74]

Even before the cessation of fighting in North Africa, development began on a new tank destroyer design. Intended to be faster and better armed than the M10, the prospective vehicle also featured a more robust suspension and an engine mounted to simplify maintenance. Limited production began even before the completion of testing to ensure the availability of sufficient numbers for combat operations in the summer of 1944. Numerous mechanical faults resulted, requiring correction and design changes before full-rate production could be achieved.[75]

The vehicle became the M18 Gun Motor Carriage. It mounted a 76-mm. gun in a partially enclosed, powered turret. It proved reliable, possessed good cross-country mobility, and could achieve speeds of sixty miles per hour. It suited Bruce's initial desire for a fast, mobile, and well-armed vehicle. In fact the rapid speed permitted the vehicle to quickly traverse open ground and displace rapidly from one firing position to another. However, compared to the M10, the M18 possessed less crew space, resulting in cramped conditions, longer loading times, and fewer main-gun rounds readily available in the turret. Moreover, the performance of the 76-mm. gun did not represent a major improvement over the 3-inch gun of the M10. Its entrance into service in early 1944 coincided with a general desire for an even more powerfully armed tank destroyer for use against the heavier German tanks then being encountered.[76]

---

[72] Cushman, "Final Report," p. 6.

[73] Waters/Bruss Interv, 29 Dec 42, p. 7; Rpt to Lt Gen Jacob L. Devers, sub: Ordnance Annex to Report of Visit Abroad, 18 Jan 43, p. 11, Item 5645, Reel 379, National Archives Project, GCM; Memo Slip Concerning Comments on Devers' Rpt, 15 Feb 43; Memo, Grogan to McCloy, 20 Mar 43, p. 9.

[74] Cushman, "Final Report," pp. 1, 3.

[75] Steven J. Zaloga, *M18 Hellcat Tank Destroyer, 1943–97* (Oxford, U.K.: Osprey Publishing, 2004), pp. 10–12.

[76] Memo, Col C. R. Landon to CG, 472.8 (ARTY), sub: User Reaction to 76-mm GMC, 9 Nov 44, Bruce Papers; Zaloga, *M18 Hellcat*, pp. 14–15.

Mock German town built at Camp Hood to support training for urban combat

In addition to the tank destroyers, combat formations in North Africa included towed antitank companies. Intended for close defense against armor, they too suffered from limited training and inexperience when they first entered combat. Lacking fire discipline, gun crews tended to engage targets at excessive ranges that revealed their location for little purpose. Therefore, they were instructed to conceal their weapons and await close-range flank shots. To prevent premature firing, unit commanders deployed their guns in locations that physically prohibited long-distance fire.[77]

Such measures became vital once the short effective range of the guns became apparent. Most companies initially used the 37-mm. antitank gun, but its popularity quickly evaporated after crews witnessed their shells bouncing off enemy tanks. The weapon could not penetrate the armor of most German tanks except at uncomfortably close ranges. By the close of the North African campaign, estimates of the gun's effective range had shrunk to one hundred yards but penetrations of frontal armor remained problematic even at that distance. Demands for a larger-caliber antitank gun resulted in the British-built 6-pounder's being delivered to American troops as a 57-mm. antitank gun. Unfortunately, it proved only marginally superior to the

[77] Cushman, "Final Report," 15 Apr 43, p. 14; Conf with Lt Col Louis V. Hightower, 1 Mar 43, p. 4, in Memo, Brig Gen Lowell W. Rooks to WD Opns Div, 21 Mar 43, Item 5612, Reel 375, National Archives Project, GCM.

37-mm. weapon it replaced and triggered requests for a still-more-powerful gun, which encouraged development of the towed 3-inch gun.[78]

The development of a towed tank destroyer addressed the desire both for a more powerful antitank gun and for an increase in towed weapons. To prevent the misuse of towed tank destroyer battalions, the Tank Destroyer Center issued special guidance to govern their employment. These instructions explained how to exploit the towed antitank gun's strengths. The weapon's vulnerability while in transit and slow emplacement rate necessitated careful reconnaissance of enemy action and predetermination of effective firing positions. Lacking the battlefield mobility of the self-propelled tank destroyers, masses of towed 3-inch guns would therefore reinforce friendly forces directly in the path of attacking tanks, forcing the latter into narrow channels of advance to be dispatched by self-propelled tank destroyers held in reserve.[79]

These instructions envisioned the "canalizing" of enemy armored assaults that McNair had once denounced as wasteful and inefficient. However, in developing both towed and self-propelled tank destroyers the Tank Destroyer Center sought to encompass both McNair's original pooling concept and division commanders' desire for improved antitank defenses. While towed tank destroyers deployed linearly in depth, a concentrated reserve of self-propelled weapons supported them.

An Uncertain Future

The criticism of the tank destroyer following the North African campaign, coupled with the mandatory conversion of self-propelled battalions into towed units, eroded the institutional status of the tank destroyer force. The continued disdain of many senior field commanders for tank destroyer units undermined the morale of tank destroyer personnel. By late 1943 transfer requests from tank destroyer units had risen to unprecedented levels. McNair's known preference for towed guns and his indication of a likely decrease in the total number of tank destroyers did little to assuage the concerns of tank destroyer personnel. The Tank Destroyer Center abounded with rumors of the disbandment of tank destroyer units, possible consolidation with

[78] Lt Col William B. Kern, Capt Thomas W. Hoban, and Capt Walter R. Geyer, "Proceedings of a Board of Officers for Recommendations for Changes and Improvements in Organization, Tactics, and Equipment," 21 Dec 42, pp. 1–3, in P. M. Robinett, "CCB, 1st Armored Division: North African Operations," Paul M. Robinett Collection, GCM; Interv with Col Robert T. Maraist, 29 Dec 42, p. 2, Item 5611, Reel 375, National Archives Project, GCM; Rpt to Devers, 18 Jan 43, pp. 11–12; Ltr, McNair to Bruce, 19 Feb 43; Ltr, Lt Gen Jacob L. Devers to General George C. Marshall, 1 Mar 43, Item 4679, Verifax 3353, National Archives Project, GCM; Second Conf with Lt Col Louis V. Hightower, 1 Mar 43, p. 2, in Memo, Brig Gen Lowell W. Rooks to WD Opns Div, 21 Mar 43, Item 5612, Reel 375, National Archives Project, GCM; Maj Gen C. P. Hall, Obsvr Rpt, p. 5, in Memo, Capt R. J. Delacroix, sub: Report of Visit to the North African Theatre of Operations, 7 May 43, Item 5612, Reel 375, National Archives Project, GCM; Cushman, Preliminary Rpt, p. 4.

[79] Tank Destroyer School, "The Employment of Towed Tank Destroyer Battalions," 3 Sep 43, pp. 1–3, Bruce Papers.

Antitank gun crew in action during training

another combat arm, and the alleged unwillingness of commanders to commit tank destroyers to combat.[80]

These rumors reflected several developments. Devers made no secret of his repeated attempts to consolidate the tank destroyers with the Armored Force. In October 1943 a proposed merging of the Tank Destroyer Center with the Field Artillery resulted in a formal analysis by both tank destroyer and artillery personnel. This study resulted in the rejection of the proposal, but it underscored the uncertainty surrounding the future of the tank destroyer force. Indeed, the expressed fears of tank destroyer personnel spurred the Tank Destroyer Center to request the War Department to issue a statement regarding its intentions for the tank destroyer force.[81]

Anxiety for the tank destroyer's future was justified. In late 1943 Army Ground Forces indicated that no additional tank destroyer battalions were required. Although McNair had sought the activation of 222 battalions in 1942, these numbers anticipated the creation of a much larger Army and the existence of a massive tank threat requiring

[80] Ltrs, Hester to Bruce, 15 Nov 43; Col Wendell Westover to Maj Gen Andrew D. Bruce, 27 Oct 43, p. 2, Bruce Papers.

[81] Ltrs, Lt Gen Lesley J. McNair to Maj Gen Andrew D. Bruce, 16 Feb 43, Bruce Papers; Bruce to Dawley, 13 Jun 44, p. 3; Westover to Bruce, 27 Oct 43, p. 2. Hist Sec, "Tank Destroyer History," p. 35.

the concentration of up to twenty tank destroyer battalions. These numbers proved exaggerated. The German tank threat diminished over time, and plans for the overall size of the Army shrank to more realistic levels.[82]

The downward adjustment of Army expansion plans led to a reduction in tank destroyers. Activation of new battalions ceased. Many battalions already in service were inactivated and their personnel transferred to combat divisions short on manpower. The Tank Destroyer Center also began to downsize, losing personnel and closing training activities. In early 1944 the headquarters underwent reduction and all training support units and organizations deactivated.

The War Department also directed the consolidation of all tank and tank destroyer training at Fort Knox. The Tank Destroyer Center successfully opposed this action, citing the more suitable maneuver and gunnery facilities at Camp Hood. Only the Officer Candidate School transferred to Fort Knox.[83]

These developments did not mark the dissolution of the tank destroyer force, but they did underscore its uncertain future. As combat operations began in Italy and preparations continued for a cross-channel invasion of Europe, the tank destroyer's role remained unclear. The general absence of large German tank masses on the battlefields of North Africa and Italy forced the Tank Destroyer Center to focus more attention on the tank destroyer's versatility and to seek missions in addition to its primary antitank role, particularly fire support to infantry and armor formations. In addition, the war against Japan was seen as another opportunity for tank destroyers to demonstrate their value in a variety of roles.[84]

---

[82] Palmer, "Organization and Training of New Ground Combat Elements," p. 428.

[83] Hist Sec, "Tank Destroyer History," pp. 36–37, 39; Palmer, "Organization and Training of New Ground Combat Elements," p. 428.

[84] Ltr, Hester to Bruce, 15 Nov 43.

13

ARMORED DIVISIONS IN BATTLE, 1944–1945

During the last two years of World War II, the U.S. Army introduced onto European battlefields fourteen additional armored divisions. Their combat experiences provided an unprecedented knowledge base for the employment and operation of armored formations. Much of this experience indicated doctrinal, organizational, and materiel flaws in the assumptions that guided early armored division development. Armored commanders generally rejected the wisdom of temporarily augmenting combat formations with specialized units pooled under corps or army control. Instead, they preferred the consistency and cohesion of larger formations independent of routine reinforcement from higher headquarters. Similarly, for most leaders, combat operations failed to validate the advantage of the extreme organizational flexibility embedded in the combat command structure. However, the wartime experience of the armored divisions confirmed the importance of combined-arms action at all levels, marking a significant break with the Army's tradition of separating organizations by tactical function.

Armored Division Doctrine

By 1944 the principles governing armored division operations reflected the formation's reduced size and incorporation of the combat command. Expressed in the Army's field service regulations and in a new armored division manual, these principles emphasized flexibility, firepower, and mobility. These characteristics made the armored division a potentially decisive influence on the battlefield. Capable of undertaking most forms of combat, since its creation in 1940 the armored division maintained its primary role: "offensive operations against hostile rear areas."[1]

Armored doctrine anticipated support from infantry divisions. The latter bore responsibility for establishing the conditions for the successful employment of the armored division. By breaching enemy defenses, securing key terrain, and engaging hostile formations in holding actions, infantry divisions created opportunities for the armored division to exploit. Once unleashed into the enemy rear area, the

---

[1] U.S. War Department (WD), Field Manual (FM) 100–5, *Field Service Regulations: Operations*, 1944, pp. 305–06; WD, Armored Command, FM 17–100, *The Armored Division*, 1944, pp. 1–2, 21, quote from p. 2.

Column of 1st Armored Division tanks at rest in Italy

armored division targeted vital installations, troop concentrations, and key terrain. There too it relied on supporting infantry to secure the objectives seized and eliminate pockets of resistance.[2]

In accomplishing these goals, the armored division relied on surprise, rapidity of action, and mass. The armored division was expected to establish a high tempo of operations that suited its flexible organization and accelerated the disintegration of hostile resistance. Although possessing considerable combat power, armored doctrine discouraged the division's employment against strongly defended or fortified positions, including urban areas. Such action risked casualties, momentum loss, and an unwarranted deviation from its primary function. The armored division was not designed to batter its way through a succession of enemy positions.[3]

In July 1944 American forces finally broke out of the Normandy beachhead near St. Lô, France, after weeks of fighting through hedgerows. Resistance collapsed after a large-scale application of air power on a narrow frontage and an aggressive infantry assault. German forces fled across France, pursued by the fast-moving columns of six American armored divisions that prevented the

[2] WD, FMs 100–5, pp. 309, 311–12, and 17–100, pp. 2, 72.

[3] WD, FMs 100–5, pp. 311–12, and 17–100, pp. 2, 26–27, 48, 91–92.

creation of a new front short of the German frontier. (*See Map 9.*) These operations caused extensive casualties and disruption to German combat formations without parallel loss to American armor. They resulted in the liberation of much of France and came to exemplify the doctrinally correct employment of the armored division.[4]

Armored doctrine also included other missions suited to the armored division's particular mix of mobility and firepower. All of them reflected the offensive nature of the formation. Pursuit, exploitation, envelopment, and the destruction of hurriedly erected defenses constituted actions suited to an organization intended for rapid, continuous movement. Acceptable defensive measures included counterattacks and delaying actions, but these missions were considered exceptional to the more general emphasis on the offense. Commanders of armored divisions considered the mission set sound, since all fourteen functions prescribed by doctrine were performed at one time or another.[5]

Armored Division Mission Set[6]

- Conduct a reconnaissance in force.
- Seize ground essential to the development of the higher commander's plan.
- Regain initiative by means of a surprise attack.
- Restore impetus to attack that has lost momentum.
- Spearhead attack against an enemy incompletely prepared for defense.
- Attack on a narrow front against a prepared position.
- Break through on a wide front against a demoralized enemy.
- Exploit success.
- Pursue a defeated enemy.
- Perform strategic envelopment.
- Attack enemy armor in self-defense and prevent disruption of friendly operations.
- Operate against lightly armored formations or installations.
- Counterattack to disrupt hostile operations.
- Execute delaying action.

The preference for decisive offensive operations notwithstanding, terrain and operational considerations sometimes forced the employment of armored divisions in less than ideal conditions. The 5th Armored Division, for example, found its combat power quickly eroded when thrust into the fighting for the Hürtgen Forest. The wooded ground and German minefields restricted the division's role

---

[4] U.S. Forces, European Theater, General Board, Study no. 48: "Organization, Equipment, and Tactical Employment of the Armored Division," 1945, p. 4, U.S. Army Center of Military History, Washington, D.C. (CMH) (hereafter cited as Study no. 48).

[5] Ibid., p. 22.

[6] WD, FM 17–100, pp. 22–23.

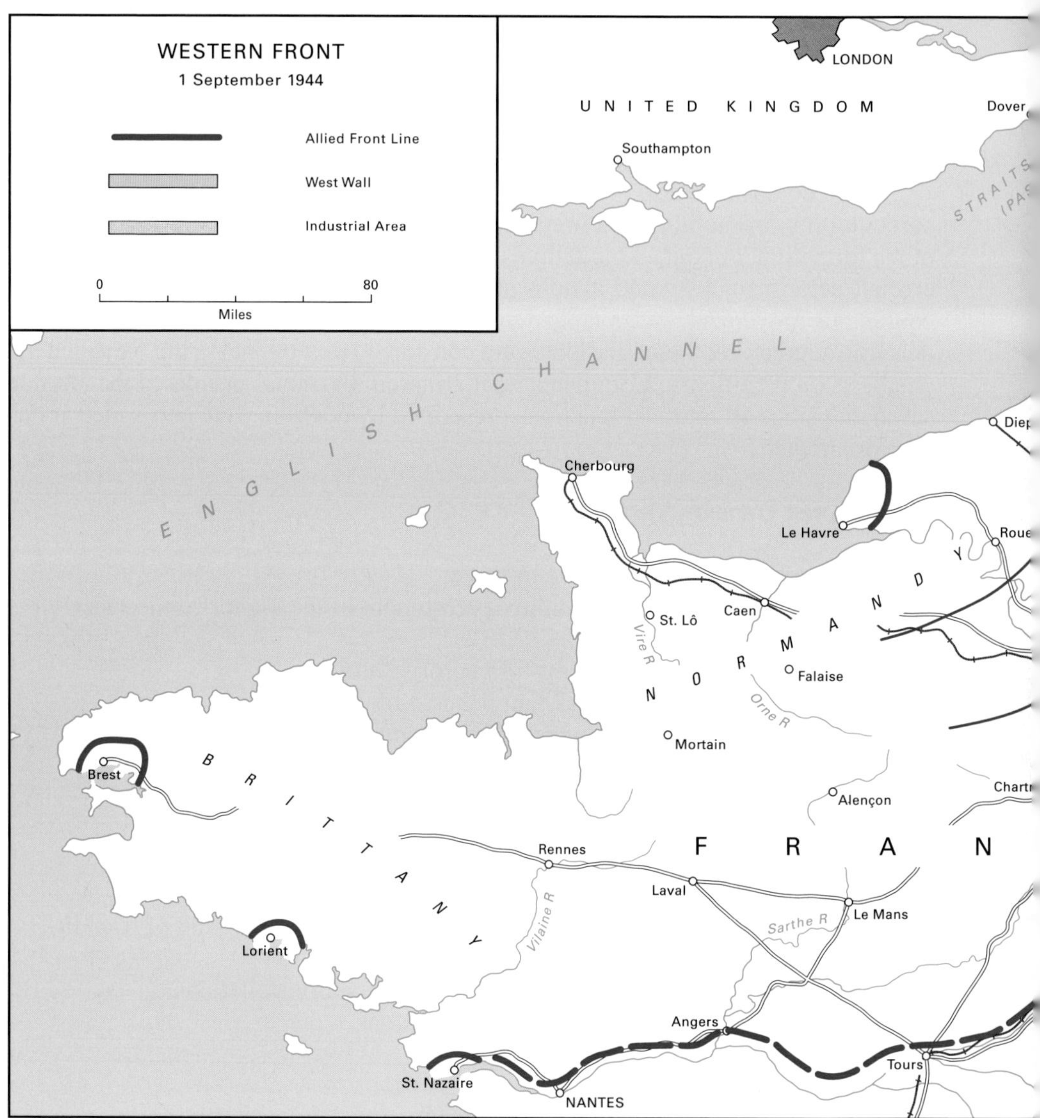

Map 9

to supporting and exploiting infantry attacks. In violation of armored doctrine, the division fought as a collection of detachments, with each combat command placed under the control of a different infantry formation. The densely wooded areas restricted armored actions; but tank units played a key role in securing clearings, where their mobility and firepower could still be used to effect. They also served as a mobile reserve. However, armored and infantry units not used to combined operations in such conditions generated tactical coordination problems and contributed to the high loss rate of armored soldiers. After sustained fighting,

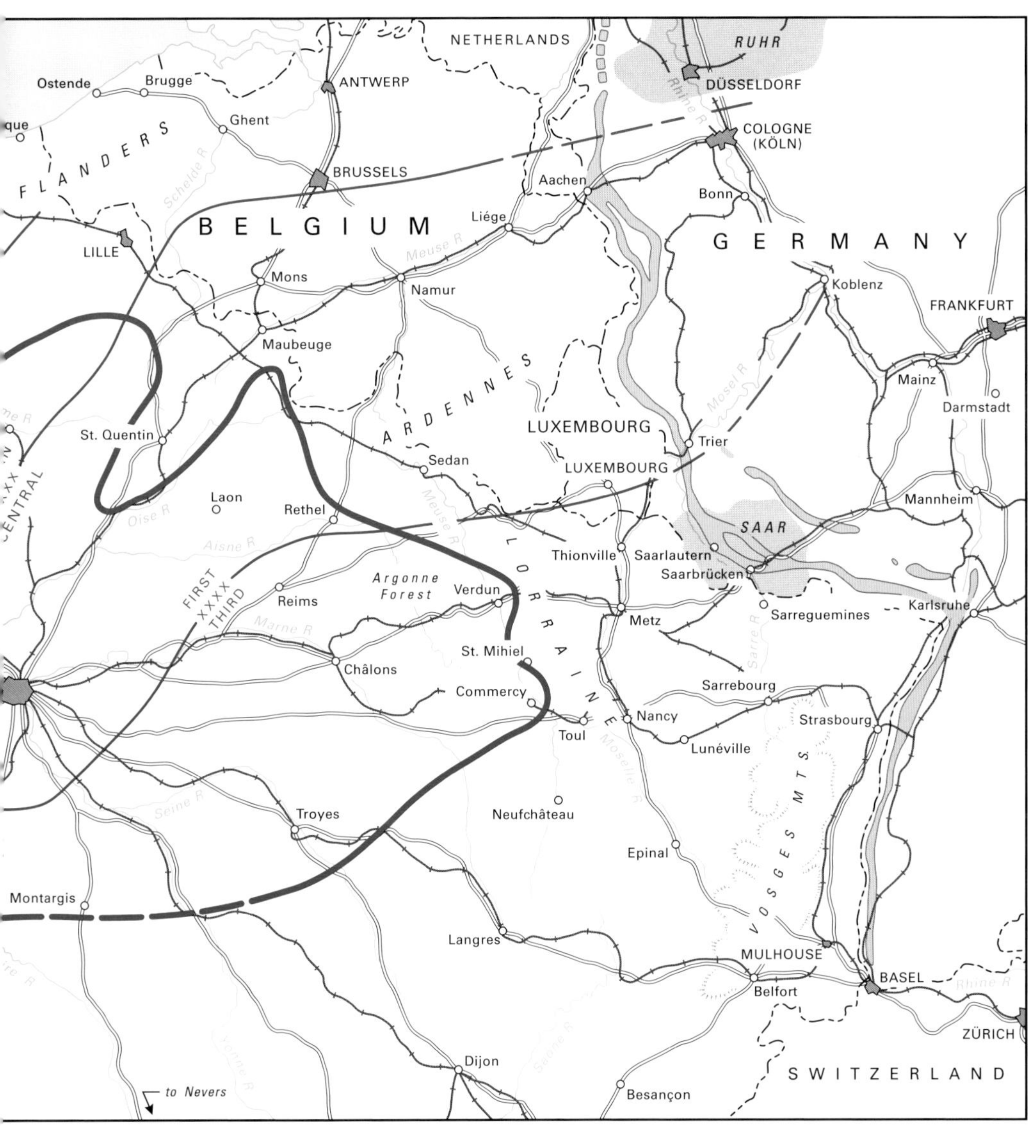

one combat command found its single tank battalion reduced to 21 tanks and its armored infantry battalion whittled to 159 men and 9 halftracks.[7]

Defensive operations posed a different challenge. They did not suit the offensive spirit of armored personnel, and they were not considered the primary function of the armored division. However, armored doctrine acknowledged their periodic

---

[7] U.S. Army Armor School, "Armor in the Hürtgen Forest, Student Report 45.1–7," 1949, U.S. Army Armor School Library, Fort Knox, Ky. Casualty statistics are from p. 163.

1st Armored Division tanks near Anzio, 1944

necessity. In a defensive role, armored units were expected to counterattack and conduct spoiling attacks to disrupt and delay enemy operations.[8] In September 1944, for example, the 4th Armored Division lay dispersed over a broad front following its double encirclement of Nancy, France. The division became the subject of a large-scale German armored attack. In the largest wartime tank battles between American and German forces, the 4th Armored Division reacted with aggressive counterattacks. During the multiday engagement, it outmaneuvered and outfought the German armor, destroying two panzer brigades in the process.[9]

The German Ardennes offensive similarly forced American armored divisions into defensive roles. In the opening days of the offensive, the 9th Armored Division became scattered amid retreating American forces. It operated as a collection of independent commands that strove to delay the Germans.[10] The 7th Armored Division was intentionally thrust into the critical road junction at St. Vith, where it conducted an effective mobile defense.[11] The 10th Armored Division also moved

[8] WD, FM 17–100, pp. 72–79.

[9] U.S. Army Armor School, *The Nancy Bridgehead* (Fort Knox, Ky.: Armor School, 1985).

[10] U.S. Army Forces in the European Theater, *The 9th: The Story of the 9th Armored Division* (Paris: P. Dupont, 1945); Walter E. Reichelt, *Phantom Nine: The 9th Armored (Remagen) Division, 1942–1945* (Austin, Tex.: Presidial Press, 1987).

[11] Staff Grp A, Sec 4, U.S. Army Command and General Staff College (CGSC), "The Battle of St. Vith: Defense and Withdrawal by Encircled Forces; German 5th and 6th Panzer Armies Versus U.S. 7th Armored Division and Attachments, 17–23 December 1944," Student Paper, May 1984,

Tank crew of the 1st Armored Division performing housekeeping chores

into the path of German forces in the early days of the offensive. It too fought an active defense that included the area around Bastogne.[12]

Armored doctrine discouraged urban combat, but it acknowledged that units might have to assault small towns and villages. In those instances armored forces

Combat Studies Institute, Fort Leavenworth, Kans.; U.S. Army Armor School, *The Battle at St. Vith, Belgium, 17–23 December 1944* (Fort Knox, Ky.: Armor School, 1984).

[12] 10th Armored Division Veterans Association, *Tenth Armored "Tiger" Division* (Paducah, Ky.: Turner Publishing Co., 1988), pp. 23–26, 58–67.

were to attempt a surprise attack, employ air and fire support to reduce the defenders, or conduct a carefully planned attack. Surprise attacks characterized by rapid movement, multidirectional assaults, and encirclement were preferred in capturing small urban enclaves. Against major cities, armored units were expected to encircle the defenses and prevent enemy reinforcement or retreat.[13]

Guidance on the detailed execution of tactical operations in cities was minimal. In Europe, the large number of cities, towns, and villages ensured the prevalence of urban combat. In the absence of effective doctrine each armored division developed its own standard operating procedures for fighting in built-up areas. During the pursuit across France, and again during the final drive into Germany, speed and surprise permitted the Allies to overrun many potential village strong points before the defenders could react. The 4th Armored Division routinely seized key terrain near towns and villages from which to fire into the urban area. Division personnel were encouraged to apply maximum firepower against towns and villages: "There is no further occasion to spare towns in our advances towards Germany. They should be plastered by artillery or air bombardment prior to the entry of our troops."[14] Tank-infantry teams then moved "rapidly into and through the town, firing at everything in sight to create terror and confusion among the defenders."[15] Against a disorganized enemy, these tactics worked well, evidenced by the capture of the French town of Commercy. There, before a battery of 88-mm. antitank guns could fire a shot, it was overrun by light tanks; the commander of the town reputedly fled "with shaving lather still on his face."[16]

Against larger cities such tactics were less likely to succeed. In such cases the role of the armored divisions lay in shaping the conditions for infantry and engineers to assault into the streets and buildings. At Nancy, the 4th Armored Division conducted a double envelopment of the city but left its reduction to supporting infantry. Similarly, at Aachen, the first German city taken by the Americans, the 2d Armored Division operated outside the city's confines and blocked German efforts to reinforce the city's garrison.[17]

American armored doctrine considered the tank's primary objective to be high-payoff targets in the enemy's rear areas. Enemy armor did not constitute such a target. Consequently, direct action against tanks was considered acceptable only as a matter of self-preservation or when a deteriorating tactical situation made such

---

[13] WD, FM 17–100, pp. 91–96.

[14] 4th Armd Div, Training Memo, 23 Sep 44, in U.S. Army Armor School, "Military History: Training/Tactics," Armor School Library.

[15] Ibid.

[16] "XII Corps Operations Notes No. 2," 7 Sep 44, in Armor Sch, "Military History: Training/Tactics" (hereafter cited as XII Corps Opns Notes no. 2).

[17] Christopher R. Gabel, "'Knock 'em all Down': The Reduction of Aachen, October 1944," in *Block by Block: The Challenges of Urban Operations*, ed. William G. Robertson and Lawrence A. Yates (Fort Leavenworth, Kans.: U.S. Army Command and General Staff College Press, 2003), pp. 68–69; Christopher R. Gabel, "Military Operations on Urbanized Terrain: The 2d Battalion, 26th Infantry, at Aachen, October 1944," pp. 1–2, U.S. Army Armor Branch Historian Files, Fort Knox; Charles B. MacDonald, *The Siegfried Line Campaign*, U.S. Army in World War II (Washington, D.C.: U.S. Army Center of Military History, 1963), pp. 251–306.

Tank recovery

action unavoidable.[18] This failure to consider enemy mobile formations as valid targets constituted a serious doctrinal fallacy. The emphasis given to operations in the enemy's rear areas and the armored division's combination of mobility and combat power made it a significant threat that an enemy could ill afford to ignore. In response to penetrations by armored formations, German doctrine called for counterattacks by mobile forces. The Germans adhered to this principle whenever available resources made it viable. The subsequent engagements pitted American tanks designed to attack soft targets against German vehicles built to engage armor.

Several factors prevented these encounters from becoming catastrophic for American armored forces. The armored division's combat command structure facilitated the rapid maneuver of multiple task forces in all circumstances. Rarely did American armored divisions commit pure tank elements to battle. Instead, tanks fought closely with tank destroyer, artillery, infantry, engineer, and reconnaissance assets as part of a task force. This team approach helped to offset the lighter armament and armor of American tanks. Air superiority also permitted regular access to air support, which the Germans could no longer expect by 1944. Finally, the quality and size of the German panzer force had diminished from the halcyon days of the blitzkrieg. German efforts to crush the Normandy beachhead through armored counterattack foundered in the face of continuous Allied air attacks, a stubborn ground defense, naval fire support, and the piecemeal employment of German tanks. Following the American breakout at St. Lô, much of the surviving German armor was destroyed in the fighting around the Falaise Pocket.

[18] WD, FMs 17–100, p. 22, and 100–5, p. 306.

M4A3s on firing range in Italy

Even after replacements and refurbishment, German armor lost its qualitative edge. Continuous fighting generated heavy, irreplaceable losses in personnel and materiel. American armored commanders, however, gained steadily in experience and capability—a development demonstrated during the September tank battles around Arracourt. Nor did German armor fare significantly better during the Ardennes offensive. Despite initial gains, American armor employed combined-arms teams to disrupt and delay the advancing German columns. Armored divisions then spearheaded the American attacks into the flanks of the German salient in the Battle of the Bulge. A total of eight armored divisions participated in these winter battles that destroyed Germany's last significant tank reserves on its Western Front.[19]

The Armored Division Organization

By 1944 the Army had a coherent doctrine to govern the employment of its armored divisions. However, two division types existed: heavy and light. The heavy armored division derived from organizational developments that culminated in 1942 and remained free from the paring influence of the Army Ground Forces (AGF) and

[19] Study no. 48, p. 6.

the Reduction Board. The heavy division embodied the desire of the Armored Force leadership to build a powerful, fully self-sufficient formation capable of sustained independent action. Like all armored divisions it dispensed with brigades, instead relying on two adaptable combat commands. It retained the regimental structure: two tank regiments, an artillery regiment, an infantry regiment, and a support regiment. Other components included an armored reconnaissance battalion, an engineer battalion, a medical battalion, and a signal company. The total strength of 14,488 soldiers and 390 tanks was distributed among four medium- and two light-tank battalions.[20]

Three heavy divisions entered combat. After the conclusion of the North African campaign, the 1st Armored Division underwent reorganization into a light division before reentering combat in October 1943. Only the 2d and 3d Armored Divisions completed the war as heavy divisions. The 2d Armored Division fought in North Africa and Sicily. Afterward it was sent to Britain, where the light and medium tank battalions of the heavy divisions were integrated into six identical battalions. The 2d and 3d Armored Divisions participated in the Normandy invasion and fought their way across France and into Germany.[21]

Throughout these operations, both heavy divisions favored standard troop assignments to each combat command. Typically, a combat command included two tank battalions; an armored infantry battalion; maintenance elements; medical support; and additional attachments of infantry, tank destroyer, engineer, and antiaircraft units. Combat Commands A and B also received the bulk of the division's organic and attached artillery support.[22]

The 2d and 3d Armored Divisions were exceptional in their organization. The remaining armored divisions bore the influence of Army Ground Forces and the Reduction Board. Each such formation included 263 tanks and 10,937 men. Smaller than the heavy 2d and 3d Armored Divisions, they became known as light divisions. They remained mobile, combined-arms formations capable of decisive action. Their principal components included thirteen battalions: three each of tank, infantry, and artillery and one each of reconnaissance, engineer, medical, and maintenance. The one-to-one ratio of infantry to tank battalions reflected analysis of foreign organizational trends. By 1943 the principal belligerents had abandoned the tank-heavy formations of the early war era in favor of a greater balance among infantry and armored assets. The light divisions emulated this trend through the reduction of tank battalions from six to three and the retention of the same number of infantry battalions. The increased proportion of infantry marked a direct response to the proliferation of mine usage and handheld antitank weapons.[23]

---

[20] Shelby L. Stanton, *World War II Order of Battle* (Novato, Calif.: Presidio Press, 1984), pp. 17–18; U.S. Army Ground Forces (AGF) Hist Sec, Study no. 27, "The Armored Force Command and Center," 1946, pp. 29–33, CMH.

[21] Hist Sec, "Armored Force Command and Center," p. 34; Stanton, *Order of Battle*, pp. 17–19, 47–52; Study no. 48, pp. 7–8.

[22] Study no. 48, pp. 7–8.

[23] Hist Sec, "Armored Force Command and Center," pp. 32–35; Stanton, *Order of Battle*, pp. 18–19.

German Panther tank knocked out in France

The light divisions also had two combat commands, but they did not retain regiments. Their smaller size and the use of combat commands with subordinate task forces obviated the need for regiments. Even in the heavy divisions, regiments rarely retained their organizational integrity in battle. Subordinate battalions were routinely distributed among different combat commands and task forces. The presence of regimental headquarters increased division overhead without improving divisional command and control. Similarly, the regiment's fixed organization contradicted the flexible and modular nature inherent to the combat command concept. The light divisions therefore possessed an unprecedented degree of organizational flexibility. Each included a collection of battalions to be assigned to the combat commands in any manner the division commander deemed appropriate.[24]

The combat command represented a modular component that could accept multiple attachments. It could also be readily task organized to fit evolving tactical situations. In the light divisions, recommendations for postwar improvement included the addition of a supply battalion to administer rations and supplies. Lacking a quartermaster unit, the light divisions encountered difficulties sustaining their units in the field and adopted a variety of ad hoc solutions. Ironically, earlier armored division organizations included such a unit, but Army Ground Forces found it unnecessary and removed it. The heavy divisions retained their supply battalions.[25]

---

[24] Hist Sec, "Armored Force Command and Center," pp. 29–35.

[25] WD Obsvrs Board, "AGF Report No. 396: Report of Visit with the 6th Armored Division," 23 Nov 44, in AGF Obsvr Board, European Theater, "Reports of Observers, ETO 1944–1945," vol. 3, C–396, Exhibit A, p. 3, U.S. Army Military History Institute (MHI) Library, Carlisle Barracks, Pa. (hereafter cited as Rpt no. 396).

Armor action in Brittany, August 1944

Both heavy and light armored division organizations included two combat commands. Designed exclusively to direct combat operations, many combat commands in fact found themselves saddled with control of service units and responsibility for supplying subordinate task forces.[26] The division headquarters also included a small staff section responsible for controlling the division reserves, but it lacked the personnel and communications equipment of the combat commands. In the light divisions, for example, this section included three officers and five enlisted personnel. An additional nine enlisted soldiers were available for augmentation as necessary. The commander of this section also served as the division's infantry training officer.[27]

In practice, both division types employed their reserve command as a third combat command, dubbed Combat Command R (CCR). It received troop assignments, managed task forces, and performed the same functions as the primary combat commands. The transformation of the reserve command into CCR occurred through improvised augmentation of personnel and communications equipment. In the heavy divisions, the infantry regiment's headquarters provided these assets. The regiment-less light divisions had to find other sources. Several formations simply diverted personnel from other tasks. The 12th Armored Division, for example, used a reconnaissance platoon, whereas the 14th Armored Division pulled the necessary personnel from a variety of duties throughout the division. However, the preferred solution lay in the use of the

[26] Ltr, Maj. Gen. Robert W. Grow to Colonel Barrows, 23 Sep 45, p. 2, Robert W. Grow Papers, MHI Archives.

[27] WD, FM 17–100, pp. 6–8.

headquarters and headquarters company of an armored group because it consisted of trained headquarters personnel familiar with armored operations.[28]

The divisional artillery structure also underwent change, but the modifications generally occurred before the armored divisions entered combat. Early armored division configurations included a regiment of artillery but no artillery representation beyond the regiment. During his tenure as chief of the Armored Force, Lt. Gen. Jacob L. Devers—a former artillerist—added an artillery commander and operations section to the armored division headquarters. Later this staff element expanded into an artillery headquarters and headquarters battery. Devers also abolished the artillery regiment, replacing it with separate battalions. These developments provided a much more flexible and responsive artillery component that permitted either centrally controlled massed fires or decentralized support to the combat commands. This responsiveness increased still further through the widespread presence of forward observers in the combat units.[29]

The light armored division reflected the AGF view that divisions should possess only those organic assets necessary for typical operations. The resultant flexible, manageable formation could deploy with considerably less shipping than the heavy division. However, deployability came at the price of combat power. Instead of temporary augmentation for select missions, the light division required permanent reinforcement. Standard attachments included a tank destroyer battalion and an antiaircraft battalion. Most commanders found the level of fire support inadequate. They sought and obtained the regular attachment of at least one battalion of self-propelled artillery and recommended still further support from heavier ordnance.[30]

The collective impact of these attachments was to restore in theater the combat power of the division that had been removed through the efforts of the Army Ground Forces and the Reduction Board. The heavy division, however, also benefited from similar attachments.[31] Already a robust organization, the accretion in strength swelled the size of the heavy division to roughly seventeen thousand men and four thousand vehicles—considerably larger than most panzer divisions by the summer of 1944. The ability of both division types to control diverse attachments attested to the versatile command and control arrangement represented by the combat command structure.

---

[28] WD Obsvrs Board, "AGF Report Number 693: Armored Notes," 1 Mar 45, in AGF Obsvr Board, European Theater, "Reports of Observers, ETO 1944–1945," vol. 4, C–693, MHI Library (hereafter cited as Rpt no. 693); Study no. 48, pp. 7–8; U.S. Forces, European Theater, General Board, Study no. 51, "The Armored Group," 1945, p. 3, CMH.

[29] Hist Sec, "Armored Force Command and Center," pp. 36–38.

[30] Ltr, Maj Gen Ernest N. Harmon to Lt Gen Lesley J. McNair, 23 Mar 44, Ernest N. Harmon Papers, MHI Archives; Rpt no. 396, Exhibit A, p. 2; WD Obsvrs Board, "AGF Report 487: Armored Notes," 30 Dec 44, in AGF Obsvr Board, European Theater, "Reports of Observers, ETO 1944–1945," vol. 3, C–487, pp. 1–2, MHI Library (hereafter cited as Rpt no. 487); HQ Armd Ctr, "Extracts From Overseas Reports Reviewed for Week Ending 25 August 1945," 25 Aug 45, p. 4, Army Field Forces Board 2, Record Group (RG) 337, National Archives and Records Administration (NARA); Study no. 48, p. 8.

[31] Study no. 48, pp. 7–8.

Tank gunner of the 37th Tank Battalion, 4th Armored Division, in September 1944

The level of organic infantry support in both division types generated universal criticism from armored commanders. Speaking of the light division organization and its reduced tank strength, 3d Armored Division Commander Maj. Gen. Maurice Rose remarked: "The new light division is little more than one combat command of this division. Granted that additional infantry is necessary for an armored division, it is stupid to think that one can increase the infantry of an armored division by reducing the number of tanks."[32] Most division commanders agreed with this sentiment and recommended the addition of up to three motorized infantry battalions for both the heavy and light divisions. Inadequate infantry support resulted in at least one division lacking sufficient dismounted strength to continue operations and simultaneously secure its initial objectives. Consequently, its forward momentum ground to a halt as the division stretched its combat power to hold onto them.[33]

[32] Rpt no. 487, p. 1.

[33] Rpt no. 396, Exhibit A, p. 2; Rpt no. 487, p. 1; Rpt no. 693, pp. 1–3; HQ, Armd Ctr, "Extracts From Overseas Reports," p. 4.

Street scene, 1944

Corps headquarters often ensured the availability of at least one additional infantry battalion for attachment to armored divisions, but the armored formations found this augmentation inadequate. The 10th and 14th Armored Divisions, for example, organized their combat commands into two task forces as encouraged by doctrine. The paucity of infantry resulted in one tank-heavy and one infantry-heavy task force. However, the 14th Armored Division engaged in sustained urban combat, where the demand for infantry far outstripped that for tanks. The tank-heavy task force possessed only limited combat value in this environment, and it played little role in some of the division's stiffest fights.[34] Attached infantry often consisted of standard line-infantry battalions rather than armored infantry. Unfamiliar with armored formations or their high operational tempo, these units did not reach their full effectiveness until they became accustomed to the needs of armored operations.[35]

Armored divisions also improvised solutions to the dearth of organic infantry. The 6th Armored Division simply diverted division personnel from other functions and redesignated them as riflemen. The 5th Armored Division converted its

[34] Rpt no. 693, p. 1; HQ Armd Ctr, "Extracts From Overseas Reports," p. 4.

[35] 4th Armd Div, "Notes on Recent Operations," 7 Oct 44, p. 4, in U.S. Army Armor School, "Military History: Training/Tactics," CS–1251–M–Army–Knox–Sep 86–2C, Armor School Library.

mortar and machine-gun crews into riflemen, whereas the 10th Armored Division followed suit with its antitank-gun crews.[36] Dissatisfaction with the level of organic infantry support led 12th Armored Division personnel to recommend a new division structure that included no tank units. Instead, infantry battalions with organic tank companies constituted the principal combat element.[37] This extreme viewpoint was not universally shared, but its sentiment reflected the general frustration of armored leaders, who found the armored division organization, particularly the light division, less than optimal.

Combat Operations

The Army fielded a total of sixteen armored divisions during the course of the war. The 1st and 2d Armored Divisions made their combat debut in North Africa. After the Sicilian campaign and Italy's subsequent surrender, only the 1st Armored Division remained in the Mediterranean Theater of Operations. Following the June 1944 Normandy landings, the 2d, 3d, 4th, 5th, and 6th Armored Divisions entered the Normandy beachhead and participated in Operation COBRA. During the ensuing pursuit across France, the 7th Armored Division entered combat. The 9th and 10th Armored Divisions joined this armored concentration as Allied forces neared France's eastern borders. In December, both of these formations conducted defensive operations during the German Ardennes offensive. During the Battle of the Bulge, the 11th Armored Division served as a mobile reserve. By late January 1945 the German attack had been defeated and American forces began operations into the Rhineland and against the Maginot Line. They were reinforced by the 8th and 12th Armored Divisions. The 13th Armored Division entered combat during the encirclement of the Ruhr Pocket, and the 14th Armored Division led operations out of southern France and into Germany. By early spring American armor was spearheading Allied drives into Germany and central Europe. The final days of the war brought the 16th and 20th Armored Divisions into combat.[38]

In all these campaigns the armored divisions fought as collections of combined-arms teams. However, the widespread application of combined-arms principles was merely a wartime phenomenon. In 1940–1941, under the direction of General Headquarters, the Army had abruptly adopted integrated doctrine and tactics in response to the success of German arms during the blitzkrieg era. The rapid change in American doctrine and organization occurred simultaneously with implementation of Selective Service, large-scale expansion of training, and changes in the Army's structure. The pace and requirements of mobilization prevented the thorough grounding of military personnel in the fundamentals of combined-arms action. Hence, commanders at all levels sought to overcome their own inexperience while training new units.

---

[36] Rpt no. 396, Exhibit A, p. 2; HQ Armd Ctr, "Extracts From Overseas Reports," p. 4; HQ Combat Command B (CCB), 5th Armd Div, After Action Reports (AARs), Aug 44–Apr 45, File no. 805–AD–404, Armor School Library.

[37] Rpt no. 693, p. 3.

[38] Study no. 48, p. 4. See Stanton, *Order of Battle*, pp. 46–69, for short overviews of each armored division's operational history.

Panzerkampfwagen IV knocked out by direct hit

Few armored commanders possessed a mastery of combined-arms principles and their application before entering combat. Such expertise was a prerequisite for fully exploiting the organizational flexibility of the combat command structure. While most officers grasped the value of molding different unit and weapon types into a single, cohesive team, they did not prefer amorphous organizations that lacked consistent definition. Hence the combat commands, designed to accommodate continuous change in response to enemy action and the operational environment, often received fixed troop assignments. This tendency restored organizational rigidity to the combat commands. By war's end many armored-division commanders were recommending a standard regimental structure in lieu of the flexible combat command.[39]

---

[39] Study no. 48, p. 24, apps. 6, 7; HQ Armd Sch, "Armored Conference Memorandum Number 4: Reference Data to Armored Conference Agenda," 3 May 46, p. O–3, Comments of Col G. M. Dean, Wartime Obsvr, European Theater of Operations, Jacob L. Devers Papers, York County Historical Society, York, Pa.

The principal exception to this trend lay in the 4th Armored Division. This formation served as the test bed for the combat-command concept. Its personnel thus became immersed in exploiting the combat-command structure and in combined-arms operations, an experience made yet more unique by the deliberate stabilization of its key personnel for two years before the formation entered combat. Not surprisingly, this division made full use of the flexibility inherent to the combat commands throughout its wartime activities.[40]

Greater acceptance and use of organizational flexibility occurred at the task-force level. Task force assignments often changed to meet specific mission needs and evolving tactical situations. Indeed, as combat experience was acquired, frequent configuration changes became routine—even in the midst of ongoing operations. Even so, some division commanders still sought consistency in the organization of task forces, routinely employing the same task-force configurations.[41]

Regardless of the degree of stabilization, combat command and task force composition normally included a mix of tanks, infantry, artillery, engineers, mechanized cavalry, tank destroyers, and antiaircraft assets. However, the ability to effectively employ these different unit types required time to acquire. Despite periodic stateside maneuvers, the battlefield served as the principal school for the conduct of combined-arms operations. Through acquired battlefield experience, armored commanders learned how best to employ the combined-arms teams at their disposal.

During the drive across France in the summer of 1944, standard practices began to emerge. Armored divisions routinely operated three combat commands, each controlling as many as four subordinate task forces. Whenever possible, the divisions functioned as a collection of fast-moving task-force columns whose separate actions and objectives were coordinated at the combat command and division levels. In France, these columns used both primary and secondary roads to keep the Germans confused as to their location and intent. At least one armored division routinely targeted telephone lines and communications centers, adding to the enemy's confusion.[42]

American armored columns operated at a pace faster than that at which the Germans could respond. The rapid, continuous action of these armored columns disrupted defensive efforts and accelerated the disintegration of German resistance.

---

[40] Memorandum, Brig. Gen. William M. Grimes to Commanding General (CG), 4th Armd Div, sub: The Organization and Employment of a Combat Team, 19 Dec 41, p. 3, Willis D. Crittenberger Papers, MHI Archives; Maj. Gen. Willis D. Crittenberger, "Unit Commanders' Meeting," 11 Apr 42, p. 2, Crittenberger Papers; Brig Gen William M. Grimes, "Notes on Combat Team Organization-Technique," ca. Jun 42, pp. 2–6, Thomas J. Camp Papers, MHI Archives; Christopher R. Gabel, *The 4th Armored Division in the Encirclement of Nancy* (Fort Leavenworth, Kans.: Combat Studies Institute, 1986), pp. 4–5.

[41] The 5th, 10th, and 14th Armored Divisions were among the formations that tended to rely on semipermanent task-force configurations.

[42] XII Corps Opns Notes no. 2, p. 3.

Tanks of the 66th Armored Regiment, 2d Armored Division, crossing an obstacle with the assistance of engineers

In Italy, the 1st Armored Division performed similar actions during the capture of Rome and the subsequent pursuit of German forces.[43]

The movement of multiple task-force columns occupied much of the combat command staff's energy. Radio supplemented by couriers provided the principal means of communication, even over long distances. The use of radio nets that corresponded to different tactical functions and command echelons refined the original communications organization pioneered by the interwar mechanized cavalry. When time permitted, security protocol mandated the use of encoded messages. In combat, however, such protective measures were often abandoned in the interest of rapid communication and clarity. Responsibility for maintaining the communications net lay with the armored signal company within the division headquarters. Oral orders were considered the norm, with written orders issued only when time permitted. Division liaison officers ensured effective coordination among the combat commands and task forces. For whatever echelon they were assigned, they served as

[43] HQ AGF, "Lessons Learned in the Battle from the Garigliano to North of Rome," 21 Sep 44, in AGF Obsvr Board, "Report of Observers: Mediterranean Theater of Operations," vol. 3, MHI Library.

the commander's representative, relaying his intent and instructions to subordinate elements. They also carried key information to the formation commander. As human conduits of information and commander intent, they played a vital role in sustaining situational awareness.[44]

Small liaison aircraft assigned to the division artillery provided an aerial dimension to coordination as they transported commanders and liaison officers among subordinate units. These aircraft were also used to coordinate the movement of task force columns from the air, a practice also pioneered by the mechanized cavalry. The 1st Armored Division used such aircraft during operations in the Po River Valley to conduct route reconnaissance, track friendly troop movements, and identify enemy strong points. The value of liaison aircraft led to recommendations to increase the number of such aircraft in the armored division.[45]

Units attached to the division posed additional challenges. They did not share the common training experience and purpose of the division's organic units. Attachments had to integrate themselves into this team environment as best they could. Their effectiveness generally improved the longer they remained attached to a formation, but their independent status meant that recognition through awards and citations did not always occur. Attached units also remained responsive to their controlling headquarters, usually a corps. The latter sometimes reassigned them without informing the division. One armored division, having made its dispositions to include attached mechanized cavalry and tank destroyers, discovered only by accident the loss of these units.[46]

The tank infantry team represented the core of the task force. Thus commanders sought to keep armored infantry close to the tanks. Doing so ensured the halftrack-mounted infantry could secure any gains the tanks made, thus sustaining forward momentum. The complementary strengths and weaknesses of the tanks and infantry provided maximum combat power and security. However, dissatisfaction with the halftrack's mobility led some commanders to favor mounting their infantry on tanks. Aware that the Germans learned on the Eastern Front to separate enemy tanks from their supporting infantry, American commanders believed that tank-mounted infantry could be carried directly onto their objective to surprise and overwhelm the defenders. This practice reduced the infantry's firepower to its small arms, because heavier weapons could not be carried in this fashion.[47]

---

[44] WD, FM 17–100, pp. 6, 29.

[45] XII Corps Opns Notes no. 2, p. 3; HQ Armd Ctr, "Extracts From Overseas Reports," pp. 3–4.

[46] 4th Armd Div, "Notes on Recent Operations," p. 4.

[47] WD Obsvrs Board, "AGF Observer Report No. 191: Notes on Interviews of Various Commanders in Normandy, August 5–10, 1944," in AGF Obsvr Board, European Theater, "Reports of Observers, ETO 1944–1945," vol. 2, C–191, p. 6, MHI Library; HQ AGF, "Battle Experiences, Twelfth Army Group," 15 Nov 44, in AGF Obsvr Board, European Theater, "Reports of Observers, ETO 1944–1945," vol. 6, p. 6, MHI Library; WD Obsvrs Board, "AGF Report No. 1120: Tactics, Organization, and Equipment, 7th Armored Division," 25 Jul 45, in AGF Obsvr Board, European Theater, "Reports of Observers, ETO 1944–1945," vol. 5, C–1120, MHI Library (hereafter cited as Rpt no. 1120).

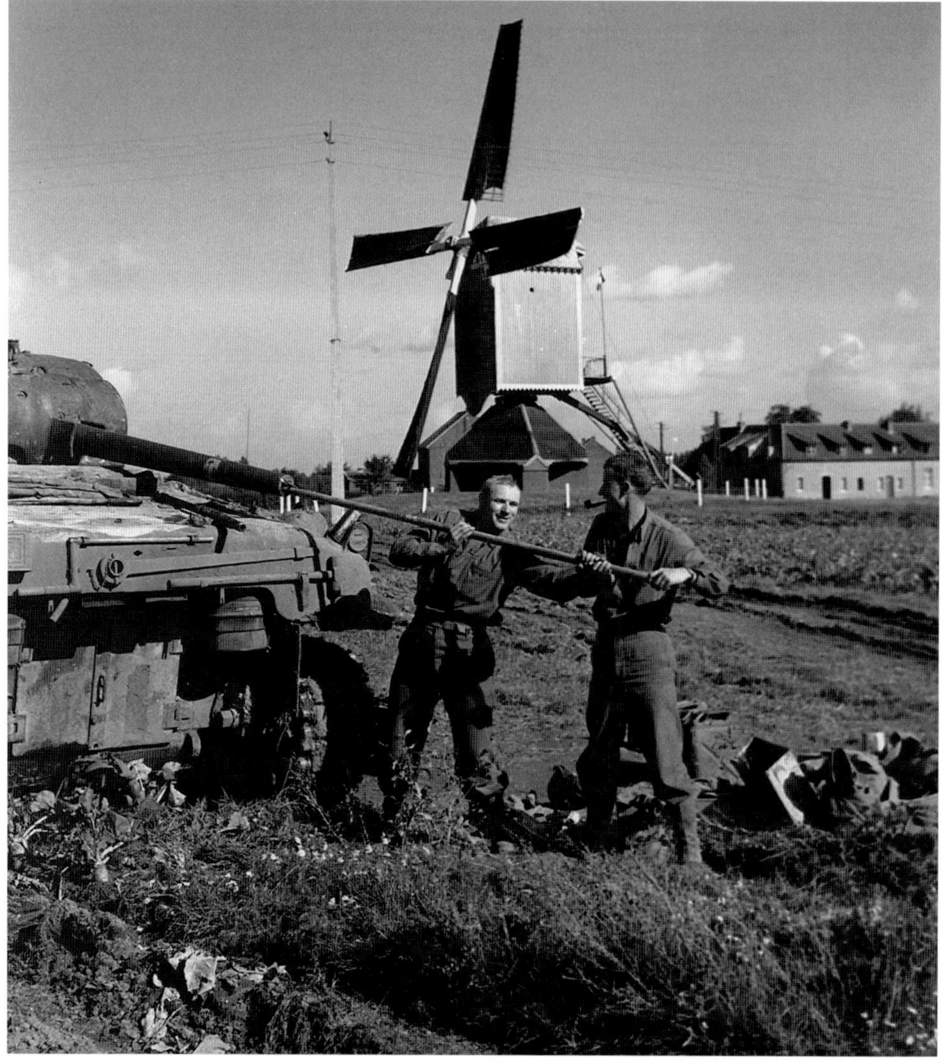

Tank maintenance in Belgium, September 1944

The 5th Armored Division carried the integration of tanks and infantry further. In June 1944, while still in England, the division commander reorganized his division. He matched an equivalent number of tank and infantry companies within each combat command. He further "married" tanks and infantry squads. Because the armored infantry platoon possessed five squads and each tank platoon included five tanks, each squad was assigned to a single tank. The division employed this reconfiguration through the end of the war. Formation personnel believed this structure maximized tactical cohesion and minimized casualties. From its entrance into combat on 2 August until the end of April 1945, the division's losses totaled

3,043 casualties and 116 tanks. The 6th and 7th Armored Divisions also entered combat within days of the 5th Armored Division yet suffered greater personnel and materiel losses during the same period.[48]

Combat operations revealed that even in the armored divisions' communication between tanks and infantry proved less than ideal. While the riflemen remained mounted, their transport's radio kept them in contact with the rest of the parent task force. Once they dismounted and maneuvered away from supporting vehicles, they lost this link. In one instance, German artillery fire forced the infantry out of their open-topped halftracks, whereupon German foot soldiers attacked them. American tanks were nearby, but the dismounted infantry lacked the means to communicate with them. The armor therefore remained idle while friendly infantry fought to survive.[49]

The ability of task-force columns to move rapidly into and through enemy rear areas depended on their ability to discover and exploit defensive weaknesses. This role fell to the reconnaissance assets available to each task force, including mechanized cavalry and available liaison aircraft. These elements normally preceded the task force and screened its movements. Information obtained through reconnaissance influenced command decisions. Hence, doctrine stressed the criticality of including reconnaissance actions in the operations planning process and providing sufficient time for their completion.[50] When the importance of sustaining forward momentum precluded the conduct of a thorough reconnaissance, armored units simply placed continuous, suppressive fire on suspected enemy positions as they advanced. This reconnaissance by fire sought to trigger an enemy reaction that revealed his position.[51]

Effective fire support also proved critical to maneuvering task-force columns in the face of opposition. Artillery moved at the same pace as the column, ready to engage on short notice. To facilitate rapid-fire missions, field observers accompanied all tank, infantry, engineer, and reconnaissance elements in addition to each headquarters. Each observer possessed a direct link not only to a particular battery but also to the parent battalion's fire-direction center. Consequently, one observer could direct the fire of either a single battery or an entire battalion.[52]

Armored Division Air Support

Task force columns often benefited from close air support. In North Africa, the process of requesting tactical air support had proven unwieldy and unresponsive to ground-force needs. In June 1943 a special board convened to revise aerial doctrine, and its actions led to the July publication of Field Manual (FM) 100–20, *Command*

---

[48] Rpt no. 487, p. 2; HQ CCB, 5th Armd Div, AARs, Aug 44–Apr 45, Armor School Library.

[49] Rpt no. 396, Exhibit A, p. 5.

[50] WD Obsvrs Board, "AGF Report No. 62: Notes from 2d Armored Division," 14 Jun 44, in AGF Obsvr Board, European Theater, "Reports of Observers, ETO 1944–1945," vol. 1, C–62, p. 4, MHI Library (hereafter cited as Rpt no. 62); WD Obsvrs Board, Rpt no. 693, p. 13; WD, FM 17–100, pp. 49–51.

[51] Rpt no. 1120; Training Memo no. 6, sub: Reconnaissance by Fire, in Rpt no. 1120.

[52] XII Corps Opns Notes no. 2, pp. 3–4.

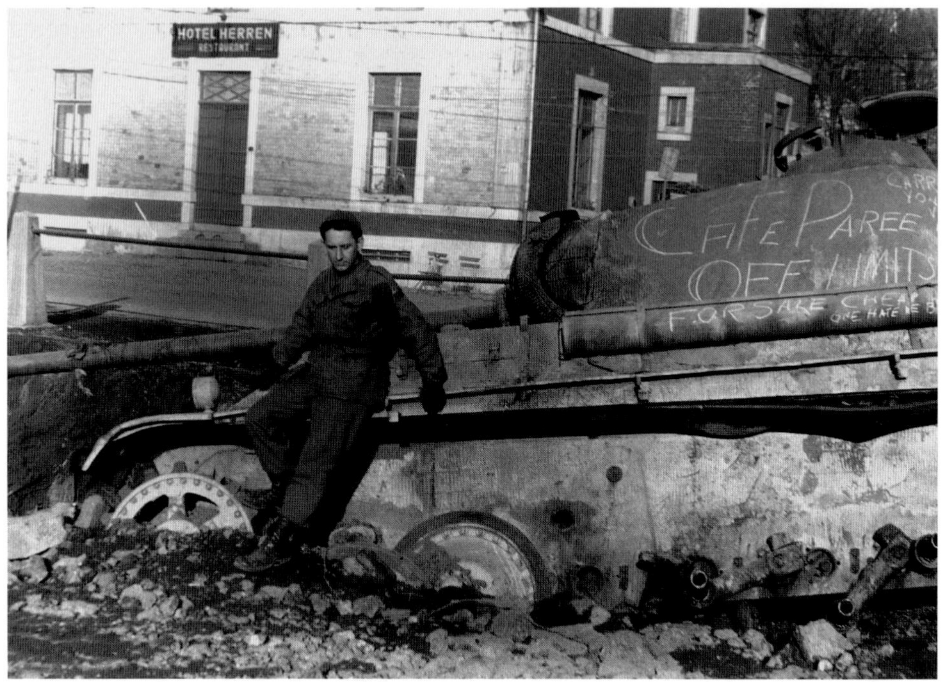

Tanker of the 32d Armored Regiment, 3d Armored Division, with a knocked-out Panther tank adorned with American humor

and Employment of Air Power. This manual offered few substantive changes and reaffirmed the low priority given to close air support missions. Consequently, the manual became the center of controversy and the focus of AGF criticism. This disagreement over the proper role of air power delayed the issuance of related doctrinal guidance. Overseas, each theater command developed its own techniques for employing air forces, which generally improved the frequency and efficacy of close air support.[53]

In Italy, the XII Tactical Air Command and the Fifth Army established close relations. Daily planning sessions helped to coordinate air and ground actions. Ground combat units submitted requests for air support to the Air Section attached to army headquarters. There, the army G–3 (Operations and Training) and the Air Command staff determined the validity of the target. Nearly half of all requests were refused, largely because they did not support army plans. Approved missions, however, tended to be much more effective. The Fifth Army Air Section maintained liaison

[53] Robert F. Futrell, *Ideas, Concepts, Doctrine: A History of Basic Thinking in the United States Air Force 1907–1964* (Maxwell Air Force Base, Ala.: Air University Press, 1971), pp. 69, 71, 90.

M5 light tank in the European Theater of Operations

officers with designated support squadrons, and experienced pilots accompanied ground combat units as flight controllers to direct the aircraft onto their targets.[54]

Offensive operations aimed at Rome's liberation benefited from these techniques. Initial attacks by ground forces forced the Germans to react and leave their fortified positions. Moving in the open, they became victims of the fighter-bomber waves operating in front of the American Fifth Army. In a single day, American pilots claimed over one thousand vehicles destroyed. Moreover, the movement of friendly ground forces disrupted German antiaircraft measures, thus reducing pilot losses. Flight controllers embedded with ground combat units demonstrated their value by consistently directing air attacks onto their correct targets, even during the fluid conditions that developed during the pursuit of German forces north of Rome.[55]

During these operations, the 1st Armored Division received the support of a fighter-bomber group. To ensure maximum effectiveness of the latter, the divi-

---

[54] HQ AGF, "Lessons Learned in the Battle from the Garigliano," pp. 13–16; Futrell, *Ideas, Concepts, Doctrine,* p. 90.

[55] HQ AGF, "Lessons Learned in the Battle from the Garigliano," p. 14.

sion made extensive use of L–5 spotter aircraft hovering over the formation's columns. Each aircraft carried an Air Force pilot and an observer from the division staff. When either ground units or the L–5 identified a target for air attack, the aircraft stationed itself over the target. It served as a beacon for the inbound fighter-bombers, establishing radio and visual communication with them. The observer and pilot then directed the strike directly onto its target; afterward, they reported the results. When the fighter-bombers were not responding to direct requests from ground troops, they attacked alternate targets predetermined by joint air and ground staffs.[56]

These improvements in air support techniques also applied to operations in France and Germany. In Third Army, for example, mission requests originated at the division or corps level. Flight controllers and the division staff selected targets and referred them to the Control Center at corps headquarters, where they were reviewed with the corps G–3. Approved targets were then transmitted to air units that conducted the mission. Pilots attached to each division controlled the flight from either the ground or an L–5 aircraft over the target. To minimize confusion, the flight controllers possessed aerial photos of the target and the same maps issued to the attacking flight.[57]

Further refinements provided advancing ground forces an unprecedented degree of air support. In the armored divisions, an air support officer accompanied each combat command. This officer rode in a tank and used a special radio for direct communication with aircraft. He maintained continuous contact with aircraft assigned to support the armored columns, thereby reducing fratricide. Moreover, during daytime movements a flight of four fighter-bombers flew cover for the column. They were relieved every thirty minutes, and the air support officer coordinated the incoming and outgoing flights. Hence, as the column advanced, the overhead flights provided immediate assistance against resistance. In this manner, the column sustained its momentum. When targets did not emerge, the aircraft attacked either targets of opportunity or preplanned alternate targets before they returned to base. The air support officer could also call in aircraft assigned to different corps areas. In these cases, direct communication with the fighter-bombers ensured their arrival over the target with fifteen minutes of receiving a request.[58]

This flexible, rapid response marked a major departure from the practices of North Africa. Moreover, the greater coordination between air and ground headquarters established a basis of mutual understanding that eroded the antipathy of the Army Air Forces toward close air support. Aircraft thus provided an aerial umbrella

---

[56] Ibid., pp. 15–16.

[57] WD Obsvrs Board, "AGF Report No. 476: Close Air-Ground Support by Fighter Aircraft," 28 Dec 44, in AGF Obsvr Board, European Theater, "Reports of Observers, ETO 1944–1945," vol. 3, C–476, MHI Library (hereafter cited as Rpt no. 476); Rpt no. 487; Futrell, *Ideas, Concepts, Doctrine,* pp. 90–91.

[58] HQ AGF "Battle Experiences, Twelfth Army Group," pp. 5–6; Rpt no. 476; WD Obsvrs Board, "AGF Report No. 598: Air-Ground Coordination," 1 Feb 45, in AGF Obsvr Board, European Theater, "Reports of Observers, ETO 1944–1945," vol. 3, C–598, MHI Library.

A tank of the 2d Armored Division in Belgium, December 1944

for the armored divisions and fulfilled a role not unlike the one originally outlined for dive bombers in early Armored Force doctrine.

Armored Materiel

The principal combat vehicles used by American armored units reflected a doctrine focused on attacking targets in the enemy's rear areas. Tank designs accordingly emphasized speed, mobility, and reliability. They did not carry the heavier armor and armament commensurate with tank engagements. Unfortunately, doctrine did not reflect the realities of the battlefield; armored units soon found themselves in engagements with German tanks.

American tanks possessed sufficient firepower for most targets they were likely to encounter in enemy rear areas. The M4 Sherman medium tank, for example, carried a turret-mounted 75-mm. gun capable of firing armor-piercing or high-explosive ammunition. When it was first fielded in 1942, this tank could compete with most German tanks. Indeed, its better automotive reliability probably made it superior. By 1944 the M4 constituted the bulk of the tank strength in the armored divisions and the separate tank battalions. However, despite a slight increase in armor protection and the provision of some vehicles with a more powerful main gun, the bulk of the

M4 fleet did not undergo significant modifications to make them more effective in tank engagements.[59]

Moreover, the quality of the M4 tank's armor initially proved inferior in its design. This flaw derived from the reliance of armor-plate manufacturers on outdated armor-penetration data gathered from prewar experiments with American tanks and antitank weapons. This data did not reflect the subsequent development of larger caliber and higher velocity antitank weapons or the parallel emergence of better antitank ammunition. Similarly, foreign achievements in these areas received scant attention. Only after combat revealed the inadequacies in American armor-plate design did changes begin to occur.[60]

In contrast, the period 1942–1944 witnessed major improvements in the ballistic protection and main-gun capabilities of German designs. German tanks were optimized for tank battles, and their doctrine encouraged confrontations with hostile armor. The *Panzerkampfwagen V* (Panther) and *VI* (Tiger I), for example, mounted high-velocity main guns for maximum armor penetration, had superior optics for long-range accuracy, offset their heavier weight with better flotation, and were more heavily armored. Both vehicles could engage and destroy the M4 beyond the latter's effective range. Even at close range, the American tank had difficulty penetrating the frontal armor of the Tiger and Panther. In action against such opponents, American armor persevered through a combination of aggressive leadership, maneuver, combined-arms action, air support, and sheer numbers—not better equipment.[61]

The increased frequency of armored battles generated interest in increasing the M4's firepower. Some M4 variants were fielded with a 76-mm. gun, but the potential value of this weapon was partially nullified by the extensive muzzle blast and smoke that surrounded the weapon's discharge, thereby identifying the tank's position. The 5th Armored Division sought to overcome these problems by pairing a spotting tank with each 76-mm. gun–equipped M4. The crew of the spotter tank reported the results of each shot fired. This practice, however, reduced the unit's firepower and could hardly be used in a fast-moving engagement with enemy tanks. German tanks did not suffer from excessive muzzle blast, and despite the greater penetrating power of the 76-mm. gun, too often it proved incapable of piercing the Tiger or Panther's frontal armor.[62]

---

[59] A total of 49,234 M4 Sherman tanks of all configurations were produced during the war, including 4,680 assault guns and 10,883 M4s carrying the 76-mm. gun. See George Forty, *United States Tanks of World War II* (New York: Sterling Publishing Co., 1983), p. 98.

[60] George B. Jarrett, "Ordnance: The Theme Song of Military History," p. 160, George B. Jarrett Papers, MHI Archives; Constance McLaughlin Green, Harry C. Thomson, and Peter C. Roots, *The Ordnance Department: Planning Munitions for War*, U.S. Army in World War II (Washington, D.C.: U.S. Army Center of Military History, 1955), p. 376.

[61] Rpt no. 487, p. 3; Rpt no. 693, p. 6; 2d Armd Div, "United States vs. German Equipment," Mar 45, Patton Museum of Cavalry and Armor Library, Fort Knox. This study resulted from General Dwight D. Eisenhower's request for an informal review of American and German equipment. The response provides a wealth of information on armored materiel from the tank crewman to the combat command commanders.

[62] WD Obsvrs Board, "AGF Report No. 385: Cavalry and Armored Report," 27 Nov 44, in AGF Obsvr Board, European Theater, "Reports of Observers, ETO 1944–1945," vol. 3, C–385, pp. 7, 18,

In response to growing concerns from the combat theaters about the inferiority of American tanks, the Ordnance Department undertook the independent development of a more powerful tank armed with a 90-mm. gun. Ultimately, this project became the M26 Pershing heavy tank, which entered combat in the final weeks of the war. Efforts to expedite the vehicle's development and fielding failed in the face of AGF opposition. General McNair did not believe the potential value of the M26 warranted the major disruption to M4 production that would have been required to establish a new tank-production line. At the time of his death in July 1944, American armor had not encountered large-scale German tank units and the frequency of tank battles remained low. With the production of improved tank destroyers in full swing, there seemed little reason to shift production emphasis to a heavy tank.[63]

In lieu of a more powerful tank, the Ordnance Department attempted to improve the ammunition used. High explosive antitank (HEAT) and high velocity armor piercing (HVAP) resulted. Both types of ammunition improved the chances of defeating heavier German armor, but they did not eliminate the discrepancy in killing power between the M4 and most German tanks and assault guns. The best results stemmed from the combination of 76-mm. gun and HVAP, but the latter's limited availability—no more than two or three rounds per tank—made its impact on the battlefield marginal.[64] White phosphorous intended for smokescreens was used against enemy tanks to blind their crews. It was also routinely used to drive infantry out of woods and buildings, where they could be eliminated by small-arms fire. HEAT also proved effective against buildings.[65]

The gyrostabilizer provided American tanks a limited ability to fire on the move. This device locked the gun tube onto a particular azimuth to assist target tracking. Its use, however, varied with units and crews. The gyrostabilizer drained batteries, interfered with radio operation, did not always provide accurate elevation corrections, and sometimes damaged the elevation mechanism. These problems led some crews to simply disconnect the device. Others used it extensively, considering its drawbacks an acceptable price for the ability to fire more accurately while in motion.[66]

MHI Library (hereafter cited as Rpt no. 385); Rpt no. 487, p. 3; 2d Armd Div, "Report on United States vs. German Armor," Mar 45, Exhibit no. 1, pp. 2, 11.

[63] Green, Thomson, and Roots, *Ordnance Department*, pp. 236–38, 278–87. For a different and critical analysis of both tank and tank destroyer development together with the clash of views among the Army Ground Forces, Ordnance Department, and the Armored Command, see Charles M. Bailey, *Faint Praise: American Tanks and Tank Destroyers During World War II* (Hamden, Conn.: Archon Books, 1983).

[64] WD Obsvrs Board, "AGF Report No. 689: Notes on Miscellaneous Munitions and Equipment (Armored and Cavalry Units)," 25 Feb 45, in AGF Obsvr Board, European Theater, "Reports of Observers, ETO 1944–1945," vol. 4, C–689, p. 3, MHI Library; 2d Armd Div, "Report on United States vs. German Armor," Exhibit no. 2, pp. 2, 11, and Exhibit no. 3, pp. 13, 34, 36.

[65] Rpt no. 396, Exhibit A, p. 1; HQ First Army, Memorandum no. 1, sub: Armored Notes: Lessons From Combat in Normandy, 19 Jun 44, in AGF Obsvr Board, European Theater, "Reports of Observers, ETO 1944–1945," vol. 2, C–110, p. 2, MHI Library; Rpt no. 385, p. 3.

[66] Rpt no. 385, pp. 7, 13, 17; Rpt no. 396, p. 7.

Track maintenance on a halftrack of the 9th Armored Division

The M5 Stuart light tank constituted the principle light tank used in both armored and mechanized cavalry units until the M24 Chaffee entered service in December 1944. Highly mobile and reliable, the M5 mounted only a 37-mm. main gun. Its light armor also made it vulnerable to most ordnance on the battlefield. Intended to support cavalry scouts or screen armored units, the M5 fared badly when confronted by German armor. Mine explosions also tended to buckle the tank's belly armor, causing it to sheer into the legs of the driver and bow gunner. By late 1944 the M5 had become unpopular among tank crews in the European Theater of Operations owing to its obsolescence. Several unit commanders recommended its removal from service, and the vehicle became relegated to secondary duties. In the different tactical environment of the Asiatic-Pacific Theater of Operations, however, the M5 continued in front-line service until the war's end.[67]

The M24 Chaffee light tank gradually replaced the M5. It carried a more powerful 75-mm. main gun that increased its ability to provide fire support to infantry and

[67] Rpt no. 385, pp. 12, 16, 19; WD Obsvrs Board, "AGF Report No. 694: Defense Against Antitank Weapons," 2 Mar 45, in AGF Obsvr Board, European Theater, "Reports of Observers, ETO 1944–1945," vol. 4, C–694, p. 2; WD Obsvrs Board, "AGF Report No. 479: Interview with Colonel S. N. Dolph, Commanding 102d Cavalry Group," 31 Dec 44, in AGF Obsvr Board, European Theater, "Reports of Observers, ETO 1944–1945," vol. 3, C–479, p. 1 (hereafter cited as Rpt no. 479); WD Obsvrs Board, "AGF Report No. 6: Organization, Employment, Training, and Equipment," Feb 44, in AGF Obsvr Board, European Theater, "Reports of Observers, ETO 1944–1945," vol. 1, C–6, p. 6; all at MHI Library.

mechanized cavalry elements. The M24's more powerful engine and better flotation enhanced cross-country mobility. Compared to parallel German light tanks, the M24 was considered superior because of its easier maintenance, gyrostabilizer, excellent visibility, and antiaircraft weapon. Popular, nimble, and reliable, the M24 proved an effective light tank capable of adequate performance in a variety of roles.[68]

Assault guns provided direct-fire support in armored and cavalry units. These vehicles resembled tanks, but their main armament was a howitzer. Assault guns advanced with tanks and infantry, entering direct-fire combat, unlike the artillery platforms stationed to the rear. Cavalry organizations used the Howitzer Motor Carriage M8, which carried a turret-mounted 75-mm. howitzer on an M5 light-tank chassis. In armored units, the assault gun was an M4 medium tank with a 105-mm. howitzer as its main armament. While this weapon could engage tanks, its armor penetration ability was low. It possessed a low rate of fire and muzzle velocity, and it lacked power traverse. Its primary use lay in the destruction of fortified or soft targets. The additional firepower of this weapon made it appreciated, but it proved just as vulnerable in combat as the more conventionally armed M4 models. Regarding the assault gun, the commander of the 69th Tank Battalion lamented: "I've had no luck with them at all. I've lost six already."[69]

In reconnaissance units, the M8 Greyhound armored car performed both reconnaissance and combat missions. This vehicle received mixed reviews from its crews. Most found it adequate and at least the equal of the German armored cars encountered. However, the vehicle's inadequate cross-country mobility received considerable criticism. Underpowered, it possessed poor flotation and an excessively large turning radius.[70] Maj. Gen. Robert Grow, commanding the 6th Armored Division, found the M8 too road bound. He undertook the replacement of his armored cars—including his own command vehicle—with the fully tracked M8 assault gun.[71] In the 2d Armored Division, too, some preferred a fully tracked replacement to the M8 armored car.[72]

Both mechanized cavalry and armored units made extensive use of the M3 halftrack. Designed as an armored personnel carrier, this vehicle proved adaptable to a variety of functions. Antiaircraft defense, gun platform, weapons carrier, ammunition supply, and ambulance versions became familiar sights in the combat theaters. The basic vehicle changed little during the course of the war. Its protection permitted passengers to move across areas dominated by enemy small-arms fire, but it proved vulnerable to most ordnance and artillery. In comparison to German

---

[68] WD Obsvrs Board, "AGF Report No. 759: Comments on the M–24 Light Tank," 25 Mar 45, in AGF Obsvr Board, European Theater, "Reports of Observers, ETO 1944–1945," vol. 4, C–759, MHI Library; WD Obsvrs Board, "AGF Report No. 1007: Mechanized Cavalry Organization and Tactics," 5 Jun 45, in AGF Obsvr Board, European Theater, "Reports of Observers, ETO 1944–1945," vol. 5, C–1007, p. 9, MHI Library (hereafter cited as Rpt no. 1007); 2d Armd Div, "Report on United States vs. German Armor," Exhibit no. 1, p. 1, and no. 2, pp. 3–4, 6.

[69] Rpt no. 62; Rpt no. 396, quote from p. 4; Rpt no. 385.

[70] Rpt no. 1007, p. 5; Rpt no. 479, p. 1.

[71] Rpt no. 396, p. 1.

[72] 2d Armd Div, "Report on United States vs. German Armor," p. 2.

M5 light tank passing a knocked-out German *Jagdtiger* in Germany

halftracks, the M3 generally proved more reliable and easier to maintain. The halftrack's cross-country mobility, however, proved less than ideal, encouraging recommendations that the vehicle be replaced with fully tracked personnel carriers to ensure transported infantry kept pace with advancing tanks.[73]

Armored Maintenance

The ability of armored units to engage in sustained combat operations depended on the mechanical state of their combat vehicles. In the armored division, responsibility for maintenance activities lay with the organic ordnance battalion. This unit included a battalion headquarters and three maintenance companies of three self-contained platoons. The ordnance battalion was designed to operate either as a single entity or as a collection of detached companies and platoons assigned to support different command echelons. The battalion headquarters retained the capability to conduct maintenance activities independent of its subordinate companies. The battalion headquarters maintained contact and control over detached elements via radio and liaison officers. In all activities, the battalion commander was "at liberty to make any grouping of men, vehicles, or equipment necessary to accomplish a given task."[74]

Often during combat operations, each command had a maintenance company or platoon. The maintenance units established forward collection points to which recovery vehicles brought damaged vehicles for repair. The nature of these locations varied from open fields to heated buildings. Security remained an important

[73] Rpt no. 487, p. 4; 2d Armd Div, "Report on United States vs. German Armor," Exhibit 2, p. 1.

[74] WD, FM 17–58, *Armored Maintenance Battalion Tactical Employment*, 1942, pp. 1–3, quote from p. 3.

M26 Pershing heavy tank

concern. The close proximity of maintenance units to combat units coupled with the tendency of armored units to bypass resistance often resulted in maintenance elements working in unsecured areas. Enemy contact sometimes occurred. Maintenance personnel received training in basic combat skills for self-defense.[75]

Liaison officers maintained contact between combat units and collection points. They also led repaired or replacement vehicles back to forward positions, routinely risking sudden enemy contact. Columns of repaired vehicles, even when they included tanks, possessed reduced combat power. Skeleton crews of mechanics and new replacement personnel operated the vehicles. Intended for different units, the preset radio frequencies did not always permit communication among the vehicles in a replacement column, complicating battle command and control.[76]

Maintenance units in armored divisions took pride in the support they provided their parent formations. The 128th Ordnance Battalion, for example, maintained a record of repairing all tanks for the 6th Armored Division within the battalion. Only completely destroyed vehicles were sent to higher echelon maintenance to the rear. Such records could be achieved only if sufficient parts were available.[77] However,

---

[75] HQ Maintenance Bn, 2d Armd Div, AARs, 24 Sep 44–2 Jun 45; HQ Maintenance Bn, 3d Armd Div, AARs, Jun 44–Apr 45; both at Armor School Library.

[76] Belton Y. Cooper, *Death Traps: The Survival of an American Armored Division in World War II* (New York: Ballantine Books, 1998), pp. 113–22. This book details the workings of the 3d Armored Division from the perspective of an ordnance liaison officer.

[77] Rpt no. 396, p. 8.

The Remagen bridge over the Rhine, captured by the 9th Armored Division, 1945

despite initial efforts to prepare stockpiles for operations in Europe before the Normandy invasion, parts shortages soon occurred. Theater reserves were quickly drained to sustain operations by both the First and Third Armies. Even so, supplies of tank tracks and engines quickly became exhausted. First Army responded by reducing its medium-tank strength by 5 percent. Higher echelon maintenance also undertook the rebuilding of engines in the field. At the tactical level, parts shortages resulted in extensive cannibalization, although this practice violated established doctrine.[78]

The drive across northern France taxed the maintenance support of the armored divisions. Maintenance teams sought to keep pace with tactical operations, continuously moving and working round the clock. Nevertheless, maintenance backlogs soon accumulated. To the shortfall of spare parts were added shortages in gasoline, oil, and lubricants. The diversion of truck transport companies from supplies to infantry transport further reduced the flow of these critical items. Stretched maintenance, parts shortages, and insufficient supply transport steadily eroded combat power. Between June and September 1944 the 3d Armored Division lost 436 medium tanks to enemy action. Of these losses, only 200 were repaired and returned to the division. Although the maintenance and supply situation eased as the front line stabilized, during the

[78] Armor Sch, "Maintenance of Armor in World War II," 1950, pp. 38–40, Armor School Library.

Tank commander

Battle of the Bulge mounted units faced a critical shortfall of antifreeze supplies, which forced combat units to improvise solutions—such as the use of alcohol or kerosene—and siphon antifreeze from nonessential vehicles. The winter's fighting also prevented armored vehicles from being rotated to the rear for long-overdue maintenance.[79]

In Italy, the 1st Armored Division experienced similar problems. Between May and July 1944 the formation remained in continuous operations with only brief respites, which adversely affected the ability to perform other than perfunctory maintenance. The state of the division's vehicles grew progressively worse, exacerbated by the extent of operations in rugged terrain, which increased the strain on engines and suspension systems. Further combat operations threatened to reduce the rate of available vehicles to just 60 percent. Even this reduced level assumed the presence of sufficient parts, particularly engines and transmissions. However, the division had suffered from ever-present parts shortages, particularly among engines, transmissions, bogie wheels, and sprockets. Replacement tanks only infrequently became available, but often they were damaged or inoperative tanks that had undergone some level of repair work. The wheeled support vehicles were in an equally poor state. Jeeps especially had high breakdown rates, and most of them had been repeatedly repaired.[80]

Despite these incessant maintenance problems, American armored units managed to continue combat operations. They did so through the extraordinary efforts of ordnance teams and the superior mechanical reliability of American-made vehicles. For example, between June and September the 4th Armored Division logged over one thousand miles; its supply vehicles traveled three thousand miles. In September the division began a period of rapid operations that climaxed in some of the largest armor engagements American forces experienced in World War II.[81] Maintenance activity tended to parallel combat in terms of periods of intense activity followed by relative lulls. The most common reasons for surges in work requirements included

[79] Ibid., pp. 44–50.

[80] Memorandum, Lt Col P. H. Brown to CG, 1st Armd Div, sub: Status of Vehicles, 4 Jul 44, Harmon Papers.

[81] Gabel, *4th Armored Division in the Encirclement of Nancy*, pp. 8, 10.

the arrival of newly trained tank crews, combat, and the general age of the vehicles, many of which remained in service for extended periods without replacement.[82]

Maintenance organizations proved flexible and able to overcome the stresses placed on them by sustained operations overseas. Combat forced them to depart from prewar concepts of operations, paralleling similar adaptations in tactical doctrine and organization. The armored divisions as a whole found themselves thrust into tank battles, urban combat, wooded terrain, and defensive engagements, although doctrine discouraged all these activities. The organizational flexibility of these organizations, however, permitted a high level of improvisation to overcome combat circumstances unanticipated during the early period of Armored Force development when much of the guiding doctrine emerged.

Through combat the armored divisions evolved into powerful, hard-hitting combined-arms formations capable of operations in most tactical environments and of effective integration of available air support. Although McNair's preference for streamlined formations that relied upon external augmentation found little favor in combat, the armored divisions gained a well-earned reputation for versatility and adaptability—qualities routinely exploited during the liberation of Europe.

[82] 2d Armd Div, AARs, 24 Sep 44–2 Jun 45.

14

ARMORED ENABLERS: MECHANIZED CAVALRY, INDEPENDENT TANKS, AND TANK DESTROYERS

The armored divisions constituted the most visible mounted presence on the battlefield, but they were supported and supplemented by mechanized cavalry, independent tank battalions, and tank destroyers. These organizations provided direct support to infantry formations and assisted the armored divisions in the accomplishment of their missions. Considered specialized assets, they were pooled in separate organizations for temporary attachment to other formations or for independent operations. However, the combat activities of mechanized cavalry, independent tank battalions, and tank destroyers suffered from doctrinal principles that did not reflect battlefield realities. Consequently, they were routinely used in missions for which they were neither organized nor equipped. The versatility inherent to each of these unit types permitted them to adapt to combat conditions but often in contravention of their doctrine. Combat operations encouraged the permanent integration of these assets into divisions.

Mechanized Cavalry

The war years marked an important transition for the Cavalry. After the creation of the Armored Force in 1940, this branch retained its responsibility for the development of horse and mechanized cavalry. Horse cavalry remained responsible for the full range of missions traditionally associated with the mounted arm, but its relevance to the war effort steadily fell. By war's end, horse cavalry had in effect ceased to exist. Conversely, mechanized cavalry became the principal focus of the branch. However, it bore little resemblance to the combat-oriented 7th Cavalry Brigade (Mechanized) of the interwar years. The organizational and operational concepts associated with that unit found expression in the new armored divisions. Cavalry mechanization thus focused on reconnaissance operations and the parallel development of light mechanized units to conduct them. Geographically, the center of cavalry development shifted from Fort Knox, Kentucky, to Fort Riley, Kansas, the site of the Cavalry School.

These developments ended the schism between mechanized and horse components. In the process the Cavalry lost the exclusive responsibility for developing mounted combat organizations. Much of its personnel served in horse cavalry

Equestrian duties at the Cavalry School, 1945

regiments and divisions. In 1942 the Army's reorganization eliminated the chief of Cavalry. Henceforth, Army Ground Forces became the controlling authority in matters of training, doctrine, materiel, and organization.

Under Lt. Gen. Lesley J. McNair's leadership, the Army Ground Forces accelerated the pace of cavalry mechanization. The 2d, 3d, 11th, and 14th Cavalry Regiments converted to mechanized units by 1943. Among the National Guard, four horse cavalry divisions and seventeen regiments were eliminated. Only seven partially mechanized and two horse regiments entered federal service. Shortly thereafter, the former became fully mechanized; the latter were dismounted and employed as infantry. Similarly, the 1st Cavalry Division transitioned to a dismounted formation before its assignment to the Asiatic-Pacific Theater of Operations. It remained there for the rest of the war and in 1945 was reorganized as an infantry division while retaining its cavalry designation.[1]

Between 1942 and 1944 mechanized cavalry units transitioned from all-purpose combat units into light reconnaissance assets. The independent mechanized cavalry regiments disappeared, replaced by units intended for either divisional or cavalry group assignment. Each heavy armored division received one armored reconnaissance

[1] Shelby L. Stanton, *Order of Battle, U.S. Army, World War II* (Novato, Calif.: Presidio Press, 1984), pp. 21–24.

Chart 21–Mechanized Cavalry Reconnaissance Squadron

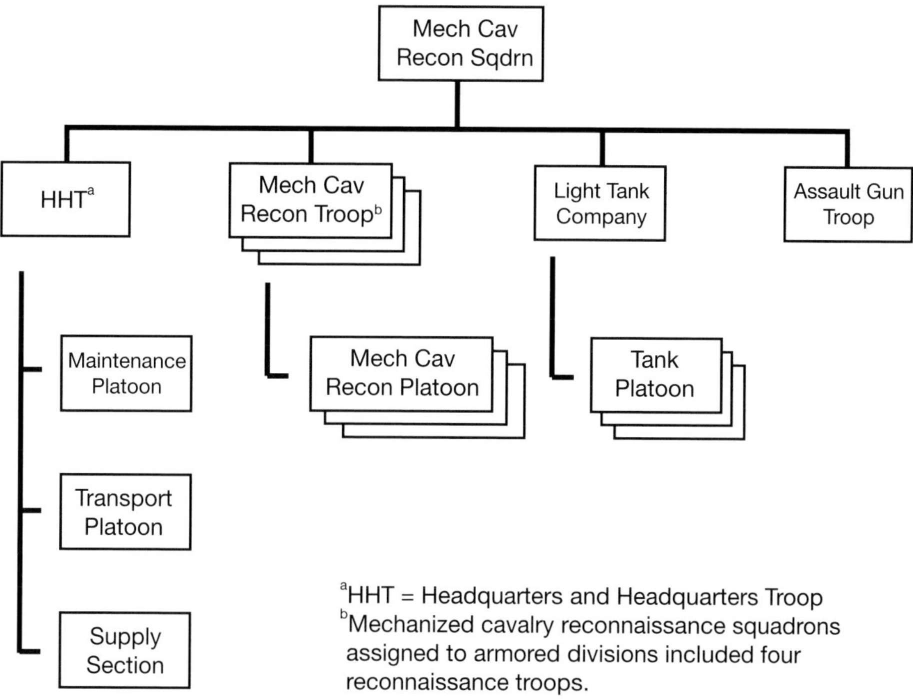

battalion, whereas light divisions received one mechanized reconnaissance squadron (*Chart 21*). A mechanized cavalry troop was also assigned to each infantry division. The cavalry groups served as corps reconnaissance assets. They included a headquarters and headquarters troop and two or more mechanized cavalry squadrons.[2]

Doctrinal changes coincided with the organizational redesign. Reconnaissance constituted the primary mission of all mechanized cavalry units. According to the 1944 field service regulations, "Mechanized cavalry units are organized, equipped, and trained to perform reconnaissance missions employing infiltration tactics, fire, and maneuver. They engage in combat only to the extent necessary to accomplish the assigned mission."[3] Mechanized cavalry units kept their parent organizations appraised of evolving tactical situations in a timely fashion, and they were expected to conduct both close and distant reconnaissance. Their doctrinal basis assumed the ability to perform reconnaissance independent of other activities. Therefore,

[2] Ibid.

[3] U.S. War Department (WD), Field Manual (FM) 100–5, *Field Service Regulations: Operations*, 1944, pp. 9–10.

mechanized cavalry units possessed high mobility and robust communications but only limited combat power.[4]

Operations in North Africa provided the mechanized cavalry's first exposure to combat. In the near debacle that befell American forces following the German attack at Kasserine Pass, the 81st Armored Reconnaissance Battalion of the 1st Armored Division lost an entire company while conducting delaying actions. Throughout the campaign the battalion performed reconnaissance, established observation posts, and mounted patrols. However, it also found itself intermittently engaged with German armor. The nondivisional 91st Cavalry Reconnaissance Squadron also served in North Africa. It performed security, static defense, and dismounted operations. The operations of both units were frustrated by the absence of accurate maps and direct confrontations with German combined-arms teams assigned to counterreconnaissance.[5]

The North African experience exposed a discrepancy between the variety of tasks actually performed on the battlefield and the narrow doctrinal emphasis on reconnaissance. Consequently, the 81st Battalion and the 91st Squadron found themselves thrust into missions they were neither organized nor equipped to perform. No constructive changes in doctrine or organization resulted; instead the problems these units faced in the performance of assigned missions were attributed to training deficiencies. The issue became further clouded by repeated assertions of the potential value of horse cavalry in North Africa. Operations in Sicily did not clarify matters because mechanized cavalry played only a limited role there.[6]

Observers noted that reconnaissance units needed to acquire information on enemy dispositions for tactical planning. They also needed to maintain contact with the enemy once established. Doing so required the ability to fight for information.[7] The jeep-equipped scout sections, however, lacked combat power. Therefore the light tanks, assault guns, armored cars, and mortars of the squadron and any attachments often supported them. These reinforced reconnaissance teams employed fire and maneuver concepts common throughout the Army. Support units fired on the objective to suppress the enemy or force him to reveal his position while maneuver elements moved on to the objective.[8] Such tactics hardly conformed to the stealthy infiltration outlined in armored reconnaissance doctrine. However, as one observer noted: "If reconnaissance units

[4] U.S. Forces, European Theater, "The General Board, Study No. 49: Tactics, Employment, Technique, Organization, and Equipment of Mechanized Cavalry Units," pp. 5–6, 1945, U.S. Army Center of Military History, Washington, D.C. (CMH) (hereafter cited as Study no. 49); WD, FM 100–5, p. 10.

[5] Matthew D. Morton, "Men on 'Iron Ponies,': The Death and Rebirth of the Modern U.S. Cavalry," Ph.D. Diss., Florida State University, 2004, pp. 266–80.

[6] Ibid. See also chs. 8 and 9.

[7] HQ, Armd Command, "Report of Observations at European Theater of Operations and North African Theater of Observations," 1 Aug 43, in U.S. Army Ground Forces (AGF), Obsvr Board, "Report of Observers: Mediterranean Theater of Operations," vol. 2, no. 35, U.S. Army Military History Institute (MHI) Library, Carlisle Barracks, Pa.

[8] HQ AGF, "Observers Report, Team No. 3," 22 Aug 43, in AGF Obsvr Board, "Report of Observers: Mediterranean Theater of Operations," vol. 2, no. 37, MHI Library.

Jeep reconnaissance patrol in North Africa, February 1943

do not overcome enemy reconnaissance units or small forward positions, the advance will be held up. Reconnaissance units have no difficulty in determining when they have reached an obstacle beyond their capabilities."[9]

In Italy, the rugged terrain and static nature of the operational environment often restricted mounted reconnaissance to the platoon level. Unable to operate according to doctrine, reconnaissance assets found employment in other roles. Scouts served as infantry in mountainous terrain, light tanks guided pack-mule trains and provided infantry support, whereas assault guns served as mobile artillery. In the 34th Infantry Division the mechanized reconnaissance troop often entered combat as dismounted foot soldiers. Even during periods of limited advances, the presence of powerful German forces prevented reconnaissance units from forging far in advance of the main body of friendly forces. One reconnaissance troop reported its routine inability to advance more than five hundred yards from its parent formation due to determined resistance.[10]

Opportunities to employ mechanized cavalry in the intended manner arose only during the pursuit of German forces following the fall of Rome and again during the final collapse of resistance at war's end. In the former case, the 81st Battalion advanced as a collection of reconnaissance teams, each including additional infantry, artillery forward observers, and at least one engineer officer in addition to the tank destroyers. Overhead, spotter aircraft acted as aerial scouts. The combat power of the mechanized cavalry was concentrated wherever possible to overcome resistance. However, the lightly armored cavalry vehicles had to be augmented with tank destroyers to cope with the isolated German armor encountered.[11]

The Normandy landings opened a new phase in mechanized cavalry operations. Between June 1944 and Germany's surrender in May 1945, an unprecedented mass

---

[9] Ibid, p. 2.

[10] HQ AGF, "Lessons Learned in the Battle from the Garigliano to North of Rome," 21 Sep 44, in AGF Obsvr Board, "Report of Observers: Mediterranean Theater of Operations," vol. 3, pp. 11–12, MHI Library; Morton, "Men on Iron Ponies," pp. 313–14.

[11] HQ AGF, "Lessons Learned in the Battle from the Garigliano," pp. 10–12; Morton, "Men on Iron Ponies," pp. 318–22.

A mechanized cavalry column stops for map consultation in North Africa.

of mechanized cavalry entered combat. This concentration included 13 cavalry reconnaissance squadrons assigned to light armored divisions, 2 armored reconnaissance battalions assigned to heavy armored divisions, 42 mechanized cavalry reconnaissance troops assigned to infantry divisions, and 1 unattached mechanized cavalry squadron. In addition, 13 mechanized cavalry groups were attached to various corps headquarters largely on a semipermanent basis.[12]

These units began operations optimized in doctrine and organization to perform reconnaissance missions. However, their actual employment quickly transcended this narrow role. Pure reconnaissance missions proved exceptional. Instead, reconnaissance normally occurred in conjunction with other activities that often involved combat. In effect, mechanized cavalry performed the traditional functions associated with the mounted arm. By 1944, however, these missions had been formally assigned to the horse cavalry, an entity that had disappeared from the battlefield.[13]

Mechanized cavalry conducted operations in all weather and terrain conditions and mounted attacks against wooded terrain, towns, and fortifications. The squadrons of the 6th Cavalry Group, for example, conducted river crossings, exploitation, and deep penetration of German lines in conjunction with armored formations; seized key terrain; provided flank security; pursued enemy forces; conducted exploitation missions; and performed reconnaissance/counterreconnaissance. An observer visit-

[12] Study no. 49, p. 6.

[13] FM 100–5, pp. 8–9; Study no. 49, p. 9.

Mechanized cavalry during the drive to Rome, 1944

ing the 102d Cavalry Group found the unit in static defense on the exposed flank of the V Corps. The unit lay dispersed over an eight-mile front manning a series of strong points and roadblocks with dismounted troopers. Its vehicles remained in service parks.[14]

Similarly, December 1944 found the 4th Cavalry Group squadrons holding part of the VII Corps' front line. The defensive posture marked a period of low activity following months of continuous operations that included amphibious assault, dismounted attacks, seizing and holding ground, patrolling, eliminating pockets of German resistance, screening, covering gaps between formations, and reconnaissance/counterreconnaissance. During the German attack at Arracourt, the 2d Cavalry Group found itself in the path of attacking armor. It conducted a successful delaying action, but its lightly armored vehicles paid a high cost in combat against German tanks.[15]

---

[14] WD Obsvrs Board, "AGF Report No. 1007: Mechanized Cavalry Organization and Tactics," 5 Jun 45, in AGF Obsvr Board, European Theater, "Reports of Observers, ETO 1944–1945," vol. 5, C–1007, p. 1, MHI Library; WD Obsvrs Board, "AGF Report No. 479: Interview with Colonel S. N. Dolph, Commanding 102d Cavalry Group," 31 Dec 44, in AGF Obsvr Board, European Theater, "Reports of Observers, ETO 1944–1945," vol. 3, C–479, p. 1, MHI Library; Study no. 49, p. 9.

[15] WD Obsvrs Board, "AGF Report No. 483: Notes on the Fourth Cavalry Group," 29 Dec 44, in AGF Obsvr Board, European Theater, "Reports of Observers, ETO 1944–1945," vol. 3, C–483, Exhibit A, p. 1, MHI Library; Hugh M. Cole, *The Lorraine Campaign*, U.S. Army in World War II

M8 Greyhound armored car in France, August 1944

Mechanized cavalry personnel sought acknowledgment for the full spectrum of missions performed. The variety of activity undertaken, including extensive dismounted combat, encouraged recommendations that cavalry troopers receive a combat badge similar to that awarded the infantry. Mechanized cavalry commanders believed that the broader mission set assigned to horse cavalry should also be applied to mechanized cavalry. Consequently, they wanted all mechanized cavalry units identified as cavalry rather than as reconnaissance organizations.[16]

The doctrinal emphasis on reconnaissance through stealth and observation received condemnation. According to Col. Edward M. Fickett, commanding the 6th Cavalry Group:

> Efforts and doctrine directed towards making the Cavalry Squadron exclusively a reconnaissance unit, not participating in combat other than as a necessity of extrication from enemy reaction or in the exceptional case of limited engagement by fire to obtain information desired, is faulty. It is evident that there is no occasion, no opportunity, and justification for the maintenance

(Washington, D.C.: U.S. Army Center of Military History, 1997), pp. 220–21; Morton, "Men on Iron Ponies," pp. 371–73.

[16] Rpt no. 479, p. 4; Rpt no. 1007, pp. 1–2; WD Obsvrs Board, "AGF Report No. 775: Mechanized Cavalry Notes," 28 Mar 45, in AGF Obsvr Board, European Theater, "Reports of Observers, ETO 1944–1945," vol. 4, C–775, MHI Library; Study no. 49, p. 20.

Dismounted patrol from the 4th Cavalry Regiment in the autumn of 1944

> in large commands of such an extremely costly, highly trained organization simply for the purpose of executing "reconnaissance."[17]

Mechanized cavalry generally had to fight for information. It therefore proved unable to perform distant reconnaissance, except where enemy resistance had collapsed. Aircraft increasingly performed this role.[18]

The War Department eventually acknowledged these concerns, but no formal changes in organization and equipment followed. Mechanized reconnaissance squadrons remained ill equipped for the missions they nevertheless performed. The unanticipated frequency of dismounted operations, for example, resulted in weapons

---

[17] Rpt no. 1007, p. 1.

[18] Ibid.; Study no. 49, p. 9.

and crews being stripped from vehicles, a practice which made the rapid resumption of mounted activity difficult. Recommendations for improvements at the platoon level included the inclusion of a rifle squad, the replacement of the 60-mm. mortars with self-propelled mortars, and improved communications suited to dismounted operations. At the troop level, suggested additions increased supply and maintenance support. Suggested squadron improvements sought more liaison officers, improved communications, the addition of pioneers, and the incorporation of a light aircraft section. Doctrine governing battlefield casualties directed units to leave wounded for personnel following to collect. Such a practice not only decreased the chances of survival, it also undermined soldier morale. Hence, it was not followed. Instead, additional medical support was sought from parent or attached units.[19]

The mechanized cavalry groups often benefited from the willingness of parent formations to attach additional combat units to them. The 3d Cavalry Group generally operated with a tank destroyer battalion. The Third Army operated four cavalry groups, each one reinforced with an artillery battalion, one or two tank destroyer companies, an engineer company, infantry, and additional wire communications. These attachments provided sufficient firepower for the groups to conduct independent operations. Similarly, the reinforced 6th Cavalry Group served as a de facto combat command that controlled its own subordinate task forces. At one time this group commanded two mechanized cavalry squadrons, an engineer battalion, an infantry regiment, three artillery battalions, two tank destroyer companies, and several tank companies.[20]

The group headquarters itself, however, proved deficient in personnel, vehicles, and equipment. It did not possess a vehicle capable of permitting effective command while moving. Radios lacked the ranges desired by commanders and staffs, resulting in the use of relay stations and slower message speeds. The minimal supply and administrative assets available were overtaxed. Nor did the headquarters possess liaison officers or military police. Such assets could be obtained only by diverting personnel from other duties.[21]

Despite these deficiencies, these headquarters provided adequate command and control over a surprisingly large number of attached units. Communication proved satisfactory, though not ideal, even among dispersed, fast-moving elements. In the 4th Cavalry Group, all subordinate units belonged to the group radio net, which was supplemented by wire communications when the unit remained in one place. Group situational awareness remained high, because new information reached all components at once. Extensive and intelligent organization of the communication means also permitted rapid fire support to all components likely to contact enemy forces. Every reconnaissance troop and attached unit was accompanied by a forward observer who maintained direct radio contact with supporting artillery. The armored

[19] Rpt no. 1007; Study no. 49, pp. 8–12, 20–21.

[20] WD Obsvrs Board, "AGF Report No. 385: Cavalry and Armored Report," 27 Nov 44, in AGF Obsvr Board, European Theater, "Reports of Observers, ETO 1944–1945," vol. 3, C–385, Exhibit A, p. 9, MHI Library (hereafter cited as Rpt no. 385); Rpt no. 483, Exhibit A, pp. 1–2; Rpt no. 1007, p. 2.

[21] Rpt no. 1007, pp. 12–18; Rpt no. 479, pp. 2–3.

car sections tuned to the frequency of the assault gun troop to ensure immediate support without elaborate and time-consuming prior planning.[22]

By war's end mechanized cavalry units had demonstrated their ability to conduct mobile dispersed operations. Their battlefield experience encouraged versatility, regardless of intended doctrine, organization, and equipment. In the process they drifted away from the pure reconnaissance emphasis for which they were designed back toward the general-purpose combat organization represented by the 7th Cavalry Brigade (Mechanized).

Independent Tank Battalion Readiness

The Army acknowledged the value of periodic armored support to infantry formations through the creation of independent tank battalions. The Army intended these units to reinforce infantry divisions for select missions or to provide a temporary mass of armor to rupture enemy defenses. Unlike the armored divisions, the independent tank battalions directly assisted the actions of the dismounted soldier at the tactical level to overcome resistance and breach enemy lines.

During the course of the war, the Army activated seventy-four of these battalions, including three battalions formed from National Guard tank companies. Two of these battalions, the 192d and 194th, were dispatched to reinforce the Philippines in 1941. They were destroyed there in subsequent operations against the Japanese. Of the remainder, thirteen battalions became amphibious tractor battalions to support landing operations, three more reorganized as special mine-clearing units, and another was equipped with flamethrower tanks. An additional battalion underwent training as airborne armor; but the concept did not materialize, and the unit reverted to its original role. Two battalions never left the United States. However, a total of fifty-two battalions provided armored support to infantry serving in the European, Mediterranean, and Asiatic-Pacific Theaters of Operation. In the European Theater alone, thirty battalions were ultimately available to support forty-two infantry divisions.[23]

Unfortunately, administrative neglect and lack of combined-arms training adversely affected the combat effectiveness of independent tank battalions. These units evolved from the General Headquarters (GHQ) tank battalions intended to provide infantry support, a mission the Armored Force considered secondary to the destruction of critical targets in the enemy's rear area. During the 1941 maneuvers, the GHQ tank battalions had often experienced difficulty in coordinating their actions with those of infantry. Proposed solutions included collocating independent tank battalions with infantry divisions, integrating tank and infantry training programs, and permanently assigning tank battalions to infantry divisions. The Army Ground

[22] Rpt no. 483, Exhibit A, pp. 1–2.

[23] AGF Hist Sec, Study no. 27, "The Armored Force Command and Center," 1946, p. 48; U.S. Forces, European Theater, "The General Board, Study No. 50: Organization, Equipment and Tactical Employment of Separate Tank Battalions," 1945, p. 4, CMH (hereafter cited as Study no. 50); Stanton, *Order of Battle*, pp. 296–302.

Tank and crew of the 741st Tank Battalion practicing dismount drill, February 1943

Forces and the Armored Force rejected all the proposals.[24]

Consequently, the independent tank battalions organized and trained on their own. Interaction with the formations they were expected to support on the battlefield proved limited to an occasional maneuver. In general, these tank units received little experience in combined-arms operations. By 1943 a gap had emerged between the effectiveness of independent tank battalions and those assigned to armored divisions. The latter benefited from a greater training emphasis on teamwork under the supervision of a divisional staff and often a representative from the Armored Force headquarters.[25]

Similar supervision eluded the independent tank battalions. They had no influential sponsor, and they did not constitute the principal focus of the Armored Force responsible for their training development. Throughout 1942–1943 the creation of new armored divisions and corps rather than independent tank battalions dominated Armored Force activity. Chief of the Armored Force Lt. Gen. Jacob L. Devers acknowledge this state, noting that "the tank battalions are now in the category of lost children and that we must take prompt action to bring them into the fold and be in closer touch with their needs and problems."[26]

Like armored divisions, independent tank battalions were formed from cadres drawn from existing battalions with similar disruption to the originating unit's cohesion. Unit training lasted thirteen weeks, but it lacked uniformity. Upon completion, each battalion participated in at least one maneuver but not generally as part of a combined-arms team. Urban operations were not addressed, and simulated combat against hostile forces gave an inflated sense of the tank battalion's power. In one instance, a unit achieved a twenty-to-one kill ratio against an opposing armored division. German combat capabilities were also not reflected in these exercises.[27]

Organizational changes to the independent tank battalions in 1942–1943 at least improved their combat power. The alterations transformed the battalions into

[24] Maj Gen Alvan C. Gillem Jr., "Report of Observations at European Theater of Operations and North African Theater of Operations," 1 Aug 43, p. 3, Xerox no. 2300, National Archives Project, George C. Marshall Library (GCM), Lexington, Va.; Hist Sec, "Armored Force Command and Center," pp. 52, 54; WD, General Staff, Ch of Inf, "Final Report of Maj. Gen. George A. Lynch: A Summary of Infantry Developments During His Term of Office," 30 Apr 41, pp. 51–54, 108, MHI Library.

[25] Memo, Maj Gen Ernest N. Harmon, sub: Notes on Combat Experience During the Tunisian and African Campaigns," n.d., p. 12, Ernest N. Harmon Papers, MHI Archives.

[26] Hist Sec, "Armored Force Command and Center," p. 46.

[27] Harry Yeide, *Steel Victory: The Heroic Story of America's Independent Tank Battalions at War in Europe* (New York: Random House Publishing Group, 2003), pp. 8–11.

Tank-infantry team in Europe

self-sufficient organizations with their own command, reconnaissance, and service support. Each battalion included a headquarters and service company, a reconnaissance platoon, one light-tank company, and three medium-tank companies. Organic support included assault guns, mortars, and a limited maintenance and supply capability. In this configuration the independent tank battalions became identical to those assigned to armored divisions.[28]

In 1943 the publication of a field manual for the independent tank battalions gave them a stronger doctrinal basis and uniform tactical principles. (*See Chart 22.*) This manual was a joint effort by Army Ground Forces, the Armored Force, and the Command and General Staff School. It emphasized the employment of the tank battalion or group as a concentrated force to ensure maximum effect on the battlefield. Tanks were to attack en masse to seize objectives, which supporting infantry secured. The manual did not provide effective guidance to govern the detailed coordination of tanks and infantry in combat.[29]

A revised version of this manual was published in March 1944. It reaffirmed the importance of using the battalion as a single mass to reinforce the supported division's main effort or to achieve a breach in the enemy's lines. The manual acknowledged the periodic necessity to detach battalion elements to support specific infantry actions, but such actions constituted an exceptional occurrence.

---

[28] Hist Sec, "Armored Force Command and Center," pp. 44–47.

[29] Ibid.

Chart 22–Independent Tank Battalion, 1943

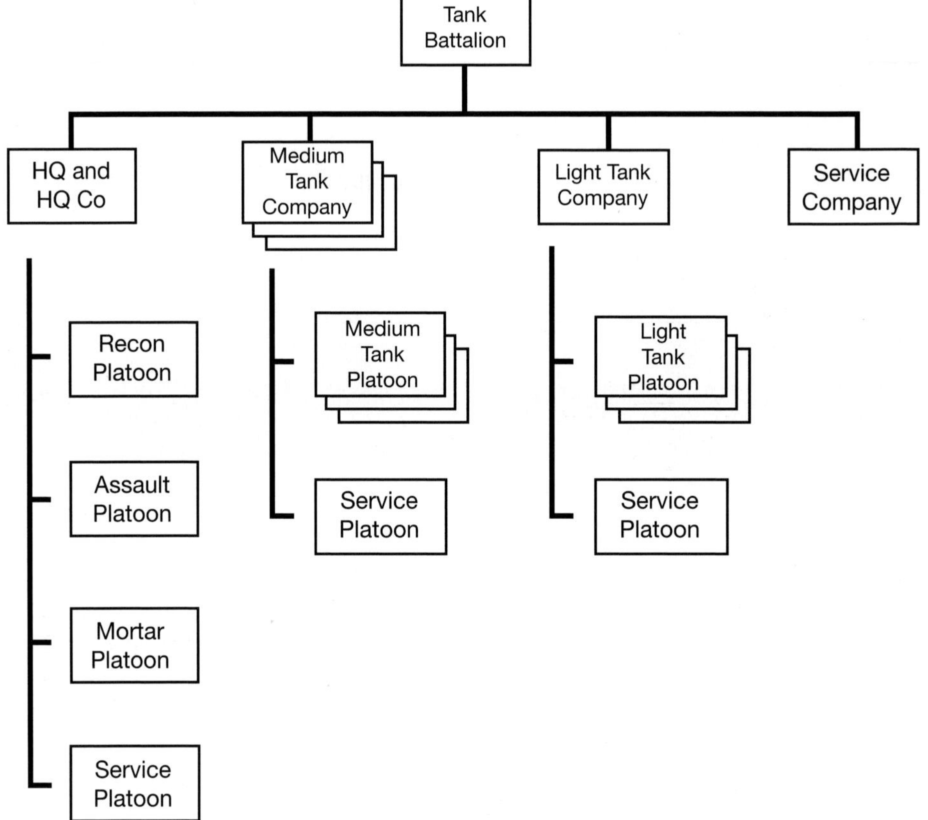

It too provided insufficient instruction for the close coordination of tanks and dismounted soldiers.[30]

Independent Tank Battalion Combat Operations

Organizational change and doctrinal definition did not adequately prepare independent tank battalions for actual combat conditions. The first encounter with German forces occurred in December 1942 during combat in Tunisia. A company of the 70th Tank Battalion was roughly handled and suffered extensive losses. The effectiveness of independent tank battalions tended to improve over time, but they could not always secure their own materiel and personnel requirements. Replacements and parts proved difficult to obtain since the independent tank battalions belonged to no division. As attachments, their needs often received a

[30] WD, FM 17–36, *Armored Employment of Tanks with Infantry*, 1944.

Tank with infantry support moving through town

low priority from senior commanders more concerned with permanently assigned organizations.[31]

The independent tank battalions also gained a reputation for ineffectiveness. Consequently, infantry divisions preferred to seek armored support from armored divisions whose tank battalions they considered better led and combat worthy. In some instances, infantry commanders requested armored division support, deliberately ignoring the presence of separate tank units already assigned. Avoidance of the independent tank battalions reflected the higher profile of the armored divisions and the attention given these formations. The second-string status afforded the independent tank battalions by the Armored Force did little to ensure they received the best personnel.[32]

In North Africa and Italy, the 1st Armored Division tried to improve the leadership and effectiveness of several independent tank battalions. It did so by replacing the battalion commanders with officers from its own ranks. Later, preparing to breakout from the Anzio beachhead, the 1st Armored Division grouped all independent

[31] Rpt no. 385, pp. 14, 20–22; Yeide, *Steel Victory*, p. 11; Memo, Harmon, n.d., p. 12.
[32] Memo, Harmon, n.d., p. 12.

tank battalions under its supervision. The formation then assumed responsibility for meeting all training, supply, and maintenance requirements.[33]

Despite these improvements, combat operations in 1944 continued to reflect difficulties in tank-infantry coordination. Combined operations by tanks and dismounted forces received insufficient emphasis in stateside training programs. Proposed solutions included pairing a tank battalion and an infantry division for combined training and employing them in combat as a team. Field commanders recommended a more permanent alignment of tank units and infantry formations, stimulated by their own combat experience and the German Army's embodiment of this concept in its panzer grenadier divisions.[34]

Tank battalions were intended for temporary attachment to infantry divisions. The effectiveness of their support increased with the length of attachment. Longer assignments improved teamwork and cohesion. Hence, where possible, corps and army headquarters in the European Theater of Operations sought to keep the same tank battalions and infantry divisions together. Regular attachment to the same infantry formation helped eliminate the perception among infantry commanders that the tank battalions were not part of the division team.[35]

Routine attachments between specific tank battalions and infantry divisions never became universal. While semipermanent attachments predominated in Third Army, some tank units experienced nearly continuous reattachment, which precluded the establishment of tactical cohesion.[36] In Italy, for example, one tank battalion underwent eleven different reattachments in a thirty-one-day period. An additional four reassignments were planned but subsequently aborted. The same unit had already logged six hundred miles during the months of May and June 1944 alone. This mileage reflected continuous operations that generated vehicle maintenance and crew fatigue problems. Unfortunately, the actual combat status of the vehicles remained largely invisible. Designated a corps asset, the unit remained on standby status until a subordinate division requested tank support. The tank battalion was dispatched, the operation conducted, and the battalion made available for a new assignment. Each new division assumed the tank unit was fresh and employed it accordingly. Consequently, the unit drifted from one mission to the next until its combat effectiveness evaporated.[37]

Poor planning and coordination only compounded the problem of continuous reattachment. Each support assignment necessitated shifting armored liaison teams,

---

[33] Ibid.

[34] Ltr, Maj Gen George S. Patton Jr. to Maj Gen Thomas T. Handy, 18 Jul 43, p. 2, Item 5645, Reel 379, National Archives Project, GCM; Gillem, "Report of Observations," p. 6; Memo, Harmon, n.d., p. 12.

[35] Rpt no. 385, pp. 10, 19, 21.

[36] Ltr, Maj Gen Ernest N. Harmon to Lt Gen Lesley J. McNair, 23 Mar 44, Harmon Papers; Hist Sec, "Armored Force Command and Center," pp. 59–60; Mildred H. Gillie, *Forging the Thunderbolt: A History of the Development of the Armored Force* (Harrisburg, Pa.: Military Service Publishing Co., 1947), p. 220.

[37] HQ AGF, "Extract from an Armored Commander's Narrative on the Italian Campaign," 11 Dec 44, in AGF Obsvr Board, "Report of Observers: Mediterranean Theater of Operations," vol. 3, pp. 3–4, MHI Library.

Knocked-out M4 Sherman medium tank

obtaining new information on friendly force plans, and developing a fresh situational analysis to guide the manner in which tanks would enter combat. These actions required time that often was not available, and they simply were not conducted. Tank battalion commanders in Italy often entered combat with little situational awareness other than what they could observe themselves. To overcome this problem, they created their own liaison officers to coordinate operations with infantry divisions, regiments, and battalions. Even this solution was nullified by the all-too-often receipt of vague, last-minute orders. Liaison aircraft, when available, offered better results. They were employed to identify friendly force dispositions, targets, and potential ambush locations.[38]

Even stabilized attachments did not ensure harmony between the tank battalion and supported infantry. Because infantry units did not routinely train with tanks, infantry officers often had little knowledge of tank capabilities or requirements. Consequently, they employed tank support without respect to their special needs and planning requirements.[39]

---

[38] Ibid., p. 1; Rpt no. 385, p. 18.

[39] HQ AGF, "Battle Experiences, Twelfth Army Group," 15 Nov 44, included in AGF Obsvr Board, European Theater, "Reports of Observers, ETO 1944–1945," vol. 6, pp. 3, 9, MHI Library; Rpt no. 385, Exhibit A, p. 19; AGF Board, "Quarterly Report," 21 Apr 44, in AGF Obsvr Board, "Report of Observers: Mediterranean Theater of Operations," vol. 3, p. 7, MHI Library; HQ AGF, "Tank-Infantry-Artillery Team," 1 Jul 44, in AGF Obsvr Board, "Report of Observers: Mediterranean Theater of Operations," vol. 3, p. 2.

Infantry officers at the battalion, regiment, and division staff levels all required better education in tank operations. Tank battalion commanders sought to improvise their own solutions. The 743d Tank Battalion, for example, divided its staff into three sections and assigned each to an infantry regiment in the division supported. These sections provided information and advice concerning armored operations. Still better results were obtained when an infantry formation undertook training with tank units. Some formations established their own training lanes and worked through tactical exercises with attached tank units. In this manner the 29th Infantry Division achieved considerable cohesion with the 747th Tank Battalion.[40]

Similarly, tank-infantry teams in the Asiatic-Pacific Theater of Operations did not always work well together, resulting in separation and combat losses. Sixth Army had several instances of tank units advancing and seizing an objective only to retreat because of the absence of supporting infantry to secure the position. Ineffective engineer support resulted in significant numbers of tanks becoming immobilized during stream crossings or destroyed by mines. Too often tanks found themselves isolated without any dismounted support. They quickly became the targets of Japanese close-assault tactics.[41]

Although tanks and tank destroyers proved effective in reducing strong points and fortified positions, infantry commanders either distrusted the weapon, as in the case of the tank destroyer, or did not understand how best to employ it. On Okinawa, the lack of confidence expressed by infantry commanders toward supporting armor undermined effective cooperation. Efforts to micromanage tank usage without regard to the recommendations of armored personnel generated friction and reduced combat effectiveness. As the island battle continued, greater cohesion began to emerge and more latitude was granted to tank commanders in the conduct of their assigned operations. Teamwork began to characterize tank-infantry action. Tanks blasted caves and ridgelines immediately before the advance of riflemen. Flamethrower tanks then followed to eliminate all vestiges of resistance.[42]

Regardless of the level of teamwork, tank-infantry teams suffered from poor communications on the battlefield. This problem became particularly acute during operations in the Normandy bocage in June and July 1944. For six weeks Allied forces struggled through several hundred square miles of fields bordered by thick hedges sunk into high embankments. These hedgerows impeded both infantry and vehicular movement, requiring ground forces to develop ad hoc techniques to breach them.

---

[40] Rpt no. 385, p. 10.

[41] HQ Armd Ctr, "Extracts From Overseas Reports Reviewed for Week Ending 18 August 1945," 18 Aug 45, p. 8, Army Field Forces Board 2, Record Group (RG) 337, National Archives and Records Administration (NARA) (hereafter cited as Extracts from Overseas Rpts, with date); U.S. Army Armor Sch, "Armor on Okinawa," May 49, p. 144, MHI Library.

[42] HQ, Armd Ctr, Extracts From Overseas Rpts, 25 August 1945," 25 Aug 45, pp. 1–2, Army Field Forces Board 2, RG 337, NARA; Armor Sch, "Armor on Okinawa." The operations on Okinawa marked the first use of flamethrower tanks by American tank units.

The Germans became adept at organizing integrated defenses in these hedgerows that transformed the enclosed farmlands into killing fields for Allied forces.[43]

The Normandy hedgerows limited tank employment to platoon and section elements. Tanks provided close fire support to advancing infantry, but the tank radios did not work on the same frequency as the handsets used by the infantry.[44] Too often planned attacks disintegrated under enemy fire. The infantry became pinned while the tanks drove off unaware of the plight of the riflemen. The inability of the infantry to communicate with the armor via radio resulted in desperate attempts to recall the tanks. Infantry climbed on the tanks and banged on the hatches, threw rocks at the vehicles, and even fired short machine-gun bursts at the turrets. None of these measures produced the desired result, particularly in the close, complex terrain of the hedgerows, where the wary tankers were more likely to consider all such activity hostile.[45]

Issuing infantry handsets to tank commanders proved more effective, but the riflemen possessed only limited numbers of such radios. Those ones lent to the tankers tended to suffer high loss rates. Some units therefore mounted on the back of the tanks field phones that linked into the vehicles' intercom systems. This setup permitted the infantry company or platoon commander to talk directly to the armored leader. The simple solution worked in combat, and it became a trademark of American tanks in the postwar years. Although common in the First and Ninth Armies, this solution to battlefield communications never became universal and problems of tank-infantry coordination plagued the Army to the war's end. Even where the field phones were available, infantry personnel were not always trained in their use. Tank crews also found that field-phone use increased the rate of radio-tube burnout and drained the vehicle's batteries. It also lowered the volume of the tank's internal communication system—a potentially serious problem in combat. In the Pacific Theater, soldiers using the field phone became sniper targets.[46]

Tank battalion combat effectiveness also depended on vehicle maintenance. These units included only limited maintenance assets. Generally, maintenance suffered from deficiencies in spare parts and tank transporters and many personnel lacked training in tank maintenance skills. The transient status of the tank battalions

---

[43] HQ First U.S. Army, "Memorandum No. 1: Armored Notes: Lessons From Combat in Normandy," 19 Jun 44, in AGF Obsvr Board, European Theater, "Reports of Observers, ETO 1944–1945," vol. 2, C–110, MHI Library; HQ European Theater of Operations (ETO), "Employment of Tanks and Infantry," 21 Jul 44, in AGF Obsvr Board, European Theater, "Reports of Observers, ETO 1944–1945," vol. 2, C–129, MHI Library; WD Obsvrs Board, "AGF Report No. 191: Notes on Interviews with Various Commanders in Normandy, August 5–10, 1944," 20 Aug 44, in AGF Obsvr Board, European Theater, "Reports of Observers, ETO 1944–1945," vol. 2, C–191, MHI Library; WD Obsvrs Board, "AGF Report No. 201: Use of Dozer Tanks and Landing of Tanks in Amphibious Operations," 30 Aug 44, in AGF Obsvr Board, European Theater, "Reports of Observers, ETO 1944–1945," vol. 2, C–201, MHI Library; Michael D. Doubler, *Busting the Bocage: American Combined Arms Operation in France, 6 June–31 July 1944* (Fort Leavenworth, Kans.: Combat Studies Institute, 1988).

[44] Study no. 50, p. 6.

[45] See Doubler, *Busting the Bocage*, for a detailed analysis of the problems posed by the hedgerows and the solutions devised by different American divisions.

[46] Rpt no. 385, 27 Nov 44, pp. 3, 5, 8, 14, 20; Study no. 50, p. 6; Armor Sch, "Armor on Okinawa," pp. 145–46.

Transporting infantry on a tank

often resulted in minimal support from the heavy ordnance companies assigned to parent corps and division formations. Continuous reattachment precluded the establishment of a steady source of parts and maintenance support. Consequently, the tank battalions faced a burgeoning maintenance problem during the course of sustained combat activity.[47]

The 746th Tank Battalion remained in continuous operations from June through November 1944, during a period when no extensive maintenance occurred. The state of the vehicles suffered accordingly. Even when sufficient spare parts were obtained, the battalion had insufficient transport for them. In combat, its recovery vehicles proved less than useful. When advanced to extract knocked-out or disabled tanks, their unique look quickly drew enemy fire. Consequently, the battalion resorted to using tanks to tow tanks. This practice saved recovery vehicles but increased the automotive wear on the combat vehicles.[48]

Many of these maintenance problems could and were overcome when a division or corps headquarters deliberately sought to alleviate them. In the XX Corps, an ordnance company was designated to serve all attached tank battalions. This

[47] Rpt no. 385, pp. 14, 20–22.
[48] Ibid., pp. 6–7, 16.

arrangement resulted in excellent maintenance support. Indeed, the level of support was considered the best in the European Theater. In Italy, the 1st Armored Division made similar provisions to sustain separate tank battalions with equally positive results. Some commanders sought a simpler solution by trying to obtain tanks with Ford engines, which were believed to require less maintenance.[49]

The problems associated with the separate tank battalions led to recommendations for their elimination in the postwar era. In lieu of a pool of battalions for attachment, the wartime experience encouraged a desire to make tank battalions organic to the infantry division. Infantry and armored leaders believed that such an arrangement would eliminate the cohesion, coordination, and attachment problems experienced during combat operations. Other recommendations included the removal of the light-tank and mortar companies and the addition of a properly equipped and trained ordnance company.[50]

These proposals aimed at improving tank-infantry coordination within the infantry division rather than the elimination of the tank support. By war's end the independent tank battalions had evolved into important assets. They had demonstrated their worth in hedgerow, wooded, and urban terrain—areas previously considered off-limits to tanks. The principal wartime difficulties included lack of combined-arms training, ineffective communications, and a doctrine that reflected prewar notions of tank massing rather than the actual needs of infantry formations. Once independent tank battalions overcame these difficulties, their effectiveness increased.

Rejection of Independent Tank Battalion Doctrine

Imbued with the doctrine of mass, the independent tank battalions deployed to theaters of operation. The notion of employing tanks in battalion or multibattalion concentrations, however, did not survive contact with infantry division commanders. Once attached to a division, the medium tanks were broken into company and platoon increments and given support missions with different infantry battalions. The most common distribution was one medium tank platoon per infantry battalion, but no universal standard applied. Within the 12th Army Group, for example, tanks were sometimes assigned to support infantry on the basis of one company per regiment. However allocated, the mission of the tanks remained the same: support the main effort as indicated by the infantry division, regiment, or battalion commander.[51]

The de facto breakup of the tank battalions into platoon parcels nullified the rationale behind the battalion's self-contained organization. The medium tank companies constituted the principal combat power of the battalion. Scattered among different infantry regiments and battalions, the tank battalion remnant possessed little intrinsic value as a combat unit. It too was split among different functions.

---

[49] Ibid., p. 16; Memo, Harmon, n.d., p. 12.

[50] Rpt no. 385, pp. 1, 6, 10, 14, 20–22; Study no. 50, p. 12.

[51] HQ 1st Inf Div, "Operations Memorandum No. 1: Employment of Tanks with Infantry," 2 Sep 44, in AGF Obsvr Board, European Theater, "Reports of Observers, ETO 1944–1945," vol. 2, C–120, p. 3, MHI Library; Rpt no. 385, pp. 1, 5, 10, 21; Study no. 50, p. 4.

Tank supporting infantry attack in the Solomon Islands, February 1943

The light tank company found employment conducting special operations for the supported division or providing an additional reconnaissance asset. Alternatively, some divisions used light-tank platoons to reinforce the medium-tank companies. However, the weak armor and armament of the light tanks limited their use in this capacity. The battalion's mortar platoon was either not employed, or it reinforced the infantry division's mortars. The reconnaissance platoon performed route and bivouac reconnaissance or liaison functions. The assault gun platoon often was organized into three sections, each assigned to a medium tank company for additional firepower.[52]

Without a unit to command, the battalion headquarters lost much of its purpose. The battalion commander served as an armored adviser to the division commander, whereas the battalion's staff continued to provide administrative support to the scattered tank units. Maintenance and supply functions became problematical, because

[52] Rpt no. 385, pp. 2, 6, 10, 11; Study no. 50, pp. 4–5.

no direct conduit existed between the battalion headquarters and the tanks. Arguably, the most effective use of the battalion staff lay in the role of liaison officers. In this capacity, they could at least participate—albeit indirectly—in the combat employment of the tank companies and platoons.[53]

Assignment of the battalion's single artillery forward observer constituted another problem. Most tank companies had no designated forward observer. Instead they relied on tank platoon leaders to call for fire missions. However, these commanders lacked training in this task, and their effectiveness varied. Recommendations to cross-train tank and field artillery officers soon resulted. In any event, the availability of artillery support could not be guaranteed, even when a trained observer was present. In the Ninth Army, for example, artillery support became a rarity after an attached observer was nearly killed on two different occasions.[54]

The dispersal of tank assets reduced the level of armored support from an entire battalion to companies and platoons. Against fortified positions, in urban settings, and in the Normandy hedgerows, tank sections constituted the principal form of tank support. Leading assaults, providing support by fire and bunker busting, and sometimes acting as reinforcing artillery were all common missions. The tanks generally moved with the infantry and engaged targets that threatened or obstructed the latter. Against fortifications they provided suppressive fire that permitted engineers to close with and destroy the defensive works. On the defensive, tanks were often assigned a sector to support and tank platoon leaders prepared contingency plans for a counterattack. Foreshadowing the Korean War experience, tanks sometimes were used as static pillboxes.[55]

In the Asiatic-Pacific Theater of Operations, tank battalions faced a different type of threat. The Japanese Army did not possess a strong tank force; its tanks were usually used in small numbers to support infantry actions. However, Japanese infantry employed a variety of techniques to destroy or immobilize American tanks. Mines were used extensively along trails used by tanks; infantry frequently attacked tanks, using surrounding jungle terrain to get close to the vehicles; ambushes staged near knocked-out vehicles targeted recovery teams. In defensive engagements with American forces, Japanese soldiers employed extensive fortifications and natural terrain obstacles, forcing attackers to expend time and casualties to remove them.[56]

American tank battalions thus found themselves employed in companies and platoons against local objectives not unlike their counterparts in Europe. They spearheaded infantry attacks, provided fire support, and used their weapons to suppress or eliminate specific positions. They also served in an artillery role, providing fire support directed by a spotter. To thwart Japanese night attacks, tank spotlights were used to highlight targets for supporting infantry to engage. Tank mobility proved

---

[53] Rpt no. 385, pp. 1, 10, 21–22; Study no. 50, p. 4.

[54] Study no. 50, pp. 6–7; Rpt no. 385, p. 1.

[55] Rpt no. 385, pp. 1–2, 8, 11, 17, 22; Study no. 50, p. 7; AGF, "Armored Notes," 18 Nov 44, in AGF Obsvr Board, European Theater, "Reports of Observers, ETO 1944–1945," vol. 6, MHI Library.

[56] HQ Armd Ctr, Extracts from Overseas Rpts, 18 Aug 45, pp. 2–3.

Tank-infantry team attack at Bougainville, March 1944

sufficient to keep pace with the infantry, but the rugged terrain in the jungles and on some of the Pacific islands often resulted in mired tanks.[57]

The Armored Group

As the war ended, so did the armored group. Intended to serve as headquarters for massed tank battalions, in fact they provided little more than planning and administrative support. No requirement for their tactical employment arose in Italy. In the European Theater of Operations, ten armored groups were assigned at the rate of one per corps. Each group bore responsibility for supervision and liaison of at least two tank battalions. However, the tank battalions remained dispersed among the infantry divisions, largely nullifying any potential influence the group headquarters might have had on them.[58]

One of the few instances of an armored group being organized to control a tactical grouping of armor occurred in the Pacific Theater of Operations. During preparations for the invasion of Luzon, several tank battalions were deliberately placed under a group headquarters. This unusual concentration was to counter the threat posed by the *2d Japanese Tank Division*. The Japanese formation possessed large numbers of tanks that could be employed offensively on the island's more

[57] Ibid., pp. 4–5.

[58] AGF Board, "Quarterly Report," 21 Apr 44; U.S. Forces, European Theater, General Board, Study No. 51, "The Armored Group," 1945, CMH (hereafter cited as Study no. 51).

open terrain. In actuality, however, the Japanese employed their tanks piecemeal in infantry support roles, rather than as a powerful, mobile counterattack force. The armored threat to American forces did not materialize, and the tank battalions of the armored group provided more conventional infantry support.[59]

In all theaters, then, the armored groups failed to perform their intended role. They proved little more than collections of headquarters staff and communications equipment. These assets were quickly employed in other duties. The group commander and immediate staff often served on a corps special staff, while its equipment supported corps liaison activities. Typical roles for the armored group as a corps staff element included operation of the corps rest center, defense of rear-areas, administration of military government functions, supervision of special schools, and the conduct of specialized training such as instruction in the use of mine rollers. The combination of trained armored personnel and their absence of a mission led to still another employment. The armored group provided the necessary personnel and equipment to make the reserve command of the armored division into a fully staffed third combat command. The armored group commander then served as an armored adviser on the corps staff. In October 1944 the 3d Armored Group became the first such organization to perform these dual roles to the benefit of the 5th Armored Division and its parent corps.[60]

From Tank Destroyer to Armored Gun

The tank destroyer experienced problems similar to those of the independent tank battalions. Its controversial debut in North Africa triggered efforts to clarify the principles governing its use. The Tank Destroyer Center revised doctrine, published a training circular, and disseminated tank destroyer information throughout the Army. However, these actions refined rather than altered tank destroyer principles. The primary mission of the tank destroyer remained the destruction of enemy armor through massed gunfire; although viable secondary roles were acknowledged, particularly that of reinforcing artillery.

In July 1944 the War Department published a new tank destroyer manual that incorporated lessons learned since North Africa. It too emphasized the destruction of enemy armor by centrally controlled tank destroyer battalions. The doctrinal emphasis on tank destruction found further elaboration in separate manuals for towed and self-propelled tank destroyer platoons. In addition, the new manuals provided general principles for the use of tank destroyers in secondary missions and better guidance for coordinated action with other arms.[61]

The emphasis on concentrated tank destroyer employment found reflection in the invasion plans for mainland Italy and France. The forces assembled for the landings at Salerno and Anzio included several tank destroyer battalions. For the

---

[59] Maj Milton T. Hunt, "Use of Armor on Luzon," Student Paper, Armd Sch, Fort Knox, Ky., 1947–1948, MHI Library.

[60] Study no. 51, p. 3.

[61] WD, FM 18–5, *Tactical Employment: Tank Destroyer Unit*, 1944; FM 18–20, *Tactical Employment of Tank Destroyer Platoon Self-Propelled*, 1944; FM 18–21, *Tank Destroyer Towed Gun Platoon*, 1944.

M10 Gun Motor Carriage in Metz, France

Normandy invasion and subsequent operations, the Army included thirty tank destroyer battalions: eleven towed and nineteen self-propelled. The large number of tank destroyers intended for France mirrored Germany's concentration of panzer formations there. To ensure sufficient strength against an armored attack, the towed tank destroyer battalions reinforced divisional antitank companies while the self-propelled units remained under corps and army control.[62]

In Italy, German mobile formations attacked the initial beachheads established at Salerno and Anzio. Tank destroyers participated in the repulse of these attacks, but they did not mass their fires in accordance with tank destroyer doctrine. Instead, they were employed by platoons to reinforce forward defenses. Once the German attacks ended and the need for antitank assets diminished, tank destroyers were used in other roles, particularly artillery.[63] A training circular distributed among forma-

[62] U.S. Forces, European Theater, General Board, Study no. 60, "Report on Study of Organization, Equipment, and Tactical Employment of Tank Destroyer Units,", 1945, p. 1, CMH (hereafter cited as Study no. 60); Martin Blumenson, *Salerno to Cassino*, U.S. Army in World War II (Washington, D.C.: U.S. Army Center of Military History, 1969), pp. 89, 115; Charles M. Baily, *Faint Praise: American Tanks and Tank Destroyers During World War II* (Hamden, Conn.: Archon Books, 1983), p. 102; Carlo D'Este, *Fatal Decision: Anzio and the Battle for Rome* (New York: HarperCollins Publishers, 1991), pp. 438–39.

[63] Maj Edward A. Raymond, "Brassing Off Kraut," *The Field Artillery Journal* 34, no. 10 (October 1944): 694–98; Christopher R. Gabel, *Seek, Strike, and Destroy: U.S. Army Tank Destroyer Doctrine in World War II*, Leavenworth Papers no. 12 (Fort Leavenworth, Kans.: Combat Studies Institute, 1985), p. 38; Steven J. Zaloga, *M10 and M36 Tank Destroyers, 1942–1953* (Oxford, U.K.: Osprey Publishing Ltd., 2002), pp. 15–16; Baily, *Faint Praise*, p. 99.

tions fighting in Italy provided local sanction for their dispersion and employment in other than antitank functions.[64]

In Normandy, the omnipresent hedgerows favored German defensive tactics and channeled vehicular movement to narrow corridors. In this environment, towed tank destroyers and divisional antitank guns proved ineffective. They could neither see nor fire over the tall hedge embankments from safe distances, forcing them to engage enemy positions at close ranges where they were vulnerable to enemy infantry. Unable to move quickly, they could not rapidly engage and displace. Consequently, self-propelled tank destroyers began to assume the role of divisional antitank protection. The absence of a large-scale tank threat and the difficulties associated with moving masses of vehicles through the bocage reinforced this reversal of centralized control at the corps and army levels. Instead, self-propelled tank destroyer battalions were assigned to infantry and armored divisions.[65]

The dispersion of tank destroyer battalions nullified tank destroyer doctrine. The embedded principles of battalion integrity, concentration, and defense in depth could no longer be applied. The tank destroyer battalion was designed as a balanced, self-sufficient force with its own reconnaissance, pioneer, maintenance, and medical support. It was intended for use as a single entity either alone or as part of a larger grouping of tank destroyers. In both Italy and Normandy, however, battalion assets were separated. Tank destroyer companies generally supported either an armored combat command or an infantry regiment, while their platoons in turn were attached to subordinate task forces and battalions.[66]

The tank destroyer battalion commander lost tactical control over his unit. His role became largely administrative, and his staff forfeited influence over planning and the tactical employment of the tank destroyer companies. These functions migrated to the company commanders, who did not possess the staffs to perform the necessary liaison work with supported units. Improvised solutions included the assignment of erstwhile battalion staff officers to each company and the diversion of reconnaissance platoon personnel to these duties.[67]

Tank destroyers found their effectiveness further limited by frequent reattachment. The development of the team cohesion necessary for effective battlefield teamwork required time that often was not available. Supported units did not always provide clear information regarding the tactical situation, resulting in at least one tank destroyer unit's becoming the victim of friendly artillery fire. Because of their temporary attachment status, tank destroyer maintenance

---

[64] HQ North African Theater of Operations, Training Memo no. 6, sub: Tactical Employment of Tank Destroyers, 11 Aug 44, in AGF Obsvr Board, "Report of Observers: Mediterranean Theater of Operations," 27 Feb–3 Dec 44, vol. 4, A–M, 58, MHI Library.

[65] WD Obsvrs Board, "Tank Destroyers Employed in Field Artillery," 13 Aug 44, pp. 3–4, in AGF Obsvr Board, European Theater, "Reports of Observers, ETO 1944–1945," vol. 2, C–163, MHI Library; Study no. 60, pp. 2, 13–14; Baily, *Faint Praise*, pp. 104–06, 114–17.

[66] Study no. 60, pp. 14–15.

[67] Ibid., pp. 15, 17.

M10 Gun Motor Carriage on the road to Paris, 1944

and personnel issues received little attention from supported units. Morale and effectiveness suffered as a result.[68]

Dispersion made the tank destroyer group and brigade superfluous. The group constituted a permanent headquarters designed to direct the operations of several tank destroyer battalions. At the start of the Normandy landings, each corps included a group headquarters. The brigade constituted a higher headquarters for two or more tank destroyer groups. In fact, these specialized headquarters rarely exercised a tactical role. They tended to perform administrative functions and helped to supply the scattered tank destroyer companies and platoons. The group commander evolved into the antitank adviser for his parent corps. Less specialized functions included rear area and corps headquarters security.[69]

While tank destroyer brigade, group, and battalion staffs struggled to find alternate missions, companies and platoons found themselves continuously employed. They regularly engaged enemy armor in small-scale actions. In the Normandy hedgerows, tank destroyers often found themselves in sudden, short-range encounters with individual enemy tanks and assault guns. In these engagements,

[68] HQ, 701st Tank Destroyer Bn, "Lessons Learned in Combat," 1 Jul 44, in AGF Obsvr Board, "Report of Observers: Mediterranean Theater of Operations," vol. 4, A–M 57, MHI Library; HQ AGF, "Lessons Learned in the Battle from the Garigliano," p. 2.

[69] Study no. 60, pp. 4–6.

M36 Gun Motor Carriage on a test track

the self-propelled tank destroyer's speed and mobility permitted it to engage, move, and reengage.[70]

In September 1944 elements of the 4th Armored Division became the target of a German counterattack near the French town of Arracourt. The fighting included some of the largest tank battles between German and American forces. Rolling terrain and ground fog favored German infiltration tactics and prevented the intervention of American air support. Nevertheless, tank destroyers supporting the 4th Armored Division used their mobility and firepower to outmaneuver and ambush German columns at close range. During several days of combat, the platoons of the 704th Tank Destroyer Battalion destroyed forty German tanks at a cost of four tank destroyers.[71]

The German December offensive in the Ardennes forced tank destroyers to conduct a series of delaying actions against multiple enemy columns. The surprise of the German operation preempted the concentration of antitank assets despite the

---

[70] Harry Yeide, *The Tank Killers: A History of America's World War II Tank Destroyer Force* (Havertown, Pa.: Casemate, 2004), pp. 126–34; George Forty, *United States Tanks of World War II* (New York: Sterling Publishing Co., 1983), p. 149; Zaloga, *M10 and M36*, pp. 15–16, 23–24.

[71] WD Obsvrs Board, "AGF Report No. 391—Notes on Tank Destroyer Activities XII Corps," 24 Nov 44, in AGF Obsvr Board, European Theater, "Reports of Observers, ETO 1944–1945," vol. 3, C–391, MHI Library; Armor Sch, "Military History Supplemental Material: 704th Tank Destroyer Battalion," Armor School Research Library; Armor Sch, "Employment of Four Tank Destroyer Battalions in the ETO," pp. 69–79, 1950, Fort Knox; Baily, *Faint Praise*, pp. 111–12; Steven J. Zaloga, *M18 Hellcat Tank Destroyer, 1943–97* (Oxford, U.K.: Osprey Publishing Ltd., 2004), pp. 17–19.

Tank destroyer attached to the 2d Armored Division, 1944

large-scale commitment of panzer forces. Instead, tank destroyer platoons battled German armor along snow-covered roads and bolstered the defense of St. Vith and Bastogne. They again relied on their mobility and firepower to engage and evade German tanks. In these freewheeling encounters, towed tank destroyers fell into further disfavor, because of their inability to adjust to rapidly changing tactical situations.[72]

The Ardennes offensive ended with heavy losses among the participating German formations. The loss of tanks and other vehicles in particular could not be recovered. As Germany's armored vehicle inventory evaporated, tank destroyers encountered German tanks with diminishing frequency. In March 1945, for example, an American intelligence assessment estimated that only forty-five German tanks and assault guns existed on the entire western front.[73]

Nevertheless, tank destroyers found the heavier armor and armament of late-war German tanks and assault guns difficult to overcome. Therefore tank destroyer crews sought flank shots, aimed at vulnerable points, or sought close-range engagements. The popularity and demand for the M36 Gun Motor Carriage also increased. This vehicle resulted from Ordnance Department efforts to upgrade the M10's armament.

[72] Armor Sch, "Four Tank Destroyer Battalions in the ETO," pp. 48–59; Baily, *Faint Praise*, pp. 116–18; Zaloga, *M18 Hellcat*, pp. 24, 33; Gabel, *Seek, Strike, and Destroy*, pp. 61–63.

[73] WD Obsvrs Board, "AGF Report No. 808—Tank Destroyer Information Letter No. 6," 4 Apr 45, in AGF Obsvr Board, European Theater, "Reports of Observers, ETO 1944–1945," vol. 5, C–808, p. 16, MHI Library (hereafter cited as Rpt no. 808). For examples of the type of small-unit engagements referenced, see also pp. 5–6 of this report.

The M36 mounted a 90-mm. gun in a redesigned turret atop an M10 chassis. It thus provided better firepower while retaining the mechanical reliability of the earlier vehicle. The Army undertook the replacement of all M10s with M36s. Those M10s made surplus were used to reequip towed tank destroyer battalions, but these plans remained incomplete at war's end.[74]

All tank destroyer guns proved effective in the performance of their secondary reinforcing artillery mission. Ironically, tank destroyers were more likely to be massed as a battalion in this role rather than in their primary antitank function. Tank destroyers used in this manner normally received support and oversight from a field artillery unit until they demonstrated proficiency in delivering fire missions.[75] Training at Camp Hood addressed artillery principles, but many tank destroyer crewmen arriving in theater possessed familiarity with only antitank operations. The Army's personnel system lacked the means to identify those soldiers trained in the tank destroyer's secondary mission. Hence, tank destroyer replacements with artillery skills did not always get assigned to units requiring this expertise. The resolution of both problems lay in the establishment of training programs improvised in theater.[76]

Terrain considerations and the limited presence of German tanks made the use of tank destroyers as reinforcing artillery commonplace. In Italy, mountainous terrain and German reliance upon successive fortified lines generated a greater demand for artillery rather than antitank support.[77] In France and Germany, tank destroyers provided artillery support to overcome prepared positions and support river crossing operations. In February 1945, for example, the XIX Corps conducted a crossing of the Roer River, reinforcing its own artillery with two tank destroyer battalions. The tank destroyers provided direct and indirect fire support against an array of preplanned targets. They were also slated to cover the flanks of the bridgehead and protect it from counterattack.[78]

Tank destroyers also found widespread employment as a general purpose weapon. Their combination of mobility and firepower made them suitable for a wide range of activities in addition to antitank and reinforcing artillery. In May 1944 Allied offensives ruptured German defenses in southern Italy and broke free from the Anzio beachhead. German resistance collapsed, and Allied forces began a close pursuit that liberated much of Italy. In these operations, tank destroyers demonstrated their versatility.

---

[74] Study no. 60, p. 2; Baily, *Faint Praise*, pp. 106–07, 115, 117; Gabel, *Seek, Strike, and Destroy*, pp. 53–54, 63. For a comparison of the fighting capabilities of the M36 and German tanks, see 2d Armd Div, "United States vs. German Equipment," Mar 45, Exhibit no. 2, Patton Museum of Cavalry and Armor Library, Fort Knox.

[75] Rpt no. 808, pp. 12–13; Study no. 60, pp. 23–24.

[76] WD Obsvrs Board, "Tank Destroyers Employed in Field Artillery," 13 Aug 44, in AGF Obsvr Board, European Theater, "Reports of Observers, ETO 1944–1945," vol. 2, C–163, MHI Library.

[77] AGF Board, "Employment of Tanks and Tank Destroyer Battalions as Reinforcing Artillery," 12 Jul 44, in AGF Obsvr Board, "Report of Observers: Mediterranean Theater of Operations," vol. 4, A–M 53, MHI Library; AGF Board, "Employment of Tanks and Tank Destroyers as Artillery," 17 Jul 44, in AGF Obsvr Board, "Report of Observers: Mediterranean Theater of Operations," vol. 4, A–M 58, MHI Library; Zaloga, *M10 and M36*, pp 15–16.

[78] Rpt no. 808, pp. 7–8; Study no. 60, pp. 7–8.

Towed tank destroyer unit training on the firing range

To cover a gap between two adjacent divisions, one tank destroyer battalion established a defensive screen. It employed its reconnaissance and security personnel as dismounted riflemen reinforced by antiaircraft machine guns removed from the tank destroyers. Most tank destroyer units, however, supported American columns that included tanks, infantry, and mechanized cavalry in their pursuit of German units. Rugged terrain limited the movement of these combined-arms teams to roads, where they encountered a succession of German roadblocks and strong points intended to slow their advance. Tank destroyers became the weapon of choice against these positions. They eliminated threats to friendly infantry and tanks and provided covering fire for their advance. In these operations, tanks and tank destroyers functioned as a team. Emerging integrated tactics soon reduced losses and exploited the relative merits of both vehicles.[79]

In Normandy, the hedgerow fighting generated demands for armored support of infantry that could not be met entirely by the independent tank battalions allocated for this task. Tank destroyers soon began to perform this role, using their main gun to suppress enemy positions and weapons.[80] Once the fighting cleared the hedgerows, tank destroyers began to support mechanized cavalry groups and to escort supplies. During the 6th Armored Division's dash across the Brittany peninsula, the formation's supply columns were forced to follow through unsecured areas subject to sudden encounters with German forces. The attached 603d Tank Destroyer Bat-

[79] HQ AGF, "Tank-Infantry-Artillery Team," 1 Jul 44, in AGF Obsvr Board, "Report of Observers: Mediterranean Theater of Operations," vol. 3, MHI Library; HQ AGF, "Lessons Learned in the Battle from the Garigliano," pp. 3–5.

[80] Study no. 60, pp. 13–14; Gabel, *Seek, Strike, and Destroy*, pp. 55–57.

Soldiers of the 7th Infantry Division with a tank destroyer on Kwajalein, February 1944

talion therefore assumed responsibility for convoy security. Its M18s could keep pace with the convoy trucks, and they possessed the firepower to cope with most threats. The 704th Tank Destroyer Battalion performed a similar role for the 4th Armored Division during the latter's race across France.[81]

Against fortified positions, the tank destroyer's high velocity, flat-trajectory armament permitted a degree of accuracy impossible to aerial bombardment or indirect fire. The tank destroyer could fire directly at apertures, doors, and other vulnerable points. These qualities made the 628th Tank Destroyer Battalion an effective tool in operations against the German Westwall. Attached to the 5th Armored Division, the tank destroyers employed both suppressive and direct fires

[81] Rpt no. 808, pp. 9–10; Rpt no. 391, p. 2; Zaloga, *M18 Hellcat*, pp. 15–17.

Tank destroyers employed in an artillery role along the Roer River, December 1944

against pillboxes. Alternatively, the vehicles maneuvered to the rear of the bunkers, concentrating their fire on armored doors. By these actions the tank destroyers permitted infantry to assault and gain entry to the fortifications.[82]

In urban areas, tank destroyers worked closely with infantry. Supporting an attack by the 34th Infantry Division on the Italian town of Lanuvio, the M10s of the 894th Tank Destroyer Battalion led the initial assault, overran a series of trenches, and engaged the occupants with their awkwardly mounted antiaircraft machine guns. The vehicles then carried infantry directly onto their objectives.[83] More commonly, tank destroyers provided direct-fire support against buildings, snipers, and antitank weapons. During the battle for the German city of Aachen, for example, tank destroyers joined small teams of soldiers equipped with rifles, machine guns, bazookas, and flamethrowers to clear individual city blocks.[84]

Towed tank destroyers also supported infantry. They displaced forward behind advancing riflemen and assumed firing positions from which they could provide antitank defense and fire support. During fighting for the German city of Colmar in February 1945, the 630th Tank Destroyer Battalion employed its halftrack transports as a maneuver force, using the vehicles' machine guns to suppress enemy soldiers. The halftracks also carried explosives for breaching walls and permitting antitank guns to be moved inside buildings. Despite these improvisations, towed tank destroyers still proved less effective than self-propelled weapons in urban environments.[85]

---

[82] Armor Sch, "Four Tank Destroyer Battalions in the ETO," pp. 17–18; Study no. 60, pp. 20–21; Gabel, *Seek, Strike, and Destroy*, p. 57.

[83] HQ 34th Inf Div, "Lessons Learned in Combat, November 7–8, 1942 to September 1944," Sep 44, in AGF Obsvr Board, "Report of Observers: Mediterranean Theater of Operations," vol. 4, A–M 89, pp. 55–56, MHI Library.

[84] For an analysis of the battle of Aachen and the role of tank destroyers as part of combined-arms teams, see Christopher R. Gabel, "'Knock 'em All Down': The Reduction of Aachen, October 1944," in *Block by Block: The Challenges of Urban Operations* (Fort Leavenworth, Kans.: U.S. Army Command and General Staff College Press, 2003), pp. 63–90.

[85] Rpt no. 808, pp. 3–4, 9.

Tank destroyer support of infantry, however, had the same coordination problems the tanks experienced. Infantry commanders did not generally understand the strengths and limitations of the tank destroyer, particularly its inability to fire while moving and its lack of an effective machine gun. Teamwork required time to develop and was prone to disruption by frequent reattachments and communication problems. Independent tank units and tank destroyers both labored through extended periods of continuous operations, but tank destroyer crewmen found their open-topped vehicles less than ideal living quarters, especially during cold or inclement weather.[86]

Soldiers from the 630th Tank Destroyer Battalion man a line of foxholes near Wiltz, Luxembourg

The few tank destroyer battalions deployed in the Asiatic-Pacific Theater of Operations faced a minimal Japanese tank threat. Many commanders sought alternate missions for tank destroyers. Among them was the 77th Infantry Division commander, Maj. Gen. Andrew D. Bruce, who first established the tank destroyer force. Eager to exploit the tank destroyer's capabilities as an armored gun, he equipped one of his divisional antitank companies with M18s and sought new roles for them. In general, though, tank destroyers acted as reinforcing artillery and provided direct-fire support for infantry. They engaged targets from safe distances to minimize the risk of close assault by Japanese infantry. During amphibious operations, they fired into fortifications from landing craft. Ashore, they became effective at deterring Japanese night infiltration of friendly positions.[87]

In all theaters, the tank destroyer's evolution into a general-purpose armored gun marked a departure from its intended role. Tank destroyers were not designed for close-range engagements with infantry. Expected to engage enemy armor from a distance, tank destroyers carried neither heavy armor nor effective secondary armament to use against infantry. Thrust into combat alongside riflemen, the open-topped tank destroyers were vulnerable to grenades, airbursts, and snipers. Lacking a bow or coaxial machine gun, tank destroyer crews resorted to side arms and grenades

---

[86] HQ, 701st Tank Destroyer Bn, "Lessons Learned in Combat"; "Third Army Staff Reports: Lessons Learned and Conclusions: Tank Destroyer Equipment," in Armor Sch, "Military History Supplemental Material: 704th Tank Destroyer Battalion."

[87] "Appendix No. II G–3 Estimate," p. 3, attached to Memo, Col W. L. Mattox to CG, Tenth Army, sub: Tank Destroyer Combat Employment, 19 Mar 45; Ltr, Maj Gen John H. Hester to Maj Gen Andrew D. Bruce, 15 Nov 43; Ltr, Maj Gen Andrew D. Bruce to Brig Gen Earnest J. Dawley, 13 Jun 44; all in Andrew D. Bruce Papers, MHI Archives. Zaloga, *M18 Hellcat*, pp. 34–36; Zaloga, *M10 and M36*, p. 37.

M10 Gun Motor Carriage loaded with personal gear, tenting, and extra gasoline for sustained operations in the field

against hostile infantry. They also sought to improve the level of armor protection by lining their vehicles with sandbags.[88]

Doctrinally, the unique antitank concept developed in 1941–1942 to govern tank destroyer use was discredited largely by neglect. The concentration of tank destroyers in battalion or multibattalion masses gave way to their dispersed employment as platoons, thereby nullifying much of the carefully crafted tank destroyer doctrine. By the war's end the de facto expansion of the tank's role to include antitank operations removed much of the rationale for a separate antitank force. The deactivation of the Tank Destroyer Center followed shortly after the war's end in November 1945.

The tank destroyer attracted more favorable attention as an armored gun. It had proven versatile in combat and agile in its ability to perform a variety of functions. Consequently, the tank destroyer experience stimulated a longstanding Army interest in a light, powerfully armed vehicle. In 1950 an Armored School study summarized the source of this interest:

---

[88] WD Obsvrs Board, "Tank Destroyers Employed in Field Artillery," pp. 4, 8; Rpt no. 391; Study no. 60, p. 27; Zaloga, *M10 and M36*, pp. 23–24.

> The self-propelled, hard-hitting weapons used by most TD [tank destroyer] units during the latter part of World War II made these organizations one of the most versatile antagonists on the battlefield. They were a quadruple threat to the enemy, being capable of maintaining a stiff defense against armor, could operate on the offensive against all hostile ground arms, supported the infantry as an assault gun, and were successfully employed as mobile artillery. The primary factor in their successful employment was the mobility inherent in the TD vehicle.[89]

The interest expressed after the war in the versatility of the tank destroyer platform was also reflected in reactions to the combat experience of mechanized cavalry and independent tank battalions. In each case, these units found themselves thrust into roles for which they were not configured. The narrowness of their guiding doctrine also proved inadequate. The result lay in the general abandonment of doctrinal concepts and widespread improvisation to meet a broad spectrum of tactical circumstances.

For each unit type, new doctrinal concepts emerged from combat to drive postwar reorganization. For the mechanized cavalry, battlefield experience led to a desire for a more robust organization capable of performing a much broader array of tactical activities. The result lay in an emphasis upon more combat power and gravitation toward a general-purpose unit with a mission set more akin to that once associated with the horse cavalry.

Tank destroyers and independent tank battalions shared similar negative experiences related to their role as separate attachments. Both unit types suffered from sustainment problems, since they were not organic to any division. Although a higher headquarters structure existed in the form of groups, tank destroyers and tank battalions generally functioned independently of them. Hence, permanent alignment with a division often became the recommended solution to their supply and administrative problems and also offered the prospect of better tactical coordination with supported units. This wartime trend marked an organizational reversal of the prewar pooling and centralization emphasis.

In general, battlefield experience identified difficulties in coordinating the actions of the armored enablers with other formations. While mechanized cavalry, independent tank battalions, and tank destroyers made an invaluable contribution to overall success in combat, they did so in spite of organizational, doctrinal, and supply difficulties. The war's end therefore brought a desire to eliminate these problems and more closely align these unit types with the formations they were expected to support.

---

[89] Armor Sch, "Employment of Four Tank Destroyers," p. 128.

15

CONCLUSION

The cessation of combat operations that followed the surrenders of Germany and Japan in 1945 triggered a massive demobilization of American forces. The Army shrank from a wartime peak of eighty-nine divisions to just ten by 1948. The number of armored divisions fell from sixteen to one in the same timeframe, and the mechanized cavalry and separate tank battalions experienced a similar downsizing. The Tank Destroyer Center deactivated, and the tank destroyer battalions disbanded. Both actions reflected wartime criticism of the tank destroyer concept and the growing versatility of the tank. Battlefield necessity thrust the tank into an antitank role; its combination of firepower, mobility, and protection undermined the need for a special antitank force. Indeed, by war's end the tank had become the preferred means of countering enemy armor. The concept of the main battle tank emerged, though this term was not yet in vogue in the 1940s.

The Armored Center inactivated. It had dwindled to little more than an advisory cell whose functions merged with those of the Armored School. The closure of the Armored Center ended the experiment begun in 1940 with the creation of the Armored Force. However, the war years demonstrated the importance of armored formations, which the Army did not intend to abandon.

In November 1946 the Armored Center reactivated, but the Army sought a more permanent means of incorporating armored organizations into its force structure. This issue was linked to the postwar status of the Cavalry, which had devolved into a hollow branch. The postwar Army retained the 1st Cavalry Division, but it was an infantry formation in all but name. Discussions concerning the future status of armor and cavalry soon gravitated toward the creation of a single mounted arm.

The immediate postwar years also triggered considerable discussion of armored organization and tactics. The wartime experience provided a wealth of combat data that the Army soon began to analyze, beginning with the General Board Reports compiled in 1945. The following year, at Fort Knox, Kentucky, an armored conference brought together armored commanders to discuss redesign of the armored division, materiel, and tactics. This event generated a consensus to increase the armored division's size and combat capability. Armored leaders generally preferred a larger, self-sufficient organization rather than the minimized light armored division of the war years. They preferred the cohesion of a permanent team organization over reliance on periodic attachments of special units for select missions. However, they retained the wartime armored division's modular, combined-arms nature and robust command and control characteristics. The net impact of postwar analysis lay in a restructuring of the armored division that increased its size to 16,000 men and 373 tanks.

Analysis of the separate tank-battalion experience indicated the need for close armor support of infantry. To avoid the coordination and training problems encountered in the war, the tank battalion became an organic element of the infantry division, which the Infantry had long advocated. Like the armored division, the infantry division tended to increase in size to provide greater combat power and reduce dependence on external attachments. These changes effectively overturned the principles embedded in the prewar triangular division, since the latter had sought to minimize formation size and encourage reliance on temporary attachments for special missions. Postwar redesign efforts for the armored and infantry divisions, however, remained largely paper drills, given the Army's reduced size. Nevertheless, both efforts derived from principles originally pioneered during the interwar years and refined on the battlefields of World War II.

Overseas, wartime organizational and doctrinal lessons found expression within the U.S. Constabulary. This organization was formed in 1946 to provide security and stability throughout that part of Germany occupied by American forces. Armored leaders played a central role in the Constabulary's creation, while the Armored School served as the model for the Constabulary School. Mechanized cavalry, armored divisions, and tank destroyers slated for demobilization provided much of the manpower and materiel necessary to create the new constabulary units. The latter drew on the wartime experience of mounted units to create modular organizations that relied on robust communications to coordinate roving patrols and checkpoints.

By 1948 the reemergence of German government and police functions reduced the need for the Constabulary's presence, while rising tension with the Soviet Union highlighted the importance of combat organizations in Central Europe. Consequently, constabulary units began to transition into more conventional tactical units. Several formed the basis of a new design: the armored cavalry regiment characterized by a modular, combined-arms organization intended to perform the full range of cavalry missions. The unit reflected the lessons learned from the mechanized cavalry experience of World War II; its nature marked a return to the versatile, general-purpose combat organization represented by the 7th Cavalry Brigade (Mechanized) in the 1930s.

In 1950 the Army Organization Act established the Armor Branch, which merged armor and cavalry development. It also provided a legal foundation for the new mounted arm, whereas the wartime Armored Force had attained only service-test status. The act resolved many of the issues of the interwar and World War II years regarding the proper roles of armor and cavalry. The new branch reflected lessons learned since the creation of the Tank Corps in 1917. It provided a central influence on armor and cavalry developments and ensured that the needs of mounted combat organizations would receive effective representation within the Army. The creation of the Armor Branch, coupled with the acknowledgment of the tank as a primary antitank system, effectively consolidated armor, cavalry, and antitank development—much as Lt. Gen. Jacob L. Devers had advocated while chief of the Armored Force.

The creation of the Armor Branch also signified the emergence of a credible armored warfare capability for the U.S. Army. Combat operations in World War II permitted the accumulation of considerable experience in the use of armored formations that became the basis for postwar developments. In the process, the U.S. became a world leader in mobile operations. This achievement marked a major milestone along an evolutionary path that began in World War I.

In that conflict, the Army first encountered the tank, a foreign invention designed to overcome the tactical problems posed by the trenches of the Western Front. The Army raced to create an American tank force, relying heavily on foreign materiel and concepts. The resultant Tank Corps' focus lay in fielding sufficient tank units to support offensive operations in 1918. Hence, the infantry support and trench-breaching roles established by the British and French were adopted with little modification by American forces more interested in the immediacy of combat rather than exploring alternate roles for armored fighting vehicles.

The lack of an analytical underpinning for the Tank Corps can be excused by wartime necessity, the circumstances under which the new force emerged, and the novelty of the tank. Unfortunately, immediate postwar developments unnecessarily constrained peacetime concept exploration. The Tank Corps' disbandment left the Army without the means to freely study tank operations and to experiment with mechanized organizations. The Infantry received exclusive responsibility for tank development and, appropriately enough, emphasized direct support to the rifleman.

Unfortunately, experimentation with tanks in other roles and the broader issue of how best to exploit the growing capabilities of armored fighting vehicles received little attention. This limitation stemmed directly from the Army's structure and the bureau system, which determined the extent and pace of mechanization. These constraints were further reinforced by public law in the form of the National Defense Act of 1920. Consequently, concept exploration lagged in the 1920s at a time when other nations, especially Britain, were dramatically expanding the horizons of mechanized capabilities and envisioning battlefields dominated by armored vehicles.

Foreign developments did finally trigger experimentation, but the potential value of the Experimental Mechanized Force and Mechanized Force became overshadowed by the danger they posed to the staffing and funding of the existing branches. This threat became more pronounced as the Great Depression dampened public support for increased military spending. The Army Air Corps' success at siphoning resources from the ground arms further reinforced opposition to a separate mechanized force. Resource issues eclipsed in importance whatever tactical value a mechanized branch might have provided the Army.

These factors underscored the U.S. Army's particular dynamics that prevented centralized, progressive mechanized development. The 1931 mechanization policy thus became a success, not because it greatly advanced the cause of mechanization but because it aligned mechanized developments with the Army's horizontal bureau structure. In effect, mechanization ceased to pose a resource threat to the branches. However, by dispersing responsibility for further mechanized development among multiple branches, each with a mutually exclusive mission, the policy did not promote the emergence of an integrated Army-wide mechanization program.

The 1931 policy did, however, permit Cavalry experimentation with tanks. The resultant 7th Cavalry Brigade (Mechanized) served as a test bed for determining how best to apply mechanization to cavalry missions and doctrine. The broad nature of the Cavalry mission set, as well as the uncertainty of the likely threat and future battlefield, encouraged development of a unique combat unit. The 7th Cavalry Brigade (Mechanized) became characterized by its flexible organization, innovative use of radio communications, revolutionary command techniques, and emphasis on combined-arms principles.

Through continuous analysis, study of foreign developments, and field maneuvers, the mechanized cavalry matured. By the end of the 1930s, the organizational, tactical, and leadership principles embedded in the 7th Cavalry Brigade (Mechanized) had begun to attract attention throughout the Army. However, the mechanized cavalry emphasis on merging tactical functions at the lowest levels contradicted the Army's traditional emphasis on separation. Outside the Cavalry, mechanized cavalry organization and doctrine became subjects of controversy rather than models to emulate. Debate over the viability of mechanized cavalry concepts intensified when the Cavalry sought to expand the 7th Cavalry Brigade into a division.

Mechanized cavalry developments also came at the cost of branch unity. In the 1930s a schism emerged in the Cavalry between proponents of mechanization and supporters of horse cavalry. This split symbolized the inherent tension surrounding the adoption of new technology and concepts that might fundamentally alter existing capabilities and their application. However promising emerging mechanized cavalry concepts appeared, they remained unproven on the battlefield. Moreover, the horse cavalry had made important strides since the World War to improve its combat effectiveness, mobility, and survivability.

For the branch leadership, the question of the relative importance of horse and mechanized cavalry had more far-reaching implications for the Cavalry. Successive branch chiefs sought to preserve the integrity of their branch by sustaining development of both horse and mechanized components without sacrificing either. Peculiarities in the bureau system interfered with their efforts and ensured the semi-autonomous development of the 7th Cavalry Brigade (Mechanized). Faced with a similar breakaway tendency by the 1st Cavalry Division and Board, each chief of Cavalry in the 1930s attempted to increase the executive authority of the office. These efforts culminated in Maj. Gen. John K. Herr's plans for a greatly expanded and consolidated cavalry arm.

The failure of these activities marked the extent to which the mechanized cavalry had secured support from key leaders within the War Department. Mechanization and the related leadership, organizational, and combined-arms principles found supporters among the senior leadership of the Army, who supported expansion of mechanization without having a clear vision of how such expansion should affect the rest of the force. Hence, the Army's senior leadership provided little guidance and no clear decision regarding the course of mechanized development. The War Department's horizontal and consensus-building nature further encouraged indecisiveness.

Consequently, while mechanized cavalry and infantry officers addressed the details of how to employ mechanization on the battlefield within their respective branches, the War Department undertook repeated studies and analysis that never led to a formal decision. The absence of clear guidance or a comprehensive plan for Army mechanization retarded American modernization efforts at a time when the likelihood of armed conflict was on the rise. Against the backdrop of the Spanish Civil War, the Italian invasion of Ethiopia, Japanese aggression against China, and German expansionism in Europe, U.S. Army mechanization remained mired in controversy and uncertainty. The lack of any foreign consensus regarding mechanized development served only to encourage competing viewpoints in the United States.

Fortunately, interwar America benefited from its geographic separation from the many regional crises erupting throughout the world. The Atlantic and Pacific Oceans ensured that military developments in Europe, Africa, and Asia did not directly threaten the United States. The nation had the luxury of observing from afar conflicts overseas while grappling with modernization issues in what could be described only as a leisurely pace.

The outbreak of war in Europe made resolution of America's impasse regarding further mechanized development critical. Germany's high-profile employment of panzer divisions and corps to overrun Poland heightened the debate surrounding the future course of American mechanization but did not resolve it. Instead, the Army opted to defer a decision until the conclusion of the Third Army maneuvers of 1940. This event demonstrated the need to create permanent mechanized divisions rather than establish them through ad hoc measures on the battlefield. The maneuvers occurred against the backdrop of the German blitzkrieg in France.

France's defeat and conclusions from the Third Army maneuvers finally ended America's mechanization debate. These events discredited French influences on American doctrine and demonstrated the importance of mechanized combat formations. The Armored Force resulted to create similar American organizations. It ended the separate development of the mechanized cavalry and the infantry tank force, and provided centralized guidance for the fielding of an American armored capability to parallel that of the Germans.

Between 1940 and 1942, Armored Force expansion occurred at a rapid pace. The Selective Service Act provided the necessary manpower, while congressional support for modernization and mobilization provided the requisite financial support. The Armored Force concentrated the Army's pool of mechanized talent and built on the experiences of the mechanized cavalry while acknowledging the importance of tank support of infantry. It provided a means of channeling personnel and materiel into new armored formations, permitting the exponential growth of U.S. armored capability.

The Armored Force successfully generated a new capability for the Army, but the means to wage mounted, mobile warfare were not synchronized with other, more traditional capabilities. No overarching vision existed to govern the interaction of the armored divisions with other Army assets in combat. The War Department initially proved incapable of providing the leadership necessary for a comprehensive integration of all Army components into a single, coherent vision for waging war.

The Armored Force's autonomy encouraged plans to establish permanent armored corps, consolidate the training of all components associated with armored formations under Armored Force leadership, and seek the overthrow of the Army's traditional reliance on the infantry-artillery team in favor of the tank and the airplane. Indeed, under Chaffee's leadership, Armored Force expansion plans were modeled on the burgeoning GHQ Air Force. The Armored Force soon symbolized a fundamental revision of the Army's method of warfighting.

This radical development path occurred largely through the absence of any restraining influence. The Armored Force emphasis on the primacy of armored formations was not unchallenged, and it faced competition from proponents of a powerful antitank force. Nevertheless, in the absence of effective central guidance from the Army senior leadership, the Armored Force pursued its own goals. While Chaffee focused his energies on building a powerful force with tactical and administrative authority, his successor, Devers, sought the concentration of all mounted-force development under Armored Force leadership.

Simultaneous with Armored Force expansion, the War Department transformed from a consensus-based, horizontal organization into a vertical, centrally directed one. This change required time to implement and occurred amid mass mobilization and hurried efforts to prepare the nation for war. General Marshall's appointment as Army chief of staff helped to stiffen the executive will of the Army leadership, but it was Lt. Gen. Lesley J. McNair's restructuring and rationalization of the General Headquarters that provided the critical integration and oversight of Army training and readiness measures. When General Headquarters transitioned into the Army Ground Forces (AGF), McNair was at last able to adopt a uniform approach to preparing the Army for combat overseas.

The emergence of the Army Ground Forces and the parallel increase in McNair's influence steadily eroded the independence of the Armored Force. Between 1942 and 1944, the Armored Force reorganized into the Armored Command and the Armored Center. Each change reflected a diminution in the influence of the Armor community, as it was subordinated to a centrally directed war effort. This development was facilitated by the Armored Force's experimental status. Lacking any legal foundation, this organization could be altered at the will of the Army leadership without congressional involvement. In addition, McNair's personal support for tank destroyers and the need to train and equip large numbers of new soldiers effectively precluded restructuring the Army around armored formations. Appending armored divisions and tank destroyers to the traditional infantry-artillery mix ensured the rapid availability of an adequate if not ideal force for the battlefields of World War II.

Increased AGF influence brought McNair's preference for streamlined organizations, pooled assets, and standardization into direct conflict with the Armored Force's embracement of self-sufficient, combined-arms combat units. Symptomatic of the changed command climate within the War Department, McNair's views prevailed. Hence, the armored corps was abolished, the armored division reduced, and armored training restricted to purely armor functions. The failure of the Armor community to sustain its position on any of these issues demonstrated its waning influence within the emerging top-down management of the war effort.

In organizational trends, the Armored Force was constrained to abandon its preference for self-sufficient divisions and to accept a smaller formation. The resultant light armored division reflected deployability concerns and McNair's preference for streamlined organizations that could be augmented as necessary. These characteristics were organizationally efficient and ensured the commitment of specialized assets only when needed. Yet, pooling created coordination and cohesion problems not easily remedied on the battlefield; it also increased divisional dependence on higher headquarters. For armored divisions supposed capable of independent operations, pooling constituted an undesirable tether to corps and army commands.

Combat discredited the pooling concept. Armored division commanders routinely sought semipermanent attachments that boosted combat power and reduced the need to coordinate for short-term augmentation. This development nullified earlier justification of a smaller division on the basis of deployability. The acquisition of additional assets in theater did not increase shipping requirements, merely the alignment of units already slated for overseas operations. Conversely, those units intended to serve as attachments—including mechanized cavalry, tank destroyers, and separate tank battalions—all encountered coordination problems. Not part of an established command chain, their needs were often neglected. The lesson from the wartime experience of armored divisions was simple: all components intended to support a formation needed to be organic. This solution eliminated the coordination and sustainment problems experienced by attachments and maximized the formation commander's ability to respond to unexpected or changing tactical situations.

The war years also demonstrated the importance of developing new concepts in conjunction with other Army initiatives and ensuring the proper dissemination of related doctrinal principles. The tank destroyer, for example, developed in isolation. Its manner of employment was not well understood outside the tank destroyer community. Consequently, it was misused by field commanders, experienced a less than stellar combat debut, and became the target of criticism throughout the war. The tank destroyer did become a valuable combat asset as a roving gun with multiple applications, but not in its intended roles as part of a special antitank unit relying on massed firepower to destroy enemy armor.

Similarly, doctrine developed without respect to actual battlefield conditions was abandoned. Both tank destroyers and separate tank battalions possessed a doctrinal emphasis on mass employment. The battalion organization was intended as the smallest tactical grouping, with a hierarchy of group and brigade headquarters to permit the concentration of several such battalions. In practice, however, supported divisions preferred to bolster the combat power of their subordinate elements by dispersing tank and tank destroyer platoons among them. This usage precluded mass employment and obviated the need for higher headquarters. It also prevented the application of the doctrinal principles associated with these special units, because such guidance embraced the battalion rather than the platoon as the smallest unit of employment.

Conversely, the inability to anticipate likely areas of operations for armored units resulted in a doctrinal void that units in combat struggled to fill on their own. Armored doctrine provided minimal guidance for the employment of mounted forces in urban environments. Tanks were generally discouraged from sustained engagements in towns and cities. However, operations in Italy, France, and Germany clearly showed the need for armored units to operate inside urban areas. Armored units thus had to develop their own principles of employment for fighting in cities through trial and error and at a cost in lives and materiel.

American armored doctrine in World War II was shaped by prewar concepts and proved slow to adapt to actual enemy warfighting methods. Armored Force doctrine embraced the tank largely as an antipersonnel weapon and discouraged tank-versus-tank engagements. Armored divisions were expected to maneuver into the enemy's rear areas and eliminate critical enabling assets such as headquarters, supply columns, and artillery concentrations. The threat posed to these targets by American armored formations could not be overlooked by German commanders. German doctrine encouraged the employment of armored units against enemy mobile formations. Consequently, the successful use of American armor tended to trigger mounted counterattacks, resulting in the very type of combat discouraged by Armored Force doctrine.

Likewise, tank destroyer doctrine reflected the tank's role in defeating masses of enemy tanks. It proved much less clear in providing guidance on how tank destroyers should combat the combined-arms tactics actually employed by the Germans. Moreover, tank destroyer doctrine failed to acknowledge the declining ability of the German armor to mount large-scale attacks. By the latter phases of the war, the absence of large numbers of German tanks on the battlefield drove commanders to seek alternate employment for tank destroyers. The result lay in the evolution of the tank destroyer into a mobile gun platform with multiple applications beyond antitank.

Doctrine drove materiel development, ensuring that fielded weapons had the capabilities desired for their intended employment. However, the failure of American armored doctrine to embrace an antitank role resulted in a tank design emphasis on mobility and reliability. American tankers thus found themselves at a disadvantage in combat with German tanks optimized for antitank operations, carrying heavier armor, and possessing more powerful main guns and better optics.

Combined-arms tactics offset the inferiority of American tanks to their German counterparts. American armor embraced the combat team approach first developed by the 7th Cavalry Brigade (Mechanized) in the interwar years, refined it, and routinely employed it in combat. Combat commands and task forces included a core tank-infantry mix supplemented by tank destroyer, engineer, antiaircraft, and artillery attachments, the whole sometimes also benefiting from close air support. This combination of capabilities provided a high degree of tactical versatility, combat power, and the ability to conduct operations effectively in most environments. This ability to adapt and succeed against varied threats on different battlefields demonstrated the superiority of combined-arms teams over more specialized organizations and formed the essence of the armored divisions' contribution to final victory in World War II.

The framework for effective combined-arms tactics lay in the armored division's organizational flexibility. The combat command structure defined in the 1943 table of organization and equipment broke from the Army's traditional emphasis on rigid unit structures. Lacking brigades or regiments, the armored division constituted a mix of tactical ingredients that could be arranged in any manner considered appropriate to its mission. Moreover, such arrangements were intended to be changed quickly and easily to meet developing tactical situations. Compared to more traditional formations, the armored division lacked form; it was an amorphous organization to be molded into a particular shape defined by the division commander.

The armored division reflected the assumption that change constituted the norm for mounted operations. Combat commands and subordinate task forces could perform a broad variety of tactical functions and through changes in their composition rapidly shift from one mission type to another without pause. However, the value of such flexibility was lost on commanders unfamiliar with combined-arms operations or lacking a clear understanding of the many different unit types and weapons capabilities within the division. Such leaders constituted much of the leadership pool initially available to the Armored Force. They preferred structure and constancy and did not immediately exploit the armored division's organizational flexibility.

The Army's tradition of separating organizations by tactical function had precluded the development of a combined-arms culture before World War II. The 7th Cavalry Brigade (Mechanized) constituted an important exception, but it was consumed in the 1940 creation and mass expansion of the Armored Force. Therefore, the Armor community had to grow its own combined-arms leaders. This process required time not generally available given the fast pace of armored growth. The battlefield rather than the schoolhouse became the principal forum for learning combined-arms principles. While many commanders did indeed master combined-arms operations, others proved less capable and less comfortable with the armored division's new look in 1943. Consequently, the principles associated with the combat commands were unevenly applied by armored division commanders. Combined-arms principles and tactics required time to digest and opportunities to practice that proved insufficient for many World War II armored leaders before they entered combat.

The wartime mechanized cavalry units, in contrast, were designed for the singular purpose of reconnaissance. In part this intent reflected the Armored Force's assumption of much of the Cavalry's traditional role. Reconnaissance remained one of the few areas left to this branch. However, the narrow interpretation attached to reconnaissance activities resulted in light organizations intended to rely on stealth and maneuver to accomplish their information-gathering mission. The specialized nature of the mechanized cavalry did not survive contact with the battlefield. These forces found themselves unable to perform their primary role without some degree of combat. Moreover, they were often required to perform a variety of additional functions more in line with prewar Cavalry missions.

Tank destroyers and separate tank battalions did possess balanced organizations with an adequate mix of capabilities to perform their respective tactical functions. However, this organizational harmony was disrupted through their employment as collections of platoons. In effect, they were dismantled in combat theaters by field commanders more concerned with bolstering the combat power of their own formations than preserving the unit integrity of an external attachment.

The separate tank battalions also suffered from their inferior status compared to the armored divisions. The latter constituted the primary focus of the Armored Force through 1942. As a result, the separate battalions suffered from training and leadership deficiencies long before they entered combat. Their role as a pooled asset limited their ability to train with the infantry formations they were expected to support in combat. The expertise developed by the Infantry in the interwar years was allowed to wane. It had to be rediscovered and relearned in the hedgerows of Normandy, the streets of Europe's cities, and the jungles of the Pacific Theater of Operations.

Unlike armored division components intended to outmaneuver enemy resistance, the mission of the separate tank battalions required them to remain in direct contact with enemy forces. Firepower and armor protection rated among the most important qualities for tanks assigned to these units. Despite the fundamental difference in their missions, the separate battalions and armored divisions used the same tank mix optimized for mobility and reliability. Similarly, the organization of the separate battalions became identical to armored division tank battalions. These measures simplified production and facilitated interaction between these armored units, but they did not enhance the separate tank battalion's ability to perform infantry support.

Materiel development during the war demonstrated the importance of teamwork. The best results occurred when Armored Force personnel, Ordnance Department engineers, and industrialists responsible for production worked closely together throughout the entire process of conceptualization, development, production, and fielding. Such interaction resulted in effective coordination of effort and early identification and resolution of problems. The development of the M3 and M4 medium tanks embodied these traits and ensured the Armor community received the platforms its doctrine required.

Where this close linkage did not exist, however, problems ensued. Initial tank destroyer designs, for example, were adversely affected by the friction that existed between the tank destroyer leadership and the Ordnance Department. Similarly, heavy tank development incurred repeated delays due first to the ambivalence of the Armored Force and later to the opposition of Army Ground Forces. Earlier, the revolutionary tank designs of J. Walter Christie had attracted Army attention, but no significant production followed. In this case, the inventor's personality obstructed development efforts. Consequently, the technology associated with Christie's tanks came to influence foreign rather than American platforms.

In one area, however, the wartime experience cemented a strong link between the Armor community and technical development. Signal communications became a vital interest to armored development, since it provided the underpinnings of effective battle command. The control of fast-moving, dispersed task forces depended on effective communications. Indeed, electronic communications had enabled the revolution in command and control techniques pioneered by the 7th Cavalry Brigade (Mechanized) in the 1930s. Principles established by this organization found further expression and expansion in the wartime experiences of armored divisions, tank destroyers, mechanized cavalry, and separate tank battalions. By war's end a symbiotic relation existed between the developments in the Armor community and the parallel evolution of signal technology.

The value attached to signal developments symbolized the importance of command and control principles to armor effectiveness. American armored divisions played a key role in the defeat of the Axis powers, but their success owed much to the way in which they were organized and how they were fought.

These formations did not possess an overwhelming technological superiority to their adversaries. Nor did materiel or technological considerations dictate the course of their development. Instead, it was the intelligent application of concepts and human resources that generated a legacy of success. Combined-arms tactics, coupled with the flexibility inherent to the combat command/task force structure and wired together via a robust communications architecture, provided the tools with which armored commanders outmaneuvered and outfought their enemies. Coupled with competent leadership, this combination provided the means necessary to overcome a doctrine that did not always reflect battlefield conditions, superior enemy tanks, unexpected tactical situations, or a resilient foe.

American armor development in 1917–1945 exemplifies the challenges inherent to the adoption of new technology and its incorporation into existing doctrinal, training, organizational, and materiel development trends. New technology requires time, analysis, and reliable performance data to ensure its most effective use and to determine training base changes. In the early period of American armored development, the tank challenged Army traditions, culture, and insular organization. Surrounded by controversy and uncertainty, determination of the best use of the tank and its optimum relation with other arms required over twenty years. This protracted timeline reflects the monetary, political, and organizational realities of the interwar years.

By 1945 the tank's battlefield influence had maximized through the adoption of combined-arms formations and principles. Integration finally replaced the separation of battlefield function institutionalized within the Army's prewar bureaus. Technological change and tactical innovation would continue to drive armored development in the postwar decades, but as part of an Army-wide evolution rather than a novelty. With the emergence of the Armor Branch, the tank and its related capabilities had not only been adopted by the Army, they had become part of its core.

Bibliography

Archival Sources

George C. Marshall Library (GCM), Lexington, Virginia

Personal Papers and Manuscript Collections: George C. Marshall; Paul M. Robinett; Mark Skinner Watson.
National Archives Project
Franz Halder Diaries

National Archives and Records Administration, Washington, D.C.

Record Group (RG) 92, Entry 1889, Office of the Quartermaster General, General Correspondence Decimal File, 1922–1935.
RG 165, Entry 10, Office of the Chief of Staff, Correspondence.
RG 165, Entry 65, Military Intelligence Division Correspondence, 1917–1941.
RG 177, Entry 39, Office of the Chief of Cavalry, General Correspondence.
RG 177, Entry 40, Office of the Chief of Infantry, General Correspondence.
RG 337, Entry 57, Headquarters, Army Ground Forces, Commanding General, General Correspondence File, 1940–1944.
RG 337, Entry 57B, Headquarters, Army Ground Forces, General Headquarters, General Staff, G–1 Section, Subject File, 1940–9 March 1942.
RG 337, Entry 57D, Headquarters, Army Ground Forces, General Headquarters General Staff, G–3 Section, Subject File, 1940–9 March 1942.

Patton Museum of Cavalry and Armor, Fort Knox, Kentucky

Library Holdings: 2d Armored Division, "United States vs. German Equipment," March 1945.

U.S. Army Armor School Research Library, Fort Knox

Armor Officer Advanced Course Student Papers
World War II After-Action Reports

U.S. Army Military History Institute, Carlisle Barracks, Pennsylvania Archives

Armored Force G–2 Bulletins

Personal Papers and Manuscript Collections: Andrew D. Bruce; Thomas J. Camp; Bradford G. Chynoweth; Willis D. Crittenberger; Alvan C. Gillem Jr.; Robert W. Grow; Ernest N. Harmon; Guy V. Henry Jr.; Hamilton Howze; George B. Jarrett; Leon B. Kromer; Raymond E. Lee; George A. Lynch; Henry C. Newton; Paul M. Robinett; Katharine Smith; Truman Smith; Orlando W. Ward; Ivan D. Yeaton.

Oral Histories: Thomas T. Handy; George R. Mather; Bruce Palmer Jr.; James H. Polk; Robert W. Porter Jr.; John K. Waters; Albert C. Wedemeyer.

World War II: U.S. Army, War Game Maneuvers

U.S. Army War College Curricular Archives

Transcripts of Lectures and Content Discussion

Student Committee Reports

Miscellaneous Reports

U.S. Army War College Records Section: Document Collections

Files 84–20, 84–17, 84–26, 84–63, 377–49

File 236–D: G–2 Information Digest, Military Attaché Reports, Germany

File 236–F: Special Bulletins: Operations in the European War

File 236–H: Tentative Lessons Bulletins: Tentative Lessons from the Recent Active Campaign in Europe

Library: Government Reports, Studies, and Training Materials

Anonymous. "Tanks or Tank Chasers?" 18 Sep, 4 Oct 36.

———. "U.S. Army Expeditionary Force, France, 1917–1919: Report Operations Tank Corps, 1918."

Armored Force. "Surplus Training Material," 3 vols.

Armored School. "Maintenance of Armor in World War II." Fort Knox, Ky.: The Armored School, Officers Advanced Course, 1949–1950.

Cavalry School, Academic Division. "Armored Cars." Fort Riley, Kans.: 1926.

———. "Mechanized Cavalry." Fort Riley, Kans.: 1932–1933.

———. "Report of Maneuvers, the Cavalry School, April–May 1934," 2 vols., 1934.

First Cavalry Division. "Report of Board of Review on Field Service Tests of the Proposed Cavalry Division Conducted by the 1st Cavalry Division, U.S. Army, 1938," 4 vols., n.d.

Lynch, George A. "Final Report of Major General George A. Lynch: A Summary of Infantry Developments During His Term of Office," 30 Apr 41.

Nehring, Walter. "Antitank Defense," 1936.

Rockenbach, S. D. "The Tank Corps," 19 Sep 19.

———. "American Tanks Since the World War," 1923.

———. "Weight and Dimension of Tanks," Feb 23.

———. "Tanks," 4 Jun 23.

Tank School. "Tank Notes," 1930–1932.

U.S. Army Ground Forces, Observer Board, European Theater, "Reports of Observers, ETO 1944–1945," 6 vols.
U.S. Army Ground Forces, Observer Board, "Report of Observers: Mediterranean Theater of Operations," 4 vols.
U.S. War Department. "Westervelt Board Report 1919."

Virginia Military Institute, Lexington, Virginia

Personal Papers and Manuscript Collection of Samuel D. Rockenbach

York County Historical Society, York, Pennsylvania

Personal Papers and Manuscript Collection of Jacob L. Devers

Government Publications

Anonymous. *The Fourth Motorized Division*. Special Service Office, 1942.
———. *The War Reports of General of the Army George C. Marshall, General of the Army H. H. Arnold, and Fleet Admiral Ernest J. King*. Philadelphia: J. B. Lippincott Co., 1947.
Ayres, Leonard P. *The War with Germany: A Statistical Summary*. Washington, D.C.: Government Printing Office, 1919.
Viner, Joseph W. *Tactics and Techniques of Tanks*. Fort Leavenworth, Kans.: General Service Schools Press, 1920.
U.S. Adjutant General's Office. *Official Army Register*, 1931.
U.S. Army Command and General Staff College, Staff Group A, Section 4. "The Battle of St. Vith: Defense and Withdrawal by Encircled Forces; German 5th and 6th Panzer Armies Versus U.S. 7th Armored Division and Attachments, 17–23 December 1944." Student Paper, Fort Leavenworth, Kans.: Combat Studies Institute, 1984.
U.S. Army Forces in the European Theater. *The 9th: The Story of the 9th Armored Division*. Paris: P. Dupont, 1945.
U.S. Congress, House. *Hearings Before Committee on Military Affairs*, 66th Cong., 1st Sess., 2 vols., 1919, vol. 1.
———. "Report of the Chief of the Tank Corps," 13 Oct 19. *War Department Annual Reports, 1919*, 66th Cong., 2d Sess., 3 vols., 1920, vol. 1.
———. "Report of the Chief of the Tank Corps." *War Department Annual Reports, 1919*, 30 Jun 20, 66th Cong., 3d Sess., 3 vols., 1921, vol. 1.
———. Subcommittee of the Committee on Appropriations. *War Department Appropriation Bill for 1931 Military Activities, Hearings*, 71st Cong., 2d Sess., 1929.
———. Subcommittee of the Committee on Appropriations. *War Department Appropriation Bill for 1932 Military Activities, Hearings*, 71st Cong., 3d Sess., 1930.
———. Subcommittee of the Committee on Appropriations. *War Department Appropriation Bill for 1933 Military Activities, Hearings*, 72d Cong., 1st Sess., 1932.
———. Subcommittee of the Committee on Appropriations. *War Department Appropriation Bill for 1934 Military Activities, Hearings*, 72d Cong., 2d Sess., 1933.

———. Subcommittee of the Committee on Appropriations. *War Department Appropriation Bill for 1935 Military Activities, Hearings*, 73d Cong., 2d Sess., 1934.

———. Subcommittee of the Committee on Appropriations. *War Department Appropriation Bill for 1936 Military Activities, Hearings*, 74th Cong., 1st Sess., 1935.

———. Subcommittee of the Committee on Appropriations. *War Department Appropriation Bill for 1937 Military Activities, Hearings*, 74th Cong., 2d Sess., 1936.

———. Subcommittee of the Committee on Appropriations. *War Department Appropriation Bill for 1938 Military Activities, Hearings*, 75th Cong., 1st Sess., 1937.

———. Subcommittee of the Committee on Appropriations. *War Department Appropriation Bill for 1939 Military Activities, Hearings*, 75th Cong., 2d Sess., 1938.

U.S. War Department. Armored Command Field Manual (FM) 17–100: *The Armored Division*, 1944.

———. Army Regulations no. 70–5: *Chiefs of Combatant Branches*, 1927.

———. *Cavalry Field Manual*, 3 vols., 1938.

———. *Field Service Regulations: Operations (Tentative)*, 1939.

———. *Field Service Regulations, United States Army*, 1923.

———. FM 17–36: *Armored Employment of Tanks with Infantry*, 1944.

———. FM 17–58: *Armored Maintenance Battalion Tactical Employment*, 1942.

———. FM 18–5: *Tank Destroyer Field Manual, Organization and Tactics of Tank Destroyer Units*, 1942.

———. FM 18–5: *Tactical Employment, Tank Destroyer Unit*, 1944.

———. FM 18–20: *Tactical Employment of Tank Destroyer Platoon Self-Propelled*, 1944.

———. FM 18–21: *Tank Destroyer Towed Gun Platoon*, 1944.

———. FM 31–35: *Aviation in Support of Ground Forces*, 1942.

———. FM 100–5: *Field Service Regulations: Operations*, 1941.

———. FM 100–5: *Field Service Regulations: Operations*, 1944.

———. *Infantry Field Manual*, 2 vols., 1931, vol. 2: *Tank Units*.

———. *Manual for Commanders of Large Units*, 1921.

———. *A Manual for Commanders of Large Units (Provisional)*, 1930.

———. *The Work of the War Department of the United States*, 1924.

———. *Report of the Secretary of War to the President*, 1933.

United States. *National Defense Act Approved June 3, 1916*, 1918.

———. *The National Defense Act Approved June 3, 1916 as Amended by Act Approved August 29, 1916; Act Approved July 9, 1918; Act Approved February 28, 1919; Act Approved July 11, 1919; Act Approved September 29, 1919; Act Approved June 4, 1920*, 1920.

Government Studies

Collins, Robert L. "Report on the Development of the Tank Corps." *The United States Army in the World War, 1917–1918: Reports of Commander-in-Chief, A.E.F., Staff Sections and Services*. Washington, D.C.: U.S. Army Center of Military History, 1948.

Harju, Craig S. "White Paper—A Study of the Maneuver Battalion Reconnaissance or Scout Platoon." Fort Knox, Ky.: Armor School, 1989.

Historical Section, Army Ground Forces. Study no. 15, "The Desert Training Center and C-AMA," 1946.

Historical Section, Army Ground Forces. Study no. 27, "The Armored Force Command and Center," 1946.

Historical Section, Army Ground Forces. Study no. 29, "The Tank Destroyer History," 1946.

Military Intelligence Division, War Department General Staff. "Intelligence Summary." *U.S. Military Intelligence Reports: Biweekly Intelligence Summaries, 1928–1938* (Microfilm). Frederick, Md.: University Publications of America, vols. 1–6.

Steadman, Ken. "The Evolution of the Tank in the U.S. Army." Combat Studies Institute, Report no. 1, 21 Apr 92.

U.S. Army Armor School. "Armor on Okinawa." Fort Knox, Ky.: Armor School, 1949.

———. *The Battle at St. Vith, Belgium, 17–23 December 1944*. Fort Knox, Ky.: Armor School, 1984.

———. "Maintenance of Armor in World War II." Fort Knox, Ky.: Armor School, 1950.

———. "Military History: Training/Tactics." CS-1251-M-Army-Knox-Sep 86-2C.

———. *The Nancy Bridgehead*. Fort Knox, Ky.: Armor School, 1985.

———. "Use of Armor on Luzon," Student Paper, Fort Knox, Ky., 1948.

U.S. Forces, European Theater. "General Board, Study No. 48: Organization, Equipment and Tactical Employment of the Armored Division," 1945.

———. "General Board, Study No. 49: Tactics, Employment, Technique, Organization, and Equipment of Mechanized Cavalry Units," 1945.

———. "General Board, Study No. 50: Organization, Equipment and Tactical Employment of Separate Tank Battalions," 1945.

———. "General Board, Study No. 51: The Armored Group," 1945.

———. "General Board, Study No. 60: Report on Study of Organization, Equipment, and Tactical Employment of Tank Destroyer Units," 1945.

Other Works

Allenby, E. H. H. Letter to the Editor, *Cavalry Journal* XXX, no. 122 (January 1921): 1–2.

Ambrose, Stephen E. *Eisenhower*, 2 vols. New York: Simon and Schuster, 1983, vol. 1: *Soldier, General of the Army, President-Elect, 1890–1952*.

Anders, Leslie. "The Watershed: Forrest Harding's *Infantry Journal*, 1934–1938." *Military Affairs* XL, no. 1 (February 1976): 12–16.

Anonymous. "The Mechanized Cavalry Takes the Field." *Cavalry Journal* XLVII, no. 4 (July-August 1938): 291–300.

———. "Notes from the Chief of Cavalry." *Cavalry Journal* XLIX, no. 4 (July-August 1940): 323.

———. "Quarter-Ton Trucks to be Distributed to Army for Field Service Tests." *The Quartermaster Review* XX, no. 5 (March-April 1941): 47.

———. "37 MM Anti-Tank Gun, M3," http://www.robertsarmory.com/37mm.htm, last accessed 7 May 2006.

Badsey, S. D. "The American Experience of Armour," *Armoured Warfare*, ed. J. P. Harris and F. H. Toase. New York: St. Martin's Press, 1990, pp. 124–44.

Baily, Charles M. *Faint Praise: American Tanks and Tank Destroyers During World War II*. Hamden, Conn.: Archon Books, 1983.

Ball, Harry P. *Of Responsible Command: A History of the U.S. Army War College*. Carlisle Barracks, Pa.: Alumni Association of the U.S. Army War College, 1983.

Beaver, Daniel R. "Politics and Policy: The War Department Motorization and Standardization Program for Wheeled Transport Vehicles, 1920–1940." *Military Affairs* XLVII, no. 3 (October 1983): 101–08.

Benson, C. C. "Armored Car Design." *Cavalry Journal* XXXVIII, no. 155 (April 1929): 196–204.

———. "Mechanization—Aloft and Alow." *Cavalry Journal* XXXVIII, no. 154 (January 1929): 58–62.

Bidwell, Bruce W. *History of the Military Intelligence Division, Department of the Army General Staff, 1775–1941*. Frederick, Md.: University Publications of America, 1986.

Black, Percy. "The Armored Force." *Cavalry Journal* XLIX, no. 6 (November-December 1940): 485–88.

———. "The Armored Force and Its Development." *Cavalry Journal* XLIX, no. 6 (November-December 1940): 485–88.

Blumenson, Martin, ed. *The Patton Papers*, 2 vols. Boston: Houghton Mifflin Co., 1972, vol. 1.

———. *Salerno to Cassino*, U.S. Army in World War II. Washington, D.C.: U.S. Army Center of Military History, 1969.

Bonsteel, F. T. "The Employment of a Mechanized Cavalry Brigade." *Cavalry Journal* XLII, no. 179 (September-October 1933): 19–26.

Bradford, W. B. "Cavalry Armored Cars: Filling the Gap at Amiens in March 1918." *Cavalry Journal* XXXIV, no. 140 (July 1925): 299–302.

Brett, Sereno E. "Tank Reorganization." *Cavalry Journal* XXXIX, no. 158 (January 1930): 30.

Camp, T. J. "The Fourth Battalion." *Infantry Journal* XLIII, no. 3 (May-June 1936): 201–07.

Canby, Charles S. "Tanks and Riot Duty." *Infantry Journal* XLII, no. 2 (March-April 1935): 162.

Canevari, Emilio. "Forecasts from the War in Spain: Lessons Based on Technical and Tactical Experience." *Army Ordnance* XVIII, no. 107 (March-April 1938): 273–80.

Carver, Michael. *The Apostles of Mobility: The Theory and Practice of Armoured Warfare*. New York: Holmes and Meier Publishers, 1979.

Chaffee, Adna R. "The Seventh Cavalry Brigade in the First Army Maneuvers." *Cavalry Journal* XLVIII, no. 6 (November-December 1939): 450–61.

Chapman, Guy. *Why France Fell: The Defeat of the French Army in 1940*. New York: Holt, Rinehart, and Winston, 1968.

Christmas, J. K. "Our New Medium Tank: A Fast, Heavily Armored Vehicle of Great Fire Power." *Army Ordnance* XXII, no. 127 (July-August 1941): 27–29.

Chynoweth, Bradford G. "Cavalry Tanks." *Cavalry Journal* XXX, no. 124 (July 1921): 247–51.

Clark, Jeffrey J. "Military Technology in Republican France: The Evolution of the French Armored Force." Ph.D. diss., Duke University, 1969. University Microfilms International Order no. 70–2147.

Coffman, Edward M. *The War to End All Wars: The American Military Experience in World War I*. Madison: University of Wisconsin Press, 1986.

Cole, Wayne S. *Charles A. Lindbergh and the Battle Against American Intervention in World War II*. New York: Harcourt Brace Jovanovich, 1974.

Cook, Don. *Charles De Gaulle: A Biography*. New York: Perigree Books, 1983.

Cooper, Belton Y. *Death Traps: The Survival of an American Armored Division in World War II*. New York: Ballantine Books, 1998.

Cosmas, Graham A. *An Army for Empire: The United States Army in the Spanish-American War*. Columbia: University of Missouri Press, 1971.

Cramer, L. W. "Portee Cavalry: An Experiment with Commercial Trucks." *Cavalry Journal* XLIX, no. 3 (May-June 1940): 254–55.

Crittenberger, Willis D. "Cavalry Maneuvers at Fort Knox." *Cavalry Journal* XLVI, no. 5 (September-October 1937): 420–26.

Crossley, Rod. "The Desert Training Center in World War II." *La Posta* 28, no. 5 (November 1997), http://www.la-posta.com/Online%20Reprints/Desert%20Training%20Center.pdf, last accessed 13 June 2006.

Cruikshank, J. R. H. "From Acre to Alepp with Allenby." *Cavalry Journal* XXXIII, no. 134 (January 1924): 52–62.

Cullum, George W. *Biographical Register of the Officers and Graduates of the U.S. Military Academy*, 9 vols. Chicago: R. R. Donnelly and Sons Co., 1930, vol. 7, Supplement, 1920–1930.

Davis, Edward. "The British Cavalry in Palestine and Syria." *Cavalry Journal* XXXI, no. 127 (April 1922): 123–29.

———. "The British Cavalry in Palestine and Syria." *Cavalry Journal* XXXII, no. 130 (January 1923): 56–65.

———. "The British Cavalry in Palestine and Syria." *Cavalry Journal* XXXII, no. 132 (July 1923): 286–95.

———. "The British Cavalry in Palestine and Syria." *Cavalry Journal* XXXII, no. 133 (October 1923): 435–44.

———. "The British Cavalry in Palestine and Syria." *Cavalry Journal* XXXIII, no. 134 (January 1924): 47–51.

Deighton, Len. *Blitzkrieg: From the Rise of Hitler to the Fall of Dunkirk*. London: Jonathan Cape, 1979.

D'Este, Carlo. *Fatal Decision: Anzio and the Battle for Rome*. New York: Harper-Collins, 1991.

Dillman, George. "1st Cavalry Division Maneuvers." *Cavalry Journal* XXXVII, no. 50 (January 1928): 63.

Doubler, Michael D. *Busting the Bocage: American Combined Arms Operation in France, 6 June–31 July 1944*. Fort Leavenworth, Kans.: Combat Studies Institute, 1988.

Doughty, Robert A. "The French Armed Forces, 1918–1940." *Military Effectiveness*, 3 vols., ed. Allan R. Millett and Williamson Murray (Boston: Allen and Unwin, 1988), 2: 39–69.

———. *The Seeds of Disaster: The Development of French Army Doctrine, 1919–1939*. Hamden, Conn.: Archon Books, 1985.

Eastmen, James N., Jr. "The Development of Big Bombers." *Aerospace Historian* XXV, no. 4 (1978): 212–13.

Edwards, Roger. *Panzer: A Revolution in Warfare, 1939–1945*. London: Arms and Armour Press, 1989.

Eisenhower, Dwight D. *At Ease: Stories I Tell to Friends*. Garden City, N.Y.: Doubleday and Co., 1967.

———. "A Tank Discussion." *Infantry Journal* XVII, no. 5 (November 1920): 453–58.

Fleming, R. J. "Mission of the Cavalry School with Comments on Modern Cavalry and Cavalry Training." *Cavalry Journal* XXXVIII, no. 154 (January 1929): 41–54.

Fletcher, D. J. "The Origins of Armour," *Armoured Warfare*, ed. J. P. Harris and F. H. Toase. New York: St. Martin's Press, 1990, pp. 5–26.

Forty, George. *United States Tanks of World War II* (New York: Sterling Publishing Co., 1983).

Fraser, William B. "Motorcycle Maintenance Problems." *Cavalry Journal* XLIX, no. 5 (September-October 1940): 450–53.

Fuller, J. F. C. "The Tank in Spain: Tactics Still Fail to Keep Pace with Technics." *Army Ordnance* XIX, no. 109 (July-August 1938): 24–27.

Futrell, Robert F. *Ideas, Concepts, Doctrine: A History of Basic Thinking in the United States Air Force, 1907–1964*. Maxwell Air Force Base, Ala.: Air University Press, 1971.

Gabel, Christopher R. *The 4th Armored Division in the Encirclement of Nancy*. Fort Leavenworth, Kans.: Combat Studies Institute, 1986.

———. "'Knock 'em All Down': The Reduction of Aachen, October 1944." *Block by Block: The Challenges of Urban Operations*, ed. William G. Robertson and Lawrence A. Yates. Fort Leavenworth, Kans.: U.S. Army Command and General Staff College Press, 2003.

———. *Seek, Strike, and Destroy: U.S. Army Tank Destroyer Doctrine in World War II*, Leavenworth Papers no. 12. Fort Leavenworth, Kans.: Combat Studies Institute, 1985.

———. *The U.S. Army GHQ Maneuvers of 1941*. Washington, D.C.: U.S. Army Center of Military History, 1991.

Gillie, Mildred H. *Forging the Thunderbolt: A History of the Development of the Armored Force*. Harrisburg, Pa.: Military Service Publishing Co., 1947.

Glantz, David M. "Observing the Soviets: U.S. Army Attachés in Eastern Europe During the 1930s." *The Journal of Military History* LV, no. 2 (April 1991): 153–83.

Green, Constance McLaughlin, Harry C. Thomson, and Peter C. Roots. *The Ordnance Department: Planning Munitions for War*, U.S. Army in World War II. Washington, D.C.: U.S. Army Center of Military History, 1955.

Greenfield, Kent Roberts, Robert R. Palmer, and Bell I. Wiley. *The Army Ground Forces: The Organization of Ground Combat Troops*, U.S. Army in World War II. Washington, D.C.: U.S. Army Center of Military History, 1947.

Gregory, Edmund B. "Motor Transport—Today." *Quartermaster Review* XXI, no. 3 (November-December 1941): 29, 72.

Griffith, Robert K., Jr. "Quality Not Quantity: The Volunteer Army During the Depression." *Military Affairs* XLIII, no. 4 (December 1979): 171–77.

Grunert, George. "Cavalry in Future War." *Cavalry Journal* XLII, no. 177 (May-June 1933): 5–10.

Guderian, Heinz. *Achtung-Panzer!* Stuttgart: Union Deutsche Verlagsgesellschaft, 1937.

———. *Panzer Leader*. New York: Dutton, 1952.

Gunsberg, Jeffrey A. "The Battle of the Belgian Plain, 12–14 May 1940: The First Great Tank Battle." *The Journal of Military History* LVI, no. 2 (April 1992): 207–45.

Harmon, Ernest N. "The Second Cavalry in the St. Mihiel Offensive." *Cavalry Journal* XXX, no. 124 (July 1921): 282.

Hawkins, Hamilton S. "Cavalry and Mechanized Force." *Cavalry Journal* XL, no. 167 (September-October 1931): 19–25.

———. "General Hawkins Notes: Conclusions Drawn from First Army Maneuvers." *Cavalry Journal* XLIX, no. 2 (March-April 1940): 163–65.

———. "The Importance of Modern Cavalry and Its Role as Affected by Developments in Airplane and Tank Warfare." *Cavalry Journal* XXXV, no. 145 (October 1926): 487–99.

Henry, Guy V. "The Trend of Organization and Equipment of Cavalry in the Principal World Powers and Its Probable Role in Wars of the Near Future." *Cavalry Journal* XLI, no. 170 (March-April 1932): 7–9.

Herr, John K. "What of the Future?" *Cavalry Journal* XLVIII, no. 1 (January-February 1939): 3–6.

Hewes, James E., Jr. *From Root to McNamara: Army Organization and Administration, 1900–1963*, Special Studies. Washington, D.C.: U.S. Army Center of Military History, 1975.

Hofmann, George F. "The Demise of the U.S. Tank Corps and Medium Tank Development Program." *Military Affairs* XXXVII, no. 1 (February 1973): 20–25.

———. "A Yankee Inventor and the Military Establishment: The Christie Tank Controversy." *Military Affairs* XXXIX, no. 1 (February 1975): 12–18.

Hogan, E. P. "The Army 'Bug': New Quarter-Ton Command Reconnaissance Car." *The Quartermaster Review* XX, no. 5 (March-April 1941): 29.

Houston, Donald E. "The Second Armored Division's Formative Era." Ph.D. diss., Oklahoma State University, 1974. University Microfilms International Order no. 75–8795.

Howe, George F. *Northwest Africa: Seizing the Initiative in the West*, U.S. Army in World War II. Washington, D.C.: U.S. Army Center of Military History, 1957.

Icks, Robert J. "Four Decades of Mechanization: Our Record of Combat-Vehicle Development." *Army Ordnance* XVII, no. 102 (May-June 1937): 331–40.

———. *Tanks and Armored Vehicles*. New York: Duell, Sloan and Pearce, 1945.

"Infantry Digest." *Infantry Journal* XLII, no. 5 (September-October 1935): 450.

Jacobs, Bruce. "The Evolution of Tank Units in the Pre–World War II National Guard and the Defense of Bataan." *Military Collector and Historian* XXXVIII, no. 3 (Fall 1986): 125–33.

James, D. Clayton. *The Years of MacArthur*, 3 vols. Boston: Houghton Mifflin Co., 1970, vol. 1.

Joyce, Kenyon A. "The British Army Maneuvers 1925." *Cavalry Journal* XXXV, no. 142 (January 1926): 17–28.

Kauffmann, Kurt. *Panzerkampfwagenbuch*. Berlin: Offene Worte, 1939.

Kennedy, David M. *The First World War and American Society*. New York: Oxford University Press, 1980.

Killigrew, John W. "The Impact of the Great Depression upon the Army." Ph.D. diss., Indiana University, 1950. University Microfilms International Order no. 60–0629.

Larson, Robert H. *The British Army and the Theory of Armored Warfare, 1918–1940*. Cranbury, N.J.: Associated University Presses, 1984.

Leach, Charles R. *In Tornado's Wake*. Chicago: Argus Press, 1956.

Liddell Hart, Basil. "Lessons of the Spanish War: An Estimate of the Military Factors: Men and Matériel." *Army Ordnance* XVIII, no. 106 (January-February 1938): 201–03.

Lininger, Clarence. "Some Trends at the Cavalry School." *Cavalry Journal* XLVII, no. 3 (May-June 1938): 233–35.

MacArthur, Douglas. "Modernization of the Army." *A Soldier Speaks: Public Papers and Speeches of General of the Army Douglas MacArthur*, ed. Vorin E. Whan Jr. New York: Frederick A. Praeger, 1965.

MacDonald, Charles B. *The Siegfried Line Campaign*, U.S. Army in World War II. Washington, D.C.: U.S. Army Center of Military History, 1963.

McGuire, E. C. "Armored Cars in the Cavalry Maneuvers." *Cavalry Journal* XXXIX, no. 160 (July 1930): 386–99.

Macksey, Kenneth. *Guderian: Creator of the Blitzkrieg*. New York: Stein and Day, 1976.

———. *Tank Warfare: A History of Tanks in Battle*. New York: Stein and Day, 1972.

Manchester, William R. *American Caesar: Douglas MacArthur, 1880–1964*. Boston: Little, Brown, and Co., 1978.

March, Peyton C. *The Nation at War*. Garden City, N.Y.: Doubleday, Doran and Co., 1932.

Mellenthin, F. W. *Panzer Battles: A Study of the Employment of Armor in the Second World War*. New York: Ballantine Books, 1956.

Messenger, Charles. *The Blitzkrieg Story*. New York: Charles Scribner's Sons, 1976.

Miller, Merle. *Ike the Soldier: As They Knew Him*. New York: G. P. Putnam's Sons, 1987.

Millett, Alan R., and Peter Maslowski. *For the Common Defense: A Military History of the United States of America*. New York: Free Press, 1984.

Mitcham, Samuel W., Jr. *Hitler's Legions: The German Army Order of Battle, World War II*. New York: Stein and Day, 1985.

Mitchell, George E. "The Rout of the Turks by Allenby's Cavalry." *Cavalry Journal* XXIX, no. 119 (April 1920): 28–43.

———. "The Rout of the Turks by Allenby's Cavalry." *Cavalry Journal* XXIX, no. 120 (July 1920): 174–205.

Morton, Matthew D. "Men on 'Iron Ponies': The Death and Rebirth of the Modern U.S. Cavalry." Ph.D. diss., Florida State University, 2004.

Nenninger, Timothy K. "American Military Effectiveness in the First World War." *Military Effectiveness*, 3 vols., ed. Allan R. Millett and Williamson Murray. Boston: Allen and Unwin, 1988), 1: 116–56.

———. "The Development of American Armor, 1917–1940." Master's thesis, University of Wisconsin, 1968.

Ogorkiewicz, Richard M. *Armor: A History of Mechanized Forces*. New York: Frederick A. Praeger, 1960.

Ohrloff, Horst. "XXXIX Motorized Corps Operations." *The Initial Period of War on the Eastern Front, 22 June–August 1941*, ed. David M. Glantz. London: Frank Cass and Co., 1993.

Palmer, Bruce. "Mechanized Cavalry in the Second Army Maneuvers." *Cavalry Journal* XLV, no. 6 (November-December 1936): 461–78.

Palmer, Frederick. *Newton D. Baker: America at War*, 2 vols. New York: Dodd, Mead and Co., 1931, vol. 2.

Patton, George S., Jr. "Armored Cars with Cavalry." *Cavalry Journal* XXXIII, no. 134 (January 1924): 5–10.

———. "The 1929 Cavalry Division Maneuvers." *Cavalry Journal* XXXIX, no. 158 (January 1930): 9–10.

———. "Tanks in Futurc Wars." *Infantry Journal* XVI, no. 11 (May 1920): 958–62.

———, and Clarence C. Benson. "Mechanization and Cavalry." *Cavalry Journal* XXXIX, no. 159 (April 1930): 234–40.

Raymond, Edward A. "Brassing Off Kraut." *The Field Artillery Journal* 34, no. 10 (October 1944): 694–98.

Reichelt, Walter E. *Phantom Nine: The 9th Armored (Remagen) Division, 1942–1945*. Austin, Tex.: Presidial Press, 1987.

Reilly, Henry J. "Proving Ground in Spain: Armament Trends as Revealed by the Civil War." *Army Ordnance* XIX, no. 114 (May-June 1939): 333–36.

Reinhardt, George C., and William R. Kintner. *The Haphazard Years: How America Has Gone to War*. Garden City, N.Y.: Doubleday and Co., 1960.
Rockenbach, S. D. "Cooperation of Tanks with Other Arms." *Infantry Journal* XVI, no. 7 (January 1920): 533–43.
———. "Cooperation of Tanks with Other Arms." *Infantry Journal* XVI, no. 8 (February 1920): 662–68.
———. "Discussion." *Infantry Journal* XXX, no. 5 (May 1927): 465–68.
Ryan, Michael. "The Influence of the Imperial Frontier on British Doctrines of Mechanized Warfare." *Albion* XV, no. 2 (Summer 1983): 123–42.
Schwien, E. E. "Cavalry Division Maneuvers, October, 1939." *Cavalry Journal* XLVIII, no. 6 (November-December 1939): 464–68.
Shirer, William L. *Berlin Diary: The Journal of a Foreign Correspondent, 1934–1941*. Boston: Little, Brown, and Co., 1941.
Spector, Ronald. "The Military Effectiveness of the U.S. Armed Forces, 1919–1939." *Military Effectiveness*, 3 vols., ed. Allan R. Millett and Williamson Murray. Boston: Allen and Unwin, 1988, 2: 70–97.
Stanton, Shelby L. *Order of Battle: U.S. Army, World War II*. Novato, Calif.: Presidio Press, 1984.
Steinbeck, John. *The Grapes of Wrath*. New York: Viking Penguin, 1967.
Surles, Alexander D. "The Cavalry and Mechanization, 1936." *Cavalry Journal* XLV, no. 1 (January-February 1936): 6–7.
10th Armored Division Veterans Association. *Tenth Armored "Tiger" Division*. Paducah, Ky.: Turner Publishing Co., 1988.
Theis, H. Jordan. "Yet Another Treasure and Problem for the Army." *Cavalry Journal* XLV, no. 4 (July-August 1936): 292–95.
Thomson, Harry C., and Lida Mayo. *The Ordnance Department: Procurement and Supply*, U.S. Army in World War II. Washington, D.C.: U.S. Army Center of Military History, 1960.
"Truck Tactics." *Infantry Journal* XLIV, no. 6 (November-December 1937): 511.
Truscott, Lucian K., Jr. *The Twilight of the U.S. Cavalry: Life in the Old Army, 1917–1942*. Lawrence: University Press of Kansas, 1989.
Watson, Mark Skinner. *Chief of Staff: Prewar Plans and Preparations*, U.S. Army in World War II. Washington, D.C.: U.S. Army Center of Military History, 1950.
Wedemeyer, Albert C. "Antitank Defense." *Field Artillery Journal* XXXI, no. 5 (May 1941): 258–72.
Willmott, H. P. *The Great Crusade: A New Complete History of the Second World War*. London: Michael Joseph, 1989.
Wilson, Dale E. *"Treat 'Em Rough!" The Birth of American Armor, 1917–20*. Novato, Calif.: Presidio Press, 1989.
Wilson, John R. M. "The Quaker and the Sword: Herbert Hoover's Relations with the Military." *Military Affairs* XXXVIII, no. 2 (April 1974): 41–47.
Wilson, Vernard. "Combined Cavalry Maneuvers." *Cavalry Journal* XLVIII, no. 1 (January-February 1939): 41–51.
Wolfe, L. R. "Standardization." *Quartermaster Review* IX, no. 6 (May-June 1940): 30–35, 61–62.

Woolley, William J. "Patton and the Concept of Mechanized Warfare." *Parameters* XV, no. 3 (Autumn 1985): 75–76.

Yeide, Harry. *Steel Victory: The Heroic Story of America's Independent Tank Battalions at War in Europe*. New York: Random House Publishing Group, 2003.

———. *The Tank Killers: A History of America's World War II Tank Destroyer Force*. Havertown, Pa.: Casemate, 2004.

Zaloga, Steven J. *M10 and M36 Tank Destroyers, 1942–53*. Oxford, U.K.: Osprey Publishing, 2002.

———. *M18 Hellcat Tank Destroyer, 1943–97*. Oxford, U.K.: Osprey Publishing, 2004.

———. *U.S. Anti-tank Artillery, 1941–45*. New York: Osprey Publishing, 2005.

———, and Victor Madej. *The Polish Campaign, 1939*. New York: Hippocrene Books, 1985.

Acronyms

AEF	American Expeditionary Forces
AGF	Army Ground Forces
CCA	Combat Command A
CCB	Combat Command B
CCC	Civilian Conservation Corps
CCR	Combat Command R
CGSS	Command and General Staff School
FM	field manual
GHQ	General Headquarters
HEAT	high explosive antitank
HHB	Headquarters and Headquarters Battery
HHC	Headquarters and Headquarters Company
HHT	Headquarters and Headquarters Troop
HVAP	high velocity armor piercing
MID	Military Intelligence Division
NCS	Net Control Station
WDGS	War Department General Staff

INDEX

☆ U.S. GOVERNMENT PRINTING OFFICE: 2008—337-644